Conflict Among Nations

ECONOMIC COMPETITION AMONG NATIONS SERIES

Series Editors

Alan Wm. Wolff, R. Michael Gadbaw,
Thomas R. Howell, and William A. Noellert

Dewey, Ballantine, Bushby, Palmer & Wood, Washington, D.C.

Paradoxically, in an era of growing economic interdependence, commercial and technological rivalry among nations is intensifying. International competitiveness has moved to the center of the U.S. public policy debate and has become the focus of increasing attention in Europe, Japan, and the developing world. This series examines the public policy issues that affect competition among nations and lead to international economic conflict. Its goals are to contribute to the policy debate by examining underlying sources of economic conflicts, providing policy suggestions for their resolution and fostering the knowledge that can make a more integrated world economy possible.

Titles in This Series

Conflict Among Nations: Trade Policies in the 1990s, Thomas R. Howell, Alan Wm. Wolff, Brent L. Bartlett, and R. Michael Gadbaw

Steel and the State: Government Intervention and Steel's Structural Crisis, Thomas R. Howell, William A. Noellert, Jesse G. Kreier, and Alan Wm. Wolff

Intellectual Property Rights: Global Consensus, Global Conflict, R. Michael Gadbaw and Timothy J. Richards

The Microelectronics Race, Thomas R. Howell, William A. Noellert, Janet H. MacLaughlin, and Alan Wm. Wolff

Conflict Among Nations

Trade Policies in the 1990s

EDITED BY
Thomas R. Howell, Alan Wm. Wolff,
Brent L. Bartlett, and R. Michael Gadbaw

Westview Press
BOULDER · SAN FRANCISCO · OXFORD

Economic Competition Among Nations Series

This Westview softcover edition is printed on acid-free paper and bound in library-quality, coated covers that carry the highest rating of the National Association of State Textbook Administrators, in consultation with the Association of American Publishers and the Book Manufacturers' Institute.

Published in 1992 in the United States of America by Westview Press, Inc., 5500 Central Avenue, Boulder, Colorado 80301-2847, and in the United Kingdom by Westview Press, 36 Lonsdale Road, Summertown, Oxford OX2 7EW

Library of Congress Cataloging-in-Publication Data
Conflict among nations : trade policies in the 1990s /
edited by Thomas R. Howell . . . [et al.].
p. cm.—(Economic competition among nations series)
Includes index.
ISBN 0-8133-1255-8
1. Commercial policy. 2. International trade.
I. Howell, Thomas R., 1949– . II. Series.
HF 1411.C5765 1992
382'.3—dc20 92-3846
CIP

Printed and bound in the United States of America

The paper used in this publication meets the requirements of the American National Standard for Permanence of Paper for Printed Library Materials Z39.48-1984.

10 9 8 7 6 5 4 3 2 1

Contents

Preface

The twentieth century has been an era of relentless upheaval. In the span of three generations, mankind has moved from the era of horse-drawn transport and gas street lights to that of supersonic transport, instant global communications, and desktop computers of extraordinary power. In the political realm, we have seen the complete disappearance of the empires that governed most of the world's territory in 1900, the emergence of over one hundred new nations, the rise and fall of vast totalitarian systems, world wars of unprecedented destructiveness, and the advent of weapons of mass destruction. The world's population, which was still primarily rural in 1900, has undergone a massive shift into urban centers, while at the same time a "green revolution" has made possible the feeding of these huge, burgeoning populations by those remaining on the land.

Set against such sweeping and dramatic events, the prosaic business of making, buying, and selling commodities and services has a tendency to be overlooked -- relegated, as it were, to the business pages of the newspaper. However, economic and commercial forces have driven many of the greatest upheavals of this century and surely will play a decisive role in shaping the next. We mean this not in a Marxist sense, in terms of struggle between economic classes, but because economic strength and political power are closely correlated. The fascist regimes of the 1940s were ultimately destroyed by the superior productive power of the United States and the Soviet Union; the collapse of Soviet power was in turn a function of the vast economic and technological superiority achieved by the western democracies in the decades after World War II. International relations in the next decade, to the extent they can now be foreseen, are almost certain to be colored by intensifying contests among those democracies for commercial advantage and technological leadership.

Although the twentieth century has been dominated by dramatic confrontations between ideological blocs, it began, and now appears to be ending, with world affairs driven by a less confrontational multipolar rivalry among a handful of mercantile powers governed by forms of parliamentary democracy and utilizing capitalist systems of industrial organization. The differences between these states are cast not in black and white (e.g., democracy/totalitarianism, capitalism/communism) but in shades of gray, these shadings are significant. Perhaps reflecting that fact, the cast of players -- the major trading powers -- has changed dramatically in the intervening nine decades. Some, like Japan and the United States, have moved by degrees from the periphery of the world stage to the center; others, like Britain and France, have moved aside, at least temporarily, as individual participants; still others, like Taiwan and Korea, have sprung up suddenly, seemingly from nowhere. This book is an attempt to examine the state of play currently as well as the strategies of some of the key players for advancing their economic interests over the next decade, as manifested in their trade and trade-related policies.

This has truly been America's century, beginning with the ebullience of Theodore Roosevelt's presidency, continuing through successful intervention in two world wars and the shaping of the postwar world, and culminating in the triumph over communism. But in the commercial sphere, there is sufficient evidence to suggest that the U.S. experience in this century resembles a parabola, reaching its apogee around 1950 and following a downward trajectory thereafter. At this writing, the United States is the world's largest debtor nation, has suffered a massive trade deficit for a decade, and confronts serious competitive problems across a broad array of industrial sectors. These trends cannot be ascribed to any single cause, but part of the explanation can be found in the sphere of trade policy as it is formulated and implemented both in foreign capitals and in Washington. Giving due regard to the importance of subjects such as education, industrial culture, and macroeconomic forces as elements in commercial success or failure, this book concentrates on trade policy -- how it is developed in six of the principal foreign trading entities, how it is likely to evolve in the next decade, and how its conduct by the United States could be usefully improved.

This book reflects the study and experience of a number of members of the International Trade Group of Dewey Ballantine, a group of 30 lawyers, economists, and trade specialists, headed by Alan Wm. Wolff, who provide legal, analytic, and economic services to U.S. and foreign clients. All of the editors and authors of this study are members of the Trade Group or were at the time the study was drafted, and this work draws on their collective expertise.

The study represents solely the analysis and conclusions of the authors, not those of the United States or any foreign government. While Dewey Ballantine represents many private sector clients, this book was not commissioned by, or subject to editorial review or revision by, any company, trade association, or other industry group, domestic or foreign, client of the firm or otherwise. All views expressed in this book are those of the authors alone and should not be taken in any way to represent the view of any client of the firm.

While the study makes extensive use of primary and secondary source materials on trade, a principal basis for the study was several hundred on-site interviews conducted with trade and industrial policymakers in the countries under study, as well as with selected academic and legal experts, U.S. government officials, and industry leaders, which were conducted between October 1989 and November 1991. A condition of these interviews was that no attribution be given for comments made during the interviews. Accordingly, in order to respect the commitments given to confidentiality, we have not footnoted text references to specific individuals, nor is the view of every individual necessarily represented in this text. This approach was necessary to ensure a level of candor on the part of those interviewed necessary to make the endeavor worthwhile.

A number of persons provided valuable assistance and insight in the preparation of this book. They include Stephen Foster, publisher of the *Brazil Watch*, who was kind enough to review and comment on the Brazil chapter, and the firm of Fischer and Foster Advogados, whose insight into the Brazilian informatics issue proved helpful to the author of the chapter on Brazil.

Many of the individuals whom we interviewed were engaged in developing and implementing policies which will determine the economic direction taken by their countries through the next decade and beyond. We are extremely grateful that they were willing to interrupt busy schedules to talk with us about the broad questions which we have attempted to address in this paper. We are also grateful to the staffs of the U.S. diplomatic missions in Tokyo, Bonn, Brussels, Seoul, Brasília, São Paulo and Rio de Janeiro, and the American Institute in Taiwan, for their assistance in arranging the interviews, sometimes on extremely short notice. Without their help this effort would have been impossible.

Thomas R. Howell
Alan Wm. Wolff
Brent L. Bartlett
R. Michael Gadbaw

Washington, D.C.

Acknowledgments

The authors would like to acknowledge the contributions of a number of individuals at Dewey Ballantine to the preparation of this book.

Much of the research upon which the book is based arises out of interviews conducted with foreign officials, industry leaders, and academics. We are grateful to Gayane Keezer, who coordinated the complicated travel schedules and arrangements which this effort required. Interviews were conducted on site by the following individuals: Alan Wm. Wolff - Brazil, Korea, Japan, Taiwan, European Community; R. Michael Gadbaw - Germany, European Community, Brazil; Jesse G. Kreier - Brazil; Thomas R. Howell - Taiwan; Brent L. Bartlett - Korea; Gregory I. Hume - Germany. Documentary research and interviews in the United States were contributed by Rosemary Gwynn, Gregory Hume, Derek Johnson, Dennis Craythorn, Catherine Stankard Levy, Thomas Kalil, Holly Glenn, and Todd Laugen. W. Clark McFadden contributed to the discussion in Chapter 10 of the system of U.S. export controls. Thomas Kalil contributed to the discussion of U.S. technology and education policy in Chapter 10. The library staff, headed by Daria Proud and including Willis Davis, William Stofega, and Leslie-Ann Kutzleb, was instrumental in acquiring virtually all of the documentary materials used in the preparation of the book.

For typing and editing of the many drafts which the manuscript required we are indebted to Annette Hatley, Joe James, Bernice Grandsoult, Marilyn Kurtz, Stella Register, Pat Brown, Dennis Curtin, Sharon von Bergener, Nancy Cernick, Joyce Harris, Debra Williams, and Cherryl Ward.

A special note of thanks and recognition is due to Annette Hatley, who, in addition to making countless revisions to the text, oversaw the production of the entire manuscript, converted the work to typeset format, and coordinated the layout and physical production of the text.

T.R.H.
A.W.W.
B.L.B.
R.M.G.

1

Introduction

Thomas R. Howell and Alan Wm. Wolff

> *Commerce, which ought naturally be, among nations, as among individuals, a bond of union and friendship, has become a most fertile source of discord and animosity.*
>
> -- Adam Smith[1]

Much has been said in recent years about the "globalization" of the world's economy -- the rapid integration of national economies into a borderless, seamless whole in which the national identity of companies and their products is supposedly becoming a meaningless abstraction. The most often cited indicators of this trend are the growing portion of global economic activity that is accounted for by international trade, huge cross-border capital flows, the existence of "global" multinational corporations and the increasingly multinational character of manufactured goods. The driving force behind this swift international integration is often said to be the economic principle of comparative advantage, with each national economy enjoying the gains from mutually advantageous trade in a world tied together with modern communications and transportation systems. In such a world, with national distinctions losing their significance, government policies which seek to affect competitive

---

1 *An Inquiry into the Nature and Causes of the Wealth of Nations*, Modern Library Edition (New York: Random House, 1937) p. 460.

outcomes are viewed as regressive, counterproductive, and ultimately irrelevant.

But while we may someday achieve such an ideal global economy, based on what Smith called the "bond of union," from the perspective of the early 1990s there remains an abundance of "discord and animosity" in international trade. One highly visible symptom of this conflict among the world's trading nations has been the unexpectedly protracted character of the Uruguay Round of Multilateral Trade Negotiations, which reflects a fundamental lack of agreement among nations on the basic issues being addressed in the Round.[2] Rather than withering away, national distinctions in the economic sphere are becoming more sharply defined. International economic conflicts are proliferating which will not be resolved either within the existing GATT framework or under such new and modified codes as may emerge from the Round. These conflicts arise out of basic structural differences in national economic systems which are coming into progressively closer contact as trade restrictions imposed at the border diminish in significance and extent.

Trade policy conflict among nations in the 1990s is not a relic of a waning era of economic nationalism, but a development which will actually grow in intensity as contact between national economies increases in scope and depth. We are witnessing today a continuation of the same prosaic struggles for national commercial advantage that have characterized the world trading system since the days of Colbert and Clive, played out in a world in which capital, technology, information and management have become far more mobile. As in those earlier times, the disputes that presently characterize trade relations among the world's trading states are not signs of disintegration of the world trading system, but conflicts over the terms of the increased integration that is unfolding. While "integration" has an auspicious ring to it, the process itself is not a cause for rejoicing for all participants in the process at all times. If the past is any guide, there is a high probability some nations will fare much better than others, as a whole, and by sector. World trade has already been "globalized" several times by technological and organizational

---

[2] The Uruguay Round is an attempt to improve the existing General Agreement on Tariffs and Trade (GATT) rules governing trade in goods and to extend the coverage of GATT regulations to international trade in services, trade in farm products, intellectual property protection, and trade-related investment issues. Success in this negotiation has proven elusive and, at the time of this writing, it appears that any agreement that parties will reach will fall short of even the modest expectations that prevailed at the Round's inception in the mid-1980s.

revolutions,[3] and the result has not been an unmixed blessing for the world's inhabitants.[4] Earlier eras of integration were riven by virtually constant conflicts over the respective roles various nations and regions would play in the evolving world commercial order. It is unlikely that this process will suddenly come to a halt in the last years of the Twentieth Century.

At present, the nations of the world confront commercial choices which, while perhaps not as stark as those of past centuries, do not differ altogether in kind. In this most recent and far-reaching "globalization," as in those of previous centuries, the biggest questions remain more or less the same: which countries and regions will emerge as the centers for the development and application of advanced technologies and the highest value-added production processes? Which will initiate technological and commercial change, and which will follow? Which will be dominant politically, based on their excelling in commercial endeavors? Which nations will have the most control of their own fate, and be most able to influence the course of world events, and which will be allotted a lesser role?

No doubt this perspective will be regarded by the majority of contemporary commentators as mean-spirited, cynical, and altogether wrongheaded. They would note the persistence of sporadic trade

---

3 A global economy was created in the sixteenth and seventeenth centuries with the advent of aggressive European expansionism, capitalist modes of commercial organization, and the long range gunned sailing ship. Another "globalization" unfolded in the eighteenth and nineteenth centuries as such previously autonomous areas as Mogul India, Manchu China, and Tokugawa Japan were incorporated, not altogether willingly, into the world trading system, driven by revolutions in communications (the telegraph, transoceanic cables), transportation (railroads, steamships), and Western military technology and organization. The British and Dutch East India Companies, the Hudson's Bay Company, and the New York merchant house of Astor were "global" companies in many ways characteristic of twentieth century multinationals. See Alan K. Smith, *Creating a World Economy: Merchant Capital, Colonialism, and World Trade, 1400-1825* (Boulder, San Francisco and Oxford: Westview Press, 1991).

4 During past periods of global integration, the great and small American Indian nations were utterly destroyed; other states and regions, such as Ireland, India, China, Ceylon, Malaya, the East Indies and the small states along the coast of West Africa, saw their native industries ruined by European manufactured goods and were reduced to various subservient roles in the emerging world system -- suppliers of raw materials, cheap labor and labor-intensive processed goods for the system's primary beneficiaries, the dynamic capitalist economies of Northwestern Europe and North America.

disputes among nations, to be sure, but would explain them according to a completely different frame of reference. A common perspective, often the favorite of economists and political scientists alike, is that most current trade conflicts can be explained as rearguard actions mounted by the forces of "parochial protectionism," a waning force in an increasingly interdependent world. According to this view, as the trading system becomes more open, domestic interest groups previously protected from foreign competition are being exposed to the forces of comparative advantage at the commercial level and are responding with pleas for their governments to restore that protection through policy measures. They are, in effect, the Luddites of global economic integration.[5] This book certainly contains evidence which tends to support this view; parochial protectionism explains, for example, the tenacious resistance of politically entrenched agricultural groups in many countries to trade liberalization, and the rigidly protectionist stance adhered to by Japan's numerous inefficient sectors (construction, retail stores, forest products and others). Such conflicts are not, it may be argued, between nations, per se, but ultimately between the forces of economic progress and conservative, entrenched interests which occur in all nations simultaneously, and in which international trade strengthens the hand of the progressive forces.

While this view is partially accurate, it explains only a portion of the trade conflicts which are occurring and are likely to occur in the 1990s, and, at that, not the most important part. The acrimonious clashes between the United States and the European Community over Airbus, for example -- which may soon become more complex as Japan's aspirations in commercial aviation reach maturity -- cannot be analyzed as manifestations of protectionism. Neither can the U.S.-Japan semiconductor wars of the mid-1980s, which may presage an era of multipolar conflict in microelectronics-based industries as an increasing number of nations struggle for advantage in the strategic information industries sector. This type of conflict arises out of government policies that seek to establish and develop new technologies, products and industries for which the constituencies consist of relatively small groupings of elite bureaucrats, interested politicians, scientists, industrialists, and engineers. Such policies produce collisions between conflicting national aspirations. There is nothing new in this; the "industrial targeting" policies being employed by Japan and Germany in aerospace, by Korea and Brazil in computers,

---

[5] This interpretation is expressed by Bhagwati: "A country that grows more rapidly than others will, on average, export at a volume and a growth rate that are hard for the other countries to accommodate without complaints from domestic industries that must bear the brunt of the adjustment." Jagdish Bhagwati, *Protectionism* (Cambridge, Mass: MIT Press, 1988) p. 63.

and by Taiwan in semiconductors have antecedents that can be traced back for generations, if not centuries, in history.

Sir Josiah Child, a 17th-century British politician, observed that "profit and power ought to be jointly considered."[6] This is still accurate today, but this proposition is not always as clearly perceived today as it was in that earlier era, nor has it necessarily been apparent to successive U.S. governments at all. In part, this is because in our own time, the centuries-old rivalry between mercantile powers has been eclipsed by dramatic, intensely ideological confrontations between totalitarian blocs and the western democracies. National commercial rivalry was disrupted by the destruction of the Second World War, and in the decades thereafter, overshadowed by larger events. But with the end of the Cold War, with the world apparently no longer to be a stage for a high drama featuring global confrontation between "freedom" and "totalitarianism," attention will turn to seemingly more mundane commercial matters. The 1990s will probably be regarded as important to historians not only as the decade when Soviet communism reached a dead end, but also as the point at which commercial competition and trade conflicts among the Western allies replaced political competition between ideological blocs as the dominant theme in international relations. Although not yet generally apparent, the outcome of this competition is nearly as significant to the United States as a nation as that of the Cold War; it will determine, in effect, whether we will remain a producer of advanced products and services, or increasingly fall behind, ceding economic leadership to others, with a corresponding decline in our standard of living and influence in the world.

THE PURPOSE AND ORGANIZATION OF THIS STUDY

In this study we attempt to look ahead at the trade policy environment of the 1990s in an effort to identify trends and likely points of international conflict, to assess the implications for the United States, and, in light of our observations, to propose some reforms in this country's trade policy. We do not believe that trade policy alone will determine the outcome of the national rivalries which we define here in rather sweeping terms. Even if one takes a broad view of what is embraced by the term "trade policy," government policies affecting trade are only one aspect of international economic competition. They are, however, an important

---

6 Rondo Cameron, *A Concise Economic History of the World* (Oxford University Press: Oxford, 1989) p. 128.

factor, because they tend to shape and define the terms on which that competition takes place.[7]

All exercises in forecasting are necessarily imperfect; many are shown by subsequent events to have been laughably flawed. Nevertheless, considerable insight into the course of future events in international trade can be gained by a careful examination of the trends of the present and the recent past. Underlying current events is the dominance of inertia in international relations; countries tend to follow existing paths, absent some abrupt external shock or internal upheaval, and this is particularly true of the advanced industrial democracies. Accordingly, the future course of events can be predicted, at least to some extent, by reference to the courses that the main actors are currently plotting for themselves, and an assessment of their ability to carry out their own designs.

A generation ago, any effort to examine the national policies shaping the international trading system would have concentrated overwhelmingly on the United States, by far the most important player. But the relative importance of the United States within the trading system, although still central, is declining, and important new actors are emerging that are imperfectly understood by us and, in some cases, even by themselves. Accordingly, in the first part of the book, Chapters 2 through 7, we have undertaken a detailed study of the trade policies of five major foreign trading powers and of the European Community, examining the bureaucratic processes through which trade policy is formulated, the political imperatives confronting policymakers, and the main multilateral, regional, bilateral and sectoral strategies likely to be pursued in the 1990s. We base this survey primarily on extensive interviews with policymakers and industry leaders in the countries under examination. These interviews took place over a two year period between November 1989 and November 1991. To a considerable degree, our assessment of the workings of these countries' trade policy bureaucracies, future objectives, and strategies reflects the assessments offered by these foreign policymakers. It also reflects, in no small part, our own experience.

---

7 While this book addresses trade policies as one aspect of economic competition among nations, trade issues intersect with a variety of other concerns, including the effects on national security of the transfer of sensitive technologies, environmental issues, energy and food security, trade in controlled substances such as narcotics, and the use of trade boycotts and embargoes as instruments of national policy. Each of these subjects warrants far more extensive treatment than we give it in a work of this scope, and we tend to address them only where they have become or are becoming significant factors in the economic competition or trade disputes between nations examined in the book.

The second part of this book, Chapters 8 through 10, is a reflection on the implications for the United States of the developments outlined in Chapters 2 through 7, with some prescriptive suggestions for reform. We base this section in part on our collective experience in the trade policy arena, and in part on the views expressed by the foreign officials and businessmen with whom we met concerning United States policies. An examination of U.S. trade policy reveals few anomalies that are not present, to a degree, in at least some other trading states, but in this country they have assumed a more extreme form.[8] These aspects of our system of government, while often rooted in U.S. historical tradition and serving other admirable purposes, have contributed to a succession of competitive debacles in the international arena since 1970. Further reversals lie ahead in the 1990s unless effective efforts are made at addressing these aspects of economic policymaking from a perspective more closely linked to the national commercial interest.

This cautionary assessment is made at a point of triumph for the United States; the world is changing in ways that validate the perspectives and objectives that have been articulated by U.S. leaders since the end of World War II. The Cold War has ended in a manner which vindicates the containment strategy that has provided the underpinning for U.S. foreign policy since the Truman presidency.[9] In the economic sphere, more nations are electing to utilize the GATT framework as a mechanism for addressing trade issues. Governments all over the world are moving toward more market-oriented policies; they are divesting themselves of state enterprises, not only in the former communist countries but in "mixed" economies like Britain and Brazil,

---

[8] Trade policy authority, for example, is fragmented in most countries, but it is unusually dispersed here, with rival political parties often controlling different parts of the trade apparatus. Most major trading states' policies are driven, to a degree, by laissez-faire ideology, but none to the extent of that of the United States. Relations between the government and the business community are often uneasy -- particularly in Taiwan and Germany -- but they do not reach the degree of mutual distrust that occurs in this country. Other trading entities make use of legalistic procedures and remedies (notably the European Community), but nowhere has this practice been elevated to such baroque extremes as here. Many countries' trade policies have an ad hoc, muddle-through aspect, but in no major trading state has government policy been as reactive and driven by random events as in the United States.

[9] Ironically this strategy was opposed to some extent by many U.S. trade policymakers and by much of the American business community, insofar as economic warfare was concerned.

reversing a previous trend toward state ownership that had become evident in the 1970s and early 1980s. Finally, even in countries which continue to practice interventionist industrial policies of the sort condemned by the United States, there is a move away from the cruder manifestations of such policies -- export subsidies, quantitative import restrictions, explicit "buy national" procurement policies. All these trends are a reflection of nations pursuing their self-interest, to be sure, but their determination as to where their interests lies can be credited, to a substantial degree, to the example set by the United States and a few other allied, market-oriented countries, most notably the Federal Republic of Germany.

It is ironic that just as the United States appears to be achieving goals that it has pursued for decades, it is suffering from a massive, chronic trade deficit, the decline of many of its advanced industries, and a broad array of structural problems that are generally lumped together under the rubric of problems of "international competitiveness." But this is not as odd as it may initially seem. The broader trade and economic goals pursued by the United States have never been designed, first and foremost, to advance national commercial interests, except to the extent that it was assumed that in any relatively open, market-driven world economy, governed by GATT-based rules and procedures, U.S. industry would inevitably prosper. Obviously, that is not happening, at least not to the extent that was anticipated. While many of the reasons for this go beyond the scope of this book, some of the answers lie in the key area of national trade policy.

BUREAUCRATIC NATIONALISM

A substantial portion of this work is devoted to an examination of how broad national policies and strategies emerge from the push and pull of competing bureaucracies and interest groups in the countries studied. Some of the most successful trading powers -- such as Japan, Korea, the European Community and Germany -- are characterized by a fragmented trade policy structure and weak horizontal mechanisms for resolving conflicts,[10] yet have generally been able to implement trade and

---

10 In Japan and Germany, for example -- two of the world's leading trading states -- there is virtually no institutional mechanism for harmonizing inconsistent positions staked out by various Ministerial power centers and their client industries. Korea not only lacks a central trade policy authority within the government, but has dispersed the function of "coordination" of trade policy (continued...)

industrial policies that have advanced the national commercial interest. This is attributable, in part to the existence within these countries of individual bureaucracies with sufficient strength to advance nationalist economic objectives despite internal opposition, and in part to an underlying consensus, transcending bureaucratic conflicts, that the successful performance of national industries in international competition, if not outright dominance, is important to the nation and should be fostered.

Each of the countries studied contains a number of key policy fiefdoms, many of which do have very clear objectives and strategies of their own -- be they protectionist, developmental, expansionist, or laissez-faire, which are not necessarily integrated into a coherent strategy embraced by the nation's leadership as a whole, and which are always subject to a greater or lesser degree of internal bureaucratic constraint.[11] The most important institutional actors in the international trade arena tend to be those individual governmental subunits that have managed to amass enough autonomy, political influence, and cooperation from private sector allies to implement at least a substantial part of their policy agendas. Japan's MITI is far and away the foremost example of such an entity; it has secured enough authority to enable it to promote the long-

---

10 (...continued)
among a diverse array of government organizations. Formal trade "policy" in Japan today consists largely of *post hoc* efforts to stamp out international fires ignited by the actions of individual Ministries and their affiliates in the private sector; the tactics of these groups are often brilliant, but the "trade policy" aspects of their efforts are often not part of a formal national strategy.

11 Thus, Japan's Ministry of International Trade and Industry has devised and implemented long-range strategies for promoting Japan's strategic industries, but it has been hampered by the frequent opposition of the Finance Ministry and at times severely obstructed by the bureaucratic machinations of other ministries jealous of their own jurisdictions. Germany's Ministry of Research has launched ambitious sectoral promotion schemes in microelectronics and computers which have been disparaged, if not undermined by the powerful Ministry of Economics. The European Communities', Directorate-General for Information Technologies and Telecommunications (DG-XIII) has been impeded in its effort to implement a strategic promotional effort in the information sector by opposition from laissez-faire elements in the bureaucracy of the European Commission, who currently enjoy a home in the Directorate-General for Industry (DG-III) as well as among the Commission's leadership. The interventionist national promotional schemes advanced by Taiwan's Industrial Development Bureau often run into ideological objections from the Board of Foreign Trade (another bureau within the same Ministry) and budgetary protests from the Finance Ministry.

range development of Japan's strategic industries, which it has done in a relatively enlightened fashion and, in at least some key areas, with spectacular success.[12] Another such bureaucracy is the European Commission of the European Community (EC), which, despite its own internal divisions and the various constraints imposed upon it by the Member States, has utilized the Single Market Initiative to achieve a sweeping array of policy objectives, not the least of which has been the informal goal of attracting, regulating and shaping foreign direct investment in key sectors like automobiles and semiconductors.[13] Each such entity is politically powerful in two respects: first, obviously, it is bureaucratically powerful, that is, it is able to achieve at least a significant part of its objectives notwithstanding the opposition of competing bureaucracies; second, it has evolved mechanisms to insulate itself, to a degree from the vagaries of partisan politics.[14]

A less tangible, but very important factor underlying the success of some bureaucracies advancing nationalist industrial and trade programs

---

12 We note here the frequent observation that "MITI's influence is declining," which has now been asserted for at least fifteen years. This is comparable to the scientific observation that technically speaking glass is not a solid but a *very* slow moving liquid. We take no position on the issue of whether MITI's influence is or is not actually declining; if it is, the process is so slow as to be not only imperceptible, but essentially irrelevant to a study that seeks to look only one decade into the future. Declining or not, with the possible exception of the European Commission, MITI is the most powerful and influential economic policy institution in the world and will remain so for the foreseeable future.

13 Agriculture ministries in Germany, Japan, and Taiwan have succeeded in sustaining highly protectionist (and highly nationalistic) trade policies in the face of considerable foreign and internal bureaucratic pressure. Brazil's Special Informatics Secretariat (SEI) has likewise struggled, with partial success, to sustain an interventionist infant-industry policy for the informatics sector even under the unsympathetic *laissez-faire* oriented Collor regime.

14 In Japan and Taiwan one party has held power for many decades; a rough consensus within the ruling party (the LDP in Japan, the KMT in Taiwan) has allowed the Ministries concerned with industrial promotion to pursue their objectives with little political interference and virtually no accountability at election time. At the same time, the Ministries associated with protected sectors (notably agriculture) have enjoyed broad latitude to maintain rigidly protectionist policies, reflecting the importance of their client industries to the ruling party's electoral base. In Europe, the Commission -- that "most undemocratic body" -- may tilt this way or that in response to shifting alignments among the Member States, but is not directly subject to the winds of electoral politics.

has been the existence of a rough consensus that national institutions should support the success of domestic industries in the international arena. This notion tends not to be articulated plainly by today's national leaders; there are few counterparts of Cecil Rhodes or Theodore Roosevelt who speak openly of "manifest destiny" in a commercial sense.[15] But the impulse exists and continues to drive policy in many of the world's leading trading states. Economic nationalism arguably underlies the European challenge to the United States in commercial aviation, the Japanese drive to dominate many high technology industries, Brazil's informatics policy, and the tenacious resistance of various national agricultural ministries to trade initiatives which, in their view, would destroy a pastoral inheritance inextricably linked with the nation's sense of itself.

Viewed against this background, the United States, which has provided most of the motive power for the postwar trading system, is something of a curiosity. By comparison with the other governments studied in this work, the American government is ancient; while the governments of all six of the foreign countries examined in this study were formed, or given most of their present form, some time after 1945, the basic foundations of U.S. government were laid down in the eighteenth century. Many of the laws, institutions and attitudes which still shape U.S. trade and economic policy took shape (some would say ossified) in the first half of this century, when there was no European Commission, no Federal Republic of Germany, and when Korea and Taiwan were colonies of a militarized, unstable Japan. While the institutions of economic policymaking in the principal U.S. trading partners have undergone revolutions since 1945, the U.S. system has continued to evolve, slowly and in a somewhat haphazard manner. The checks and balances built into the system by the Founding Fathers, nurtured by subsequent generations suspicious of government power, have for the most part prevented the growth of autonomous economic bureaucracies like MITI with freedom to pursue an activist commercial policy.[16] For the most part, the government has functioned as a regulator of business behavior, not a booster of U.S. commercial success.

---

15 An exception is Brazil, where a vision of national greatness, which persists in spite of all the nation's troubles, is a strong motivating force, especially within the powerful Foreign Ministry.

16 To the extent such bureaucracies have come into being here, with power to influence some aspects of commerce -- notably in the areas of defense and agriculture -- they have pursued objectives consciously unrelated to the international commercial success of U.S. manufacturing and services industries.

As a result, moving into the twenty-first century the United States arguably carries heavier ideological and institutional baggage than any of the other countries examined.

Several of our recommendations for reform of U.S. trade policy relate to the creation of a centralized executive department for managing civilian trade, technology and commercial matters, staffed by a cadre of trained career officials, with a series of institutional links to the private sector. Recognizing that the separation of powers is an embedded aspect of our system, we suggest that the problems this phenomenon tends to produce in trade could be mitigated, to a degree, by systematic rotation of personnel through the various key Congressional and Executive institutions, as well as by the creation of a closer consultative process between the two branches. Both of these steps are necessary to restore a sense of mutual confidence between the Executive and the Legislative Branches. Like comparable bureaucracies in the foreign countries studied, the new department would need to be at least relatively autonomous; that is, to be able to act without excessive constraints imposed by other departments, and to be insulated from the wholesale purges of personnel (who are replaced by political appointees) which take place in the wake of national elections. The chronic turnover of staff and officials that constantly and severely undermines the functioning of the U.S. trade bureaucracy would be offset by the establishment of a viable lifetime career option for such individuals. We recognize that there has been little stomach for reorganization of the trade functions of the U.S. government, and that Congressional committee jurisdictions and competing private sectoral interests make these issues unduly complicated, but this does not make the proposal less valid, nor the need for change any less compelling.

THE RULES OF THE INTERNATIONAL TRADING SYSTEM IN THE 1990s

Since at least the Middle Ages (and, according to anthropologists, from the time of tribal warfare) mankind has sought to establish rules to govern and circumscribe intergroup conflicts, recognizing that such conflicts cannot be averted altogether. There have been similar attempts down through the centuries to establish international norms governing at least certain aspects of international economic competition.[17] Following

---

[17] The Fifteenth Century Papal demarcation of the world into spheres of influence between Spain and Portugal is one example; Britain's crusade to stamp out the slave trade in the Nineteenth Century is another; the generalized adoption of the (continued...)

World War II, there was an ambitious effort, led by the United States, to establish a comprehensive system of multilateral institutions and rules governing international commercial activity. The General Agreement on Tariffs and Trade (GATT) emerged from this process, a multilateral agreement which established certain agreed principles relating to the sort of commercial matters normally included in commercial treaties.[18] Even so, the widespread adoption by the world's leading trading nations of certain practices called for by the GATT (reciprocal, bound tariff reductions; extension of general most-favored nation treatment; and phasing out of quantitative restraints) gave enormous impetus to the growth of world trade. The GATT was subsequently refined and expanded through the adoption of multilateral codes expanding on and interpreting certain aspects of the original agreement (such as antidumping and subsidies), and extended to areas outside the ambit of that agreement (e.g., government procurement, and civil aircraft).

Most studies of international trade relations center on the GATT and its codes and agreements, how it is working, how it can be improved, and what problems lie ahead if the momentum toward refinement of the GATT system cannot be sustained. The Uruguay Round negotiations, for example, have spawned numerous warnings that the failure of the Round would presage an unraveling of the GATT system itself, perhaps followed by a generalized regression into protectionism and a global economic collapse. We disagree. A survey of officials within each country studied

---

17 (...continued)
Most-Favored Nation principle by the European powers in the 1860s is another. Following the First World War, there were not only efforts to establish comprehensive international institutions, notably the League of Nations, to help prevent or at least limit future wars, but also some fitful efforts to establish multinational arrangements that would mitigate the commercial conflicts which, rightly or wrongly, were seen as contributing causes of the war. One such effort was the interwar establishment of the International Steel Cartel to regulate international competition in this strategic industry; another was the unsuccessful attempt by the League to secure adoption of a general Most-Favored Nation Clause. Most of these fragile efforts, of course, were overwhelmed and disappeared in the crucible of the Great Depression and the Second World War.

18 A parallel effort to establish an International Trade Organization (ITO) of the United Nations foundered, with the result that an international body formally charged with administering multilateral trade rules has evolved in stages rather than being formally created. While the GATT (which has a Secretariat and staff in Geneva) is often regarded as such a body, the GATT was, and remains, fundamentally only a contract between nations, subject to varying interpretations and lacking an effective means of resolving fundamental disputes.

reveals, without exception, that each country's leadership bases its strategy on a greater, not diminished, use of the GATT institutions in the 1990s.[19] Based on these strategic decisions, made for a variety of reasons in a disparate array of countries, we conclude that rather than fading into irrelevancy, as many warn, the GATT is likely to move closer to assuming the role of a forum for resolving international trade disputes envisioned by its founders than has ever been the case in the past. The GATT system will grow in importance whether or not the Uruguay Round is pressed to a successful conclusion.

In any event, we do not center our analysis on the GATT system at all, but on the maneuvering for advantage of some of the most important actors within this system (as well as one, Taiwan, on the fringe of and seeking to join it.) Regrettably the GATT is not structured to regulate important aspects of this competition, and, perversely, its selective strengthening, in areas such as dispute settlement, is not necessarily beneficial to the commercial interests of the United States. Contrary to a prevalent impression, the GATT is not an institutional mechanism for enforcing basic U.S. economic beliefs and values around the world, but a negotiated agreement among disparate states about how some aspects of their commercial relations shall be managed. In some areas, a broad consensus has been reached, extending across many nations, on a definition of desired or acceptable conduct, and it is precisely in these areas that the GATT has been the most effective, in some cases dramatically so. But there has never been agreement among the "contracting parties" about a number of the fundamental questions that lie at the root of the conflicts that are described in this book. Should governments, for example, be allowed to promote strategic industries with massive subsidies? Can governments sanction cartels which pursue strategic international objectives through means which would be illegal

---

[19] Japan is successfully making use of GATT dispute-resolution procedures as an element of its trade strategy -- a departure from past behavior. The European Community has shifted from a longstanding postwar attitude toward the GATT characterized by obstructionism to a position more supportive of the GATT and this might increasingly be the case if agriculture is successfully included within the GATT's disciplines. Taiwan is placing enormous political capital behind its effort to accede to the GATT and is conforming its trade regime to GATT discipline in anticipation of full membership. Brazil, long reluctant to employ GATT-based import regulation arrangements (tariffs, antidumping) is phasing out administered protection in favor of such mechanisms. Mexico recently joined the GATT. These trends will continue regardless of the outcome of the Uruguay Round, simply because a broad array of nations has recognized and accepted that the GATT regime serves -- or potentially can serve -- their own national interests.

in the United States? Can an advanced developed country like Japan justify continued government sponsorship of "infant industry" promotional schemes traditionally employed by developing countries? Can a company in a developing country infringe a U.S. patent and freely export infringing products to the United States? The U.S. answer to all of these questions is "no," but this view is by no means shared by all of the contracting parties, and on some fundamental points, the United States is virtually isolated. At the same time, the other parties to the GATT resent and fear the U.S. propensity to act against practices which it regards as "unfair", sometimes vigorously and with little forewarning, through the application of its own national trade remedies -- the much decried phenomenon of "U.S. unilateralism." In their view, the problem is not their own policies, but the American response to them, which again, in their view, should be curtailed by new GATT rules.

Given the fact that there is no real international consensus as to what constitutes acceptable behavior in the pursuit of national interests, the GATT cannot be said currently to represent a mechanism for enforcing a comprehensive set of shared economic and industrial policy values. Absent mutual consensus on the values and rules which are being enforced, the elaboration and strengthening of GATT dispute resolution mechanisms cannot succeed in mediating fundamental conflicts arising out of the pursuit of national commercial advantage. In this context, the current headlong flight of the GATT contracting parties into adoption of new dispute resolution procedures is a premature move which will not only foster further controversy but may ultimately weaken the fabric of the GATT itself. This effort is based on two mistaken assumptions: first, that it will regulate economies that are essentially similar and share congruent objectives; and second, that it will administer rules that are already well-developed.[20] Unfortunately for the United States, for all the current worldwide shift toward an appreciation of the efficacy of market forces, the predominant foreign view is that government support for industry is acceptable conduct, while offsetting trade measures are not. Our own trade policy system, with its emphasis on overt legal measures rather than informal administrative actions, is uniquely susceptible to attack by generally unsympathetic supranational review bodies. Surrender to such bodies of this country's ability to act unilaterally, in effect a major surrender of sovereignty, would be a dangerous mistake.

---

20 The analogy is to a system of criminal justice that establishes mechanisms for meting out justice to wrongdoers, but with the definition of wrongdoing not only left unclear, but subject to widespread disagreement, and with punishable "crimes" determined on a case-by-case basis according to the tug and pull of shifting political forces.

At the same time, it would be equally unwise to turn our backs on the GATT as an instrument for regulating certain commercial and industrial policy practices which we regard as harmful and with respect to which some common ground with the major trading states may be possible. The new codes governing intellectual property and services under discussion in the Uruguay Round are examples. In addition, it is quite conceivable that certain subjects which are of growing concern to the world trading system but which are not addressed under existing GATT rules or in the Uruguay Round could be brought within GATT disciplines. The need to establish agreed international rules on the acceptable limits of private commercial behavior is perceived in many nations in addition to the United States and could be a subject of discussion in a multilateral forum like the OECD and ultimately, the next GATT Round. Similarly, the tangle of problems posed by mercantilistic approaches ("industrial targeting") to industrial and commercial expansion is now a matter of pressing concern to many nations and could conceivably be the subject of a broader initiative one principle benefit of which could be better integrating Japan into the world trading system. Such new actions would require a decision by the United States to invest a substantial amount of political capital, but no more than has been sunk into the Uruguay Round (with respect to issues, such as agriculture, that are arguably less central to the long run national interest.)

PUBLIC POLICY AND PRIVATE ENTERPRISE

Some of the most controversial and fundamental political disputes of the past two centuries have revolved around the subject of industrial organization -- that is, what sort of structures should be established to organize and run production processes, which, with each passing decade, have become more capital and technology intensive. Who should own the means of production, on what terms, subject to what constraints, and directed to what ends?[21] In the United States, a somewhat schizoid

---

21 By the time the United States achieved its independence, the European innovation originally known as the joint-stock company was already well established and had begun to assume a variety of expanding functions. A century later, "capitalism" had become the world's most dynamic system of economic organization, but in the process, it accumulated a long record of abuses, including the horrors associated with rapid industrialization, low wages with appalling working conditions, child labor, and the depredations "trusts," cartels, and monopolies. In reaction to these developments, attitudes took root in the (continued...)

public perspective has evolved, extolling "free enterprise," on the one hand (often associated with small business, the family farm, and Yankee tinkers who develop ingenious innovations), but condemning and seeking to constrain, even pulverize, the concentrations of industrial power that seem to be the natural consequence of unbridled entrepreneurialism. Public revulsion at "trusts" and "big business" at the end of the nineteenth century gave rise to an antitrust tradition that remains one of the centerpieces of U.S. economic policy; in similar disgust with financial chicanery on "Wall Street" and the bank failures that were a hallmark of the Depression, Congress enacted legislation which limited the extent to which banks could play a direct role in industrial organization. If anything, the experience of the 1980s -- of junk bonds and bank deregulation -- has served only to reinforce these feelings.

Most of the countries studied in this work industrialized after the United States, and more often than not industrial growth was initiated as much by the state as by private capitalists. Little or no political tradition evolved in which the government was seen as a public bulwark against "big business;" on the contrary, the state played a major role in organizing and launching enterprises in Meiji Japan and, much later, in Japan's former colonies, Korea and Taiwan. Virtually all of Brazil's main industrial sectors were spearheaded by state enterprises. Even in Germany, which has a tradition of "industrial self government," in the early years of this century national and local governments collaborated with banks and entrepreneurs to assemble massive concentrations of industrial power. In most of these countries, not only was a close industry-government nexus accepted but various industrial combinations designed to limit competition -- that is, the "trusts" that alarmed turn-of-the-century Americans -- were viewed as simply another legitimate means of organizing production and marketing functions. Large industrial groups often headed by major banks and linked by extensive cross shareholdings evolved in Germany (the *Konzerne*) and in Japan (the *zaibatsu*), and cartels were extremely common in the industrial culture of both countries.

---

21 (...continued)
nineteenth century which continue to shape the way in which productive enterprises are organized, owned, and regulated. Britain's political agenda is still driven, to a substantial degree, by the class antagonisms that arose out of that country's brutal industrialization. The Soviet Union, China and the nations of Eastern Europe have been the unhappy objects of a vast, failed experiment in state ownership of the means of production which was itself a reaction to the perceived evils of capitalism.

After World War II, the United States exported its philosophy to the conquered Axis powers. The *Konzerne* and *zaibatsu* were broken up, local antitrust authorities patterned on the U.S. model were set up, and the virtues of unbridled free enterprise were expounded. To paraphrase a former MITI bureaucrat, this grafting of an alien organism onto the body politic of both Japan and Germany provoked something of an allergic reaction. Antimonopoly enforcement in Germany proved to be weak (by U.S. standards) and virtually nonexistent in Japan. Large industrial groups were reconstituted in both countries as the focus of U.S. power and influence shifted to the fight against world communism. Both Germany and Japan proceeded to develop a broad array of internationally competitive industries, many of which went on to inflict severe competitive setbacks on U.S. companies. At the same time, U.S. efforts to constrain and in some cases break up some of its premier companies continued; IBM, for example, was the subject of a massive antitrust investigation in the 1970s, at the very moment that MITI was organizing *keiretsu*-based electronics firms to challenge IBM in computers.[22]

In the late 1980s, U.S. policymakers began to perceive that there were a number of competitive problems confronting U.S. firms that could be traced to various aspects of industrial structure. The *keiretsu*, it seemed, were often more than a match for even very big U.S. companies. German bank-affiliated industrial groups were extraordinarily adept at competing for large engineering and capital equipment projects in developing countries. Vertical relationships between various U.S. makers of production equipment, components, and downstream end products were poorly developed, characterized by arms-length dealing and even hostility.[23] Small and medium U.S. firms had difficulty organizing themselves into successful consortia or export associations to achieve scale economies. This situation did not simply happen; we have in fact largely achieved the industrial culture which we have been seeking for a century, reflecting the efforts of generations of antitrust crusaders and regulators. The question now is how much suited that culture is to international

---

22 Even in recent years, following some relaxation of antitrust enforcement, a number of U.S. designers of integrated circuits have concluded that it makes more sense to enter into joint production arrangements with Taiwanese or Korean firms (with corresponding surrender of technology) than with other U.S. firms because of antitrust risks.

23 See, for example, U.S. International Trade Commission, *Global Competitiveness of U.S. Advanced Technology Manufacturing Industries; Semiconductor Manufacturing and Testing Equipment* (USITC Pub. No. 2434, September 1991).

competition in the 1990s, where U.S. firms are pitted against competitors who organize themselves in a fundamentally different way.

National Multinationals

As recently as the 1970s, American multinationals were regarded internationally with a mixture of admiration and apprehension, as both the wave of the future and a threat to national autonomy. Moving capital, technology, and people of many nationalities around the world and across national frontiers in a fluid manner, able to organize production, distribution, and marketing with extraordinary efficiency, U.S. multinationals generated a vast analytic literature, not all of it entirely positive. The global companies, it was warned, were really stateless, amoral, and devoted to objectives known best to themselves; unchecked, they could reduce national governments to a state of dependency or irrelevance, influencing and even overthrowing governments as might serve their purpose.

Such concerns seem oddly dated now. The golden age of multinationals never quite arrived, and is now palpably receding. While the U.S. has more multinationals in the 1990s than it did in the 1970s, these firms -- and other non-U.S. multinationals -- have not only not been able to dominate governments or economies of other major trading nations, but have often been compelled by foreign governments to implement investment and technology transfer policies that are driven by governments, not firms. The massive investment rush in Europe which has accompanied the Single Market Initiative was driven by fear of exclusion from, and a desire to be part of, the Single Market, encouraged by the bureaucracy in Brussels, rather than by the decisions of multinational firms based on the optimal timing and location for new plants. The transfer by U.S. information technology firms of technology to Korean enterprises does not always reflect a decision by company management that this is a wise commercial move -- quite the contrary -- but on occasion is due to pressure from the Korean government, which makes such transfer the price of market access. Government exertion of leverage against foreign multinationals is not, of course a new phenomenon, but governments are employing it in a more sophisticated manner, to achieve specific national objectives.[24]

---

24 Traditionally, multinational corporations have been able to play off localities and governmental subunits against each other to secure entry on preferential terms. One example of this phenomenon is the "bidding wars" that pit U.S. states against each other to attract foreign investment through tax breaks, infrastructural (continued...)

The supposed threat posed by "stateless" multinationals has been eclipsed since the mid-1980s by the emergence in the global arena of national, some would say nationalistic industrial groups, the most prominent of which are the Japanese *keiretsu* and *keiretsu*-affiliated firms. The *keiretsu* are organized in a way which effectively prevents foreign penetration; they possess enormous internal financial resources (incorporating, as they do, some of the largest financial institutions in the world) and have a tradition of collaborating with the Japanese government and with other Japanese industrial groups to achieve strategic objectives. If American multinationals were once regarded as instruments of "U.S. imperialism," the *keiretsu* are now coming to be seen as instruments of Japanese economic domination of sectors and markets. But the *keiretsu* are not the only manifestation of this phenomenon. The Korean *chaebol* resemble the *keiretsu* in many ways, including their impenetrability to foreign interests and the willingness and ability to function as arms of Korean industrial policy. Major German multinationals are virtually impervious to takeovers or penetration by foreign firms. Taiwan has few multinationals, but the state is seeking to promote the creation of larger enterprises and the assist them in "going global;" significantly, such support is conditioned on the firms' retaining a clear economic nexus with Taiwan itself. France's huge state-owned Usinor-Sacilor steel concern is "going global" with an acquisition spree of foreign steel producers and distributors which would not have been possible without the massive infusions of state aid which it received in the 1980s. These developments do not herald the waning of the global corporation, only the idea of the increasingly stateless global corporation

---

24 (...continued)
benefits, and the availability of land and facilities on concessional terms. Increasingly, however, national governments are managing this process to prevent such competition and to ensure that foreign investment -- while perhaps still subsidized -- is consistent with national industrial objectives. Japan, in particular, tightly regulates inward foreign investment. MITI negotiates understandings with prefectural governments to prevent them from competing with each other with incentives to attract foreign investment, regulates and monitors the incentives, and participates in negotiations between foreign firms and potential Japanese joint venture partners to secure the best terms for local Japanese firms. U.S. State Department Center paper. *Japanese Investment in the United States* (October 1989). In the European Community, the Commission has begun to regulate incentives offered to foreign investors and regions to forestall interregional bidding wars, and has applied strong leverage to foreign firms investing in the Community to utilize an extremely high level of EC content, to avoid "screwdriver" assembly operations in favor of full scale manufacturing facilities, and to transfer high skill, high value-added functions into the Community.

that once dominated the writings and imaginations of so many economists and political scientists.[25]

Old and New Protectionism

In the postwar era (and indeed for generations before it), nations which sought to promote specific industries or to achieve particular trade objectives utilized a fairly standard array of policy tools. Markets were protected with border measures such as tariffs, quantitative restrictions, import licensing schemes, and restrictive bilateral arrangements. Designated industries were promoted through measures such as direct subsidies, preferential allocation of capital, the establishment of state enterprises, tax preferences, and government-directed industry rationalization. Exports could be stimulated through export subsidies, competitive devaluations of the national currency, and the imposition of export performance requirements on the subsidiaries of foreign multinationals. Such practices are still common in the 1990s, although some of them are declining in their significance and extent.

At present, official trade restrictions imposed at the border are waning in significance and extent as a policy measure. The European Community is phasing out the system of "gray" bilateral restraints that have restricted its imports from the Far East and Eastern Europe. Newly-industrializing countries like Taiwan and Brazil, which have commonly utilized protection to foster domestic industries, are reducing the restrictiveness of quantitative measures in favor of GATT-based import regulatory mechanisms such as tariffs, antidumping and safeguards procedures. Japan has eliminated virtually all quantitative restrictions and high tariffs outside of those pertaining to a few inefficient protected sectors (such as agriculture). While in part the movement away from border measures

---

25 In the view of some economists and political scientists, "strategic alliances" between multinationals will usher in the golden age of borderless commercial activity that was once to be the province of the stateless multinational. That is unlikely. Some strategic alliances represent a banding-together of firms against a larger common challenge (such as IBM-Siemens in response to Japan's growing dominance of semiconductor memories, and perhaps Mitsubishi-Daimler-Benz in response to U.S. dominance of commercial aviation). Others simply reflect a continuation of competition by other means, and can be lethal for the participants, who may see their technology and manufacturing functions, and perhaps eventually their customers, absorbed by a stronger "partner." Governments are frequent participants in "strategic alliances," both to strengthen the bargaining leverage of their national firms and to guide the alliance along a path consistent with broader national objectives.

reflects pressure from the liberal trading states, exerted bilaterally and through the GATT and other multilateral fora, the most significant element underlying the shift is the recognition that border measures are often ineffective and counterproductive,[26] and, where this is not the case, protection can be implemented in ways that do not entail the same political cost as overt official restrictions. Protectionism is not dead, but simply assuming new forms.

Japan, for example, has evolved what is far and away the world's most effective system of protection, while at the same time, increasingly assuming the public posture of a nation that has eliminated most of its trade barriers. By the 1990s the function of protecting the domestic market against foreign imports and investment that was exercised primarily by the government has devolved almost entirely onto private industrial groups -- the *keiretsu*, de facto cartels, restrictive distribution networks, associations of domestic producers with a mutual interest in limiting access to the domestic market, and less coordinated, but equally effective, private restrictions on trade often manifested as a strong tendency to buy from traditional domestic suppliers.[27] In some cases (textiles, steel) Japanese industrialists have even negotiated their own

---

26 Restrictive border measures have proven counterproductive in a variety of contexts. In general, border measures tend to shield a domestic sector from international competitive pressure, thus reducing the incentive to remain competitive; in addition, trade restrictions may prevent domestic industries from acquiring steel, electronic components and other similar intermediate industrial products on competitive terms, placing downstream industries at an international disadvantage. Examples of such ineffective trade restrictions include the European and Brazilian information industries and the farm sector in most of the countries examined in this book.

27 In some cases, the protectionist function is transferred to private firms in conjunction with purported "liberalization" measures. In gasoline, for example, MITI secured enactment of a law in 1986 which was portrayed publically as a liberalization measure, despite the fact that under prior law, free importation of refined petroleum products was already allowed. The new law set up a system of licensed importers under which the criteria for licensing included possession of domestic refining and storage capacity, effectively limiting the class of potential importers to exsiting petroleum refiners, who were organized in a cartel. The law was enacted to block further imports by independent firms; it "thus eliminated the slightest possibility that small companies. . .would enter the downstream market and disrupt the industry cartel." Frank W. Upham, "The Man Who Would Import: A Cautionary Tale about Bucking the System in Japan," in *Journal of Japanese Studies* (1991), reviewing Sato Taiji, *Ore wa Tsusansho ni barasareta!* ("I was Butchered by MITI") (Tokyo: Tairyusha, 1986).

voluntary restraint arrangements with foreign industries, limiting imports into Japan. Because the GATT rules and most U.S. trade remedies are designed to discipline *government* intervention in the market, the assumption by Japanese industry of responsibility for trade protection has removed much of the leverage of the U.S., the European Communities, and other nations which emphasize a rule-based approach to trade, to overcome or control such techniques. Moreover, as Japanese firms globalize their manufacturing operations, the buy-national propensities of the Japanese industrial groups become even harder for other countries to attack on a national basis; for example, if Japanese manufacturing firms in Thailand procure components primarily from other Japanese firms, is that fact a trade issue which is properly addressed to the Japanese government, to the government of Thailand, or to any government?

Another more sophisticated form of protectionism is evolving in Korea and the European Community, where a variety of formal and informal incentives are being applied to subsidiaries of foreign firms to adopt high levels of local content in their manufactured products.[28] These measures not only increase the demand base for domestic components and materials supplies, but, by compelling foreign firms to "design in" their products and work with local suppliers to improve quality, result in an upgrading of the technological competence of local producers. In Japan, of course, while MITI and other government agencies once exhorted Japanese industry to utilize domestic content, such promptings are no longer necessary; the large Japanese industrial groups have a strong preference for national products, and MITI finds itself, ironically, in the formal role of booster of the incorporation of foreign components to blunt foreign criticism of Japanese private protectionism.

Technology and National Competitiveness

National industrial policies have traditionally featured a technological aspect; the steel industry promotion schemes implemented by Japan, France and Italy in the first postwar decades, for example, featured government support for the development and adoption of new production technologies. By the 1980s, as competition between the advanced nations shifted toward technology-intensive industries in which research and

---

28 Brazil has employed a variety of local content requirements for many years; these have enjoyed mixed success, at best, perhaps because of the initially low level of development of many local industries. Even in the European Community, these measures, like formal protection, may prove ineffective with respect to the results desired -- fostering a competitive domestic industry -- but nevertheless are trade distortive and harmful to others.

development accounted for a substantial proportion of total cost and often determined competitive outcomes, the promotion and acquisition of industrial technology became more central to national economic strategy, and much more sophisticated. Government-funded, industry-government research consortia have been launched in every country examined in this book, generally in an atmosphere tinged with the sort of economic nationalism that used to accompany the founding of a national airline or steel mill. In addition, governments have implemented sophisticated strategies to lure research activity, regardless of the nationality of the scientists or firms, to locations within national boundaries, on the assumption that benefits from this activity diffuse throughout the local economy and society. Governments are groping for ways to restrict the outward flow of technology, where this is seen as desirable, and to circumvent such restrictions when they are imposed by others.

Key bureaucracies within all six of the entities studied in this book have repeatedly cast aside whatever laissez-faire compunctions they may otherwise hold in order to promote frankly national strategies in the advanced technologies.[29] These policies, pursued to their logical conclusion, will not only produce continuing erosion of U.S. technology leadership across a broad spectrum of industries, but are likely to deliver a series of dramatic shocks to the United States in the 1990s. For example, the Airbus consortium is likely to challenge Boeing's position as the world's only producer of 400-plus seat transcontinental aircraft of the B-747 class. In the mid-1990s Japan is likely to launch a series of space spectaculars, including a manned space shuttle, and may begin to eclipse the troubled U.S. space program in a number of areas, such as materials processing in space. Taiwan and Korea will establish and expand a niche presence in product areas that were virtually a U.S. preserve ten years ago -- e.g., software, application-specific integrated circuits, and small computers.

Transnational conflicts will erupt in the advanced technologies because the current array of national aspirations are inconsistent, there are no agreed international rules to apply, and there are no viable established

---

[29] West Germany, for example -- a strong proponent of government nonintervention -- makes dramatic exceptions in the areas of semiconductors, commercial aviation, and supercomputers. Japan is pouring government resources into an astonishing range of leading technologies, including exotic materials, superconductivity, micromachines, and space exploration. Taiwan and Korea lag only a short distance behind the world leaders in some key areas of semiconductor technology. Brazil, in spite of reforms, continues to grant informatics, telecommunications and related sectors special consideration in terms of market protection and government assistance.

mechanisms for resolving conflicts in a mutually agreed manner. Current GATT dispute resolution procedures are hopelessly inadequate and cannot be perfected absent an underlying consensus among the major trading powers as to the delineation of acceptable industrial policy and commercial behavior. What likely lies ahead are bitter bilateral rows, resolved through ad hoc settlements reflecting the relative strength of the parties to such arrangements -- in short, in some respects, a continuation of the trade conflicts previously seen in autos and steel, but moving up the technology spectrum, requiring remedies far more complex than the administration of protection alone.

THE COUNTRIES

The Japan Problem

One of the principal sources of trade conflict in the 1990s is, to borrow a term coined by Dutch journalist Karel van Wolferen, the "Japan Problem." The aggressive, state-backed commercial expansionism of Japanese companies, the rapid technological strides of Japanese industry, and the relative impenetrability of the growing Japanese market are viewed with concern in every other advanced industrial country, and with alarm in some. The country's institutions and economic relationships are arranged in a manner which consistently favors production over consumption, whether in agriculture or the high technology industries. For decades these arrangements have not been challenged by any significant organized group in the country.

Somewhat paradoxically, while Japan's political economy is remarkably cohesive in terms of basic values and shared assumptions, it is also institutionally fragmented, and therein lies at least part of the explanation for the seemingly constant economic conflicts in which Japan is embroiled around the world. Japan is sharply segmented into autonomous power centers which consist, at a minimum, of a Ministry and a group of client industries, and which may also incorporate a segment of the electoral base of the ruling Liberal Democratic Party (LDP). Because of the peculiar organization of Japanese institutions, these quasi-feudal bureaucratic/industrial combines are generally not really answerable to anybody -- the voters, higher political authority, an independent, critical press, or even to each other. They tend to formulate and implement their own trade and industrial policies more or less independently; these may range from pure protectionism to efforts to achieve world domination of a particular industry or group of industries. The policies of every power center, from the protectionism of the farmers and the construction industry to MITI's technological promotion efforts, are intensely nationalistic, but there is no institutional mechanism for melding them into a single national economic policy which considers the interests of Japan as an entirety rather than those of individual interest groups. Foreign pressure, *gaiatsu*, acquires this role by default; when the foreign backlash against the actions of a particular Japanese interest group becomes too intense, some sort of ad hoc response is cobbled together, usually pursuant to informal arrangements worked out among bureaucrats, industrialists, and LDP political leaders.

Japan's leading export industries are dominated by *keiretsu*-affiliated firms which have traditionally looked to MITI for guidance and support. Since the 1960s, MITI's industrial promotion policies, applied in an industrial milieu dominated by the *keiretsu* and characterized by weak-to-nonexistent antitrust enforcement, have resulted in aggressive investment programs and export drives in a succession of industries, including shipbuilding, ball bearings, motorcycles, steel, televisions, various textile products, and semiconductors. The result has often been the severe weakening or even destruction of foreign industries; the impression has been created, in the words of a MITI Vice Minister "that Japanese enterprises have a fiercely offensive-type nature, as embodied in the expression 'fast as the wind and plundering like fire.'"[30] The foreign response has generally been to impose trade restrictions on Japanese firms, with MITI generally cast in a mediating role, attempting to moderate both the excesses of Japanese firms and the severity of the foreign response. MITI acts, in a sense, as its own antidote; many of its policy measures are designed to mitigate, directly or indirectly, the friction that is a natural consequence of its own domestic policy measures.

For decades Japan has been said to be in the midst of, or at least on the verge of, fundamental, sweeping change (frequently in response to criticism of the country's industrial polices and structural characteristics.) In fact, during the past several decades, Japan's political and economic institutions haven't changed very much, and a good case can be made that its current direction will remain largely the same throughout the next decade. In the eyes of Japan's policymakers, her course has not been proven to be a failure. The history of Japan's success is well known. Its growth rate led the OECD, its inflation rate has been the envy of most nations, its productivity growth has been high, its competitiveness in those areas in which it has placed emphasis is either second to none on closing on first place rapidly. Its banks dominate the list of the top ten

---

30 Naohiro Amaya, "The Ethics of *Wa* and Logic of the Antimonopoly Law," in *Bunjei Shunju* (December 1980).

in the world. Its rate of investment in plant and equipment exceeds that of the United States, with half the population. Thus there is no feeling on the part of Japan's leaders that there is any cause to change its policies dramatically -- not even because the living standard of its people lags those of those of Europe and the United States. If there is some disquiet in Japanese government circles, it is because the policies Japan employs, of maintaining an illiberal economy when it comes to imports, of fostering export waves which incidentally seriously injure the industries of others, of taking proportionately less of the burden of world trade (in terms of accepting the manufactured goods of others) than of any other developed country, leads to an endless series of confrontations with others. And in a world no longer preoccupied with the political contest between world communism and democracy, the tolerance for carrying the burden of Japan's mercantilism will be much diminished. Therefore the pressure will be much greater for Japan to find means of accommodation with the rest of the trading world.

Japan's accommodation will take two forms. One is the continued slow convergence of policies towards those of its trading partners. The other is the search for interface mechanisms between differing forms of capitalism that cannot coexist in complete harmony. If there is one insight that the SII[31] process has afforded its more astute participants, it is that Japan and the United States do differ, that those differences give rise to conflict, and that the current rate of convergence between the United States and Japan is too slow to avert a continuing series of explosive confrontations.

The pace of change has always been the central question in U.S./Japanese relations. It determines whether there will be unmanageable conflict between the United States and Japan or a break that seriously damages the relationship. The problem has always been that the pace of change has been too slow (e.g., Japan removing its tariff protection on autos in the late 1970's only when it was fully competitive in autos, while allowing other barriers to keep most automobile imports out of Japan[32]). Rather than accelerate the pace of Japan's liberalization beyond that which is comfortable for Japan's manufacturers, Japan has repeatedly chosen to

---

31 Structural Impediments Initiative negotiations commenced between Japan and the United States in the spring of 1989.

32 In 1988, the year of the Seoul Olympics, Japan allowed in some 120 Hyundai automobiles. That total was quickly brought down to seven in the following half year, it was said that Japanese consumers would not have wanted them anyway. The Japanese consumer was not given an opportunity to make this judgment himself or herself, however.

blunt trade friction by restraining its exports (e.g., to the U.S. and Europe in automobiles), and more recently by investing in manufacturing facilities in the end-markets. Such actions may ameliorate the immediate sources of conflict, but do little to resolve underlying differences.

The realization has emerged from the schooling of SII and the events in Eastern Europe that while it is absolutely clear that the market economy is better than complete central planning, in the eyes of Japanese officials, this does not mean that a completely free market economy is an ideal form of promoting growth and stability either in Japan or in the world generally. There is therefore a perceptual gulf between Japanese and U.S. negotiators which is difficult to bridge -- each side believes that its form of economic organization is superior. Even if Japanese society were as guilt-driven as their Western counterparts, Japanese officials would not feel a strong need to be apologetic. In these differing perspectives lies the basis for unceasing conflict.

Americans fail to understand how different the two countries are, although both are market economies. One Japanese official said that if two identical seeds of commercial activity were planted in the two soils, in Japan and in the United States, the resulting tree would differ in shape. As long as they grew without coming into contact with each other, all would be well, but if they touched, some intervention would be necessary to prevent conflict.[33] For policymakers there are two basic rational choices -- to facilitate the convergence of these different kinds of market economies,[34] or alternatively, to take the differences as given, and build an international system in which the two forms of market economy can co-exist. Accommodation between Japan and the United States needs to be reached via reforms at several levels: 1) government relations with the private sector, 2) relations among firms; and 3) relations between firms and their workers. Fully peaceful coexistence between the United States and Japan requires changes to occur in each country at each of these levels. This reality has yet to be contemplated by American or Japanese decisionmakers. It means that the United States' goal of relying solely on a GATT modeled along its current lines, which assumes that all the contracting parties are equally market driven, is mistaken. The current GATT system does not provide explicity for interface mechanisms required

---

33 Interview with Foreign Ministry official, November 1991.

34 This is the path that the European Community has chosen with respect to reconciling the differences among its Member State economies. But that harmonization is driven by political and economic imperatives that are absent in U.S. - Japan relations.

for the coexistence of economic systems as different as Japan and the United States, and those which do exist -- antidumping and countervailing duties -- are misguidedly being weakened in the name of fostering harmony and free trade. Thus, while efforts should continue to be pursued toward convergence, it has to be recognized that the actual point of convergence is indefinitely distant, and may even be theoretical. If this conclusion is freighted with value judgements, it is easy for most non-Japanese to find Japan more at fault than her competitors. But the fact is that United States' policies -- disregarding the needs of its productive enterprises and excessively oriented toward current consumption -- are also very much major causes of the uneasy disequilibria that characterize Japan's international trading relations.

One key to a less troubled economic coexistence will be to accelerate a pragmatic examination of the strengths and weaknesses of the U.S. and Japanese economies in the promotion of high technology industries against a background of increasing demands of these industries for huge amounts of capital, increasing short product life-cycles, and the need for interfirm, and government/industry cooperation. The ideal competitive model lies somewhere between those employed in these two countries. There are strengths and drawbacks to either. The likely conclusion is that a combination of policies is needed which will bring the two countries along converging paths, but tempered by a recognition that the period of mutual transition may be indefinite. Therefore, intensive, conscious management of the relationship (not synonymous necessarily with management of trade and investment) will be needed. Current U.S. and Japanese efforts in the Uruguay Round do not take this need into account, and in some ways may -- in the name of systemic improvement -- actually result in a lessening of the tools available for maintaining amicable relationships not only between Japan and her trading partners, but between and among all major trading states.

A New Europe, a New Germany

The European Community is currently not only in the process of forming a Single Market among its members, but of integrating a vast ring of peripheral states more closely into its institutions and economy. The European Free Trade Association (EFTA), once a sort of counterpoise to the EC, has opted to associate itself more closely with the Community through formation of the European Economic Area (EEA), and appears destined to be absorbed into the European Community through the accession of most or all of its members in the 1990s. Another rival economic bloc, the Soviet-sponsored Council for Mutual Economic Assistance (CMEA or COMECON) has disintegrated along with the communist regimes of Easter Europe, and the Community is entering into comprehensive association agreements with the countries which are likely to lead to the accession of at least three of them (Hungary, Poland, Czechoslovakia) around or shortly after the turn of the century. Finally, the Community is actively pursuing negotiations with the nations of the Mediterranean littoral designed to draw them into closer economic relation with the Community, albeit stopping short of full membership. These events have been accompanied by German reunification and the trend toward the establishment of a de facto German economic sphere of influence throughout Eastern Europe and what was once the western Soviet Union. While U.S. and other European enterprises are active in this region, German capital, management expertise and technology predominate. Both of these developments -- the imminent expansion of the EC and the prospect of a vast German-dominated economic zone in the East -- have prompted a good deal of anxiety, the former primarily outside of the Community, the latter mainly within it.

The United States has taken a position that is generally supportive of EC expansion, but the formation of an economic colossus which may stretch from Ireland to the Urals alarms many policymakers in the Far East, and the events of the late 1980s and early 1990s suggest that their concerns are not altogether irrational. The basic worry is that the protective net of trade and investment policy measures which currently surrounds the Community will be cast around a much larger region, limiting non-European firms in existing and prospective markets. It is a basic tenet of the Community's public position that such fears are groundless, even silly. But the Single Market Initiative itself has been accompanied by Commission deliberations over a sweeping range of Community economic rules which affect trade, but which have been characterized by the Commission to the U.S., Japan and other external trading powers as "internal EC matters." Under such circumstances, while the Commission has certainly taken into account the views expressed by the U.S. and others as the directives implementing the Single Market were formulated, it has not regarded itself as under any obligation to do so. As the Community expands to 20 or even 30 members, countries representing a substantial proportion of the world economy will, in effect, be removed from a position of dealing directly with other third countries on trade-related issues; many of those issues will become "internal EC matters."

A key question for both the EC and its trading partners as the Community expands is the role Germany will play in the greater EC. German commitment to open markets, government non-intervention and laissez-faire principles has never been as completely unqualified as its government and industry spokesmen sometimes suggest, but is nevertheless, to a considerable degree, both genuine and deeply rooted. Outside of agriculture Germany has been one of the most forceful advocates of economic liberalism within the EC, although its influence has been partially offset by the southward expansion of the Community in the 1980s; Spain, Portugal and Greece are much more likely to embrace protectionist initiatives, and their accession may have served to strengthen the *dirigiste* elements within the Community. Arguably, the EFTA countries -- wealthy and oriented, to a degree, toward liberal economic policies -- will serve to tilt the balance back in Germany's direction; in addition, further in the future, Poland, Hungary and Czechoslovakia may follow Germany's lead should they become full members. It is conceivable that a growing German influence within the EC would ensure that the Community opens outwardly as well as inwardly.

Several factors, however, limit Germany's role as a force for liberalism within the Community. First, an increasing amount of Germany's attention is turning inward, absorbed with the enormous tangle of economic and social problems associated with reunification; it is in no position, at the time of this writing, to undertake crusades. Second, while German economic liberalism is genuine, it does not always prevail at the policy level, reflecting the fact that Germany is part of a supranational economic bloc where protectionist impulses are often given effect. The Germans very often protest market protection measures initiated by the French and Italians, but do not necessarily have their way in every case, nor are such failures necessarily detrimental to German industry -- "sometimes it's nice to lose," as one German industry association executive put it.[35] Finally, the rise of Japanese economic and technological power has given rise to a movement in German political and industrial circles, not yet in a position to decisively shape national policy, which advocates a more direct role for government in mobilizing a national response to the Far Eastern challenge.

New Trading Powers: Korea, Taiwan, Brazil

Three of the six major foreign trading entities examined in this book were only marginal players in the world trading system as recently as 1970. Brazil, perennially characterized as a "sleeping giant," underwent an extraordinary industrial expansion in the 1970s, and having accumulated a huge foreign debt in the process, attempted to export its way back to solvency in the 1980s. While these changes have embroiled Brazil in an extensive array of trade disputes with virtually all major industrialized

---

35 Interview, 1990.

western nations, there is no question that Brazil has managed to shoulder its way into the ranks of the major trading states. Similarly, twenty years ago, Korea and Taiwan were little more than assembly platforms for U.S. multinationals, whose primary advantages were cheap labor and a congenial regulatory climate. Today, after twenty years of phenomenal industrial expansion and export growth, these countries have their own multinationals and offshore assembly platforms (in Southeast Asia and Latin America) and are mounting a significant competitive challenge to Japan and the United States in the advanced technologies.

These accomplishments, particularly those of the Far Eastern states, simply defy superlatives, and pose interesting questions as to how and why some countries succeed while others fail at the task of industrialization. Yet at the beginning of the 1990s, all three of these countries are confronting the fact that as their economies mature, they can no longer pursue the neomercantilist developmental strategies which proved so successful through the mid-1980s, featuring import protection, export subsidies, and extensive government involvement in the allocation of capital, technology, and other resources. In Brazil, reflecting growing concerns over the high rate of inflation, consumer unrest, and declining competitiveness of an industrial base with limited access to imported parts, equipment and technology, the Collor regime has undertaken an effort to open the economy to the world. In Korea, the government has moved to internationalize the economy as part of an effort to shift from a perceived overemphasis on textiles and heavy industry toward a more sophisticated, technology-intensive industrial profile. Taiwan, confronting a critical labor shortage, an environmental crisis, and eroding competitiveness, is dismantling most of its trade barriers and encouraging inefficient domestic industries to move offshore, rationalize and/or restructure as the economy is reoriented toward high technology manufacturing, design and sophisticated services.

The internationalization policies being pursued by these newly industrializing trading powers are sufficiently dramatic that they tend to obscure the fact that these countries have by no means abandoned the pursuit of national commercial advantage, but simply discarded some old tools in favor of more sophisticated and effective new ones. The Korean government has privatized much of the banking system and eliminated import licensing requirements and quotas, but Korean bureaucrats continue to utilize administrative guidance to discourage Korean trading companies from expanding imports of consumer goods, to encourage Korean firms to favor domestic components and production equipment, and to nudge banks into directing capital toward the government's industrial development priorities. Taiwan's government institutions are employing a number of sophisticated, innovative policy mechanisms to facilitate the overseas expansion of domestic industries, which include establishment of industrial parks and distribution infrastructure in Europe and throughout (or elsewhere in) Southeast Asia, the deployment of foreign exchange reserves overseas to facilitate local investment by subsidiaries of Taiwanese firms, the governmental creation and spinoff of new high technology firms, and the use of government funds to acquire equity positions in foreign technology-intensive firms. In Brazil, where the Collor government is still struggling, with some difficulty, to dismantle the old industrial policy regime based on high levels of protection and export subsidies, the shape of the new policy tools remains unclear; initially, the government's approach appears to be a more judicious, carefully targeted application of protectionist and export-stimulating measures formerly employed in a sweeping fashion.

If the 1990s are witnessing the crumbling of the Soviet bloc, they are also seeing increasingly deep fissures in the "Third World," which, in the area of trade policy, has traditionally adopted an ideological, confrontational posture toward the advanced industrialized nations comparable to that of the former Soviet and Chinese blocs. Of the countries examined here, Taiwan and Korea arguably now have more in common with Europe, Japan and the United States than with most developing countries; their membership in the OECD, while not imminent, is under discussion; they are emerging as net contributors to multinational lending institutions like the Asian Development Bank; and, as their overseas activities become more extensive, Korean and Taiwanese capitalists operating in developing countries are becoming the objects of local resentment formerly reserved for western business interests. Brazil has by no means pulled itself up from poverty to the same degree, but under Collor it has broken with the ideology of the old "Third World" coalition in an attempt to forge closer ties with Europe, Japan, and the United States.

New Directions for the United States

There is so much that the United States has done well. It has created an experiment in democracy that has lasted several centuries, building, in general, a healthy homogeneity out of diversity. It has put together a market system that has delivered a higher standard of living for a longer time for a greater proportion of its people than any other country in world history. It has led much of the rest of the world to emulate its political and economic precepts to a significant degree. Under its leadership, an international trade and payments system has been put together that has brought a longer period of general worldwide peace and improvement in standards of living than any other in this century. In these circumstances, with policies apparently well-tested, and with successes so marked, it could be argued that there is no better plan to consider than to stay the course. This book advances the somewhat heretical view that U.S. trade policy is in need of wholesale review, that by another set of measures it must be judged to have failed repeatedly, and that unmodified it will not serve the United States well in future years. While the authors subscribe to many of the general verities and pieties of the laissez-faire ideology, recognizing its contribution to the post-World War II growth in world trade and enhanced income levels to which this trade gave rise, there are fresh questions to be asked and answered, and policy changes adopted if the United States -- and ultimately the world trading system -- are to fare well in the next century.

The U.S. technological and commercial lead is slipping in too many areas not to suggest that American trade policy is in need of revision. Over the centuries the Chinese evolved a belief that when a certain art or skill had reached the peak of perfection -- in paintings, in decoration of porcelain, in the design of ships -- one should cease trying to develop it further. In the West, the Aristotelians were unable to surpass their master's philosophy for centuries. In the United States, ossification in relationships which to some degree determine international competitiveness has resulted from the belief that government and industry have little or nothing to contribute to each other, and that in fact this process would be actively harmful. Trade restrictions are applied by legalistic formulae, to counter dumping or subsidization, without an understanding of the breadth of the problems faced. In fact, this nominally laissez-faire approach often leads to repetitive doses of restrictions on trade, as the remedy does not effect a cure.

This book does not call for revolutionary change, but for the application in government of science, logic, and pragmatism to problems of international competition in the same way that businesses succeed by applying these tools to their own problems. For example, if it is concluded that Japanese industrial organization has conferred on Japanese producers of semiconductors a substantial commercial advantage, then a menu of measures in response should at least be discussed as a matter of national priority. If Detroit is suffering from an aging workforce with companies encumbered with pension liabilities, which Japanese "transplant" producers in the United States do not share, the public policy aspects of that unequal competition also need discussion. Indeed, the current notion that all forms of foreign investment in the U.S. economy are an unmixed blessing to be encouraged deserves to be debated. Opening up such issues carries with it an assumption that does not underlie current policies. That is that the nature of the goods and services that the economy is called upon to produce will affect the country's standard of living and capability of the nation to provide for its defense. There is in fact a national commercial interest -- a concept not to be found in any U.S. administration's policy papers within the memory of those currently living.

This book poses the question of whether current U.S. trade policy without change serves the national interest, and answers the question in the negative. To persist in the current course, which, beguilingly enough, has had much to recommend it, would in fact be folly.[36] This is not to say that the U.S. should not pursue coverage of agriculture, trade related investment restrictions, intellectual property rights and services by GATT codes. These negotiating efforts should be continued and even redoubled. But the part of the scoreboard that needs an occasional glance from the playing field is not how many agreements have been reached, new markets opened, new rules put into place, but also whether America is in a position to take equal advantage with others of the opportunities presented, and if not, to find that mix of policies which will enable it to do so. World commerce is not a game played solely out of altruism. Some degree of conflict is inherent in the system. Becoming poorer at the game, a less effective competitor, will only increase the acrimony of the international competitive process, and ultimately undermine the probability that a liberal international trading system can be maintained. America's global role in 21st Century depends on finding the proper solutions to two problems -- its failure in those internal policies which underlie international competitiveness, and its failure to find an adequate means of dealing with competition which results from industrial organization abroad which differs from our own. Some of the cure lies in changing ourselves; part lies in creating bridging policies for dealing with others who differ in ways which are not tolerable, and yet it is in our interest to continue to trade with them.

---

36 "Wooden-headedness, the source of self-deception, is a factor that plays a remarkably large role in government. It consists of assessing a situation in terms of preconceived fixed notions while ignoring or rejecting any contrary signs. It is acting according to wish while not allowing oneself to be deflected by the facts. It is epitomized in a historian's statement about Philip II of Spain, the surpassing woodenhead of all sovereigns: 'No experience of the failure of his policy could shake his belief in its essential excellence.'" Barbara Tuchman, *The March of Folly*, Ballantine Books, 1984.

THE FARM PROBLEM

A substantial portion of this study is devoted to the politics of trade in agricultural products in some of the major trading states. This does not reflect the judgment that farm trade is central to the long-run strategic economic interests of the United States or any of the other nations studied. Agriculture commands an important place on the agenda of the main international trading states primarily because domestic policies of many trading nations makes agriculture an area of continued conflict. For decades successive U.S. administrations have expended an extraordinary amount of energy and political capital in an effort to open agricultural markets to U.S. farm exports; the United States has made its assault on the EC's Common Agricultural Policy the centerpiece of its entire Uruguay Round negotiating effort. The results achieved to date are in no way commensurate with the enormity of the U.S. effort. Moreover, by electing to give such a high priority to issues such as the sale of rice to Japan, by default the United States places less emphasis on other issues which are arguably more central to the national commercial interest. While U.S. negotiators prod Japan in the Uruguay Round over rice, that country's targeting of high technology industries, for example, is not even on the agenda.

Farm trade is an emotionally-charged, highly politicized issue in all of the foreign trading entities examined in this study, with the exception of Brazil. Farmers are well organized and politically deeply entrenched, reflecting, to a degree, the relatively recent character of industrialization in East Asia and much of Western Europe.[37] This means that even minuscule concessions to the U.S. on trade carry with them an extremely high price. Japan, for example, has been maneuvered into making the prospective offer of liberalizing a small fraction (3 percent) of its rice market -- a concession which is perhaps fraught with symbolism for the Japanese but inconsequential in commercial terms -- as its main proffered concession in the Uruguay Round. Japan's industry should rejoice at this outcome. Conversely, this Japanese concession is unlikely to result to any signficant net economic benefit for the United States.

This is not to say that the liberalization of farm trade is not worth pursuing, only that the pursuit should not blind U.S. leaders to the broader national interest. All of the nations studied are already in the

---

[37] The reapportionment of voting to reflect mass migration to cities has not proceeded as quickly in countries like Japan and Taiwan as has been the case in the U.S., with the result that rural voters tend to enjoy a disproportionate say in national elections. In addition, many city dwellers were born on farms, have relatives there, and consider themselves "farmers at heart."

process of liberalizing their farm sectors in any event, for reasons related to their own perceived national interests. This process is unfolding slowly, reflecting not only the resistance of conservative elements but the recognition that gradual adjustment is preferable to the dislocations associated with revolutionary change. Pressure by the United States, including trade retaliation, the countering of export subsidies with similar measures, and the application of most of the other weapons in the U.S. policy arsenal has perhaps accelerated the process, but only slightly. A rethinking of U.S. priorities in this area is overdue.

ORGANIZING PRINCIPLES FOR WORLD TRADE

There are three relevant approaches for considering how best to construct a trading system. These are multilateral (approaching the global), regional (including, on occasion, specific bilateral arrangements), and national.

The Multilateral (Global) Trading System

There are a variety of reasons why building a global trading system makes sense. It is economically the most efficient organizing principle. Adam Smith and David Riccardo laid the theoretical basis for this approach. Those countries which have a comparative advantage in one product will find it advantageous generally to trade that product for another produced with greater comparative advantage abroad, rather than producing it themselves. Therefore, there are no greenhouses in Maine for the production of bananas. There are very few advocates (the Green Parties in Europe may be an exception) who do not subscribe to the basic principle that openness to world trade is generally beneficial.

The multilateral trading system was to serve a political purpose as well. Nations which were free from physical want would be more likely to be resistant to the political extremes of fascism and communism, and more likely to choose democracy. It was also a humane system, at least to the degree that countries which organized themselves efficiently should generally be better off for participating in it. While there would be exceptions for regional and pre-existing preferential arrangements, the multilateral trading system was designed for global integration, hedging in the exceptions with limitations, fostering widespread economic integration for all those willing to participate. There were also simple, pragmatic reasons for adopting a multilateral system. To open markets through a series parallel bilateral negotiations was at best time-consuming and at worst difficult if not bordering on the impossible. When there were multiple suppliers of the same good, and each supplier wished to be treated as a "most-favored-nation", it made sense to try to gather periodically, in large, multi-sided negotiations and try to work out tariff levels in general meetings of the all those desiring to do so. It was a logical extension to begin to use these great convocations to address other barriers to trade and other general rules of the game as tariff walls declined.

Forty five years later, the multilateral approach can be judged to have served its original postwar purposes. And with the collapse of world communism as an economic system, and the removal over time of most historic preferences, the multilateral approach is in fact becoming global -- with one important exception.

Common Markets, Free Trade Areas, and Bilateral Deals

In the early days of the GATT, there were clear memories and remaining vestiges of great colonial preferential trading systems (e.g., the Imperial Preferences associated with the British Empire). The GATT grandfathered the surviving preferential systems (which subsequently succumbed to the needs of European integration) and limited new preferential arrangements by holding (after an initial series of struggles), that preferences had to be reciprocal and sweeping in scope. In effect, but for the Generalized System of Preferences for developing countries, and a few other development-based exceptions (e.g., the Caribbean Basin Initiative), exceptions from the GATT were required to take the form of complete removal of barriers among participating states, through either a customs union (with a common external tariff) or a free trade area (in which each nation continued to maintain its own external tariff). Now, for the first time since the early post war period, the multilateral trading system is again being threatened by regional trading arrangements.

In one sense, the largest preferential exception to the multilateral trading system at its outset, although it was never viewed as being so, was the United States. It was not a legal exception, of course, because it was a single country. It was just one of the building blocks of which the multilateral trading system was to be made up of. But it was very large, comprised of constituent units some of which have more "exports and imports" than most other countries in the world, and itself accounted for most of the GATT contracting parties' GNP when the GATT was formed. Nevertheless the multilateral system worked, because the United States was in fact very open to the goods of other countries, and in time the countries developed to make the system truly multilateral rather than mainly a series of parallel bilateral trading relationships with the United States.

Now, two growing exceptions to multilateralism are being proposed. The first of these is the North American Free Trade Area (NAFTA), possibly to be followed by the creation of a Western Hemisphere Free Trade Area (WHFTA). The second is the continuing enlargement of the European Common Market, together with a European Economic Area (EEA).

The North American Free Trade Area began as a U.S.-Canada Free Trade Area, and was exactly the kind of exception to the GATT's most-favored-nation (MFN) rule that was contemplated by the drafters of the GATT. This is an example of regional economic integration that will be more trade-creating than trade-diverting (that is moving trade away from others), and makes both global and local economic sense. There are reasonable arguments why, even though the economies differ greatly, an extension of free trade area concept between Mexico and the United States makes sense from most GATT contracting parties' perspectives. There is already substantial integration of the two labor markets (legal and otherwise), as well as economic integration at the border. There are political arguments for the NAFTA as well, but these are not relevant to the GATT. The WHFTA has some lesser political arguments, but little in the way of GATT justification. The region is large and diverse. The economies have less to do with one another than does either Europe or Japan with the United States. Equal, and equally ill-founded, arguments can be made for a U.S.-ASEAN (Association of Southeast Asian Nations) or Pacific Basin free trade area as for a free trade area consisting of the nations of this hemisphere.

At a certain point, regionalism damages multilateralism, and as by their nature free trade areas must have some preferential, that is, discriminatory, aspect to them. The course of growing world-wide economic efficiency would be reversed with the re-introduction of major, trade-distorting preferential arrangements.

Of greater consequence to the multilateral trading system than the notion of a discriminatory Western Hemisphere arrangement is the creation of a single European trading bloc. For decades, the strongest single national proponent of European integration has been the United States, or at least none has been stronger. This is partially rooted in economics -- our own states do well not to have customs barriers between them, why should Europe be a checkerboard of small customs territories? But the primary American motive for backing European integration has always been political. As economic causes gave rise to forces which twice convulsed the world in war in this century, some preferential trading arrangement has appeared to be a small price to pay for political stability. This argument was also used to justify U.S. support for preferential European trading relations with Greece and Turkey three decades ago --

to solidify NATO and counter Moscow's attempts at turning the West's flank. America's political expediency in fostering these arrangements was seen later as an error when Europe carried its preferences to the countries of the Mediterranean, to Africa, and to a host of former colonies. Finally, a row with the United States called a halt to Europe's preferential arrangements (the limits were established in the Casey-Soames Agreement).

The European Single Act (or "EC 92"), in accordance with the most expansive views of its supporters, seeks political, monetary, and general economic union for the current 12 member states of the European Community. This sent a shiver down the spine of the ECs long-term trading partners, the members of the European Free Trade Area (EFTA). It set off a rush by these countries toward integration into the European Community. If it makes economic sense for there to be a United States of America, why not a United States of Europe? But this is not what is being proposed at this stage. Rather, it will be a very large group of countries not only engaging in tariff-free trade among themselves, but setting standards in common, and harmonizing other aspects of their economic regulatory systems. The trade discrimination will precede political integration, and may never be followed by it. There has been little or no debate in the United States or in the GATT as to what the consequences are for the future of the multilateral trading system of regional integration of these vast proportions. (If these developments were seen to foster, rather than delay, global integration, however, they would probably win widespread support.)

There is more to the possibilities of a European Common Market than anyone would have dreamt of just a few years ago. It is easily assumed now that some day, Poland, Czechoslovakia and Hungary might be members, and what about the Baltics, and the Ukraine, and the Russian Republic? The United States does not seem to have given much thought to what the organizing principles ought to be for the highly desirable incorporation of the former Eastern bloc countries in the world economic system. But what form should the joining of East and West take? Should it be multilateral? Or in the name of the same expediency that began with Greece and Turkey and ended in a conflict between the EC and the U.S., should it be primarily regional? The United States, caught in the confusion of its own little-thought-through scheme for the Americas, is hardly in a position to enter this debate from a high GATT moral plane.

In this confused picture, enter the Prime Minister of Malaysia, who has concluded with some logic, that if sweeping regional integration is good for Europe and for the Western Hemisphere, that the same approach must perforce make good sense for East Asia (the Pacific Basin excluding

Canada, Australia, New Zealand and the United States)[38] as well. Fortunately, at this stage, this notion has been rejected by Japan, and is clearly seen as being unwelcome by the United States, Australia and New Zealand. If the world's trading system's building blocks are to be regional, then what of the GATT as a multilateral institution? Could it not be replaced by an inter-regional secretariat and council? Would this be a better organizing principle than multilateralism? But what sense does it make that standards be harmonized, for example in the first instance between Sri Lanka and Singapore, between the United States and Paraguay, and between Poland and Spain, and government procurement and trade in services be opened on that same regional basis, before these benefits are made more widespread? Is there any logic that justifies these "local" approaches to be found in transportation costs or ease of communications, or close linkages between these sets of economies? Would these regional pacts in fact be a good precursor to grand global integration?

In fact the pursuit of regional trading blocs must be rejected. This approach risks dividing the world and limiting world trade rather than expanding it. It is inefficient. It does not make much sense. It is contrary to the visions of the architects of a very successful post World War period of reconstruction and development. It is dangerous. Its consequences deserve a much greater policy attention in the United States and abroad.

Nation-States

The third and last of the three organizing principles of trade is national. It is the oldest. There are few barriers to trade between Maine and California, perhaps other than some relatively minor phytosanitary restrictions (which should apply by growing region rather than by state in any event) and barriers to trade in services. It is likely that these latter will erode as barriers to international trade in services are removed. Questions over national treatment will be raised as to whether some higher standard must be met than equivalency with the most limiting practice of political sub-units. This is an issue which has been addressed in connection with foreign banking in the United States for years.

Difficult as the remaining questions of intramural national integration for trade purposes are (e.g., as in trade in the professions or in banking), the greatest challenge for any nation in international trade will lie in being internationally competitive, maximizing the benefits of international

---

38 It is not clear why the Indian Subcontinent should not also qualify.

trade and tempering its adverse affects.[39] Singapore and Japan have known for some time that they must do so, as in varying degrees have others. The United States is dimly becoming aware of this Darwinian fact, which is the ineluctable consequence of a generally open international trading system. In an open world economy, nations compete for capital, human talents and technology. Increasingly, many countries are likely to have stable governments interested in providing a positive environment for investment from all sources. They will increasingly have comparable physical infrastructures (or at least in a given country some of its deficiencies will be offset by some lower costs), transportation and communications barriers will cease to be a strong factor for the location of production. In a world of many strong commercial competitors -- a situation which has never before existed in an open world trading system -- most factors that can be shaped by collective action within the nation will have to be a matter of common domestic concern for both government policymakers as well as for businessmen. These include: the education system (from training in modern production skills to assuring adequate supplies of those holding advanced degrees in electrical engineering and applied physics), the physical environment (those who have special advanced skills find Taiwan unattractive as a place to raise families), the tax system (e.g., as it has effects on the cost of capital and the pursuit of research and the commercialization of new technologies), and the infrastructure for the 21st century (such as computer networks).

In a world that was cordoned off into national markets by tariffs and quotas, or one in which the main competitors were destroyed by war or not yet industrially developed, national complacency could seemingly be afforded without cost. Now each nation's attention must be riveted on two objectives -- whether the international playing field is in fact level and whether the quality of the home team (including the contribution of foreign investors) is all that it should be. If one were grading the United States on these two objectives, we would be given about a C+ in effort to the first, and would have flunked the second -- that is, being competitive, but for the fact that we started so far ahead. In the future

---

39 *Yononaka no hito ni okureo torinubeshi*
Susuman toki ni susuma zariseba.

We shall fall behind
Our fellows in the world
If, when we should advance
We make no move at all.
-- Emperor Meiji --

"The world continually moves on, and one who fails to make the effort required by each new day will remain in place and be left far behind his peers." Thirty-one syllable *waka* -- obtained by Omikuji (Poem drawing) at Meiji Jingu, Tokyo.

achieving both objectives will take more conscious effort. This book is largely about how each of several major trading nations, and the European Community, has approached the challenge of participation in an increasingly open international trading system, particularly with respect to their trade policies.

2

Japan

Alan Wm. Wolff and Thomas R. Howell

By the end of the decade of the 1980s, Japan had emerged as the central paradox of the world trading order. In virtually all major Western nations, policymakers debated what to do about the "Japan problem," and the most significant new industrial and trade policies implemented in these countries were largely if not wholly responses to the growing competitive and economic challenge emanating from Japan.[1] Yet despite the proliferation of alarmist theories about a Japanese master plan to achieve world economic dominance,[2] or of a "strategic, mercantilistic

---

[1]Major trade and industrial policy initiatives launched since 1987 that can be traced to the Japanese challenge include the formation of semiconductor research consortia in the United States (Sematech) and the EC (JESSI); the enactment of the Omnibus Trade legislation in the U.S. in 1988; and the initiation of major national high technology promotional programs by Germany, Taiwan, and South Korea. Even the European Community's Single Market Initiative can be traced, in part to mounting concern over the need to respond to the Japanese challenge.

[2]For an extreme example of this genre see Andrew J. Dougherty, *Japan: 2000* (University of Rochester, Draft, February 11, 1991); see also Marvin Wolf, *The Japanese Conspiracy* (1988); comments of Thomson President Alain Gomez in *Le Monde* (April 20, 1991).

state" pursuing dynamic comparative advantage,[3] the country whose rapid gains in technology and trade are forcing the world's leading trading nations to reexamine and restructure their own longstanding approaches to economic policy does not appear to have an explicit strategic national objective of its own, or even a set of institutions that would make direction of such an undertaking possible. Ironically, perhaps the most dynamic force for change in the Japanese body politic does not arise from any Japanese source at all but from abroad -- *gaiatsu*, "foreign pressure," demands by the major trading states that Japan temper the industrial policies, competitive practices and domestic structural arrangements that have produced such dramatic competitive success.[4]

Japan is in many ways a remarkably cohesive society, with *wa* (harmony) emphasized at virtually all levels of social interaction and throughout the postwar era, a rough consensus has existed among the nation's industrial and political leadership that industrial expansion should be a paramount national objective. At the same time, Japan's political economy is so sharply segmented that the country cannot be said to have a clearly defined national trade policy at all, only an aggregation of sectoral policies bound together, if at all, primarily by an abiding underlying nationalism. The vertical cleavages between Japan's economic sectors are intensified by the complex, myriad interlinkages between the sectors and their bureaucratic and political patrons; indeed, feudal analogies are sometimes used to characterize the powerful, autonomous groupings in which a Ministry, its client industry, and their political supporters in the Liberal Democratic Party (LDP) are bound together in alliances of mutual interest and interdependence. To a considerable degree, each of these groups develops and implements its own industrial and trade policies without regard to an overall national strategy. The horizontal institutional mechanisms that might rationalize and harmonize intergroup conflicts and inconsistencies in the interest of forming a cohesive national position are underdeveloped. *Wa* is sustained, in substantial part, simply by avoiding confrontation of intergroup structural contradictions which are potentially divisive, at least until some powerful force -- such as economic disruption or strong external pressure -- renders

---

[3]The phrase was originated by Kent Calder, who questions the validity of the mercantilistic state model in *International Pressure and Domestic Policy Response: Japanese Informatics Policy in the 1980s* (Princeton Research Monograph No. 51, 1989), p. 3.

[4]Many Japanese policy experts interviewed agreed that *gaiatsu* is the dominant element in Japanese trade policy. Interviews with Foreign Ministry officials; senior Keidanren executive; Economic Planning agency official; MITI officials.

such an approach untenable. In this milieu *gaiatsu* performs a crucial function, forcing autonomous groups to achieve a consensus, usually mediated by the leadership of the LDP, in order to avoid harm to the nation.

While the spectre of a "Japanese conspiracy" to achieve economic hegemony, orchestrated by a high command of bureaucrats and industrialists, has alarmed a number of Western observers, the reality -- a country in which enormous, frequently aggressive private aggregations of industrial power are imperfectly regulated by a fragmented array of clientelistic ministries -- poses its own set of problems for the world trading system. Implicit in Japan's reliance on *gaiatsu* to force fundamental policy changes is a larger inability of the country's leadership to set an agenda for Japan's participation in the world trading system commensurate with the country's economic size and strength, or even to control the domestic forces that increasingly spill over into the international arena. The actions of Japanese industrial groups, if not manifestations of a national strategy, are nationalistic and expansionist, and the failure to control them ultimately becomes a policy of sorts, if only by default. One official even drew an analogy to the 1930s, when the political leadership had difficulty controlling the actions of the Kwantung Army in Manchuria, and was eventually dragged into an open-ended conflict with China, the European powers and the United States.[5] Japan is the initiator in international trade not because of the vision, planning and boldness of its political leaders -- far from it -- but because of the extraordinary competitive advances of its industrial groups, nurtured by supportive government polices, which have forced other trading nations to adopt defensive strategies and increasingly, to reassess their own basic economic assumptions.

TRADE POLICY BACKGROUND

The International Political Context

Despite emerging signs of estrangement in the 1980s, the centerpiece of Japan's foreign policy remains the multifaceted relationship with the United States. While the foundation of this relationship is the 1951 security treaty, which provided the basis for stability in the Pacific basin during the Cold War, Japan has worked in close partnership with the U.S. in numerous other key areas, including the coordination of

---

[5]Interview with a Foreign Ministry Official (1990).

macroeconomic policies within the Group of Seven major industrialized nations (G-7), joint efforts to correct exchange rate misalignments, the provision of aid to developing countries, efforts to ensure political stability in the Philippines, gathering and sharing of intelligence on China and the Soviet Union, and even the financing of the U.S. budget deficit. The two countries are increasingly bound together by a massive web of investment, trade, educational, cultural and personal ties. The relationship with the U.S. has overshadowed all of Japan's other international relations to such an extent that the end of the Cold War -- the original *raison d'etre* for the security treaty -- has resulted in a considerable amount of uncertainty and anxiety among Japan's leadership over the future of the relationship and Japan's place in the world.

Despite what appears from a foreign perspective to be a position of unassailable strength, the Japanese have felt insecure about their strategic position. For decades, no visitor to Japan could escape being constantly reminded by Japanese officials that the country is a resource-poor island which must import most of its raw materials and energy, and therefore must export processed products in order to support its population and sustain its standard of living. This background, while less pronounced is not wholly absent today. Japan's vulnerability to disruption of trade is periodically driven home by events; many older Japanese recall how the United States used an economic embargo as a means of strategic coercion in the 1930s and 1940s, and the oil shocks of the 1970s and the Gulf War have served as reminders of Japan's resource vulnerability. Japan's sense of insecurity has not disappeared with the end of the era of bipolar U.S.-Soviet confrontation, which has created a fluid international political environment; with American polls showing that a majority of U.S. citizens regard Japan as a greater threat than the Soviet Union (when the latter still existed in 1989), many Japanese officials have expressed concern over a backlash from the U.S. arising out of trade problems and Japan's relative lack of support for the Gulf War effort. Some recent Japanese fears seem far-fetched -- that the fiftieth anniversary of Pearl Harbor in 1991 was to have been accompanied by a wave of anti-Japan feelings in the U.S.,[6] that U.S. consumers would boycott Japanese cars because of Japan's failure to send combat troops to the Gulf,[7] and that U.S. congressmen who voted against President Bush on the use of force in the Gulf would have sought to stir up anti-Japanese feelings to "dodge criticism" of their own dovish

---

[6]Interviews with Japanese officials.

[7]*Mainichi* (March 24, 1991).

stance[8] -- but they illustrate the extent to which anxiety over the state of the U.S. relationship colors the thinking of the Japanese leadership.[9] While bilateral U.S.-Japan strategic and trade issues have never been directly linked in negotiations, linkage in fact exists and partially explains the posture taken by the two countries on trade matters; the U.S. usually makes demands, while Japan must conciliate, delay and in many cases make grudging concessions on those trade matters which assume a profile sufficiently large to jeopardize the strategic relationship.[10]

Japan's obsession with the U.S. is itself a source of worry for an increasing number of Japanese leaders who believe Japan's real future lies in closer relations with its Asian neighbors in the last several years has been growing sharply. The volume of Japan's trade with the East Asian NICs and ASEAN and Japanese investment is rapidly transforming the economies of a number of Southeast Asian countries.[11] However, Japan has not articulated clear political or trade objectives for Asia, and frequently appears in conflict between its U.S. ties and those nearer home.[12] Despite a growing interest in and commitment to Asia, it has proven difficult for Japan to articulate a clear policy beyond vague support for regional cooperation. Japanese officials are sensitive to deeply-rooted Asian suspicions over their intentions, and have developed a cultural bias in the post-War years (for Japan, this refers to World War II) against putting forth bold proposals in the international arena that

---

[8]*Nihon Keizai Shimbun* (March 19, 1991).

[9]Characteristically, the end of fighting in the Gulf was followed by a "visit-to-U.S.-rush of influential politicians" (most prominently Prime Minister Kaifu himself) eager to shore up the relationship and ascertain U.S. strategic thinking in the post-Cold War era. *Yomiuri* (March 21, 1991).

[10]In 1991, in the wake of the Gulf War, Japan was considering opening its market for the large scale procurement of defense products, despite the fact that many segments of its domestic arms industry were not yet internationally competitive; an LDP leader commented that "we should keep U.S. arms production lines running. . .to maintain U.S.-Japan Security ties." *Nikkei Weekly* (June 22, 1991).

[11]*Nihon Keizai Shimbun* (March 12, 1991).

[12]These pulls were highlighted in the spring of 1991 when Prime Minister Kaifu was torn between his desire to meet with President Bush on security issues and his prior commitment (already canceled once) to visit ASEAN countries sensitive to Japan's disregard of their concerns. *Nihon Keizai Shimbun* (March 10, 1991).

might raise suggestions of another Greater East Asia Co-Prosperity Sphere.[13]

The Domestic Political Context

Despite the frequent turnover of Japanese prime ministers, there is an extraordinary degree of continuity in Japanese politics. The LDP -- a conservative, pro-producer party -- has retained power since the immediate postwar era, and has maintained stable, growth-oriented economic policies for over thirty years. The center and left parties have traditionally been such marginal factors in the political equation that as a practical matter Japanese politics is dominated by internecine struggles between various LDP factions rather than partisan competition. Moreover, the political leadership has been shown to have relatively limited influence over Japan's large industrial groups or the Ministerial bureaucracies allied with those groups. Thus, although the Recruit scandal raised at least the possibility that the LDP's monopoly on power might be broken in the future, officials believe that even a coalition government would not produce a radical shift in Japanese trade policies because those who took power would confront the same domestic and foreign pressures as the current leadership. On specific trade disputes affecting industrial products, most Japanese officials regard political considerations as unimportant; the Diet does not have the resources or the inclination to monitor and affect the tactical policies of the ministries.[14] An independent, critical press, which might serve as an alternative check on such groups, has not evolved.[15]

---

[13]Japan has cautiously begun to assert itself politically in the region, primarily to support initiatives designed to alleviate its greatest current worry, instability. Many Japanese officials express anxiety over unrest, particularly in China, that could "flood Japan with boat people." The Foreign Ministry has been working behind the scenes to promote a peaceful political settlement of the civil war in Cambodia, pressing the various factions and regional governments to make concessions to facilitate peace.

[14]Exceptions to this general rule are found in several "politicized" sectors, such as wood products and agriculture, where individual Diet members take a strong interest in the day-to-day progress of trade negotiations, and in sectors where LDP Zoku (policy groups) have formed to monitor trade issues.

[15]See generally Karel van Wolferen, "The Japan Problem Revisited," in *Foreign Affairs* (Fall, 1990).

Several political trends are under way in Japan which are noteworthy because they may ultimately affect Japanese positions on long term trade issues. One is the emergence and growing influence of a large group of government and business leaders who formally favor a liberal trade regime and internationalization (*kokusaika*) of Japan's economy. The internationalist group includes most of the leading officials and staff of the Ministry of International Trade and Industry (MITI), the Ministry of Foreign Affairs, the Tariff Bureau within the Ministry of Finance, the leadership of the Keidanren (association of Japanese industries), and the executives of most of Japan's world class manufacturing firms.[16] It would be misleading to characterize most of these individuals as free trade purists, blind to national interests; for many of them, their ability to embrace a liberal trade and investment policy is based, in part, on the awareness that structural factors will prevent large scale foreign economic penetration of the Japanese economy. One recent observer has drawn a distinction between the strong support which exists in Japan for "superficial internationalization" (involving import of foreign technology, exchange programs, tourism and similar activities) and "profound internationalization," which is perceived as threatening.[17] One official characterized the views of the new internationalists as driven by pragmatism rather than free trade ideology, per se; because Japanese industry has become, for the most part, highly competitive, a liberal trading regime works to Japan's advantage: "We now favor free trade, openness to investment. It serves our interests. If we had a $50 billion trade deficit, we would definitely be protectionist. Our policy in the future is unpredictable because of our pragmatism." While such views are not universal in Japan, they provide a basis for the success of liberal policies which could not have been implemented as recently as a decade ago, and which might again prove unworkable in a more uncertain economic climate.

A second change cited by Japanese officials is the "graying" of Japan, which will become more acute as the 1990s progress and could manifest itself in Japan's trade policies in a number of ways. The retirement of a generation of Japanese is expected to diminish the savings rate and

---

[16]Interviews with MITI and Foreign Ministry officials (1990).

[17]Kenneth B. Pyle, "Japan's New Internationalism: Struggling with the Burdens of History," in Yamamura, ed., *Japanese Investment in the United States* (1989) p. 285.

increase spending, which will diminish Japan's external imbalances.[18] Industry will be under growing pressure to redeploy to Southeast Asia, since the country's insularity will probably not permit it to meet growing labor shortages through immigation. Some officials believe that the leadership of the Keidanren and other influential groups is getting "too old" and implied that this is undermining their effectiveness on public-policy issues.[19] Whether or not this is accurate, a generational shift in Japanese trade leadership will occur in the 1990s. One experienced American observer of Japanese trade policy believes that the younger generation of top Japanese officials will view the United States more as a competitor than as an ally or senior partner as has been the view of Japanese bureaucrats since the War. This attitude is likely to be manifested through a posture which is less deferential to the U.S. and less willing to countenance compromises on trade issues which are seen to be contrary to Japan's interests.

The Economic Context

Japan has the second largest economy of any western nation, and is rapidly overtaking the U.S. in many indicia of economic strength, including productivity, level of technology and net capital investment. Successive LDP governments have facilitated this growth through policies of explicit promotion of key industries, control of interest rates and "rationing" of credit to designated sectors, regulation of interfirm competition, and -- particularly since the second oil shock -- government promotion of commercial research and development.[20] Several broad economic considerations currently dominate the thinking of Japanese trade officials. Perhaps most important at present is foreign direct investment by Japanese firms; the flow of direct Japanese investment into

---

[18]Interview with a MITI trade official (1990) and Foreign Ministry Official (1991). See also Wayne M. Morrisson, "Japan's Changing Population Structure: Projections and Implications," in Joint Economic Committee, U.S. Congress, *Japan's Economic Challenge* (October 1990).

[19]Interview with a mid-level MITI official, (January 1990). The official implied that the direction of Keidanren policy could probably be better understood if one studies the Japanese system of appraising and promoting of younger executives within the organization.

[20]MITI, Subcommittee on Industrial Finance Problems of the Central Division Committee, Industrial Structure Council, *Kongo No Nozomachii No Arikata Ni Kansaru Hokolu* (September 29, 1982).

foreign economies has increased phenomenally since 1986, and Japan now has the fastest growing stock of foreign assets in the world. While the Japanese government is encouraging this process as a means of diminishing trade friction, from a Japanese corporate perspective the rationale for such investments is quite sound. Japanese corporations are generally flush with capital; the high yen increases manufacturing costs in the home islands in relation to such costs abroad and makes non-yen assets relatively cheap; and numerous competitive advantages are fostered by producing close to foreign markets.

A second broad, trade-related economic consideration is the remarkable degree to which Japan's emergence as a technological innovator, particularly in basic technologies, is providing further impetus to Japanese competitiveness. Japan's economy is moving rapidly away from low-cost, high-volume production and towards high value-added innovative new products and services.[21] The content of Japan's current capital spending boom is decidedly forward looking. According to one analysis, 30 percent is being committed to the development of new products and services; 30 percent to new means of product development, design, production, and distribution;[22] and 40 percent to capacity expansion -- with half of this amount being targeted for goods and services not available 5 years ago.[23] This trend can even be seen in mature industries such as steel, which is concentrating on developing new steel materials for innovative applications as well as high technology materials such as silicon, amorphous alloys and carbon fibers.[24]

A third broad economic trend affecting Japan's thinking in trade is the rapid development of the Pacific Rim newly-industrializing economies, particularly Korea and Taiwan, which are emerging as significant rivals.

---

[21]See generally "Strategy for Technology in the Year 2000," *Nen E No Gijutsu Senryaku* (November 13, 1990) (JPRS-JST-91-035-L); MITI, *Trends and Future Tasks in Industrial Technology* (September 1988).

[22]For example, Japan's auto industry hopes to design and develop new models in half the time with half the staff for a quarter of the cost by 1993.

[23]Kenneth S. Courtis, "The Third Economic Miracle." *Business Tokyo* (November 1989) p. 47. Courtis concludes that "only 20 percent of capital investment [is] being channeled to the economy of the past. All of the rest is for building an economy that did not even exist at the beginning of the 1980s."

[24]"Aggressive R&D Plan by Nippon Steel," in *Trigger* (March 1991); *Purometeusu* (September-October 1985); *Jihyo* (April 1986); *Jidosha Gijutsu* (August 1985); *Zaikai Tembo* (December 1985).

The "boomerang effect," in which Korean and Taiwanese industries have utilized Japanese assistance to become major competitors of Japan in industries like steel and electronics has had a pronounced impact on Japanese commercial investment decisions and strategic planning, driving many firms to diversify into higher technology, higher value added product areas.[25] In many sectors, including the advanced technologies, Japanese leaders regard Korea with more apprehension than they do the U.S. or the E.C.

Finally, there remains the troublesome, unresolved issue of the country's external imbalances. Many Japanese officials believe the health of U.S.-Japanese trade relations will be heavily dependent on the direction of Japan's external trade balance, particularly the merchandise trade balance with the United States. Officials are divided, however, over the future of the imbalances themselves. Some believe that the shifting geography of Japanese production will begin to reduce the imbalances, or that the greying of the Japanese population will result in more Japanese capital remaining in Japan. Others feel that the respective savings-investment imbalances in the United States and Japan are not likely to change significantly -- therefore no reduction in the trade imbalance is likely. Although the precise implications of these perceptions for trade policy are unclear, trade statistics -- which are carefully scrutinized by MITI and other ministries -- appear to be a useful indicator of Japanese sensitivity to potential U.S. trade actions.

The Industrial Context

The so-called Structural Impediments Initiative (SII), a bilateral U.S.-Japan investigation of possible underlying causes of the trade imbalance, has thrown considerable attention on Japan's industrial structure, which has come to be regarded by many in the U.S. and Europe as itself a leading if not primary cause of "the Japan problem." The issue of "structure" has many facets, but one of the most important is the fact that much of Japan's manufacturing and services economy is organized into *keiretsu*, large industrial groups bound together by cross shareholdings of equity, interlocking directorates, commercial and financial relationships,

---

[25]The rapid development of South Korean and, to a smaller extent, Taiwanese MOS-memory semiconductors has contributed to the decision by large Japanese semiconductor manufacturers to diversify into more specialized, technology-intensive products like microprocessors and ASICs (custom-made Application Specific Integrated Circuits). See Dataquest Newsletter, "International Semiconductor Trade Issues -- Dominance, Dependence, and Future Strategies" (1989).

and *jinmyaku* (personal connections). The best known of these groups, the *kin-yu* (financial) *keiretsu*, are huge, diversified combinations each of which is grouped around a major commercial bank; a second type, the *kigyo* (enterprise) *keiretsu* consists of dozens of hundreds of specialized interlinked firms engaged in a related enterprise such as automobiles, electronics, or steel; a third type, *ryutsu* (distribution) *keiretsu* consists of wholesale and retail distributors controlled by a major manufacturer. These groups dispose of enormous financial, technological and human resources and have repeatedly demonstrated impressive staying power in international competition, absorbing hundreds of millions of dollars in losses, where necessary, in order to establish, sustain and expand a presence in strategic markets.[26] The *keiretsu* also frequently enjoy market power within Japan -- the ability to control prices and other terms of competition, to allocate market shares, and to limit or prevent entry by outsiders.

While it is beyond the scope of this paper to delineate the trade strategies of the leading *keiretsu*, a word about their broad international strategy is appropriate here. These enormous entities have become significant centers of economic power and decisionmaking in their own right, a fact which concerns some Japanese leaders as well as foreign competitors. Since the onset of *endaka* (strong yen) at the end of 1985, it is evident that most of the large *keiretsu*-affiliated firms have embraced a competitive strategy which may be termed "one-way globalization" -- that is, the internationalization of Japanese production through investment in overseas manufacturing, assembly, service and support operations. Japanese-owned offshore manufacturing facilities which ship finished products to Japan are competitive with newly-industrializing country products and reduce Japan's external imbalances but -- because of their control by the *keiretsu* -- do not disrupt private domestic market-regulating arrangements. Offshore manufacturing facilities now serve as low cost "export platforms" for sales into industrialized markets; in addition to the

---

[26]The six major financial *keiretsu* (Mitsubishi, Mitsui, Sumitomo, Fuyō, Sanwa and Dai-Ichi Kangyo) collectively account for about 18 percent of the net profits of all Japanese business, and employ about 5 percent of Japan's work force. The Mitsubishi Group is the largest industrial conglomerate in the world, and the leading *keiretsu* banks are no the largest private financial institutions on earth. Each *keiretsu* contains a major trading company which is among the leading entities of its kind in the world. *keiretsu*-affiliated firms in sectors ranging from metals to electronics to engineering are the leading companies in the world. U.S. International Trade Commission *U.S. Global Competitiveness: The U.S. Automotive Parts Industry* (USITC Pub. No. 2037, December 1987); *Wirtschaftswoche* (April 5, 1991).

cost advantage, in many cases the use of such platforms may serve as some cover for the Japanese origin of the product, making these products more acceptable abroad, and reducing bilateral trade imbalances.

The globalization strategy is "one way" in its character -- that is, foreign investment in Japanese companies is not welcome, and in fact is frequently regarded with considerable antipathy. The *keiretsu* are organized in a system of cross-shareholdings which prevents takeovers by outsiders. The infrequent forays by foreign investors (such as T. Boone Pickens) involving attempted acquisitions of a *keiretsu*-affiliate are met with intense opposition and are unlikely to succeed.[27] To be sure, foreign investors can and do establish their own manufacturing facilities and dealer networks in Japan, but the extraordinary cost of land and a wide range of structural problems -- including resistance by the *keiretsu* themselves -- limit the extent to which such inward investment is likely to "globalize" Japan's economy.

While most of Japan's export industries consist of *keiretsu*-affiliated firms, Japan's economy is actually dominated by small enterprises which lack the *keiretsus*' resources, connections, and international competitive power -- a so-called "second economy" which is labor-intensive, relatively inefficient, and encumbered by an intricate array of archaic business practices. Over three quarters of Japan's employment is accounted for by small and medium enterprises (SME); while some of these enterprises are affiliated with *keiretsu* as subcontractors or through ownership ties, the vast majority are small mom-and-pop operations lacking connection with big business. Similarly, while some SMEs are high technology enterprises or are capable of competing internationally, most SMEs are not only not competitive by world standards but could not, as presently organized, withstand a real opening up of Japan's economy to foreign competition.

Japan's antitrust policy has important trade-related effects both for *keiretsu*-affiliated firms and the "second economy." The country has no antitrust tradition predating the U.S. Occupation and in fact places considerable value on cooperation in the commercial arena. The Antimonopoly Law was enacted under the Occupation and was originally based on U.S. antitrust principles; perhaps not surprisingly, over time it

---

[27]See generally "Barriers to Foreign Direct Investment in Japan: Crossing the Regulatory and Cultural Minefield to Successful Mergers and Acquisitions," in 24 *Vanderbilt Journal of Transnational Law* 155 (1991). Pickens acquired a stake in Koito Manufacturing Company, an auto-parts maker belonging to Toyota's enterprise *keiretsu*. Despite a 26 percent equity stake in the company he was able to obtain no seats on the Company's 20-member board of directors. Toyota, with a 19 percent stake, effectively controlled the Company. *Japan Economic Journal* (July 7, 1990); *Reuters* (February 15, 1991); *Vanderbilt Journal*, pp. 160-165.

has become riddled with exceptions which permit the formation of cartels under a wide variety of circumstances. The Japan Fair Trade Commission (JFTC) does not enforce the law in a manner which could be characterized as vigorous or even adequate by U.S. standards, and its writ simply does not run in a number of sectors which are under the jurisdiction of powerful Ministries -- the electronic information industries, steel, and financial services. As one former MITI official commented with respect to financial services,

> *The Japan Fair Trade Commission (JFTC) never looks into the financial system. The banks have been the most cartel-minded. Ministry of Finance (MOF) is the most powerful agency. From the 1980s banking and MOF have become more liberal. However, a Ministry of Finance official being appointed to chair the JFTC makes the robber the chief policeman.*[28]

Weak antitrust enforcement has made possible the "privatization of protection" -- the de facto protection of the domestic market on a sector-by-sector basis by private groups through restrictive distribution arrangements, import-regulating cartels, pressure on customers and distributors, and similar measures (See below). The Japanese government has committed itself to more vigorous enforcement of the Antimonopoly Law in the Structural Impediments Initiative, and has increased the personnel and budget resources of the JFTC and undertaken a number of specific institutional reforms. The U.S. government,[29] however, has expressed concern over the "overall lack of progress. . .[t]he Government of Japan has not yet strengthened sufficiently its Antimonopoly enforcement regime so that it will effectively deter collusive anticompetitive practices that exclude foreign competition in the Japanese market. . . ."[30]

Current Import Regime

In terms of formal import restrictions, Japan arguably has the most open market of any major trading nation. Japan's trade is governed by the Foreign Exchange and Foreign Trade Control Law of 1949, which

---

[28]Interview, 1990.

[29]*Joint Report of the U.S. Japan Working Group on the Structural Impediments Initiative* (June 28, 1990).

[30]Comments of the U.S. Delegation, *First Annual Report of the U.S.-Japan Working Group on the Structural Impediments Initiative* (May 22, 1991).

originally provided the legal basis for a system of comprehensive protection, but which has been successively modified to provide for a system of "freely conducted foreign exchange, foreign trade and other external transactions." Tariffs on imports of industrial products are relatively low (simple average rate of 5.3 percent in 1989) with high tariffs applicable in only a few significant product areas (clothing, footwear, leather, and some food and agriculture products). Most agricultural products are protected by quantitative restrictions (rice, certain dairy and fish products), tariff quotas (tomato products, pineapples) or high tariffs (beef). Formal quantitative restrictions apply to only a few non-agricultural products (such as silk and coal).[31] Japan generally does not apply antidumping or countervailing duties or invoke safeguards measures.[32]

Formal trade protection measures are not widely used by Japan because, under the circumstances, they would be superfluous. Outside of a few sectors (agriculture, forest products) criticism of Japan's import regime has not been centered on formal trade restrictions but on technical standards requirements, informal government actions which limit imports and on a wide array of "structural" barriers to imports. MITI and other ministries have employed "administrative guidance" (*gyoseishido*) to limit imports in the past, although this practice appears to have declined somewhat both in frequency and effectiveness. Voluntary restraint arrangements restrict a substantial volume of imported products, primarily from developing countries, although many of these are based on industry-to-industry agreements rather than government measures.[33] Most importantly, *keiretsu* groups, formal and informal cartels, and restricted distribution systems present substantial barriers to imports and are a

---

[31]Report by the GATT Secretariat, *Japan: Trade Policy Review* (November 1990).

[32]Japan has never invoked GATT Article XIX (Safeguards). It has adopted procedures for antidumping and countervailing duty actions. It has initiated several countervailing duty and antidumping investigations, but all of these cases were terminated before duties were imposed. Report of the GATT Secretariat (1990), Nos. 147-50; GATT, *Information on Implementation and Administration of the Agreement*, ADP/1/Add. 8/ Suppl. 1, February 18, 1987.

[33]See discussion of MITI policies, below.

principal reason for Japan's relatively low level of manufactured imports.[34]

THE TRADE POLICY PROCESS

While many outsiders believe that all of Japan's trade policy functions are concentrated in the Ministry of International Trade and Industry (MITI), MITI is simply the most influential of several ministries with plenary authority over trade matters. By statute MITI controls imports and exports, formulates and coordinates the implementation of trade policies, and oversees most of the domestic industrial policies that have an impact in the trade arena; its exercise of these functions arguably make it the most powerful trade bureaucracy in any major developed or newly-industrializing state. However, the Ministry of Finance is responsible for tariffs, the budget, and trade-related policies affecting the financial services sector, and is in a position to block MITI's initiatives in with respect to tariffs and industrial promotion. The Ministry of Foreign Affairs is formally responsible for the conduct of negotiations with foreign governments. The Ministry of Agriculture, Forestry and Fisheries is responsible for trade policies affecting the industries under its jurisdiction, which include the entire agriculture sector, most wood products, and fish. Many other ministries hold authority to make trade-related policies for the industries overseen by them; thus, for example, MITI has little influence over trade-related policies affecting the construction industry, airlines, and the procurement of defense, telecommunications, medical and educational equipment.[35]

Three aspects of Japanese trade policymaking are rather singular. First, Japanese policy positions are negotiated, rather than decided by a central authority. Second, the trade policy process is highly fragmented and issue-specific. Third, foreign political pressure, or *gaiatsu*, is by far the

---

[34]See "Concluding remarks by the chairman of the [GATT] Council, Mr. Rubens Ricopero, in the Council Meeting on the Trade Policy Review of Japan" (August 1-2, 1990, in *GATT Trade Policy Review: Japan 1990.*

[35]Every Ministry involved in trade policy maintains contact with a variety of advisory councils which consist of executives from lending Japanese companies, academics, bankers, and union officials. The most significant and well known of these groups is MITI's Industrial Structure Council, which advises the Ministry on long range questions of industrial policy, but most major Japanese sectors have an advisory council working closely with the staffs of the Ministry relevant to the sector.

single greatest cause of trade-policy decisions in Japan; indeed, in most cases *gaiatsu* is the catalyst that sets Japan's trade policy process into motion.

The Process of Negotiation

As with most other matters in Japanese society, trade-policy positions are the result of a complex negotiating process rather than mere bureaucratic mediation. Although a number of interministerial consultative bodies exist which address trade matters,[36] there is usually no single locus of decision-making power on trade, nor a final authority to arbitrate internal disputes.[37] Attempts to exert cross-sectoral pressure on trade issues at the ministerial level are not only virtually unknown but regarded as inappropriate.[38] "It is axiomatic in Japanese politics that established interests should be respected to the maximum extent." [39] As a result, even if protection of a specific farm sector entails major foreign relations costs for Japan's strategic export industries, there is usually little that even MITI or the Keidanren, can do about it other than offer

---

[36]The Councillor's Office on External Affairs in the Prime Minister's Cabinet was created in 1986 to coordinate policies on specific international issues; other organizations include the Ministerial Conference for Economic Measures and the Trade Conference. These entities perform a liaison function between Ministries and the Cabinet. GATT Secretariat (1990), Point 55.

[37]". . .Japan does not have a central coordinating entity to oversee the formulation of trade policy; therefore coordination must take place through interministerial negotiations, the pace of which is determined by the slowest ministry involved." Chikara Higashi, *Trade Policy Formulation in Japan* (New York, Westport and London: Praeger, 1983) p. 58. See also George C. Lodge and Ezra F. Vogel, *Ideology and National Competitiveness* (Harvard Business School Publishers: 1987) pp. 141-172.

[38]Okimoto (1989) cites an incident in 1984 in which a Keidanren subcommittee on agriculture recommended trade liberalization in the farm sector. The Hokkaido Agricultural Cooperative asked for an apology and organized a boycott of products of several of the companies whose heads sat on the Keidanren subcommittee (Sony, Daiei and Ajinomoto). The chairman of the subcommittee resigned and, with the Sony and Daiei executives, made apologies. "Not even Keidanren, Japan's biggest and most prestigious business federation, whose membership includes virtually all blue-chip corporations, could trespass on the policy domain of a smaller, economically less central, but politically autonomous sector."

[39]Interview with a Foreign Ministry Official (1990).

sympathy to the foreign interest affected. Most studies of the Japanese trade policy process emphasize its seemingly haphazard nature. Bunroku Yoshino describes the Japanese trade policy decision-making process as complex, amorphous, with form often superseding substance:

> *Indeed, the Japanese policy-making process can be compared to the ritual of carrying a shinto portable shrine at a village festival. Many participants in this exercise seem to enjoy the sheer hoisting and pushing . . .[b]ut none knows which way the shrine is heading, for some are pushing it forward and while others are pulling it backward. After some hours, however, people will realize that the shrine has moved a few hundred yards down the main street, making all the participants happy that they have been able to join in this great event of the village festival.*[40]

In a trade policy context, "hoisting and pushing" is accomplished through strong ties and frequent contact among bureaucrats and between bureaucrats and industry leaders. On a routine basis, there is almost daily contact between ministry officials at the director and deputy-director level with the executives of the key Japanese firms.[41] Much of this contact is after business hours, and the implicit objective of such contact is to develop a consensus on questions facing the industry.[42] Discussions among ministries are carried out on a horizontal plane; directors deal with other directors, deputy directors with other deputy directors, and so on. The status of the Ministry of Finance, however, is one level higher than that of other ministries, so that a deputy director in MOF deals with the directors in other ministries. When a trade policy consensus is unobtainable at the lower bureaucratic levels, or fails to adequately address the *gaiatsu* that initially sparked the discussions, the dialogue is elevated to higher levels of the bureaucracies and the companies involved.

---

[40]Yoshino Bunroku, "Japan and the Uruguay Round" in Henry R. Nau, ed., *Domestic Trade Politics and the Uruguay Round* (Columbia University Press: 1989) p. 113. Yoshino-san was Vice Minister of the Ministry of Foreign Affairs.

[41]Interview with MITI and Finance Ministry officials (1990). MITI officials meet with manufacturing companies under their supervision, MOF officials meet with financial institutions, Ministry of Construction officials meet with construction firms, and so on.

[42]Interview with a Finance Ministry official (1990). See the discussion of MITI's informal meetings with industry officials in Daniel Okimoto, *Between MITI and the Market* (Stanford University Press: 1989).

The buck often stops at the highest levels of the LDP, with the formation of a "Joint Headquarters," embracing the government and the LDP leadership, to resolve a specific issue.[43] Once a consensus is reached, it is implicitly binding on the parties affected. As a result, while it often appears that MITI is commanding private industry to take a given action, in fact the administrative guidance is actually the embodiment of a policy agreed upon by the relevant circle of bureaucrats and industry officials.

Fragmentation

As a corollary to the role negotiation plays in Japanese trade policy development, the process by which Japan's trade policies are formulated is usually limited to the issue the trade policy is intended to address, producing a fragmentation on a number of levels. Within the government, lines of authority and responsibility on trade policy differ from issue to issue. Japan has no central negotiating authority; as noted, MITI, ostensibly the ministry with responsibility for trade matters, has final authority over only a select number of trade-policy issues, while ministries like Construction and Agriculture dominate trade policy in the sectors under their jurisdiction. While MITI and parts of MOF are generally more internationalist in outlook, it is hard to characterize even these agencies as either protectionist or liberal, since their positions often change "in accordance with the dictates of the bureaucratic struggle for survival."[44] Finally, MOF often holds effective veto power over trade-policy changes recommended by other ministries; because MOF is more

---

[43]The Maekawa Report, which set forth a blueprint for internationalizing Japan's economy, was the product of a Joint Headquarters for the Promotion of Economic Structural Adjustment in 1986. In 1989 the Joint Headquarters for Adjustment of Price Differentials between Domestic and Overseas Markets was established to address the issue of consumer price differentials between the Japanese and foreign markets. In 1985, the Action Program for Improved Market Access was generated by the Government-Ruling Parties Joint Headquarters for the Promotion of External Economic Measures. GATT Secretariat (1990), Point 56.

[44]Chalmers Johnson, "MITI, MPT, and the Telecom Wars," in Johnson, Tyson, and Zysman, eds., *Politics and Productivity: How Japan's Development Strategy Works* (Ballinger: 1989) p. 221. Michael Blaker writes, "Domestic political habits and practices bear greatly on Japanese negotiating behavior. Its fragmented, inner-directed government processes, in which participants tend to put their own interests above all others, have an onerous impact on negotiating performance, and especially on timing, flexibility, and speed." "Probe, Push, and Panic," in Robert A. Scalapino, ed., *The Foreign Policy of Modern Japan* (University of California Press: 1977) p. 69.

conservative than MITI, officials characterize the MITI-MOF relationship as one in which MITI proposes and MOF disposes.[45] "MITI has the big ideas, whereas the Ministry of Finance is very conservative." [46]

At the political level, the determinants of Japanese trade policy become even more complex. Depending on the sector and issue, political players with near-veto power over trade-policy matters can include business organizations, industry cartels individual companies, Diet and LDP factions, as well as factions within the formal bureaucracies. As a result, Japanese officials often express contradictory opinions regarding the trade policy power of a given group, which vanish once specific trade issues are identified. Such fragmentation of trade policy authority creates even greater confusion over issues that overlap (or fall in the cracks between) various groups or ministries. As Kent Calder observed:

> *. . .on broad, complex questions of global economic management, or on issues created by emerging technology or economic transformation where bureaucratic responsibilities have yet to be defined, ministerial jurisdiction is often unclear, and internal conflict over how to proceed is often strong.*[47]

Because Japan's trade policies are not determined through a predictable process, forecasts of how the government will finally act on a given trade-policy matter can only rarely be based on the opinion of a single individual or group. While different issues are decided upon by different constellations of political players, both public and private, domestic political forces can play a decisive role in determining the outcome of trade-policy negotiations between the Japanese government and foreign governments.[48] While such forces are clearly an important factor in trade-policy outcomes in every country, the role these forces play in the Japanese context is unusual; of those trade-policy negotiations between

---

[45]Interview with a former MITI Vice Minister (1990).

[46]Interview with a Finance Ministry official (1990).

[47]In telecommunications policy, for example, MITI and MPT have fought incessantly to assert jurisdiction over value-added networks, the privatization of NTT, the setting of product standards, protection of software, satellite procurement, "teletopias" and "new media communities", and telecommunications research and development. Johnson (1989) p. 221.

[48]For two case studies illustrating this complex fragmentation of decisionmaking, see Kent Calder, *Informatics Policy* (1989).

Japan and a trading partner that are deemed "successful" from the partner's point of view, the outcome is often a solution to a domestic political problem facing the Japanese government that might be only tangentially related to the trade policy problem. Identifying those areas of trade policy disputes in which domestic political forces can become serendipitously aligned with (or coincidentally opposed to) the demands of trading partners is thus a key to accurately predicting the direction of Japanese trade policies in the 1990s. During the 1970s and 1980s the Ministry of Trade and Industry (MITI) agreed to "rationalize" or manage several industries subject to trade disputes with the United States and Europe, including textiles, steel, automobiles, and semiconductors; in each case the policies adopted by the Japanese government were taken in part to ameliorate a trade-policy dispute and in part to curtail what Japanese government and industry officials considered "excessive competition" characterized by overcapacity among the domestic competitors. Several issues which are currently the subject of trade-policy disputes between Japan and her trading partners -- particularly the United States -- follow a similar pattern.

Importance of *Gaiatsu*

Most changes in Japan's trade policies over the past two decades can be traced to foreign political pressure, usually originating from the United States.[49] Although this fact is not a matter of controversy among experts on Japanese policy, it is striking to note how prominently *gaiatsu* figures in conversations with Japanese trade officials; when discussing the future course of Japanese policy, they almost always assess the policy under consideration in terms of the policy's effect on foreign pressure.[50] Japanese officials and academics agree that it is important to attempt to satisfy U.S. trade policy demands to some degree, even when the Japanese consider such demands unreasonable, in order to keep the overall U.S.-

---

[49]Former MITI Vice Minister Amaya observes that almost all Japanese liberalization initiatives have been taken in response to U.S. pressure. See Pyle, p. 283.

[50]Although the reasons behind *gaiatsu*'s importance in Japanese policy-making have well-known origins in Japanese history and have been widely examined elsewhere, it is interesting to note that Japanese officials are quick to invoke the imagery of the Meiji Period, Admiral Perry, and General MacArthur, when discussing the motivations behind even tactical changes in Japan's external trade relations. It is apparent from conversations with Japanese officials that Japan's fear of once again being isolated in the international community is deeply rooted and affects trade policy on a continuing basis.

Japan relationship healthy. The Structural Impediments Initiative (SII) between the governments of Japan and the United States is a clear example of the unusual character of Japanese trade policy. SII's themes are somewhat removed from the traditional concept of trade (competition policy, distribution relationships, *keiretsu* relationships) and some nations might regard the U.S. attempt to tell Japan how to restructure its domestic economy as an infringement on sovereignty (ameliorated, to a degree, by U.S. willingness to discuss its own "structural" problems such as the budget deficit); SII is a trade policy negotiation, however, in the sense that it is motivated solely by U.S. dissatisfaction with the current bilateral trading relationship. Japanese officials implicitly view the initiative as a political necessity to satisfy a foreign (U.S.) request for Japanese action on the trade problem; they do not invest much hope that even an outcome which is favorable from a U.S. perspective would actually effect a reduction in the trade deficit.[51]

The foreign political pressures that tend to dictate Japan's trade agenda themselves arise in reaction to three interrelated aspects of Japan's trading relationships. First, Japan's import barriers to foreign products lead to recurrent foreign calls for import liberalization. Although Japanese import tariffs or quotas are no longer a major source of trade friction over manufactured products, nontariff barriers against imports of foreign products exist throughout the Japanese economy, often supported by elements of the bureaucracy, if not by official policy. Second, the high volume of Japanese exports affecting foreign industries, often in areas in which imports into Japan are highly restricted, is a major source of concern among Japan's trading partners. The foreign backlash against Japanese exports is sometimes based solely on sheer export volume and pricing practices -- regardless of the government role -- but usually the foreign complaint also singles out Japanese government policies that provide alleged "unfair" support for such exports[52] and the so-called

---

[51]One Japanese Finance Ministry official said that the effects of SII would take five, ten, fifteen, or twenty years, and that even those aspects that are positive for Japan will not affect the trade imbalance. One top MITI official said that it is difficult to accomplish much with SII because of political opposition to its various elements. Interviews (1990).

[52]Although this study avoids subjective characterizations of what constitutes "fair" or "unfair" trading practices, the issue is not irrelevant to assessing the direction of trade relationships. For example, allegations of "unfair" trading practices often appeal to GATT definitions, and therefore a complaint by a trading partner might carry more weight in bilateral trade negotiations. For an interesting academic

(continued...)

"laser beam" nature of Japanese exports, concentrated in narrow product areas with a highly destructive impact.[53] Foreign criticism of Japanese exports practices is often linked to the import-barrier problem discussed above; in several sectors, for example, protection allegedly allows Japanese firms to enjoy price-controlling power at home, to extract economic rents, and to achieve economies of scale abroad through aggressive export pricing. Finally, Japan's overall trade surplus can be considered a policy issue separate from the sectoral problems of imports and exports.[54] Industrial policies that have directly or indirectly served to foster exports and limit imports have contributed to Japan's substantial trade surplus; the imbalances, in turn, have given impetus to trade policy reactions by Japan's trade partners.

TRADE STRATEGIES

Because of the decentralized, fragmented nature of Japanese trade policy formulation, it is somewhat misleading to describe the mix of policies undertaken by the government of Japan as a trade strategy at all. One Japanese official referred to Japanese trade policymaking as "moving from crisis to crisis" and a Japanese academic said that Japan's strategy for the 1990s was to "muddle through," an attitude which is common among Japanese officials.[55] Over the short term, Japanese trade officials often do appear to be engaged in little more than damage control, seeking to resolve specific sectoral spats as they arise. However, over the long term, Japanese officials are encouraging structural changes in the Japanese economy designed to create an environment that is less likely to create trade policy tensions with Japan's trading partners. They perceive two broad, long-term, interrelated economic trends that are working in Japan's favor in this regard; first, they believe, Japanese foreign direct investment

---

[52](...continued)
discussion of "fair" and "unfair" definitions, see Andres F. Lowenfeld, "Fair or Unfair Trade: Does It Matter?" *Cornell International Law Journal* (Summer 1980) Vol. 13, pp. 205-219.

[53]For a European analysis of this phenomenon, see EC Commission, Directorate-General Internal Market and Industrial Affairs, *Industrial Targeting Strategies, With Particular Reference to the Electronics Industry* (January 1990) (working paper).

[54]Interview with a Japanese think tank advisor (1990).

[55]Interviews with Economic Planning Agency's Foreign Ministry officials (1990).

will alter trade patterns in a manner which will diminish friction, and second, evolutionary internal structural changes will allow reform of Japan's protected sectors in a manner which will permit their phased opening to the world. A third element is the abandonment of contentious areas as sectors targeted for export performance (textiles, steel) and movement into higher value-added higher technology products. The long run trade strategy of the internationalists within Japan's bureaucracy is to encourage these developments, in some cases utilizing *gaiatsu* as a policy tool to effectuate change.[56]

Structural Reform

In the 1980s the issue of structural reform of Japan's economy underwent a transition from a vague expression of hope for the future to an agenda for action supported by significant segments of the bureaucracy, the LDP, and the business community. While *gaiatsu* was an important catalyst, an equally important factor was the belief by many Japanese that structural reform of the economy would make Japan much more competitive internationally; some U.S. businessmen have lent credence to this view by grousing that U.S. pressure on Japan results in reforms that "only makes them stronger."[57] The seminal document outlining the likely direction of structural reform is the so-called Maekawa Report, which was submitted to the Prime Minister in 1986.[58] It recommended that Japan undertake a fundamental transformation of its traditional policies for economic management: the country should move away from a development strategy based on export-led growth to domestic demand-driven growth, and it should attempt to improve market access and increase imports of manufactured goods. The Maekawa Report was not universally well received by Japan's leadership, but it has had a definite impact; elements of the Report were incorporated into a five-year plan adopted by the Cabinet in 1988 which emphasized the reduction of external imbalances through stimulation of domestic demand, establishment or continuation of financial incentives for imports, and elimination of a variety of standards and procedural barriers to

---

[56]Interviews with present and former Foreign Ministry and MITI officials (1990).

[57]USITC, *Phase II: Japan's Distribution System and Option for Improving U.S. Access* (USITC Pub. No. 2327, October 1990) p. 4-8.

[58]*Report of the Advisory Group on Economic Structural Adjustment for International Harmony* (submitted in April 1986).

imports.[59] Further restructuring, particularly in the retail sector, is taking place pursuant to the 1990 accord reached with the U.S. in the Structural Impediments Initiative.[60] In 1990, Japan implemented the "Comprehensive Import Expansion Measures," eliminating tariffs on over 1,000 items, establishing preferential financing and tax breaks for imports, encouraging private firms to boost imports.

Such "structural" reforms are open to the charge that they do little to effect true restructuring and, in some cases, are identical to similar "reforms" that were taken in response to *gaiatsu* decades ago. MITI's recent proposal to utilize the corporate tax system to encourage imports, hailed by some observers as a measure setting this market access initiative apart from prior efforts, in fact has close antecedents in a by now long-forgotten 1972 plan to "bring about effective changes in the country's external economic relations." The increased public spending on infrastructure projects undertaken pursuant to the 1990 SII accords has close parallels in MITI's 1972 proposal that the "government should make further improvement to infrastructures while seeking to restore equilibrium to international payments."[61] However, a distinction exists between formalistic gestures toward structural reform taken purely in response to *gaiatsu* and measures taken not only to foreign pressure but also benefitting domestic interests pursuing their own agendas using *gaiatsu* as a lever. Most of the significant domestic trade-related structural reforms of the past decade -- the restructuring of the telecommunications and financial services sectors and now, apparently, of beef imports and retail stores, fall in the latter category.[62] One Japanese observer,

---

[59]Interview with a former MITI Vice Minister (1990).

[60]*Joint Report of the U.S.-Japan Working Group on the Structural Impediments Initiative* (June 28, 1990).

[61]The 1972 program directed the Japan Export-Import Bank to extend subsidized import financing to the importation of manufactured goods. A reprint of the 1972 plan can be found in Takashi Shiraishi, *Japan's Trade Policies* (Atlantic Press, 1989).

[62]The retail store sector, in which large domestic retailers and some manufacturers are moving to exploit opportunities created by U.S. - initiated liberalization, is addressed below. The liberalization of beef imports has already given rise to a proliferation of discount stores for meat and barbecue products, organized by entrepreneurs who are distributing "mountains" of beef from the U.S. and Australia to restaurants, small and medium retailers, and individuals in direct competition with the domestic beef suppliers. *Nihon Keizai Shimbun* (January 14, 1991). In

(continued...)

commenting on the structural reforms undertaken in the mid and late 1980s under Prime Minister Nakasone (which included deregulation and privatization of the tobacco monopoly and telecommunications), concluded that "every step was made hand-in-hand, with or under the prodding of, the Reagan Administration."[63] But those which succeeded had important Japanese private sector backing.

Globalization

Apart from fostering domestic reform, the other "long run" aspect of Japan's trade strategy is the encouragement of overseas investment by Japanese firms, particularly in manufacturing facilities. Japanese firms manufacturing abroad can lessen the numerical imbalances by reducing foreign imports of Japanese products, by producing abroad and shipping to a third-country market, and by manufacturing Japanese goods abroad and then "reverse importing" them into Japan; such arrangements allow Japan to consume its own products while reducing the apparent trade deficit.[64] In 1989 MITI "asked" Japan's 50 largest companies to submit five-year plans for balancing their imports and exports. Japanese companies trying to boost imports are likely to achieve this objective by "reimporting" Japanese goods produced by the company or a sister company within the *keiretsu*, rather than importing foreign goods.[65] One Japanese official believes that overseas Japanese production is likely to reach the same levels as the percentage of American-owned and European-owned production that occurs outside national borders, currently 20 percent and 15 percent, respectively. According to the official, Japanese overseas production is still at four to five percent.

Japanese foreign direct investment may ameliorate some traditional aspects of trade friction while giving rise to new foreign concerns. As

---

[62](...continued)
telecommunications, the elimination of NTT's monopoly opened up opportunities for domestic firms to establish value-added networks (VANs), mobile radio systems, and other services in competition with NTT.

[63]Naoki Tanaka in *Economic Eye* (December 1987), cited in Pyle (1989) p. 282.

[64]Interviews with former MITI and Foreign Ministry officials (1990).

[65]The term "reimporting," although widely used, is somewhat of a misnomer. The imported goods are Japanese by virtue of the ownership of the company that produced them, but the goods themselves had not been imported before as the term might suggest.

noted previously, Japanese globalization is almost entirely a one-directional affair, involving Japanese investment in other countries, a fact which has subjected Japan to criticism as the volume of its investments has increased.[66] Foreign acquisitions of Japanese companies in a number of key sectors are precluded by law;[67] the *keiretsu* structure impedes foreign acquisitions; and MITI reportedly negotiates understandings with prefectural governments to prevent them from competing with each other to offer incentives to offset foreign investment.[68] One Japanese official allowed as how globalization is currently one-directional, but at some future point, a "phase 2 globalization" would see large scale foreign investment in Japan.[69] A U.S. State Department Center Paper observed in 1989 that Japan "has by far the most protectionist stance of developed capitalist countries toward foreign investment. . . . [I]t is the hands-down winner at blocking foreign investment."[70] Apart from the issue of reciprocity, establishment of local Japanese manufacturing facilities abroad -- particularly in the United States and Britain -- has generally been welcomed by citizens, localities and national governments as a source of jobs, capital, and technology, as well as offering lessons in management style and labor-management relations. On the other hand, the rush of Japanese transplants into Europe in anticipation of the Single Market Initiative, coupled with retrenchment by large European firms and the acquisition of high profile firms like ICL, has provoked a level of anti-Japanese sentiment in Europe that is more intense at present than during the decades when Japan's sales in Europe were based primarily on direct exports.[71] In addition, the propensity of Japanese transplants to source

---

[66]Japanese firms concluded 404 overseas mergers and acquisitions in 1989. In the same year there were only 15 foreign acquisitions of Japanese companies. *Vanderbilt Journal* (1991), p. 166.

[67]No foreign company may own more than 25 percent of a "technologically innovative" company. Investment is restricted by law in agriculture, fishing, forestry, space technology, aviation, oil and gas, mining, tobacco, and leather products. USTR, *Foreign Trade Barriers* (1991).

[68]U.S. State Department Center Paper, *Japanese Investment in the United States* (October, 1989); *USTR, Foreign Trade Barriers* (1991).

[69]Interview with a senior MITI official (1990).

[70]*Japanese Investment in the United States* (1989).

[71]See generally "The Battle for Europe," *Business Week* (June 3, 1991).

components from other transplants -- in effect, exporting the entire *keiretsu* structure abroad -- is coming under criticism in both the United States and in East Asia.[72]

Multilateral Trade Strategy

Japan has always occupied a rather curious position in the multilateral trading system. The GATT system works greatly to Japan's commercial advantage, but it has also served as a reminder of Japan's relative isolation in the world. Japan joined the GATT in 1955, but many of the GATT contracting parties concurrently applied GATT Article 35 to Japan, which permits a party to refuse to conduct GATT-based trade relations with another contracting party.[73] While this discriminatory treatment was gradually phased out during the following decades, many contracting parties proceeded to restrict imports from Japan pursuant to discriminatory bilateral restraint arrangements which were arguably inconsistent with the letter and spirit of the GATT.[74] These measures were justified on the grounds that Japan's own market was not truly open and that such extraordinary measures were appropriate. In a 1987 GATT meeting, Japan was subjected to attacks not only by the U.S., but by countries from all over the world for its agricultural policies, leading a Japanese social critic to lament Japan's status as an international outcast with no real friends.[75] Adding to Japan's sense of isolation, it was usually defeated or forced into a compromise to forestall defeat when another contracting party invoked GATT dispute resolution procedures against it.[76] Japan has therefore traditionally kept a low profile in the

---

[72]See generally Kozo Yamamura, ed., *Japanese Investment in the United States: Should We Be Concerned?* (Seattle: University of Washington, 1989).

[73]Ryutaro Komiya and Motoshige Itoh, "Japan's International Trade Policy, 1955-84," in Inoguchi and Okimoto, (1988) p. 178.

[74]See *Nihon Keizai Shimbun* (February 8, 1989).

[75]Yayama Taro in *Seiron* (March 1988), cited in Kenneth Pyle (1989) p. 270.

[76]Between Japan's accession to the GATT in 1955 and the end of 1990, a total of sixteen complaints were brought against Japan pursuant to GATT Article XXIII; of these, thirteen led to establishment of a panel, and of the thirteen, eight were settled prior to a panel finding. Of the five cases that resulted in panel reports, the results in four were adverse to Japan. GATT Secretariat (November 1990), Points 335-338.

GATT, pressing few initiatives and trying to avoid review of areas where domestic political imperatives -- as in agriculture -- have created indefensible policies. The U.S. has used its influence to keep Japan's practices from being subject to broad attack within the GATT.

Through the 1980s, the ministries of the Japanese government have been engaged in a strenuous internal debate over whether to invoke Japan's GATT rights to defend its export interests. In 1987, when the U.S. applied trade sanctions to certain Japanese exports in response to Japan's noncompliance with the U.S.-Japan Semiconductor Arrangement, MITI and the Foreign Ministry were each divided internally on whether to "take the United States to the GATT;" at that time, the decision was reached not to take on the U.S. in a multilateral forum. MITI officials who pressed for a GATT challenge to the U.S. sanctions were also countered by Ministry of Agriculture officials who "wanted a quiet settlement" of ongoing disputes over market access for beef and citrus fruit.[77] In 1989, however, Japan brought and successfully prosecuted a case in the GATT against the European Community for applying its antidumping rules against Japan's assembly facilities in the EC, with the result that the Community is being compelled to modify its antidumping regulations. Similarly, in the spring of 1991, Japan warned that it would take its erstwhile patron, the U.S., to GATT dispute resolution if the U.S. International Trade Commission imposed sanctions pursuant to Section 337 against Seiko Epson in a dispute over static random access memories (SRAMs).[78] It indicated it would take the EC to the GATT if it proceeded to increase antidumping duties on Japanese compact disk players where importers were found to have absorbed the original duty rather than raising their prices.[79] Japan has now also successfully defended a case in the GATT; the Canadian government recently complained that Japan utilized differing tariff levels for different species of wood products; Japan prevailed, as the GATT panel hearing the case found that this practice was within Japan's rights.

---

[77]Interview with a former MITI Vice Minister. More broadly, Japan's posture of being a vulnerable junior partner is currently undergoing significant change. For the first time, Japan recently introduced its own resolution in the United Nations in competition with a U.S. initiative. The subject was driftnet fishing, and the Japanese government decided that it was better to risk some international costs of bucking the majority view and the position of its American patron than to accept immediate and serious adverse economic consequences for its fishermen, with attendant domestic political costs. Interview with a Foreign Ministry official (1990).

[78]*Nihon Keizai Shimbun* (March 12, 1991).

[79]*Nikkei Weekly* (August 24, 1991).

These actions have required Japan to overcome not only its traditional reticence to assume a high profile in the GATT, but a cultural bias against litigation; GATT has been perceived as a sort of court, recalling the pre-Meiji period when courts were "used as a mechanism for repression against the common people."[80]

Japan's new assertiveness in using GATT mechanisms has been paralleled, to a degree, by its use of the Uruguay Round as a forum for advancing several specific trade objectives of its own. Japan was one of the original proponents of the new Round, although its primary concern was the overall invigoration of the multilateral system rather than specific changes in GATT rules. However, as the Round has unfolded, Japan has pressed for rules that would limit the use of antidumping, rules of origin, and safeguards measures as mechanisms for restricting Japanese exports, and has sought to strengthen multilateral dispute settlement procedures as a way to limit other parties from acting unilaterally, as the U.S. has done under Section 301. Nevertheless, while Japan's recent activity in the Uruguay Round represents a change from its past posture, its profile still remains comparatively low profile for an economic power of its size. In part, this reflects its vulnerability with respect to agriculture and its desire to "hide," if possible, behind European intransigence on this issue. In addition, outside of agriculture, Japan is not being asked for significant concessions; its tariffs are already relatively low, and its industrial targeting practices and structural barriers to foreign products -- criticized in the U.S. and the EC -- are not at issue in the Round. Finally, Japan is simply unaccustomed to making major sacrifices for the sake of the international system; as a MITI Vice Minister expressed it in 1986, "Japan has usually considered the international economic order a given condition and looked for ways to use it."[81]

The collapse of the Round in December 1990 and the onset of the Gulf War, however, threw into question whether a country with Japan's structure and stake in the multilateral system could sustain a posture based on merely keeping a low profile and offering no meaningful concessions in the one area where concessions were sought. When the Round adjourned in December 1990 with no agreement, second only to the EC's stance on agriculture, Japan was singled out for criticism for its unwillingness to make any significant sacrifice in order to restore momentum to the negotiations. These events, coupled with apprehension over a possible adverse reaction to Japan's low profile in the Gulf War,

---

[80]Interview with a Foreign Ministry official (1990).

[81]*Look Japan* (September 10, 1986), cited in Pyle (1989) p. 282.

forced a reassessment of GATT position on Japan's leadership; by the spring of 1991, the most influential members of the LDP were preparing a proposal for limited concessions on rice imports to be offered up in the context of a successfully-concluded [82] But this was no more than a response to *gaiatsu* -- that is, a limited strategic retreat.

Looking beyond the Uruguay Round, there is considerable interest in the U.S. and Europe private sectors in developing multilateral rules that would regulate Japanese industrial targeting and the competitive behavior of Japanese industrial groups, possibly through initial discussions in the OECD leading to an eventual agenda item in the next multilateral Round. Somewhat surprisingly, Japanese officials, who might be expected to react to such proposals defensively, are not entirely adverse to them. One influential MITI official indicated that many Japanese companies were becoming multinational in character and that "an international worldwide antitrust policy will be needed to control them in the late 1990s. . .there must be a means to control even Japanese companies when they misbehave." [83] Japanese officials also do not reject proposals for the development of multilateral disciplines on industrial and competition policies. They indicate that issues such as those being addressed in the Structural Impediments Talks could be shifted into a multilateral forum such as the OECD; this may be preferable for Japan since the exercise would probably involve hammering out multilateral rules applicable to all nations rather than the development of disciplines on Japan only.

Regional Trade Strategy

Japan, virtually alone among leading industrial nations, does not belong to any preferential regional customs union or free trade area. At the same time, Japanese investment in East Asia has now reached such proportions that some observers believe that Japan will achieve a de facto trading bloc in East Asia through the dominance of local economies by large Japanese industrial groups;[84] imports of manufactured goods from

---

[82]*Nihon Keizai Shimbun* (March 14, 1991).

[83]Interview with a MITI official, 1990.

[84]As of 1990 over 4,500 Japanese firms or joint ventures were operating in other East Asian countries, employing nearly one million workers; over 100,000 Japanese expatriates were deployed overseas to support these operations. East Asian countries not only have become highly dependant on Japanese firms for parts and components, management services, and production equipment but on Japanese (continued...)

these countries are rising dramatically, largely reflecting offshore manufacturing operations by Japanese firms.[85] The expansion of regional trading arrangements in Europe and North America has naturally raised the question whether Japan will seek to formalize its Asian ties through formation of a customs union, free trade area, or some other institution designed to promote regional economic integration.

There is little enthusiasm in Japan for formation of an Asian bloc and little expectation that one will materialize in the foreseeable future. The new organization for Asian Pacific Economic Cooperation (APEC) has provided much of the focus for discussion of this issue, but does not appear to be evolving toward much more than another regional forum for discussion. Japanese officials see it developing into a "loose, consultative" group similar to the OECD rather than an EC-style trading bloc; the fact that it includes the U.S. and Canada makes it an unlikely vehicle for a new regional bloc or any other economically significant structure. Most officials believe that APEC will be best suited for such activities as data exchange and, later, discussions over import-barrier reduction on a most-favored-nation (as opposed to regional, common-market) basis. One official believed action would take place only at meetings, e.g., there would not be a large permanent staff conducting ongoing business.[86]

A primary obstacle to East Asian economic integration is political, the numerous conflicts and systemic differences that divide the nations of the region.[87] There are numerous active, unresolved territorial disputes of the sort no longer relevant in a Western European or North American context; two East Asian nations, Korea and China, are divided between communist and capitalist regimes; and civil wars or internal insurgencies are under way in Burma, Cambodia and the Philippines. The PRC is unstable and a source of considerable worry; one Japanese official felt that

---

[84](...continued)
trading companies to organize and direct their own export efforts. "The Rising Tide: Japan in Asia," *Japan Economic Journal Special Supplement* (Winter, 1990).

[85]Interviews with Japanese ambassador to a Southeast Asian country; MITI official (1990).

[86]This would make APEC resemble a more diffuse G-7, rather than the OECD. It is clear, however, that Japan would prefer that the organization have less structure than that which is envisioned by the other non-English speaking members. Several officials noted this, but one official noted that Australia, the United States and Japan were opposed in their proposal for an APEC secretariat.

[87]Interview with a senior Japanese bank official (1990).

it would be important to include the dynamic economies of Taiwan and Hong Kong in any regional Asian grouping, but exclude the PRC for political reasons, and he noted that this would be "very difficult (a Japanese expression equivalent to "impossible")." In addition, the disparities in levels of development are much greater in East Asia than in the "northern" and "southern" Member States of the EC.[88] There is moreover, clear recognition among Japanese officials that Japan is considered to be threatening by the other Asian countries, which is likely to weaken Japan's resolve to see an APEC formed which it would dominate. A backlash is already perceptible throughout East Asia against Japanese economic expansion and its various manifestations.[89] For this reason, one official noted that it was "convenient" for Australia, but Japan, to have raised the original idea for APEC.[90]

Bilateral Trade Strategy

Japan's two key bilateral trading relationships are with the United States and the European Community. The importance of the U.S. tie will remain paramount in the 1990s; despite a flurry of recent discussions over Japan-EC ties and expanding Japanese investment in the Community, this relationship is explicitly described by many Japanese officials as secondary in importance in terms of Japanese trade policy formulation in the 1990s -- "our future cannot lie with Europe."[91] Expansion of trade relations

---

[88]Interview with former senior MITI official (1990).

[89]Common complaints include Japanese companies' failure to transfer technology to other Asian countries, exploitation of cheap labor, failure to promote Asian nationals to senior management positions within Japanese companies, environmental damage, and the failure of the *keiretsu* to draw on local sources for services, parts, and other inputs. *Japan Economic Journal* (Special Supplement, Winter, 1990).

[90]Significantly, Japan has reacted coolly to Malaysia's proposal to create an East Asia Economic Grouping (EAEG), which would exclude the U.S., Canada, Australia and New Zealand. The U.S. opposition to this proposal probably plays some role in Japan's attitude, but Japan is also worried that its participation in the bloc-like entity proposed by Malaysia would undercut its ability to call upon the EC and the U.S. to maintain the multilateral liberal trading order. Another concern is the burden of which an Asian bloc would place upon Japan to absorb an increased volume of imports from its Asian neighbors. *Asahi* (March 14, 1991): *Nihon Keizai Shimbun* (March 12, 1991).

[91]Interview with a Foreign Ministry official (1990).

with the Soviet Union is impeded by Japanese skepticism over Soviet economic prospects as well as the continuing impasse over Soviet occupation of four Japanese islands off Hokkaido; relations are unlikely to expand substantially in the next decade.[92] While the collapse of communism in Eastern Europe has opened up potential new markets in that region, Japanese business has adopted a cautious attitude toward large scale commitments in light of the difficulties involved.[93] As one Japanese analyst put it in 1991;

> *The biggest problem of all for these countries [in Eastern Europe] is that they have no economic means of carrying on trade. To put it more bluntly, they don't have any money. . . . It would be foolhardy. . .to rush our troops into the fray without planning. To borrow another military metaphor, we might as well wait for the German companies to clear the minefields, although that's a terrible way to put it.*[94]

Japan and the European Community. While Japanese officials rank the European connection well below that with the U.S. in importance, the EC's Single Market Initiative has compelled both the government and Japan's export industries to devote an increasing level of attention to European issues and strategy. Many Japanese officials see European integration as eventually producing an economic colossus that embraces not only all of what is now the Community, but also the EFTA countries, Eastern Europe, and perhaps parts of the western Soviet Union. This entity, with 600 to 700 million people, would dwarf the United States and Japan and would be in a position to dominate the world economy.[95] The Japanese regard this "greater EC" with a mixture of apprehension and opportunism; the new entity would be a formidable competitor but also the world's biggest market. Japan's principal response has been direct investment in the EC to avoid being shut outside the walls of what could become a fortress.

---

[92]Interview with a Finance Ministry official; Comments of Finance Minister Ryutaro Hashimoto in *Kyodo* (00:28 GMT, June 24, 1991).

[93]*Frankfurter Allgemeine Zeitung* (June 6, 1991) (FBIS-WEU-91-137).

[94]Takao Negishi, "From Speech Made to Import-Export Committee," in *Denshi* (September 1990) (JPRS-JST-91-031-L).

[95]"Japan has no great concrete interest in Eastern Europe." Interviews with Foreign Ministry official and a senior Japanese bank executive, 1990.

Although the leadership of both the EC and Japan have long embraced the liberal principles embodied in the GATT, a significant percentage of the total volume of EC-Japan trade has been managed through "gray" arrangements which fix quantitative limits on Japanese exports to individual Member States and, in some cases, to the EC as a whole.[96] While the gray measures limit some relatively inconsequential products (such as tuna fish) they also restrict many products that constitute the core of Japan's export sector -- autos, steel, machine tools, consumer electronics products, precision instruments.[97] The gray arrangements with the Member States are being phased out, but, in some cases, replaced with new gray measures at the Community level. In March 1988 Japan notified the GATT of 156 residual quantitative restrictions maintained by EC Member States against Japan; following a series of bilateral discussions, the Community proposed to drop 68 of its quantitative restrictions if Japan would drop its GATT challenge to the remaining quotas. Japan agreed to this provided that "further reasonable progress" was made toward eliminating these limits on trade; EC-Japan consultations on this subject are now held on an annual basis.[98] Japanese officials believe that rhetoric notwithstanding, Japan-EC relations will have a strong managed trade component for many years to come.

The relevance of residual gray restrictions, however, has declined as Japanese commercial strategy has shifted from one based on direct exports to investment within the Community; indeed, while the governments have been engaged in negotiations over border measures, hundreds of Japanese companies have been "going over the wall," acquiring European

---

[96]The Member States reached "separate deals with Japan in flagrant disregard of the Treaty of Rome. Such breaches in the common commercial policy are widespread and probably touch each Member State of the Community, but they are usually kept fairly quiet. (A very public exception is provided by Ambassador Missoffe's statement in a press interview published on 6 January 1981 to the effect that France had decided itself to deal with trade issues with Japan rather than relying on the institutions of the European community.) The consequence had been a tendency to sidestep the EC-Japan relationship -- on cars and electronics, to cite the most widely publicized examples -- by arranging industry-to-industry or State-to-State undertakings." Benedict Meynell, "Relations with Japan: The Problem and the European Community's Response," in L. Tsoukalis and M. White, eds. *Japan and Western Europe* (New York; St. Martin's Press, 1982).

[97]*Nihon Keizai Shimbun* (February 8, 1989).

[98]EC Commission, *EC-Japan Relations*, MEMO 32/89 (June 2, 1989); GATT Doc. L/6530 (July 31, 1989), Point 58.

firms and establishing manufacturing facilities inside the Community. Japanese investment has accelerated in part because of the view that the Single Market will enhance business opportunities, but primarily because of Japanese perceptions that EC 1992 -- regardless of assurances to the contrary -- will result in a net increase in the level of EC protection. As one Japanese observer commented in late 1988, "For manufacturers. . . integration represents the building of a wall around the massive EC market. Unless Japanese companies can somehow establish a full-scale presence there before the gates slam shut, they are likely to be excluded from the Community and thereby to lose one corner of the triangular global market formed by Japan, North America and Europe."[99] Because Japan's strategy is driven by investment rather than exports, the most controversial aspects of 1992 with respect to Japan relate to the evolving EC rules which affect foreign subsidiaries and joint ventures operating on EC soil. The Commission has taken measures designed to channel Japanese investment and impose some constraints on the nature of the activities undertaken by Japanese firms in the EC. The principal EC policy tools affecting Japanese inward investment are addressed in the EC chapter of this paper -- a variety of formal and informal measures to encourage local content, stricter rules of origin, and the application of antidumping duties to "screwdriver plants."

The Japanese believe that these policies are being formulated with little transparency and, in many cases, in a "legal vacuum,"[100] placing a premium on access to the political process itself and on alignments among the Member States on key issues. The Japanese have secured an important ally in Britain, which is increasingly bound to Japan through ties of mutual interest based on Japan's assistance in revamping Britain's

---

[99]Koichi Hori, "Getting Ready for EC 1992" in *Voice* (November 1988), translated in *Economic Eye* (December 1988).

[100]*Business Tokyo* (January 1989). For example, in early 1989 the EC determined that Ricoh photocopiers made at its California screwdriver plant were not "U.S." products under the EC's rules of origin, and were therefore subject to a 20 percent antidumping duty. The Treaty of Rome provides that the origin of a product is where the last "substantial transformation" occurred, but interpretation of this term has been nebulous at best. A MITI official complained of the EC that "they are just making up a rule to suit themselves." *European Report* No. 1469 (February 4, 1989). Similarly, in May 1989, the Japanese electronics industry protested an initiative under way in the EC to classify camescopes (video cameras with a video player incorporated which can also project an image on a screen) as videoplayers. This administrative change would raise the tariff on camescopes from 4.9 percent to 14 percent. *European Report* No. 1499 (May 27, 1989).

industrial base.[101] Germany and the Netherlands are also generally supportive, reflecting a combination of liberal trade philosophy, self-confidence in the face of the Japanese challenge, and a growing web of strategic alliances between major Japanese and German industrial groups.[102] Twenty-five percent of Japan's total investments in the EC are concentrated in the Netherlands, where firms such as Fujitsu, JVC, Canon and Sony have established distribution centers.[103] In addition, sensitive to the importance of European perceptions of them, the Japanese have sought to allay fears that they are "moving in and taking over;" most Japanese inward investment in the EC has involved acquisition of shares in existing enterprises or formation of joint ventures with EC partners. *Dochakuka*, adapting to local conditions or "going native" has become a watchword for Japanese companies operating in Europe.[104] Hostile takeovers have been avoided.[105] While EC officials initially pressed reluctant Japanese-owned firms to increase their local content, the Japanese quickly shifted to a practice of voluntarily moving to a high level of local sourcing. As one commented, "[R]egardless of the presence or absence of regulations, the important thing is to raise the local procurement rate. . . . [L]et us quickly abandon the mentality of trying to

---

[101]Encouragement of Japanese investment has become a principal element of British industrial policy. Conservative policies toward labor and the economy have proven to be an added incentive for Japanese firms. Nissan's controversial Bluebird plant at Sunderland was at the time Japan's largest single investment in Europe; Nissan now plans to expand the Sunderland plant's capacity more than sixfold. In 1989 Toyota announced plans to establish a $1.2 billion plant in Britain. Yamazaki, the world's leading manufacturer of machine tools, has established the most modern machine-building plant of its type in Britain with "generous assistance from the British government." *Nihon Keizai* (February 8, 1989); *L'Usine Nouvelle* (October 8, 1987); *Sankei Shimbun* (February 3, 1989).

[102]Nissho Iwai has joined Metall Gesellschaft to cooperate in nonferrous metals, steel, machinery, chemicals and finance, and to jointly pursue markets in Eastern Europe; and in 1991 Toyota and Volkswagen announced a comprehensive arrangement for joint research and development. Mitsubishi has jointed Daimler-Benz in a wide-ranging strategic alliance involving autos, aircraft and electronics. *Nikkei Weekly* (June 29, 1991).

[103]*L'Espresso* (June 6, 1991).

[104]Yoh Kurosawa, Deputy president, Industrial Bank of Japan, in *Voice* (November 1988), translated in *Economic Eye* (December 1989).

[105]*Actualidad Economica* (November 28, 1988).

get country-of-origin recognition with as little local procurement as possible. We are not Tokaido highwaymen."[106]

The French and Italians have been the most vigorous critics of Japanese investment in the EC. While Franco-Italian resistance to Japan is influenced substantially by the automobile issue, both countries are traditionally more protectionist in outlook than other Member States; they are more reluctant to write off individual industrial sectors and see the need to compete with Japan's disciplined work ethic as a threat to their way of life. The concentration of Japanese investments in a few strategic sectors (machine tools, electronics, autos) is seen as particularly threatening.[107] The Japanese have worked hard to improve their position. In early 1989 MITI set up a group called the "Committee to Promote Investment Between Japan and France," headed by Sony's Akio Morita, to sponsor a series of bilateral Japan-France private sector conferences.[108] Direct Japanese investment in both countries is expanding, although from a relatively small base. Seiko Instruments has announced a plan to build Europe's most advanced facility for liquid crystal displays (LCDs) in Italy in a joint venture with Olivetti.[109] Mitsubishi will manufacture mobile phones in France, despite "red tape, bureaucracy and regulations," to help forestall a political backlash against Japan.[110] There is some evidence these Japanese efforts are at least partially succeeding; French officials have assured their Japanese counterparts that Japanese investment is welcome in France, and are reported to be reconsidering their basic posture.[111] Even France's "iron lady" Prime Minister, Edith Cresson, who has been blunt in her criticism of Japan, also talks about the need to encourage Japanese investment in France, although she would prefer that this investment be limited to industries which do not exist in France currently.[112]

---

[106]*Denshi* (September 1990) (JPRS-JST-91-031-L).

[107]*Far Eastern Economic Review* (May 18, 1989).

[108]*Sankei Shimbun* (February 28, 1989).

[109]*Media Duemila* (March 1990).

[110]*Business Week* (June 3, 1991).

[111]*Sankei Shimbun* (February 28, 1989).

[112]AFP (21:14 GMT, June 20, 1991).

The accession to the Community of the Mediterranean countries in the 1980s, particularly Spain, exacerbated the EC's anti-Japanese tendencies. Spain's traditional stance toward Asia has been characterized as one of "thinly disguised protectionist ardor."[113] As of early 1989 it maintained more residual quantitative restrictions on Japanese imports than any other EC Member State, limiting imports of steel, machine tools, televisions, radios, motorcycles and glass products.[114] Spain backed France and Italy in the fight to impose strict local content rules on Japanese cars made in Britain. In addition, because of its special relationship with Latin America, Spain has tended to favor a reduction of EC aid to Asian countries in favor of Latin America, and may be expected to press this position with respect to trade issues as well. However, as with France and Italy, Japanese investment in Spain is rapidly growing; Toyota, Fujitsu, Sanyo, Sony, Bridgestone and NEC have established or expanded major operations in Spain, particularly in Catalonia, and these investments are apparently inducing Spain to temper its longstanding antipathy.[115] Spain has provided incentives for such investment; *Nikkan Kogyo* observed in 1990 that "since a country like Spain does not have its own industry an observation with which some Spaniards may differ Spain is inclined to allow the Japanese business, which has already made inroads into Spain, to become an aid recipient.[116] In a 1991 visit to Japan, Spanish Prime Minister Gonzalez disavowed a protectionist agenda and not only made a strong plea for Japanese investment in Spain, but argued that his country offered greater economic advantages than Britain, the first choice of Japanese investors.[117]

Japan and the United States. The United States occupies such a central role in Japan's trade relations that most of the discussion of Japan's trade policy in this chapter relates primarily and in many cases exclusively to the U.S.-Japan relationship. Nevertheless, several specific general observations about the relationship and Japan's trade policies are

---

[113]*Far Eastern Economic Review* (January 12, 1989). Spanish attitudes could color the EC position toward Japan, particularly as Spaniards are coming to occupy important posts in the EC bureaucracy.

[114]*Nihon Keizai Shimbun* (February 8, 1989).

[115]*Actualidad Economica* (November 28, 1989).

[116]*Nikkan Kogyo* (August 22, 1990) (JPRS-JST-90-069-L).

[117]*Asahi* (May 23, 1991); *Nihon Keizai Shimbun* (May 22, 1991).

appropriate here. First, despite the importance both the U.S. and Japan place on the overall political relationship, neither government has articulated or pursued a clearly defined set of trade objectives with respect to the other apart from managing individual conflicts as they arise. Even the periodic, broad initiatives undertaken by the U.S. in which the Treasury takes a prominent role (attempts to realign the exchange rate, liberalization of financial markets, MOSS negotiations, SII) have been attempts to channel U.S. domestic political pressures rather than manifestations of a broader vision of U.S.-Japan trade relations. The very formlessness of the bilateral relationship makes it difficult to predict its course -- it is to a large degree shaped by forces external to the economic policy bureaucracies of either country, specifically commercial developments and the political pressures they foster, manifested in trade complaints filed by U.S. companies and initiatives for new trade legislation. If the domestic pressures ease, for whatever reason, the U.S. government usually drops a given item from its agenda. This pattern will continue in the 1990s, although the specific sectors which are subjects of dispute may change as Japan moves up the technology spectrum; the potential for conflict now exists even in such traditional U.S. strongholds as pharmaceuticals, aerospace, and mainframe computers. These conflicts are unlikely, however, to produce any larger rupture because the community of interests between the two countries is too strong, "[I]t is almost impossible for the United States and Japan to fight with each other. . . . We are like Siamese twins. We share the same body although we may not like each other."[118]

One of Japan's principal responses to periodic, seemingly unpredictable demands emanating from the U.S. has been simply to seek to delay decision on any given issue. This is a natural outgrowth of the lack of a broader, longer-term U.S. trade policy toward Japan; the agenda is constantly changing, and many U.S. demands, if put off for awhile, simply go away. The U.S. has no career trade bureaucracy comparable to that of MITI; most of USTR's staff and leadership turns over entirely in any given five-year period, with corresponding loss of continuity and institutional memory. Priorities and administrations change. While U.S. pressure on a sectoral issue can reach great intensity at a given point in time, the pressure -- and the government's attention -- is usually short-lived, and can be defused, where necessary, through well-timed concessions. Once an agreement is reached, there is frequently no meaningful follow-up on the U.S. side, reflecting the reassignment of personnel to other matters once a dispute is "resolved," so that in commercial terms it becomes

---

[118]Interview with a former MITI Vice Minister (1990).

evident over time that Japan has actually conceded very little. One former U.S. negotiator observed in 1990 in the wake of the SII accords that "it will take a lot of hammering away to get the Japanese to keep their commitments" and this may mean going to them "day-after-day and week-after-week."[119] In many cases, this does not occur.

When looking ahead to the coming decade, it is clear that important segments of the U.S. trade policy community perceive that there is a "Japan problem," although there is no consensus about the exact nature of the problem, much less what to do about it. In the 1980s the Reagan Administration emphasized the exchange rate as the principal mechanism for improving the bilateral imbalance; specific problem areas were addressed in the so-called MOSS (market oriented selected sector) talks and through the conclusion of sectoral arrangements in autos, semiconductors, and steel.[120] SII, the most recent comprehensive U.S. effort to address the "Japan problem" arose out of the Super 301 provisions of the U.S. trade legislation enacted in 1988, which required the President to designate priority countries and sectors for action. In order to satisfy Congressional critics of Japan, who complained that the Administration had limited itself in Japan's case to a short list of formal government barriers rather than embedded structural problems, the Administration established the SII forum as a mechanism for addressing structural aspects of the Japanese economy that were believed partially responsible for the trade deficit. In effect, SII was as much an effort to channel domestic U.S. pressure on the Administration to do something about Japan as it was to come to grips with the "Japan problem."[121] The SII talks culminated in a final report of the two governments which recommended a series of structural measures to be taken by each country to reduce the bilateral imbalance.[122] The SII Working Group will continue to meet

---

[119]USITC, *Japan's Distribution System* (1990), p. 4-3.

[120]See generally USTR's *Annual Report of the President of the United States on the Trade Agreement Program.*

[121]One former U.S. negotiator described SII as "either incredibly naive or clever depending on how you look at it. If the thought was an attempt to change Japan's system, it was naive. It if was to defuse political tension, it was brilliant." USITC, Phase II: *Japan's Distribution System and Options for Improving U.S. Access, U.S.I.T.C. Pub. No. 2327* (October 1990), p. 4-1.

[122]*Joint Report of the U.S.-Japan Working Group on the Structural Impediments Initiative* (June 28, 1990).

periodically, discuss implementation of the Report, and negotiate follow-up measures.

Japanese officials are skeptical that the SII process will resolve the bilateral tensions in trade.[123] A 1990 investigation by the U.S. International Trade Commission, which surveyed experts, businessmen and government officials, likewise concluded that SII would not produce short-term gains in exports, although it prompted some favorable comments about the negotiating process itself and the conclusion that there could be long term benefits from the agreement. U.S. negotiators did in fact succeed in striking resonant chords among Japanese consumers and some domestic business interests, which was probably a factor underlying some Japanese concessions, particularly in the retail area. Many U.S. businessmen, in particular, expressed the view that SII would simply make Japan's economy stronger by eliminating structural inefficiencies, underscoring the fact that SII is being used as a lever by advocates of systemic reform in Japan -- "the U.S. piggybacked onto the interests that were advocating change, including large retailers, big business and consumer groups."[124] The first annual report by the SII Working Group indicates that the process, to date, has not come close to resolving "the Japan Problem;" while incremental progress was noted in numerous areas, notably the revision of the *Daitenhō* (Large Retail Store Law), the U.S. government indicated that it was "disappointed with the overall lack of progress," particularly the limited change in enforcement of the Antimonopoly Law.[125] One U.S. businessman even complained that the revision of the *Daitenhō* was "the fig leaf used by SII negotiators to cover up what would otherwise be a largely worthless agreement. . . after initially billing the negotiations as addressing broad issues associated with the structure of the Japanese economy. . .the SII negotiators got desperate, so we got the Large Scale Retail Store Law."[126]

The principle outcome of the SII talks is the confirmation of the belief of the Japanese participants that there is little of a fundamental nature that can or will be done to alter the factors which underlie both the trade imbalance and individual trade disputes. For the Americans, however, SII has been something of an education in the true nature of the trade

---

[123]Interview with a senior MITI official (1990).

[124]USITC (1990) p. 4-2.

[125]*First Annual Report of the U.S.-Japan Working Group on the Structural Impediments Initiative* (May 22, 1991), Comments of the U.S. Delegation at p. 7.

[126]USITC, *Japan's Distribution System* (1990) p. 4-2.

problem (although the lesson is 90% wasted, as the U.S. officials directly involved will move back to the private sector having served a few years in government.) It is clear that continued bilateral friction in the 1990s is inevitable because the underlying contradictions in the economic relationship between the two nations have not been resolved. A significant portion of the U.S. business community has begun to call for "a comprehensive rethinking of American economic goals and objectives, especially as they relate to Japan."[127] While new, superficially sweeping initiatives in the mold of SII may be attempted, the focus of friction in the 1990s, as in prior decades, will be individual sectors. Japan's response to U.S. *gaiatsu* will likewise be implemented on a sector-by-sector basis, and can therefore most usefully be examined as in the context of the sectoral strategies addressed in the following section.

SECTORAL TRADE POLICIES

Japan's trade policy lends itself to examination on a sectoral basis more readily than that of any other major trading state. Given the absence of effective "horizontal" institutional mechanisms for balancing sectoral interests to achieve an overall national trade strategy, Japan's position on trade issues is largely the sum of the policies adopted by various autonomous sectoral power centers, each of which consists of a key ministry, the industry under its jurisdiction, and, in some cases, the relevant members of the LDP. Stanford Professor Daniel Okimoto has established a useful typology for examining Japanese sectors, dividing them into politically "tied" and "untied" categories. The politically "tied" sectors are, with a very few exceptions, not internationally competitive; their basic trade objective is continued trade protection, and their strategy -- if it can be called that -- consists mainly of maintaining the political strength within the LDP and the relevant ministries necessary to sustain a protectionist stance in the face of foreign pressure.[128] With the

[127]Letter from Jerry J. Jasinowski, President, National Association of Manufacturers, to President Bush (March 13, 1991).

[128]Okimoto divides Japan's "political" sectors into two types. In "clientelistic" (Type I) sectors, support groups in each sector (agriculture, small businesses) provide votes and political contributions to the LDP in return for subsidies, lenient treatment of tax evasion and favorable tax treatment, trade protection and other government benefits. In "pork barrel patronage" (Type II) sectors (construction, telecommunications) benefit from large scale public procurement by specific (continued...)

exception of small retail stores, the bureaucratic patron of these sectors is a ministry other than MITI. The politically "untied" sectors include virtually all of Japan's leading export industries, which have traditionally looked to MITI for guidance and support. Most of these industries have benefitted from MITI's industrial promotion policies, and in many cases, their inroads into international markets have brought them into collision with foreign commercial interests. Their trade objective is almost always continued expansion, particularly in the more technology-intensive product areas. The strategies and tactics employed by the export sectors themselves are frequently perceived by foreign industries as rapacious and predatory; much of MITI's trade policy is therefore aimed at restraining these tendencies and averting punitive foreign countermeasures. Thus, somewhat ironically, MITI's efforts in the international arena are, in significant part, directed at containing the forces that its own extraordinarily successful domestic promotional policies have helped to unleash on the world economic scene.

While most Japanese officials believe that trade friction will be ameliorated over the long run by the evolution of Japan's economy and the globalization of production, they are constantly confronted with short-run problems -- with acrimonious and potentially dangerous sectoral disputes. The mechanisms employed by the Japanese government to contain those disputes have evolved into an identifiable and predictable set of policy tools, measures which, while often characterized as Japan's "trade strategies," are more properly regarded as tactical devices designed to mitigate friction and diminish foreign pressure over the short run. The single most important policy tool -- the management of exports -- is addressed in the discussion below of MITI and the export sectors, since managed exports are almost exclusively a mechanism employed by MITI. Several other common stratagems, however, are applied not only by MITI but by other ministries, and are worth noting.

Shift Bilateral Disputes to a Multilateral Forum

In several areas where the U.S. had pressed Japan on difficult market access issues, Japanese policymakers have considered shifting the dispute into some multilateral forum, such as the Uruguay Round or GATT dispute resolution procedures. Under bilateral pressure from the U.S. on rice imports, Japan moved the dispute to the GATT, and a similar tactic

---

[128](...continued)
ministries are channeled by the industry back to the LDP in the form of political contributions. From the standpoint of trade policy the distinction between these two types of "political" sectors is not particularly significant.

was considered in the 1985-86 semiconductor dispute. This stratagem not only delays resolution of a dispute but may have the effect of blunting a U.S. thrust altogether. In a multilateral forum, Japanese trade barriers may well be considered in the context of barriers which exist in many other countries rather than *sui generis*, and U.S. "unilateralism" may be perceived by other GATT members as equally or even more problematic than the practice which is the subject of the original U.S. complaint. A few officials noted that Japan's inability to give a direct "no" to U.S. trade policy demands may in the future make it preferable to take the United States to a neutral forum whenever the Japanese government believes it is unable to make concessions, or when the government needs to point to multilateral pressure for reform -- as opposed to American pressure -- when making trade concessions. Given Japan's recent successes in the multilateral arena, its trade negotiators are likely to make greater use of multilateral mechanisms in the 1990s. However, this will be tempered by the understanding on the part of Japanese officials that Japan would be vulnerable in a multilateral review of its industrial targeting policies and its non-application of its competition laws in cases involving private anticompetitive behavior.

Privatize Protection

Until very recently, most foreign pressure on Japan to open its markets has focused on formal legal barriers to imports and investment. However, during the past twenty-five years Japan has successfully diminished this pressure by allowing or fostering the transfer of most market-protecting functions from the government to the private sector. The privatization of protection arguably confronts foreign governments with little in the way of overt Japanese government action that is inconsistent either with GATT norms or the provisions of national unfair trade remedies, which are generally directed toward governmental acts and policies.

Privatization of protection has been under way since the late 1960s, when Japan liberalized most forms of foreign investment and dismantled many of the formal import restrictions that had been established in the immediate postwar era. Concurrently, however, Japanese companies, encouraged by the government, rapidly put into place the *keiretsu*-based system of intercompany shareholdings, "keeping foreign capital out by means of stock-securing maneuvers. . . . The main reason almost no Japanese companies have been absorbed by foreign capital is that each corporate group met the capital liberalization with its own stock-defense program."[129] The liberalization of imports and investment in the Japanese computer, software and semiconductor industries in 1974-76 was accompanied by a crash MITI-directed effort to implement "liberalization countermeasures" featuring the establishment of strong interfirm links in research, production and sales by Japanese firms.[130] In many other industries facing import pressure between the late 1960s and the mid-1980s, formal import restrictions were replaced by import cartels, exercise of import restraint by large Japanese trading companies, and pressure on distributors by large domestic manufacturers. In at least some of these instances, such as textiles and gasoline, these private import-restricting arrangements are known to have been encouraged by MITI.[131]

Japan has been praised by some informed observers because it "has not resorted to the imposition of voluntary export restraints (VERs) on foreign producers to prop up its declining sectors."[132] This is not accurate; MITI has in fact negotiated a number of VERs, but has simply done so in a manner which is far less overt than that of the United States.[133] More importantly, however, this governmental function, too, has been largely privatized -- Japanese industrial groups confronting import pressure go directly to foreign industries and negotiate their own VERs, bypassing governments altogether. In 1982, for example, Nippon Steel secured a commitment from Korea's Pohang Iron and Steel Company to

---

[129]Hiroshi Okumura, "The Closed Nature of Japanese Intercorporate Relations" *Japan Echo* 9 No. 3 (1982) p. 61, cited in Okimoto, *Between MITI and the Market* (1989) p. 104.

[130]*Nihon Keizai Shimbun* (June 15, 1973), January 24, 1974); *Nihon Kogyo* (June 25, November 29, 1973) *Nikkan Kogyo* (March 20, 1974) *Asahi Shimbun* (July 22, 1975).

[131]With respect to textiles see *Yomiuri* (May 12, 1974); *Nihon Kogyo* (March 13, 1975, August 13, 1974); *Nihon Keizai Shimbun* (October 18, 1975). For a comprehensive account of MITI-sponsored privatization of protection in the gasoline market (in January 1986) see Frank K. Upham, "The Man Who Would Import: A Cautionary Tale about Bucking the System in Japan," in 17:2 *Journal of Japanese Studies* (1991), pp. 323-343.

[132]Okimoto (1989), p. 109.

[133]Thus in 1984 MITI secured a pledge from China with respect to textile sales to Japan "that they would not disorder supply and demand, not export at low prices and not sell to those buying on speculation." This pledge appears to have stabilized Chinese import volume and prices. Similar pledges were extracted from Pakistan and Korea in the early 1980s. *JTN Weekly* (March 15, 22, 1985); *JTN* (June 1983).

limit its exports to Japan (which had been "unsettling" the market) to 180,000 tons per quarter.[134] A similar agreement was reached in 1979 between Japanese steel producers and Taiwan's China Steel, under which the latter agreed to limit its exports to Japan to an agreed quantity and price.[135] By 1991 these arrangements had evolved into a stable system of voluntary restraints; a trade journal reported that

> *[I]t is common knowledge that every quarter officials from POSCO and Nippon Steel (the latter represents the Japanese majors) meet in either Tokyo or Seoul to discuss coming quarter export prices (to Japan and elsewhere) and quantities. Similar talks are held between the Japanese and [Taiwan's] China Steel. Years ago, [Brazil's] Siderbras was apparently included in this open secret agreement. . . . Although both POSCO and CSC have their own marketing policies, what they agree to is essentially a commitment to "orderly marketing" in Japan.*[136]

An association of Japanese steel importers was set up in 1984 to ensure "orderly" marketing of imported steel, and this group negotiated import quotas directly with foreign steel producers[137]. In 1986 Japanese steel producers reportedly reached an agreement with Korea's Inchon Iron and Steel with respect to the volume and price of that company's exports of structural shapes to Japan.[138] In 1983 the Japan Spinners Association conducted industry-to-industry talks with Korean producers which culminated in a Korean agreement to voluntarily restrain exports to Japan to 270 thousand bales per year for three years; as a result, Korea would "no longer export massive volumes of cotton yarn at low prices [to Japan]."[139] In a recent case involving Korean knitwear, MITI did not want to negotiate a governmental VER, so it allowed the private sector to make the arrangement under MITI's advice.[140]

---

[134] *Nihon Keizai Shimbun* (February 11, 1982)

[135] *Japan Metal Bulletin* (June 23, 1979; December 15, 1981)

[136] *Metal Bulletin Monthly* (May, 1991).

[137] *Japan Metal Bulletin* (February 16, June 26, 1984)

[138] *Metal Bulletin* (October 7, 1986)

[139] *Japan Economic Journal* (April 26, 1983)

[140] Interview with a Foreign Ministry official (1990).

While virtually all of the market-protecting functions that were exercised by MITI in the 1960s with respect to the industries under its jurisdiction have by now devolved onto private industrial groups, recent trade negotiations involving other ministries suggest that privatization of protection will remain an important Japanese trade technique in the 1990s as foreign pressure mounts against Japan's remaining legal import and investment barriers. In the negotiations over admitting U.S. firms to bid on construction contracts for the Kansai International Airport (KIA), for example, the Ministry of Construction took the position that KIA -- whose funding and staff were primarily derived from the government -- was not a governmental but a "private" entity and therefore not subject to the requirement of open bidding and tender.[141] Similarly, the Ministry of Posts and Telecommunications has taken the position in trade negotiations that the government telephone monopoly, Nippon Telephone and Telegraph (NTT), although arguably a government entity, has been "privatized" and is thus no longer subject to the bilateral U.S.-Japan agreement opening up its procurement to competitive bidding.[142]

The privatization of protection has been one of Japan's most successful trade tactics. The United States, which has been the principal source of *gaiatsu*, primarily aims its trade policy initiatives at foreign government actions which distort markets and restrict trade. Throughout the 1980s the U.S. government was losing this handle on Japan even as the bilateral trade deficit worsened; U.S. industries seeking relief from alleged Japanese market barriers were urged by the U.S. government to "find some connection with the Japanese government" or the U.S. would be unable to act. By the late 1980s the U.S. government had been largely reduced to complaining of "structural" impediments to market access; the Japanese government has won at least some sympathy outside Japan by arguing that these U.S. concerns involve private commercial and domestic issues

---

[141]Of KIA's 120 billion yen capital, 20 billion was supplied by private sources and 100 billion by the national and local governments; 7 of KIA's 151 employees were drawn from the private sector, the rest from the government; KIA's choice of directors, financing, construction decisions and annual business plans must be made by the Ministry of Transport or subject to its approval. Ellis Kraus and Isobel Coles, "Built-in Impediment: The Political Economy of the U.S.-Japan Construction Dispute," in Kozo Yamamura, ed. *Japan's Economic Structure: Should it Change?* (Society for Japanese Studies, 1990), p. 343.

[142]The government will retain at least a one-third bloc of NTT stock and must approve any changes in its budget, business plans, rates, and Board of Directors. NTT Annual Report (1989); *Nihon Denshin Denwa Kabushiki Kaisha Huan Kankei Shiryo* (101st Diet Session, April 1984).

and are an inappropriate subject for government-to-government trade negotiations.

Grant Selective, High-Profile Access

For many years MITI and other Japanese ministries have used their influence to facilitate entry by select foreign firms into the Japanese market. The beneficiaries are typically world-class competitive entities which are extremely influential in their home countries and within the circles of their own industries. Typically these firms gain business in Japan which is highly profitable and which confers considerable prestige on them worldwide for having have "cracked" the Japanese market; at the same time they frequently become advocates of "understanding" on trade issues, or at least counsel avoidance of brinkmanship over points of bilateral friction. These firms are virtually never allowed to become dominant in any Japanese product market, and their own entry into Japan is usually not paralleled by broad-based entry by other foreign firms. Thus, Bechtel has been permitted to bid on a number of high profile construction projects, but the construction market has not been opened to most U.S. and Korean firms or, for that matter, to Bechtel itself.

Selective, high profile access for influential foreign firms serves several purposes. First, it is an easy way of demonstrating that Japan's critics are wrong and that if a foreign competitor is good enough, it can succeed in Japan just like domestic firms. Thus Toyota has entered into an arrangement to distribute Volkswagens through its dealer net in Japan, "motivated mainly by political considerations" -- the need to counter European criticism of Japan's market barriers at a time when Japanese auto firms were engaged in a major expansion effort in the EC.[143] Second, it placates influential foreign firms that might otherwise agitate for a political response to Japan's closed markets. Third, by allowing the influential foreign firm into a closed Japanese market, the firm will discern benefits to itself of keeping the Japanese market closed to other competitors, and may act accordingly, or at least refuse to support new market access initiatives. Because Japanese prices are typically very high, the business which these firms gain in Japan is very profitable, and the favored firms are reluctant to jeopardize it by advocating liberalization measures which might simply open the market to their own competitors. Finally, the degree of limited success achieved even by very large and

---

[143]*Nikkei Weekly* (July 6, 1991).

prestigious foreign entrants can demonstrate to smaller potential entrants the futility associated with doing business in Japan.[144]

The stratagems described above -- shifting bilateral disputes to a multilateral arena, privatization of protection, and selective, high-profile market access -- can be observed across the broad spectrum of Japanese industrial sectors, and may even be said to be typical of the country as a whole. Other strategies, however, are more sector-specific. MITI has evolved a series of sophisticated mechanisms designed to alleviate trade friction in the export-oriented manufacturing sectors under its jurisdiction which are highly sensitive to international political realities. Most other Ministries, by contrast, are parochial and have no objective more broad than to protect the industries under their jurisdiction from foreign competitive pressure; their trade "strategies" often constitute little more than more obstruction and delay, backed by political muscle. Given these considerations, one might expect that Japan's bilateral trade disputes would be centered around the "political" sectors rather than the reverse, MITI's "export" industries, as in fact is the case. In reality, however, MITI's domestic industrial policies, applied in an industrial environment dominated by the *keiretsu*, repeatedly spill over into the international arena in ways which provoke the most intense foreign criticism and dramatic policy responses.

MITI and the Advanced Industrial Sectors

The most important Japanese industries, from an international perspective, are those under MITI's jurisdiction, which comprise virtually all of Japan's internationally competitive industries, ranging from mature sectors like textiles, steel and autos to emerging industries like the information technologies, new materials, biotechnology and factory automation. These industrial sectors are relatively free from political entanglements; big business makes huge contributions to the LDP, primarily through the Keidanren, but its expectations are not specific economic rewards (such as government contracts) but a set of government policies which provide a good environment in which business can function.[145] MITI thus enjoys considerable flexibility in developing and

---

[144]The experiences of Cargill's and IBM Japan are examples of this phenomenon. See *Wall Street Journal* February 24, 1990; *East Asia High Tech Review* (June 1991).

[145]See generally Okimoto (1989) The political contributions of big business to the LDP are substantial. The Keidanren annually sets an umbrella target for political funds from the business community and designates how much each industry

(continued...)

implementing relatively rational industrial policies, generally free of the sort of political pressures that have characterized industrial policy in countries like Britain, Spain and Italy.[146]

The industrial sectors subject to MITI's jurisdiction are generally organized within the *keiretsu* system, which has given MITI certain advantages in implementing industrial policy.[147] The *keiretsu* give MITI multiple mechanisms for influencing private sector behavior efficiently, which include huge horizontal and vertical networks within which communications are good; banks whose lending policies may be influenced by government signaling; dominant firms with leading market

---

[145](...continued)
should contribute on the basis of an elaborate, computerized allocation formula, the so-called "Hanamura List." In 1989, the LDP asked the Keidanren for donations totaling 13 billion yen. This aid is not linked to any particular political quid pro quo but reflects the recognition of the business community of the importance of the LDP's hold on power. In addition to these overt donations through the Keidanren, "secret donations to Diet members belonging to specific groups, based on the enterprises' own individual judgment, are also rampant." These so-called double-donations are reportedly most common by enterprises which also have the largest donation shares on Hanamura's List, so that these industries can be assumed to wield the greatest influence with the LDP. The donations are characterized by the Keidanren as "an insurance premium for the defending of the free economy" and "one of the pillars which have been supporting the long-lasting LDP Administration." *Tokyo Shimbun* (February 6, 1989).

[146]The LDP leadership and the Diet are usually not significant players in trade matters under MITI's jurisdiction (for example, autos, steel, semiconductors), except on the rare occasions that MITI feels compelled to seek special legislation. Labor unions and consumer groups have essentially no voice in trade policy. Accordingly, in these sectors, the principal actors determining Japanese trade policy are MITI bureaucrats and representatives of the affected industries themselves, often working through trade associations and industry-government coordinating and consultation councils. Okimoto (1989).

[147]This phenomenon is partially an evolutionary one; MITI's organizational predecessor, the Ministry of Munitions, worked closely with the zaibatsu groups to facilitate wartime production, and some of these relationships survived the war, the Occupation, and the restructuring of the industrial groups. Subsequently, however, MITI commonly turned to large *keiretsu*-affiliated firms to undertake the development of infant industries (microelectronics, computers, new materials) with the result that these industries have evolved primarily within the *keiretsu* structure. Finally, in some cases, MITI has acted to forge links between smaller independent firms and *keiretsu*-affiliated firms in order to strengthen the "industrial structure" for purposes of international competition.

shares who can forge a consensus with the rest of the industry; and a large number of horizontal industry associations in which MITI officials play an active role.[148] Working with the *keiretsu* groups, MITI can mobilize massive financial, technological and human resources toward particular objectives with a relatively minor commitment of government funds, and with a degree of formal government regulation which is very small by international standards.

However, the existence of the *keiretsu* structure has had a number of idiosyncratic effects in the trade policy arena. One manifestation of these effects is the fact that MITI, alone among the trade ministries of the leading trading nations, generally does not administer policies designed to provide legal trade protection to the industries under its jurisdiction, and instead devotes considerable effort to promoting imports. This is not because these industries do not need protection -- many of them do, particularly those facing competition from Korea -- but because, as noted above, the *keiretsu*-based firms administer their own regimes of protection which are far more effective (and less controversial) than most governmental systems. As a result, MITI is almost never called upon by beleaguered industries to expend international political capital by invoking the Escape Clause or to apply antidumping and countervailing duty measures, and is seldom placed in the awkward international posture of defending protective policy measures for certain vulnerable industries while espousing free trade as a general proposition.[149] However, while "privatized protection" has offered some obvious advantages, it appears to have become a decidedly mixed blessing. Although the various private structural barriers to foreign penetration were in many cases established with MITI's participation or at least tacit approval between the late 1960s and mid-1980s, these barriers are now in some cases an embarrassment

---

[148]See Okimoto (1989), pp. 16-19.

[149]It is true that, as noted previously, MITI has occasionally implemented covert measures through the use of informal voluntary restraint arrangements and administrative guidance, but these cases appear to have been exceptional, involving situations where the private industrial groups' protective nets have failed, resulting in an import surge and "confusion" in the domestic market. In textiles, for example, import surges in 1973-74, 1978-79, and 1984-85 produced alarm in Japanese industry circles; in each case MITI stepped in, requesting trading companies to conduct "orderly" imports, establishing import monitoring systems, and using its leverage to secure voluntary price and volume restraints by foreign firms serving the Japanese market. *Nihon Keizai Shimbun* (October 18, November 28, 1975); *JTN* (December 1978); *Japan Economic Journal* (December 19, 1978); *JTN Weekly* (March 1, 15, May 3, 1985).

(when they become the focus of international criticism) and in others a drag on Japanese industrial development (when they prevent or retard restructuring of declining sectors). Moreover, while MITI enjoys considerable influence over the private sector firms under its jurisdiction, having surrendered much of the control over the import-regulating function to private industrial groups in the past, it is now not always able to prod them into a greater degree of openness toward foreign products even when trade policy or competitive imperatives so require. Thus, somewhat paradoxically, by the 1990s MITI has evolved into one of the industrialized world's only import-promoting trade ministries, seeking ways to pressure, cajole, persuade and financially induce the *keiretsu* firms to procure more foreign products.[150]

In trade, MITI seen by some observers as being the prisoner not only of a legacy of protection but of its own past and current domestic industrial policies, which have "unintended and perverse" consequences in the international arena -- condemning MITI to a "cycle of intermediation and further industrial policy measures which produce still other distorting effects and demands for intermediation."[151] MITI's industrial promotion policies have enjoyed dramatic success in elevating the competitive power of many Japanese industries. Unfortunately for Japan, these policies, which have been the catalyst for Japanese industry actions, have had extraordinarily disruptive consequences in international markets, embroiling MITI in a seemingly endless succession of serious trade disputes. The symptoms of the problem are by now well known and documented; in sectors prioritized by MITI, an extremely rapid buildup of capacity occurs, frequently leading to excess capacity, a rapid fall in prices, and an "avalanche" of exports which may disrupt, injure or even destroy foreign producers. In foreign markets, in the aftermath of

---

[150]The Import Expansion Measures program is the latest, and perhaps most formal of MITI's efforts since the mid-1980s to boost imports. Previously, MITI's actions primarily took the form of administrative guidance. At the end of the 1980s, MITI ran an informal program to set company-by-company import targets and export restraints both to reduce sectoral tensions and improve overall trade figures. By its own description, MITI's new program, announced in January 1990, "seeks to be a mirror image of the export promotion program established in the 1960s by Japan." The government proposed to eliminate over 1,000 tariffs currently covering about $13 billion in imports; grant tax credits linked to increases in imports for individual firms; subsidize import loans totaling $1.6 billion from government-controlled lending institutions; and create government programs to educate Japanese consumers and encourage purchases of foreign products.

[151]Okimoto (1989), p.7.

"export avalanches," foreign competitors may exit the market, diversify away from products dominated by Japanese firms, or seek an accommodation with the Japanese through joint ventures or acquisition by a Japanese company. Trade litigation is common. Such episodes have occurred at intervals since the 1950s in industries ranging from textiles to motorcycles, cameras, ball bearings, flat-rolled steel, oil country goods, telecommunications equipment, television receivers, semiconductor memory devices, and high purity silicon. Export drives have occurred not only in "priority" sectors but in many "structurally depressed" industries suffering from excess capacity such as synthetic fabric, acrylic staple, wire rods, and bar steel.[152]

Japan's recurrent export drives, which have had a disruptive impact on a number of important European and U.S. industries, have given rise to much foreign criticism and underlie the various theories about "Japanese conspiracy" to dominate world markets. In fact, while there are discrete examples of collusion within some individual Japanese industrial groups to achieve aggressive export objectives,[153] Japan's periodic export drives, rather than reflections of any organized strategic plan, usually appear to be the unintended side effects of commonplace industrial policy measures applied in a singular milieu. MITI's policies are prosaic by world standards, involving the usual mix of R&D subsidies, preferential financing, antitrust relief, tax breaks and other measures comparable to those employed in many advanced and developing countries. However the existence of *keiretsu* groups produces effects that are distinctive; when MITI identifies a priority sector, usually in close consultation with *keiretsu* firms, there occurs a rush by rival groups to enter the new field and establish a strong position. Because of the so-called *wan settu* principle, under which each major *keiretsu* seeks to maintain one enterprise in each key sector, each group tends to mobilize its resources to back its own entrant, with the result that five, eight or even twelve firms may simultaneously enter the field, frenetically expanding capacity and cutting prices to expand market share. When this "excessive competition" spills

---

[152]See *Nihon Keizai Shimbun* (February 23, 1976); *Japan Metal Bulletin* (June 13, December 19, 1981, October 9, 1982); *Mainichi* (September 14, 1974); *Free China Weekly* (November 8, 1978).

[153]See Kozo Yamamura and Jan Vandenburg, "Japan's Rapid Growth Policy on Trial," in Yamamura, ed. *Policy and Law Issues of the Japanese Economy* (University of Washington, 1987); T. Howell, W. Noellert, J. Kreier and A. Wm. Wolff, *Steel and the State* (Boulder and London: Westview, 1988).

into export markets, the result is a characteristic "export avalanche."[154] The tactics employed by Japanese firms to expand their sales during such periods has brought condemnation from Japanese as well as foreign observers.[155] The culmination of episodes of "excessive competition" in the domestic market is usually formation of a cartel, with explicit or implicit support from MITI, which stabilizes market shares.[156] While such cartels are designed as a remedy for "excessive competition," they arguably feed the problem over the long run by reducing the risk of overbuilding; if all players know that a cartel will be formed at the end of the day, the risk of overinvestment is reduced and the incentive to expand is enhanced by the prospect of a larger share of a cartelized market.[157]

To be sure, not all Japanese capacity-expansion races and export drives are rooted in MITI's policies; the *keiretsu* structure is quite capable of fostering such phenomenon on its own, without any apparent prompting by the government. "Disorderly" exports of the sort that injure foreign industries generally occur in areas of the Japanese manufacturing sector that are, for whatever reason, not organized; the abrupt emergence of "excessive" competition may reflect the emergence of a new product area in an established industry where market shares and relationships have not yet been defined (such as oil country tubular goods in the 1970s and 1980s); breakdown of existing cartel arrangements under the pressure of recession (as in steel in 1970-71); entry of new competitors or other

---

[154]*Japan Economic Journal* (August 30, 1977).

[155]For European comments critical of Japanese export tactics, see *Süddeutsche Zeitung* (March 21, 1990); *Elektro-Anzeiger* (February 1983); *L'Espresso* (June 6, 1991).

[156]MITI facilitates cartel-like arrangements in a number of industries characterized by overcapacity through the publication of production "guideposts" forecasting the aggregate output for a coming period which will suffice to sustain "supply-demand balance." Japanese producers in the affected industry conform their output volume to the MITI guideposts by curtailing their output by a common percentage, decreasing available supplies and creating an environment conducive to stable prices. For examples of de facto cartels facilitated through MITI guideposts, see *Japan Metal Bulletin* (September 19, 26, 1987) (reinforcing bars); *Yomiuri Shimbun* (September 4, 1986) (polyester filament); *JTN* (November 1981) (cotton yarn); *Japan Metal Bulletin* (March 26, 1987) (crude steel); *Nihon Keizai Shimbun* (April 24,1986; March 31, October 10, 1987) (semiconductors); *Nihon Keizai Shimbun* (May 12, 1990) (pulp and paper). On the philosophy underlying these measures, see comments of Naohiro Amaya in *Bunjei Shunju* (December, 1980).

[157]Yamamura (1982).

destabilizing factors; or the emergence of entirely new industries or industrial areas such as advanced materials, biotechnology, and optical communications. The spectacular overbuilding of seamless pipe capacity by Japanese steelmakers in the late 1970s and early 1980s apparently originated not from MITI's prompting but from a race by four producers to expand production in what seemed to be a promising new field.[158] Japanese automakers have frequently disregarded MITI's guidance and mapped out their own investment strategies, sometimes provoking disputes with Japan's trading partners. Nevertheless, an indication by MITI that a particular product or sector is where Japan's future lies is frequently enough to trigger an investment stampede.

Thus, in trade, over the past two decades MITI has repeatedly been seen struggling to contain the forces to which its own industrial policies have given the initial impetus. During the massive steel export drive of 1975-76, for example, which provoked an acrimonious dispute with the United States, MITI was frantically -- and unsuccessfully -- urging Japanese steel firms to conduct "orderly" exports to avoid dumping charges.[159] MITI played a similar role in 1985-87 as it sought to curtail dumping by Japanese semiconductor producers.[160] In any event, whether or not its own policies have been the proximate cause of an export drive, it is usually in the aftermath of such episodes that MITI begins to forge a true trade policy for the affected sector. Somewhat ironically, foreign government action, in the form of trade litigation, sanctions or restrictions gives MITI greater leverage over its own industry than it previously enjoyed; its calls for "orderly" exports have more weight when the alternative is the prospect of exclusion from foreign markets. MITI generally enters into an agreement with a foreign government pledging voluntary export restraint (VER), and ensures the formation of an informal or legal export cartel to facilitate compliance; in some cases this merely entails extension of domestic cartel arrangements into the international arena.

Export restraint is also useful as a mechanism to deflect foreign pressure for access to the Japanese market, a demand which, for various reasons, MITI may find it difficult to satisfy. MITI typically takes the position in negotiations that while market access is a "very difficult"

---

[158]*Nikkei Sangyo* (September 12, 1981); *Japan Economic Journal* (March 16, 1982); *Japan Metal Bulletin* (March 15, April 24, 1979; July 12, 1980; April 2, 4, July 2, 28, August 13, November 5, 1981).

[159]*Nihon Keizai Shimbun* (November 23, 1975).

[160]*Nihon Keizai Shimbun* (April 24, 1986); *Asahi Shimbun* (March 20, 1987).

proposition, some form of export restraint can be arranged. In many cases this is enough for hard-pressed foreign producers and their governments. Even when demands for market access persist, MITI has been able to argue, not without success, that such demands do not reflect what a U.S. industry "really wants," which is protection.[161]

Japanese producers have generally been amenable to VERs, which are regarded as preferable to the alternatives -- permanent quotas, tariffs or even embargoes imposed by importing nations. VERs are generally temporary, allow Japanese firms considerable flexibility in exporting, and enable them to shift their export mix toward higher value-added products, increasing their profits. They commonly strengthen their position in a target market by acquiring firms which have been weakened by dumping or whose owners are demoralized by the prospect of further Japanese incursions.[162] In addition, VERs are uniquely easy for Japanese industries to implement; producers are frequently cartelized domestically and possess the institutional mechanisms and industrial traditions which are necessary to organize exports, like domestic sales, in an "orderly" manner. "There is a perverse irony in the relationship between the exceptionally large number of VERs imposed on Japanese industry and Japan's institutional capacity to accommodate foreign demands that VERs be practiced."[163] At present, MITI monitors a wide range of Japanese manufactured exports and frequently takes preemptive action when those exports are seen as potential sources of trade friction. One Japanese official commented that MITI should be renamed "Ministry of Managed Trade and Industry."

Japan's trade relations in the MITI-administered sectors thus in many respects mirror competition in the domestic market: in established sectors relations are relatively stable, reflecting longstanding market-regulating arrangements, but ferocious, "excessive" competition is constantly erupting at the margins. Trade friction tends to be very intense at the outset, with alarmed foreign producers and governments scrambling to prevent the

---

[161]In the 1985-86 U.S. Japan semiconductor dispute, the principal demand of the U.S. semiconductor industry was improved access to the Japanese market. During the negotiations, despite repeated protestations to the contrary, U.S. industry representatives were assured by MITI officials and representatives of the Japanese semiconductor industry that "we know that you don't really want market access, but protection in your own market."

[162]See Yamamura, "High Growth Policy on Trial" (1986)

[163]Okimoto, "Political Inclusivity: The Domestic Structure of Trade," in Takashi Inogushi and Daniel Okimoto, *The Political Economy of Japan*, Vol. II, p. 316.

total destruction of their industries; however the period of extreme friction is relatively short -- one or two years -- and is followed by many years of relatively stable trade under VER arrangements, punctuated by renewed friction only when the arrangements lapse, are disputed, or are rendered inadequate by changes in technology and markets. The bitter U.S.-Japan carbon steel trade dispute took place in 1976 and 1977; in the fourteen years since 1977 (which were characterized by voluntary export restraint by Japan), while disputes have occasionally flared over specific Japanese actions, the steel sector has not seen another major bilateral trade confrontation. At the same time, while exercising export restraint, Japanese firms have used direct investment, joint ventures and other global measures to progressively enhance their international competitive position. The same pattern is observable in autos, semiconductors and other industrial sectors whose trade relations are managed by MITI.

It is fairly clear both from discussions with Japanese officials and actions taken by the Japanese government that MITI will continue to rely on management of exports through formal and informal quotas set by MITI or through negotiations with either the foreign government or the foreign industry itself. One Japanese official stated bluntly "we must accept managed trade in the short term" with the United States and the European Community. Another official acknowledged that MITI is restraining excess capacity in a number of industries for fear that the resulting exports would increase trade tensions. Such actions have been widespread within Japan in recent years, and there is some evidence that private companies have moderated their investment plans in response to MITI.[164] In the summer of 1987, MITI announced that it would start a detailed investigation of export pricing practices of Japanese corporations, to begin in April 1988. According to press accounts, MITI officials said

---

[164]In August 1989, MITI asked 11 Japanese automakers to moderate their investment in capacity, on the grounds that a slowdown in the domestic market would trigger another export drive. Not all companies complied, but in October, Mazda announced that it would cut planned production capacity at its new plant in Hofu, Yamaguchi Prefecture, from 240,000 units to 150,000. Also in 1989, Japan's Fair Trade Commission began to investigate charges that seven or eight of Japan's major electronics companies formed a cartel to fix production and prices. The cartel was allegedly formed after MITI told VCR manufacturers to reveal their production plans. Because 70 percent of Japanese households already own VCRs, MITI was concerned that a softening domestic market would lead Japanese companies to increase exports. Sony and Funai Electric, the two companies which are not alleged to have participated in the cartel, were the only two major companies to have increased their shipments and market share during the first half of 1989. *Jiji Press Ticker Service* (August 15, 1989; *Asahi News Service* (August 4, 1989).

that they would "force exporters to adjust their pricing policies or implement export controls." MITI officials also said that they might intervene in production and investment plans if they were out of line with worldwide supply-demand conditions.[165] MITI announced this policy in reaction to a number of antidumping investigations that had been initiated by the United States (such as forklift trucks) and the European Community (semiconductors, computer printers). In 1990 three Japanese automakers reportedly modified their plans for investment in new plant after MITI asked them to limit investments to areas that would not result in increased exports.[166] A senior MITI official said that "excessive competition", low pricing, and aggressive pursuit of market share were responsible for much of the trade tension between Japan and its trading partners.[167] MITI has also sought to manage disclosure of information about Japan's technological advances; when NEC announced in 1989 that it had developed the world's fastest supercomputer, it drew

---

[165]In October 1988, MITI announced that it would draft 5-10 year projections of worldwide supply-demand conditions in nine major industries, including automobiles, electronics equipment and industrial machinery. MITI said that the projections (to be released in the spring of 1989) would be used to avert trade friction with Japan's trading partners. In September 1989, MITI asked several dozen major automobile, machine tool and electronics goods manufacturers to curb their exports. MITI was concerned that the lower value of the yen would have increased Japan's exports to the United States. MITI was worried that this would heighten U.S.-Japan trade tensions during the spring 1990 round of Super 301 determinations, the final stages of the Structural Impediments Initiative and the run-up to the 1990 Congressional elections. "MITI Seeks Curbing of Exports -- Automobiles and Electronic Equipment; Concerned over Worsening of Japan-U.S. Friction," *Tokyo Shimbun* (September 20, 1989).

[166]*BNA International Trade Report* (February 21, 1990).

[167]"Uproar Prompts MITI Pricing Checks", *Japan Economic Journal* (July 4, 1987). On August 24, 1987, an advisory panel to MITI called for new policies to reduce trade friction caused by six of Japan's export-oriented industries (VCRs, automobiles, telecommunications equipment, semiconductors, machine tools and copiers). These policies included joint industry/MITI supply and demand forecasts and, if necessary, curbs on exports, production and investment. The report was greeted with some skepticism by the private sector. Some companies were concerned that export curbs could damage their competitiveness vis-a-vis European and Asian firms. "MITI's remedy for Japan's exporters gets cool response from industry," *Japan Economic Journal* (September 5, 1987).

a rebuke from MITI which said "why do you provoke the U.S. at a time when it is thinking of implementing Super 301?"[168]

MITI's Industrial Policies. If MITI's industrial policies are a catalyst for channeled investment by Japanese industrial groups into key sectors, then its current sectoral promotional priorities arguably have considerable predictive value in identifying the sectors where trade friction is likely to erupt in the 1990s. Conversely, if, as many observers believe, MITI's influence over Japanese industry is diminishing, it would follow that MITI' current priorities may not be particularly relevant indicators of where Japanese industry is going in the 1990s. Concededly there is certainly evidence to support the latter view. Some Japanese trade officials argue that MITI is like a poverty agency that has cured poverty, and point out that many large Japanese companies are not only internationally competitive but can finance their research and development and capital investments with their own resources, without government assistance.[169] The globalization of Japanese companies enables them to remove a substantial portion of their operations from MITI's domain altogether.[170] However, despite such observations, MITI's current sectoral promotional priorities are probably the best indicator of where Japanese industry will commit its formidable resources in the 1990s and hence, where trade friction is likely to erupt. The "decline of MITI" has been exaggerated; Karel van Wolferen goes so far as

---

[168]*Nihon Keizai Shimbun* (April 23, 1989).

[169]The liberalization of the Japanese banking system, and the consequent rise of its commercial orientation, is loosening one of the reins MITI has indirectly had over the direction of industry. "Many large Japanese corporations now have access to the Euromarket for capital and have to lessen their dependence on loans from their Japanese banks." F.M. Rosenbluth, *Financial Politics in Contemporary Japan* (Cornell Press: 1989) p. 225. "Privately and sometimes even publicly, scientists, engineers, and some of the nation's top executives say they depend far less than ever" on MITI. David E. Sanger, "Mighty MITI loses its grip." *New York Times* (July 9, 1989).

[170]For example, Sony's bid to participate in DARPA's high-definition television project and Toyota's announced goal to expand auto production by 200,000 in the United Kingdom stimulated some criticism abroad. In response, Masahira Maeda, the general manager of MITI's industrial structure division, said "We need to take effective measures to prevent Japanese firms from causing friction in foreign markets. But we have no legal means to control them outside our national borders." Katsuro Kitamatsu, "MITI fights to hold influence as Japanese firms go global." *Japan Economic Journal* (April 1, 1989).

to characterize it as the "myth of slipping control," commenting that "the idea of Japanese industry wrestling with the bureaucracy in order to escape from its grasp is, quite simply, false. . .Japanese officials, weary of foreign criticism about controlled trade, applaud these views and help spread them."[171] Many Japanese officials inside and outside MITI believe that Japanese enterprises cannot disregard MITI's guidance. Moreover, even if one embraces the notion of MITI's declining influence, its industrial promotion priorities remain an excellent indicator of the strategic direction of Japanese industry simply because these priorities were evolved through intensive consultation between MITI and industry. "The government usually does not act until there is enough agreement between it and the concerned firms for a consensus to be declared, whatever the relative influence of government and business in reaching the agreement."[172] MITI's developmental objectives, in other words, are roughly congruent with those of the *keiretsu* firms themselves.

If Japan's trade policy frequently has a stumbling, reactive, ad hoc quality, the industrial development strategy overseen by MITI is, by world standards, a model of rational, long range strategic planning, and has served as the prototype for the developmental strategies implemented by Korea and Taiwan. MITI's broad industrial strategy has remained the same since the first oil shock and the pollution scandals of the early 1970s. Japan will become "a nation based on technology" (*gijutsu-rikkoku*); it will move toward an industrial structure which will be based on the high technology industries, an "informationized society" (*joho-ka shakai*). The technology-based industries have a number of characteristics that distinguish them from the traditional industries: (a) they will not depend on imported raw materials or energy and they will not significantly pollute the environment; (b) they will be technology-intensive; (c) they will be highly automated and will place a premium on highly skilled and educated workers to oversee development and production. Four "basic" technologies will be promoted because of their "far reaching ripple effects" across many other advanced sectors: biotechnology, advanced materials, semiconductor devices with new functions, and superconductivity.[173]

---

[171]Karel van Wolferen, *The Enigma of Japanese Power* (New York: Knopf, 1989) p. 394.

[172]Robert Wade, *Governing the Market: Economic Theory and the Role of Government in East Asian Industrialization* (Princeton, 1990), p. 326.

[173]MITI, "Development of Basic Technologies," in *The Vision of MITI's Policies in the 1980s, 1981*; MITI, *Mid-Term Report of the Industrial Superconductor Technology Development Roundtable* (August 24, 1987).

Most Japanese officials believe that the transformation of Japan into a high-technology economy is the best way to counter the advance of the newly-industrializing economies (NIEs).[174] At the same time, Japan will not abandon its declining sectors such as textiles and nonferrous metals. These industries will be transformed and revitalized by diffusion of advanced technology, intensive R&D and investment in automated plant that will deprive NIEs of their labor-cost advantage. Where necessary, MITI will wink at low visibility protectionist measures employed by industry to stall inroads by the NIEs and enable crisis sectors to restructure and modernize.

The promotional tools employed by MITI include, most importantly, subsidies for research and development as well as coordination of research efforts; in addition, MITI uses tax incentives (with cooperation from MOF) and direct and indirect loans to encourage investment in high risk technologies that the private sector might otherwise neglect.[175] Where necessary, MITI has established training programs and has sought to encourage "international cooperation" in research areas where Japan is perceived to be weak. MITI may also work to restructure industries to enhance their international competitiveness; a good recent example of this is its efforts with respect to fine ceramics and semiconductor equipment and materials firms, where it encouraged the formation of capital and commercial links between these firms and large Japanese electronics enterprises.[176] Large scale subsidies are rare, although MITI may encourage banks or large Japanese enterprises to bail out failing firms in strategic areas.

---

[174]MITI, *The Vision of MITI's Policies in the 1980s* (1981).

[175]As a MITI official described it in 1987, MITI subsidizes R&D in high technology in areas which have "wide-ranging influence on the economy, society and technology," but require a long time to implement, "fields in which the size of the risks involved and the capital required for development surpass the capacities of private industry," fields in which the needs of the economy are very pressing, and areas where institutional coordination is required. Kazuyuki Motahashi, MITI Machinery and Information Industries Bureau, in *Kikai Shinki* (January 1987); "Strategy for the Year 2000," in *Nen E No Gijutsu Senryaku* (November 13, 1990) (JPRS-JST-91-055-L).

[176]Ikuo Tomita, MITI, "Administrative Policy in the Field of Fine Ceramics," in *Ceramics Japan* (August 1987); *Shukan Daiyamondo* (September 7, 1985); Jon Sigurdson, *Industry and State in Partnership in Japan* (Lund: Research Policy Institute, 1986).

MITI's industrial priorities, and those of Japanese industry, have changed over time, but not dramatically. From the perspective of 1991, based on the current and proposed policies of MITI and the investment behavior of Japanese enterprises, it is possible to identify a number of Japanese sectoral priorities which coincide with advanced industries of particular importance to the United States and/or to the European Community, and are therefore likely to be flashpoints in the 1990s. They are: the entire information industry, including semiconductors, computer systems, software, peripherals, high speed computers, advanced imaging systems, digital telecommunications systems, and personal computers; biotechnology; commercial and military aviation; advanced materials; and the space industry. In some sectors, such as advanced consumer electronics (camcorders, video discs, VCRs) there may be little trade friction simply because Japan is already completely dominant. In addition, the auto industry, because of its vast impact on the economies of industrialized nations, is like to be a source of trade friction despite the fact that trade in this sector already is, and will continue to be, heavily managed. The situation and prospects for these sectors are addressed briefly below.

The Information Technologies. The principal focal point of MITI's effort to transform Japan into a technology-based society is the electronic information sector, which embraces computers, data processing, telecommunications, and the various subsectors that support these industries -- peripherals, semiconductors, advanced imaging systems, semiconductor manufacturing equipment, electronic materials, software. The boundaries of this sector are indistinct and becoming more so; the advent of digital technology is leading to a convergence not only of computers and telecommunications systems, but of these industries and advanced consumer electronics products, factory automation systems, and even products such as automobiles and duplicating equipment. Because Japan is competitively strong in virtually all of these sectors already, and gaining in relative competitiveness, MITI's developmental efforts in this field are being regarded with increasing concern in many advanced and newly-industrializing countries. Some observers even speculate that despite its continuing wide lead in basic computer science, the United States faces the prospect of a loss of leadership to Japan in the information field over the long run.[177]

---

[177]This assessment is based not only on Japanese technological gains but on market trends; IBM, Wang, Cray and Data General have suffered commercial setbacks in the late 1980s and early 1990s, and Honeywell and Control Data have largely (continued...)

Japan's drive to catch up with the United States in the information field underlies a substantial proportion of its government trade and industrial promotion policies of the 1970s and 1980s. Disputes that have erupted over Japanese policies in software, microelectronics, and supercomputers reflect facets of this larger effort to achieve world leadership in computers. While by most measures the U.S. remains ahead in the computer industry overall, most informed observers see the Japanese gaining ground rapidly, and the industry will remain a major area of confrontation between Japan and the U.S. in the 1990s.[178] Fujitsu, in particular, is undertaking aggressive expansion moves; it has acquired ICL of Britain and reportedly plans to absorb its longtime U.S. affiliate, Amdahl, "thus eliminating wasteful competition and putting the combined entity in a position to achieve a 20 percent share of the world computer market."[179]

---

[177](...continued)
abandoned the computer industry. Moreover, the Japanese producers have substantial leverage over U.S. computer firms because of their near-monopoly on DRAMS and other critical components. Skeptics point out that the Japanese trail the U.S. in microprocessor technology, software, systems integration, and after-sale service.Japanese penetration of the U.S. computer market is small but growing. Japanese share of the U.S. PC market has grown from 5.8 percent in 1985 to 13 percent in 1989. Japanese laptop computers are competing successfully against U.S. desktops. *Business Week* (October 23, 1989); McKinsey & Company, *The 1990 Report on the Computer Industry* (1990).

[178]Japan's computer industry is dominated by six *keiretsu*-linked companies that were organized by MITI in the 1960s to counter the seemingly overwhelming strength of IBM; originally MITI considered merging these firms to create an enterprise of requisite scale, but settled for a loose collaborative arrangement, with joint R&D and allocation of a variety of production and sales areas. The six firms have grown into economic powerhouses in the information field, but some vestiges of the cooperative arrangements of the 1960s and 1970s remain, including the division of the industry between makers of IBM and non-IBM compatible equipment and the practice of pooling major R&D tasks in industry-government consortia. In addition, the industry has a legacy of protectionism and aggressive acquisition of foreign technology, and disputes over these issues still color U.S.-Japan trade relations in this sector.

[179]*Nikkan Kogyo* (July 24, 1990) (JPRS-JST-90-069-L).

The current flagship promotional R&D efforts sponsored by MITI and NTT in computers have been widely reported.[180] These large scale projects, however, while highly visible, are probably less significant than the numerous government-sponsored projects in specific technology areas relevant to computers and computer systems -- optoelectronics, automated production of software, neutral networks, synchrotron lithography, flat panel displays, and supercomputer systems. Japanese technological gains in these sub-areas of computer science have been matched by dramatic market gains by Japanese computer firms in subsegments of the computer market -- semiconductor devices, printers, floppy disk drives, and more recently, personal computers and desktop workstations. The principle areas of conflict are likely to be in such sub-areas where Japanese gains threaten U.S. leadership.

Semiconductors. Semiconductors are not only a subsector of the information industry, but one of the four "basic" technologies identified by MITI in the 1980s which enhance the competitiveness of all Japanese industries. MITI, its ancillary financial institutions and NTT have devoted major promotional efforts to this industry since the early 1970s, with virtually all of the aid going to established *keiretsu*-affiliated electronics firms, which have themselves made massive resource commitments to this industry. Formal import and investment restrictions were eliminated in 1974-76 but U.S. firms have continued to complain about structural barriers which have limited U.S. sales in Japan.[181] Recurrent export drives by Japanese firms in commodity memory devices culminated in widespread Japanese dumping, market exit by a number of U.S. producers, extensive trade litigation in 1985-86, and a bilateral agreement regulating

---

[180] MITI is currently sponsoring the so-called Sixth Generation Computer Project at a budget which has been projected as high as $1.6 billion. The project will emphasize massively parallel processing and radical components technology (optical circuits and wafer scale integration). *New Technology Week* (January 22, 1991). Meanwhile, NTT is spending over $550 million to develop an advanced computer for its Information Network System (INS), an advanced digital communications network using optional communications technology. See generally Martin Frannsmann, *The Market and Beyond: Cooperation and Competition in Information Technology in the Japanese System* (Cambridge: Cambridge University Press, 1990).

[181] Semiconductor Industry Association, *Japanese Market Barriers in Microelectronics* (1985).

trade for the period 1986-91, the U.S.-Japan Semiconductor Arrangement.[182] The U.S. imposed trade sanctions on Japanese electronics products in 1987 in response to alleged Japanese noncompliance with the market access and antidumping terms of the agreement.[183] After that date, Japanese dumping largely ended and Japanese firms began a major effort to facilitate expanded sales by U.S. semiconductor firms in Japan. The Arrangement was renewed for another five years in 1991, with principal emphasis placed on improved market access for foreign firms in Japan.

In the 1990s Japan's trade conflicts in semiconductors are less likely to arise over traditional trade issues such as dumping than out of the Japanese industry's growing world dominance in the microelectronics field. Japanese firms are achieving monopoly or quasi-monopoly status in a variety of areas of components technology, materials, and semiconductor manufacturing equipment.[184] As Germany's high technology spokesman Ingolf Ruge complained in 1989, "The goal of the Japanese. . .is a world monopoly on chips, a prospect which many non-Japanese observers regard with apprehension."[185] The Japanese firms' ability jointly to regulate their output and sales of semiconductors

---

[182]*Arrangement Between the Government of Japan and the Government of the United States of America Concerning Trade in Semiconductor Products* (September 2, 1986). Most U.S. producers of dynamic random access memories (DRAMs) exited the market in 1985 after experiencing heavy losses. The U.S. government made affirmative findings of dumping with respect to Japanese sales of 64K DRAMs, 256K DRAMs, and EPROMs. The U.S. semiconductor industry also brought a Section 301 action against Japan based on denial of access to the Japanese market. *Erasable Programmable Read Only Memories from Japan; 64K Dynamic Random Access Memory Components from Japan; 256K and Above Dynamic Random Access Memories from Japan.*

[183]Proclamation by the President, *Increase in the Rates of Duty for Certain Articles from Japan* (April 17, 1987).

[184]Japanese monopolies or near-monopolies exist with respect to ceramics packages for integrated circuits; glass blanks for photomasks; fused quartz; emitter-coupled logic (ECL) random access memories; electron cyclotron resonance (ECR) etchers; active matrix displays; state-of-the art automated testing equipment for integrated circuits, certain models of advanced wafer steppers and a number of other types of semiconductor manufacturing equipment. General Accounting Office, *U.S. Business Access to Certain Foreign State-of-the-Art Technology* (September 1991).

[185]Cited in *Der Spiegel* (April 24, 1989).

was demonstrated in the late 1980s,[186] and a number of U.S. and European firms complained of "strategic withholding" of critical components and microelectronics equipment by their Japanese suppliers.[187] These developments have raised serious concerns in Europe and the U.S. over the strategic implications of loss of self-sufficiency in microelectronics, and what, if anything, can be done about it. In Europe, in particular, a movement has developed among industry circles to ensure European autonomy in microelectronics, if necessary through overtly protectionist and interventionist measures,[188] although the direction that Europe will take is very much in doubt.[189] In the 1990s, MITI will continue its current efforts to minimize foreign backlash by encouraging Japanese firms to exercise restraint in investment in existing facilities and in their acquisitions of foreign microelectronics firms. Because of the strategic nature of the semiconductor industry, however, continued friction with the U.S. and the EC is likely in the 1990s.

Advanced Displays. Advanced display systems for computers and high definition television (HDTV) are regarded as one of the most promising and strategically important electronic technologies of the 1990s. MITI and the Japanese electronics producers have made a large commitment to fostering next-generation displays, particularly liquid crystal displays (LCDs). MITI's financial affiliate, the Japan Key Technology Center, is

---

[186]Beginning in mid-1985 Japanese producers of DRAMs began jointly curtailing their output in order to stabilize prices and improve profitability. MITI began reinforcing these efforts with production "guideposts" in the spring of 1986. These joint actions (which took place both before and after the Semiconductor Arrangement was concluded in September 1986) ultimately led to sharp price increases, spot shortages of DRAMs, and enormous profits for Japanese firms, which controlled nearly 90 percent of world DRAM by 1988. See *Nihon Keizai Shimbun* (December 4, 1985; April 24, 1986; March 31, 1987; October 10, 1987); *Sankei Shimbun*, (December 5, 1985).

[187]L.M. Thorndyke, ETA Systems, Inc., *Supercomputer Systems Markets* (October 28-29, 1985); Siemens complained in 1986 of "an embargo policy on the part of the competition. . .Japan is no longer delivering certain components for solid state lasers today." *Handelsblatt* (March 17, 1986).

[188]*European Report* No. 1608 (August 4, 1990).

[189]The French are perhaps the most wary of Japan but are nevertheless now debating welcoming Japanese investment into France. The EC is divided, but apparently by moving away from protectionism. See generally Chapter 7.

funding a large scale industry-government R&D project to develop LCDs, and several Japanese firms have entered volume production.[190] The competitive approach being taken by the large Japanese electronics producers is similar to that in semiconductors; a Toshiba executive indicated in 1989 that "we are prepared to accept red ink for the first five or six years. . . . From the experience of our semiconductor business we have learned that one has to take a long term perspective to do business with this kind of product."[191] The strategic character of LCDs enhances the likelihood of trade friction:

> *The stakes in the LCD race are staggering; for the new generation displays will be driven by a core of visual processing electronics comprising most semiconductor technologies. As business strategists on both sides of the Pacific have long pointed out, the economic power that controls LCDs will control the driver electronics. The production economies of scale then will make the LCD suppliers the dominant market force in commercial and industrial electronics of the 1990s.*[192]

In 1990 U.S. flat panel display firms brought an antidumping action against Japan which culminated in imposition of stiff antidumping duties on active matrix LCDs, which are the mostly likely choice for use in the next generation of color laptop computers.[193] While U.S. and Japanese companies may ultimately develop a collaborative approach to LCDs -- IBM and Toshiba are jointly developing flat panel technology -- the competitive significance of this sector may make the 1990-91 antidumping action a harbinger of future U.S.-Japan conflict in this area.

Computer Procurement. Disputes over government procurement of large computers are likely to continue in the 1990s, if only because there is no real unified Japanese government position on the issue. While MITI has jurisdiction over industrial policy for the computer industry, most of

---

[190]MITI, *Dawn of the Age of Giant Electronics* (August 10, 1989); *DQ Monday* (June 19, 1989); *Senmon Koshukai Koen Ronbunshu* (January 1990) (JPRS-JST-91-002).

[191]*Japan Economic Journal* (December 23, 1989).

[192]*Electronics News* (April 23, 1990).

[193]Duties of 62.67 percent were imposed on imports of Japanese active matrix liquid crystal displays. Duties on three other types of flat panel displays ranged from 0 to 7 percent. *High Information Context Flat Panel Displays and Subassemblies Thereof from Japan (ITA 91-48)*; *New Technology Week* (July 15, 1991).

Japan's government procurement of computers is administered by other Ministries, and there has been a chronic bias in favor of made-in-Japan machines. As a general proposition, government procurement of computers is politicized, with many Japanese makers employing "old boys" (OBs) -- former officials of the Ministries to which sales are sought. The U.S. government has criticized Japan's lack of an independent bid test procedures, pre-selection of vendors without open solicitation, lack of procedural transparency, and a variety of other practices that tend to perpetuate a system which favors domestic machines.[194] A bilateral accord was negotiated in 1990 with respect to supercomputers, and one U.S.-made supercomputer was subsequently procured by a government entity, but the Japanese government computer market remains effectively protected.

Commercial and Military Aircraft. MITI has been promoting commercial and military aircraft development as a strategic priority for many years. The principal Japanese aircraft firms are large *keiretsu*-affiliated heavy industrial concerns for whom the production of airframes and engines and components occupies only a small percentage of resources. These firms have produced helicopters, military aircraft and small commercial aircraft under license to U.S. firms; they have also gradually come to produce a large proportion of Boeing's aircraft parts, and are engaged in a variety of joint development and co-production arrangements with European and U.S. firms. Such joint production arrangements came under scrutiny in the FSX affair, in which Japan was criticized for its desire to design and produce its own close-support fighter rather than buy F-16s from the U.S. Among other things, the FSX affair underscored the fact that MITI's long range objective is to establish Japan as an independent manufacturer of commercial and military aircraft. Japan's growing prowess in areas such as new materials, electronics, engine technology, and metalforming, where the industry is bound together through *keiretsu* ties and cartel relationships, make this a realistic prospect.[195]

---

[194]Office of U.S. Trade Representative, 1991 *National Trade Estimate Report on Foreign Trade Business*; IDC Japan, Ltd., *Foreign Computer Manufacturer Participation in the Japanese Government Sector* (February 26, 1990).

[195]The Japanese aviation industry is described as a "friendship club" (*nakayushi kurabu*) within a "village society" (*mura shakui*) based on mutual knowledge (*touka*). Collaboration is common in R&D, facilitating technology diffusion; a division of labor occurs at the production stage. See R. Samuels and B. Whipple, "Defense Production and Industrial Development: The Case of Japanese Aircraft, in C.

(continued...)

There is clearly significant potential for future U.S. trade friction in this sector. MITI is already promoting development of a 75-100 seat prop-jet, and has asked Japanese manufacturers to subcontract out work on this project to China and Southeast Asian countries who are seen as potential future customers.[196] It has announced an R&D effort to enable Japan to manufacture supersonic transport aircraft early in the 20th century, and is funding methane-fueled engine development, composite materials resistant to high temperatures, wind tunnels, test chambers, and other technologies required for an SST.[197] At some point, probably in the 1990s, Japan will begin commercial sales of domestically developed small passenger aircraft; later it will enter the market with larger aircraft and ultimately, supersonic passenger jets.[198] Boeing will be vulnerable to strategic coercion since it will be dependent on its Japanese competitors for the parts needed to make its own planes.[199] Over the long run, the U.S. is likely to react to the incursions of this new "targeted" industry with charges of unfair trade; more immediately, FSX-type disputes over the co-production of defense aircraft are likely to recur. Japan's expanded defense plans for the 1990s will call for items ranging from AWACs aircraft to airborne tankers for refueling and even aircraft carriers with vertical-takeoff jets. The U.S. could sell these items to Japan or co-produce them with the Japanese, but Japanese officials, stung by the fallout from the FSX affair, are likely to shun co-development in favor of all-Japanese type projects. The JDA is likewise becoming more

---

195(...continued)
Johnson, J. Zysuman and L. Tyson, eds., *Politics and Productivity*, (Ballinger, 1989); *Kabushiki Nippon* (August 5, 1987); Ogawa Kazuhisa, *Mata Hitomi Goku ni Sureta Anzen Hosho* (July 1989), translated in *Japan Echo* (Autumn, 1989).

196*The Economist* (November 11, 1989).

197MITI is currently pursuing an R&D effort designed to enable Japan to produce supersonic transport aircraft early in the 21st century; it is funding methane-fueled engine development, composite materials resistant to high temperatures, wind tunnels, test chambers, and other technologies required for an SST.

198*Aerospace* (May 1988); *JITA News* (May 1989); *Sankei Shimbun* (August 17, 1989); *Aviation Week and Space Technology* (October 9, 1989).

199At present about two thirds of the value of a B-747 comes from outside suppliers, a substantial portion of which are Japanese. Boeing has turned to such suppliers to avoid the cyclical risks associated with expansion, and to diminish pressure on its work force; the work load was a major factor in a strike which shut Boeing down in 1989. *The Economist* (November 11, 1989).

enthusiastic about the autonomous development of military aircraft technology, which could in turn bring renewed U.S. criticism.[200]

Biotechnology. In 1981 MITI unveiled a national program for the promotion of biotechnology, and in the early 1980s biotechnology became one of Japan's leading industrial development priorities.[201] To date most market entry has been by large, *keiretsu*-affiliated companies in fields such as chemicals, beverages and food.[202] Outside of a few areas, such as fermentation, Japan lags behind the U.S. in technology level and has sought to catch up through an aggressive technology acquisition effort, characterized, in part, by provision of capital to small U.S. biotechnology firms in return for technology.[203] Based on current trends, trade friction in biotechnology is likely to be centered on conflicts over intellectual property rights. Biotechnology originated in the United States and the Japanese have long suspected that the U.S. has designated biotechnology a strategic industry and "was weaving about it a new and unprecedented network of protective patents."[204]

The likelihood of friction is most evident where Japanese efforts have reached the commercialization stage -- the use of biological processes to produce medicines. Japanese firms are making several types of Interferon

---

[200]*Nihon Keizai Shimbun* (August 11, 1989).

[201]MITI's promotional measures in biotechnology include subsidies for joint R&D and establishment of a number of R&D centers. Areas of particular emphasis include recombinant DNA, bioreactors, and large scale cell cultivation. A number of other Ministries are competing with MITI for influence in this field, including construction, Agriculture, Health and Welfare and the Science and Technology Agency. See generally *Symposium Report on Government and Private Sector Joint R&D Projects* (January 1988); *JTECH Panel Report on Biotechnology in Japan* (June 1985).

[202]Akihiro Yoshikawa, *Japanese Biotechnology: New Drugs* (BRIE, January 1988) and The Japanese *Challenge on Biotechnology: Industrial Policy* (BRIE, September 1987).

[203]Thirty-six (36) of these tie-ups are summarized by Yoshikawa (1987) based on *Sekai no Baio Kigyo 500-sha* (Tokyo: Nikkei - McGraw-Hill, 1986).

[204]One basis for this concern was the so-called Cohen-Boyer patent, which gave the U.S. firm Genentech broad patent rights over recombinant DNA technology, and a U.S. Supreme Court case which ruled that inventors of new microorganisms could be granted patent protection. S. Tatara, *Indenshi Sangyo Kakumei* (Tokyo: Bunjei Shungu), cited in G. Saxonhouse, "Industrial Policy and Factor Markets: Biotechnology in Japan and the United State," in Patrick and Meissner, eds., *Japan's High Technology Industries* (1986).

and Hepatitis-B vaccine for commercial sale using biological production methods.[205] They have drawn heavily on U.S. and European technology to achieve their current level of development and have already become involved in disputes over patent infringement.[206] Chugai Pharmaceutical, working jointly with Sankyo-Kirin Brewery, used U.S. technology to develop its own manufacturing capability to produce EPO, a drug used to treat renal anemia; in 1989 the U.S. company Amugen Inc. brought a Section 337 action against Chugai, alleging violation of its EPO patent. The drug TPA, which is used to treat blood diseases, was first marketed by the U.S. firm Genentech, but two Japanese groups subsequently developed a production capability for TPA; Genentech sued them for infringement of its TPA patents.[207]

Advanced Materials. MITI has identified new materials as a strategic basic technology not only because of its potential ripple effect on other advanced sectors, but because it offered an area where companies in older, depressed industries could move into high technology. When in the early 1980s MITI designated new materials as a priority sector and began actively encouraging market entry, a rush of large firms entered the field from sectors such as mining, metals, glass, chemicals and cement.[208] A "ceramics fever" swept Japan in the early 1980s as companies surged into the field of fine ceramics.[209] A similar surge into the high purity silicon field occurred in the late 1980s (resulting in massive overcapacity.) MITI has provided a wide range of support measures, including the formation of joint research and engineering associations, financial support for joint R&D, establishment of the Japan Fine Ceramics Center (JFCC) to conduct

---

[205]Nikko Research Center (1989) p. 328.

[206]Shionogi & Co. has begun producing human-type insulin made through gene recombinant technology acquired from Eli Lilly, Sumitomo Pharmaceutical has begun producing alpha-interferon made under license from a British firm.

[207]These included Asahi Chemical and a joint arrangement between Kyowa Hakka Kogyo and Mitsubishi Kasei, which licensed TPA technology from Genentech.

[208]*Toshi Keizai* (October 1985); *Nikko Materials* (March 1986); *Purometeusu* (September-October 1985).

[209]A popular book on the topic of fine ceramics sold 50,000 copies in Japan in a period of several months. National Materials Advisory Board, *High Technology Ceramics in Japan* (1989).

R&D, promote standardization, and diffuse technology, and encouragement of industry restructuring.[210]

Trade friction in at least some advanced materials sectors is virtually certain in the 1990s. As in other high technology sectors, there have already been skirmishes over intellectual property issues, and these will very likely intensify.[211] The simultaneous rush of large *keiretsu*-based firms into "hot" new materials areas has already produced several instances of frenetic Japanese expansion culminating in a global shakeout and consequent Japanese domination of world markets, and there is no reason to expect this pattern to change. A closely related issue is raised by the foreign perception that Japanese firms are moving to dominate strategic materials sectors, both by out-investing U.S. and European makers and by absorbing them through acquisition and merger. Ceramic packages for integrated circuits, for example, are now virtually a Japanese monopoly, and Japan's growing dominance of high purity silicon and silicon wafer production has begun to provoke concern in the United States.[212] Because of the strategic importance of many advanced materials sectors, Japan's growing market presence will almost certainly provoke U.S. and European countermeasures in the 1990s.

Space. MITI does not currently hold exclusive jurisdiction over Japan's space development effort, but its role is expanding at the expense of other Ministries as Japan's commercial space industry matures. The principal sponsor of Japan's space program has thus far been the Science and Technology Agency (STA) which provides about 80 percent of total government funding through its public corporation, the National Space Development Agency (NASDA). Several other government entities can influence Japan's space development effort through their procurement of satellites. MITI, however, has used its jurisdiction over the commercialization of new technologies as a lever to expand its role in the

---

[210]*Kagaku Kogyo Nippo* (July 25, 1990) (JPRS-JST-91-034-6); *Shinkinzoku Kogyo* (January 1987); *Ceramics Japan* (November 1986, August 1987); National Materials Advisory Board; *Nihon Keizai Shimbun* (August 11, 1990).

[211]In 1980 Carborundum charged Kyocera with violating U.S. patents for silicon carbide sintering technology, and Allied Corporation has charged Hitachi Metals with infringing its patents for amorphous metal alloys. *Nikkan Kogyo* (November 7, 1990) (JPRS-JST-90-069-L).

[212]Defense Science Board, *Task Force on Semiconductor Dependency* (November 30, 1986); "Below the Iceberg's Tip; The Loss of Domestically Owned Silicon Wafer Supply," *Dataquest Research Newsletter* (February 1989).

space field; on the basis of its relationship with financial institutions such as the Japan Development Bank, the Key Technology Center and the Export-Import Bank, it has channeled financial assistance to the growing commercial space sector.[213]

Although Japan's first rockets were built with parts and technology licensed from the U.S., NASDA has developed and used a rocket launch vehicle, the H-1, which is more than 80 percent domestically made, and which features an inertial navigation system and cryogenic propulsion technology that is all Japanese. It is now building a bigger rocket, the H-2, with no U.S. technology which is designed to be cost-competitive with the U.S. space shuttle; launch of the H-2, which could come in 1993, will put Japan in launch services competition with the space shuttle and the EC's Ariane.[214] The H-2 program has suffered a series of setbacks, including a 1991 explosion during a test that killed an engineer, but the government remains determined to launch the rocket in 1993.[215] In satellites, as in rockets, Japan has weaned itself from an early dependency on U.S. technology, and has made such rapid gains that some observers predict it will catch up with and pass the U.S. by the mid-1990s. The Japanese government has used an overtly nationalistic procurement policy to stimulate indigenous capability in satellites, allocating the market largely to Mitsubishi (communications satellites), NEC (weather satellites and some broadcast satellites) and Toshiba (broadcast satellites).[216]

Japan's 1983 *Long Range Vision on Space Development* contained an express prohibition against procurement of foreign satellites; this meant that the country's first communications satellite, launched in 1983, cost three times as much as similar or better satellites that could have been brought from the U.S.[217] One Japanese official's perspective on the issue was that "NTT. . .plans its satellites well in advance of orders. They are designed before launch. They can't buy off the shelf. . .but America's view is that you give us black boxes, you won't collaborate with us -- you

---

[213]G.A. Eberstadt, *Japan's High Frontier; Viewing the Space Program as Industrial Policy* (Harvard University A.B. Thesis, 1989); S.K. Vogel, *Japanese High Technology, Politics and Power* (Brie Research Paper #2, March 1989).

[214]*Purometeusu* (January 1987).

[215]*Nikkei Weekly* (August 24, 1991); *Nihon Keizai Shimbun* (May 21, 1991).

[216]Vogel (1989), p. 61; *Purometeusu* (January 1987).

[217]Johnson, "Telecom Wars" (1989), pp. 223-25.

force us to develop our own satellites."[218] The government's buy-national posture reflected a lobbying effort by the Keidanren, which normally takes an internationalist posture on such matters; here though, a Keidanren committee headed by NEC's Kobayashi Koji recommended development of indigenous satellites rather than their procurement from the U.S., with the long range objective of exporting satellites to Europe and the U.S. by the mid-1990s. Following U.S. protests to the Keidanren and the government, the Japanese government ruled that private firms could buy U.S. satellites but that the government entities could not if such purchases interfered with national development objectives. Despite such measures, which have resulted in a number of private joint ventures with U.S. firms for provision of satellite communications services and sale of a substantial volume of U.S. parts for use in Japanese satellites, Japan's satellite market remains dominated by government procurement, which will exclude U.S. and other foreign products.[219] U.S. pressure in this area will likely be stonewalled while Japan moves forward with its development effort; one reason NASDA is rushing the H-2 project is to place Japan in the position to counter U.S. demands by pointing out, with some degree of credibility, that with an all-Japanese launch vehicle and all-Japanese satellites, U.S. products and services are no longer needed.[220] The Japanese can complain, with some justification, that the problems encountered in cooperating with the U.S. in projects such as NASA's troubled Freedom Space Station, warrant a stand-alone national effort in space.[221]

As it presses ahead with expanding its bureaucratic domain at their expense, MITI has used satellite trade disputes to criticize both of its rivals in space, MPT and STA, for contributing to trade friction. MITI announced in 1989 that it would sponsor development of a "self-returned unmanned spaceship," with launch set for 1994; it has already secured full jurisdiction over several new space R&D projects, and is girding for a struggle with STA over control of the H-2 program, having established its own "Space Utilization Research and Examination Committee" to expand

---

[218]Interview with a Foreign Ministry official (1990).

[219]*Nihon Keizai Shimbun* (May 29, 1989); Johnson (1989); , pp. 224-25; USTR, *Foreign Trade Barriers* (1989), p. 104.

[220]"It is necessary to make the launching of the H-2 in 1993 successfully, as scheduled, partly in order to prevent such troublesome friction from arising." *Nihon Keizai Shimbun* (October 30, 1989).

[221]*Nikkei Weekly* (June 29, 1991).

its current role in space.[222] Should MITI succeed in wresting control of a major portion of Japan's launch vehicle and satellite programs from its rivals, Japan's overtly protectionist policies will probably be softened and given a more international dimension, without, however, any significant diminution of the basic drive to achieve technological parity with the U.S.

Japan's launch of the H-2 rocket sometime during or after 1993 is likely to have a significant impact on U.S.-Japan relations. At a minimum it will probably foreclose the prospect of a significant expansion in the sale of U.S. space products and services to Japan. More importantly, it will put an ascendant Japan in direct competition with the troubled U.S. space program, and in a position to compete with or surpass the U.S. in exotic areas ranging from materials processing in space, geostationary communications platforms to minerals mining on the moon.[223] It will open opportunities for Japan to make its own dramatic moves in space. A 1987 STA survey of 1017 exports in 17 Japanese government departments resulted in predictions that Japan would achieve space objectives according to the following rough timetable: unmanned probes of distant planets, 1998; industrial production in space, 2003; manned Japanese on the moon, 2010; manned Japanese landing on Mars, 2013.[224] While these predictions may or may not in fact be borne out by events, the political and emotional impact of such achievements on the U.S. could be comparable to the Soviet launching of Sputnik in 1987.

Automobiles

The auto industry remains of such central importance to every major industrialized state that it is likely to be the subject of continuing state intervention and of international disputes throughout the 1990s. At the beginning of the 1990s, there was global overcapacity in the industry, reflecting not only recession but the establishment and expansion of Japanese transplant operations in Europe and North America. With Japan's market share progressively expanding and several U.S. and European car makers experiencing major difficulties, MITI was seeking to avoid a backlash against Japanese vehicles, using its traditional tool, voluntary export restraints. However, given the increasingly global

---

[222]*Kikai Shinko* (August 1990) (JPRS-JST-91-052-6); Eberstadt (1989) , pp. 115-16; *Nihon Keizai Shimbun* (August 25, 1989).

[223]See generally Eherstadt (1989) , p. 47.

[224]*Aerospace Japan* (December 1987).

nature of the Japanese auto industry, it is an open question whether MITI's traditional policy measures will be adequate to forestall major friction in this sector.

Motor vehicles are Japan's largest source of export income -- $48 billion in 1988 -- and a principal element in Japan's favorable trade balance. By the close of the 1980s, Japan's automobile industry had arguably become the most competitive in the world; six of the world's top twelve automakers are Japanese, and Japanese automotive technology and manufacturing techniques have given the industry a competitive edge, particularly in the high volume cars at the lower end of the product line.[225] While in the past the Japanese government has provided substantial assistance to the auto industry -- most importantly, virtually complete protection from import competition into the mid 1980s, but also financial support -- its main role in the 1990s will be as a mediator of international trade disputes. No major auto producing nation has allowed completely free imports of cars, and Japan's export drive in automobiles has compelled MITI to negotiate bilateral restraint arrangements on behalf of its industry. Japan currently exercises voluntary export restraint pursuant to formal or informal agreements with the United States, Canada, Sweden and the EC.[226]

In the 1980s, facing proliferating trade restrictions, Japanese automakers shifted from a strategy based on direct exports to one emphasizing local production in "transplant" facilities inside the U.S. and the EC, a trend which accelerated with the strengthening of the yen after 1985 and the EC's move toward formation of the Single Market. In the U.S. by 1990, the capacity of the transplants had reached 2 million units annually; at the

---

[225]The reasons for Japan's success in autos have been exhaustively analyzed elsewhere, but they include a protected home market during the industry's growth years, rigorous attention to manufacturing processes and product quality, and successful conduct of labor-management relations. See generally Hiromichi Mutoh, "The Automotive Industry," in Komiya, Okuno and Suzumura (1988) and Booz, Allen & Hamilton, *The Effects of Foreign Targeting on the US Automotive Industry* (May 1985).

[226]GATT Doc. 1/6530 (July 31, 1989). Even West Germany and Sweden which have no formal restrictions on auto imports, have reached informal arrangements pursuant to which Japan exercises export restraint. GATT, Secretariat, *Trade Policy Review: Japan* (Number 1990), Point 324. Since 1986 MITI has monitored auto exports to the EC, checking each to see whether individual carmaker exports are below the levels of prior years; if overshooting occurs, the producers are directed to balance the figures the following month; in 1990, the indicative EC target volume was 1,237,000 units.

same time, direct exports declined, with total shipments falling well below the voluntary limit of 2.3 million units in every year after 1988.[227] The Japanese industry has periodically urged MITI to inform the U.S. government that the voluntary restraint would not be followed, but MITI has consistently extended the restraint to avert trade friction.[228] MITI's insistence on retaining the export quota has more than symbolic importance; under the current quota arrangements, second rank Japanese producers like Isuzu, Suzuki and Daihatsu have minuscule quotas, and if quotas were removed, MITI fears that these firms will launch an export push to the U.S., "possibly rekindling strife with the U.S. industry and government."[229]

Even with existing restraints, such a scenario appeared to be materializing in 1990-91. During the preceding year the leading Japanese automakers were engaged in dramatic expansion moves in both the U.S. and the EC. Toyota was particularly bullish, with an "expansionist philosophy" and a stated goal of capturing ten percent of the global auto market.[230] In the U.S., Toyota, whose "enthusiasm for increasing its car sales. . .was extraordinary," was reported to have paid about $100 million in dealer incentives in one three-month period in 1990; Honda, attempting to keep pace, gave incentives to its dealers "on an unprecedented scale," but concluded that it was "not tough enough to. . .cope with Toyota."[231] In the EC, nine Japanese automakers were in the process of establishing or expanding existing local manufacturing operations -- Nissan, Toyota, Mitsubishi, Mazda, Honda, Daihatsu, Isuzu, Suzuki and Subaru.[232] These initiatives prompted sharp criticism in the EC, where automakers argued they did not enjoy reciprocal access in Japan, and in the U.S., where an antidumping action was brought against Japanese minivans. MITI continued to urge restraint on Japanese automakers, with

---

[227]In 1991, total shipments were expected to fall 0.5 million units short of the 2.3 million voluntary limit. *Nihon Keizai Shimbun* (January 5, February 8, 1991) *Yomiuri* (January 8, 1991).

[228]*Nihon Keizai Shimbun* (January 5, 1991); *Kyodo* (January 10, 1989).

[229]*Kyodo* (January 10, 1989).

[230]*Nikkei Weekly* (July 6, 1991).

[231]*Nihon Keizai Shimbun* (January 6, 1991), citing Honda Vice President Shoichiro Irimajiri.

[232]*Handelsblatt* (May 13, 1991).

some effect in 1991 as the leading producers appeared to be in the process of curtailing their growth plans.[233] MITI vigorously pressed Japanese makers to hold down their exports, particularly to the EC, to avoid jeopardizing ongoing market access negotiations with the Community.[234]

The disputes which have developed in the 1990-91 already suggest several crucial trade issues that are likely to face Japan in autos in the 1990s. Most importantly, there is the question of whether cars produced in Japanese transplant facilities will be treated as local-origin for all purposes, or potentially subject to trade restrictions notwithstanding their local manufacture. It is a generally accepted proposition in international commerce that locally-produced products are entitled to national treatment regardless of the nationality of the producer. However, the 1991 EC-Japan agreement on autos resulted in Japanese acceptance of quantitative limits on its transplant sales through 1999, and U.S. automakers reportedly asked President Bush for similar treatment of locally-produced Japanese cars in the U.S.[235] In negotiations with the U.S., MITI remained adamant in its adherence to the principle that "locally manufactured automobiles are American automobiles" and should not count against the 2.3 million quota, but in light of the 1991 EC arrangement, the issue cannot be regarded as completely foreclosed."[236]

A second key issue relates to the local content of autos manufactured in the transplants. As Japanese firms have negotiated with Member States to establish transplant facilities, they have been required to agree to fixed percentages of local content; the U.K. asked Nissan to reach a specified percentage of local content by 1991, France compelled Fuji Heavy Industries to rewrite its business plan for a Subaru plant by imposing local content requirements, and France and Italy have threatened to treat Nissan vehicles made in the U.K. as "Japanese" for import quota purposes unless they contain 80 percent local content. Under such pressure, the Japanese transplants have gone to a very high level of EC content, and are moving in a similar direction, albeit more slowly, in the U.S., where local content legislation has periodically been considered by the Congress. By

---

[233] *Nikkei Weekly* (July 6, 1991).

[234] *Nihon Keizai Shimbun* (March 5, 1991). Toyota bridled at this pressure but by mid-1991 appeared to have accepted a more conservative sales strategy. *Nihon Keizai Shimbun* (February 9, 1991); *Nikkei Weekly* (July 6, 1991).

[235] *Nikkei Sangyo Shimbun* (March 27, 1991).

[236] *Nihon Keizai Shimbun* (March 27, 1991).

the mid 1990s MITI expects the U.S. transplants to be utilizing 75 percent local content.[237] However, the transplants have done this, in substantial part, simply by bringing in transplanted version of their own supplier networks from Japan, so that the result is not necessarily an increase in sourcing from established U.S. and EC firms. The migration of the *keiretsu* structure into the domestic U.S. and European economies, particularly in a key area like autos, has already raised antitrust and other policy concerns.

A third issue is the degree of openness of the Japanese auto market. While formal import restrictions have largely been eliminated, import penetration in Japan has been remarkably low (under 2 percent until 1986). Reasons include the control of the dealer network by the producers, who inhibit dealers from handling imports, strict standards and testing procedures, and differentiated commodity taxes.[238] The Europeans have been particularly vigorous in demanding "reciprocity" in market access, and as a result, several Japanese carmakers have agreed to handle European imports through their dealer nets.[239] Such moves, however, are not tantamount to a more generalized market opening -- Korean sales in Japan, for example, are virtually nil -- and Japan is likely to experience criticism on this issue for the remainder of the decade.

Finally, Japanese firms are developing revolutionary new technologies, such as four wheel steering and electric cars, that could well destabilize competition in autos in the coming decade. While U.S. and EC firms are also exploring these technologies, the Japanese firms have demonstrated a propensity to move forward quickly from the developmental phase into mass production, and are poised to enter promising new areas on a large scale. Toyota is preparing to sell at least 6,000 electric cars in California by 1998, and to expand this effort to other states in subsequent years.[240] Conversely, as a Japanese journal noted in 1991, because of recent losses U.S. firms have "hardly any room to squeeze out funds for attack-type investments, such as the development of new models, rationalization,

---

[237]Interview with a MITI official (1990).

[238]See Eric Batzer and Helmut Laumer, *Marketing Strategies and Distribution Channels for Foreign Companies in Japan* (Boulder: Westview Press, 1989) pp. 177-95; GATT Secretariat in *Trade Policy Review: Japan* (November 1990), point 327.

[239]*Nikkei Weekly* (July 6, 1991).

[240]*Tokyo Shimbun* (February 6, 1991).

etc."[241] The impact on trade relations of large scale Japanese commercialization of one or more new technological concepts, which may render U.S. and EC products and physical plant obsolete, could be dramatic.

Political Sectors

A major feature of the Japanese economy is the existence of manpower-intensive, inefficient sectors which, somewhat paradoxically, coexist with the nation's highly competitive export industries. They include construction, agriculture, fishing, forest products, telecommunications, education, defense procurement, electrical power, retail stores, transportation, tobacco, health care, financial services, medical equipment and a number of other large sectors. To the extent these sectors are affected by trade, they tend to be protectionist in outlook. They enjoy strong political backing not only because of the large number of people employed but because of special institutional arrangements that have evolved between these sectors and the LDP during the past four decades. In the political sectors a powerful triangular alliance is formed between an industry which can mobilize votes and political funds, a government ministry, and the LDP itself, which can be quite resilient in the face of pressure for trade liberalization, and is likely to resist calls from other ministries (MITI, MOF, the *Gaimusho*) for flexibility and reform.[242] The ministries that administer the political sectors are concerned, above all, with protecting the welfare of the industries within their jurisdiction (which may provide landing places for *amakudari* bureaucrats from the ministries).[243] Internationally-minded officials do not exercise significant influence within any of these organizations, and, as MITI officials frequently point out, these ministries are often insensitive to the international implications of their domestic policies. In part this is because most politically-tied sectors do not export significantly (exceptions are telecommunications and shipbuilding) and are therefore not vulnerable to trade retaliation. The protected sectors' position is enhanced by the widely shared view in Japanese politics that established interests should be respected to the maximum extent possible.

---

[241] *Nikkei Sangyo Shimbun* (March 27, 1991).

[242] Interviews with MITI and Finance Ministry officials (1990).

[243] Commonly translated as "descent from heaven" -- indicating the stature held by bureaucrats who "descend" into jobs in the private sector.

In 1990, at least five major political sectors were subject to foreign (primarily U.S.) pressure for liberalization -- agriculture, construction, telecommunications, small retail stores, and processed wood products. Japanese reluctance to make significant concessions in these sectors has been directly linked to political factors, and, to a greater or lesser degree, to electoral politics. The LDP could not retain its hold on power without the support represented by the political sectors, and indeed, its loss of its majority in the Upper House in 1989 was partially attributable to erosion of support among farm groups angered by the LDP's trade liberalization measures in agriculture. Significant trade concessions by Japan in any of these sectors will have major political costs and will be extremely difficult to achieve under any circumstances, but particularly whenever the ruling party's grip on power appears less sure. Through the 1990s Japan will continue to resist foreign demands for liberalization of these sectors, although not without a profusion of incremental, often token liberalization measures designed to defuse foreign pressure. Such measures will permit foreign sales which may be significant in dollar amounts but which, above all, do not force fundamental systemic change. To the extent true change occurs it is likely to be through a combination of strong forces within Japan (such as the demand for more efficient land use) and foreign pressure.

The approach to trade taken by the politically-tied sectors generally does not rise to the level of "strategy;" it usually consists of a sequence of ad hoc tactical moves by individual Ministries and their industry allies with no purpose more grand than to fend off foreign pressure and delay liberalization. This is not to demean the actions taken -- Japanese tactics have generally been skillful and successful -- but they seldom comprise elements in a larger scheme for promoting industry adjustment, rationalization, or broader national economic interests. Tactics include attempts to shift disputes to multilateral trade negotiations (without, however, much sense of how the issue will ultimately play out multilaterally); small and incremental "liberalization" measures accompanied by public relations measures hailing "market opening;" and dramatization of incidents centered on quality and health and safety problems associated with imported products -- a week seldom passes in Japan without several press accounts about problems or tragedies caused by defective imported automobiles, faulty aircraft parts, tainted food and the like. If pressure for liberalization becomes too intense, the affected industry can fall back on the fact that it forms a key element in the LDP's power base; an apparent government movement toward opening agriculture markets was effectively chilled in this way in 1989-90.

It is beyond the scope of this work to trace the Byzantine relationships which characterize each of the political sectors and their effect on trade.

However, a brief survey of three such sectors, agriculture, construction and retail stores, illustrates certain common features. In all of these sectors, the U.S.-Japan dialogue appears immutable: the U.S. demands fundamental systemic change and Japan responds with specific concessions, usually with not insubstantial commercial value but which fall far short of the reforms sought by the U.S.; the U.S. makes further demands and the cycle beings again. Because the affected Japanese sectors usually have no significant export interests, possess an unassailable domestic political base, and are relatively impervious to pressure from internationalist institutions like MITI and the Keidanren, they have no real incentive to undertake fundamental reform. Thus, while it is difficult to predict precisely which industries within MITI's jurisdiction will be the subject of trade friction in the year 2000, it is a reasonably safe conclusion that agriculture, construction and retail stores will remain a major source of trade conflict throughout the decade.

Agriculture

Japan's agricultural production is dominated by part-time farmers cultivating small plots of land.[244] The farm sector is inefficient and much of it survives in its present form only through import protection and government price support programs, which extend to about 70 percent of Japan's agricultural output.[245] Japan's system of electoral districts gives disproportionate power to rural voters, which is reflected in their over-representation in the national government; in some cases a rural vote may carry three times the weight of an urban vote, and while the main urban centers of Japan account for over 40 percent of the national population, they elect less than 20 percent of the members of the Diet.[246] The LDP's ability to dominate the rural districts has proven

---

[244]Over 85 percent of Japanese farm households receive more income from other forms of work than from farming.

[245]R.S. Jones, "Political Economy of Japan's Agricultural Policies," in *World Economy* (March, 1989).

[246]Okimoto (1989) p. 183. In the urban Fourth District of Kanagawa Prefecture, there are three times more people per Diet Member than in six districts of the rural Nagano Prefecture. In the 1982 election, a vote cast in the predominantly rural 5th District of Hyogyo Prefecture carried more than three times the weight of a vote in the urban 4th District of Chiba Prefecture; the Hyogo candidate won a seat with 81,375 votes and the Chiba candidate needed 321,351 to win. R.H. Moore, *Japanese Agriculture: Patterns of Rural Development* (Westview: 1990).

the key to its unbroken hold on power since the U.S. Occupation -- in Lower House general elections, the LDP generally captures up to 90 percent of the seats in the rural districts, whereas it usually wins only about 25 percent of the seats in the metropolitan districts.[247] The rural vote accounts for over half of the LDP's total representation in the Diet; of all the LDP members elected to the Lower House in 1980, 60 percent came from rural prefectures.[248] Accordingly, no LDP government has been willing to accede to trade liberalization measures sufficiently sweeping to jeopardize their rural electoral base.

Rural politics are dominated by a politically powerful organization known as Nokyo, a de facto agricultural *keiretsu* which embraces the Central Union of Agricultural Cooperatives (Zenchu) and all of its roughly 4500 subsidiary cooperatives, affiliated organizations and federations, and local offices. The Nokyo is the principal mechanism through which farmers are brought into economic relationship with the central government and the rest of Japanese society, and it is also a powerful machine for delivering the vote in the rural districts to supportive politicians. The local Nokyo units buy farmers' products and market them through Nokyo trading companies; the Nokyo also sells the rural population most of the tools, seed, and fertilizer which it needs for farming, and provides credit, welfare, warehousing, insurance, health, and other services.[249] The government's payment for virtually the entire rice harvest goes to the Central Bank for Agriculture and Forestry, where it "circulates in all the sections of the Nokyo organization like blood, supplying nourishment to each segment."[250] The bank transfers the rice money through the Nokyo credit federation directly to the savings accounts of the individual rice farmers, where it can be loaned by Nokyo banks.[251] The central Nokyo bank reserves about half the deposits for outside investments, and when a general meeting of Nokyo members endorses a campaign, the bank may automatically deduct contributions from each savings account to support the campaign -- a mechanism which enables the Nokyo to finance massive publicity campaigns, for example, on the perils of imported food products. While the Nokyo is sometimes

---

[247]*Japan Economic Journal* (July 8, 1989); Okimoto (1989).

[248]Moore (1990) p. 163.

[249]*Food Policy* (August, 1988); Van Wolferen (1989) pp. 60-63.

[250]H. Ishikawa, cited in Van Wolferen (1989) p. 62.

[251]Moore (1990).

viewed as a spokesman for farmers, Von Wolferen (1989) and Hayami (1988) argue that its real client is itself; it does not necessarily represent farmers' interests and serves as a mechanism to forestall independent political action by farmers.[252]

The Nokyo organization is a powerful and often irresistible force in rural elections. The Nokyo visits each rural household at least twice during each election and indicates which candidate is the Nokyo's choice; it holds meetings of local farm groups at which its favored candidates are announced; and it may organize rallies and send Nokyo employees, their wives and children to boost campaign staffs -- in Miyazaki Prefecture, for example, the Nokyo supplies 3,000 campaign workers free of charge.[253] In addition to electioneering, The Nokyo sponsors a number of Diet members' *zoku*,[254] the largest of which is the Agricultural Policy Research Association. The Nokyo officials represent the organization directly in meetings of the *zoku*, and there are regular personal contacts between Nokyo leaders and party leaders; The Nokyo uses every channel and point of access into the policy-making process, in addition to the mass mobilization activities it mounts in public arena.[255]

The Nokyo has traditionally functioned as a machine for delivering the rural vote to the LDP, alhtough its interests and those of the ruling party are not congruent. Local Nokyo units occasionally back opposition candidates or alternative LDP candidates in opposition to the candidates put forward by the national party leadership, but these actions are

---

[252]"Even if the total income of farm households may increase by trade liberalization through an increase in their off-farm income, that is of no benefit to Nokyo. . . . Probably the greatest myth of Japanese agriculture today is the slogan that Nokyo is of the farmers, by the farmers, and for the farmers." Y. Hayami, *Japanese Agriculture Under Siege* (New York: St. Martin's Press, 1988); Van Wolferen (1989) p. 60.

[253]Because open electioneering is prohibited by law, the visits and meetings are held under the guise of some other purpose, such as the announcement of a new kind of insurance, but the Nokyo's candidate of choice is identified. Van Wolferen (1989) p. 64.

[254]*Zoku* are roughly analogous to partisan policy groups and caucuses in the U.S. Congress. They are groups of Diet members who follow the issues and concerns of a particular sector such as telecommunications or construction, as well as the policies of the relevant Ministry.

[255]A. George and E. Saxon, "The Politics of Agricultural Protection in Japan," in Anderson and Hayami, eds., *The Political Economy of Agricultural Protection* (Sydney: 1986).

exceptional.[256] The linkage from such "grass-roots" political power to agricultural trade policy is both clear and deeply embedded. The Nokyo organization vigorously resists any initiative to open the Japanese market or to promote structural adjustment in agriculture. In fact, a fundamental pillar of rural support for the LDP has been the party's willingness, through MAFF to embrace a protectionist trade policy in agriculture. "[A]griculture protection policies are entrenched deeply in vested interests -- above all, the powerful Nokyo organization with its alliance with MAFF and LDP stands ready to fight against any move towards trade liberalization."[257] The Nokyo has forged a very successful alliance with urban consumers, using publicity campaigns to play on the fear of food additives and chemicals in imported foods, with the result that consumer groups like the Housewives Association have criticized the proponents of trade liberalization.[258]

The Ministry of Agriculture, Forestry, and Fisheries is the vehicle through which the Japanese government both provides support for domestic agriculture and fends off foreign pressure for agricultural trade reform. MAFF's position is opposed by powerful ministries like MOF and MITI. MOF's opposition to current agricultural policy is based on the financial drain agriculture places on the national budget. For MITI, Japan's protectionist agricultural trade policies are an embarrassment in its efforts to promote the international interests of Japan's strategic manufacturing industries. However, to date, neither of these otherwise powerful ministries has even begun to break the political alliance that maintains the government's deep support for domestic agriculture, despite occasional efforts to alter the terms of the debate.[259]

It is difficult to characterize Japan's approach to trade in agriculture as a "strategy" at all; in effect Japan has simply waged a rear guard action through a series of tactical gambits designed to fend off foreign initiatives

---

[256]Van Wolferen (1989) p. 64.

[257]Hayami (1988) p. 125.

[258]George and Saxon (1986) p. 107. In 1988 the group representing domestic agriculture produced a video that showed deformed children, human fetuses and monkeys and questioned whether imported food was safe. The video was distributed through local Nokyo subunits and video stores. *Billings Gazette* (March 29, 1988).

[259]For example, witness the consequences of MITI Minister's January 1990 remarks to the press that Japan could no longer resist foreign pressure to liberalize its rice market, discussed below.

to open the market. Many Japanese officials hope that Japan's agriculture sector can be rationalized and become internationally competitive over the long run; some even see Japan emerging as a major agricultural exporter. But as Agriculture Minister Kondo commented at the end of 1990, "I cannot say by when, but it is necessary to put a brake (on market liberalization as much as possible at this time, carry through internal measures considerably quickly, and realize rational agriculture about which there is no anxiety in the future."[260] From MAFF's perspective, this approach has worked fairly well, although entailing costs for Japan in the form of periodic defeats in the GATT, where *gaiatsu* in agriculture has taken the form of multilateral dispute settlement to a degree that is uncommon in other sectors. Japan's policies in this area are an easy target; GATT panels are unlikely to rule in Japan's favor, and less political capital need be expended in negotiations if formal rulings against Japan can be secured. In the face of a series of adverse GATT rulings (and the pendency of other GATT cases where its prospects for success were poor) Japan has been compelled to phase out quantitative restrictions in sector after sector; in general, however, it has concurrently raised tariffs to extremely high levels, committing itself to phased, partial reductions thereafter. In dairy products, for example, after the GATT Council in 1988 adopted a panel report in a case brought by the United States, finding that Japan's quantitative restrictions were inconsistent with the GATT, Japan eliminated quotas on processed cheese but raised the tariff to 60 percent, to be reduced by stages to 40 percent by 1991. Similar measures were taken with respect to beef, some types of fruit juice, sugar products, catsup and a number of other products.[261]

The most politically sensitive agricultural trade issue is rice, which has an emotional hold on many Japanese heavily tinged with nationalism.[262] A 1989 poll showed that nearly 80 percent of all Japanese were opposed to liberalization of imports,[263] and in September 1988, both Houses of the Diet unanimously passed a resolution opposing liberalization of rice imports. Japan has been unwilling to eliminate

---

[260]*Nihon Keizai Shimbun* (December 31, 1990).

[261]GATT, *Japan: Trade Policy Review* (November 1990), Point 242.

[262]The Japanese view themselves as a nation descended from rice farmers, with many cultural roots in the communal rice farming society. In addition, recalling the U.S. blockade in World War II and the oil embargo of the early 1970s, there is a concern with self-sufficiency in food.

[263]*Kyodo* (13:06 GMT, June 9, 1989).

quantitative restraints on rice imports, and has responded to U.S. pressure by shifting the issue into the Uruguay Round negotiations. This gambit was successful in a number of respects: it induced USTR to reject two Section 301 petitions filed by U.S. rice producers; it placed other countries in the spotlight with Japan, notably the EC, enabling Japan to depict itself as relatively liberal in world terms (a large importer of soybeans and wheat and a non-practitioner of export subsidies); and it enabled Japan to make common cause with the EC on some key issues, such as the need to preserve family farming. However, whatever the short run benefits of this approach, it has involved significant risks. Having aroused U.S. expectations of significant reform in the Uruguay Round, the Japanese government found that political pressure placed high domestic costs on making significant concessions in the Round.

The domestic pressure to resist further concessions on rice was actually becoming more intense at the end of the 1980s. In 1989 the LDP suffered a series of sharp defeats in special elections in rural districts, followed by the loss of its majority in the Upper House in July.[264] The LDP's defeats reflected not only voter dissatisfaction but the extent to which opposition parties have moved to capitalize on the LDP's vulnerability on the farm issue.[265] The JSP strongly advocated a protectionist policy in 1989, including tighter restrictions on imports and retention of the existing system of price supports.[266] This resulted in some unusual political

---

[264]In June an LDP candidate was defeated in an Upper House special election in Niigata, a major rice-producing prefecture and a traditional base of LDP support. In a gubernatorial election in the same prefecture during that month, the LDP candidate won such a narrow victory that it was regarded as a "moral defeat." In February 1989, in a special election in Fukuokua Prefecture, which has a large rural population, an LDP candidate lost by a wide margin to a JSP candidate. Finally, in the July 1989 elections, the LDP lost its majority in the Upper House; a key element in its defeat was the gains made by the opposition in traditional LDP rural strongholds. *Japan Economic Journal* (July 8, 1989); *Kyodo* (17:45 GMT, July 23, 1989).

[265]The trade issue was the most important of a number of rural grievances with the LDP which came to a head in 1989. The Recruit and Uno-womanizing scandals alienated voters. More significantly, the LDP had supported a policy of reform of the price support system for rice which resulted in reductions in the price of rice for two consecutive years -- a policy that was sufficiently unpopular that the government decided to freeze rice prices in fiscal 1989, seeking to forestall further erosion of rural LDP support prior to the Upper House elections in July. Finally the government sponsored a plan to promote the gradual reduction in the acreage under cultivation for rice, another unpopular measure.

[266]*Kyodo* (08:40 GMT, July 24, 1989).

alignments, with local Nokyo units -- traditionally conservative LDP supporters -- working loosely with the Socialists to elect opposition candidates. A number of local Nokyo units openly and successfully backed opposition candidates in the Upper House elections, citing, in particular, their dissatisfaction with the LDP's moves toward trade liberalization in agriculture.[267] While this alignment did not appear to represent a permanent change in the balance of political power in the rural prefectures,[268] the JSP and other opposition parties have demonstrated that they can capitalize on LDP weaknesses through alliances with traditional sources of LDP support.[269] Even prior to the 1989 elections the government was forced to abandon its policy of reduction in price supports, a measure which failed to placate rural voters. Reflecting these political pressures, there was a stiffening of opposition by Japanese bureaucrats and politicians to any suggestion of further market opening. In the wake of the July elections, MAFF officials commented that they were "concerned" that the LDP's defeat "could result in a standstill in the process of liberalizing Japanese agriculture by allowing the protectionist opposition to have a larger say in fashioning farm policies."[270] In late 1989, Prime Minister Kaifu pledged that he would honor resolutions passed by the Diet opposing liberalization of rice imports. The new Agriculture Minister, Michihiko Kano, acknowledged that the LDP's setbacks in the July elections were due in part to the unpopular agricultural policies undertaken by the LDP; one of his

---

[267]*Japan Economic Journal* (July 8, 1989); *Asahi* (August 31, 1989).

[268]One local Nokyo spokesman who collaborated with the JSP commented that his organization had some misgivings about "joining hands with the JSP," but that "if we did not have the support of the JSP we could not possibly win." He indicated that "It is not that we have severed our connections with the LDP. However, unless it produces new policies toward farm households, 60 to 70 percent of them will not return to the LDP. . . . However, conservative blood flows in our veins. . . . The sense of relying on the political party in power is especially strong. Our big task from now on is how to repair our relations with the LDP and appeal our demands to it." *Asahi* (August 31, 1989).

[269]The JSP has advanced a proposal opposing the government's plan to reduce rice acreage, which is consistent with the Nokyo's opposition to the plan. *Tokyo Shimbun* (October 21, 1989).

[270]*Kyodo* (July 24, 198).

principal objectives is to make MAFF more "reliable" to Japanese farmers, meaning a more uncompromising posture on trade.[271]

The rice issue underscores one of the principal structural weaknesses in the Japanese government, the weakness of "horizontal" institutions cutting across ministerial boundaries which can produce compromises in areas where one ministry's positions are creating unacceptable costs for Japan. In the case of rice, MAFF's intransigent posture (supported, to be sure, by major elements of the LDP) placed significant strains on the Uruguay Round, in which Japan stood to gain far more in general than it would lose by opening its rice markets, and raised the prospect of foreign retaliation against Japanese exports. In the absence of a powerful executive with a final say over such issues, and with MAFF relatively impervious to pressure from other ministries, there was no clear institutional mechanism for resolving this issue. Thus, in 1990 MITI Minister Matsunaga remarked that Japan could no longer resist liberalizing its rice market; he was publicly rebuked by MAFF and the Zenchu, Prime Minister Kaifu told a cabinet meeting he strongly regretted Matsunaga's remark, and Matsunaga himself backed away from his original comments.[272]

Developments in early 1991 raised the prospect that the rice issue might be resolved through intercession of the leadership of the LDP, with significant concessions on rice imports being offered in the context of a successful conclusion of the Uruguay Round. A number of influential LDP politicians began to speak, "as if orchestrated by some hidden conductor," in favor of partial liberalization of rice imports as part of a larger Uruguay Round agreement; these included former Prime Minister Takeshita, LDP power broker Shin Kanemaru, and Prime Minister Kaifu.[273] There were reports that the government was contemplating a limited opening of the domestic market (e.g., 10 percent) to imported rice as a bargaining chip in the Uruguay Round negotiations. However, mass protests by Japanese farmers were held in response to these moves, and by the summer of 1991, the proponents of liberalization were reportedly backing away from their position. A significant factor, in addition to the

---

[271]*Kyodo* (January 4, 1990).

[272]Bureau of National Affairs, *International Trade Reporter* (January 24, 1990).

[273]*Nikkei Weekly* (July 6, 1991); *Washington Post* (May 29, 1991). Former Agriculture Minister Tsutomu Hata, the head of the LDP agriculture *zoku*, indicated that a partial opening of the rice market could be accepted so long as there was a "guarantee as not to lead gradually to complete liberalization in the future." *Sankei* (January 11, 1991).

predictable resistance from farm interests, was the slackening of *gaiatsu*; the Uruguay Round negotiations appeared bogged down around issues to which rice suddenly appeared peripheral; and post-Gulf war anger at Japan had not materialized as feared.[274]

Regardless of how the rice issue is resolved, the issue dramatizes the larger problems inherent in liberalizing the "political" sectors. Whatever happens with respect to rice, the nation's top leaders cannot come together to orchestrate similar measures in the hundreds of more prosaic product areas, ranging from construction services to wood products, where powerful ministries allied with protectionist domestic constituencies work together to restrict imports. Absent extraordinary circumstances, the LDP leadership will not intervene in these areas and there is no institutional mechanism through which other elements of the bureaucracy and business community can seek a moderation of policies which may, on balance, be inconsistent with Japan's broader foreign policy and economic interests.

Construction

The construction industry and its affiliated politicians and bureaucrats arguably constitute the most powerful protectionist bloc in any Japanese sector. The industry itself is enormous: Japan has over 500,000 construction companies employing over 5 million people. Many of these firms are small enterprises that support local communities as their constituents.[275] The industry accounts for over 15 percent of Japan's GNP. It has been characterized as a sort of "unemployment countermeasure" which can absorb large numbers of Japanese who might otherwise be unable to find work.[276] The primary nexus between the construction industry and the LDP is a system of bid rigging known as *dango*, which is based on collusive relations among political, governmental and industrial circles in public projects and quasi-public projects."[277] According to Van Wolferen, if a construction firm wants to bid on a

---

[274]MAFF Minister Kondo charged that in proposing liberalization, "LDP leaders had not understood what was going on in the Round." *Nikkei Weekly* (July 6, 1991).

[275]*Nihon Keizai Shimbun* (October 5, 1989).

[276]*Japan Economic Journal* (March 26, 1988).

[277]Director of Japan Institute of Architects Masayoshi Yendo in *JEI Report* (January 6, 1989).

project, it begins by bribing a powerful LDP politician, who will recommend that the government steer the project to the firm.[278] The lead firm convenes the other candidates for the job at a session (*dango*) in which the actual work is divided and parceled out among the candidates to ensure that all of the firms in the "joint enterprise body" get a piece of the project. The lead firm then submits a bid with the price based on inside cost information received from government officials; the other firms set all of their bids above this price.[279] According to Japanese press accounts the companies sometimes pool a part of the contracted price and make secret political donations to LDP politicians with ties to the construction industry.[280]

Besides the *dango* system itself, there are many other ties between the ruling party and the industry. The construction industry pays more political contributions to the LDP than any other industry except banking;[281] moreover, it accounts for 10-15 percent of all large-account contributions of 20 million yen or more. According to Japanese press accounts, with respect to large scale public construction projects such as

---

[278]Of the roughly 100 bribery scandals that occur in Japan each year, over half involve construction firms. For specific examples of bribery by construction enterprises, see *Tokyo Business Today* (February 1987). In 1988 the *Asahi Shimbun* uncovered an internal "pre-bidding" list at the Ministry of Construction which listed "most likely candidates" among construction companies for specific awards; these were companies that had already completed the dango process and were in communication with the Ministry over who should win the contract. Confronted with the procedure, which made a sham of competitive bidding, a former Ministry official said only that "The Construction Ministry is not the only case. I think that public-works ordering organs throughout the country are doing things like that." *Asahi* (December 30, 1989).

[279]Van Wolferen (1989).

[280]*Tokyo Shimbun* (February 6, 1989). A number of specific cases involving *dango* have come to light in recent years. In December 1988, 105 Japanese contractors were caught rigging bids for work at a U.S. navy base and were suspended by the Construction Ministry for bidding on public works for two months. "The penalized executives apologized, swore not to do it again, and agreed to draw up a plan to stop it. Few believed them." In 1989 the Japanese press disclosed a dango arrangement, called "Sennari-Kai," involving 18 companies bidding on TV receiving facilities ordered by the Osaka Prefectural Office, which allocated contracts among the members based on a mutually agreed points system. *Engineering News Record* (March 16, 1989); *Mainichi* (Osaka Edition) (April 3, 1989).

[281]*Tokyo Shimbun* (February 6, 1989).

dams and highways, traditionally a fixed percentage of the funds expended on each project were channeled directly to the LDP, or specifically, to the Tanaka faction of the LDP, which "had a virtual stranglehold on the Ministry of Construction."[282] In 1988 *Nihon Keizai Shimbun* estimated that 80 percent of all 425 LDP Diet members had close ties with the construction industry.[283] The children of a number of prominent LDP politicians (including former Prime Ministers Takeshita and Nakasone) have married children of construction executives. The construction industry also wields enormous clout at election time. Local political organizations under the control of the Construction Ministry can coordinate elections in virtually all of Japan's election districts, and they vigorously support former construction officials running for office.[284] The sheer volume of the Construction Ministry's spending makes it one of Japan's most powerful ministries, and the Minister of Construction is in an excellent position to attract "political" funds.[285] The Ministry receives a larger share of the general accounts budget than any other ministry (8-14 percent) and about 25 percent of the "second" budget, the Fiscal Investment and Loan Plan (FILP). It issues licenses to the entire construction industry, and directly or indirectly supervises most of the roughly 500,000 public works projects undertaken in Japan each year.

The principal barrier to foreign participation in the domestic construction market is the complex Japanese system of awarding public works contracts, which contrasts sharply with the open U.S. system. In Japan, to bid on any part of a project, a company must be registered with the Ministry, which ranks each firm according to factors such as its ability, past performance, business record and other similar factors; based on these rankings, about ten firms are invited to submit bids, with the "low" bidder winning. This system enables the Ministry to manipulate the firms that are even eligible to bid on a contract for its own purposes; big firms are

---

[282]With Tanaka's decline in health, his faction's control over the Ministry broke down and was largely taken over by the Nakasone faction of the LDP. *Tokyo Business Today* (February 1987).

[283]*Japan Economic Journal* (March 26, 1988).

[284]The Construction Ministry coordinates at election time with flood-prevention unions that are found in most of Japan's populated valleys. Finally, the construction companies provide electoral support for the LDP through the *Koenkai*, local organizations that establish and maintain vote-getting networks, and lend secretaries and cars to LDP politicians. Van Wolferen (1989) p. 117.

[285]Van Wolferen (1989) p. 115.

kept from bidding for small projects, "excessive" competition is prevented, and only "qualified" firms are invited to bid. The system is not only vulnerable to corruption and favoritism, but works to exclude foreign firms from even the opportunity to bid on most projects. Many foreign firms, for example, are not eligible to register with the Ministry because to do so they must have demonstrated their competence through prior work experience in Japan -- an impossibility given their inability to register.[286] U.S. negotiators' principal objective in the 1980s was to persuade Japan to adopt an open bidding system comparable to that used in the U.S.

The Japanese construction industry itself and its bureaucratic allies in the Construction Ministry have vigorously opposed foreign participation in the Japanese construction market, and the industry's influence within the LDP is so great that the Japanese government is unlikely to assent to wide-ranging liberalization regardless of the amount of *gaiatsu* which is applied. According to a Japanese critic of the system, reform would require elimination of the joint enterprise body system, its replacement with a system based on market principles, and "vigorous legal enforcement, including civil actions and criminal prosecutions."[287] The Construction Ministry has made no moves toward establishing a new system,[288] and "politicians having close relations with the construction industry will certainly have their say if the Americans seriously call for liberalization, even of local public works projects that have direct bearings on election results."[289] A deep-seated Japanese concern is that changing to an open, U.S.-style bidding system would not only result in the failure of many small construction firms but an influx of low-cost construction companies from Korea, possibly using cheaper foreign workers -- which could destroy much of the Japanese industry.[290]

---

[286]Krauss and Coles (1990) p. 341-42.

[287]M. Yendo (1989).

[288]*Asahi* (April 14, 1989).

[289]Hiroyoshi Aoki, President of Aoki Corp., in *Japan Economic Journal* (March 26, 1988); *Washington Post* (June 1, 1991).

[290]Krauss and Coles (1990) p. 346. As of April 1991 nine Korean construction firms had received licenses to do business in Japan; they had won eight private sector projects but no public works projects. Korean workers could not be used on these projects without revision of Japan's Immigration Control Law. *Japan Economic Journal* (April 13, 1991).

The Japanese negotiating strategy in construction has been to preserve the system itself more or less intact while defusing periodic U.S. pressure through small, incremental concessions on specific projects, which are hailed with considerable fanfare.[291] Project-specific concessions have been augmented by government gestures and statements emphasizing the open nature of the market; the Ministry points out that *dango* is illegal and that it punishes it; the Japan Federation of Construction Contractors (JFCC) states that the government is "strictly" implementing the Antimonopoly Law and does not tolerate the practice of *dango*, "and that the JFCC is "very conscientious in ensuring compliance with the Antimonopoly Law among its members."[292] At the same time, they argue that U.S. construction firms have not made the level of commitment to serve the Japanese market which is necessary to succeed, and that this is perhaps the real reason for the poor U.S. results in Japan to date.[293]

U.S.-Japan trade friction in construction is likely to continue through the decade of the 1990s. The Construction Ministry, backed by its industry and political allies, is not now under great pressure to modify the closed bidding system that protects virtually all of local construction market, and the strategy of throwing a few projects to the Americans to dissipate *gaiatsu* has thus far arguably been successful. The U.S. will continue the pressure, if for no other reason than to secure additional projects which, while falling short of market opening, are nevertheless valuable for U.S. firms. While the JFTC's actions against *dango* have been cited as indicators that the system is slowly changing, those actions are arguably indicative of the government's lack of zeal to eradicate *dango*. The Commission cited a group of Japanese firms for rigging bids for the U.S. Navy facility at Yokosuka; it fined the firms and wanted to suspend them from bidding on all government projects for six to nine months. The Ministry of Construction intervened to reduce the period to one

---

[291]Bechtel has become a member of a 10-company joint enterprise body which will construct Haneda Airport's terminal building, and has been awarded a consulting fee by the Trans-Tokyo Bay Highway Company. Scherr has won 10 percent of the "Yokohama Port Future" project. Some European and Korean firms have also begun to secure small projects in Japan. U.S. architects have found a substantial market for design work in Japan. In 1991, confronting trade sanctions, Japan agreed to allow U.S. firms to bid on several dozen additional major projects, including a resort, hospitals and airports. *Nihon Keizai* (May 23, 1989). *Asahi* (April 14, 1989); *Engineering News Record* (April 13, 1989).

[292]*Jiji Press Ticker Service* (March 16, 1989).

[293]*Nihon Keizai Shimbun* (May 23, 1989).

month -- to be applied during the slowest month of the year -- and lifted the ban just before bids were due on the $12 billion trans-Tokyo Bay bridge project were accepted.[294] As the *Asahi Shimbun* summarized the situation on April 14, 1989,

> "*[T]o look back at the situation over the past one year, there are seen no attempts for improvement in the liberalization of the main parts of the construction work itself, the monetary amount of which is big, reflecting the intentions of the influential members of the LDP, whom the construction industry circles call the 'voice of Heaven,' even though making some concessions toward hard line and loud-voiced arguers. . .*"

Retail Stores

Like construction, the retail store sector will continue to experience significant foreign pressure for liberalization in the 1990s, but with somewhat better prospects for real opening. With the exception of farmers, small shopkeepers are probably Japan's most powerful conservative electoral bloc. The shopkeepers, together with their families, account for about 20 million votes, most of which are cast for the LDP, although Komeito also enjoys significant support. The shopkeepers, like the farmers, enjoy a certain mystique, being seen as the social glue which holds together the large Japanese cities that have grown up since the War. The LDP particularly depends on the shopkeepers in urban areas, where it is comparatively weak; retailers are active and effective at canvassing for elections. As the chairman of the National Shopkeepers Promotion Association comments, "the big stores stuff the politicians with money, but we have the power of 20 million votes."[295] The retail store owners' bureaucratic support is found in MITI's Small and Medium Enterprise (SME) Agency, a politicized enclave within a relatively apolitical ministry.[296] MITI directs loans to SMEs through private banks,

---

[294]*JEI Report* (March 17, 1989). Similarly, in 1989 the Construction Ministry cited six Japanese firms for rigging bids on a part of the Kansai Airport project. The penalty was a one month suspension from bidding on construction projects in Western Japan. *Reuters* (September 20, 1989).

[295]*Financial Times* (February 27, 1989).

[296]MITI's role in providing financial assistance to SMEs reflects an early 1970s bid by the Japan Communist Party to woo small business support. The LDP responded by increasing MITI's SME budget by 600 percent, to 240 billion yen, and (continued...)

depending on the guidance of a veritable army (over 25,000) of "small business advisers" who screen loan applications. These advisers' wages are half paid by MITI and half paid by prefectural governments and the local chambers of commerce. Through this system the government effectively reaches a segment of the electorate by channeling money to them. According to some analysts such programs are essentially defensive in character, to prevent inroads by the JSP or the JCP among the SMEs.[297]

The retail sector's protection from foreign inroads is founded on the *Daitenhō*, or Large Retail Store Law. The law originally designed was to provide for a smooth adjustment by small retail stores to the opening of nearby supermarkets and large retail outlets; however it has evolved into a mechanism for thwarting the opening of big stores altogether. By its terms the law requires anyone opening a large store (over 1500 sq. meters) to submit an application to MITI five months before the planned opening; proposed medium-sized stores (500 to 1500 sq. meters) must be reviewed by prefectural governments before an application is submitted to MITI. After the filing, the information is circulated to affected retailers and officials review the impact of the store opening; if the impact is seen as major, officials can recommend that the opening be delayed. Applications for new stores above 1500 square meters must also be reviewed by an advisory body, the Council on Large Scale Retail Stores, while smaller stores must be reviewed by similar councils established in the prefectures. The Council on Large Retail Stores must in turn take into account the views of the Council for Coordinating Commercial Activity (CCCA), a body made up of consumers, scholars, and the local Chamber of

---

[296](...continued)
elevating the SME bureau within MITI to Agency status. Patrick and Bohlen, "Small Family Enterprises," in Yamamura and Yasuba, eds., *The Political Economy of Japan* (1989) Vol. 1, p. 369.

[297]Patrick and Bohlen (1989) p. 369. It would be inaccurate to characterize MITI's role with respect to SMEs as simply seeking to protect this sector. MITI's basic objectives lie in the opposite direction, encouraging structural changes that lead to greater efficiency in the Japanese economy. However, political pressures are sometimes such that if MITI does not implement policies to strengthen threatened SME sectors, the Diet will enact its own protectionist legislation, or the LDP will face large-scale SME defections to other parties. MITI is thus engaged in a balancing exercise in which it must nudge various SME sectors toward structural reform while sweetening the process through financial assistance, antitrust protection, and the delay of measures that would expose SMEs to greater competitive pressure.

Commerce. Local pressure groups have exploited this complex structure to block the opening of large retail stores altogether.[298]

The U.S government has made the *Daitenhō* a major subject of discussion in the Structural Impediments Initiative and a number of large U.S. retail chains, including Seven-Eleven and Toys 'R' Us, have made a substantial commitment to penetrating the Japanese market. Despite the political strength of the shopkeepers, U.S. efforts in the retail sector are more likely to produce significant results than in most of the other "political" sectors because *gaiatsu* can be employed in conjunction with domestic pressures for change of the current system. The political strength of the small store owners is partially offset by the large retailers and the Keidanren, many of whose members have a direct economic interest in improving the efficiency of the retail system and who are also large financial contributors to the LDP. In addition, Japan's consumers have begun to awaken to the substantial and in many cases outrageous disparities between Japanese prices and the world price for many items; the LDP must increasingly balance traditional electoral concerns over the retailers' vote against a potential backlash by consumers who associate their own high prices with the LDP's "money politics." Moreover, some Japanese communities have begun to seek large stores in their localities, in some cases supported by small and medium shopkeepers who have become convinced that the larger outlets will draw more customers for their own business.[299] Japanese manufacturers, who are often linked to domestic distributors, have begun to discover that the opening of chains like Toys 'R' Us in Japan is not necessarily all bad; such chains are multinational in character and constitute a potential vehicle for

[298]While under the *Daitenhō* the opening of a new store is supposed to take five to seven months, at the end of the 1980s the average time for opening a new store was seven to eight years and in some cases as long as 15 years. Under official MITI guidelines the CCCA was supposed to provide its recommendation to the Council on Large Scale Retail Stores in three weeks. Local merchants, however, lobbied for and eventually succeeded in securing an official role for an informal body called a "pre-CCCA," which was required to approve items such as the size of a store and its business hours before an application could be filed with MITI. Compounding the problem, local retailers established another group, the "pre-pre-CCCA," which was required to be consulted before applications could be filed with prefectural governments. The procedures of the pre-CCCAs and the pre-pre-CCCAs lacked transparency and time limits, and were characterized by large retailers as vehicles for harassment, the extraction of concessions, and extensive delay. Obviously many potential retailers, confronted with this obstacle, simply did not make the effort. *JEI Report* (November 10, 1989).

[299]USITC, *Japan's Distribution System,* p. 4-8.

distributing Japanese manufactured products to many other countries.[300] Finally, the stranglehold which small businesses have established on this area of the Japanese economy is being eroded, ironically, by small-and-medium entrepreneurs who are finding ways to undercut Japan's artificially high prices and bring "bargains" to consumers.[301]

Partly for these reasons, overhaul of the *Daitenhō* became the centerpiece of the SII negotiations and was held up as an example of the overall success of the talks. The reality is more mixed. Reform of the law has served to highlight the abiding strength of the "structural" resistance to change as well as the fact of change itself. In 1990 Prime Minister Kaifu announced that the *Daitenhō* would be phased out over a three-year period, but the ensuing political uproar forced him to back away from this proposal. (MITI asserted that retention of the law was necessary to enable it to influence the result of the reforms in favor of liberalization.) Under a compromise reached in the SII talks, Japan agreed only to revise, not abolish the law; the maximum waiting period was to be reduced from three years to one in 1991; three "exempted zones" would be set up in Japan where the law would not apply at all; opening or expansion of stores of up to 1,000 meters was exempted from coordination procedures, and the CCCA system was to be abolished and replaced by a review by MITI's Large Scale Retail Store Council.[302] In the wake of these reforms, the U.S. government noted in its 1991 SII report that new store openings had doubled in one year, that MITI was "processing these applications in a smooth and transparent manner," and that U.S. and other foreign retailers were moving to enter the Japanese market.[303] Toys 'R' Us moved forward with an ambitious plan to open 100 outlets in Japan over the next decade, stirring up considerable controversy, as a new "coming of the black ships."[304] Retailers joined together to secure limits on the floorspace available to Toys 'R' Us outlets; while the U.S. chain was progressively overcoming these problems, Japanese and foreign

---

[300]"Japanese toymakers drool at the prospect of supplying Toys 'R' Us." *Japan Economic Journal* (February 16, 1991).

[301]Mari Mishima, "A Distribution Revolution Begins," *Ekonomisuto* (May 31, 1988), translated in *Economic Eye* (September 1988).

[302]"Report by the Japanese Delegation," SII *First Annual Report,* Item III. 3.(1)(b).

[303]"Comments of the U.S. Delegation," SII *First Annual Report,* p. 12.

[304]*Japan Economic Journal* (February 16, 1991).

toymakers expressed fear of selling to Toys 'R' Us and incurring the wrath of Japanese wholesalers, who might then boycott their products.[305] Nintendo, for one, was large enough to disregard such pressures and enter into a direct sale arrangement with Toys 'R' Us.[306]

Retail stores are likely to remain on the bilateral trade agenda through the decade of the 1990s, although if present trends continue, by decades end a number of U.S. chains will be well established in Japan. Resistance is likely to be sustained by groups of local shopkeepers on a town-by-town, even store-by store basis, requiring the U.S. government to maintain constant pressure to prevent backsliding. An atmosphere of crisis reportedly pervades some communities potentially affected by the changes, and "MITI is trying to determine the best way to consult with the localities and alleviate the pressure;" one U.S. government official even suggested that the specific number of large stores that will actually be permitted to open "had already been agreed to long before SII."[307] One U.S. academic has predicted that the "corruption and intimidation associated with" the *Daitenhō* will continue at the grass roots level through mechanisms such as intimidation of officials and shopkeepers sympathetic to large stores and landowners who might sell out to them."[308] One unknown is the effect of the relaxation of the *Daitenhō* on large domestic retailers; one scenario postulates that these enterprises, not U.S. chains, will be the primary beneficiaries of the restructuring, and will come to dominate the retail sector in the same manner that *keiretsu*-linked firms now dominate many manufacturing sectors.

CONCLUSION

While considerable attention and foreign criticism has been directed toward the role played by the Japanese government in the country's extraordinary commercial and technological success, Japan's involvement in a seemingly endless succession of trade disputes is as attributable to too little government as to too much. The government has actively promoted industrial expansion but has proven not just passive but arguably absent altogether in important areas of commercial and economic policy where

---

[305]*Japan Economic Journal* (November 24, 1990; February 16, 1991).

[306]*Nikkei Weekly* (June 29, 1991).

[307]USITC, *Japan's Distribution System* (1990) p. 4-8.

[308]USITC (1990) p.4-8.

governments are expected exercise authority. A country whose external commercial policies are largely the sum of the individual policies of autonomous sectoral power groups, most of which have no objective other than the perpetuation of trade protection and mutually beneficial systems of political patronage cannot exercise much leadership within the international trading system, a fact underscored by Japan's low profile in the Uruguay Round. A system of government that depends on foreign pressure to provide the basis for consensus among its component parts invites continual foreign "bashing," simply because it becomes evident to outsiders that bashing provides the motive power for securing results from the system, however imperfect the results may be.

Japan's institutional weaknesses will become more problematic in the 1990s as Japanese industries and industrial groups become even more powerful and assertive. These industries are inadequately regulated by international standards; in many cases they have captured the Ministry which oversees them and are not truly accountable to any higher authority or rules of competitive behavior other than those which the industries choose to adopt themselves, or which are intermittently forced upon them by foreign complaints, threats and retaliatory action. It is not truly remarkable that practices like *dango,* boycotts, cartels and pressure tactics applied to importers and distributors have proliferated in such an environment. To be sure, MITI has learned to moderate the worst excesses of the industries under its jurisdiction through use of methods such as administrative guidance and export cartels, but in a modern economy such opaque and discretionary measures cannot substitute for a real antitrust regime uniformly applied to the economy as a whole and a clear delineation of the limits of acceptable commercial conduct, backed by the prospect of uniform enforcement. A government which cannot adequately discipline its domestic commercial enterprises ultimately invites the imposition of such discipline from the outside. Many of Japan's current leaders recognize this. But given Japan's current institutional structure, the embedded strength of vested sectoral interests, the aggressive moves underway by Japan's export sectors, and the glacial pace of domestic structural reform, trade friction with Japan's trading partners -- "the Japan problem" -- is likely to continue through the 1990s and beyond the turn of the century.

3

Germany

Thomas R. Howell and Gregory I. Hume

For a country of its size and commercial importance, Germany has kept a remarkably low profile in the international trade arena. At the end of the 1980s, West Germany, not Japan, was running the world's largest trade surplus.[1] Yet while the "Japan problem" was generating heated political debate, extensive editorial comment, and hundreds of books, studies and monographs, there was not only no comparable concern over a "German problem" in trade, but little interest in German industrial and trade policies at all. In the United States, only a handful of books were published on the German industrial system between 1980 and 1990. The Office of the U.S. Trade Representative's annual report on trade barriers, which cites a long list of formal and structural barriers in Japan, never contains more than a few entries for Germany, a shorter listing than for such second-rank trading states as Egypt, the Philippines and Mexico.[2] While the Federal Republic's low level of visibility is attributable, in substantial part, to the competitive strategies of its firms and to liberal trade policies, both of which have served to minimize trade friction, it also reflects a certain deliberate stance. Sensitive to their neighbors' historic fears, the Germans have found it prudent to avoid confrontation and controversy in the trade arena, to emphasize their European identity, and

---

[1]GATT International Trade 1987-88, Volume II (Geneva: General Agreement on Tariffs and Trade, 1988) Table AC 3.

[2]USTR, *1991 National Trade Estimate on Foreign Trade Barriers.*

to allow virtually all of their specific trade concerns to be managed by the institutions of the European Community.

Germany's low profile is now harder to sustain. German reunification, coupled with the collapse of the Soviet sphere in Eastern Europe and the imminent breakup of the Soviet Union itself, has thrust Germany onto the center of the European stage as a potential economic and political superpower. German influence in Eastern Europe, quietly developed through commercial contacts and technical assistance over the past several decades, has taken on a new significance as the former Soviet satellites and republics seek western economic and political alignments. Germany's impressive economic strength is now receiving greater attention, with European observers expressing concern that the Community economy will be dominated by Germany's formidable industrial groups: "Germany's European neighbors fear its powerful industries will conquer their markets from a home base made almost inviolable by entrenched and often intangible defenses."[3]

The Germans themselves are less sanguine about their own national prospects. Reunification has brought with it a welter of problems, including high unemployment and growing unrest in the former East Germany, increased taxes, an influx of refugees from all over Eastern Europe, and an ugly wave of anti-foreign violence. The Chairman of the Free Democratic Party, Otto Graf Lambsdorff, observed in late 1991 that reflecting the fiscal strains of reunification, the current federal budget deficit, five percent of GNP, was "more than the frequently criticized U.S. deficit."[4] The state-owned industrial sector in the new Länder (states) in the East has simply fallen apart, and economic conditions in 1991 were appalling, at least by West German standards. A study published by the Kiel Institute concluded that:

> *After the drastic decline in production and employment as a consequence of economic and monetary union, there are no signs of recovery in the East Germany economy during the winter half of the year 1991. Many things even point to a further deterioration. . . . All in all, general world economic conditions are now less favorable for the east German economy*

---

[3]*New York Times* (August 18, 1991).

[4]*Welt am Sonntag* (October 31, 1991) (FBIS-WFU-91-201).

> *than at the time of the implementation of the economic and monetary union. . . . The situation of east German industry gives cause for alarm.*[5]

However, while Germany is preoccupied with reunification, many of its leaders recognize that its most serious long-run challenges come from outside the Continent. Germany's position as a leading trade and economic power rests on the international competitiveness of its leading industries. While these have demonstrated extraordinary skill in adapting quickly to changes in the world economy, long-run German industrial preeminence is threatened by Germany's apparent inability to remain abreast of Japan and the U.S. in the advanced technologies that will determine international competitiveness in the next century. A recent study by the German Research Ministry concluded that German industries were falling behind Japan and the United States in the innovative technologies that would determine future market position in key sectors like machinery, computers, metals and photographic equipment.[6] A Foreign Ministry official, Konrad Seitz, provoked widespread comment in the business community with his 1991 book, *The Japanese-American Challenge*, which argued that German prosperity was threatened by its lagging position in a "third industrial revolution" being driven by five new technologies: information technology, biotechnology, new materials, new energy technology, and space. "We need a new Japanese-style industrial policy for high technology," argued Seitz, "one which combines two normally conflicting tasks with each other: competition and government promotion of industry."[7] But these views are as yet outside the mainstream of German economic thinking; indeed, while their views on most economic matters are characterized by a rough consensus, the country's industrial and political leaders are deeply divided over how to respond to this perhaps most fundamental challenge.

---

[5]First Report in Joint Study by the German Institute for Economic Research, DIW, and the Institute for World Economics at the University of Kiel, published as DIW Report, Number 12, Berlin, 21 March, 1991: "The Macro- and Micro-economic Structural Adjustment Process in Eastern Germany," reproduced in *Wochenbericht* - DIW (March 21, 1991) (FBIS-WEU-91-112) (hereafter DIW *Eastern Germany*).

[6]*Wirtschaftswoche* (April 5, 1991) (JPRS-EST-91-014).

[7]Interview in *Wirtschaftswoche* (April 5, 1991) (JPRS-EST-91-04); see also interview in *General-Anzeiger* (September 27, 1989).

TRADE POLICY DETERMINANTS

The Economic Setting

Trade plays a more important role in Germany than in any other major industrialized nation, including Japan. In 1988 the nation's merchandise exports and imports were equal in size to roughly 45% of GNP, a ratio that was dramatically higher than those for the U.S. (16%) and Japan (15%). The export orientation of the German economy is considerably greater than that of either the U.S. or Japanese economies: exports accounted for roughly 26% of West German GNP in 1988, but only 7% of U.S. GNP and 9% of Japanese GNP.[8] In 21 of the past 25 years (including 1989), West Germany ran a current account surplus, which in recent years has become extremely large. While Japan's surplus is roughly 2.8% of its GNP, West Germany's surplus was roughly 4% of its GNP,[9] making it the leading "surplus" nation within the world economy on the eve of reunification.

Competitively, at the beginning of the 1990s Germany was relatively strong in all major established industrial sectors. That fact has been attributed to Germany's ability to diffuse new technologies rapidly through its industries; its skilled work force with a long tradition of craftsmanship; a relatively high degree of cooperation between industry, banks, labor and government; and the niche strategy emphasizing product quality and specialization pursued by most German industries. A striking feature of the German economy is the proliferation of small and medium-sized manufacturing firms, the so-called *Mittelstand.* Whereas in some countries (such as Taiwan and Japan) smaller firms are often regarded as impediments to international competitiveness, requiring restructuring and consolidation, in Germany, even in the most internationally competitive sectors, small and medium firms play an important role. In part, this may reflect the basic German competitive strategy of pursuing high value, low volume niche markets and generally avoiding head-to-head confrontations with Asian firms in commodity product areas; more fundamentally, the small firms tend to be innovative, technologically advanced, well managed and highly adaptable.

Large industrial groups also play an important role in German industry. Daimler-Benz, Germany's largest group, is a sprawling, diversified entity with over $40 billion in annual revenues, 380,000

---

[8]IMF, *International Financial Statistics*, (August 1989).

[9]IMF, *International Financial Statistics: Yearbook 1989*, pg. 370/1.

employees, and manufacturing operations which include aerospace, automobiles, consumer electronics and arms production; Germany's largest bank, Deutsche Bank, holds a 28.1 percent stake in the company. The steel industry is dominated by five large firms that have extensive cross-sectoral holdings in coal and shipbuilding. Large firms account for a significant portion of total German production in all of Germany's leading industries, and in particular automobiles and electronics.

Germany's manufacturing economy is centered on three "core" industries in which German firms are highly competitive internationally, chemicals, automobiles, and machinery. In all of these industries, advanced technologies and manufacturing processes (many of them of foreign origin) are widely diffused and the industries rank among the world leaders. German trade performance and international competitiveness has been generally solid, but not nearly as successful, in "old" industrial sectors (textiles, steel, shipbuilding) and in "emerging" industries (computers, semiconductors, biotechnology and aerospace). One of the principal questions facing German industry in the 1990s and beyond is whether it can maintain its current international competitive standing through a strategy based on induction and internal diffusion of advanced technologies if Germany itself is not at the forefront of the countries pursuing those technologies.

If the West German economy is extraordinarily strong by world standards, that of the former East Germany is a shambles. Reunification and the introduction of a market economy have resulted in severe economic dislocation throughout the new Länder formed from the old German Democratic Republic. Many former state enterprises have collapsed, and as of mid-1991, new structures had not yet been created which were sufficient to replace the old ones. "From the very beginning the enterprises in East Germany had nothing with which to counter the onrush of western competition, neither domestically nor in foreign western countries."[10] Unemployment in the new Länder in February 1991 was 787,000, with another 1.9 million people working part time, "a kind of disguised unemployment."[11] Bonn was channeling massive aid to the East, but its impact had not yet been felt, in significant part because of the organizational problems associated with spending it in a rational manner. "Money is available in many fields, however the bottlenecks are

---

[10]*Europe "Brief Notes"* No. 1134 (March 1991).

[11]*Wochenbericht - DIW* (March 21, 1991) (FBIS-WEU-91-112).

the administrations which need to learn to use these means quickly and flexibly."[12]

The strain of supporting the restructuring of the East German economy was manifested in increased taxes, rising inflation, and Germany's first monthly balance of payments deficit since the beginning of the 1980s, in January 1991.[13] However, the West German economy appeared capable of sustaining the burden of reunification without significant difficulty. Demand from the new Länder has actually created a boom for many industries in West Germany. Finance Minister Waigel commented in July 1991 that

> *Our economy is in good shape. It reached a growth rate of about 4.6 percent in the first six months of this year, business and industry are very competitive, and equity financing of enterprises is higher than it has ever been before. Regarding stability, we still hold an excellent place in Europe. The German Federal Bank is pursuing the correct monetary and currency policy, and financial policy is under control.*[14]

Industrial Organization

While German economic ideology emphasizes laissez-faire, "behind this facade, German officials and businessmen take for granted a degree of industrial concentration and interfirm cooperation that seems strange to U.S. eyes and often goes relatively unnoticed."[15] German "industrial solidarity" is deeply rooted in the traditions of modern Germany and has survived all of the upheavals of this century. Germany's industrialization in the latter nineteenth and early twentieth centuries was characterized by a close working relationship between banks, the state, and large

---

[12]Minister-President of Schleswig-Holstein in *Berliner Zeitung* (July 27-28, 1991) (FBIS-WEU-91-147).

[13]*Europe/Brief Notes No.* 1134 (March 1991).

[14]Interview in *Süddeutsche Zeitung* (July 30, 1991) (FBIS-WEU-91-147).

[15]Christopher S. Allen, "The Underdevelopment of Keynesianism in the Federal Republic of Germany," in Peter Hull, *The Political Power of Economic Ideas: Keynesianism Across Nations* (Princeton: Princeton University Press, 1989), p. 266; see also Gerard Braunthal, *The Federation of German Business in Politics* (Cornell: Ithaca, 1965).

industrial groups (*Konzerne*) and associations (I.G.s or cartels).[16] Cartels -- not illegal until the Allied occupation -- were a basic form of industrial organization and self-regulation; there were 1,500 in Germany at the end of World War I, 2,700 in 1931 and 6,000 at the end of World War II. Under the Nazis the government assumed control of the economy, frequently utilizing the *Konzerne* and cartels as instruments for implementing their policies. The Allied occupation at the end of the War saw a concerted effort to break up the *Konzerne* and cartels which "dismantled hundreds of viable plants, disrupted supply networks, and broke many of the links between the agricultural and industrial sectors."[17] While Germany's postwar tradition of opposing government intrusion in the economy may well reflect a reaction against the command economy which existed during the War, "many Germans saw the Allied controls as even more oppressive than those of the Nazis," and those controls "contributed to an atmosphere in which enthusiasm for state intervention was quite limited."[18] Thus, while U.S. antitrust concepts did take root in Germany, they did so in rather poor soil. Ludwig Erhard, strongly backed by the Americans, secured the enactment of anticartel legislation in the 1950s, but the legislation was one of Germany's most controversial legislative initiatives of the 1950s, took six years to enact, and was riddled with major loopholes and exceptions when it finally became law.[19] The Bundeskartellamt (Federal Cartel Office), set up by the new law, enforced it very cautiously; it approved all but a handful of the mergers which came before it. In effect it has had "to accommodate itself to a setting in which economic concentration is not only quietly

---

[16]The *Konzerne* were entities linked by share ownership; the I.G.s were associations of separate companies joined by contractual arrangements and other formal and informal agreements. The banks tended to specialize in specific industrial sectors; they owned shares of stock in industrial concerns, organized cartels, and founded new firms. Conversely, industrialists sat on the boards of their affiliated banks. A Dresdner Bank official commented in 1908 that "in Germany our banks are largely responsible for the development of the Empire, having fostered and built up its industries." Kenneth Dyson, "The State, Banks and Industry: The West German Case," in Andrew Cox, ed. *State, Finance and Industry* (New York: St. Martin's Press, 1986).

[17]Allen (1989), p. 269.

[18]Allen (1989), p. 269.

[19]Peter J. Katzenstein, *Policy and Politics in West Germany: The Growth of a Semisovereign State* (Philadelphia: Temple University Press, 1987).

tolerated but actively embraced."[20] Its influence has further diminished with the Single Market Initiatives, which transfers much of the authority which it wielded over large industrial combinations to Brussels.

Against this background, postwar German industry has been characterized by a degree of industrial concentration and cartelization that perhaps falls short of that of the pre-1945 era, but is nevertheless pronounced, certainly by U.S. standards. Firms in major industries take care to refer to each other continually as competitors, but "informal cartel-like arrangements" have not disappeared.[21] Large mergers and acquisitions by major firms (Siemens, Daimler-Benz) have been allowed to proceed. Banks, insurance companies, and industrial concerns are linked through a maze of interlocking directorates and cross-shareholdings of stock: "so many firms are interrelated that it is hardly possible to pick one's way through the network any more. When shareholders form large groups, it grows denser yet. The threads come together in the major banks and insurance companies."[22] A strong tradition of "industrial solidarity" is present in many manufacturing sectors, which on occasion is manifested in what U.S. antitrust authorities would regard as outright cartels, in the old-fashioned sense of that term.[23] At the same time, this tradition has not necessarily reduced the competitiveness of German industry and in some cases has arguably enhanced it, facilitating a joint

---

[20]Peter J. Katzenstein, *Policy and Politics in West Germany: The Growth of a Semisovereign State* (Philadelphia: Temple University Press, 1987), p. 88.

[21]Wyn Grant, William Paterson and Colin Whitston, *Government and the Chemical Industry: A Comparative Study of Britain and West Germany* (Oxford: Clarendon Press, 1988), p. 90.

[22]"Cartel Germany: Competition in our Ranks is Being Curbed," in *Der Spiegel* (August 26, 1991) (FBIS-WEU-91-192).

[23]One example of this phenomenon was the so-called rolled steel joint sales agencies (*Walzstahlkontore*) established by German steel firms in 1967. Under these arrangements, 29 steel firms were organized into four "agencies" which marketed all the steel manufactured by these producers, assuming that each generic product would be sold at a uniform price. The agencies fixed production quotas for each member and facilitated the distribution of purchase orders among companies to spread the burden of a recession in sales. See Klaus Stegemann, *Price Competition and Output Adjustment in the European Steel Market* (Tübingen: J.C.B. Mohr, 1977).

German response to foreign competition.[24] As a French industrialist commented with admiration, "The West German producers. . .know how to exploit to their best advantage a dual principle of free competition and collective discipline to present a hard competitive front."[25]

The Institutional Setting

The German federal government's authority over trade and industrial policy matters is so constrained from below, above, and within that it is questionable whether it could implement a Japanese-style industrial promotion strategy even if it were inclined to do so. Below the federal level, a substantial proportion of German sovereign power over economic, science and industrial policy resides in the Länder, who are also charged with implementing most federal policies outside of defense, currency, and foreign policy "on behalf of" the federal government; implementation of federal policies must be negotiated with the Länder, which are significant centers of power in their own right. In addition, a substantial part of the power normally exercised by sovereign states over economic matters have been or are being transferred from Bonn to the EC authorities in Brussels. This process is leaving the German government with only limited formal legal authority over trade.[26] The federal government's role in trade policy is evolving into that of a mere political subunit -- albeit a highly influential one -- within a larger European confederation. As such it is increasingly a misnomer to speak of German trade policy, per se, rather

---

[24]Using again the example of the *Walzstahlkontore*, the joint sales agencies established a scheme jointly subsidizing exports at prices below prevailing domestic prices in a manner which spread the export loss among all members. The *Kontore* agreements provided (Clause 25) that steel firms that supplied products to the joint sales agencies for export sales should receive the actual export price plus a subsidy (*Exportausgleich*) paid jointly by the *Kontore* members, calculated at 75 percent of the difference between domestic and export prices in the month of sale. See B. Roper, *Rationalisierungseffekte der Walzstahlkontore und der Rationalisierungs-gruppen* (Berlin: Duncker and Humblot, 1974).

[25]Jacques Ferry in *Metal Bulletin* (November 28, 1978).

[26]Germany retains the power under Article 115 of the Treaty of Rome to implement border measures to counter deflections of trade or "economic difficulties" resulting from differing national commercial policy objectives. It retains the power to grant industrial and agricultural subsidies, but subject to EC review. It can, as a practical matter, negotiate "gray" arrangements such as Voluntary Restraint Agreements (VRAs) with external trading partners. It retains a national membership in the GATT and a number of other multilateral organizations.

than the German position on trade issues manifested within the broader Community institutions. A reflection of the gravitational shift in the locus of trade policymaking is the fact that young Germans are no longer opting to undertake a career in the national trade bureaucracy; the opportunities are seen as lying in Brussels rather than in Bonn.

The federal government's ability to act decisively is further diffused by the peculiar institution of "Chancellor democracy," under which each ministry has the final say over policies in its particular area of jurisdiction. While the Chancellor takes part in trade policy discussions, he does not possess formal power to overrule his ministers, and in areas of interministerial conflict must instead plead, cajole, muster political pressure, or simply continue discussion of the issue at hand. As a result, the Ministry of Economics, which has principal jurisdiction over trade policy and which is a bastion of economic liberalism, is able to speak with virtually complete authority -- almost always as a free trade advocate -- on behalf of the broad constellation of industries which fall under its jurisdiction. Conversely, when an industrial sector (such as telecommunications or agriculture) or an industrial activity (research) falls under the jurisdiction of a different ministry, there is virtually nothing the Economics Minister can do -- other than persuasion and the exertion of political pressure -- to influence that ministry's policy. The Chancellor can mediate interministerial disputes but cannot necessarily resolve the inconsistent policies which frequently result.

In trade, an important consequence of the German system of ministerial primacy is the incoherence of positions being advocated by Germany within the European Community on trade in manufactured goods, on the one hand, and on farm trade issues (and several other exceptional sectoral issues) on the other hand. Germany's hard-line protectionist stance in agriculture tends to undercut its free trade position on most other issues, and thus, by weakening Germany's voice within the Community, probably results in a less liberal overall EC trade posture. As a prominent German economist explains, "West Germany uses up much of its politico-economic capital in Brussels urging increased agricultural protection."[27]

The Political Setting

German politics has been dominated by two large centrist parties, the Christian Democrats (CDU) and the Social Democrats (SPD), each of which has held political power for a substantial period during the postwar era.

---

[27]Frank D. Weiss, et al., *Trade Policy in West Germany* (Kieler Studien: 1988) p. 76.

The CDU, the more conservative of the two, is based around a core of Catholic support, particularly in the South, but has become a much broader party embracing numerous interest groups; it now has a labor wing with close ties to the unions, a business wing representing industry and the financial community, and groups representing refugees, small businessmen, women and students.[28] Its history as the ruling party during the *Wirtschaftswunder*, as the architect of compromise between industry and labor, and as an enemy of communism have all served to broaden its appeal to German voters. On economic issues the CDU has stood for principles of "social capitalism" or the "social market economy," that is, free enterprise tempered by institutional mechanisms to ensure an acceptable level of social welfare. An important offshoot of the CDU is the conservative Catholic Bavarian Christian Social Union (CSU), the party of the late Franz-Josef Strauss, which has maintained a frequently stormy working alliance with the CDU.[29] The two parties form a joint parliamentary party in the Bundestag (the CDU/CSU), but the CSU is in all other respects a separate party with its own organization and agenda.

The SPD, heir to the German socialist tradition, has progressively abandoned its original positions based on class struggle and become a *Volkspartei*, moving very close to the centrist policies espoused by the CDU, although showing a greater disposition to intervene in the economy and a relatively greater concern for social welfare.[30] On economic issues the SPD favors, in general, a greater degree of government intervention in the economy, and expansion of social welfare programs and benefits for labor.

The Free Democratic Party (FDP), or Liberal Party, has never received more than about 10 percent of the popular vote, but has held the balance of power between the CDU and the SPD and has been able to parlay this into a disproportionately large role in governing the country -- and significantly for the present analysis, it has been extremely influential in the areas of trade, economic and agriculture policy. The FDP joined with the CDU in governing coalitions between 1949 and 1966; in 1969, it switched to align itself with the SPD, enabling that party to hold power until 1982. After 1982 the FDP was again been aligned with the CDU in a governing coalition. Reflecting its pivotal role, and its interest in economic issues, the FDP has typically held more than 20 percent of the

---

[28]Katzenstein (1987) p. 36.

[29]I. Derbyshire, *Politics in West Germany from Schmidt to Kohl* (Sandpiper, 1987) pp. 12-14.

[30]Derbyshire (1987), pp. 14-15.

ministerial posts and has dominated the Ministry of Economic Affairs, which is critical to industrial and trade policy.[31] The FDP's balancing act has drawn both the CDU and the SPD toward the political center, since in its coalitions with each party it has forced them to adopt more centrist positions to accommodate their ally.

Trade Policy Setting

There is a broad consensus within German society in favor of free trade and open markets. This reflects the fact that Germany's principal industries (in terms of revenues and jobs) are heavily export dependent; the continued prosperity of the Germany economy is thus linked to the maintenance of a stable, liberal international trading order. Free trade enjoys support not only from the majority of the business community but from the nation's leading labor unions, including IG Metall, probably the world's largest trade union. A consensus nearly as broad exists that governments should not intervene in industrial matters through sectoral subsidies, interference with output, investment and pricing decisions, and other similar measures. The government's proper role is seen as provider of a stable infrastructure in which economic activity can occur through measures to foster education, basic research and the sciences, and a transportation and energy infrastructure.

Germany's embrace of free trade has both intellectual and practical bases. Most German economists, economic officials, and business leaders subscribe, with relatively few qualifications, to the modern neoclassical economic theory that free trade is beneficial to all. At a practical level, Germany is faring extremely well under the current relatively open international trading order; German industry has proven highly competitive internationally across a broad front of sectors, and German prosperity has been based in large part on the success of German export industries. These realities are apparent not only to the business community but to the labor unions and the public generally. As a result, support for free trade in Germany is not only broad, but fairly deep; Germany did not significantly retreat from its basic posture even during the recession of the early 1980s, which forced a significant restructuring on several major industrial sectors.

Despite Germany's commitment to a free trade regime with a minimum of state intervention, much of the focus of Germany's actual trade and industrial policy has been directed toward areas where departures have occurred from this basic ideal. In agriculture and telecommunications,

[31]Derbyshire (1987), pp. 15-16.

politically powerful domestic constituencies have induced successive federal to adopt protectionist agendas, although in telecommunications this pattern appeared to be breaking down at the end of the 1980s. The Ministry of Research (BMFT) subsidizes high technology R&D and has sponsored overt sectoral promotion policies in the information technologies. The Länder, usually more sympathetic to the problems of particular sectors than Bonn, have spawned a broad array of industrial policy measures which are not consistent with the federal government's philosophy, and these tendencies are increasing as the power and autonomy of the Länder grows relative to that of the federal government. Finally, an often-reluctant federal government has been drawn, by political imperatives and broader national concerns, into a series of interventions at the two extremes of Germany's industrial spectrum, the sectors of declining competitiveness (agriculture, steel, shipbuilding, coal) and the emerging sectors (microelectronics, computers, aviation). Such interventions have been the principal source of friction with Germany's trading partners.

A few exceptions to Germany's free trade posture in its mainline industrial sectors should be noted. The German market is protected, to a degree, by structural characteristics -- longstanding interfirm relationships, informal cartels, and preferential procurement arrangements. A counselor at the U.S. Embassy in Bonn remarked in 1991 that "there is no official policy, but there are a number of 'small p' protectionist features here. I don't question the Kohl government's sincerity. The senior officials believe in competition. The bureaucracy is a different matter."[32] In a few documented cases, the government itself has acted to restrict trade. Between 1971 and at least 1988 Japan maintained a "unilateral commitment" not to seek more than 10 percent of the German color TV market, Germany maintained an import quota on Japanese tableware between 1960 and at least 1988.[33] In 1981 Japan offered a "firm forecast" to the Commission and to German Economics Minister Lamsdorff that Japanese car exports to the German market would not grow by more than 10 percent in that year; despite official denials, "it is widely believed, in Germany as well as elsewhere, that Japan was prompted to act by Germany."[34] In 1990 an executive from Nissan Deutschland stated that

---

[32]John W. Bligh in *New York Times* (August 18, 1991).

[33]GATT Doc. No. L/6530 (1989), p. 170.

[34]J. Pierce, J. Sutton, *Protection and Industrial Policy in Europe* (London: Routledge and Keegan Paul Ltd., 1985), p. 63; see also Frank Weirs, *Trade Policy in West Germany* (Tübingen: J.C.B. Mohr, 1988), p.12.

Japanese auto exports to Germany were being voluntarily restrained.[35] A Fiat executive commented in 1991 that "in Germany the Japanese already have 15 percent of the market, but it is a quota somehow agreed upon, even if only verbally, by the two countries."[36] Although the existence of these restrictions has been denied, the Japanese share of the German auto market has never exceeded 15 percent, a phenomenon which led the EC Commission's Martin Bangemann to remark sarcastically in 1991 about a "miracle, a second German miracle," in which Germany has succeeding in putting a ceiling of around 15 percent on imports of Japanese cars while there is no official agreement."[37] Finally, the government-backed credit insurance institution, Hermes-Kreditversicherungs-AG, covers exports or credits for export against unforeseen commercial risks, a form of export subsidy "if a foreign client goes broke (commercial risk), a country imposes a ban or payments because of a shortage of foreign currency (political peril), then the central government, as Hermes' guarantor, pays the company for its losses."[38]

However, such interventions have been exceptional and have produced a relatively low level of bilateral conflict, certainly nothing like the nasty sectoral rows which have characterized Japan's relations with the U.S. and the EC. Indeed, the primary criticism levelled at Germany by the U.S. is not related to Airbus or chips but to a macroeconomic concern -- that Germany has an economy which is not expanding at a pace fast enough to mitigate international trade imbalances. The German economic authorities have repeatedly made it clear that they are unwilling to boost domestic demand through expansionary monetary and/or fiscal policies[39] and have placed the onus for reducing the nation's current account

---

[35]The Director of Nissan Motor Deutschland stated that in the absence of voluntary restraints the Japanese share of the German auto market would be 20 to 25 percent instead of 15 percent. "Autoimporteure blicken auf ein Rekordjahr Zurück," *Frankfurter Allgemeine Zeitung* (February 24, 1990).

[36]Massimo Mucchetti in *L'Espresso* (July 21, 1991) (FBIS-WEU-91-156).

[37]*Europe* No. 5497 (New Series) (May 24, 1991).

[38]*Kölner Stadt-Anzeiger* (February 16, 1991). The Gulf War, and associated losses in Kuwait and Iraq, have reportedly required payout of several billion Deutschemarks to firms suffering loss of export sales. "Many firms which have exported to Iraq are now glad they have an export guarantee. . . . No commercial insurance company would have entertained the idea of insuring exports to Iraq. . . ." *Europe* No. 5497 (New Series) (May 24, 1991); see also *Frankfurter Allgemeine Zeitung* (April 5, 1991).

[39]*See* Reuters News Service, September 21, 1989.

surplus on the shoulders of the nation's trading partners, who are asked to control their domestic demand and boost their savings rates. However, conservative macroeconomic policies simply do not have emotional or political implications comparable to those associated with Japan's aggressive moves to dominate strategic industrial sectors.

TRADE POLICY PROCESS

Germany embraces the concept of free trade, and as a result, there is little in the way of an identifiable German national trade policy. The Federal government maps out broad economic goals relating to international trade, but it is exceptional for specific aspects of the nation's trade policy to be stipulated at the federal level. Trade policy is determined primarily at the industry level, framed largely in commercial terms, with the government's role only to ensure that a suitable environment exists for industry to be successful.[40] As a practical matter, Germany's trade policy is drawn up and executed by five sets of private and/or regional institutions: the large commercial banks, the industry organizations [*Verbände*], several large German multinationals, the regional governments [*Länder*], and the skilled-worker-dominated trade unions. The Federal government is generally limited to formulation of broad trade-related economic guidelines, a task which is performed by the Ministry of Economics.[41] The government's hands-off approach to trade, coupled with the existence of powerful private industrial groups and associations, has in effect led in some sectors to the "privatization of protection" rather than a truly open market, although this phenomenon is not nearly as pervasive as in Japan. The *New York Times* observed on August 18, 1991 that the "banking, insurance, electrical utility and chemical industries. . .operate as virtual cartels. It is often impossible for a foreign company to enter those markets without a German partner."[42]

---

[40]*See* Christopher S. Allen, "Germany: Competing Communitarianisms", in *Ideology and National Competitiveness*, ed. George C. Lodge and Ezra F. Vogel (Harvard Business School Press, 1987), pg. 88.

[41]Since almost 90% of German exports consist of manufactured products, trade policy is essentially synonymous with manufacturing trade policy.

[42]Ferdinand Protzman, "Greetings from Fortress Germany," in *New York Times* (August 18, 1991).

The Ministry of Economics

Although, the Ministry of Foreign Affairs is legally responsible for Germany's international trade policy, this function has been almost completely assumed by the Ministry of Economics, which exercises responsibility over industrial policy matters.[43] With respect to trade policy which affects the vast majority of German manufacturing industries, no other ministry has any substantive say, even the Ministry of Finance, although all interested ministers are formally involved in interministerial committees on every measure at every level. The Ministry of Economics has consistently been a stronghold of liberal economic views, beginning with the first Minister, Ludwig Erhard. The ministerial portfolio has been held by the FDP since 1972, and the bureaucracy of the Ministry tends to support the liberal views of the Ministers themselves. The Ministry does contain offices for particular industries, and a certain amicability has grown up between the industry desks and the sectoral associations with which they deal. However, the industry offices are all in one department, whereas other departments (Foreign Economic Policy and especially the Basic Principles Department) tend to avoid sectoral concerns in favor of a broad view of what is in Germany's best interests.

The Verbände

The German industrial associations (*Verbände*) play a significant role in the formation of national trade and industrial policy. The two major West German *Verbände* are the Bundesverband der Deutschen Industrie eV (BDI -- Federation of German Industry), which represents German manufacturers, and the Deutscher Industrie-und Handelstag (DIHT -- Association of German Chambers of Industry and Commerce).[44] German

---

[43]The role of the Foreign Ministry in the trade policy formulation process increased in recent years due to the fact that the leader of the Free Democrats, Hans-Dietrich Genscher, was also the Foreign Minister. In effect, Genscher's role as leader of the FDP mandated that he be taken seriously by Economics Ministry officials (almost all of whom are members of the FDP). Now that Otto Lambsdorff has assumed the leadership role within the FDP, however, the trade policymaking power wielded by the Foreign Ministry is likely to diminish significantly.

[44]The BDI represents German manufacturers; it has a sectoral structure (with 34 associations representing various manufacturing sectors) and a direct mandate to represent the interests of German industry. Its board is made up of industry CEOs who volunteer to ensure that the businessman's point of view is reflected in the

(continued...)

Basic Law provides for interest groups to be heard when major policy decisions are made, and these two organizations[45] frequently play a formal consultative role; their views, formal and informal, on economic issues are widely solicited throughout the German government. In addition, the positions on trade adopted by these umbrella organizations tend to provide guidance for their membership to a far greater degree than is the case with U.S. organizations such as the Chamber of Commerce -- "most industries take their cues on trade policy from the BDI."

Both of these organizations tend to favor free trade and oppose protectionism of any sort. Reflecting the difference in their client bases, the DIHT is generally more committed to free trade and economic liberalism than is the BDI;[46] according to one of its officials, the DIHT considers itself to be the "most [economically] liberal institution in West Germany", which surely makes it one of the most liberal major business groups in the world. The BDI occasionally tolerates special trade measures on behalf of constituent industries which have come under

---

[44](...continued)
organization's policy decisions. It has a number of standing committees, including an influential Foreign Trade Committee (Aussenwirtschaftsausschuss); each of the 34 member associations delegates 1-2 representatives to this committee, which meets 1-2 times per year to develop consensus positions based on discussion papers generated by the BDI staff. The DIHT is a more diverse organization. Membership is voluntary and open to all commercial (not just industrial) organizations in Germany; its membership is broader and more fluid. Policy for the regional chambers is set by the DIHT leadership in Bonn. Although there is a fair amount of overlap between the roles of the BDI and the DIHT within the trade policymaking process, there are some important distinctions. Membership in the BDI is a) mandatory for all industry associations within West Germany, and b) limited to such associations. Membership in the DIHT, on the other hand, is purely voluntary and open to all commercial associations within the FRG. Thus, while the BDI represents the interests of West German industry per se, the DIHT's client base in considerably broader and more fluid.

[45]West Germany's industries are also represented by sectoral industrial associations. In most cases, on trade issues, these associations allow the BDI to speak for them, primarily in deference to the expertise of the BDI's 220-member staff (exceptions are the textile and iron-and-steel associations). Another organization consisting of businessmen (as well as academics), the Aussenwirtschaftsbeirat, advises the Ministry of Economics on economic and trade issues, but it does not enjoy the level of influence of the BDI.

[46]Most of the DIHT's members do not compete directly with imports, so it is more prepared to embrace free trade.

foreign competitive pressure; thus, while not commonplace, the DIHT and BDI may hold different positions on particular trade issues.

By keeping in close contact with Ministry of Economics officials and meeting with those officials on a regular basis, the leadership of the BDI and DIHT remain continuously and directly involved with the development of that Ministry's policy positions. The BDI communicates regularly with the German and EC GATT delegations and often holds parallel meetings with the German negotiators during negotiations in Geneva. While the opinions of BDI and DIHT officials are valued highly by the Ministry of Economics, instances do arise in which the position taken by the Ministry differs considerably from that favored by one or both of the industry organizations. In such instances, both the BDI and the DIHT do not hesitate to lobby Brussels directly in an attempt to try to overrule the decisions made in Bonn. Such activity is generally reserved for occasions in which the organizations feel extremely strongly about an issue, however, and the position on that issue adopted by the Ministry of Economics is unacceptable to one or both of the organizations.[47] The DIHT has complained to the Community, for example, about its aggressive use of antidumping measures, and the BDI has gone directly to the Commission to register its opposition to safeguard measures. Reflecting the fact that Brussels rarely, if ever, adopts industrial trade measures which are more liberal than those proposed by the FRG government, the BDI and DIHT are fighting an uphill battle when they lobby Brussels directly. European Community officials reportedly do not like being directly lobbied by German industry groups, particularly the DIHT.

The Major Commercial Banks

West Germany's three largest commercial banks -- Deutsche Bank, Commerzbank and Dresdner Bank -- play a substantially larger role in the German economy than do their counterparts in most other industrialized countries. Indeed, the ability of the banks to intervene in cimplex industrial matters such as the collapse of a large firm, the restructuring of a crisis sector, or the financing of massive foreign projects effectively relieves the government of the necessity of doing so, and contributes to

---

[47]A recent example of this was the controversy over the "screwdriver assembly" provision adopted by the Community. The DIHT was strongly opposed to that provision, and when the FRG government decided to support the measure, that organization lobbied Brussels intensively. "This was a big issue for us. We were unwilling to stand on the sidelines and watch it be adopted without a fight." Interview with a DIHT official, March 1990.

the federal government's ability to adhere to a laissez-faire posture in most situations.[48] All of these banks combine the functions of deposit banks and investment banks, making long term loans to industry as well as issuing shares and floating debenture loans for companies.[49] Although the banks play no formal role in the trade policymaking process, they exercise a significant degree of informal, behind-the-scenes influence that has actually led casual observers and critics to exaggerate their power and importance.[50] The banks are permitted by law to own equity stock in the companies to which they lend and to hold directorships on these companies' boards -- for example, the largest German bank, Deutsche Bank, owns 40 percent of Daimler-Benz, its principal client and the largest West German company.[51] Thus, according to some German analysts, Germany has "three MITIs," the banks. One analyst observed in 1986 that

> *A bank like the Deutsche can stand at the center of a web of industrial interests, with. . .some 140 representatives on supervisory boards, proxy votes to the value of some DM 70 billion, excellent internal organization, managers. . .of world stature and earning annually more in dividends from its industrial shares alone than it pays out to its own shareholders. Most important of all is the cumulation of modes of industrial interests by bankers: shareholdings, proxy voting, floating shares, credit business and presence on supervisory boards.*[52]

---

[48]Dyson (1986) p.138.

[49]Dyson (1986) p.131.

[50]West Germany's major banks are viewed by many people both inside and outside of the FRG as having far too much power. Indeed, in recent years there has been quite a groundswell of support among West German politicians (including Otto Lambsdorff, previously Minister of Economics and currently leader of the liberal Free Democratic Party) for provisions which would limit the power of banks (presumably by limiting the size of their equity holdings in clients). Banking executives are not worried about this threat, however, since they feel that it is based on emotional reactions rather than careful analysis of the situation.

[51]German banks not only own equity shared directly, but may exercise proxy rights for shares on deposit for their customers. In addition, pursuant to the practice of *Leihstimmen*, one or more banks may loan voting rights of shares held by them to a bank specializing in the affairs of a specific company or sector. Dyson (1986) p.129.

[52] Dyson (1986) p. 133.

Some of the more extreme characterizations of the banks' pervasive influence in the German economy are probably overstated. There is a fair amount of competition between the three largest banks, so there is little prospect that they could formulate joint policy or form a "bankers' cartel." They are in a position, through their lending policies, to ensure that their clients do not engage in "excessive" head-to-head competition, a form of influence that has reportedly been employed in the steel sector. Most West German companies, however, are "much too proud" to allow themselves to be controlled, or even heavily influenced by their banks, according to bank officials. Perhaps most importantly, the three major banks do not have the resources, human and otherwise, to accomplish anything like the sort of strategic influence over industry exercised by MITI. As is the case with banks in the United States and elsewhere, the bulk of these banks' staff are engaged in financial activities; none of the banks has a sizeable staff of economists, and none spends much time analyzing the intricacies of West German industry's competitive dynamics.[53]

The close ties between the major banks and their corporate clients exist primarily, indeed, in most cases exclusively, at the Advisory Board level. It is commonplace for executives from Deutsche Bank, Dresdner Bank and Commerzbank to sit on the Advisory Boards of those banks' respective clients.[54] Since the principal role of Advisory Boards is to choose corporations' Executive Boards, these bank executives have a fair amount of power in deciding who will assume leadership positions within the FRG's major corporations. Advisory Boards play a limited role in companies' strategic decision-making, so bank executives are generally quite removed from any sort of control over their clients' competitive strategies.[55] The bank executives' influence on trade policy, therefore,

---

[53]It would be grossly inaccurate for anyone to claim that within the major West German commercial banks there is a feeling that, for example, "what is good for Deutsche Bank is good for the FRG." Interview with a senior bank official, March 1990.

[54]Interview with a senior bank official, March 1990.

[55]West Germany has one of the strongest "old boy" networks in the world, and the banks are prominent in that network and thus in a position to express their views within it. The late Alfred Herrhausen provided the consummate example of how banking executives are able to use their "old boy network" contacts to influence corporate (and, in Herrhausen's case, even national) policymaking decisions. Most German observers, however, regard Herrhausen as something of an aberration rather than the norm.

is indirect and manifested over the longer term; that is by helping to choose the leaders of German business, and so to assure that the private sector will not deviate from its current, strongly-held free-trade orientation.[56]

The Länder

The regional governments, or Länder, within West Germany play an active role in the trade policymaking process through their inclusion in the roundtable discussions involved in that process. They partially own certain firms (and therefore have a stake in how those firms perform) and are directly responsible for the implementation of economic growth plans; accordingly, the Länder tend to participate actively and wield a fair amount of influence within those policy discussions.[57]

The trade policies of the various Länder tend to be functions of the political parties dominating those governments and the industrial composition of the Länder which they are representing.[58] The governments dominated by the SPD tend to favor trade policies which are somewhat less free market-oriented than those favored by those dominated by the CDU. Moreover, in those Länder in which agriculture predominates (such as Lower Saxony), the government is more supportive of protectionist trade policies, while the governments of states in which advanced manufacturing predominates (such as Hesse) tend to advocate free trade to a far greater extent. The one exception to this rule is the state of Bavaria, in which both agriculture and advanced manufacturing have solid footholds. The Bavarian government tends to advocate policies

---

[56]The basis for the banks' pro-free trade stance is the fact that the major West German corporations, who are the banks' principal clients and whose financial welfare is therefore extremely important, tend to not only export a great deal, but also import a great deal (from their foreign subsidiaries). This trade stance is rarely made public, however, because the banks are for the most part only involved in private sector, company-specific trade policy discussions, not public sector trade policy discussions. Hence, the banks' trade positions are in fact more akin to strategic business plans which deal with corporations' international trade, not the desirability of a particular set of trade measures.

[57]*See* Christopher S. Allen, "Germany: Competing Communitarianisms," in George C. Lodge and Ezra F. Vogel, eds., *Ideology and National Competitiveness* (Harvard Business School Press: 1987).

[58]It should be noted that these two factors are by no means mutually exclusive. *See* The Economist Intelligence Unit, Business International, *West Germany: Country Profile, 1989/90*, p. 20.

which are more in line with agricultural interests than with industrial interests.[59]

Inevitably, parochial concerns are manifested more dramatically at the Länder level. Since the late 1970s several Länder have engaged in interventionist policies in order to boost the exports of the small and medium-sized firms within their jurisdictions.[60] Even those Länder which are dominated by the CDU are unlikely to be as free trade-oriented as either the Federal Ministry of Economics or the *Verbände*. Lothar Späth, the CDU minister president of Baden-Württemberg, has even put forward an argument in favor of government intervention in the development of "strategic" industries.[61]

The Multinationals

The European Communities' Single Market Initiative was intended, in part, to facilitate the formation of world class European companies capable of standing up to the Japanese and American internationally. Germany already has an impressive roster of such firms -- Daimler-Benz, Siemens, Hoechst, Bosch, Bayer, Volkswagen, and others. As French and Italian

---

[59]It appears that if a Länder has anything more than a negligible amount of agricultural constituents, then it will attempt to appease those constituents by tailoring its trade positions to fit their interests.

[60]The government of Baden-Württemberg led the way in the late 1970s by setting up an export promotion agency which sponsored overseas exhibitions of products from that state. The success of that agency prompted both the Bavarian and the North Rhine-Westphalian *Länder* to initiate similar agencies. The *Verbände* have criticized these export promotion policies because they feel that extensive *Länder* activity on behalf of small and medium-sized firms may well undermine the *Verbände*'s role within the process of trade policy formulation. Gary B. Herrigel, "Industrial Order and the Politics of Change: Mechanical Engineering", in ed. Peter J. Katzenstein, *Industry and Politics in West Germany* (Cornell University Press: 1989) p. 212.

[61]See Winfried Fuest and Peter-Rüdiger Puf, "Erfahrungen Mit der "Neuen Industriepolitik," *Wirtschaftsdienst* (September 1989) p. 457. Minister Späth's essential point is that the state should play an active role in facilitating the adjustment of small and medium-sized firms to the production of new technologies. In order to do this, he argues, the government must reinterpret its traditional responsibility for the maintenance of economic infrastructure to include all those institutions and services (such as universities and research institutes) which are concerned with the development and dissemination of information about new technologies and overseas markets. Herrigel (1989) p. 212.

firms concentrate on mergers with other European firms to prepare for the Single Market, the large German firms are not only undertaking further intra-European expansion but entering into wide-ranging strategic alliances with some of the leading competitors in Japan and the United States. Daimler-Benz, itself an extraordinarily diversified organization, has entered into a multifaceted alliance with the largest industrial combination in the world, Mitsubishi -- "nothing less is involved than the worldwide future of the automobile, aviation and space, and electronics industry."[62] Siemens, the only European firm to have stood its ground against Japan in semiconductor competition, has entered into a pact with IBM for the joint manufacture of dynamic random access memories (DRAMs).[63] Volkswagen has concluded a joint arrangement with Toyota which will enable it to market its vehicles in Japan through the latter's dealer net.

The German multinationals establish their own competitive strategies and seek to induce the government, or at least part of it, to support them; because of their sheer size, these firms can perceptibly affect government policy decisions. For the most part, the big companies simply reinforce the national commitment to free trade -- they have little choice but to support the open international trading regime that is a prerequisite to their existence in their current form. They do, however, pursue government support, generally not overt trade protection, but subsidies for R&D, procurement preferences, lenient antitrust enforcement, and financial backing for particularly risky and expensive investments such as commercial aviation and semiconductor manufacturing.

The Public Policy Institutes

There are five public policy institutes in West Germany which are 50 percent funded by Länder governments and 50 percent by private organizations. While these institutes are independent and are not in any way organizationally linked to the government, several of them maintain close ties to various branches of the government. In particular, the Kiel Institute, which traditionally has been the most economically-oriented of the think tanks, has become closely associated with the Ministry of Economics and for that reason has come to play an important role in

---

[62]*Industriemagazin* (May 1991) (JPRS-EST-91-014).

[63]*NTIS Foreign Technology* (August 13, 1991).

German trade policy formation.[64] The Kiel Institute, and in particular its director, Professor Herbert Giersch, acts as the Ministry of Economics' conscience on most issues. Kiel is a bastion of pure economic liberalism and for that reason is constantly reminding the Ministry of what the FRG's economic policy should be.[65]

The Unions

In contrast to the experience of other industrialized nations, German labor unions have never emerged as a significant force for protectionism, a key fact given the power of the unions within West Germany. Membership in a union is not obligatory and union agreements apply to all employees within an industry whether they are union members or not. Nevertheless, the majority of workers below the senior management level are union members. Analogous to the Verbände discussed above, the German labor unions are organized along industry lines with an umbrella organization, the Deutscher Gewerkschaftsbund (DGB - Federation of German Trade Unions), overseeing the whole group's interests as a whole. Many of the senior members of these component unions cultivate contacts at high levels of the state and federal governments, so the unions exercise a strong voice in the formulation of overall government policy -- and trade policy in particular. The union movement as a whole supports free trade, reflecting a widespread recognition that German jobs depend on exports. IG Metall, the largest single union, has continued to embrace free trade despite serious job losses in a number of the metal industries in the past decade.

---

[64]Periodically, that Ministry presents the Institute with a range of topics it plans to examine in the coming months. The scholars at Kiel are under no obligation to work on any of those issues; however, should one or more of the scholars decide to pursue one of the topics indicated by the Economics Ministry, then the Ministry will provide funds for the necessary research. Any work done by Kiel on research funded by the Ministry of Economics is likely to end up in a ministry speech and/or publication. At the same time, however, there is also a great deal of work done by Kiel which is not funded by the Economics Ministry but which nonetheless ends up in speeches and publications provided by that ministry. Interview with Kiel Institute official, March 1990.

[65]Interview with a senior trade official in the Federal Ministry of Economics, March 1990.

TRADE-RELATED OBJECTIVES

Germany's main objective in trade is conservative -- to maintain and expand the current liberal world trading regime, based on agreed multilateral rules and institutions, which is seen as the basis for the country's prosperity and future economic well-being. Germany also has subordinate trade-related objectives dictated by industrial policy and parochial political concerns, which are not always consistent with Germany's primary goal. These include a desire to mitigate external competitive pressure on the nation's agricultural sector long enough to permit restructuring; development of world-class aviation, information, and biotechnology industries, if necessary through sectoral promotional methods not fully consistent with the prevailing liberal economic ideology; and securing a degree of international acquiescence in "buffering" measures which will permit a phased withdrawal from certain declining sectors, particularly shipbuilding.

Germany has consistently embraced free trade under coalitions headed both by the CDU and the SPD, and this is unlikely to change in the 1990s regardless of the party in power and notwithstanding the effects of reunification. In fact, German policy is likely to become even more free-trade oriented during the next decade because the sectoral contradictions which have complicated German positions are likely to diminish in significance. The extraordinary power of the farm lobby, which has sustained a protectionist government posture in agriculture, is likely to diminish sufficiently to permit at least a partial liberalization of farm trade by the end of the 1990s. The political significance of the declining sectors is waning as the number of workers in those sectors drops. Telecommunications, traditionally one of the most heavily protected enclaves in the German economy, is undergoing a major restructuring which is opening up market opportunities for foreign firms, particularly in telecommunications services. In the high technology sectors which the government seeks to promote, border measures are generally perceived as inappropriate and counterproductive (although procurement preferences remain a policy tool); the principal promotional technique is R&D subsidies, which, depending on their manner of application, are not inconsistent with a policy of open markets.

Paradoxically, even as Germany's trade policy posture becomes more liberal, by the early 1990s its market will be more protected, reflecting EC-wide trade and procurement measures implemented in conjunction with the Single Market Initiative. As of 1991, the German auto market, previously protected only by an informal understanding with Japan, is subject to EC-administered quotas, and telecommunications procurement -- just opening up with the Bundespost restructuring -- will be subject to local content requirements imposed at the Community level. Some influential German firms (Volkswagen, Ford) have supported new protective measures at the EC level; however, the majority of German government officials and industry leaders genuinely disapprove of the EC's new protectionist measures and can be expected to oppose such measures within the Community's policy deliberations during the coming decade.

TRADE STRATEGIES

Many German officials are bemused when asked to describe their country's "trade strategy." A typical response is that Germany does not have a trade strategy, does not need one, and that nobody spends time thinking about such issues in Bonn. Upon further reflection, officials indicate that Germany has fared very well through a strategy -- if it can be called that -- of simply adhering to principles of liberal non-intervention while seeking to strengthen the multilateral institutions governing international trade.

There is no major industrial country in the world, except perhaps the Netherlands, where the commitment to free trade is broader and deeper than in Germany. This commitment is based on self interest, to be sure -- Germany is one of the world's principal exporting nations -- but also on a sense of optimism and self confidence that borders on arrogance. The Germans believe in themselves and their economic system. German "strategy" in trade consists largely of an effort to keep other governments from interfering with the market mechanism, an approach based in substantial part on German recognition that their industries will almost always prevail in a laissez-faire environment. The principal German trade policy tool is thus the pursuit of multilateral constraints on government intervention in the market, whether these are EC codes against industrial subsidies or GATT rules aimed at limiting unilateral trade actions by the United States. Incongruously, Germany must simultaneously seek to deflect the application of comparable norms to its own agricultural sector.

The decade of the 1990s is unlikely to see increased activism on the part of the German government in the trade arena. Even prior to reunification the Germans were fond of characterizing their role in the world trading system as a passive one; preoccupation with the merger of the two Germanies is likely, if anything to increase this passivity, at least over the short run. The government does not intervene in trade frequently and, in their view, the world would be better off if other governments followed the German example. Moreover, most specific interventions affecting German industry are already laid by the Germans at the door of the European Community, a tendency which will, if anything, increase in the 1990s.

Multilateral Trade Strategy

Germany regards the GATT and its ancillary institutions as central to its economic interests. The GATT framework has made possible the expansion of German trade in the postwar era; German economic officials note that although the GATT is by no means perfect, "no system could be conceived which would work better." Germany's multilateral objectives are therefore profoundly conservative, to preserve the status quo and perhaps improve it with careful tinkering. The government has three basic objectives in the Uruguay Round negotiations. First, and most importantly, the Germans want to prevent the collapse of the Round or any other outcome that would weaken the GATT system itself. Second, the government would like to see GATT rules revised and expanded to economic activity not currently regulated by GATT rules; the government supports a GATT regime for services and, in particular, intellectual property protection which is seen as important as traditional German industries (chemicals, pharmaceutical) became more technology-intensive. Finally, the government would like to see strengthened multilateral constraints on "bilateralism" and "unilateralism," which are seen as weakening the whole GATT system; this could be achieved by increased use of the GATT dispute-resolution procedures and adherence to the decisions of those panels by the contracting parties.[66] The government opposes use of the EC's version of Section 301, the New Commercial Policy Instrument, and would like to see multilateral restrictions placed on the United States' use of Section 301.

The integrity of Germany's support for the GATT is compromised, to a considerable degree, by its protectionist stance in agriculture, a principal contributing cause of the collapse of the GATT Ministerial in December 1990. The Germans would like to finesse the issue of trade protection in agriculture in a manner which does not jeopardize the stability of the GATT institutions, but they are walking a fine line.[67] In 1990, Germany

---

[66]Interview with a senior trade official in the Federal Ministry of Economics, March 1990.

[67]Economics and Finance Ministry officials as well as the Chancellory itself take the position that the Uruguay Round is too important to be derailed by farm issues. The Agriculture Ministry is obviously less committed to such compromise, but its officials allow that some concessions will be required to bring the Uruguay Round (continued...)

was prepared to agree to a phaseout of farm subsidies and protection, particularly if the final termination of such practices was put on an indefinite timetable or made subject to interim review in several years. German officials have warned that the United States should not demand an immediate cessation of farm support programs, but this is because they want to avoid being placed in a position where they must choose between sacrificing significant segments of their farm sector, on the one hand, and the Uruguay Round, on the other hand.

Germany and the Community

Germany is a major player in the world's largest regional trading bloc, the Community, whose creation and expansion has placed substantial strains on the GATT system since its inception. Because German leaders are committed both to the GATT and to European integration, they constantly seek to minimize the inherent tensions between the two regimes. They have taken positions in the policy debates within the European Community designed to reduce potential protectionist effects of the 1992 process,[68] and have taken pains to assure foreigners that EC 1992 will not create a Fortress Europe and does not portend a breakup of the world into trading blocs.

Germany's role with respect to other Member States is increasingly less that of a trading partner than that of a mere component in a larger economic system.[69] Transnational mergers, joint ventures and investment have already significantly blurred national distinctions within the Community. If and when European Monetary Union (EMU) is

---

[67](...continued)
negotiations to an acceptable conclusion. Interview with senior officials in the Ministries of Economics and Agriculture, and the Federal Chancellary, March 1990.

[68]Interview with a senior trade official in the Federal Ministry of Economics, March 1990.

[69]As EC integration proceeds, Germany is able to pursue as "domestic" (i.e., internal) objectives which, in an international context, would be considered trade objectives. For example, the Germans have pressed hard for the establishment of greater discipline on subsidies by the Commission, an effort that has by no means met with complete success, but which has nevertheless had some curtailment in the volume of subsidies.

achieved, trade between Member States[70] will no longer be international in any meaningful sense, but interregional, like trade between New England and the Midwest. The divisions between German and EC trade policymaking functions are becoming similarly indistinct, and are proceeding toward a point where all significant trade-policy decisions will be made in Brussels, albeit influenced from Bonn; indeed, in theory Germany is no longer free to pursue any independent trade policies. Trade policy is perhaps the best example of European integration which has occurred to date; it is the policy area in which the greatest shift toward Brussels from national capitals has already occurred. While some Member States continue to implement "gray" policy measures independently, Germany generally disapproves of and refrains from such actions which, in any event, are becoming less common and more difficult to implement.[71]

The regional trade issue confronting Germany is thus not what its own trade policy toward Europe will be, but the extent to which it can influence the formation of trade and economic policies within the EC institutions. West German observers have long complained that the country has not wielded influence in Brussels commensurate with its size and importance.[72] In part, Germany's underrepresentation is built into the system of qualified majority voting, which gives Germany ten votes, the same as France and the U.K., which are smaller in population. France's perceived dominance of the Community institutions is attributed in part to the fact that it assigns highly qualified individuals to defend French interests whereas Germany has used Brussels "as a retirement home for worn-out politicians and dubious bureaucrats." While this phenomenon is changing as the Germans commit increasing attention and talent to the EC policy process, a number of factors will continue to limit German government influence on trade policy at the Community level. Perhaps most importantly, German reunification will absorb substantial German attention and resources at least through the mid-1990s. In addition, the Single European Act eliminates the old system under which one recalcitrant Member State could block adoption of a policy in favor

---

[70]Germany's "trade surplus" will dramatically shrink, or at least become less visible, as the German economy is merged with that of the European Community. Fifty-four percent of Germany's manufactured exports go to other EC states, and trade with the EC accounts for roughly half of the current German trade surplus. GATT, *International Trade 1988-89*, Table A-9.

[71]Interview with a senior official in the Ministry of Economics, March 1990.

[72]Interview with a trade official at the Washington embassy, March 1990.

of decisionmaking by majority vote, which tends to dissipate the political power of the larger states. Even though Germany usually enjoys the support of the Netherlands, Denmark, and Luxembourg, it can be outvoted on key issues.[73] Germany is seeking to advance non-trade related agendas in connection with completion of the Single Market, particularly adoption of Germany's strict environmental and health standards and social benefits as the European norm.[74] This effort is driven, in significant part, by a concern over competitive disparities which could result if other EC companies do not need to meet such standards. EC adoption of German standards, however, will impose substantial costs on non-German firms and will require tradeoffs with other Member States if it is to be achieved, limiting Germany's room to maneuver on trade issues. Finally, Germany's liberalized positions on trade are compromised by its hard-line protectionist posture on farm issues.[75]

At the heart of the move toward European integration is the special relationship between Germany and France, which arguably gives the Community its essential momentum.[76] Despite fundamental differences in trade and industrial philosophy, the two countries share a consensus over the need to confront international competitive challenges on a "European" scale, even at the expense of national autonomy and pride. They have worked together to promote "European" competitive responses in the information technologies, in commercial aviation, and in a number of other key fields. The inherent strength of the Franco-German axis has enabled the two countries to bypass, where necessary, EC structures altogether in order to achieve goals deemed to be of overriding importance. If anything, reticent, particularist attitude of Britain has effectively reinforced the central role of the Franco-German alliance and dominance of the EC.

It is the French, not the Germans, who have provided the main impetus for the Single Market Initiative. While German officials universally endorse European integration, they have displayed a palpable

---

[73]Interview with a senior official in the Ministry of Economics, March 1990.

[74]Interviews with a Federation of German Industry official, March 1990 and a former Ministry of Agriculture official, February 1990. See also Werner Ungerer, "Deutsche Interessen in und an der Europaeischen Gemeinschaft," *Aussenpolitik* (April 1986) p. 370.

[75]Interviews with a Kiel Institute official, February and March 1990.

[76]"The Odd Couple," *International Management*, 20, (February 1989).

lack of excitement over the EC 1992 process itself.[77] German industry has already achieved most of the benefits that the Single Market is designed to confer on European firms, and government officials and industry spokesmen are confident that Germany will prosper whether or not the 1992 effort is completed. Politicians from the ruling CDU/FDP alliance who speak on behalf of business interests believe that the European Community's 1992 program will improve the competitiveness of West German industries by encouraging deregulation, privatization, and an end to the state's "excessive" influence.[78] On the other hand, SPD politicians, together with the labor unions they represent, fear that European Community's 1992 program will lower West German social standards.[79] Union leaders also worry that their influence will diminish as labor and capital become mobile across national borders, particularly if they lose the right of co-determination (i.e., worker participation on supervisory boards and in corporate strategic planning) which has been a mainstay of the West German economic tradition.[80]

In the 1990s, the issue of Community enlargement could fracture the Franco-German relationship, with uncertain consequences for the future of the Community. Germany has endorsed not only the accession of EFTA countries, but of the Baltic States, declaring its readiness to take responsibility for preparing these countries for membership status.[81] Accession of such new members would tend to strengthen Germany's existing voting bloc to the detriment of France. Accordingly the French, backed by the Commission, have succeeded in deferring consideration of new members until 1993, and may well resist expansions which may undercut their traditional leadership role.

---

[77]Germany has been more sluggish than a number of other states in implementing EC Directives approved by the Council of Ministers. Bureau of National Affairs, *International Trade Reporter* (September 13, 1989).

[78]Published interview in *Sueddeutsche Zeitung* (December 10, 1988) (FBIS-WEU-88-241); See also Bureau of National Affairs, *Daily Report for Executives* (June 16, 1989).

[79]*Daily Report for Executives* (June 16, 1989).

[80]Robert J. McCartney, "The Fight Over Jobs in a Unified Europe," *The Washington Post* (January 15, 1989). See also U.S. Chamber of Commerce, *Europe 1992* (1989) pp. 35-44.

[81]*Berlingske Tidende* (October 23, 1991) (FBIS-WEU-81-209); *Die Presse* (September 23, 1991) (FBIS-WEU-91-186).

Germany and Eastern Europe

Germany has been establishing a de facto commercial sphere of influence in Eastern Europe (including the Soviet Union) since the 1970s, but the implosion of Soviet power abruptly invested the German presence in these countries with a larger potential significance. Over the short and medium term, the states of Eastern Europe are looking primarily to Bonn to provide financial support, technical and organizational advice, and infrastructural renovation to restore their wrecked economies. The expansion of western commercial ties with the eastern European countries is impeded by their massive debt, their primitive financial, communications and transportation infrastructures, and their general state of disarray, and only the Germans appear capable of extending help on the scale required. German public and private institutions have taken the lead in stepping into this difficult situation; in 1991, German firms had concluded more joint ventures with Polish enterprises than companies from the next three countries (Sweden, Austria, U.S.) combined.[82] These actions entail significant commercial risks. A Japanese observer commented in 1990 that:

> *In the old days Germany took up arms against the East. Now instead of arms it has taken up the power of technology and the power of the mark. Today, driven by their dauntless spirit, Germans are willing to go into situation where you can't even count on water coming out of the spigot. A Frenchman will tell you plainly that he will not go where there is no wine. But a German, he is ready to go anywhere. Everywhere you look, Germans are at work. Who then is building bridgeheads for the future and deploying forces in Eastern Europe? Nobody is. Nobody except the Germans. If you take a walk through Eastern Europe today, you will frequently find yourself in a place where only German can be heard. The Americans are hopeless. The Japanese are worse than hopeless. The conclusion we have to draw here is that Germany is the only nation which has the know-how to carry on trade with Eastern Europe.*[83]

In the 1990s Germany will act as the patron of at least the most advanced Eastern European countries, Poland, Hungary and Czechoslovakia, and the Baltic States. It will work to arrange EC and international financial packages for them; it will sponsor their bids for

[82] *Frankfurter Allgemeine Zeitung* (July 19, 1991) (FBIS-WEU-91-159).

[83] Takao Negushi in *Denshi* (JPRS-JST-91-031-L).

accession to the EC; and its firms will take the lead in refurbishing their enterprises and infrastructure. While these moves may raise apprehensions in some European circles, Germany activities in Eastern Europe will in all likelihood prove beneficial to the international trading system. The new non-communist regimes are already proceeding down the German economic path, favoring market-oriented, liberal economic policies and an open trading regime. No other country or group of countries is in a position to supply the financial, managerial and technical assistance on the scale required to facilitate this transformation. To be sure, German firms will be in the best position to reap economic benefits when these countries begin to prosper, but with German firms having made the initial large investments and taken most of the risks, this can hardly be regarded as inappropriate.

Bilateral Trade Strategy

German bilateral strategy, ironically, is to eschew bilateralism to the extent feasible in favor of multilateral and regional arrangements. This posture has worked reasonably well for Germany so far and remains feasible so long as no individual country begins to loom as a major threat to German interests. German government and industry leaders see only one trading partner -- Japan -- as seriously threatening, and even in this case, they are divided over the degree and nature of the actual threat. Many other countries, including some EC member states, notably Italy, are seen as the source of market-distorting intervention measures, but the Germans find such actions annoying rather than a source of real insecurity. The United States, while basically a stable partner, is viewed as prone to unpredictable outbursts of unilateralism, but requiring steadying rather than potentially provocative countermeasures. Problems associated with all of these countries, the Germans feel, could be managed if every country could be induced to follow a set of reasonable multilateral rules of good behavior. The risk -- not perceived as great by many Germans -- that German industry could be eclipsed by other nations in an open trading environment should be addressed, if at all, through comparatively noncontroversial industrial promotion measures (research subsidies, worker training) rather than through trade restrictions.

Germany's membership in the EC has served as an excellent foil for deflecting bilateral trade pressure. When confronted with foreign demands that Germany enter into negotiations over a point of bilateral friction, the Germans respond that they cannot do this legally -- while their government can conduct informal discussions and "fact finding" sessions, only the Commission has the authority to conduct negotiations on trade matters. A bilateral fight with Germany thus means taking on the whole Community; the EC is not only much bigger than Germany, but not particularly disposed to yield to foreign pressure or threats, and likely to respond to trade retaliation with vigorous countermeasures.

Germany and Japan. Japan is the one trade-related subject with respect to which German self-confidence and commitment to liberal principles now wavers. German policymakers and industrial leaders admire many Japanese attributes and most of them believe that German industry can compete effectively with Japan. There is a general conviction, however, that Japan does not play by the international rules -- or rather, that it avoids per se violations of GATT rules but pursues policies which are inconsistent with the spirit and intent of the GATT. Japanese targeting or "laser beaming" of particular industries and government intervention in the market are widely and severely criticized; even diehard free traders express bitterness over the destruction of the German camera industry.[84]

Although there is a rough consensus within the German trade policy community that Japan constitutes, at a minimum, a serious challenge to Germany, there is no general agreement as to what, if anything should be done about it. Passivity, in the German case, is not synonymous with inaction, since in the absence of strenuous German protests, Member States like France and Italy often succeed in securing adoption of managed trade measures with respect to Japan; Germany is often more than happy to "sit back and allow France to engage in Japan-bashing on its behalf."[85] A more activist faction, however, which includes officials at the BMFT and leaders of the electronics industry, advocates government subsidies for R&D, special procurement measures, and other policies designed to promote German competitiveness in the advanced technologies. Some Ministry of Economics officials, however, regard such programs as excessively costly, relatively ineffective, and a waste of effort because "the Japanese have perfected these technologies already anyway."[86]

One official whose thinking is probably representative indicates that the rubric of international trade policy is inadequate for addressing Japan's actions within the world economy because current international rules do not adequately address competition policy. He would like to see

84Interviews with senior officials at the Federal Chancellory, the Ministry of Economics, and the Federation of German Industry, March 1990, and an American official familiar with German thinking on the issue.

85Interviews with a German academic and a senior bank manager, March 1990.

86Interview with a Federal Chancellory official, March 1990.

international rules drawn up which would deal with Japanese pricing strategies and the manner in which Japanese firms acquire dominant shares of the world market; such rules would very likely be applicable to other East Asian NICs as well. Noting that it will be extremely difficult to address these issues in the Uruguay Round, he believes that when the Round is completed, the OECD (or some other multinational body) should devote substantial resources to examining these issues. As a starting point, this official would like to see recommendations on restrictive business practices drawn up within the Uruguay Round.[87]

Germany's likely trade-related strategy toward Japan during the next decade will avoid confrontational positions. In EC trade policy deliberations, the German government will rarely if ever advocate managed trade policies toward Japan, and in most cases will oppose them; its opposition, however, will be sufficiently tepid in some cases to permit implementation of such policies by the Commission. At the same time, the German government will work with the United States and other OECD nations to develop multilateral rules governing industrial targeting, restrictive business practices, predatory dumping, and other aspects of Japanese competitive behavior's subjecting such practices to multilateral discipline will be a major German objective in the next round of multilateral trade negotiations. In the sphere of industrial policy, the government will tacitly support strategic moves by German companies, such as the Daimler-Benz/Mitsubishi alliance, which result in technology transfer to German industry, which direct Japanese thrusts away from German markets, and which provide the basis for negotiated access to the Japanese market. In addition, the government will continue to subsidize R&D in the advanced technologies, not with the objective of overtaking Japan, which is seen as impossible, but of remaining sufficiently abreast to avoid technological dependency. German industry will seek joint ventures with U.S. R&D consortia, such as SEMATECH, and with leading U.S. high technology firms such as IBM.

Germany and the United States. The most striking feature of the U.S.-German bilateral trade relationship is the relative lack of conflict given the large volume of two-way trade and the chronic bilateral German export surplus. This is attributable to several factors. First, trade issues have been overshadowed by security concerns, including joint military arrangements to defend Western Europe and issues relating to transfer of technology to the Soviet bloc and regimes regarded as unfriendly by the

---

[87]Interview with a senior trade official, Federal Ministry of Economics, March 1990.

U.S. (Libya, Iraq).[88] Second, the points of actual friction in the trade area are relatively few. The recent U.S. Republican administrations and the CDU/CSU/FDP coalitions in Bonn share a working commitment to principles of economic liberalism and to the GATT system -- the two governments "agree about 75 percent of the time."[89] Indeed, German and U.S. government views on trade issues are often substantially more congruent than those which exist between Germany and its fellow members in the EC. In addition, Germany's trade surplus is not perceived as particularly adversarial or threatening. It exports on a broad product front; it is known for high quality, high-priced export products rather than high volume, low-priced exports that foster market disruption and the destruction of industries. Germany is open to most forms of U.S. exports and investment. Moreover, the so-called "locomotive debate" over Germany's chronic reluctance to stimulate its economy has never aroused much popular or political interest in the United States; the issues are poorly understood and the German position of fiscal conservatism does not, at first impression, appear to strike Americans as particularly outrageous or unreasonable. Finally (with the possible exception of aircraft), German competitive strategy in the advanced technologies, an area characterized by a relatively high level of government intervention, emphasizes alliances and cooperation with U.S. firms rather than the displacement or conquest of U.S. industries.

While trade conflict has been relatively rare, Germans tend to be quite critical of U.S. trade policies and attitudes. U.S. trade policy is seen as erratic, tending toward protectionism and actions inconsistent with U.S. GATT obligations; above all, the U.S. propensity to act unilaterally is constantly criticized. Recent U.S. actions under "Super 301" legislation were roundly denounced as crude and a threat to the GATT system ("blind in one eye and short sighted in the other").[90] America's trade problems are seen as more a function of failing to satisfy consumer preferences; U.S. politicians

---

[88]Arguably Germany's lax national security controls on the export of sensitive technologies has generated more friction with the U.S. than any trade dispute during the entrie postwar era, including the rows over Airbus, argiculture, and telecommunications. From a German perspective, the permissive attitude taken by the government toward the freewheeling activities of some German exporters merely reflects the abiding national belief that the government should not intrude into the commercial arena.

[89]Interview with a trade official posted with the Washington embassy, March 1990.

[90]*Handelsblatt* (May 9, 1989).

> *[H]ave no wider horizon than foreign leaders in East Bloc states who also do not understand why Western consumers simply do not want products from socialist production. Not all, but some U.S. products certainly live up to East Bloc standards in terms of sloppy manufacture and quality that is aimed at rapid wear.*[91]

Such carping, however, is rarely translated into direct German actions to counter or frustrate U.S. bilateral initiatives, just as German criticism of Japan's protectionism and "laser beam" strategies generally does not escalate into government-to-government confrontation.

Sectoral irritants in the U.S.-German relationship have been remarkably few given the scale and scope of trade, and most involve complaints by U.S. authorities over German practices which deviate from the norm of nonintervention and open markets. The most potentially volatile source of conflict in the 1990s is probably in commercial aviation, where continuing German government support of the Airbus consortium, a chronic source of friction, could degenerate into a major bilateral brawl. Most other bilateral problems arise in protected German sectors -- medical devices, agriculture, telecommunications and heavy electrical equipment. Germany is likely to counter U.S. pressure in these areas (as it has done in telecommunications) through a strategy of partial concessions and attempts to shift the dispute away from Germany and into the Community institutions.

Sectoral Trade Strategies

German policymakers generally oppose sector-specific industrial policy and sometimes even deny that such policies exist. It is true that the competitive success of such mainstays of the German economy as chemicals, autos and machinery arguably makes a sector-specific promotional policy unnecessary. In the past, the federal and *Länder* governments have implemented sectoral policies in several traditional industries which have fallen into difficulty -- coal, shipbuilding, steel -- but the consensus today is that the better course lies in allowing such industries to adjust mainly on their own, as the textile sector did in the 1970s. Large-scale, sector-specific intervention at the federal level is now limited to a relatively few "political" sectors (agriculture and, to a rapidly diminishing degree, telecommunications) and to the high technology sectors, where some segments of the industrial policy community have

---

[91]*Handelsblatt* (May 30, 1989).

succeeded in mobilizing public resources to combat the perceived challenge from Japan.

This is not to say that sectoral promotional policies cannot be identified in many German industries, including mainline sectors like autos. A large volume of federal and *Länder* aid is provided to many German industries, but it is usually administered "with a sprinkling can" -- in the form of a very large number of comparatively small grants, loans and tax breaks for activities such as research, environmental compliance, training, transportation, adaptation of new technologies, and "regional development." Such assistance -- unlike the large scale subsidies to failing firms commonly seen in other Members States -- generally does not provoke foreign criticism and almost never becomes a trade issue. The German industrial policy measures most likely to generate trade friction in the 1990s are in the relatively few sectors where support measures are substantial and where they arguably have a major, readily apparent trade distorting effect.

Agriculture

The farm sector presents Germany with its most intractable trade policy issue. The politics of farm trade have driven successive coalition governments to endorse trade and subsidy policies that are wholly at odds with Germany's liberal economic philosophy. The roots of German agricultural protectionism are multifaceted; intertwined bureaucratic, political and cultural aspects make a complete elimination of trade restrictions unlikely in the foreseeable future. At the same time, even many of the defenders of the current policies recognize that some significant degree of liberalization is inevitable, probably within the decade, and they seek to influence the timing of such measures rather than the ultimate outcome.

The Ministry of Agriculture dominates German agricultural trade policy and represents Germany on agricultural issues within the EC. The Ministry's considerable power is attributable to the German system of ministerial responsibility, which enables each ministry to conduct its policies in a relatively autonomous fashion, and to the political strength of the farm lobby, which manifests itself whenever the Ministry's positions come under attack. On trade, the Ministry's position has been to support continued protection, in the form of the EC variable levy (which imposes prohibitive tariffs) and subsidies, but with some allowance for a graduated reduction in such measures. The Ministry's position is somewhat more moderate than that of the German farmers, whose association favors an open-ended, rigid adherence to the status quo. The Ministry takes the position that an "immediate" end to agriculture support policies within the European Community is "not manageable," but that a more gradual reduction of support measures (including trade protection and subsidies) is appropriate.[92] In mid-1991 State Secretary for Agriculture Walter Kittel stated that while measures to reduce EC farm production surpluses were appropriate, "measures must be taken through adequate external protection against non-EC countries so that the quantitative reductions will not be undermined."[93]

All Ministries in the Kohl government are in agreement that German farm policy will be one of phased liberalization. At issue is the pace, and to a lesser extent the nature, of that liberalization process. One Chancellory official suggested in 1990 that it was much easier to predict what Germany's farm trade policy will be at the beginning of the twenty-first century than what it will be at the beginning of 1991. The ultimate determining factor will not be the economic rationality of a particular

---

[92]Interview with a senior trade official with the Ministry of Agriculture, March 1990. The Ministry has supported an agreement within GATT providing for a gradual phasing down of farm subsidies within the European Community for a five year period, with a stipulation that at the end of that period there would be another set of negotiations to determine whether a continuation of the phasing-down process for another five years is in the Community's best interests. This "five-plus-five" approach is seen as preferable to an automatic 10 year phaseout of all EC farm subsidies. A Ministry official indicated that Germany could agree to an automatic 10 year phaseout of all farm subsidies if it were necessary to bring the GATT negotiations to a conclusion, but if the economic situation within the European Community worsened over the following five years, the German government would not abide by the agreement; hence, a five-plus-five formulation was superior. The Ministry's position is based on its assessment that some concessions on agriculture are inevitable. This is due in part to the sheer economic cost of current farm support programs at a time when the absorption of East Germany and the development of Eastern Europe is substantially increasing demands on German resources. In addition, agriculture is no longer the priority that it once was for the government; the political focus of the nation is on reunification, not farmers and their problems. Finally, political pressure for liberalization is growing stronger, both from external sources (other EC Member States, the United States and the Cairns Group) and internally, from inside all federal ministries including the Agriculture Ministry itself. Finally, the Ministry readily admits that from a purely economic perspective (for example, using a cost-benefit analysis) the CAP is not worthwhile and should be scrapped.

[93]*Süddeutsche Zeitung* (July 23, 1991) (FBIS-WEU-91-159).

course of action but the ability of the farmers to maintain their current political strength in a rapidly-changing environment.[94]

Interministerial skirmishing on agricultural issues has thus far been acrimonious but inconclusive. The Ministry of Economics has argued strongly for greater flexibility on agriculture to facilitate a successful Uruguay Round.[95] In the interministerial staff-level discussions of prospective farm policy, the Ministries of Economics and Finance are harshly critical of the Agriculture Ministry's policies. Periodically this criticism is regarded as sufficiently obnoxious that mid-level officials in the Agriculture Ministry complain to the Minister, who in turn complains to the Chancellor. The Chancellor speaks to the other Ministries about the political realities underlying the farm issue and asks them to cease their pressure on the Agriculture Ministry. This leads to a momentary abatement in criticism but interministerial bickering resumes when the Economics and Finance Ministries are confronted with new problems in their respective spheres arising out of German farm policies.

The Farm Lobby. The German farmers' political assets are formidable. They have their own powerful lobbying organization and, effectively, their own client political party (the CSU) as well as considerable strength in two other parties; their own client state government (Bavaria); and their own powerful ministry, as well as considerable support within German society at large. They have been able to employ these assets in coalition politics to secure policies which have largely insulated them from external competitive pressure.

Farmers comprise an important component of three parties -- most notably the CSU in Bavaria, but also the CDU and the FDP, which draws

---

[94]Interview with an agricultural official in the Federal Chancellory, March 1990. The West German government's current (and likely future) position on agriculture is perhaps best described by the following anecdote (as related in an interview with a Federal Chancellory official in March 1990): "In the midst of a fishing trip that they are on together, Stalin, Roosevelt and Churchill each catch a fish. All three of the fishes however are still alive when they reach the shore. The three men are therefore forced to kill their fish. Roosevelt, taking the initiative, decides to kill his fish by banging its head against a rock. Churchill is aghast at this method of execution, labelling it 'barbaric'. Instead, he executes his fish by cleanly cutting the head off with a sharp knife. Stalin in turn reacts with outrage to Churchill's method of execution, labelling it 'unnecessarily brutal'. Stalin then proceeds to gently caress his fish for several minutes until it has died of asphyxiation." German farmers are likely to experience the latter treatment in the form of a gradual phaseout of protection and supports.

[95]Minister Jürgen Möllemann in *Die Welt* (March 18, 1991).

a small, but important component of its support from farmers.[96] The farm vote has been a key element in every West German election since the formation of the federal republic. All three center-right parties are reluctant to support any policy measures that would alienate farm support, and one of these parties, the CSU, is effectively a farmers' party. If farmers feel that these parties have been insufficiently supportive, they threaten to stay away from the polls at election time (many small farmers boycotted the Bundestag elections in early 1987. DBV officials point out that the "era of big majorities has passed," with small minorities ruling the day and able to exert pressure at key points -- the farmers being a prime example.[97]

Farmers are even more powerful at the *Länder* level of politics than at the federal level. They dominate the political life of Bavaria and enjoy strong support in several other *Länder*. The fact that *Länder* elections are held every six months puts the government (and the Ministry of Agriculture) under continual political pressure to uphold farmers' interests. The farmers' local strength also means that agricultural interests are well represented in the Upper House of the Bundestag.[98] The Bundestag's Agriculture Committee is dominated by members who are either farmers themselves or pro-agriculture in their outlook. This Committee is in a good position to provide support for the Agriculture Minister in the event that his policies come under attack by other ministers.[99]

The farmers' association, the Deutscher Bauernverband, is one of the strongest and most effective lobbying groups in Europe. It has about 750,000 members and represents over 90 percent of all Germans engaged in full-time agriculture, the highest ratio of membership of any interest group in the federal republic.[100] Even the DBV's opponents pay tribute

---

[96]Even when the CDU/CSU coalition was out of power during the late 1970s, the FDP was able to secure the Ministry of Agriculture, and its longstanding Agricultural Minister, Josef Ertl, maintained protection for the farm sector. Interview with a German trade association official.

[97]Interview with an analyst with the German Farmers Association, March 1990.

[98]Interview with a representative of the German Industry and Trade (BDI and DIHT), March 1990.

[99]Interview with an official responsible for European issue, Federal Ministry of Economics, March 1990; Bulmer and Paterson (1987) p. 73.

[100]Simon Bulmer and William Paterson, *The Federal Republic of Germany and the European Community* (Allen & Unwin: 1987) p. 157.

to its organization and lobbying skills, and its ability to convey its positions to the German public.

The Ministry consults regularly with the DBV, and few, if any, major agricultural policy decisions are made without some input from the DBV; the Ministry has, in effect, been "captured" by the farm industry. The DBV's political clout within the CDU/CSU and the FDP has meant that successive Ministers of Agriculture have come from agricultural backgrounds and have been sympathetic to farm interests. Moreover, the technical level officials within the Ministry of Agriculture are heavily dependent upon the information and statistics which the DBV has at its disposal and furnishes to these specialists. The specialists, who play an important role in the agricultural policy-making process, are therefore often predisposed to supporting the agricultural consensus.[101]

The farmers' principal asset, however, is perhaps not institutional but attitudinal. Germans tend to depart from the norm of economic liberalism when agricultural issues are considered; the farmers' stance thus enjoys a surprising degree of support throughout German society. A large majority of the German population believes that the FRG must maintain self-sufficiency in food, particularly older Germans who recall the deprivations of the Second World War and the immediate postwar period.[102] In addition, Germany's Catholic and Evangelical churches, both of which play an important role in the formation of public views on many political issues, are strongly identified with agrarian fundamentalism of the sort promoted by the CDU/CSU. The farm is seen as the "backbone of Christian civilization," fostering independence, family relations, and a sense of closeness to nature and the basic rhythms of life. The churches believe that German agricultural policy must support the independence of the family farm.[103] Moreover, over twenty percent of the population of the Federal Republic consists of former refugees from largely agricultural areas like East Germany, East Prussia and the Oder-Neisse territories. In the early years of the Federal Republic there was a general

---

[101]Bulmer and Paterson (1987).

[102]Ministry of Economics official. This perspective was articulated by a member of the Bundestag: "*In such an area as food we must not fully rely on imports. It would be fatal if the Community were to open its markets and we would become dependent upon imports, for this would surely lead to situations we could not control politically.* Gisela Hendricks, "The Politics of Food: The Case of FR Germany," *Food Policy* (February 1987).

[103]Hendricks (1987).

sense that the loss of the eastern lands would require West Germany to subsidize agriculture indefinitely to compensate for that loss.[104]

While consumers might be expected to form a natural constituency protesting policies which result in higher food prices, this in fact has not proven to be the case. The Arbeitsverband der Verbraucher (AgV), the consumers' lobbying group, has criticized German agricultural policies and occasionally organized boycotts against individual producers. Its activities have failed to spark a groundswell of consumer protest, however, in part because the farm lobby has succeeded in demonstrating its own concern for consumers by stressing both the environmental benefits from a healthy German agricultural sector and the high quality of German agricultural products. Significantly, consumers within the FRG are far more concerned about the ecological safety, pureness and quality of the agricultural products that they buy than they are about the prices of those products.[105] This tends to produce an attitude toward trade which is protectionist in impact, if not intent (for example, support for the ban on hormone beef).[106] In addition, the CDU/CSU frequently point out that the FRG's agricultural polices benefit German consumers as well as German producers.[107]

Factors for Change. Despite the entrenched political position of the farmers, a number of actual and potential factors for change exist which will gradually diminish the farmers' political strength, and ultimately provide the basis for more liberal policies. A loose coalition between industry and agriculture ("iron and rye") has dominated German trade policy since the 1890s, with industry tolerating trade protection and high prices for agriculture in return for farmers' support for industry concerns (such as free trade in manufactures and policies which foster low input costs). This coalition is unraveling as international pressure highlights the basic contradictions on trade issues between the manufacturing and farm sectors.[108] The BDI has taken the lead in calling for a reform of current German agricultural policy, although the DIHT is also a vociferous critic of German agricultural policy and purports to be delighted with about

---

[104]Bulmer and Paterson (1987) p. 157.

[105]See, for example, "Ich bin ein Grüner," *Wirtschaftswoche*, (October 6, 1989).

[106]Interview with an Agricutural Counsel in the Foreign Ministry, March 1990.

[107]Hendricks (1987) p. 42.

[108]Interview with a senior Kiel Institute official, March 1990.

U.S. pressure on Germany with respect to agriculture.[109] Until recently the BDI took no firm position on agricultural trade issues because some of its constituent industries (for example, chemicals and sugar) had close commercial links with agricultural interests: the agriculture industry acquiesced in a chemical fertilizer cartel, for example, so the chemical industry stood by the farmers.[110] When the entrance of Spain and Portugal into the European Community led to U.S. trade retaliation against EC manufactured exports as well as farm products, however, a rough consensus was reached within the BDI that West Germany's protectionist stance in agriculture jeopardized German exports. This view was subsequently reinforced by the Uruguay Round negotiations, which led BDI members to conclude that the GATT negotiations "are being held hostage to agricultural interests."[111] The BDI therefore published several papers which were highly critical of the CAP,[112] and challenged the DBV directly in discussions of agricultural policy.[113] The result was "quite a dog-fight between the agriculture lobby and the industry lobby."[114]

German reunification altered the immediate political situation in a manner which tended to diminish the power of the agricultural lobby; a prominent member of the DBV conceded this point in March 1990.[115] The CDU/CSU gained substantial political strength at the expense of the SPD in 1990 while both the Greens and the Republicans failed to mount a viable political challenge; as a result, the center-right parties' dependency on the farm vote has probably lessened.[116] However, over

---

[109]Interview with a Director at the Association of German Chambers of Industry and Commerce (DIHT), March 1990.

[110]Interview with a senior Kiel Institute official, March 1990.

[111]Interview with a senior Ministry of Economics official, March 1990.

[112]In particular: Bundesverband der Deutschen Industrie e.V., *Agricultural Policy: Some Thoughts on Reform in a Market Economy* (Cologne: Industrie-Förderung GmbH, January 1988) (henceforth BDI).

[113]Interview with a Ministry of Economics official, March 1990.

[114]Interview with a DIHT official, March 1990.

[115]Interview with a policy analyst with the German Farmers Association, March 1990.

[116]Interview with a senior economic official in the Federal Chancellery, March 1990.

the longer term, the impact of reunification on the farm question is less clear. According to one view, given the sheer size of the farm sector in the former GDR, the political hand of the German farm lobby will be strengthened. Conversely, others argue that the addition of the GDR farm sector to the Community agriculture market will further increase the cost of the Common Agricultural Policy, making fundamental reforms that much more likely. A third issue is whether integration of the GDR into the CAP will result in a net increase in agricultural products produced (a function of the level set by the CAP for the total farm output of a united Germany); should net output increase, there is an increased likelihood of a larger volume of subsidized EC farm exports, which would exacerbate trade friction.[117]

It is not inconceivable that perceived disparities in federal policies toward farmers in the old and new Länder could result in a farm movement divided along an east/west line. As of mid-1991, conditions on the farms of the new Länder were so bad that the immediate issue was simply the ability of the agricultural sector to survive at all in this part of Germany. Ninety-seven percent of the farmland under cultivation in the East had been organized under state production associations; with the collapse of communism, these entities had no idea what products to produce or in what quantities, or how to market them, and according to Brandenburg's Minister of Agriculture, three quarters of the former state production associations faced imminent bankruptcy in 1991. Privatization efforts stalled, in part, not only because of bureaucratic delays but because many East German farmers no longer wished to remain in the eastern Länder or in the agricultural profession.[118] Eastern farmers could not compete with those in the Western Länder and were reportedly plowing under crops for which no markets could be found; large numbers of dairy cattle were slaughtered because East German farmers feared they would fare badly in the CAP's quota allotments.[119] With the abandonment of large areas formerly under cultivation, the "countryside is becoming a wilderness and the abandoned fields are in danger of becoming prairies".[120] Instead of even "the crude beginnings of a pan-German agriculture concept," with western and eastern farmers forming a more

---

[117]M.A. Freney and Rebecca S. Hartley, *United Germany and the United States* (National Planning Association, 1991) p. 38.

[118]*Frankfurter Allgemiene Zeitung* (July 24, 1991) (FBIS-WEU-91-156).

[119]*Stuttgarter Zeitung* (February 1, 1991).

[120]*Der Spiegel* (August 19, 1991) (FBIS-WEU-91-176).

powerful political bloc, the bitter view in the East was that Bonn was deliberately rigging its farm policies to "serve the interests of the producers in the old Länder."[121]

Finally, two major divisions have opened up within the farm lobby in the Western Länder, between big and small farmers and between "Green" farmers and large-scale users of chemicals. The large farmers benefit most from the price support system associated with the CAP and defend the CAP more vigorously. The small farmers tend to favor income supports over price supports. The larger farmers (who tend to be grain producers) have a greater prospect of becoming competitive on a world scale; many of them would survive a restructuring and consolidation of the farm sector, whereas the smaller farmers would not.[122] The small farmers are extremely bitter because they believe that the current CAP benefits the big farmers, but it is the small farmers who deliver the votes. A second fault line in the farm lobby divides "Green farmers" -- usually, but by no means always smaller farmers -- from heavy users of pesticides and chemical fertilizers. Green farmers have formed a loose coalition with urban consumers concerned about the health quality of their food.[123] This group supports "sustainable agriculture" and limits on the use of fertilizers and pesticides. The German farmers and other groups with similar concerns could well affect trade policy by pressuring the German government to establish stringent national healthy standards for imported food. The imposition of such standards could lead to trade conflicts similar to the hormone beef dispute as foreign agricultural products that have been grown with fertilizers and pesticides are subjected to increased restrictions.[124] These divisions in the farm movement -- which recently led to an abortive breakaway movement from the DBV -- are unlikely to affect trade policy directly over the short term since all factions currently

---

[121]*Deutsches Allgemeines Sonntagsblatt* (June 21, 1991).

[122]Interview with a senior agricultural official in the Federal Chancellery, March 1990.

[123]This coalition was at least partially responsible for the introduction of the set-aside program by the Ministry of Agriculture, which took farmland out of production.

[124]Interview with a former high-level bureaucrat in the Ministry of Agriculture, March 1990.

support a protectionist stance.[125] A serious rupture between big and small farmers could, however, diminish the political clout of the farm lobby as a whole and afford the government more flexibility in moving toward a liberal trade posture.

External pressure on the FRG over agricultural trade is a significant factor for change in the country's current policies. The BDI and DIHT are emphatic that foreign pressure, for liberalization, especially from the United States, is effective and should be increased.[126] The DBV corroborates this view, in a negative manner, by expressing irritation that U.S. interests are "in bed with" the Economics Ministry on farm issues, a "dangerous" situation for Germany.[127]

Regardless of the party in power, government support for farmers -- including trade protection -- is likely to decline substantially over the next decade, with the most dramatic change coming after 1995. There being "no future for small farmers within the European Community",[128] the government will seek to foster rationalization of the agricultural industry. There are indications that the current government support system will be increasingly based on income supports rather than production supports.[129] The government will accede to a greater degree of trade

---

[125]Interview with a former high-level bureaucrat in the Ministry of Agriculture, March 1990. The DBV is dominated by large farmers and its policies tend to reflect their views. Recently most of the small farmers within the DBV as well as a number of large farmers interested in environmental issues (so-called "Green farmers") broke away to form their own lobbying organization, the Deutsche Bauernbund, whose primary objective was to secure a more "equitable" distribution of agricultural supports within the FRG. However, the new organization, lacking the DBV's established political and financial infrastructure, simply collapsed. Nevertheless, the incident illustrates the fact that while it remains the farmers' principal lobbying organization, the DBV suffers from substantial internal strains.

[126]Interviews with officials at the BDI and DIHT, February and March 1990.

[127]"How do you think the Americans would like it if the DBV began to join forces with the textile lobby or some other protectionist lobby in the U.S.?" Interview with a DBV official.

[128]Interview with a senior economic official at the Federal Chancellery, March 1990.

[129]Interview with a foreign trade official at the Ministry of Economics and "Ich Bin Ein Grüner," *Wirtschaftswoche* (October 6, 1989).

liberalization by the EC[130] but may insist on more stringent health and quarantine requirements. Most of these changes will not begin until after the current "period of flux" is past, however, and the government will remain cautious of alienating farmers until the most destabilizing aspects of reunification have been resolved.[131]

Telecommunications

The extent to which telecommunications will remain a trade issue for Germany in the 1990s depends largely on the extent to which the liberalization of telecommunications equipment and services, initiated in May 1989 is actually carried out, and the outcome of EC revisions on telecommunications procurement procedures under consideration.

During the 1980s, the U.S. and Germany differed sharply over the practice of the Bundespost (the government postal and telecommunications monopoly) of favoring German suppliers in its procurement of equipment and its restrictions on access by foreign firms to the German network. The Ministry of Posts and Telecommunications, which exercised jurisdiction over the Bundespost, traditionally protected it against outside pressure but in the late 1980s began to more toward partial deregulation, reflecting not only external pressure but the concern that the existing restricted system would result in German telecommunications' gradual loss of international competitiveness. In 1989 the Ministry of Posts and Telecommunications announced reform legislation which resulted in the breakup of the old Bundespost into three entities, including one with jurisdiction over telecommunications (Deutsche Telekom). Concurrently, most telecommunications services formerly monopolized by the Bundespost were opened to competition, and the market for customer premises equipment was liberalized on July 1, 1990. Foreign companies were permitted to participate in all telecommunications activities that are open to competition.[132] Telekom

[130]"The FRG must accept that many agricultural products can be produced more efficiently elsewhere. . . . [These products] should be imported from other nations in order to boost the FRG's industrial exports to those of other nations." Interview with an agricultural official in the Federal Chancellery, March 1990.

[131]Interview with a senior economics official in the Federal Chancellery, March 1990.

[132]Christian Schwarz-Schilling in *International Trade Reporter* (May 17, 1989). For example, as a result of the reforms any private firm wishing to provide data links

(continued...)

retains a monopoly on the provision of telephone service and the public telecommunications network.

The German government position on these changes is that they have eliminated any potential for further trade friction in this sector.[133] In the view of government officials, Germany has moved from being one of the EC's most closed telecommunications markets to one of the most open. Indeed, the new liberal German licensing requirements for telecommunications services have been criticized by France, which supports a more restrictive licensing scheme.[134] In 1990, the Office of the U.S. Trade Representative reported that the German market for telecommunications services was opening and that "U.S. firms have already made inroads."[135]

Nevertheless, the structure of the partially-deregulated market suggests that substantial potential for trade friction remains. In mid-1991, 18 months after its formation, despite some privatizations (satellites, cellular phone systems) "the majority of Telekom's business is still dominated by the same cadre of government functionaries. . . . Telekom's president and its management board do not have enough authority to act independently of the government."[136] Telekom, like the Bundespost, controls its own procurement of telecommunications equipment for the German voice telephone network, and much of the equipment needed to operate this network is the type of product in which U.S. firms were most competitive -- "core" items like switching and transmission equipment. The old Bundespost procured virtually all such equipment from a constellation of smaller German suppliers, and it is likely that Telekom will retain a strong national bias, particularly in the strategic area of central office

---

[132](...continued)
to West German firms can do so by registering with the government, and several companies (BASCOM, BAFG, INFO AG) have begun to set up internal networks with companies for data transmission services.

[133]Interviews with officials at the Ministry of Economics and the German Embassy in Washington, March 1990.

[134]*Financial Times* (April 19, 1990).

[135]USTR, *1990 National Trade Estimate on Foreign Trade Barriers*, p. 72.

[136]*German Brief* (June 12-18, 1991).

equipment.[137] Indeed, according to one recent estimate, because of prior procurement commitments, only about 10 to 15 percent of the West German market for central office switching equipment will even be contestable in the 1990s, with the remainder already locked in by German firms.[138] Should a continuing "buy German" attitude be manifested overtly, the issue of procurement could flare into major friction with the United States, particularly because the rewiring of East Germany's telecommunications system will involve huge procurements and represents a major potential market for U.S. suppliers.[139]

The political forces which opposed deregulation did not evaporate with the 1989 reforms and may act as a brake on further liberalization, particularly of the telephone network itself and the equipment for that network. The SPD has positioned itself as an opponent of deregulation and vowed a tenacious rear guard action against further change. The union which represents telecommunications workers, the Deutsche Postgewerkschaft (DPG) opposed deregulation and will resist further moves to liberalize Telekom's services and procurements.[140] There is some continuing apprehension over deregulation within the CDU and CSU as well, since a substantial portion of Germany's telecommunications suppliers and subcontractors are CDU constituents. Many telecommunications equipment suppliers are based in Bavaria, and reflecting their influence the CSU opposed deregulation. While Siemens' position has softened, reflecting its increasingly international outlook, the smaller suppliers remain concerned over the impact of liberalization.

Support for the telecommunications reforms within the FRG itself remains somewhat less than wholehearted, reflecting the fact that the

---

[137]USTR warned in 1990 that "access to West German equipment markets may . . .be slowed by traditional procurement and product approval practices." 1990 *National Trade Estimates*, p.72.

[138]P.F. Cowley, "Telecommunications," in Gary Clyde Hufbauer, ed., *Europe 1992: An American Perspective* (The Brookings Institution: 1990) Table 4-6.

[139]The estimated cost of establishing a modern telecommunications network in East Germany is DM20-30 billion. Telekom has awarded Siemens and SEL a grant of DM250 million to establish 18 switching centers of 2000 lines each, but this will provide only a small fraction of what is needed. *Financial Times* (1990).

[140]The DPG has traditionally been so powerful that "all the way up to the Federal Chancellor there are people who want to avoid a conflict with the DPG." K. Morgan and D. Webber, "Divergent Paths: Political Strategies for Telecommunications in Britain, France and West Germany," in *9 West European Politics* 56, 69 (October 1986).

telecommunications sector is considered to be a component of the public infrastructure within Germany.[141] People view the nation's telecommunications service in much the same way as the postal service, the utilities and the railways; monopolization of the telecommunications sector by a government-controlled entity is therefore not necessarily viewed in a negative light, and fees paid by users of the telecommunications service are generally regarded as being a form of indirect taxes.[142] Since Germans are strongly opposed to paying taxes to foreigners, there is a natural aversion to opening up the domestic telecommunications sector to foreign firms, no matter how much more efficient those firms might be.[143]

The EC Commission has proposed a directive on telecommunications procurement which would force all monopoly providers of telecommunications services to adopt competitive bidding procedures, which would affect Telekom's procurement practices. Under the proposed directive, however, procuring entities would not be required to accept bids from non-EC suppliers: "EC supplier" would be defined by a 50-percent local content test. Although they did not allude directly to these new rules, German officials suggested that if U.S. firms wanted to gain access to the West German telecommunications market, they would be advised to rely less on direct exports to that market and more on developing a local presence in that market. They were careful to point out, however, that U.S. firms should adopt such a strategy simply as a sound business practice, not as a response to the changing EC regulatory environment.[144]

Autos

Officially Germany has no trade or industrial policy in the automobile sector, but because of its importance to the German economy, the government cannot ignore the industry if it drifts into competitive difficulty. While not well known or publicized, the *Länder* provide a

---

[141]Interview with a senior Ministry of Economics official, March 1990.

[142]Indeed, such a monopoly is seen, in many cases, as being beneficial for the nation insofar as the government is able to maintain direct control over the services being provided.

[143]Interview with a senior Ministry of Economics official, March 1990.

[144]Interviews with BDI and Ministry of Economics officials 1990.

considerable volume of subsidies to the industry,[145] and, as already noted, the federal government appears to have negotiated a voluntary restraint arrangement with MITI in the early 1980s. Autos are in fact the primary sector in which Germany has been able to benefit from its curious posture as an advocate of free trade within a larger confederation with protectionist tendencies. The German auto industry depends on exports to achieve economies of scale and has traditionally been a vigorous proponent of open markets, a position fully supported by the Ministry of Economics. At the same time, the German industry has benefitted tremendously from national restrictions on Japanese auto exports to Italy, France, Spain and the United Kingdom, which have helped preserve these markets for German sales. Significantly, as the EC's trade regime in autos was restructured, the German auto industry simultaneously came under increased competitive pressure from Japan and tempered its traditional free trade position in favor of "transitional" EC-wide quotas on imports from Japan.

The German producers of standard vehicles, Ford and Volkswagen, have been most seriously affected by Japanese competitive pressure and led the German industry's move toward a more protectionist stance. Volkswagen's Chairman, Karl Hahn, advocated a "transitional period before the Japanese have access to our markets," and supported a Franco-Italian position favoring interim pan-EC quotas.[146] In addition, although its trade position remains considerably more liberal than that of Volkswagen, Mercedes-Benz also suggested that perhaps trade curbs against the Japanese are not such a bad idea. As Toyota and Nissan upgraded their production lines and began to target the upper end of the auto market with the Lexus and Infiniti models, Mercedes became concerned. In late 1989, Edward Reuter, Chairman of Daimler-Benz AG, expressed hope that the abolition of EC import quotas on Japanese autos could be delayed.[147] Mercedes-Benz Chairman Werner Niefer admits

---

145 *European Report* No. 1495 (May 13, 1989).

146 Mr. Hahn now serves as a policy advisor to President Mitterrand of France. Interview with a DIHT official, March 1990. *European Report* No. 1510 (July 5, 1989); 1524 (September 30, 1989).

147 "VW Head Favors Continued Restriction on Auto Imports," *Kyodo News Service* (October 6, 1989).

that, "It's not a BMW with a 12-cylinder motor but cars like the Lexus and Infiniti that scare me."[148]

Over the longer term the German auto industry is aware that it cannot rely on government policy measures to preserve its market position. The relationship between Daimler-Benz and Mitsubishi apparently represents an effort on the part of Mercedes-Benz to slow the entry of additional competition into its traditional markets. In effect, with Toyota and Nissan threatening the luxury model market in Europe, Mercedes-Benz appears to be seeking to guide Mitsubishi's future development within the automotive sector towards truck production for Eastern Europe and away from car production for Western Europe (which is Mercedes' primary market), while at the same time providing Mercedes with improved access to the Japanese market. If this strategy is successful it could well prefigure a future trend in German trade policy within the automotive sector and perhaps other sectors as well; namely, the use of international joint ventures to avert future losses in market share.[149]

Commercial Aircraft

Germany is a key player in Airbus Industrie, the controversial consortium of European commercial aircraft manufacturers. A subsidiary of MBB (a publicly-held German firm), Deutsche Airbus, holds a 38 percent equity stake in Airbus Industrie, and has received substantial subsidies from the German government. Two other German participants in Airbus, Bölkow and Messerschmidt, have also received Airbus subsidies. Total German subsidies for Airbus between 1967 and 1991 were estimated by the U.S. Trade Representative as $7.8 billion, with $3.5 billion disbursed.[150]

In 1988 the German government announced that it would privatize MBB by selling a controlling share of the company to Daimler-Benz for $2.1 billion. To sweeten this arrangement for Daimler, the German government offered the following incentives: (a) restructuring of existing obligations of the Airbus group, including forgiveness/writeoff of MBB's past Airbus-related losses; (b) a guarantee of exchange rate risks worth $1

148"Infiniti and Lexus: Characters in a German Nightmare," *Business Week* (October 9, 1989).

149Interview with a Kiel Institute official, March 1990. See "Car Maker Spreads Its Wings," *Financial Times* (April 23, 1990) p. 40; "Mitsubishi, Daimler Pick Up Pace of Talks on Joint Ventures," *The Wall Street Journal* (May 17, 1990) p. A15.

150Office of U.S. Trade Representative, *National Trade Estimates* (1989) pp. 66-69.

billion; (c) a commitment that the federal government would acquire a 20 percent stake in a new MBB civil aircraft company; and (d) about $2.0 billion in support for the Daimler-Benz/MBB merger.[151] The exchange rate guarantees provide that Daimler-Benz will receive the agreed subsidy amount if the dollar falls to DM1.60 or lower -- so that the international competitive impact of a weakening dollar would automatically be offset by the subsidy.

Bonn views the sale of MBB as a way to improve the competitiveness of its aircraft industry while redirecting government resources into other aerospace priorities. It recognizes that successful aircraft manufacture requires huge economies of scale, and with this purchase, Daimler-Benz acquires 60 percent of West Germany's aerospace industry, the domestic strength needed to compete on an international level.[152] It will also begin a restructuring of the industry, a process which Bonn supports.[153]

The U.S. government has criticized Airbus subsidies for many years, questioning, for example, whether the subsidies granted by Germany and three other EC governments are consistent with the GATT Agreement on Trade in Civil Aircraft. The Bush Administration reacted with particular vehemence, however, to the exchange rate guarantees for Daimler-Benz since these measures appear designed to undercut the work of the Group of 7 to correct the U.S. trade deficit through joint action on the exchange rate.[154] The U.S. initiated formal GATT proceedings against the EC in 1991, citing the German exchange rate scheme; this was seen as "less confrontational" than a Section 301 action.

Friction between the U.S. and Germany is likely to continue and even intensify in this sector in the 1990s because this is one of a relatively few areas in which Washington's and Bonn's interests are fundamentally divergent. The Germans will not relinquish a position in commercial aviation; they are eager not only to capture market share from the Americans but to counter Japan's emerging aviation industry and to exploit potential opportunities in the Soviet Union.[155] Given the huge

---

[151]Office of U.S. Trade Representative, *1991 National Trade Estimate on Foreign Trade Barriers* (1991).

[152]"Merger Proposal Splits West Germans," *Chicago Tribune*, July 9, 1989.

[153]"Bonn Official Sees Aviation Competition from Japan," Reuters, February 17, 1989.

[154]*Journal of Commerce* (October 2, 1989).

[155]Reuters (February 17, 1989).

economies of scale in this industry, it is unlikely that even a very large entity like MBB working in concert with other European firms will be able to compete without extensive additional government support, whether overt or covert. These imperatives place Germany on a collision course not only with longstanding U.S. economic doctrine but with major and vital U.S. commercial interests.

Information Technology

The German information technology sector has been the subject of intensive soul-searching by the ministries, companies, industry organizations and banks that make up West Germany's trade policy community. There is a general recognition that the Federal Republic lags behind the United States and Japan in information technology, and even the most ardent free-traders express concern that Japan plays by different rules in the international trading system. A debate is under way over what, if anything, should be done; and three schools of thought have emerged. The first, fully convinced that West Germany's information technology industry is not competitive with the U.S. and Japanese industries, argues that West German companies both can and must catch up to their competitors, if necessary through use of R&D subsidies and even trade protection. The major proponents of this school are the Ministry of Research and Technology (BMFT) and elements within Siemens, by far the largest and most important of West Germany's information technology companies.[156]

The second view agrees that West German companies lag behind their U.S. and Japanese competitors and that this gap should be closed. However, it argues that government subsidies through publicly-funded R&D are neither appropriate nor effective, and that the job must ultimately be done by industry itself.[157] The most important trade policy actors favoring this school of thought are West Germany's two

---

[156]BMFT provides direct subsidies for R&D to virtually all information technology fields. Generally these consist of grants or soft loans which cover 50 percent of a project's cost. BMFT's 1989 budget for R&D programs was DM 7.7 billion. While many of these are relatively small grants sprinkled among small and medium firms, BMFT has also funded large-scale efforts like the Siemens-Philips Mega-Project to commercialize the 4M DRAM and 1M SRAM. BMFT has also drawn up comprehensive promotional plans involving a wide range of stimulating measures -- procurement policy, tax benefits, R&D subsidies, and other forms of government aid.

[157]Interview with a senior German bank official, March 1990.

major industry organizations -- the Federation of German Industry (BDI) and the German Chamber of Industry and Trade (DIHT).

The third school acknowledges the superiority of the American and Japanese information technology industries but argues that the gap is unimportant. Therefore, although West Germany could conceivably catch up, it should not bother to try.[158] Domination of the information technology industry is not critical to a nation's well-being; in fact, high technology in general rarely accounts for more than 10 percent of a nation's GNP -- and Germany should continue to focus its efforts on consumer goods, the "cash cows" of most developed economies.[159] Moreover, it is argued, West Germany benefits by letting the United States and Japan spend billions of dollars developing sophisticated information technology products, which it can then import at low prices. This school concludes that the process of "catching up" would be enormously costly and ultimately not worth the effort, given the advantages to West Germany of specializing in other products.[160]

Many of West Germany's most prominent trade policymakers subscribe to the third school of thought, particularly those working at the Ministry of Economics and in the leading banks. It is these two groups that most vehemently criticize the BMFT's R&D programs. One senior manager at the Dresdner Bank complains that the BMFT has thrown money at a problem -- the information technology gap -- that does not require a solution.[161] A high-level Ministry of Economics official has denigrated the ESPRIT project, arguing that the costs far outweigh the benefits.[162] Even a top Chancellory official believes that West Germany should resist the high technology research projects that the BMFT advocates.[163] These policymakers instead agree that West Germany's information technology strategy ought to remain "diffusion-oriented" rather than "development oriented."[164]

---

[158]Interview with a senior economist with a major German bank, March 1990.

[159]Interview with a Ministry of Economics official, March 1990.

[160]Interview with an economic official in the Federal Chancellery, March 1990.

[161]Interview with a senior German bank official, March 1990.

[162]Interview with a senior Ministry of Economics official, March 1990.

[163]Interview with a Federal Chancellery official, March 1990.

[164]Interview with a senior German bank official, March 1990.

Given Germany's peculiar economic policy structure, it is quite conceivable, indeed, likely, that this debate will not be resolved during the next decade since there is no immediate external or internal pressure on the various parties to the debate to compose their differences. The BMFT is free to continue subsidizing its R&D projects, subject only to the normal budgetary constraints that all Ministries confront. The Economics Ministry can carp about BMFT's efforts, but it is not in a position to block them. Even in the event German industry decides to seek trade protection, the Economics Ministry does not constitute an insurmountable obstacle, since the industry can take the matter to Brussels. Nevertheless, if the Japanese industrial and technological ascendancy increases, as seems likely in the 1990s, the school of thought headed by the BMFT is likely to gain in strength and support.

WHITHER GERMANY?

German reunification and the end of Soviet power in Eastern Europe have, perhaps not surprisingly, stirred up a considerable amount of speculation over possible German ambitions for political dominance in Europe. While these concerns are understandable, given their historic context, they are not only in all likelihood unfounded, but tend to obscure more important questions about Germany's future role in the international economy, its competitive strategies, and the part which it will play in two critically important supranational institutions, the European Community and the GATT. Notwithstanding the existence of some domestic protectionist constituencies, Germany has traditionally been one of the most important champions of liberalism and multilateralism in the international trading order. Arguably, the principal risk posed to the international Community by German reunification is not that of political revanchism, but that the Federal Republic will be so preoccupied with the process of absorbing the new Länder that it will not be able to pull its weight within the EC and the GATT during a critical period in the early and mid-1990s. This is not a hypothetical concern; notwithstanding disclaimers by Messrs. Kohl and Genscher, every major ministry focused primarily on reunification in 1991, and the Ministry of Economics reportedly transferred staff and resources from the Uruguay Round negotiations and European integration to deal with problems arising out of reunification. Arguably, given its role as a pillar of liberalism, German reticence and self-absorption pose greater risks for the international community than German assertiveness.[165]

An economic question of key importance is posed by the ongoing debate over how to enhance Germany's competitive position in the industries of the future. Germany has the potential to become another Japan, and is groping for the right combination of economic doctrine, industrial structure and government policy measures to make this happen. There is a growing awareness that something must be done differently. One German official commented in 1991 that while demand from the new Länder was creating an economic boom in western Germany,

> *in the middle of the boom we don't notice that some companies -- our semiconductor and computer firms -- are recording increasing losses and are threatened by failure or takeover by Japanese and Americans. While in our consciousness there is only more Germany and at most Europe and the Gulf, in the silent battle the Japanese are monopolizing the key technologies of the 21st Century in the world market.*[166]

As the Japanese shadow has grown longer over Europe, the German constituency favoring large scale subsidies and other departures from the liberal economic norm has grown larger.[167] At the same time, German multinationals like Daimler-Benz are pursuing their own competitive strategies based on globalization of production and international strategic alliances. The prospect of a new German competitive strategy which merges these seemingly "conflicting" elements -- industrial policy and the autonomous actions of world class multinational firms, backed by a sophisticated financial system -- is being considered in Germany. As Conrad Seitz observed in 1991, "A MITI in Bonn or Brussels, which drafts

---

[165]Interview with a Ministry of Economics official, March 1990. One example of the potentially pivotal role Germany could play in the trade arena is offered by Community enlargement. The Germans have actively supported Austria's petition for accession and will lobby within the EC institutions for further expansions to embrace other EFTA countries and ultimately, several Eastern European states. As the U.S.-EC clash over the accession of Spain and Portugal demonstrated, these future enlargements could precipitate a full blown transatlantic trade war unless the new member states are absorbed without a net increase in external protection. German assertiveness on this point will be crucial to the outcome.

[166]Conrad Seitz in *Wirtschaftswoche* (April 5, 1991) (JPRS-EST-91-014).

[167]See comment of SPD economics spokesman Wolfgang Roth in *Wirtschaftsdienst* (September 1989); Conrad Seitz in *Wirtschaftswoche* (April 5, 1991) (JPRS-EST-91-014).

visions for the future of the European information economy and society and brings together the European industry for large research and development projects, would not be a bad thing."[168] Maybe not, but there is no question that a Germany, or a German-led Europe, organized along such lines would be an extremely powerful entity, fully capable of challenging Japan and the United States in the competition for world markets.

---

[168]Interview in *Wirtschaftswoche* (April 5, 1991) (JPRS-EST-91-014).

4

South Korea

Brent L. Bartlett

Korea has been characterized by many analysts as a newly-industrializing country whose spectacular success is attributable to its market-driven, increasingly liberal economic policies, and by many others as a mercantilistic state whose rapid industrialization and success in export markets have been primarily government-driven. This disparity of views reflects the fact that both elements are manifested in what may be characterized as a "lurch-and-halt" approach to economic policy. The *dirigiste* government apparatus alternates between taking bold steps toward liberalization and backsliding into more protectionist policies. Although the overall direction is toward greater openness, the country's course is not a steady one and the pace of change is fitful and uncertain.

The trade-policy events that unfolded in Korea during the first year of the 1990s contained all of the dramatic elements found in the evolution Korean trade policy. This period repeated a cycle that observers of Korean trade policy had seen before and are likely to see again in the coming decade: Korea announces and partially implements trade-reform measures; discomfort among Korean interest groups affected by the reforms leads to sporadic backsliding, although the government's official role is never clear; foreign trading partners, particularly the United States, responds to the developments with displeasure and vague threats of retaliation; finally, Seoul provides increased foreign (mostly U.S.) access to Korean markets in selected areas and announces new trade reforms and partially implements them.

As 1990 began, Korea was in the midst of another trade-liberalization program. Tariffs were scheduled to be phased-down over a five-year period and the so-called liberalization ratio, or the percentage of goods for which no import license was required, had reached 99.5 percent. To avoid being cited by the U.S. government as a "priority country" for U.S. trade action, the Korean government was accelerating trade reforms in telecommunications and agriculture, and had strengthened enforcement measures against violations of foreign-owned intellectual property rights.

A backdrop to these announced reforms, however, was an economy that was deteriorating rapidly, at least by Korean standards. Exports were off 17 percent from the previous quarter while imports were at an all-time high. The huge trade surplus Korea enjoyed in 1988 was gone by the first quarter of 1990 as the trade balance fell into the red for the first time since the mid-1980s. Domestically, inflation was accelerating and labor costs stood more than 25 percent higher than a year earlier, eroding Korea's international competitiveness. Real growth, although respectable by developed-country standards, had slowed to about half the rate of the 1980s.[1]

The first sign of policy action in response to these developments was a surprise cabinet shake-up in March 1990. Key economic officials who had argued that the time had come for Korea to adopt more balanced growth policies, including greater resources for social programs, were replaced by the perennial champions of Korea's dauntless pro-export, pro-growth strategies. Soon the face of Korea's trade policies began to change.[2] An "anti-luxury campaign" emerged targeted at foreign goods, although Korean officials denied involvement claiming that it was a spontaneous movement on the part of the public to return to more traditional Korean values of thrift and self-sufficiency. There were widespread reports of imported goods being removed from department stores while imports of big-ticket items, such as American cars, slowed to a trickle. Foreign exporters to Korea began lodging complaints that the usual difficulties in clearing Korean customs suddenly grew worse. In June, the government announced that the five-year tariff-reduction schedule would be postponed for one year.

The U.S. reaction to these reports was swift. American officials shelved ongoing negotiations between Seoul and Washington to establish a permanent bilateral working group to resolve sectoral trade disputes. Several high-level meetings were held to communicate Washington's unhappiness with these trade policy trends, including Korea's opposition to U.S. proposals on agricultural liberalization in the Uruguay Round.

---

1 International Monetary Fund, *International Financial Statistics*, various issues.

2 For detailed contemporaneous reports in English of the shake-up, see *Korea Times* in the weeks following the March 10 announcement and the analysis in Korea Trade & Business, "Korea Inc.: Going for Growth Again" (April 1990) p. 23.

By early 1991 there were signs that the episode was coming full circle. The Korean government took several steps to forestall further trade frictions with the United States. Seoul announced that foreign companies could own retail sales networks within Korea and that four foreign firms -- two American and two British -- could operate in the Korean securities market. The Ministry of Foreign Affairs announced that keeping U.S.-Korean trade relations on track was its top priority for 1991. Korean officials told their U.S. counterparts that the anti-luxury campaign would henceforth be called the anti-consumption campaign so as to not discriminate against imports, although at least one U.S. official wondered how the Korea government could rename what it said was a spontaneous public movement.[3]

TRADE POLICY BACKGROUND

From the late 1950s to the early 1980s, Korean trade policies were little more than supporting measures for Korea's heavily interventionist industrial policies, and the Korean government's industrialization goals constituted the single force driving Korean trade policy. During this period, the government's overall strategy of export promotion and import substitution was sustained by strong export subsidies, directed domestic credit, strict import barriers, rigid exchange-rate and capital controls, and what the World Bank termed "a host of finely-tuned, export-promoting instruments."[4]

Around 1980, however, two forces for trade liberalization emerged. First, calls for the liberalization of the Korean economy arose from several non-political quarters in 1982. The Korean Development Institute (KDI), the influential advisory body to the government's powerful Economic Planning Board (EPB), and the Ministry of Finance (MOF) both advocated a more liberal direction for Korean trade policy. The causes behind the shift toward trade liberalization by Korean planners at the turn of the decade were complex. Contributing factors include the second oil shock, the political instability surrounding the assassination of President Park, and the mounting financial problems at both the industry- and economy-

---

3 "Changing Tunes," Korea Trade & Business (February 1991) p. 24.

4 World Bank, *Managing the Industrial Transition* (Washington, D.C.: World Bank, 1987) p. 29.

wide levels.[5] Simultaneously, the World Bank and International Monetary Fund (IMF) proposed trade-liberalization measures in conjunction with Korea's debt-reduction efforts. These international organizations lent objective credibility (and some degree of financial leverage) to the arguments of those within the Korean government calling for trade reform.

Second, many foreign governments responded to Korean trade policies with a variety of trade measures of their own. Prior to 1983, Korea was almost free from trade friction with its trading partners.[6] Korean officials then discovered that Korea was not immune from foreign trade-remedy laws. As the decade of the 1980s progressed, foreign pressure came to both reinforce and overshadow the indigenous Korean advocates of liberalization.

The United States soon emerged as the predominant force driving the Korean liberalization. According to Park Un-Suh, Korea's chief trade negotiator during this period,[7] the turning point was an affirmative 1983 antidumping finding by the United States against Korean color televisions[8] -- a major Korean export -- which caused "dismay and anger" among Korean officials who had previously considered the United States "a friendly ally and even a generous big brother."[9] Park argues that such foreign pressure both accelerated the process of trade reform and "helped

---

[5] World Bank (1987) p. 48. Perhaps most importantly, Western-educated, liberal-oriented economists began to dominate the ranks of Korea's technocratic elite in the influential think tanks. See Kim Kihwan and Chung Hwa Soo, "Korea's Domestic Trade Politics and the Uruguay Round," in Henry R. Nau, ed., *Domestic Politics and the Uruguay Round* (Columbia University Press: 1988) p. 136. Kim and Chung are researchers at the Ilhae Institute, an economic think tank in Seoul. This paper is by far the best single survey of the Korean trade-policy process.

[6] There was one U.S. antidumping case brought against South Korea in 1980, and none in 1981.

[7] Park Uh-Suh recounts his experiences as Director-General of MTI's Industrial Policy Bureau in his 1989 Korean-language book, *At the Field of Trade Friction.* Park was among Korea's top trade negotiators from 1981 to 1987.

[8] As a result of the 1983 investigation, the antidumping margin imposed was 14.64 percent in 1984 and 34.84 percent in the 1985 review. Trade negotiations had occurred during the 1970s on, for example, footwear exports to the United States, but such talks were generally resolved without major conflict.

[9] United States International Trade Commission, *Operation of the Trade Agreements Program* (Annual Reports 1981 to 1989).

Koreans realize the importance and seriousness of trade negotiations for the first time."[10]

Soo-Gil Young, senior official at the Korea Development Institute, articulated the turning point somewhat differently, but again the United States was at the forefront.

> *President Reagan brought with him on his visit to Korea in November 1983 the first of a series of market-opening request lists. Since then, high-profile bilateral trade negotiations have continued, and trade liberalization under pressure from the United States has become an established practice in Korea.*[11]

The following year South Korea agreed to join the U.S. voluntary restraint arrangement (VRA) to avoid antidumping and countervailing duties on steel products. During the rest of the 1980s, Korea faced 77 antidumping allegations from GATT signatories, as well as mounting pressure from the United States to liberalize other sectors, particularly agriculture. Forty-six of these allegations were found to be valid. Korean officials have also linked the rise in U.S. pressure in the early 1980s to the Korean merchandise trade balance which turned in Korea's favor in 1982.[12] In 1989, Korean officials conceded to a series of liberalization measures in order to avoid being cited on the U.S. government's Priority List of unfair traders under the Super 301 authority.

Korean trade policies in the 1990s will continue to reflect a balance of pressures. On the one hand, trade policies are seen by many Korean officials as supporting measures for domestic industrial objectives. On the other hand, influential Korean planners and Korea's foreign trading partners support substantial trade liberalization. The extent to which this balance leads to true liberalization of the Korean trade economy is a matter of wide dispute, however. Many Koreans argue that the liberalization has been rapid and is now nearly complete, whereas the number of foreign trade-related complaints against South Korea remains

---

[10] *Business Korea* (June 1989) p. 40.

[11] Soo-Gil Young, "Economic Relations Between the U.S. and Korea," in Thomas O. Bayard and Soo-Gil Young, eds., *Economic Relations Between the United States and Korea: Conflict or Cooperation?* (Washington, D.C.: Korea Development Institute/Institute for International Economics, 1989) p. 120.

[12] Korea Development Institute, *Major Indicators of the Korean Economy* (Seoul: Korean Development Institute, May 1987).

high -- South Korea was among the top three targets of Super 301 complaints filed in 1989 and 1990.

To understand this apparent contradiction it is important to distinguish between the liberalization of Korea's formal trade regime and the government's continued use of informal trade-related measures to restrict imports and promote exports. On the one hand, there can be no question that a great deal of liberalization has occurred with respect to Korea's formal trade regime. In particular, the government has reduced the average import tariff rate by over half and gradually increased the "liberalization ratio," or the percentage of import products not on the so-called Restricted List, to near 100 percent. On the export side, Korea no longer uses extensive export subsidies[13] and since the mid-1980s has moderated its use of direct production subsidies. The World Bank has characterized the 1980s as a period of "cautious liberalization"[14] for Korea's formal trade regime as the government's use of conspicuous border measures was curtailed. Korean officials argue that these indicators demonstrate that Korea has liberalized more rapidly than any other country at a comparable stage of development, and has moved faster in some areas than was called for by foreign pressure.[15] There is little dispute that Korean trade reforms have been significant.

Despite this progress, it should be noted that several significant formal trade barriers remain. In particular, the Korean government has largely exempted agriculture from liberalization of formal import restrictions.[16] Korea also is under pressure from the United States to reduce tariffs on wine,[17] automobiles,[18] electronics,[19] and telecommunication

---

[13] The Korean government claims that the Korean Export-Import Bank now follows OECD Arrangement guidelines.

[14] World Bank (1987) p. 48.

[15] See a wide variety of press reports surrounding Rho's 1989 visit to Washington, D.C.

[16] The primary example is Korea's beef-import quota, which a GATT panel -- formed at the request of the United States, Australia, and New Zealand -- has ruled unfairly discriminates against foreign beef. As a result of recent negotiations with the United States, this quota has been raised. For a complete discussion, see Agricultural section, below.

[17] The threat of U.S. trade sanctions, as well as the possibility that Korea might be designated an "unfair trading country" under the "Super 301" section of the 1988

(continued...)

equipment.[20] Moreover, Korea maintains a blatantly GATT-illegal ban on more than 200 Japanese imports including automobiles, in an effort to protect domestic industries and reduce Japanese exports to Korea.

The broad liberalization of Korea's formal trade regime has, however, highlighted the wide variety of remaining informal trade-policy instruments used by the Korean government. As a major study of Korean trade barriers concluded in 1986:

> *For almost two decades now Korea has attempted to promote its image as a market economy with a relatively liberal attitude toward imports. This stands in marked contrast, however, with the views held by most foreign businessmen who attempt to actually penetrate the Korean market. Their familiarity with the "nuts and bolts" of the Korean import regime leads them to characterize it as essentially restrictive and full of hidden obstacles.*[21]

Five years later, a review of the many contentious trade conflicts between Korea and its trading partners -- usually the United States -- clearly indicates that, at minimum, there is a widespread perception that the true "openness" of the Korean economy is far from complete, despite the removal of most formal barriers. A recent publication by the American

---

17 (...continued)
Trade Act, led Korea to liberalize wine imports. Under the terms of the accord signed on January 18, 1989, Korea doubled its import quota for all wines immediately and by 1990 it is to have eliminated all restrictions on imports. Tariff reductions on wine will continue through 1993.

18 As part of a market-opening program in February 1988, Korea bowed to U.S. pressure and reduced tariffs on autos from 50 percent to 30 percent. Later that year, it lifted its import ban on foreign (non-Japanese) cars with engines greater than 2,000 cc.

19 As a result of foreign pressure, Korea has agreed to lower its electronics tariffs from 21 percent in 1989 to 8 percent by 1993.

20 In 1989, USTR identified Korea as a priority country for negotiations aimed at opening the Korean telecommunications market to U.S. exports. Trade barriers cited included import tariffs on telecommunications equipment. Although negotiations are still underway, Korea has accelerated its tariff reductions on certain telecommunications items.

21 R. Luedde-Neurath, *Import Controls and Export-Oriented Development: A Reassessment of the South Korean Case* (Boulder: Westview Press, 1986) p. 89.

Chamber of Commerce in Korea stated that "While tariff reductions are always welcome, tariffs are among the less significant problems facing U.S. companies trying to export to Korea."[22] Trade statistics reflect this difficulty. Less than five percent of Korea's imports are finished consumer goods.

Although the development of these issues in the 1990s will be examined below, it is important to recognize that points of dispute over Korean trade policies have evolved over the past decade from a few large issues -- tariffs and import restrictions -- to a wide variety of less easily defined or identified trade-related measures.

TRADE POLICY PROCESS

The development and implementation of Korean trade policy is best understood on three levels. First, there is the Korean government's formal trade policy structure. Second, there is the informal trade policy process in which trade policies are often developed and implemented. Third, there are the important, quasi-governmental trade policy powers of the private sector.

Formal Trade Policy Structure

The Economic Planning Board (EPB) is a "super-ministry" chaired by the Deputy Prime Minister. Its official power stems from its control of the national budget and its authority over Korea's Five-Year Economic and Social Development Plans, the master plans for the economy. On trade matters, the EPB acts mainly as a policy coordinator among the other, less powerful, ministries and to the extent it develops its own policies, these policies often reflect a compromise position among competing ministries.[23] The EPB is heavily staffed with Western-educated, liberally-oriented officials and, because it has no specific "constituency," the EPB is insulated from domestic political pressure more than the other relatively shielded ministries. As a result, the EPB is the most

---

22 American Chamber of Commerce in Korea, *United States-Korean Trade Issues* (Seoul: April 1990) p. 1. Other exporters voice similar complaints. European Community interests have argued that it is imprudent to grant Korean companies greater access to the EC market until EC exporters have reciprocal access to Korean markets.

23 This coordination role is performed through the EPB's International Economic Policy Coordination Office. See Kim and Chung (1988) p. 137.

economically liberal[24] of the ministries. The head of the EPB is the Deputy Prime Minister, who is unquestionably the single most influential economic official in the Korean government.

There are countervailing pressures against liberalization within the EPB, however. First, unlike Korea' Ministry of Foreign Affairs, the EPB is free from substantial foreign pressures for further liberalization. Second, the EPB has a broad view of the country's development, and often adopts strong policy positions on such issues as greater economic equity and the development of strategic industries.

The Korean government has several advisory think tanks that operate as extensions of the formal bureaucracy which, over the years, have had considerable effect on Korean trade policy.[25] The EPB has authority over two of these. The Korea Development Institute (KDI) is by far the most influential and liberal of the government's many advisory institutes. Although the KDI does have an international economics division, it focuses mainly on long-run, macroeconomic policy issues[26] and has not established itself as a consistent source of trade policy options for the Korean bureaucracy. The increasing importance of the trade dimension in Korean economic policy -- and the perceived failure[27] of the KDI to properly address it -- lead the EPB to form a new advisory institute, Korea Institute for Economic Policy (KIEP), which specializes in international economic policy matters.

---

24 *Liberal* in the sense of advocating deregulation and a greater role for market mechanisms.

25 Aside from the day-to-day relationships between the bureaucracy and the advisory bodies, it is important to note that these think tanks have traditionally been "breeding grounds" for top government officials.

26 "[T]he KDI makes policy recommendations from the perspective of broad national interest, and its approach to trade issues is distinctly liberal. It is worth noting that the KDI played a major role in formulating the nation's trade liberalization program." Kim and Chung (1988), p. 140, footnote omitted. The KDI has as part of its broad portfolio the task to "analyze the implications of rising protectionism in developed nations and evaluate potential policy responses." *Korea Development Institute 1989: Organization and Activities* (Seoul: KDI, 1989) p. 7.

27 The EPB's dissatisfaction with KDI's trade-policy performance was alluded to by both KIET and KDI officials during interviews.

Next to the EPB, the Ministry of Trade and Industry (MTI)[28] is the most powerful of Korea's ministries. EPB sets Korea's economic course with MTI's help, then turns much of the steering responsibility back over to MTI. The ministry has de jure authority over most trade-related matters, both through its role as the administrator of industrial development policies (which are largely export-oriented) and through its jurisdiction over trade regulations and negotiations.

Because of its sector-specific viewpoint, MTI's "horizontal" policies (such as import restrictions) are often orchestrated to support the industries it has targeted for development. MTI's dual responsibility over industry and trade has led to "an inherently split-minded approach to trade issues," which will be explored below.[29] In general, this split-mindedness has meant that the Ministry as an institution supports liberalization, but at a slower pace than does the EPB. As a result, MTI is often criticized by both ends of the economic reform spectrum. On the one hand, MTI is often seen by opponents to liberalization as "appeasers" on trade-policy matters, so the Ministry's bureaucratic position is hurt when other nations, particularly the United States, appear at the root of specific policy reforms. On the other hand, according to Brandt, ". . . there is a certain amount of in-fighting within the bureaucracy, with the Ministry of Trade and Industry often mounting a delaying action against the powerful forces for economic change represented by the Economic Planning Board. . . ."[30] MTI also has authority over the quasi-autonomous Korean Trade Commission (KTC), which performs a role similar to that of the International Trade Commission in the United States by determining whether imports alleged to be dumped or subsidized are "injurying" Korean industries.

Korea's Patent Office, whose role in trade policy matters stems from trade frictions over Korea's intellectual property regime is also under MTI authority. The Korea Institute For Economics and Technology (KIET) is under the authority of MTI and can be considered the microeconomic counterpart to the EPB's KDI, and is primarily responsible for formulating industrial policies. Consequently, KIET is less liberal on trade matters than KDI.

---

28 Sometimes called *MOTI* (moe-tee) or the *Trade and Industry Ministry*.

29 Kim and Chung (1988) p. 137.

30 Vincent S.R. Brandt, "Korea," in George C. Lodge and Ezra F. Vogel, eds., *Ideology and National Competitiveness* (Cambridge: Harvard Business School Press, 1987).

The Ministry of Finance's (MOF) role in Korean trade policy stems from its authority over import tariffs, including import-relief measures such as countervailing and antidumping duties. When a Korean industry files a petition with the Korean government that alleges that certain subsidized or dumped imports are causing injury to that industry, the Customs and Tariff Deliberation Committee, under supervision of MOF, determines whether relief duties should be imposed. The KTC determines whether there has indeed been "injury" to the domestic industry -- a GATT prerequisite for such trade relief -- and generally advises MOF on the appropriate level of duties to impose. MOF also has direct responsibility for management of the Korean *won*[31] and for liberalization of Korea's financial system. The Ministry has publicly supported financial reform, including trade reforms in financial services, but has stopped short in several areas of taking substantive actions. This waffling is probably due in part to the MOF's varied, and sometimes conflicting, policy responsibilities and in part to the bureaucratic tendency to not give away power. In addition, the MOF often underestimates the "adjustment costs" of reform and quickly reverses itself when these costs become apparent. For example, in the early 1980s the MOF attempted to withdraw subsidized credit lines from large industrial firms that had been targeted for development over the previous decade, but when sagging exports and financial problems within heavy industry threaten the economy as a whole, "the government intervened heavily irrespective of its announced intentions to the contrary, in financial allocation decisions."[32]

The Ministry of Foreign Affairs (MOFA) affects Korean trade policy in four ways. The Ministry "lends its traditional expertise in conducting international negotiations" to other Korean entities engaged in trade talks; "injects a foreign policy perspective" into Korea's trade-policy process; gathers trade-related information and channels it back to Seoul;[33] and uses its diplomatic posts abroad, particularly in the United States, for public relations efforts to forestall adverse trade policy actions taken by foreign governments. Within the economic-policy process, MOFA is

---

31 By virtue of control of the financial system, the MOF is responsible for liberalization of Korea's financial system, which has substantial implications for trade in services, particularly with the United States. See Bureau of National Affairs, *International Trade Reporter* (October 26, 1989) p. 1414.

32 World Bank (1987) paragraphs 4.21-4.22.

33 Kim and Chung (1988) p. 138.

consulted on trade matters but does not participate regularly.[34] As with many Foreign Ministries, MOFA's "diplomatic responsibilities make the ministry more sensitive to the concerns of Korea's trading partners and less beholden to the views of domestic industry."[35] As a result, the MOFA is inclined to favor liberalization of Korea's trade regime. MOFA's limited influence in trade policy, however, implies that foreign pressure on the MOFA loses some of its force as it filters back to the government's trade-policy apparatus.

There are several other Korean Ministries that have authority over specific areas of trade-related policy. In particular:

- The Ministry of Agriculture and Fisheries (MAF) has responsibility over agricultural trade, including import tariffs and phytosanitary codes. Within MAF is the National Plant Quarantine Service (NPQS), which has become the focal point for many U.S.-Korean disputes over agricultural import barriers.
- The Ministry of Health and Social Affairs (MHSA) has an analogous role in the pharmaceutical sector, which is also an area of trade policy friction.
- The Ministry of Construction (MOC) holds that wood housing is inherently less safe than concrete and steel housing, so it uses its regulatory procedures[36] to sharply curtail the demand for, and therefore imports of, wood products.

These Ministries, along with those of Culture and Information, Home Affairs, Education, and Labor, are often called the "paternalistic" ministries in the Korean tradition of society and government. The paternalistic ministries see government as a provider for Korean society -- in Confucian rather than socialistic terms -- and economic liberalization threatens that role. In addition, bureaucrats within these ministries tend to be more nationalistic and perceive trade liberalization as concessionary.

---

[34] "When foreign trade issues are involved, the minister of foreign affairs is invited to take part in the discussions [in inter-minister councils]." Kim and Chung (1988) p. 139.

[35] Kim and Chung (1988) p. 138.

[36] Most construction financing in Korea is controlled by the Ministry of Construction. Raphael Jim Kim and B. Aach, "Study of Non-tariff Barriers and Building Code Barriers for Timber Frame Construction in Korea," unpublished industry report (Jeans Design and Development, Inc., March 1987) p. 8.

Aside from MAF, the paternalistic ministries lack focused influence when considered in isolation, but their power can manifest itself in two ways. First, these ministries can lobby as a coalition within the government's trade policy process to the extent they are allowed to participate. Second, and perhaps more importantly, each of the paternal ministries have jurisdiction over some aspect of trade policy, either directly or indirectly. For example, MAF has been an obstacle to liberalizing agricultural imports because of its strict and often complicated sanitary standards for imported food.

Until recently, the National Assembly had little influence over trade matters. In general, bureaucrats wrote wide-ranging laws economic laws that were rubber-stamped by the Assembly and then broadly interpreted by the bureaucracy in the implementation of policy.[37] The National Assembly does have key committees that are counterparts to economic-policy ministries, as well as interested panels such as the Committee on Finance, Committee on the Budget, and so on. As will be discussed below, the Assembly's role in trade policy formulation is becoming less passive, although this role is more as a "spoiler" than as a source of trade policy options.

In theory, trade policies -- as with economic policies in general -- are set by the Economic Minister's Council (EMC), which is chaired by the Deputy Prime Minister and comprises the key ministries with responsibility on economic policy matters. The EMC and its ad hoc twin, the Economic Ministers' Consultative Council (EMCC),[38] are the main forums for resolving policy disputes among the ministries. According to Kim and Chung, "[The EMCC] is where the really decisive policy battles take place. . .[the EMCC] is convened on an ad hoc basis to resolve

---

[37] "The National Assembly legislates in huge generalities, and at the same time delegates authority to the bureaucracy to fill the precise meaning at its own discretion. Laws invoking such vague concepts as 'excessive competition' or 'deemed desirable' are enacted, and it is left to officialdom to interpret them." Sang Hyun Song, *Introduction to the Law and Legal System of Korea* (Seoul: Kyung Mun Sa Publishing, 1983) p. 518. In one interview, a senior MTI official noted that the Minister of MTI reports frequently to National Assembly committees, but that they do not play a direct role. A former high-level MTI official gave the impression that he did not give much thought to the Assembly.

[38] Both Councils have the same membership: the Deputy Prime Minister, who chairs the Council and heads EPB; and the ministers of MTI, MOF, MAFF, energy and resources, communications, transportation, construction, labor, and science and technology. The MOFA minister takes part in trade discussions of the EMCC. Kim and Chung (1988) p. 139.

particularly sensitive issues, or in the event of 'crisis,' when the government need to act immediately on a policy problem."[39] The EMCC has no legal force, so any decisions taken within an EMCC meeting must be approved at a full EMC quorum. On a more routine basis, the EMC meets once a week to screen proposed changes in the law before proposals go before the full cabinet and, if approved there, the National Assembly. Meetings with ruling-party officials are, according to a former minister, "infrequent."[40] When such meetings do take place, the DLP's policy coordination council is usually the forum.

At the most general level, Korean trade policies are a reflection of the government's broad objectives for the economy, as set forth in periodic multi-year plans, particularly the Five-Year Plan for Economic and Social Development. Individual sectors -- such as textiles, steel, aircraft -- often have their own custom-made multi-year plans and Special Laws that provide more detailed guidance to the bureaucracy. Although these plans and laws provide solid insights into the general thinking of Korean economic officials and the direction in which these officials wish to carry the economy, they usually do not set forth the precise trade-related policy actions the government will undertake.

Informal Trade Policy Process

Despite this formal bureaucratic structure, South Korea's trade policy process is still in its infancy, and many of the country's trade policies continue to be formulated in an ad hoc manner.[41] Several aspects of the Korean trade policy structure contribute to the ad hoc nature of the trade policy process. First, there is no central trade policy authority within the Korean government. This means that there is no Korean counterpart to the White House's USTR -- there is no single bureaucratic group that has the authority and the resources for formulating and articulating the Korean government's trade policies.

There are myriad trade policy "coordinating" offices throughout the government. Although there is a wide variety of trade-related bureaucratic components (including many within EPB and MTI) that

---

39 Kim and Chung (1988) p. 138. This assessment is confirmed by officials within the MTI, who said that the EMC (and by implication the EMCC) is "very strong" in arbitrating disputes.

40 Interview, March 1990.

41 The U.S. Department of Commerce official described the trade-policy process within the Korean government as "not very institutional."

would appear from their titles to constitute a central authority for trade policy-making, the very existence of more than one such group indicates the lack of a central authority or a clear division of responsibility -- even the responsibility for coordinating Korean trade policy is divided. For example:

- The EPB has an International Economic Policy Coordination Office that is nominally tasked with formulating "common positions from the competing views of the ministries." Although the power of the EPB can be brought to bear in bureaucratic disputes over a given trade issue through this Office, the Office does not appear to furnish the Korean government with a means for strategic policy development.[42]
- One high-level official officially responsible for certain trade matters said that he has neither the formal authority nor the informal bureaucratic weight to develop and implement trade policies under his portfolio independent from other elements of the Korean executive branch, and therefore performs a coordinating role.[43] One former MTI minister noted that MTI "has no tools" in the trade policy area, as opposed to Finance and Agriculture which control tariffs and quotas.[44]
- A key MTI official concerned with U.S.-Korean trade-policy matters said the attitude in other ministries -- particularly MAF and MOHSA -- during the coordination of trade policy positions is that international trade conflicts are "your job -- not my job," despite the fact that these other ministries have authority over the policies in dispute.[45]

The Korean government has periodically attempted to provide greater centralization to its trade-policy structure, with limited success. During the mid-1980s, for example, trade negotiations were handled by the International Economic Policy Council (IEPC) with members from various

---

[42] Interviews with a senior official reponsible for bilateral trade matters and a high-level EPB official who is responsible for reaching interagency consensus on economic matters. March 1990.

[43] Interview, March 1990.

[44] Interview, March 1990.

[45] Interview, March 1990.

Korean ministries concerned with trade matters. The IEPC was dissolved in 1986 and was considered to be a failure by Park Un-Suh because of its mismanagement in coordinating a unified Korean position on trade matters. The Korean experience with the IEPC might have contributed to the absence of a central trade-policy body since that time. In the late 1980s the government established the Foreign Trade Policy Council (FTPC), which is chaired by the minister of MTI and includes vice-ministers from economic ministries and private-sector representatives. The FTPC has no de jure authority and performs an advisory role only. An inter-ministerial committee was formed specifically for the Uruguay Round negotiations, but it has not played a conspicuous role.

Finally, most trade policy tools are held by bureaucratic elements responsible for industrial policy. As outlined above, Korean government officials gave scant attention to trade policies separate from industrial policies prior to the early 1980s. Officials had not been considering trade policies from a broader political perspective until faced with trade policy conflicts with other nations. Consequently, the Korean government has not developed a strong trade-policy apparatus distinct from its industrial-policy structure.

Different government organizations often proclaim policy positions on a given trade issue that do not reflect a unified government policy. This is a longstanding problem in various arenas of Korean public policy, and has been particularly acute in the trade policy area. Former Korean negotiator Park Uh-Suh has argued[46] that lack of a single government voice in trade negotiations has been a "serious problem" for the Korean government, and that different ministries often want to initiate trade talks based on their own strategies. Consequently, trade policies are developed through negotiations among a wide range of bureaucratic units in various government organizations, and the officials responsible for resolving a trade dispute are often not the officials with the power to make the required changes in policy. This has weakened the government's ability to both formulate and implement trade policy.

The Korean government's preparation for the Uruguay Round demonstrates the ad hoc nature of Korean trade policy formulation. Because there is no central trade authority, the government formed a special inter-ministerial committee, headed by the EPB and staffed by working level officials from various trade-related ministries, to formulate Korea's Uruguay Round position. A parallel structure was formed at Seoul's mission to Geneva. Not only was it necessary for the Korean government to create a special apparatus to deal with the Round, but

---

46 Park Un-Suh (1989).

workings of the apparatus itself were somewhat informal. As Kim and Chung described it, "In actual practice, of course, the division of labor. . .is fluid at best."

For example, both MTI and MOFA officials claim "responsibility" over technical matters, such as safeguards, at the Uruguay Round negotiations.[47] Despite the official division of responsibilities for Uruguay Round between MTI and MFA, the Korean position paper on antidumping and countervailing duty (AD/CVD) reforms were written by Suk-ho Sonu, a division director at KIET. Sonu was asked to draft the position paper because of his experience in trade matters and because his work was known by the Assistant Minister for trade at MTI, and his role in developing Korea's Uruguay Round policy position was not related to his official position at KIET. Indeed, one official noted that Sonu would have probably drafted the AD/CVD papers regardless of what post he held within the government.[48] A similar example of how Korean trade policy is often developed by key personalities, rather than responsibilities being given based on job titles, is the role Park Uh-Suh played as a top trade negotiator from 1981 to 1987. Park was Director General of the Industrial Policy Bureau -- not formally a trade-policy organization. According to Park, he was chosen because, in large part, he had spent time at Korea's consulate in New York.

Similar stories have emerged more recently. In negotiations over import barriers against foreign agricultural products, MFA took the lead role away from MAF in the Korean team conducting the bilateral talks with the United States.[49] Moreover, public disagreements between the

---

[47] Kim and Chung (1988) claim that MTI bureaus are responsible for technical matters in multilateral negotiations, citing safeguards and non-tariff barriers as two examples (p. 165). A top trade official in MOFA claims that Korea's negotiating position on "legal" and "technical" matters are the responsibility of the Economic Affairs Division of MOFA. Such issues would include safeguards and antidumping codes. Interview, March 1990.

[48] Dr. Suno has a Ph.D. and attended Wharton business school for several years, speaks and writes fluent English, which probably contributed to his being asked by Kim Chol-Soo to work on an multilateral trade-policy matter such as the Uruguay Round. Dr. Suno appears to be an "up and comer" in Korea's trade policy, although he is reputed to have an academic slant in his approach to trade problems.

[49] Interview with an American embassy official in Seoul. MAFF's minister, Kim Shik, was the spokesman and negotiator for the Government of Korea in its refusal to liberalize its beef regime during talks with U.S. Ambassador Carla Hills in October 1989. *Journal of Commerce* (October 11, 1989) p. 1.

key economic ministries over the direction of economic policy was a contributing factor for the March 1990 cabinet reshuffle.[50]

There is also a serious disconnect between the enactment of a trade policy by high-level officials and its eventual implementation by mid-level officials.[51] Mid-level officials have wide discretionary powers that do not require formal legal authority. Within the Korean government the bureaucracy has the latitude to enact a broad range of regulations without legislative empowerment by the National Assembly. These regulations govern many aspects of imports (including both import tariffs and import licensing), exports, cross-border investment, technology agreements, and so on. Even within these regulations, the various ministries have considerable authority. For example, within the overall liberalization goals arising from the government's plans and the EMC's decrees, MAF promulgates regulations governing the import of agricultural goods, investment by Korean enterprises in foreign agriculture-related projects, and foreign investment in Korean food-related businesses. The Finance Ministry can use its discretion over foreign exchange allocation to guide imports and regulations governing the entry of foreign banking and insurance firms. As a result, regulations are often promulgated without undergoing the inter-ministerial process the passage of a law would require. Moreover, even written regulations are not necessary for effective government action in trade related areas -- the bureaucracies' use of administrative guidance is widespread. Conversely, many recent trade agreements -- such as those on intellectual property rights -- require active government enforcement, which is often not forthcoming. Again, the problem usually lies in the distinction between those who negotiate the trade agreement (normally MTI and MFA) and those who must implement the agreement. As a result, official Korean commitments to a trading partner to liberalize a certain industrial sector are sometimes not heeded by the bureaucrat who wields authority over that sector. The Korean government itself acknowledged this problem in the Commission Report, stating that "[t]he consequent gap between nominal and effective

---

50 Statement by Pot Pil-soo, reported in major Korean dailies after the reshuffle, March 20, 1990.

51 A former high-level MTI official noted the difficulty of communication and authority between the Minister and his bureaucracy. He said that a Minister "must be able to read the wind" of what is happening at the bureaucratic levels within his ministry. Interview, March 1990.

measures of import liberalization undermines the government's import liberalization policy. . ."[52]

It is important to appreciate the subtly and sophistication with which Korean bureaucrats can effect a specific trade policy goal outside formal channels -- and therefore outside the normal scope of trade-policy negotiations with foreign trading partners. For example, during particularly intensive export drives, the Korean government will -- informally -- link the volume of loans that flow from government-influenced Korean financial institutions to the *chaebol* to the export performance of the *chaebol's* general trading company (GTC). This can work as an effective export subsidy, whereby losses sustained by uneconomic exports are compensated by the reward of cheap domestic loans.

There are signs that Korea's trade policy process is becoming less ad hoc, however. As noted above, the Korean government has, over the years, tried to provide a more formal structure for trade policy development within the government, and these attempts are continuing. In January 1990, for example, EPB created a new research institute designed specifically to focus on international trade policy matters. The new organization, called the Korea Institute for Economic Policy (KIEP), was created as a result of what EPB officials considered to be the increasing importance of trade policy and the inability of the KDI to properly address trade issues given its current resources.[53] According to an official at the KDI, employment at KIEP is rather selective with officials from KDI, KIET, and other research organizations being hired away at "double" their previous salaries.[54] KIEP is still in its formative stages, and has yet to produce a publication.

The creation of the Korean Trade Commission discussed above, also demonstrates an effort to formalize thrade policymaking and parallels the liberalization trend within the Korean trade sector, as the government "anticipates possible disruptions to the domestic market as Korea further opens its market to domestic competition."[55] It is important to recognize the limitations of the Foreign Trade Commission in trade policy formulation. The Commission is an ad hoc group drawn from the bureaucracy and chaired by an MTI Assistant Minister. Therefore, it does

---

52 Commission Report, p.30.

53 Interview, March 1990.

54 Interview with a KIET official, March 1990.

55 Kim and Chung (1988) p. 138.

not develop trade policy as would, for example, USTR in the White House nor does it have the judicial autonomy of the ITC. Nevertheless, the creation of the Foreign Trade Commission and of KIEP are significant steps toward making Korean trade policy formulation more rigorous and transparent. Presumably, Commission decisions will be subject to multilateral trade rules to which Korea is a signatory, such as the GATT antidumping and countervailing duty codes. As for KIEP, the Korean government appears to be devoting sufficient effort for KIEP to develop a respected cadre of trade policy professionals within the new institute.

Trade Policy Powers of the Private Sector

Any assessment of Korean trade policy must recognize the quasi-governmental trade policy powers held by the Korean private sector. Such power arises from both Korea's concentrated industrial structure and the quasi-governmental authority granted to private entities. Although estimates and measurements vary, over half of Korea's manufacturing output is accounted for by the top half-dozen diversified industrial groupings, or *chaebol*, and powerful industry associations facilitate the private sector's ability to exercise an enormous degree of control over the foreign trade dimension -- imports and exports -- of their own industry.

On the export side, for example, the Electronics Industry Association of Korea (EIAK) in 1989 "offered" to resolve the many dumping allegations against Korean electronics producers by European Community manufacturers by enforcing industry-wide limits on exports and instituting a price floor on Korean electronics exports to the Community.[56] The Korean government was not integrally involved in this resolution. EIAK, as well as other private associations, have the power to grant or withhold export licenses.[57]

On the import side, a peculiar obstacle to a more open trade regime is the power granted to private industry within the administration of Korean trade policy to block certain imports. For example, one story appeared in

---

56 *Financial Times* (April 1989).

57 Young J. Kim, Executive Director of Goldstar, described one example. "Another consequence of the U.S. trade law proceedings is the establishment of government guidelines on the export price of consumer electronic goods in the United States. Each year, the government receives guidelines for export prices. Items that do not meet the guidelines are not granted an export license by the Electronic Industry Association of Korea." "The Impact of U.S. Trade Law Actions on Business Decisions in Korea," *Michigan Journal of International Law* (University of Michigan Law School, Winter 1990) p. 455.

Korea Trade & Business regarding the role of industry in the "reform" of a government import program. Noting that exemptions from a certain import ban could previously be obtained by local governments, the article stated:

> *This process has delayed the import of samplings and caused public petitions. To cut this red tape, the Trade-Industry Ministry authorized the Korean Society for Advancement of Machinery, the Electronics Industry Association of Korea, the Korea Automobile Manufacturers Association, and eight other related organizations to grant import permission on those items or samplings.*[58]

Although this is a de jure liberalization to the extent that the government is abdicating import decisions to the private sector, the interest of these collective industry organizations is to maintain the de facto import restrictions on these products. This is but one case exhibiting the widespread Korean practice of allowing industry associations to set product standards for imports and to control the flow of goods across the border.

Another mechanism by which the *chaebols* can control trade on an industry-wide scale are their general trading companies (GTCs). The GTCs are licensed by the Korean government to import or export specific goods, and both the import-competing industry and the bureaucracy[59] can use this control to operate an ad hoc trade policy.[60]

TRADE POLICY DETERMINANTS IN THE 1990s

In many respects, Korea is still a young country and will be facing the challenges of political and economic maturation as the 1990s proceed. At the political level, South Korea is in the midst of a watershed political transition, the most likely outcome of which is a greater role for popular forces within the government. Although it is well beyond the scope of

---

58 "Reduction of Import Source Diversification System," *Korea Trade & Business* (June 1989) p. 28.

59 For example, GTCs have been occasionally put under government pressure to reduce imports of luxury goods.

60 It is believed among U.S. businessmen in Korea that this is mechanism through which the Korean government has put pressure on importers to reduce the flow of foreign consumer goods to the Korean domestic market. See discussion, below.

this book to fully assess these political developments, certain aspects of Korean political trends in the 1990s will be critical to Korea's trade policies. The political turmoil facing Korean leaders in 1990 is likely to have conflicting effects on Korean trade policy, but the net result of more populist economic policies is likely to weigh against a more liberal Korean trade regime. On the one hand, reducing the economic and political power of the *chaebol* is a primary demand of both radical and mainstream critics of the ruling party. On its face, meeting such demands would entail greater influence for consumers and small importers in trade policy, which presumably would accelerate market openness. As the American Chamber of Commerce in Korea stated it, ". . .the government is now unable to pursue growth-oriented policies as efficiently as in the past because of the increased because of the increased political considerations associated with democratization. Executive Branch decisions are subject to scrutiny by the press and the National Assembly."[61]

On the other hand, a broad spectrum of evidence indicates that Korea's liberalization efforts would suffer as a result of greater populism. First, trade liberalization has not been driven by a broad consumer movement within Korea -- indeed, liberalization has faced popular opposition -- and any diffusion of political power away from the bureaucracy would not add much support for further liberalization. For example, in early 1990 the *Korea Economic Daily* conducted a survey of 1,000 citizens over twenty years of age regarding import liberalization. According to the poll, 22.9 percent were in favor of Korea's current import liberalization program whereas 40.6 percent were against. Males, those with higher incomes, and those with higher educations tended to be more in favor of liberalization. Overall, 80.8 percent of the respondents opposed the decontrol of agricultural, forestry, and fisheries imports.[62] Second, on the contrary, embedded in the recent political turmoil is a significant amount of economic nationalism and its predictable consequences for more open import policies.[63] This conclusion is reinforced by the fact that recent political turmoil in Korea has chronologically, if not logically, followed an increase in economic turmoil. Third, agricultural liberalization, in particular, is one area where there is

---

61 American Chamber of Commerce in Korea (1990) p. 3.

62 "Patriotic Consumerism," *Korea Trade & Business* (April 1990) p. 40.

63 What were formally the opposition parties -- and what are now factions within the ruling party -- do not have well-formulated trade-policy positions. Officials within these factions are critical of liberalization, but do not present formal alternatives.

little disagreement among observers (including Korean officials) that increased democracy is almost certain to mean a strengthening of protectionist forces.[64] Fourth, because the popular movements within Korea are anti-*chaebol*, it therefore could be argued that policy actions taken against *chaebol* in areas unrelated to trade, such as the recent restriction on real estate speculation would occur with a series of quid pro quo in areas of trade policy. Examples include greater indirect export subsidies, extended infant-industry protection, and weak enforcement of intellectual property rights, each of which the public is indifferent towards or even supportive. Fifth, a stronger trade policy role for the National Assembly could create obstacles for trade policy reformers within the bureaucracy. Several sources indicate that the Assembly's role is growing, albeit from a low base.[65] Again, the Assembly's constant polemics against the *chaebol* in favor of smaller enterprises is likely to restrain liberalization as -- other factors remaining equal -- infant-industry protection must be extended to even weaker Korean enterprises. Finally, the rise of anti-American sentiment that has paralleled the calls for greater democracy among many Korean citizens can only serve to make the Korean government more reluctant to undertake liberalization measures that are, in many Koreans' eyes, exercises in subservience to the United States. Given that the primary force for Korean liberalization is the government of the United States, this trend also weakens the prospects for liberalization.

In 1988, Kim and Chung speculated that

> *Clearly, the demands for a more open, participatory policy-making system will have to be accommodated in some fashion, and this will have important implications for the way trade policy is made. . .this trend is already evident today, and it suggests that narrow, parochial interests will have a greater say in the making of trade policy in the years ahead.*

The authors then concluded that, "The anticipated changes in Korea's political life do not augur well for the future of market opening in Korea."[66]

---

64 See discussion on agriculture below.

65 One official who must obtain funds to carry out Korea's industrial policy stated that the Assembly's demands for more resources for social programs was reducing the available funds for industry. He notes that politics influences policies unlike ever before. Interview, March 1990.

66 Kim and Chung (1988) p. 147.

In sum, it is likely that the political machinations Korea will face in the 1990s -- other things remaining equal -- will probably slow, but not permanently reverse, the trends toward a more open Korean economy. Although there are a large number of factors weighing against liberalization as a result of greater popular democracy, the degree to which the popular will on trade matters is likely to remain circumscribed in the 1990s by the Korean authorities will act to restrain substantial backsliding.

As an episode within the longer-term political transition, the March 1990 cabinet reshuffle is more of an indicator of the fundamental political forces driving Korean trade policies in the 1990s than a force unto itself. Over the past decade there have been calls within the Korean political system for greater social and economic equity that threaten to temper Korean export objectives over the longer run. After years of apparent single-minded determination of Korean policy to industrialize the country, the government's economic planning documents are peppered with the words balance, stability, diversification, equality, and democratic. President Rho and former EPB Minister Cho Soon were particularly outspoken in this regard. When Cho assumed office in January 1989, he urged the government to pay more attention to the politically sensitive problem of economic inequality by saying that the government's agenda would focus on ". . .balanced development and better distribution of wealth, rather than quantitative export-dependent growth."[67]

Government officials in the late 1980s cited several goals in conflict with a resolute export drive, such as reduced economic concentration in

---

67 *Far Eastern Economic Review* (February 9, 1989) p. 51.

the *chaebols*,[68] higher standards of living (as opposed to simply high incomes),[69] and more balanced regional development.

The March 1990 cabinet reshuffle demonstrated the political weakness of a Korean balanced-growth, moderate-export policy. Just prior to the cabinet reshuffle the former MTI minister, Han Seung Soo was reported to have "dismissed rumors of an imminent change in direction to re-emphasize exports at the expense of income redistribution and other social goals."[70] The same day Cho formally denied rumors that the government was about to make export growth top priority. Within six weeks both Cho and Han were replaced, however, and the new MTI minister, Park Pil-soo, immediately announced that "Without economic growth led by exports and investment, it is impossible to promote national welfare and fair distribution of wealth."[71] Indeed, the selection of Park Pil-soo was a strong indicator that the ruling party had settled on a strongly pro-export stance -- Park was an early advocate of the government's export drive in the 1970s and has remained a champion of the cause.

---

68 The government hopes to "de-concentrate" the economy away from the conglomerates that dominate. Despite its stated goals to achieve this goal, the government has been entirely unsuccessful in its past efforts, with economic concentration actually increasing. See *Korea at the Crossroads: Implications for American Foreign Policy* (Council on Foreign Relations, Inc. and the Asia Society, Inc.: 1987). "In Korea, concentration of economic power by conglomerates is severe." Presidential Commission on Economic Restructuring, *Realigning Korea's National Priorities for Economic Advance* (1988) p. 71 (hereafter, *Commission Report*). Despite the stated goal of increasing the role of market forces in the early 1980s, the government's actual responses to crises usually involved forced mergers and nationalizations, assigning the resulting enterprises monopoly status. "It is clear from these [restructurings] that Government has bypassed competitive solutions in most of its restructuring operations. Reluctance to permit market forces to guide adjustment on the surface seems to be inconsistent with policy emphasis on liberalization." World Bank (1987) Vol. I, p. 50.

69 The final chapter of the *Commission Report*, designed to set the direction for Korea's overall path, is entitled "Improving the Quality of Life," and "improvements in the population's welfare" is a key objective in the current Five-Year Plan. See also Department of Commerce Incoming Telegram, *Seoul 12852* (November 26, 1986) paragraph 10.

70 "Korean Minister Says Trade Won't Override Social Goals," *Journal of Commerce* (February 9, 1990) p. 5A.

71 "Trade Minister Stresses Tech Development," *Korea Times* (March 20, 1990).

Overall, the importance of the political events of early 1990 extend beyond the trade policy measures announced in the wake of the reshuffle. The reshuffle itself demonstrated that the pro-growth, pro-export forces within Korea's current political elite dominate those factions calling for greater social-based economic policies -- although the disagreements tend to be a matter of degree.[72] As noted above, Korea's backsliding away from further liberalization efforts confirms the early indications from the new cabinet.

A counterbalancing force to economic nationalism that might keep liberalization on track is Korea's "graduation" from its developing-country status. From a statistical point of view, Korea already ranks among the world's lower-tier developed economies in terms of income and production. Moreover, the composition of its economy is rapidly moving away from that of an LDC -- Korea now ranks third in the production of semiconductors behind Japan and United States.

Perhaps more importantly, Korea is being held to industrial-country standards in its trade policies.

- In October 1989, the Korean government -- with its trade surplus and underappreciated won -- "disinvoked" its developing-country status as an Article 18b country under GATT provisions.[73]
- Effective January 1989, the United States removed Korea from its Generalized System of Preferences list, citing Korea's economic success and trade competitiveness.
- Effective January 1988, the European Community took Korea off its Generalized System of Preferences list because Korea did not

[72] Even in the late 1980s, when government planning documents emphasized social goals, the long-term importance of Korea's pro-export policies were evident "between the lines," and social development was often viewed as simply another supporting element to rapid growth. The Commission Report begins by noting the problem of social inequities for further industrial development, "In the process of rapid industrialization the increased discontent of the underprivileged as a result of accelerated urban-rural, interclass and regional disparities has deepen social conflict, and has emerged as a bottleneck to further development. Therefore it important to emphasize the necessary policies to redress various social imbalances as well as to sustain economic growth in order to become a truly advanced economy."

[73] Article 18b of the GATT allows developing countries with unstable currencies and massive external debt to regulate imports as necessary to manage balance-of-payments difficulties.

extend the benefits of a U.S.-Korea intellectual property accord to European companies.

- By the mid-1990s Korea could become a full member of the Organization of Economic Cooperation and Development (OECD). Formal discussions with the OECD are already underway, and Korean officials think acceptance is likely if the Korean economy continues its current development trajectory.[74] Until the Korean government resumes its trade policy reforms, however, progress is likely to be slow on OECD acceptance, particularly if the United States links the two issues.

As a result, the Korean government faces more pressure from abroad to reform its trade policy regime. For example, Korea can no longer justify its beef quotas as an Article 18b exception, which will affect the course of Korea's agricultural strategy in the 1990s.

On the bilateral front, political attitudes on the part of Korean officials -- both public and private -- toward Japan and the United States already plays a major role in Korean trade policy. In particular, Korean officials -- both public and private[75] -- are extremely wary of Japanese dominance of Korea and the Pacific Rim, while anti-American sentiment is far more likely to be rising in the coming years than declining. It is extremely difficult to assess the breadth, intensity, and implications of anti-American sentiment in South Korea, and this book cannot focus on this issue. It is unlikely, however, that the rise of populist Korean political institutions and the decline of North Korea as a perceived threat to South Korea will coincide with an easing of anti-American polemics.

The shape of Korean trade policies in the 1990s will also depend on two broad economic factors. First, there are underlying shifts in Korea's economic position in the international marketplace that are encouraging Korea's officials to "restructure" the economy. Second, there are what many Korea observers refer to as "the numbers" -- namely, the trade-balance statistics and the quarterly GNP figures. In addition to these two

---

74 One MTI official cited a threshold of 6 percent GNP growth for the economy remaining "on track." Interview, March 1990.

75 Interviews with MTI and EPB officials, March 1990, as well as discussion on other occasions with officials at Goldstar, Samsung, Hyundai, and Daewoo. The goal of moving the Korean economy away from the Japanese economy was a constant theme. One top *chaebol* official said that Japan is like a duck on the water -- it appears to be calmly floating on the surface but there is constant activity underneath.

factors, the Korean government is -- ironically -- wary of a possible economic overheating.

Government officials are keenly aware of Korea's changing role in the international economy, and their economic and trade policies are a reflection of this awareness. In particular, the Korean economy is losing two key competitive advantages that have sustained its economic development until recent years. First, Korean industries can no longer depend on a pool of inexpensive labor for assembly-type mass production industries. Over the past several years Korean businesses have been squeezed by rising labor costs[76] at home -- largely an outgrowth of the rising expectations accompanying democratization -- and rising competition from the other Pacific Rim NICs, primarily Taiwan, Hong Kong, Singapore, Thailand, and Malaysia. Second, Korean industries that export or compete with imports no longer enjoy historical exchange-rate advantages. Over the past few years Korean authorities have been under pressure from Washington to maintain the *won* at a higher level. In addition, the depreciation of the Japanese yen against the U.S. dollar has undercut Korea's competitiveness with respect to Japan.[77] Finally, despite the commercial benefits of a cheaper *won*, Finance Ministry officials are wary of the inflationary effects.[78]

Another factor that Korean officials consider important for the longer-range performance of the Korean economy is the saturation of its traditional markets. Specifically, the Korean economy can no longer stake its double-digit growth on textiles, heavy-metal industries such as steel

---

[76] There is an apparent contradiction in the Korean labor market, namely that labor costs have been rising rapidly at a time when there is a large flow new workers to the market. See A. Amsden, *Asia's Next Giant* (1989) p. 189.

[77] Given the Korean and Japanese bilateral trade pattern, this change in the *won*-yen rate's more important for Korean-Japanese competition in third markets -- particularly the United States -- rather than for bilateral trade.

[78] The inflationary effects of a cheap-won policy are particularly complicated during the present period. Inflation would be the result more of hot-money flows on the Korean capital account rather than the usual trade effects of higher import prices. In the eyes of MOF officials, the ongoing liberalization of the foreign investment sector, coupled with the political problems of the Rho government already faces over domestic real estate speculation by the *chaebol*, further undercuts the government's flexibility to pursue a cheap-*won* policy.

and shipbuilding,[79] or the assembly-intensive phase of consumer-goods manufacturing in which there is increasing competition from other Pacific Rim economies.

When asked about the prospect for the pace of trade liberalization in Korea, interviewees often noted the importance of the growth and trade-balance statistics -- collectively referred to as "the numbers."[80] In recent years, both of these numbers have not looked good for liberalization, and the outlook for the early 1990s is not bright. Growth of the Korean economy has slowed from its double-digit pace of the 1980s down to around six percent in 1990. Although this growth rate appears healthy from an outside perspective, it is considered a recession by Korean standards. First, many Korean officials argue that the influx of 400,000 entrants to the workforce each year requires double-digit growth.[81] Second, slower growth has prompted the business community -- particularly the *chaebols* -- to agitate for pro-growth policies. Indeed, this was probably the dominant proximate cause of the March 1990 cabinet reshuffle. The importance of exports to the Korean economy means that the deterioration of Korea's export surplus is considered a serious problem in its own right, regardless of its consequences for specific industries. In addition there remains a "debtor mentality" among officials that are concerned about the country's debt-service capabilities.

These two numbers carry a political importance that exceeds their economic importance, at least in the short run, and Korean officials seem to recognize the circularity of Korea's economic and political problems. Korean officials leave the impression that they view export performance as a leading indicator of Korea's future prosperity and social stability, and that the current labor problems within Korea foreshadow further export problems. In short, officials see the larger picture as a virtuous circle: "Korea must grow and export to pay the workers so they will work so

---

79 Shipbuilding is undergoing a renaissance internationally, and Korean shipbuilders are in a strong position, but planners are not likely to stake Korea's long-term future in this area.

80 "[T]he temptation for the Korean government to backslide on its [trade liberalization] commitments will be strong in light of Korea's economic slowdown." American Chamber of Commerce in Korea (1990) p. 3. In March 1990, an American embassy official accurately predicted the import restrictions that occurred within weeks.

81 An MTI official is the source of this figure, and said that he believes that this is contributing to the rising role of politics in economic and trade policies. Interview, March 1990.

that Korea can grow and export. . . . " Given this relationship, there is likely to be a strong correlation in the 1990s between the performance of "the numbers" and the extent the Korean government pursues a liberal trade policy.

Ironically, another economic factor of concern to Korean policy-makers that will affect Korea's trade policies is the "overheating" of the economy, or sectors thereof. Two areas emerge as critical:

- *Consumer Demand.* The Korean government has never encouraged rampant consumerism. The 1988 Presidential Commission Report stated that the "Redistributional policy should be approached from two directions; through the improvement of the distribution system itself, and through rational management of the people's demands," and the Report also lists "preventive measures against excessive popular desires."[82]
- *Capital-Driven Inflation.* Over the past decade, Korean monetary officials have waged periodic battles against inflation, and this continues to be an important priority in Korean financial circles. The connection of this concern on trade policy is in the financial-services trade sector, trade-related investment measures, and the *won* exchange rate. Indirectly, official apprehension over inflation will restrain the government from rapidly increasing financing to export-related industries.

These concerns are likely to mean continued government restraint on both financial liberalization and imports as foreign consumer products, to be discussed in more detail below.

Another key economic factor is the pronounced trade-partner imbalances. The Korean trade economy is heavily concentrated in imports from Japan and exports to the United States. This situation is an important determinate for Korean trade policies because of the consequences Korean economic officials see for Korea of such dependency relationships. The Korean export economy, which is largely based on assembly manufacturing operations, is highly dependent on Japanese

---

[82] Emphasis added. Nowhere in the 47-page chapter on improving the quality of life in the President's Commission Report is there any mention of increased access to foreign goods, or even the use of import liberalization to reduce domestic prices. In fact, the chapter even states that "the government should protect both farmers and city dwellers through a stable supply of daily necessities and an improvement in the distributional structure of agricultural products, while tightening price controls on monopoly goods which enjoy no foreign-goods competition."

production equipment and upstream components -- which the Japanese have used for their own commercial advantage. For example:

- Japanese VCR manufacturers provide Korean VCR exporters with several critical electronic components. The Japanese have used this leverage to mandate to Korean exporters that the prices of Korean VCRs shipped to the United States do not undermine Japanese sales in the U.S. market.
- Because the ratio of input components to the number of final systems products is in many cases fixed, and because Japanese companies supply 100 percent of some critical components to Korean manufacturers, Japanese *keiretsu* use Korean parts orders to accurately gauge Korean design, investment, production, and marketing strategies on a product-by-product basis in areas in which they compete.[83]
- Japan's uses its monopoly status over input components to keep Korean profit margins at a minimum. Korean government officials claim that Japanese suppliers intentional link the price of the part to the price of the final Korean product, thereby returning a greater share of the revenues back to Japan and forestalling Korean R&D expenditures in product areas that would challenge Japanese producers.[84]

The Japanese use of such tactical maneuvers must be seen against the background of the historical Korean animosity toward the Japanese. During a discussion on trade policies, for example, one Korean official reflected that historically Japan has used the Korean Peninsula as a springboard for its Asian conquests.

On the export side, Korea's heavy dependence on the U.S. market is seen by officials as an Achilles Heal for the Korean economy. Korea's trade surplus -- with the United States -- which is in remission is widely recognized as corrosive to Korea's long-run interests in maintaining a strong strategic relationship with the United States, and as placing the Korean entire economy at the mercy of future U.S. trade actions.

---

83 Interview with an American business consultant in Seoul, March 1990.

84 Interview with a senior KIET official, March 1990.

TRADE-RELATED OBJECTIVES

South Korea's trade-related objectives in the 1990s can be summarized in four broad categories: export-based economic growth; diversification of Korea's exports in terms of both product and partner; a restructuring of the Korean economy, particularly toward high technology products; and continued strong relations with the United States. Alone, these broadly-defined objectives cannot determine the direction of individual Korean trade polices. Understanding these trade-related objectives, however, provides a connection between Korea's trade policy determinants -- outlined above -- and the specific Korean strategies in the trade arena -- outlined below.

Export-Based Economic Growth

Korea's fundamental objective of export-based economic growth, which has been exhaustively discussed over the past three decades, will continue to be a fixed star of Korean policies for the 1990s. Although any discussion of Korean trade policies must acknowledge this objective, the objective itself is rather generic and cannot provide a great deal of insight into the direction of specific Korean policies. What should be noted, however, is that the March cabinet reshuffle marked the beginning of a renewed government emphasis on exports.[85] Given the trade policy determinants outlined above -- in particular, the industry's recent experience with a poor performance of "the numbers" -- it is likely that the government will maintain this objective well into the 1990s.

Diversification of Korean Trade

A trade-related government objective that has been in place for several years and will continue to shape Korean trade strategy is the diversification of Korean exports, both in terms of partner and product.[86] As noted above, Korea's unbalanced trade profile is a key determinate in Korean trade policy. Korean planners hope to increase exports to Japan and imports from the United States, as opposed to reducing trade with either, and the government is taking steps to diversify the share of its trade away from both Japan and the United States, and sees increased

---

85 The headline of *Korea Trade & Business* captured the spirit of the post-reshuffle outlook: "Export Drive Once Again." (April 1990).

86 See discussion of Import Source Diversification program, below.

trade with the rest of the world as complementing its efforts to strengthen Korea's standing in the international community.[87]

Both industry and government are working to expand the range of products that Korea exports. This is a corollary to diversification of trading partners. Korean officials hope to elevate the Korean economy above the level of large "assembly operation" for foreign -- mostly Japanese -- components into finished goods that are then sold to abroad -- mostly to the United States. Only by upgrading its own production capabilities in upstream components and manufacturing equipment can Korea reduce its reliance on Japanese technology and parts,[88] and by expanding its export base the country can export to a wider number of non-U.S. customers abroad.

Restructuring of the Korean Economy

With few exceptions, "economic restructuring" in the Korean context is a policy designed to move the economy away from its traditional products (such as textiles, heavy industry, and assembly manufacturing) toward a wide range of high-value-added, high-technology products. This restructuring objective is closely related to the diversification objective, whereby planners hope to foster a greater Korean capability in product design, upstream inputs, manufacturing equipment, as well as the ability to manufacture the final product. This is a Korean industrial objective that will generate a variety of trade strategies to support it. Although it is beyond the scope of this book to outline the many industrial programs the Korean government has and will put in place, it is important to recognize that despite the liberalization efforts it has taken with regard to its domestic economy, the government still intends to intervene on a systematic basis through industrial targeting (see sectoral section, below).

The existence of interventionist industrial policies, coupled with the fact that many trade policy tools are in the hands of mid-level government officials who are responsible for implementing these industrial policies, implies that the Korean government will continue to intervene in the trade sector despite liberalization intentions from a more philosophical standpoint. Indeed, many of the trade strategies Korea is likely to pursue in the coming decade will be an outgrowth of the restructuring effort.

---

87 *Commission Report* (1988) p. 17.

88 See discussion of plans for the electronics industry, below.

Strong Relations with the United States

Despite these first three parochial economic objectives -- growth, diversification, and restructuring -- the Korean government will continue its efforts to maintain a strong relationship with the United States. The importance of this factor mandates that it be included in any list of Korean trade-related objectives. As documented above, the United States has been the dominant force driving Korean liberalization, and although many of the trade strategies outlined below run counter to the basic thrust of U.S. policies toward Korea, those officials at the top of the Korean government are unlikely to jeopardize the relationship for specific interventionist trade policies it would otherwise undertake.[89] Korean planners will strive to keep trade actions by the United States at bay.

TRADE STRATEGIES

To meet the country's trade-related objectives, the Korean government is likely to resume its liberalization of South Korea's formal trade policy regime when the Korean economy regains a substantial portion its previous vigor -- when "the numbers" look better to Korean officials from a political standpoint. The significant exceptions to liberalization will be agricultural imports and trade with Japan. Despite this progress on the formal level, however, the Korean government will continue to use its informal trade policy instruments to diversify Korean trade away from Japan and the United States, and to restructure the Korean economy away from traditional industries toward high technology. Korea will respond to the bilateral trade frictions that arise in the 1990s with a policy of managed trade, strategic investment, and further liberalization measures.

As measured by import tariffs, import quotas, and restrictions on foreign investment, the Korean economy will soon be as open as those of the industrialized countries, although the remaining formal barriers will be weighted heavily against manufactured imports. On the export side, it is unlikely that the Korean government will resume its use of direct

---

[89] As the *Commission Report* stated the problem, "The internationalization of the Korean economy requires an outward-looking development strategy. However, at the same time, the country most be cognizant of the ill effects that accompany export-driven growth. Consequently, policies should be formed to hedge against said adverse effects." (p. 3). More specifically, the *Commission Report* later notes that, "international trade tensions are threatening to damage Korea's relationship with her most important ally." (p. 4).

export subsidies as a remedy to the economy's recent trade-balance problems. Similarly, the Korean legal regime governing trade-related issues, such as government procurement practices and the protection of intellectual property rights, is moving closer to the developed-country standard. Even with the many economic and political changes facing Korean policymakers, these trends are likely to be sustained in the 1990s.

Two key aspects of Korean trade policy are not likely to undergo formal liberalization in the 1990s, however. First, because of the strength of domestic political forces opposing the opening of the Korean agricultural industry to foreign competition, this sector is likely to remain largely closed even after the 1997 deadline for agricultural liberalization.[90] Second, Korean officials have no intentions of dismantling the blatantly GATT-illegal Import Source Diversification program, which bans over 200 Japanese imports.[91]

Moreover, Korean government officials will continue to use their informal but powerful leverage over industry to intervene in Korea's trade sector in the 1990s. The Korean bureaucracy will continue to use administrative guidance to discourage Korea's general trading companies from rapidly expanding consumer imports, and to encourage Korean manufacturers to use domestic components and production equipment. The Korean government can enforce such administrative guidance through the bureaucracy's influence over domestic capital flows, licensing of trading rights, government procurement preferences, and a wide array of subtle pressures that can be applied to domestic businesses. In addition, the bureaucracy can indirectly restrict certain imports through standard-setting regulations -- particularly in the area of food safety and phytosanitary testing -- and import-financing rules that discourage imports. Although the use of direct export subsidies has been abandoned, the government has a variety of programs and plans to support strategic export industries in the 1990s. In particular, the government is targeting high-technology industries for expansion through a combination domestic subsidies, directed private credit, substantial R&D assistance, discriminatory government procurement, and government-backed inducement of foreign technology to domestic high-technology projects.

This apparent contradiction between formal liberalization and the persistence of informal trade intervention can be explained by several factors. First, the forces behind Korea's recent formal trade reforms do not affect informal trade-related measures to the same degree. Korea's formal

---

90 See discussion of agricultural policies, below.

91 See Korea and Japan section, below.

trade policy reforms were driven by foreign pressure -- largely from the United States -- and the emergence of influential, reform-minded economists at the top levels of the Korean government. As a result, conspicuous trade-intervention policies -- such as tariffs, quotas, and export subsidies -- were easily identified and removed. Korea's informal trade-related measures, by contrast, are less transparent by definition and often implemented at the discretion of middle-level bureaucrats. Such bureaucrats are responsible for the development of specific domestic industries, rather than general economic reform, and are therefore less responsive to liberalizing influences coming from either higher levels of the bureaucracy or from abroad.

Second, despite its sincere commitment to economic reform, the Korean government officially endorses many of the economic objectives that such informal trade measures are designed to achieve. In the short run, the political turmoil attributed by Korean officials to the deterioration of Korea's trade and growth performance has translated into informal government measures -- sanctioned at the highest levels -- to slow imports and speed exports, and this stance is likely to persist for several years. Over the longer run, the official government objective of restructuring the economy toward high-technology will result in a wide range of trade-related actions, including import protection, discriminatory government procurement, and subsidies to strategic export industries. Ironically, formal liberalization could increase the bureaucracy's use of informal measures as "tools of last resort," although the development of more transparent trade-remedy procedures, such as antidumping and countervailing duty actions, could relieve some pressure on informal import protection.

Third, the quasi-governmental trade policy powers of Korea's private sector will continue to play an important role in Korean trade policy in the 1990s. These powers -- which allow the private sector to restrict imports unilaterally -- result from the heavy concentration of the economy in the *chaebol*, the channeling of imports and exports through a few general trading companies, a closed domestic distribution system, and the government-sanctioned authority of industry associations over certain trade matters.

The dichotomy between formal liberalization and the persistence of informal barriers is likely to lead to confusion and debate over whether the Koreans are indeed liberalizing. For example, the International Trade Reporter recently stated that "While paying lip service to free trade,

Koreans have acted as aggressive "economic nationalists."[92] Although it is clear that the Korean government has done far more than just give lip service to reducing formal barriers, the pervasive web of informal barriers will continue to be a problem for those attempting to export to the Korean market. Whether these commercial problems will translate into trade policy disputes between governments depends on the priority trade has among Korea's trading partners, particularly the United States.

Multilateral Trade Strategy

South Korea's role within the GATT is changing along with the economy's changing role within the international trading system, perhaps with Korea adopting GATT policy positions more characteristic of developed countries'. Korean officials have not given great consideration to Korea's post-Round positions with respect to the GATT, but observers have linked Korea's commitment to the GATT to success of the Uruguay Round. "Success" is defined as progress in those areas of prime importance to Korea -- namely standstill and rollback, the strengthening of dispute settlement procedures, the tightening of safeguard procedures, and the constraints put on countervailing duty and antidumping procedures. From the Korean perspective, GATT has been abused by the developed countries, and the rise in developed country "protectionism" against Korean exports can be almost exclusively traced to GATT-sanctioned countervailing and antidumping remedies taken by developing-country importers -- with the notable exception of Japan -- against Korean trade practices. As a result, Korea entered the Uruguay Round with the objective of stemming these responses.[93] Kim and Chung have written that ". . .if domestic support for the Uruguay Round is to be maintained, this commitment [to standstill and rollback] will have to be fully honored in the course of the negotiations."[94]

It is not clear what a lessening of Korea's commitment to the Uruguay Round -- and by implication the GATT -- would mean, however. Indeed,

---

92 "South Korea's Emergence as Trading Power Increases Pressure for More Open Markets" *International Trade Reporter* (August 29, 1990) pp. 1345-1347.

93 MTI official Kim Jong-Kap noted in a November 1989 speech given at an American symposium on U.S.-Korean trade that foreign CVD actions were no longer a concern to Korea because subsidization was eliminated by the government, but that antidumping actions remained problematic because the United States used them as a form of "procedural protectionism."

94 Kim and Chung (1988) p. 153.

there are reasons to believe that Korea will continue to look to the GATT as an important trade policy forum in which Korea must participate. Those Korean officials who favor many of the trade liberalization measures called for by the United States privately argue that it is politically easier for them to cite GATT pressure, which is considered less political and therefore less of a threat to Korean sovereignty by the Korean populace. Moreover, Korea's graduation from the developing world has meant that the country can no longer benefit from the trade-liberalizing effects of GATT on the developed countries while standing under the protection of Article 18b. As a result, Korea's official position on GATT-sanctioned exceptions to free trade for LDCs is likely to weaken and move closer to the positions of the developed-country governments. Similarly, Korea's trade policy structure is maturing to the point where the Korean government itself is likely to make greater use of GATT-sanctioned trade remedies, such as countervailing duties, antidumping measures, and safeguard actions, and therefore Korea might be less inclined to weaken these remedies within the GATT.[95] As a result, opportunities might exist for the United States to bring South Korea in as an ally on a wider range of GATT-related issues in the 1990s, regardless of the outcome of the current Round.

Regional Trade Strategy

South Korea's regional trade policies in the 1990s will be centered on the new organization created for Asian Pacific Economic Cooperation (APEC) in which Korea is a member. APEC is forcing South Korean officials to better articulate Korea's regional trade policy. Any analysis of Korea's specific role in APEC suffers from the fact that a formal policy position on APEC is still under development. Nevertheless, discussions with Korean officials indicate that Korea's regional trade policies will not change significantly, and the outlines of Korea's specific policy positions within APEC can be discerned. Several salient points are evident:

- *Korean support for APEC is solid.* Korean officials are eager to go forward with APEC, even if the direction of such an organization

---

95 S.K. Lee, Pohang Inn and Steel Company's (POSCO) regional director for the United States, stated at a speech in the United States that the company views countervailing duty actions as "an accepted cost of doing business in the United States". POSCO is therefore unlikely to staunchly protest a strengthening of the GATT CVD code. "The Impact of U.S. Trade Law Actions on Business Decisions in Korea," *Michigan Journal of International Law* (University of Michigan Law School, Winter 1990).

is not clear. One official said that regional cooperation -- namely APEC -- will be Korea's "major focus"[96] after completion of the GATT Round.[97]

- *The role of Japan is a concern.* Looming large in Korean thinking about APEC is the role Japan would play. Korean distrust of Japanese motives in the region runs deep, and it is clear that the Korean officials do not want APEC to further Japanese dominance of the region. Indeed, when asked what Korea's primary objective in APEC is likely to be, one official provided a discourse on the "Japan problem."[98]
- *APEC should not be a "fortress Asia."* While he was MTI Minister, Han had made clear that he felt any regional pact such as APEC should be "non-discriminatory and non-exclusive."[99] The reasoning behind this stance is apparently that other regional pacts -- such as EC 1992 and the North American Free Trade Agreement -- might exclude Korean exports, and an exclusionary APEC would

---

[96] Interview with a senior EPB official, March 1990.

[97] A Blue House official said that Korea's role in APEC will be "active." Interview, March 1990. Korean support for APEC, at least prior to the reshuffle, also appeared to be strong within the Foreign Ministry and the MTI. Both MTI Minister Han and Foreign Minister Choi expressed support for APEC, Han stating that ". . .if countries in this region successfully chart a course for cooperation within the region, it could well be adopted by other regions as a global model." "Growing Emphasis on Cooperation in the Asian-Pacific Region," *Korea Trade and Business* (December 1989) p. 23. Choi noted after the first APEC meeting in November 1989 that " . . .we cannot fail to open a new chapter in the history of the Asia-Pacific area. Let us seize this momentum and carry it into the Pacific century." "Support Grows For Asia-Pacific Trade Bloc," *Reuters Business Report* (November 6, 1989).

[98] Interview with a KIET official, March 1990. When asked about Korea's objective within APEC, a top EPB official stated that it was important to make the United States and Canada understand that Japan is not subordinated to the United States and Canada, but that Japan is a competitor, and that Korea can play a partnership role to balance Japan. The Asian perception of Japan carries baggage from their mutual history.

[99] *Financial Times* (June 15, 1989) Section 3, p. 5.

help foreign trading blocs justify their own exclusionary practices.[100]

- *APEC should have OECD-like informality.* Unlike the GATT, however, Korean officials do not envision an APEC with a highly formal structure. One top MTI official foresees APEC as little more than an organization for exchanging ideas on, for example, pollution.[101]

Official Korean thinking has not progressed beyond these generalities, although the formation of KIEP and the conclusion of the Uruguay Round are likely to accelerate the process of policy formulation on this issue. Some policy specifics can be inferred from Korea's overall trade policy position, however. First, given the suspicion Korean officials have regarding Japan, Korea will probably take special care to keep the U.S. government strongly involved in APEC as a counterweight to Japan, and perhaps attempt to be seen as a U.S. ally on a wide range of issues.[102] Second, Korea is likely to favor GATT-like reciprocity within APEC because, among the NICs, Korea has been on the forefront of trade liberalization. Third, judging by Korea's rhetoric toward the Association of South East Asian Nations (ASEAN), Korea will probably try to use APEC as a vehicle to promote foreign direct investment and its corresponding intra-industry trade.

---

[100] It is clear from other statements that the Soviet Union, North Korea, and China would not, however, automatically be welcomed into APEC by South Korea. On a related note, one top presidential advisor said that EC 1992 might spur Asian unity. Interview, March 1990.

[101] Interview, March 1990. The official noted that APEC is "not an European Community." He said that it is very difficult to form regional groups, and this effort is likely to take more than ten years. A top economic advisor to the President said that APEC would be "looser than a formal type" of organization such as the EC because of the different values and historical circumstances among the Asian countries.

[102] An EPB official emphasized that Japan has been moving closer to other Asian countries and away from the United States. Interview, March 1990. A presidential advisor said that he believed that the Japanese were "agonizing over their own role" in APEC, and that the 1990s will be a decade of Japan "groping" to determine its role in the international community. Interview, March 1990.

Bilateral Trade Strategy

There are four bilateral relationships that are important from a Korean trade policy perspective: the United States, Japan, the European Community, and the newly reformed countries of Eastern Europe. In short, Korea wants to shift its trade surplus away from the United States, its deficit away from Japan, and to expand it trade relations with the rest of the world. As a result, Korea's trade strategies with each of these partners is best understood by recognizing the interrelationships among the individual bilateral relations. When discussing any one of these relationships with Korean officials, the other trading partners quickly emerge in the conversation. As the *Financial Times* wrote, "[T]he point emphasized in Seoul is that the key to reducing trade friction lies in eliminating Korea's long-standing trade deficit with Japan. Fears about that deficit fuel the accumulation of surpluses elsewhere."[103] Indeed, the Korean government's most blatant program for controlling Korean trade -- the Import Source Diversification program -- is aimed at modifying the pattern of trade among all of its partners.

It is also interesting to note that Korean trade policy officials tend to think in bilateral terms. When asked to list top trade policy priorities, the United States always topped the list, with the rest of the issues consisting of some combination of the EC 1992 program and Korea's "Northern Policy"[104] -- with an occasional reference to the Uruguay Round.

Korea and the United States

By far the most important relationship South Korea has is with the United States.[105] As noted above, the United States government has

---

103 "Seoul Dancing to U.S. Tunes," *Financial Times* (June 15, 1989) p. IV.

104 This is the label for South Korea's relations with North Korea and related communist countries. Because of its heavily political nature, Korea's Northern Policy does not appear to have significant implications for Korea's trade relations with the rest of the international trade community despite its appearance on such unofficial lists of priorities. During the interviews, for example, Korean officials found it difficult to draw a connection between the Northern Policy's trade elements and Korea's overall trade policies.

105 This fact is beyond serious dispute, and will not be supported further here. When asked what Korea's top five trade-policy priorities were, one top government official responsible for trade-policy matters said that the relationship with the

(continued...)

been the main force for liberalization of the Korean economy, and therefore the direction of this bilateral relationship is likely to determine much of Korea's overall trade policy future. Because the United States is likely to continue taking the initiative in U.S.-Korean trade policy discussions, however, and due to the wide variety of potential bilateral trade issues, it is hard to predict future of the relationship -- much depends on U.S. moves.

It is possible, however, to assess the broad outlines of Korean trade relations with the United States in the 1990s because the current conditions of U.S.-Korean trade friction are unlikely to abate for several years. First, points of contention between Korea and the United States are likely to include those trade-related policies discussed above -- such as informal import barriers, indirect export promotion measures, enforcement of intellectual property rights, and the foreign-investment regime. In other words, disputes are likely to center on "functional" issues, as opposed to sector-specific concerns. Second, the possible combination of import barriers, domestic overcapacity, and a U.S. recession could lead to a sharp rise of dumping cases brought by U.S. producers against Korean exporters. High-profile candidates for dumping cases include automobiles and semiconductors. Third, the persistence of Korea's formal and informal barriers to agricultural imports will probably simmer through the 1990s and reemerge as a major bilateral issue as the 1997 deadline for liberalization approaches, unless there is a significant change in the domestic politics surrounding this sector. Of the 39 Super 301 complaints filed by U.S. interests against South Korea in 1990, 20 were on agricultural products. Indeed, tensions could immediately resume if Uruguay Round fails to resolve the agricultural issue or if there is an agreement to which the Korean government does not fully adhere.

Finally, if the evolution U.S.-Japanese relationship is any guide, the Korean *chaebol* structure itself might emerge as a bilateral trade issue as

---

[105] (...continued)
United States is "always number one." Interview, March 1990. When other officials discuss any aspect of Korean trade relations, statements are often prefaced by noting that United States will remain Korea's first trade-policy priority. Although it was clear during the interviews that the individuals making these statements were careful to emphasize the importance of the United States because the questions were put by Americans, there is little question that officials are sincere in their statements.

has the Japanese *keiretsu* structure.[106] As discussed above, Korean manufacturing is concentrated in a few *chaebol* and the limited channels of import-export trade are vested in a few GTCs controlled by the *chaebol* and subject to bureaucratic influence. The anticompetitive, trade-distorting effects of these structures could become more apparent to U.S. officials as the more obvious interventionist government trade policies are liberalized away. Indeed, given the strong sentiment among the Korean populace against the *chaebol*, trade-distorting anticompetitive activities might be an easy target for U.S. negotiators.

Because of the importance of the U.S. relationship, the Korean government will continue to devote substantial effort to keeping frictions to a minimum. As noted above, this is a key trade-related objective. This objective is in conflict, however, with the objectives of export-based growth and a restructuring the economy toward high-technology manufacturing. Korean actions to minimize U.S.-Korean trade conflict can be characterized as a three-stage "defense," although Korean officials themselves do not necessarily view their actions as having this structure.

Avoid Provoking the United States. Korean officials point to a number of government policies designed around minimizing U.S. trade policy responses. For example:

- *"Functional" Industrial Targeting.* As outlined in the high-technology section below, the Korean government is taking great care to not provide product-specific production or export subsidies that would be clearly countervailable under U.S. trade law. Korean officials acknowledge that such industry-promotion policies are tailored to avoid trade frictions.[107]
- *Monitoring Exports.* MTI bureaucrats and industry association officials are likely to continue monitoring Korean exports of products that might be particularly sensitive from a trade policy standpoint, such as electronic components. Implicit price floors or quantity ceilings are likely to be imposed occasionally, and

---

106 Technically, the industrial structure of Japanese industry was not the point of debate between the U.S. and Japanese governments. Rather, the Japanese government's lax enforcement of regulations governing anticompetitive practices of these structures, and the consequences for U.S. exports, were at issue.

107 Interviews with senior officials at MOFA and MTI, and with a senior advisor to the Presdient, March 1990.

enforced through the informal powers government and industry officials have over exporters.

- *Encouraging Some U.S. Imports.* The Korean government's efforts to promote U.S. imports -- particularly of goods for which Korea is heavily dependent on the Japanese -- will continue. The two main mechanisms for such promotion are the Import Source Diversification program and specific tax breaks given to companies that use American capital equipment.[108]
- *Promoting Joint Ventures.* Korean officials believe that the wide range of U.S.-Korean joint ventures reduces bilateral trade frictions.[109] "Turning friction into cooperation" was the theme of MTI minister Han's visit to Washington in early 1990. The prime example of this is automobiles, where KIA and Ford, Hyundai and Chrysler, and Samsung and General Motors have partnership arrangements. MTI bureaucrats believe that such cooperation in other areas -- semiconductors, consumer electronics, overseas construction, and spacecraft were mentioned -- would have both commercial and trade policy benefits.[110]
- *Overseas Investment.* The Korean government encourages investment in both the United States and third-country markets, although it is difficult determine to what extent defusing U.S. trade friction plays a role in this policy. The future of this policy might change if Korea's recent current-account problems become chronic -- thereby reducing the pool of Korean capital. Moreover, a sharp uptick in domestic unemployment might put pressure on policy makers to bring capital back to Korean soil. Finally, some Korean officials fear that the 1988 Omnibus Trade Act made this strategy

---

108 For example, the Korean government provides a tax break and tariff exemptions for semiconductor capital equipment purchased from U.S. sources.

109 U.S. companies use trade-policy mechanisms to affect the contract terms on alliances, however, so the causation is two-way. This phenomenon will be particularly germane in the 1990s given that many of the "trade" issues that are taking on a greater importance in U.S.-Korean relations are in the investment area. For example, informal government mandates that foreign access to Korean land be "bought" with technology transfer from the foreign entity to the Korean partner, or the "localization" of the purchase of specific inputs from Korean sources.

110 Note that such ventures, especially in high-technology areas, would also help Korean companies upgrade their technical capabilities -- another trade-related Korean objective. Interviews with senior MTI and KIET officials.

less viable because it imposed tighter sanctions on third-country dumping.[111]

It should be recognized that there are those in the Korean trade policy community who acknowledge that the best way to mitigate U.S.-Korean trade frictions is to fully liberalize the Korean economy. One MTI official responsible for bilateral relations with the United States noted that U.S. trade relations with both Canada and West Germany are generally healthy despite large trade deficits, and he attributed this to the laissez faire policies of those two governments.

Greater Efforts at Bilateral Dialogue. As a result of Korea's 1990 backsliding on trade liberalization, the United States broke-off talks with the Korean government that were aimed at establishing a joint U.S.-Korea trade policy discussion committee.[112] The committee would focus on defusing potentially divisive trade conflicts between the two governments and is the kind of trade forum with which Korean officials are most comfortable. Consequently, Korea is likely to invest a great deal of energy in this new forum should it be created.[113]

Korean officials have long emphasized their wish to keep U.S.-Korean trade difficulties out of the public limelight. From the popular Korean perspective, liberalization policies adopted by the government represent Korean submission to U.S. authority -- which puts officials who genuinely favor liberalization in a politically difficult situation. Moreover, Korean officials often feel that Korean policies are "misunderstood" by foreign observers -- particularly U.S. government and company officials. On the broadest scale, trade officials frequently cite the pace of Korean liberalization when compared to other developing countries, and assert that the only real policy differences between U.S. and Korean officials are over the timing of future reforms. In public, Korean spokesmen have long stressed that Korea is not "another Japan" in the trade realm, arguing that the Korean economy is both more open and less powerful than Japan's.

---

[111] "Korean Offshore Assembly Operations Threatened," *Korean Trade and Business* (November 1990) p. 36.

[112] Formally known as *The Joint Committee on Commercial Cooperation.* The Committee will focus on specific sectoral concerns. Interview with a U.S. Department of Commerce official (June 1990).

[113] Korea's success in avoiding Super 301 status in 1989 was largely due to the back-door negotiations that took place between Korean and U.S. officials, which probably enhanced Korean appreciation for such a private dialogue.

Korean officials are likely to use the new bilateral forum as a platform to make well-honed presentations along these lines.

Similarly, the Korean government is likely to substantially raise its trade-lobbying efforts within the United States in the 1990s. The Korean embassy in Washington has long urged Seoul to hire American lobbyists to respond to U.S. allegations of unfair Korean trade practices, according to a Korean embassy official.[114] Yet until recently Korea has kept a low profile in Washington since the "Koreagate" scandal of the late 1970s, relying on sending government and industry officials from Korea to discuss issues directly. Since 1988, however, the Korean government has hired trade policy lobbyists from one Washington law firm to counter the Treasury Department's findings that the Korean government has manipulated the *won* exchange rate and accusations that the Korean steel industry is heavily subsidized.[115] Such increased lobbying efforts would be consistent with the maturation of the Korean trade policy process. Indeed, one American embassy official in Seoul said that KIEP is likely to be used to develop better public relations on trade matters.[116]

More Managed Trade. A probable outcome of both Korea's efforts to avoid trade conflict with the United States, coupled with its emphasis on dialogue, is an increased in managed trade, rather than an abandonment of Korean government intervention in trade. An example was the outcome of the U.S.-Korean controversy over beef quotas, in which the settlement did not lead to an abolishment of government beef restrictions, but merely an increase in the foreign quota. The nature of those trade disputes most likely to occur in the 1990s points toward continued Korean government intervention in trade, albeit to satisfy U.S. pressures. Potential areas of managed U.S.-Korean trade in the 1990s include:

---

114 "Korea Stunned by U.S. Traders," *Legal Times* (April 17, 1989) p. 4. Jeng Woo Kil, first secretary of the economic section at the Korean embassy in 1989, stated that "We are losing time. . . . We have to follow the rules of the game in Washington."

115 The Washington D.C. office of Reid & Priest prepared these reports and the Washington firm of Arnold & Porter has several Korean corporate trade clients and is considered a leading candidate for running a government lobbying campaign. "Kid Korea Grows Up," *National Journal* (July 1, 1989) p. 1685.

116 Interview with a U.S. embassy official in Seoul, March 1990.

- *Government Procurement.* Korean officials might seek to deflect U.S. pressure over discriminatory government procurement practices by ensuring that, for example, U.S. telecommunication firms are selected to provide some equipment to the Korean Telecommunications Authority.
- *Restraints on Exports.* Although the Korean government fought against Korea's inclusion in the U.S.-imposed voluntary restraint agreement on steel exports, Korean officials were resigned to the idea of such a managed solution to the steel-export problem. A similar but informal understanding could emerge regarding automobile or semiconductors, even if such actions are taken unilaterally by Korean officials eager to cool U.S.-Korean tensions over a sharp rise in exports to the U.S. market.
- *Discriminatory Policies Favoring U.S. Products.* As noted above, the Korean government will continue to promote certain U.S. imports through the Import Source Diversification program and its tax and tariff policies. For example, in April 1991, the Korean government allowed four foreign firms to enter the securities business in Korea. Two licenses went to U.S. firms and two went to U.K. firms. None of the four Japanese firms that applied were allowed in, and observers cite strong U.S. and U.K. trade policy pressure as the deciding factor.[117]

As in the 1980s, a substantial part of Korean "strategy" with the United States will be simply to acquiescence to U.S. trade policy demands. Ongoing examples of this include tariff reductions on manufactured goods, de facto as well as de jure liberalization of agricultural imports, enforcement of foreign-owned intellectual property rights, and so on.

Even when agreements-in-principle are reached between U.S. and Korean negotiators, secondary disputes are likely to linger over the pace and the enforcement of reforms. Korean enforcement of promised trade-related reforms will be a chronic problem in the 1990s because most of the reforms will involve the elimination of informal, non-transparent practices, such as intellectual property protection, discriminatory government procurement practices, and enforcement of regulations governing anticompetitive activities.

One of the most discouraging informal barriers facing foreign exporters to Korea is the bureaucratic red tape that surrounds imports. One trade journal referred to the Korean Customs Administration as "a den of

---

117 "Bowing to U.S. and U.K. Trade Pressure," *Korea Trade and Business* (April 1991) p. 49.

frustration for foreign business" because of the layers upon layers of forms and official approvals that must be obtained before a good can be brought into the country. Business people we have talked to complain that for many goods the customs officials seem to display no interest in approving some foreign merchandise despite the lack of any formal government restriction against their import. An American Chamber of Commerce reported that 73 percent of its members surveyed complained of unnecessary customs delays, 33 percent found "major difficulties" in importing spare parts, and a high 9 percent said that their goods had been damaged by customs officials. Such barriers are difficult to negotiate away at the government-to-government level.

Korea and Japan

The degree to which Japan affects overall Korean trade policy development should not be underestimated. The combination of Koreans' historical antipathies toward Japan and the Korean economy's current dependence on Japan is both slowing Korea's overall trade liberalization and keeping Korean import policies biased in favor of the United States.

Korea's Economic Dependence on Japan. Japan is Korea's dominant source for critical manufacturing technologies and inputs, which contributes to Japan's longstanding role as Korea's largest source of imports and its chronic trade deficit with Japan. Japanese companies then use their control over critical components in Korean products to call the shots on prices and volumes in markets in which the Korean and Japanese compete -- such as the United States.[118] Moreover, Japanese companies often know how many electronics products their Korean competitors are planning to make because the Koreans must let their Japanese suppliers know how many key components will be required. Finally, because Japanese suppliers have a virtual monopoly over some key parts, they are able to set parts prices so as to effectively set the profits the Korean producer can make. One Korean official even claimed that government support for semiconductor R&D was necessary because the Japanese parts suppliers would not allow Korean producers enough revenues to conduct

---

118 This phenomenon widely believed to be true among those in the electronics trade in Korea. For example, one report states that "Samsung has refrained from undercutting Japanese camcorder prices in the United States because the company relies on Japanese suppliers, industry sources say." "Under Attack on All Fronts" *Financial Times* (July 1990).

their own R&D.[119] Such economic dependence looms large in Korean officials' minds given Korea's high-tech plans. On the investment front, Korean officials worry that their economy will be deeply penetrated by Japanese investment.

Korea's Policy Reaction to Japan. The Korean determination to fight Japanese intrusion into their economy has resulted in the Import Source Diversification (ISD) program which, in a rather ad hoc manner, bans over 200 Japanese products in a blatant violation of the GATT.[120] Korean officials do not foresee an end to the ISD program.[121]

Conversely, the Korean government is not likely to go on the offensive to liberalize the Japanese market as the United States has tried. Although one U.S. official said that the Korean government has "given up" on Japan from policy standpoint,[122] it is not clear that the government has ever tried to force a change in Japanese import barriers, which officials believe are largely informal rather than border measures. A top EPB official said Japanese market is "closed" due to non-tariff barriers and said that there is "no price elasticity" and that the Japanese just "purchase certain amount [of foreign goods]" and that penetrating "takes time."[123] Consequently, Korean government policy towards Japan in the 1990s is likely to be defensive -- keep Japanese goods out but do not help Korean businesses get access to the Japanese market.[124] One area that the Korean planners are hopeful is in Korean competition against Japan in third markets where Japanese restrictions do not rule.[125]

---

119 Interview with a senior KIET official, March 1990.

120 In particular, restrictions on imports must be executed on a most-favored-nation basis unless trade remedies are being used against goods that are "unfairly" traded in terms of the GATT.

121 Interviews with senior officials at EPB and MTI, March 1990.

122 Interview with a U.S. official in Seoul.

123 Interviews with an official at EPM and a professor of Economics at Sogang University, March 1990.

124 Discussions with Korean *chaebol* officials make it clear that the Korean private sector still sees substantial long-term opportunities in Japan.

125 Interview with a senior EPM official.

The Korean government encourages (through the tax code, for example) the use of American capital equipment over Japanese equipment. Nevertheless, Hyundai semiconductor officials have noted that they are shifting to Japanese equipment because of the relative strengths of Japanese equipment despite their reluctance to increase ties with the Japanese.

Korea and the European Community

Korean officials -- in both government and industry -- view the European Community as a natural outlet for expanded Korean manufactured exports, which would help Korea meet its objectives of trade-partner diversification and maintaining strong relations with the United States.[126] Korea will continue to deal with EC trade difficulties as it has in recent years -- by expanding its manufacturing presence within the EC and Eastern Europe and by carefully managing Korea's exports to the Community -- but trade policy discussions are likely to be more formal in the 1990s as recently established channels for dialogue mature.

Contentious Bilateral Trade Relations. Korean exporters are keenly aware that bilateral trade relations with the Community have been particularly contentious in recent years. According to MTI estimates, in 1989 more than 40 percent of Korea's exports to the Community as measured by value were restricted by either antidumping actions or voluntary restraint agreements. Moreover, Korean exporters believe that recent EC Commission decisions -- such as the rules-of-origin regulations -- do not bode well for Korean access to the EC market, particularly in such competitive Korean products as electronics and electronic components. Past relations and the current direction of EC directives have led Koreans to view EC 1992 as the creation of fortress Europe.

Lee Sang Seol, former KOTRA representative to Brussels, told the *Far Eastern Economic Review* that "[a]fter 1992 everyone will have crammed into Europe and if you are the last on the bus you will not get a good seat."

---

126 "The positive aspect [of EC 1992] would be the fact that Korea will be able to expand exports to the EC, diversifying away somewhat from its heavy links to the markets of the United States and Japan." KOTRA, *Korea Trade & Business* (April 1990) p. 28. A top Ministry of Foreign Affairs official specializing in international economics matters put EC 1992 as number three on the list of Korean trade priorities, after the United States and the Uruguay Round, while a top trade official at KDI put EC 1992 at number two after the United States. Interviews, March 1990.

One MTI official opined that "a fortress Europe after 1992 is certain."[127]

A good outline of Korean fears was given in *Korea Trade & Business*, an organ of KOTRA:

> *the negative effect [of EC 1992] will be that the EC is likely to take protectionist actions against Korea, along with other nations, with which the EC is running a trade deficit. . . . The EC will put pressure on Korea to open its services and government-procurement markets. Such pressure will grow as Korea is positioned to join the OECD membership and further liberalize its capital and financial markets. The EC will place a quantitative restriction on Korea and halt the provision of GSP privileges. The EC will strengthen it vigilance on Korea by imposing antidumping and countervailing duties. . . . The EC will demand that Korea protect EC copyrights and industrial property rights.*[128]

Investment in EC. From the Korean perspective, the EC problem and solution are simple, if not easy. As one American observer aptly summarized Korea's EC policy: "Koreans see EC 1992 as a Fortress Europe with Korea inside."[129]

Although estimates of the level and rate of Korean investment in the Community vary, it is clear that there is a Korean push to establish a presence behind any potential EC import walls. In early 1989, MTI forecast that by 1992 there would be over 100 trading and manufacturing operations in the Community owned by Korean interests -- more than double the 1989 figure.[130] All of the major industrial groups have invested in substantial manufacturing operations in Europe, particularly in the areas of consumer electronics, which currently dominate Korea's exports to Europe. A similar sectoral drive could soon began in the automobile area, according to press reports, with Hyundai and Daewoo

---

127 "Seoul Searching: South Koreans Protest Against Unfair Treatment," *Far Eastern Economic Review* (May 1989) p. 73. This characterization of the Korean attitude was confirmed in nearly every interview and is the view that government and company officials espouse repeatedly in the press.

128 "The Korean Perspective: Single, Unified, Integrated EC," *Korea Trade and Business* (April 1990) p. 28.

129 Discussion with U.S. embassy official, Seoul.

130 *Far Eastern Economic Review* (May 18, 1989) p. 73.

setting up wholly-owned plants or joint ventures for either entire vehicles or automobile components.[131]

Korean investment within the Community is being assisted by individual Member States that are working to induce foreign investment before the 1992 deadline, when Member governments will be prohibited from making efforts to attract such investments. A number of governments have made formal presentations to high-level Korean officials in government and industry,[132] and "European representatives [are] making frequent visits to Korea."[133]

In addition to the trade policy causes of Korean investment within the EC prior to 1992, it should noted that rising labor costs in Korea -- which reduces relative labor costs in Europe -- and the importance of the Community as an export platform for Eastern Europe are contributing to Korea's recent rise in foreign direct investment in the Community.

Managing Korea's Exports. The Korean government, Korean industry associations, and individual exporters have reacted to EC trade policy actions against Korean exports with actions that could be considered managed trade. For example:

- In 1988, with antidumping suits against Korean microwave ovens and televisions still pending, the EC imposed provisional antidumping duties on Korean VCRs. Shortly thereafter, the Korean government called on its electronics industry to curb sharply its exports of televisions and VCRs to the Community.
- In January 1989, the Electronics Industry Association of Korea announced that it would continue monitoring its members' sales to ensure that exports of televisions to the EC did not exceed 1988 levels. It also agreed to limit its microwave oven exports to 2.5 million units per year.

---

131 Note that Hyundai has taken advantage of the U.S.-Canadian Free Trade Area agreement with its plant in Canada producing vehicles for the U.S. market.

132 In 1989, the governments of France, Italy, Portugal, Ireland, Greece, the Netherlands, and West Germany all made concerted efforts to attract South Korean investment within their respective borders. "EC Rushes for Investment Before 1992 Deadline," *Yonhap* (June 14, 1989) and "Netherlands Offers to Help Korean Businesses Advance to EC," *Jiji Press* (September 6, 1989).

133 *Business Korea*, "Countdown to 1992" (November 1989) p. 63.

- February 1989, the EC accepted "price undertakings" -- a Korean commitment to not ship below a set price -- from Korean VCR exporters.

This pattern is likely to continue in the 1990s. The Koreans, however, are aware of scrutiny from the EC Commission, and are reportedly acting accordingly. In April 1990, a top semiconductor official in Korea's MTI wrote:

> *. . .Korea must begin by managing the price and quantity of semiconductors exported to the EC.* ***At the request of Japanese makers,*** *the EC Executive Commission reviewed whether Korean makers sell their products below cost. . .Korean semiconductor makers are thus urged to be cautious due to possible dumping allegations from the end of this year [1989] when the global price of semiconductors is forecast to tumble.*[134]

Indeed, the three elements of Korea's EC "counter-strategy" in the semiconductor area, as outlined by this same MTI official,[135] are indicative of Korea's overall trade strategy to defuse pressures:

- ". . .management of price and quantity of semiconductors exported to the EC;"
- "Korean makers need to advance into the EC by setting up plants to project Korea's image as an insider of Fortress Europe. . .it is, therefore, necessary to secure a beachhead in specific European nations including Spain and Great Britain before 1992;"
- ". . .the Korean government must formulate an official position on the international standard code on the country of origin."

Such trade management is likely to be facilitated through a more formalized EC-Korean dialogue. In early 1990, Korean and EC officials established delegation offices in Brussels and Seoul, respectively.[136] This constitutes an attempt by both sides to institutionalize the annual meetings that have been held between EC officials and MOFA since 1984.

---

134 Kim Ho-Won, "EC Unity: Korean Semiconductor Industry Needs Counter-Strategies," *Korea Trade & Business* (April 1989) p. 35, emphasis added. Mr. Kim is Deputy Director of the Electronic Parts and Components Division of MTI.

135 Kim Ho-Won (1989) p. 35.

136 *Business Korea* (November 1989) p. 63.

Although the dialogue is ostensibly political, most of the bilateral issues between Brussels and Seoul are economic in nature and this forum bears watching for the trade-related demands that are likely to be made from the EC side and the deals that might be struck as a result.

EC officials have repeatedly said that Korea's best strategy for access to the EC market is to open the Korean market to EC products.[137] There is little evidence, however, that EC pressure has been directly responsible for any market-opening measures by the Korean government. The only effect on Korea of EC accusations seems to be a series of trade shows sponsored by Korean associations to demonstrate that it is possible to export to the Korean market from the Community.[138]

Korea and Eastern Europe

Korean *chaebol* are also making substantial efforts to develop markets for Korean products in Eastern Europe. Korean exporters see several advantages. First, greater East European sales would contribute to the Korean objective of export diversification. Second, Korea sees Eastern Europe as a market with relatively unsophisticated tastes which lessens the Korean commercial disadvantage with respect to Japan and the United States, and one in which Korea and its export competitors will be starting with on a level playing field -- as opposed to other markets in which Korean see the Japanese or Americans as already established.[139] Third, although never explicitly stated by Korean officials, Korean companies are not as constrained by technology-control restrictions, such as COCOM, and therefore have somewhat of an advantage in technology exports, according to U.S. business competitors. Finally, Korean government officials are eyeing stronger trade relations with former communist

---

137 In July 1989, Frans Andriessen, vice president of the EC Executive Commission, told the *Korean Herald*, "The most important thing is that Korea should open its market to European operators as we are opening up our market to their Korean counterparts." (July 18, 1989) p. 2.

138 See, for example, "EC Stalks the Korean Tiger," *Business Korea* (November 1989) p. 67.

139 Hungary is the toehold for Korean companies. Samsung, Daewoo, and Lucky Goldstar have branch offices in Budapest and Samsung has a 50:50 joint venture to produce color televisions. On the political level, diplomatic relations were established in February 1989 and President Rho's 1989 visit was the first by a South Korean president to a Communist country.

countries as an element in Seoul's strategy to isolate North Korea economically and politically.[140]

Sectoral Trade Strategies

There are three sectors that will figure prominently among the trade issues that are likely to be contentious between Korea and its trading partners in the 1990s. First, despite government promises that agriculture will be liberalized, it is highly unlikely that the Korean economy will be more open in the 1990s to the import of raw agricultural products or even many processed foods. Second, the Korean government's objective to move the economy toward high-technology production is likely to lead to a variety of trade and industrial strategies that could, in turn, trigger sporadic trade disputes. Finally, as formal trade barriers come down in many other sectors, barriers in the financial services sector are likely to become more apparent to Korea's trading partners.

Agriculture. For several reasons, Korea's agricultural trade policy in the 1990s will stand somewhat apart from its trade policies in other areas. First, Korea's agricultural import barriers have been a major source of trade tension between the United States and Korea. Second, a protectionist agricultural policy is supported by every significant element of the Korean political system. Even reform-minded technocrats in, for example, the KDI and EPB recognize the political futility of widespread agricultural liberalization. Third, unlike many other sectors that the Korean government protects from international competition, the agricultural sector is clearly a declining industry in which Korea has no comparative advantage.

Disputes over agricultural issues between the United States and Korea have been routine over the past decade. U.S. complaints range from formal barriers -- such as the outright ban of beef imports -- to informal barriers such as phytosanitary restrictions that discriminate against foreign imports. These bilateral disputes demonstrate the essential role U.S. pressure has played in those agricultural reforms Korea has agreed to undertake.

Ongoing disputes are mostly over the many non-tariff barriers used by the Korean bureaucracy to exclude foreign agricultural products at both the raw and value-added levels. As an American Chamber of Commerce policy paper complained:

---

140 The "Northern Policy."

While significant progress has been achieved since mid-1988. . .overall progress has been undermined by the imposition of new non-tariff barriers. These include nonscientific food safety and phytosanitary barriers, contradictory product inspection procedures, and "unofficial quotas" on customs clearance.[141]

Korea has a self-proclaimed 1997 deadline for agricultural liberalization, but it is unlikely that Korea's agricultural sector will be competitive enough to withstand market opening or that political sentiments would favor such an opening.

Yet, there is almost no indigenous support for significant agricultural liberalization in Korea.

- *Farmers.* At the center are, of course, the farmers themselves. Farmers feel that Korea's economic boom excluded rural areas, although they continue to enjoy a disproportionate share of political influence due to the high representation of farm constituencies. Farmers have also strengthened their influence through organized interests groups. In particular, in March 1989 they formed the Chonnongnyon, the national alliance of farmers' movements.[142] In at least one case, that of the National Livestock Cooperatives Federation, a beef farmers organization, the interest group was created by the government, but is now reportedly out of its control.[143]
- *Urbanites.* Aside from the obvious concerns of the import-competing rural sector, protection of the domestic agricultural sector is favored by the urban class, the majority of whom are only one generation away from the farm and, in any case, are highly nationalistic on farm-related issues.[144] On a closely related note,

---

141 American Chamber of Commerce (1990).

142 Singdong-A, (April 1989) pp. 416-433.

143 There is some evidence that the farmers are divided among themselves. The National Farmer's Council, one of the three largest farmers' groups before the creation of the Chonnongyon, refused to join the new group.

144 Interview with a USDA official, Seoul, March 1990.

the intelligentsia also oppose liberalization on nationalist grounds.[145]

- *Opposition Movements.* The various opposition groups strongly support the Korean farmer. Six opposition lawmakers,[146] in angry response to U.S. protests over beef import bans, demanded that Rho scrap his plan to visit Washington in 1989. The rural movement has attracted sympathetic interest groups as well. The radical student movement has embraced the farmers' cause, and students have joined farmers at rallies protesting foreign imports.

At the most fundamental level, the Korean government wants to maintain a viable domestic agricultural sector. It prefers to achieve this through the development of a rural sector strong enough to compete fairly with imports, but will protect domestic producers if this proves unworkable.

In light of this objective, the Korean government approach to agricultural trade in the 1990s will be threefold. First, the government will continue to pour resources into upgrading its agricultural competitiveness. Over the past several years, government spending on agriculture has grown more rapidly than overall government outlays in an effort to bolster the sector and the government is hoping that future efforts will relieve the need for import protection. As one top Korean economic planner stated that "the solution to the agricultural problem will depend on internal reforms."[147] Specifically, the government is implementing a program to increase efficiency by raising the size of the average Korean farm.[148] Second, the government will probably continue to placate foreign governments by undertaking formal liberalization at the margin, while claiming that full liberalization can wait until 1997. This is likely to involve a significant degree of managed trade, as in the beef example where the quota was raised rather than abolished. Third, the government (or perhaps more accurately, elements of the

---

145 Nau (1988) pp. 135.

146 They were Rep. Kim Yong-shin, Yi Sang-oh (PPD), Pak Kyong-su, Pah Tae-kwon (PDP), Yun Chae-ki, Chong Il-yong (NDP). Although political realignments have brought some opposition under the government party.

147 Interview with an EPB official, March 1990.

148 The government has, for example, created a special credit facility to allow current farmers to buy surrounding farms and consolidate. Interview with an EPB official, March 1990.

government) will rely on informal trade barriers -- such as those cited by the American Chamber of Commerce document -- to keep foreign agricultural goods from flooding the Korean market. This tactic is likely to persist regardless of the policies adopted by the ruling party because of the great deal of discretionary power that resides at the lower levels of the bureaucracies, particularly in MAFF, which can use non-transparent standards procedures to defeat formal liberalization.

As the 1997 deadline approaches, it is likely to become apparent to all parties -- domestic and foreign -- that even formal liberalization is politically unworkable.[149] Unless there is a major shift in domestic sentiment, the Korean government is likely to create an excuse to postpone formal liberalization into the next century.

High Technology. Korea's efforts to develop its high-technology industries -- such as computers, semiconductors, and telecommunications -- is central to Korean government economic planning in the 1990s. Although many of the blueprints that government officials have drawn up do not specifically call for trade policy changes, the broader industrial plans will undoubtedly have trade effects that could give rise to trade disputes.

Telecommunications has been the first major area of high-tech conflict between Korea and the United States. On February 21, 1989, USTR Carla Hills identified Korea as a priority country for telecommunications negotiations aimed at opening the Korean telecommunications market to U.S. exports. Trade barriers cited included import tariffs on telecommunications equipment, standards and certification-related procedures, government procurement practices, and restrictions on value-added services.[150]

---

149 One powerful Agricultural Committee official and PPD member stated that the opening of the Korean agricultural market by 1997 was "impossible." Interview with a member of the Agriculture and Forestry Committee (opposition) of the National Assembly, March 1990.

150 Following six rounds of discussions, President Bush, taking into consideration the progress Korea had made on liberalizing its telecommunications sector, in February 1990 extended the negotiating period for another year. Among the problems cited in the initial report, three have already been resolved. Korea has accelerated its tariff reductions on certain telecommunications items. It has agreed to apply for coverage under the GATT Government Procurement Code and to include its major telecommunications contracts under the code. It has taken significant steps to provide for non-discriminatory standards-making, testing and (continued...)

Trade friction in the telecommunications area might be only the first of several high-technology sectors subject to U.S.-Korea trade dispute in the 1990s: after more than a year of research and policy debates, the government unveiled its Seven-Year High-Technology Development Plan.[151] The Plan calls for the government to undertake a wide variety of measures -- including $5.6 billion in government expenditures -- to promote seven high-technology products.[152] The government is aiming for a 60 percent increase in Korea's share of world high-technology exports by 1994 and a 130 percent increase by 2000.[153] Of the seven targeted products, only microelectronics is currently a significant Korean export. The Plan explicitly calls for the development of Korean high-technology industries at all levels, from "upstream" products such as semiconductor manufacturing equipment, through electronic components, to "downstream" goods such as high-definition television and medical equipment.

For example, according to the Plan, over the next seven years the government will provide $1.83 billion for the development of Korean microelectronics products, to be channeled through a variety of government financial institutions and a new High-Tech Industry

---

150 (...continued)
certification requirements. Korea has until February 1991 to phase out or eliminate its barriers to trade in telecommunications services before facing the possibility of sanctions. *International Trade Reporter*, various issues. GATT, *Review of Developments in the Trading System*, various issues.

151 "Seven Year Program Introduced: High-Tech Industry Gets Helping Hand," *Korea Trade and Business* (March 1990) p. 10. "Won 3.6 Trillion Will be Invested in Electronics Industry," *Korea Times* (February 8, 1990) p. 8. Information about the plan was leaked to the press as early as September of 1989, and there were conflicting press accounts of the goals, resources, and mechanisms of the Plan prior to its announcement. MTI and MOST are currently working to develop a comprehensive "special law" to support high-technology industries. The Economic Planning Board, however, favors "strengthening current measures," rather than implementing heavily interventionist subsidy program common in the 1970s and early 1980s. An official government document will be available in July of 1990 that will outline measures to support the high-tech industries. Interview with a senior EPB official, March 1990.

152 Semiconductors, new materials, mechatronics, bioengineering, fine chemistry, optics, and aircraft.

153 The Plan identifies funds in *won*. A 700 *won*/dollar exchange rate was used for these calculations.

Promotion Fund; provide a series of tax incentives and administrative guidance to induce an additional $3.36 billion of private-sector investments in microelectronics; and create an "industrial estate" in Chunchon city for the assembly of semiconductors, computers, and optical equipment.[154] Other measures in place include a reduced tariff rate on imported equipment if the equipment is used in selected high-technology applications; tax benefits for certain high-technology joint ventures; and institutional support for engineering education and manpower training in targeted high-tech fields.[155]

There are already some signs that such high-technology programs and their export consequences could be the source of increasing trade friction in the 1990s.

- In October 1989, Carla Hills "warned that [Korean] government subsidies for specific industries would serve to be a cause of trade friction."[156]
- Some top executives of American semiconductor companies have hinted that they might bring antidumping cases against Korean electronics manufacturers that have recently emerged as major exporters in the semiconductor memory market.
- Several of the issues that are continuing sources of trade policy contention between Korea and the United States -- such as import tariffs, intellectual property protection, and regulations governing

---

154 Since the Plan was announced, the government has unveiled other measures. According to a February 1990 news report, "Plans were announced to increase by 500 billion won [$714 million] in the special loans for facility investment to 1.5 trillion won [$2.14 billion]. Loans to domestic firms suffering from accumulating inventories can use inventory as collateral. Electronics firms are asking for 201.6 billion won [$288 million] in technical development funds for R&D projects." Note that this constitutes a subsidy to production capacity, rather than R&D. "Support for Auto Makers, Electronics Firms," *Korea Economics Journal* (February 26, 1990), emphasis added.

155 "Plans for Massive Investment in High-Tech," *Hanguk Kyongje Sinmun* (July 1, 1989) p. 3.

156 Yu Hee-yol, Director for Policy Planning at the Ministry of Science and Technology, in "Hi-Tech Strategies for the '90s," *Korea Times* (February 7, 1990) p. 9. In addition, another Korean official responsible for long-range economic planning said that the R&D subsidies were emphasized in large part because they were not proscribed by the GATT Subsidies Code. Interview with a KIET official, March 1990.

foreign investment -- are particularly acute in the high-technology areas.

As noted earlier in this chapter, Korean government planners hope to move the economy away from its traditional manufactured products toward a wide range of high-value-added, high-technology products. Similarly, the top executives of the *chaebol* see the high-technology path as the only course for their companies. The only two forces that are countervailing the government's high-technology push are foreign pressure against government intervention to support targeted industries and domestic popular resistance to further government support for the unpopular *chaebol* -- support that is an integral part of government efforts to develop Korea's high-tech capabilities.

Another political dynamic that should be recognized is the infighting among the various Korean bureaucracies. In theory, MTI is responsible for developing overall industry plans and implementing the production aspects of those plans, whereas MOST is confined to research and development of new technologies. Because "high-technology" can be considered both "industry" and "technology," however, jurisdictional disputes between MTI and MOST are rampant in this sector.[157] As a result, the EPB often arbitrates bureaucratic disagreements. In general, MTI and MOST are more in favor of direct government support of high-tech industries (with each Ministry wanting the authority over the programs), while the EPB prefers more subtle promotion measures.[158]

Aside from a long list of specific export and production targets set by the Korean government in the area of high-technology, Korean planners' objectives are simple: Meet industrial targets without provoking foreign retaliation. Taken as a whole, the promotion measures demonstrate the Korean government's philosophy for strengthening the Korean high-technology industries. There are two main themes. First, there is a heavy emphasis on government support for research and development projects, as opposed to widespread subsidies for production or exports. Second, most of the support measures are subtle and indirect, and do not involve

---

157 Several officials either raised this point themselves or acknowledged the persistence of infighting when queried. Interviews with MTI officials responsible for industrial policies and relations with the United States, a senior EPB official, and a former Minister, March 1990.

158 A clear example of bureaucratic infighting occurred over the recent development of the Seven-Year High-Tech Plan. Announcement of the Plan was delayed for several months as the EPB acted to resolve disputes.

direct transfers from government funds to specific semiconductor companies.

There are two reasons that Korean policies have these characteristics. First, the Korean government is consciously trying to avoid trade policy frictions with its major trading partners, particularly the United States.[159] According to Yu Hee-yol, Director for Policy Planning at the Ministry of Science and Technology,

> *Industrial and export targeting, which is bound to invite trade friction, should be excluded. . .we will not provide direct support for the high-tech industry in order not to conflict with the principle of the subsidies code of the GATT and the currently ongoing Uruguay Round negotiations. The U.S. trade representative, Carla Hills, during her visit to Korea last October, also warned that government subsidies for specific industries would serve to be a cause of trade friction.*[160]

Second, both industry and government officials understand that Korea's foremost shortcoming in the high-technology area is its daunting technological weakness.[161] As a result, the government views R&D support as more than a highly effective tool for promoting the high technology industries, such support is considered necessary for its long-term survival.

Despite the emphasis on indirect government support for high technology, however, there are widespread signs that the government is continuing to provide capital subsidies through various facilities, including its control of the banking industry, while trying to keep the

---

159 Interviews with two EPB officials responsible for interagency affairs, march 1990. A former MTI minister said that the government cannot provide direct support "as you know," only functional support. Interview, March 1990.

160 "Hi-Tech Strategies for the '90s," *Korea Times* (February 7, 1990) p. 9. In addition, another Korean official responsible for long-range economic planning said that the R&D subsidies were emphasized in large part because they were not proscribed by the GATT Subsidies Code. Interview, March 1990.

161 Nearly every government planning document related to the semiconductor industry has as its focus the need for Korean industry to close the technology gap with the United States and Japan. See Steers, et. al., *Chaebol: Korea's New Industrial Might* (Harper & Row: 1989) p. 83. Indeed, understanding the individual company's technology needs -- and the strategies they are employing to overcome their technical deficiencies -- is key to understanding their overall commercial capabilities, constraints, strategies, and objectives.

programs quiet.[162] Moreover, U.S. industry officials in Korea believe that operating subsidies might also occur, although evidence is scarce.

The government's definition of high technology often extends to advanced applications for older industries. For example, *Metal Bulletin* recently reported that the

> *Korean steel industry has formed a united front -- with quiet government backing -- to develop the next generation of steel technologies. . . . How much money the Korean government is injecting into the scheme is unclear: industry officials in Seoul would not comment, saying this could lead to charges from abroad that the Korean steel industry is being subsidized by the government which they say is not the case.*[163]

This curious passage is typical of the tone Korean officials take when discussing specific subsidies. Officials often deny that an industry is government subsidized, yet they are hesitant to give details of government support for industries because of the sensitivity of the subsidies issue among foreign governments.

Financial Services. As the Korean economy moves into the ranks of the industrial countries, the services sectors are likely to become more important as trade issues. In the Korean case, financial services has already been a point of contention and is likely emerge as among the more important sources of friction, particularly with the United States. The trade policy politics the Korean financial services industry is unusual because of the pervasive control the government has over the industry -- the financial institutions themselves do not constitute an independent political force.[164] As a result, liberalization of this sector does not face the same opposition from an independent, import-competing, private-sector group of firms and therefore, the wishes of Korean government planners are likely to hold sway.

---

162 Many of the obvious capital subsidies are related to the government's establishment of an industrial estate in Chunchon city for the assembly of semiconductors, computers, and optical equipment.

163 "Korean Steel Learns Lessons from Japan," *Metal Bulletin* (August 13, 1990).

164 Despite the privatization of most Korean banks in the 1980s, the Ministry of Finance maintains inordinate control -- either directly or indirectly -- over Korean banking activity. For example, through the MOF's Office of Supervision, the government still appoints key bank officers.

Forces for liberalization are coming from several directions. First, as one American official noted, Korean companies that require capital to operate "want competition" in the financial sector. Unlike the Japanese *keiretsu*, the Korean *chaebol* do not normally have a bank as a member of the corporate family. Second, the United States has complained about Korea's closed financial services market on a bilateral basis.[165]

> *More areas will be open to foreign investment in coming years, partly because of pressure from abroad, partly the force of local companies to compete with MNCs and also to stimulate incorporation of foreign high-tech know-how via direct investment.*[166]

Counterbalancing these forces, however, are the bureaucrats in the Ministry of Finance and the Economic Planning Board who hope to keep so-called hot money out of the Korean economy, fearing a return to the inflationary early 1980s when the Korean money supply skyrocketed. According to U.S. economic officials in Seoul, Korean officials are wary of foreign capital flowing in rapidly from major money centers. Moreover, from a bureaucratic standpoint, it is likely that MOF officials are loath to give up their traditional power over the Korea's financial institutions.

Because of the ease with which informal barriers can be covertly erected in the financial-services field and the reluctance of Korean officials to liberalize capital flows, it is likely that financial services will become a textbook case where formal barriers will continue to disappear with little progress being made by foreign firms trying to enter and remain in the Korean market.

Intellectual Property Rights. Intellectual property rights is another key area where the gap between formal liberalization and the endurance of discriminatory informal policies is substantial. Over the past several years the Korean government has been the leaders in upgrading and strengthening de jure intellectual property rights. Yet a woalk through a Korean shopping district makes clear the irrelevance of many of the new laws to foreign companies' efforts to stop violations of their protected

---

165 Indeed, current disputes between the United States are largely over financial-services issues. "On the U.S. hit list are sectors such as accounting, insurance, banking, brokerage, transport and farm products." "South Korea's Emergence as Trading Power Increases Pressure for More Open Markets," *International Trade Reporter* (August 29, 1990) pp. 1345-1347.

166 Business International, *Worldwide Financial Regulations: South Korea*, various issues.

properties -- there is a cornucopia of fake Rolexes, photocopied foreign books, and pirated video tapes. One government trade official admitted that neither the government bureaucrats nor Korean business understand the very concept of intellectual property rights. He said that it is difficult for the average Korean making T-shirts to believe that someone owns a picture of Batman -- "Batman is Batman."[167]

Intellectual property violations in the high-technology industries could be a growing source of friction between the United States and Korea in the 1990s as Korea targets more high-tech industries. Already the U.S. government has expressed dissatisfaction over Korea's repeated postponement of a Chip Protection Act to ensure that the maskwork designs used to produce a semiconductor are either purchased properly or developed independently in Korea.

CONCLUSION

Overall, the liberalization of South Korea's formal trade policy regime will be nearly complete in the 1990s, with the significant exceptions of agricultural imports and trade with Japan. Despite occasional backsliding, Korea has been among the most successful trade-policy reformers among the late-industrializing countries. Indeed, regardless of what drives or slows Korean reform, Korea has been on the leading edge of the wave of market-based liberalization that swept through the international political economy in the 1980s. Despite this progress on the formal level, however, the Korean government will continue to use its informal trade policy instruments to diversify Korean trade away from Japan and the United States, and to restructure the Korean economy away from traditional industries toward high technology. Korea will respond to the bilateral trade frictions that arise in the 1990s with a policy of managed trade, strategic investment, and further liberalization measures.

---

167 Interview with top MTI official, March 1990. In the same conversation, however, the official said that complaints of intellectual property violations were "way down" after the laws were put into effect.

5

Taiwan

Thomas R. Howell and Holly Glenn

It has been expedient, for a variety of reasons, for a diverse array of nations, international organizations, institutions and individuals to ignore Taiwan. This will no longer be possible in the 1990s. Taiwan is now one of the world's leading trading states, and one of the richest. In twenty years Taiwan has transformed itself from an offshore assembly platform prized mainly for its cheap labor into a country capable of designing and manufacturing leading edge application-specific integrated circuits, and one of the world's leading manufacturers of personal computers.[1] Indeed, eighteen million Taiwanese are arguably achieving success in the electronic information industries that compares with that of 320 million Europeans. Taiwan's businessmen are establishing a sphere of commercial influence in Southeast Asia and in South China that may constitute the only real counterpoise to Japanese influence in that part of the world.

Yet Taiwan's success is awkward for many people, institutions, and nations. Most obviously, its very existence is a continuing rebuke to the communists in Beijing, upstaging their revolution and demonstrating how China itself might have developed under a different economic system. Taiwan is politically inconvenient for the large number of countries that seek to curry favor with the Peoples' Republic, or at least avoid its displeasure, forcing them to adopt a variety of unorthodox institutional arrangements in order to maintain some sort of relationship with Taipei. The GATT has put Taiwan's application for membership on the "back

---

[1]*Far Eastern Economic Review* (December 13, 1990); *Business Week* (September 25, 1989).

burner," notwithstanding the fact that the only real obstacle is the opposition of the Peoples' Republic, which, unlike Taiwan, has shown little inclination to embrace GATT principles. The World Bank barely acknowledges the existence of Taiwan, a large potential contributor, choosing to embrace the convenient fiction that it is merely a province of China. Similarly, Taiwan's economic achievements have occurred in something of an academic vacuum -- with a few noteworthy exceptions,[2] scholars and academic institutions have found it imprudent to risk Beijing's irritation by devoting more than passing attention to its "lost province."

The Taiwan experience poses problems for orthodoxies other than communism. A massive body of Western neoclassical economic thinking attributes East Asian commercial success to economic policies which have emphasized free markets, open trade, and small government, and the International Monetary Fund and the World Bank, "being among the more passionate supporters of the free market theory of rapid growth, have prescribed liberalization and privatization as the cure for underdevelopment and stagnation in the third world." However, as has been underscored by recent analysis, the island achieved its success not by adherence to laissez-faire principles, but through an approach featuring government "guidance" of the market mechanism and an interactive collaboration between government and business. Taiwan's developmental effort was characterized by indicative planning, targeting of strategic industries, government-launched flagship companies in key industries like semiconductors and steel, import protection, investment restrictions, export promotion, and rationing of preferential credit to key industries.[3]

If Taiwan's accomplishments are a source of discomfort for others, they have produced surprisingly little satisfaction among the Taiwanese themselves. The island's very growth has produced so many undesirable side effects that the developmental strategy which fostered it is no longer sustainable. These include environmental pollution so severe that it is producing social unrest; a growing scarcity of key resources, including, above all, that of skilled manpower; trade friction arising out of neomercantilist trade practices; financial instability manifested in wild

---

[2]See, in particular, Robert Wade, *Governing the Market* (Princeton: Princeton University Press, 1990); "Dirigism-Taiwan Style" in *IDS Bulletin* 15(2), (1984); "East Asian Financial Systems as a Challenge to Economics: Lessons from Taiwan," in *California Management Review* 27(4), (Summer, 1989). See also Walter Arnold, "Science and Technology Development in Taiwan and South Korea," *Asian Survey* (April 1988); Robert G. Sutter, *Taiwan: Entering the 21st Century* (1988).

[3]Wade (1990) p. 5.

gyrations of the stock market and bouts of speculation; an appreciating currency; and stagnating international competitiveness. Confronting the "Taiwan crisis," the island's leadership, convinced that a radical reorientation of national priorities is in order, has mapped out a long range industrial strategy designed to transform its economy from one based on light manufacturing and a few heavy industries into a high technology economy by the year 2000. This effort involves abandoning at least some of the tools which have played an important role in Taiwan's success, most notably trade protection. Important aspects of the new program include massive spending on infrastructural improvements, sweeping trade liberalization, internationalization of Taiwan's economy, and diversification of traditional trade relationships away from the United States, on the export side, and Japan, on the import side. These bold objectives are being pursued, however, at a time when the nation's political process is becoming more democratic and potentially volatile, raising the question whether the government will enjoy enough flexibility and autonomy from political pressures to implement its policies fully.

TRADE POLICY BACKGROUND

The Economic Context

Taiwan is perceived by its leaders to be in a state of crisis -- in effect, at an economic dead end after years of rapid development and concentration on heavy industry and export promotion.[4] Taiwanese officials frequently speak of the country's need to enter into a new "phase" similar to the past phases of import substitution, export promotion, and industrial expansion. Development has given rise to massive pollution and a wide range of other quality-of-life problems. The nation is experiencing "environmental riots" in opposition to new industrial expansion. Educated people are migrating in search of better living conditions. Heavy industry is running out of land for new facilities. Land prices have escalated dramatically, and labor is scarce, restive, and no longer cheap. The trade surplus with the United States is declining, a source of relief in policy terms but also a concern, since it underscores the eroding competitiveness of Taiwan's traditional export

---

[4]Interview with MOEA official. See also preamble to CEPD, *Perspective of the Taiwan Economy to the Year 2000*; comments by Vice President of China Institute of Economic Research in *Liaowang Overseas Edition* (July 17, 1989) (FBIS-CHI-89-144).

industries.[5] The solution to this tangle of problems is seen as a transformation of Taiwan's economy in a manner similar to that undertaken by Japan at the beginning of the 1970s. The country must abandon labor-intensive and pollution-intensive sectors or move them offshore, and shift into knowledge-intensive, high value-added, non-polluting industries, which lend themselves to automation. This change, however, gives rise to anxiety over the "hollowing out" of the economy.

The "Taiwan crisis" has an important financial component. The nation has accumulated massive foreign exchange reserves. The country's high savings rate (30 to 50 percent) coupled with a much lower investment rate (now about 20 percent) results in excessive liquidity. To make matters worse, the strengthening of the New Taiwan Dollar (NT$) against the dollar has caused a massive inflow of funds hitherto held in overseas deposits by Taiwanese businesses. Taiwan's relatively undeveloped financial sector has been unable to absorb this money. Because of the limited investment opportunities in Taiwan, there was an extraordinary influx of funds into the stock market, which caused wild gyrations in stock prices. In the late 1980s, the lure of "fast money" on the stock market attracted astounding numbers of small investors and drawing people away from industry and other productive endeavors. Then, between February and October 1990, the market collapsed -- falling by 80 percent, with average daily trading volume dropping by 89 percent.[6] Adding to these concerns, inflation, which had been virtually nonexistent for nearly a decade, was increasing significantly at the end of the 1980s. Part of the solution is seen as internationalization of the financial system, which, it is hoped, will open up investment opportunities and foster the growth of a mature financial services sector.

At the end of 1990, the government adopted a new Six-Year Plan for the economy which features massive outlays of $476 billion to upgrade the island's infrastructure with projects such as urban mass transit systems for five cities, coal-fired power generators, a fourth nuclear power plant, a north-south super-highway, five water reservoirs, 120,000 public housing units, a high speed rail link between Taipei and Kiaohsiung, and industrial development sites at 18 locations around the island. The plan is also designed to reduce the island's trade surplus; exports are to grow by 46 percent, but imports by 60 percent. Industrial pollution is to be cut

---

[5]Export competitiveness has been progressively declining since the second oil shock in 1981. OECD Working Party Report (1990) p. 24.

[6]The Economist Intelligence Unit, *Taiwan Country Profile, 1990-91*, cited in U.S. International Trade Commission, *Operation of the Trade Agreements* (42d Report, 1990) p. 137.

by 80 percent. The plan, although criticized as overly ambitious, too expensive and too reliant on government action, was nevertheless regarded as an important direct response to the "Taiwan crisis" itself.[7]

The Political Context

Taiwan's domestic and international political relations are still overshadowed by issues that remain unresolved since Chiang Kai-Shek and his Kuomintang Party (KMT) fled the mainland in 1949. The KMT imposed a harsh authoritarian role on the island, with martial law remaining in effect for thirty-eight years; native Taiwanese were excluded from most governmental KMT posts. Externally, Taiwan adopted a policy toward the Peoples' Republic of China (PRC) based on the "three nos" -- "no contact, no negotiation, no compromise." Taiwan's government prohibited any official contacts with the PRC, and based its international relations on its claim to be the true government of China. By the 1980s these rigid policies were producing growing domestic unrest, particularly among native Taiwanese, and had resulted in Taiwan's virtual diplomatic isolation, with only a few dozen countries (the most important of which were South Africa, South Korea, and Saudi Arabia) maintaining diplomatic relations.

Domestically, the authoritarian character of Taiwan's government began to change when Chiang's son Chiang Ching-Kuo became president in 1978 and began making major political concessions to the Taiwanese majority. Taiwanese were brought into the party, and by the mid-1980s native Taiwanese made up a majority of the KMT's membership. At the end of 1985, Chiang designated Lee Teng-hui, a Taiwanese KMT member, as his successor, and upon Chiang's death in 1988, Lee became Taiwan's first native-born president; he subsequently consolidated his position by assuming the acting chairmanship of the KMT. While avoiding a direct confrontation with the old guard KMT members, he elevated pragmatic, liberal technocrats to leadership positions, many of them with PhDs from foreign universities. Some (but not all) of these were Taiwanese; by 1990 about half of the ministerial posts in the Cabinet and over a third of the seats in the powerful KMT Central Committee were held by Taiwanese.

Under martial law opposition parties were banned. Nevertheless, in 1986, the government did not interfere when a loose group of political activists formed the Democratic Progressive Party (DPP). While the DPP

[7]U.S. Department of State Telegram, November 14, 1990, Taipei, Message Reference No. 7570, cited in USITC, *Trade Agreements Program* (1990) op.cit., p. 140; *Far Eastern Economic Review* (February 14, 1991).

was dominated by native Taiwanese, it also included mainlanders, and its principal unifying theme was not Taiwanese nationalism per se but opposition to one-party rule and demands for democratic reforms which would culminate in true majority rule. At present, as these issues come to the fore, the old cleavages between mainlanders and Taiwanese are declining in political significance.

The KMT has reacted to the rise of an organized opposition party by introducing democratic reform measures which have tended to preempt the DPP agenda, and by undertaking reform of the KMT itself. The "period of communist rebellion" was declared ended in May 1991, and the "temporary measures" pursuant to which the island had been governed since 1949 were revoked, removing the primary obstacle to constitutional government.[8] In 1991 the government abolished the sedition law, which had been an instrument of repression under martial law, and established a timetable to replace the senior legislators who had held office since the last elections on the Chinese mainland in the late 1940s with an elected National Assembly.[9] The "old guard" of the KMT is still powerful; it includes members of the army's high command, old mainland legislators, and key members of the KMT Central Committee. They are opposed by President Lee, who has sought to broaden the KMT's political base and transform the party into a center-right coalition analogous to Japan's LDP. A key faction of the KMT is a group of "young Turk" Taiwan-born legislators, who advocate legalization of relations with China and a fully elected Parliament.

The liberalization of Taiwan's domestic political system has been paralleled by a more pragmatic, subtle, and successful approach to the two-China issue in international diplomacy. Taiwan is now using its economic strength to reinforce its international political situation, and has placed Beijing on the defensive with so-called "flexible diplomacy," which accepts special relationships and arrangements with countries that also have diplomatic relations with the PRC. Taiwan has established trade offices in Canada, Britain and Australia that function essentially as consulates. Taiwan has set up an "External Economic Aid Fund" which has been used as a lever in achieving some substantial diplomatic gains.[10] France has established a U.S.-style "Institute" in Taiwan as Taiwan purchased French planes for its air force. These moves have

---

[8]*Far Eastern Economic Review* (May 9, 1991).

[9]*Far Eastern Economic Review* (April 11, May 30, 1991).

[10]*Ta King Pao* (February 3, 1989) (FBIS-CHI-89-024).

generated counterpressures by Beijing designed to thwart Taiwan's efforts to expand its relations. Beijing accuses Taiwan of using "silver bullets... to buy the hearts of the people and to develop diplomatic relations."[11] In December 1988, the PRC's Foreign Ministry issued a statement expressing "grave concern" over Taiwan's "elastic diplomacy."[12] In 1988, China sent a cable to Malaysia reminding it of its one-China policy after Malaysian Premier Aziz visited Taiwan.[13] Taiwan's massive expansion of investment in the Philippines has prompted actions by the Chinese Embassy in Manila to protest Taiwan's moves to enhance its official standing, particularly the draft Taiwan Relations Act. In 1987, the increasing number of Filipino officials visiting Taiwan prompted President Aquino to issue an executive order banning such visits and the return visits of their Taiwanese counterparts.[14] However, the balance began to tip in Taiwan's favor in the wake of the PRC's suppression of the Tiananmen Square protests. In 1990, for example, Canada and Australia -- major Beijing trading partners -- substantially upgraded their offices in Taipei, "a slap in the face for [the PRC] whose diplomatic protests are increasingly being ignored."[15]

Current Trade and Investment Regime

During the initial phases of its industrialization, Taiwan protected domestic industries with high tariffs and import licensing requirements, and exports were subsidized through a variety of fiscal incentives. Import restrictions are now being rapidly dismantled. The average nominal tariff rate was over 30 percent in the early 1980s; it had fallen to under 20 percent by 1987, with most of the cuts coming on manufactured products.[16] In July 1989, the government announced that between 1990 and 1992, the effective duty rate would be reduced from 5.7 percent to 3.5 percent, the average of the industrialized members of the OECD, and the

---

[11]*New York Times* (October 15, 1989).

[12]*Kyodo* (September 9, 1988).

[13]*Far Eastern Economic Review* (February 2, 1989).

[14]*Far Eastern Economic Review* (February 2, 1989).

[15]*Far Eastern Economic Review* (November 29, 1990).

[16]OECD, Working Party of the Trade Committee, *Trade Relations With Developing Countries* (confidential, March 2, 1990) (hereafter, "OECD Working Party Report.")

average nominal rate would be reduced to seven percent.[17] Principal sectors affected will be consumer products and some agricultural and capital goods. Upon GATT accession, 94 percent of Taiwan's tariff items will be bound at a maximum rate of 30 percent; the ceiling for the remaining 6 percent will not exceed 50 percent.[18] High tariffs remain on most agricultural products (up to 40 to 50 percent ad valorem on imports of processed foods and fresh fruit), plywood (up to 20 percent) and small passenger cars (40-42 percent).

Quantitative import restrictions based on prior approval procedures have been dramatically reduced in the 1980s; however, at the beginning of the 1990s a substantial number of import commodities remained subject to import licensing requirements by the Board of Foreign Trade (BOFT) or by licensing units authorized by BOFT (such as banks).[19] Pursuant to this mechanism, an importer must apply to a bank for a license to import an officially permissible item; the bank must check to see if it is on a so-called "secret list" issued by the Board of Foreign Trade, which consults the Industrial Development Bureau (IDB) of the Ministry of Economic Affairs. Although the procedure is rather murky, the importer is apparently asked to provide evidence that domestic suppliers cannot meet his terms on price, quality, service or delivery terms. While the prior approval mechanism applies to a relatively small proportion of Taiwan's import trade, it has been particularly important in affording a form of flexible protection to infant industries with large capital requirements -- notably petrochemicals, chemicals, steel, heavy machinery, machine tools, bearings and forklift trucks.[20] Most agricultural imports are subject to

---

[17]Taiwan lowered its average nominal tariff rate to 9.7 percent in 1989; however, scheduled reductions for 1990 failed to pass the Legislative Yuan. USITC, *Trade Agreements Program* (1990) op.cit., p. 141.

[18]Government of Taiwan, *Memorandum on Foreign Trade Regime of the Customs Territory of Taiwan, Penghu, Kinmen and Matsu* (January 1, 1990) (hereafter, *GATT Memorandum)* p. 16. In addition to tariffs, Taiwan applies special levies to certain grain imports.

[19]These items included auto parts (such as radial car tires), stainless steel cutlery, and food products such as whole ducks, cattle fish, unbaked coffee, apples, citrus fruits, octopus, and savory.

[20]Wade (1990) pp. 128-35; *Metal Bulletin* (September 28, 1982); unclassified Department of Commerce Cable No. R-2181352 (July 1983, Taipei); Josephine Wang, "A General Overview of Import Regulation (Taiwan)" in *East Asian Executive Reports* (May 1986).

prior approval requirements; in other cases, in order to obtain a license, other regulatory approvals must first be secured (cosmetics, medical equipment). Importation of some products is banned altogether.[21]

Taiwan controls foreign investment in its economy pursuant to the *Statute for Investment by Foreign Nationals.* Foreign investment is channeled into areas that enhance the skill and technology-intensity of production.[22] Foreign investment which supports this objective (such as investment in high technology and capital-intensive industries) is actively encouraged with tax holidays, tariff exemptions, accelerated depreciation, preferential financing, and a variety of other incentives. Conversely, foreign investment in over 50 types of businesses is prohibited altogether, including the acquisition of most types of agricultural land and investment in refining of gasoline and diesel fuel; electric power and other utilities; home construction; most forms of transportation; real estate brokerage; telecommunications; and radio and TV broadcasting. Investment in a large number of other industries is subject to approval by government authorities.[23] The government has in the past decade reportedly conditioned its approval of some types of foreign investment on a commitment by the investor to export a designated percentage of its output.[24] The rationale offered for these continuing constraints on investment is that Taiwan's limited land area and resources require regulation of the types of investment that will occur.

Two government organizations, the Industrial Development and Investment Center and the Joint Industrial Investment Service Center, attract desired foreign investments, while a separate organization, the Investment Commission, reviews proposed investments in Taiwan by foreigners.[25] The Commission is subordinated to the Ministry of

---

[21]These include peanuts, rice, small red beans, and animal offal. U.S. Department of State Telegram (Nov. 6, 1990), Taipei Message Reference No. 7347, cited in USITC, *Trade Agreements Program* (1990) op.cit., p. 141.

[22]OECD Working Party Report (1990) p. 24.

[23]These include coal mining, petroleum extraction, pharmaceuticals, banking, securities, insurance, audio tapes and records, and the manufacture of some types of telecommunications equipment. Industrial Development and Investment Center, *Negative List for Investment by Overseas Chinese and Foreign Nationals* (October 1989).

[24]Wade (1990), p. 155.

[25]Wade (1990), p. 205.

Economic Affairs (MOEA) but staffed by representatives of all government agencies concerned with foreign investment in Taiwan.[26] This group functions, in effect, like the Committee on Foreign Investment in the United States (CFIUS), but with more teeth -- it has the authority to deny an investment application. It reviews about 40 applications in a biweekly meeting; most are approved. There are no fixed criteria for which investments will or will not be approved. Rather, the group's decisions tend to reflect the government's current thinking and priorities; for example, it is unlikely that applications for investments in heavily-polluting industries will be approved at present or in the future.[27]

TRADE POLICY DETERMINANTS

Institutional Actors

Taiwan's ultimate trade policy decisions have traditionally been the province of the "economic cabinet," which consists of the Ministers of Economic Affairs, Finance, and Foreign Affairs, the Chairman of the Council for Economic Planning and Development (CEPD) and the Governor of the Central Bank of China.[28] The decision-making process is becoming more diffused, however, as other actors, such as the private sector and the Legislative Yuan, gain a greater voice. The Council of Agriculture exercises a virtual veto over trade measures that might adversely affect certain farm sectors. The role of the key ministries in the process is summarized below.

The President. Teng-hui Lee is a proponent of trade liberalization and privatization in the domestic economy. His key ministers in the economic sphere share this philosophy. While the president does not normally involve himself in day-to-day economic decisions, he has demonstrated the ability and willingness to remove those people who he believes are

---

[26]Bodies represented include the Finance Ministry, the Central Bank, the Environmental Protection Agency and the Ministry of Transport. Interview with a MOEA deputy director general.

[27]Interview with MOEA official; Industrial Development and Investment Center, (1990); *IDIC Stands for Services to Investors in Taiwan, Republic of China* (October 1989).

[28]Interview with an American academic specializing in Taiwanese economic policy (1989).

slowing down the liberalization process.[29] As long as Lee remains in office, Taiwan is unlikely to depart from its current program of liberalization, internationalization, and diversification.[30]

The Board of Foreign Trade (BOFT). While BOFT is only a subordinate division of the MOEA, its influence on trade policy formation is acknowledged throughout the government. It is commonly understood that "[T]he Director General of BOFT makes the real decisions on trade."[31] As a result, the Minister of Economic Affairs himself has very little to do or say about foreign trade policy.[32] The principal reason for BOFT's influence is the fact that Taiwan's expertise on the minutiae of trade and international legal matters is heavily concentrated in the ranks of BOFT staff. Most other ministries lack the staff and expertise to challenge BOFT on substantive grounds, although they may do so on the basis of political or industrial development concerns.

Bureaucratically, the BOFT has defused and weakened opposition to its free-trade oriented policies. Its principal opponents are the Council of Agriculture, which seeks to protect the farm sector, and, to a lesser degree, the Industrial Development Bureau of the MOEA, which sometimes seeks to protect strategic sectors. BOFT staff chairs 7 or 8 interagency working groups on issues like services, intellectual property, investment, agriculture, and customs duties, which are attended by staff from the Ministries of Finance, Foreign Affairs, Transportation, Interior, the Council for Agriculture, and other concerned agencies. The BOFT uses these meetings to educate the other ministries on trade issues and to air

---

[29]One example of the changing balance is the opening up of airline competition. The state-owned China Airlines, together with its allies in the air force, opposed the sale of routes to Evergreen Airlines. President Lee interceded on behalf of Evergreen to ensure a more competitive pattern of service (although the Chairman of Evergreen was a friend of the President, and the action led to charges of favoritism). Interview with an American academic specializing in Taiwanese politics.

[30]Interview with an American academic specializing in Taiwanese politics (1990).

[31]Interview with a senior CEPD official (1990) Wade (1990) suggests that the Industrial Development Bureau (IDB) instructs BOFT on matters such as import protection for strategic industries. This may have been the case in the period studied by Wade (1970s and early 1980s) but at present BOFT appears capable of holding its own with the IDB in disputes over import policy.

[32]Interview (1990).

potential objections and opposition. The BOFT staff has used Taiwan's GATT application as a lever with these agencies; it used informal interagency working groups to discuss the implications of GATT accession. At these sessions BOFT staff asked each other agency to engage in "self-criticism," identifying those aspects of its policies which were inconsistent with GATT principles. As this educational process unfolded, BOFT staff noted that a perceptible softening of the other agencies' positions on trade protection occurred.[33]

Although BOFT plays an extremely important role in the trade policy formation process, its relative influence appears to be eroding somewhat. With liberalization, the policy instruments that it once wielded--such as control over import licenses--are disappearing. The progressive democratization of Taiwanese society ultimately acts as a check on BOFT policy decisions which could provoke a public backlash; that fact has enabled the Council of Agriculture, for example, to forestall the rapid liberalization of the farm sector favored by BOFT.

Industrial Development Bureau. The IDB, like BOFT, is an arm of MOEA; it is charged with implementing sectoral development plans and has also acquired a variety of routine regulatory functions which, it is sometimes observed, impede its efforts at industrial promotion. The IDB may prescribe a variety of incentives to promote sectors regarded as national priorities; these include support for research and development, subsidies and fiscal incentives, and trade protection. It screens applications for loans from government and parastatal credit funds, organizes export cartels, and exercises a degree of "administrative guidance" over industry to effect the government's promotional plans.[34] As the government's principal institutional advocate of protectionist actions to support local manufacturers, the IDB is periodically embroiled in policy disputes with BOFT.

Council for Economic Planning and Development (CEPD). CEPD until recently was an advisory body to the cabinet engaged in economic planning; it gained ministerial status in 1987. Numerous Taiwanese

---

[33]Interview with an MOEA deputy director (1990). Significantly, despite its important role, BOFT staff morale appears to be low. The workload has increased as Taiwan's trade has expanded, and the pay has not kept pace. Turnover has been high, with many staff members seeking positions in the Securities and Exchange Commission, seen as a stepping stone to a lucrative position in the private financial sector.

[34]Wade (1990), pp. 201-208, describes the IDB in considerable detail.

officials and U.S. observers compare CEPD's functions with those of the Office of the U.S. Trade Representative (USTR), an analogy which is correct only to a degree. Both organizations play an interagency coordinating role on behalf of the President/Prime Minister. Both have clashed periodically with the cabinet department charged with responsibility for industry (Commerce in the United States and MOEA in Taiwan), reflecting jurisdictional ambiguity. However, important differences exist between CEPD and USTR. CEPD chairs interagency policy deliberations involving all economic issues, not just trade, so its coordinating role is broader than that of USTR. In contrast to USTR, CEPD conducts long range planning for Taiwan's economy, drawing up One-, Four-, and Fifteen-Year Plans that sketch out general directions in which the economy is expected to move. These plans are generally indicative rather than normative, but CEPD can employ a variety of policy tools not available to USTR to encourage results which are consistent with the plans' forecasts. Finally, CEPD has no trade negotiating role comparable to that of USTR, and generally defers to BOFT on trade matters that do not involve significant interagency conflicts.[35] On the other hand, CEPD has been quite active in developing coherent Taiwanese policies and strategies to deal with specific trade problems that affect fundamental national interests (such as relations with the United States and relations with the European Community).

An example of the CEPD's coordinating role on trade matters is the so-called "small committee" or task force on U.S. relations, which is called the Sino-American Committee in press accounts. This ad hoc interagency body was set up by CEPD in the mid-1980s at the request of the Cabinet as U.S. trade pressure on Taiwan was increasing; its purpose was to engage the relevant ministries in discussions about an appropriate response. The Vice-Chairman of CEPD chairs the small committee, which meets infrequently, usually when serious problems are looming with the United States. In March 1989, when the United States considered action against Taiwan under Super 301, the small committee developed the "Detailed Action Plan for Strengthening Economic and Trade Ties with the United States," setting forth a sweeping set of liberalization and economic restructuring measures as well as providing for increased procurement from the United States.

---

[35]CEPD has virtually no staff dealing specifically with trade issues, although its Economics Research Department performs staff functions with respect to trade when necessary. CEPD also borrows staff from BOFT and the Finance Ministry as needed.

The Private Sector and the China External Trade Development Council (CETRA). Taiwan's political economy has traditionally been dominated by the KMT and the bureaucracy and has been characterized by a rather adversarial relationship between the government and the private sector.[36] Under Teng-hui Lee this relationship is changing, and the activities of Taiwan's private sector are coming to play an increasingly important role in driving the country's trade policy. While the government does set broad goals for the economy (and offers incentives toward those goals), the private sector, to a degree, develops its own trade policy and ultimately pulls the government along. Taiwan's businessmen roam the world looking for new markets and trade opportunities, constantly testing the limits of the government's controls; generally, they will do or attempt anything that is not explicitly prohibited by the government. Thus, the private sector has led the way in opening up market opportunities in Eastern Europe and is aggressively pursuing investment opportunities in the PRC. As a general matter, the private sector takes the lead in developing new relations with the more advanced countries; the government takes the lead with respect to poorer countries.[37]

The government is rapidly acceding to the business community's role as initiator of new trade opportunities and has partially institutionalized role in trade policy formulation in the unique public-private China External Trade Development Council (CETRA), which is helping to bridge the traditional gap between the government and the private sector. CETRA is a government entity in the Ministry of Economic Affairs (MOEA), but its capitalization is provided 50 percent by the private sector and 50 percent by the government. All of its operating funds are furnished by the private sector, so that its officials recognize that they "work for the businessman, not the government."[38] It is a point of pride for CETRA officials that they maintain constant daily contact with the business community and understand its actual needs.[39]

---

[36]Walter Arnold, "Science and Technology Development in Taiwan and South Korea," *Asian Survey* (April, 1988).

[37]Interview with a senior MOFA official, March 1990.

[38]CETRA's board of directors has 33 members; of these, only 5 are government officials appointed by the Prime Minister, the rest being leaders of various key Taiwanese industries, which make large financial contributions to support CETRA's activities.

[39]Interview with a senior CETRA official, March 1990.

Much of CETRA's staff and budget is devoted to trade promotion activities: organization of trade shows and fairs, provision of information to potential importers and exporters, trade missions to potential markets, and various activities designed to showcase Taiwanese products.[40] However, it also plays an important and growing role as the spokesman for Taiwan's business community in the trade policy deliberations of the government. In so doing, it is helping to offset a longstanding weakness of Taiwanese industrial policy formation: the relative absence of a close industry-government working relationship and consultative process.[41] To be sure, while individual industry associations may go directly to BOFT and MOEA to raise their particular concerns, these groups often do not adequately represent their industries,[42] and CETRA "always has a better line into the government."[43] CETRA is always consulted when the MOEA submits a trade policy proposal to the Prime Minister for Cabinet review because it is responsible for promoting export and import trade; and unlike MOEA, it is in extremely close contact with the business community and can "speak with authority about the actual difficulties which businessmen face."[44] CETRA's views are also important in

---

[40]CETRA, *CETRA Trade Promotion Activities 1989-90* (1990); *Taiwan Products* (August 1989).

[41]Arnold (1989).

[42]Taiwan has over 150 trade associations, and the leaders of many of these associations are members of the Legislative Yuan. However, "one would be quite mistaken to perceive these trade associations as functional equivalents of interest groups in liberal-democratic settings because they are controlled by the ruling party ... which normally staffs the secretariat of these trade associations." Their function is primarily one of information dissemination and policy implementation. Arnold (1989) p. 212.

[43]Several of Taiwan's sectoral trade associations are influential in the formulation and implementation of trade policy. The Textile Federation, for example, administers the country's system of textile export quotas and staffs the government's textile negotiating teams. Similarly the government relies heavily on the views of the Machine Tool Association in managing that industry's program of export restraint. On the other hand, while Taiwan's auto makers have good connections in the Legislative Yuan, their association, the Taiwan Transport Vehicle Manufacturers' Association, has largely been excluded from government liberalization over economic policies affecting the auto industry. Arnold (1989) p. 206.

[44]Interviews with officials at CETRA, CEPD, and MOFA, March 1990.

determining which strategic industries should be the focus of the government's promotional measures.[45]

The Council of Agriculture (COA). The COA has jurisdiction over Taiwan's policies affecting crops, livestock, forestry and fishing, it has overseen the development of the farm sector through a series of long term plans. Its officials are generally from farming backgrounds themselves and see the Council's role as representing farmers' interests. While acknowledging that Taiwan has obligations to the world trading community, their basic orientation is protectionist.[46]

Although BOFT chairs trade delegations when agricultural issues are discussed, COA makes most of the final decisions on quota and tariff issues except when an unusually controversial issue is presented (usually as a result of U.S. pressure.) Those issues are referred to CEPD for resolution, usually to the Sino-American "small group." COA consults the Finance Ministry on tariff changes and MOEA on quota issues, but "the Council makes much of the [final] decision." Decision-making at COA involves the Chairman and a special committee of the six department heads; arbitrary actions by the Chairman without the consensus of this committee are rare.[47]

In trade policy matters that affect agriculture, COA generally does not oppose liberalization outright, but seeks to delay it.[48] Its principal bureaucratic opponent is BOFT, although most of the other key ministries and entities (Foreign Affairs, Finance, CEPD, CETRA) are usually in sympathy with BOFT's position. Despite this alignment, COA's positions frequently prevail because of the government's sensitivity to the political implications of liberalization. Taiwanese farmers have demonstrated and rioted on several occasions in reaction to liberalization measures; such actions, inconsequential by U.S. standards, have profoundly upset

[45]Interview with an American academic.

[46]Interview with a senior CEPD official, March 1990.

[47]Interviews with two senior Council of Agriculture officials, March 1990.

[48]COA officials insist that the council does not have too much basic disagreement with BOFT. "We recognize that liberalization is a must. The question is the time span." BOFT officials tend to corroborate this perspective; they indicate that in private, COA officials concede the correctness of the BOFT market-oriented, pro-liberalization philosophy, but argue that political factors limit their ability to implement such policies abruptly. Interviews with MOEA and Council of Agriculture officials.

Taiwan's leadership. In addition, there is a concern that if liberalization is pushed too far too fast, the Legislative Yuan could rebel and attempt to block the government's trade program.[49]

Ministry of Finance. The Finance Ministry has jurisdiction over several of the tools which other ministries need to wield in order to implement trade and industrial policy including tariffs, the tax code, the national development bank, and the Executive Yuan Development Fund. Its position toward trade in manufactured goods is generally free trade oriented and non-interventionist. Thus, it consults with BOFT on proposed tariff cuts but generally does not oppose them; conversely, it is in a position to thwart, or at least force modification of, various initiatives of the Industrial Development Bureau of MOEA which are seen as too interventionist and industry specific. MOFA's position, for example, has forced MOEA to accede to major revisions in the Statute for Encouragement of Investment. MOFA is more conservative, however, with respect to liberalization of the financial sector.

Ministry of Foreign Affairs (MOFA). Because trade plays an important role in Taiwan's diplomacy, MOFA takes an unusually close interest in trade matters; there is a "marriage of convenience between foreign and economic policies." It is particularly sensitive to the international political implications of trade issues; in matters involving the United States, for example, it seeks to contain U.S. protectionism; it supports "buy-American" missions, is sensitive to U.S. concerns on counterfeiting and intellectual property rights, and seeks to differentiate Taiwan from Japan in U.S. perceptions.[50] A number of MOFA officials supported trade liberalization long before it became the official policy.[51]

MOFA is in the process of establishing its own economic department. The purpose of this new department will be to maintain liaison with other ministries on trade and economic matters and to ensure that MOFA is fully advised on such issues, given the close linkage between Taiwan's

---

[49]COA's bureaucratic position will be strengthened soon when an administrative reorganization consolidates some new functions under its jurisdiction; the Council will become a Ministry, although that fact in and of itself is not regarded as particularly significant. Jurisdiction over farmers' organizations will be transferred from the Ministry of the Interior to the new Ministry, and as noted, COA has ambitious plans to build a politically active national farm organization.

[50]Interview with a U.S. official familiar with the issue.

[51]Interview with a senior MOFA official.

diplomacy and trade.[52] Other ministries do not appear to regard this development as a jurisdictional threat.[53]

The Legislative Yuan and the Political Parties. As Taiwan's democratization continues, the role of the Legislative Yuan in trade matters is becoming more important. The Executive can no longer conduct trade policy with a completely free hand. Its major trade policy decisions and actions are subject to oversight and approval by the legislature.

However, while virtually all observers agree that the Legislative Yuan's trade role is becoming more important, its significance is still more prospective than actual. Because of the nature of the Yuan's committee structure, no powerful trade committees have emerged comparable to the House Ways and Means and the Senate Finance Committees.[54] The Yuan's trade committees are starting to develop trade staffs, but the staffs thus far do not have expertise comparable to that of the trade staffs in the U.S. Congress. Most of the Yuan's energy thus far has been absorbed by debates over basic political issues, such as democratization.

Trade is not yet a party issue in Taiwan. The opposition DPP styles itself as a populist party, and its constituents are drawn from groups which are potentially adversely affected by trade liberalization -- farmers, blue collar workers and small businessmen. Some DPP politicians have taken stands on particular economic issues; for example, the mayor of Kiaoshiung, a DPP member, led the fight against Formosa Plastics' proposal to locate a new naphtha cracker in his city. However, DPP expertise in trade matters is minimal at present. "Trade is a very technical thing, and they don't know much about it yet."[55] Its contacts with BOFT to date, for example, have been largely limited to information

[52]Interviews with a senior MOFA official and a senior official from the North American Affairs department of BOFT.

[53]Interview with a senior MOEA official.

[54]The Yuan's committees have no seniority system. Junior members can and do serve as chairmen of committees; there is no stability among the committee membership, which is characterized by constant turnover. This works against the evolution of powerful, expert committees willing and able to become involved in the complexities of international trade.

[55]Interview with a senior official of the Third Department of MOEA.

gathering; the DPP "doesn't have a view on trade yet, they are just following developments."[56]

Similarly, the "KMT never gets involved in trade matters," although KMT politicians occasionally criticize the government for being too soft in responding to U.S. demands.[57] The Party's obsession with the retention of political power has "led to benign 'political' neglect of the operational aspects of industrial policy."[58] The KMT's operational arm exists to win elections and dispense patronage, rather than to formulate policy. People are chosen from the KMT to serve in the Executive Yuan, but policy is determined in relation to their government positions rather than their party role. The party platform only sets forth certain broad economic policy guidelines (for example, liberalization, improvement of the investment environment, intelligent use of foreign exchange reserves, reduction of the export surplus), and the party platform itself has little significance for purposes of actual policy formation.[59]

Trade's current status as a non-partisan issue is almost certain to change in the next decade. Trade issues have given rise to outbursts of popular anger, such as the recent "turkey parts" riot (sparked by a decision to liberalize imports of U.S. turkey parts), which have clearly upset the current leadership. The course on which Taiwan is now embarked -- liberalization and internationalization -- will inevitably force adjustment on many areas of Taiwanese society, particularly small businesses and farmers, which will generate a degree of unrest. In a democratic society (which Taiwan is becoming) such conflicts are eventually channeled into the political arena and become partisan issues. At present both the KMT and the DPP criticize the government for trade concessions,[60] and it is not unlikely that the Legislative Yuan, like the U.S. Congress, will be characterized by advocates of a more assertive economic nationalism in both political parties.

Labor Unions. Labor unions have been increasingly effective in securing wage concessions, but they do not wield much political power in Taiwan. In contrast to Korea, there is little union militancy. Many of

---

[56]Interview with a senior official of the Third Department of MOEA.

[57]Interview with a senior CEPD official.

[58]Arnold (1989) pp. 181-82.

[59]Interview with a senior CEPD official.

[60]Interview with a senior MOFA official.

the unions are "company unions" which are partially co-opted by company management. The principal issues for most unions are wages, the size of year-end bonuses and working conditions, not trade or trade-related issues.[61] Labor's clout is growing; Taiwanese leaders are concerned that labor's wage demands are becoming "unreasonable" -- that is, that wages are going up faster than increases in productivity.[62] Management's basic strategy -- to move manufacturing offshore and automate onshore production -- might be expected to increase disaffection among workers. However, Taiwan's labor shortage and extraordinarily low unemployment rate suggest that workers displaced by these changes can be rapidly reabsorbed by the economy, minimizing the prospect for widespread discontent over the impact of industrial restructuring on the blue-collar work force, a concern in Korea, where rising unemployment is feared.

The Process in Action

Most trade-policy initiatives originate at the Board of Foreign Trade (BOFT). The BOFT is currently divided into six departments (themselves segmented into sections) with responsibility delegated according to geographic areas and particular functions. A seventh department will soon be created when a section in the Third Department dealing with multilateral organizations is upgraded to department status.[63]

Most ideas for new trade policy initiatives are generated by the section chiefs within each BOFT department. The section chiefs meet with their departmental deputy directors to brainstorm about their ideas, and ultimately, to generate departmental proposals. At this phase the BOFT staff also informally consult other Ministries and, where appropriate, the Council of Agriculture, to ascertain the existence and extent of potential opposition to the proposal. If an issue is regarded as particularly significant, a "green paper" on the issue is circulated within the government and to scholars and businessmen for comment and revision

---

[61]The wave of strikes before the February 1989 Lunar New Year, for example, centered around labor demands for huge year-end bonuses, sometimes more than their annual salaries.

[62]Interview with a senior official of the Central Bank of China.

[63]The BOFT Departments are: (1) Imports; (2) Exports; (3) North America, Western Europe and multilateral organizations; (4) Developing countries, Eastern Europe, Soviet Union, and trade promotion; (5) Supervision of traders (to avoid damage to Taiwan's reputation through counterfeiting and other practices) and dispute settlement; and (6) Relations with the PRC.

based on those comments.[64] The proposal is ultimately submitted to the Director General of BOFT for review and adoption, and then to the Minister of Economic Affairs for adoption by the Ministry; as a practical matter the Minister usually defers to BOFT's expertise and signs off on the proposal.[65]

Conflicts within the Ministry of Economic Affairs are fairly common between BOFT and the Industrial Development Bureau (IDB) which has responsibility for promoting industrial development. The IDB frequently is reluctant to accede to a completely open trade regime, particularly with respect to infant industries and traditional key industries undergoing structural adjustment.[66] With respect to "small spats," BOFT and the IDB are encouraged to work out their differences through "exchanges of views" at the Deputy Director General level; big conflicts, which are rare, must be arbitrated by the Vice Minister of MOEA. Typically these disputes are resolved by allowing some residual protection for specific industries, but with IDB directed to establish a timetable for liberalization. Such intra-ministerial disputes are expected to become less frequent as the number of protected sectors shrinks; the IDB will increasingly use fiscal incentives rather than border measures to foster key industries.[67]

A trade policy proposal adopted by the Ministry of Economic Affairs is submitted to an interagency review process chaired by CEPD for discussion.[68] The relevant affected Ministries are asked to make their

---

[64]With respect to proposals for tariff cuts, an *ad hoc* committee consisting of representatives from BOFT, the Industrial Development Bureau of MOEA, the Council of Agriculture and the Ministry of Finance reviews all proposals. Initially BOFT proposes a list of tariff cuts which it circulates to these other bodies; after some haggling among the various ministry staffs, a consensus list is drawn up and sent up the decisional chain within the MOEA for final approval by the Minister. This process tends to head off inter- and intra-ministerial conflicts at higher levels in the decision-making process.

[65]Interviews with three senior MOEA officials.

[66]Interviews with two MOEA officials.

[67]Interview with a senior MOEA official.

[68]The international council chaired by CEPD meets every Wednesday.

views known.[69] CETRA is also asked to give its views on the proposal from the standpoint of the business community.[70] Most interministerial disputes are worked out at this stage, with the CEPD serving as a mediator. When the CEPD inter-ministerial council reaches its conclusions, they are reported to the Prime Minister, who refers them to his weekly Cabinet meeting. Usually if a trade policy proposal is supported by CEPD and the Ministry of Economic Affairs, it is adopted by the cabinet. Particularly important issues must be referred to the Legislative Yuan for consideration and in some cases, adoption of enabling legislation.[71]

Taiwan's trade goals are set in conjunction with short (1-year) medium (4-year) and long term (15-year) plans for the economy drafted by the (CEPD) in consultation with government ministries, the private sector, and the academic community.[72] The plans are loose guidelines rather than rigid prescriptions and often "do not match reality," but they do give an indication of government priorities and goals.[73] The plans always have a trade component, reflecting the government's view that trade policy is an aspect of broader industrial policy. While Taiwan's trade objectives are not always spelled out in their entirety in the plans, the plans do offer a good indication of the broad direction of government thinking.

---

[69]On trade issues, the relevant ministries may vary somewhat. For example, on tariff issues the views of the Ministry of Finance are particularly important; on telecommunications issues, the Ministry of Communications is important; on intellectual property issues, the Ministry of the Interior is the key ministry, and so on. Interview with a senior CEPD official.

[70]Interview with a senior CETRA official.

[71]Interviews with officials at MOEA (Third Department), CETRA, and CEPD.

[72]The long-term plan for the years 1986-2000, adopted in 1986, is summarized in CEPD's *Perspective of the Taiwan Economy to the Year 2000*. The tenth 4-year plan will begin in 1990-93.

[73]For example, Taiwan experienced 7 percent economic growth in 1989 -- "we didn't plan for that, our target was much lower." Interview with a senior MOFA official.

TRADE-RELATED OBJECTIVES

Taiwan's specific trade-related objectives in the 1990s are designed to further a broader economic goal: to make a qualitative leap from an economy based on medium-technology light industries, and, to a lesser degree, on traditional heavy industries, to one based on high technology, high value added, non-polluting industries and services, enabling Taiwan to enter the ranks of the advanced countries by the year 2000. Trade-related objectives that will be pursued in connection with this basic goal are as follows:[74]

- *Liberalization.* Most trade and investment restrictions will be removed to the extent that this is politically feasible and not inconsistent with basic concerns such as national security, financial stability and prevention of further deterioration of the environment.
- *Internationalization.* Taiwan's economy will be more fully integrated into the world economy through liberalization of the financial system and membership in international economic organizations (particularly the GATT). The government will foster the development of Taiwanese multinationals and encourage overseas investment by Taiwanese firms through a variety of policy measures.[75]
- *Diversification.* Taiwan will seek to diversify its export trade away from the United States toward the European Community, Japan, and newly developing markets in Southeast Asia, Eastern Europe, the Soviet Union, and ultimately the PRC. It will seek to diversify import trade away from Japan toward the United States and the European Community.

---

[74]Interviews with senior MOEA, MOFA, and CEPD officials; CEPD, *Perspective of the Taiwan Economy* and CEPD, *Highlights of the 1989 Economic Development Plan for Taiwan, Republic of China* (December 1988).

[75]The government will: (a) provide for investment loss reserves up to 15 percent of overseas investment under the draft *Statute for Upgrading Industries*; (b) establish overseas industrial parks, trade centers, and take other infrastructural support measures for Taiwanese businesses investing overseas; and (c) deploy Taiwan's foreign exchange reserves into Taiwanese branch banks in overseas markets to provide a source of capital for Taiwanese firms investing in those markets. Interview with a senior Central Bank of China official; *Lee and Li Bulletin* (March 1990).

- *Continued Expansion.* Expansion of both exports and imports will be pursued to support the increases in Taiwan's technology level and standard of living which are sought by its leadership. Domestic demand rather than export growth, however, is seen as the primary source of economic growth.[76]

Taiwan's broader national objectives -- both in and out of the economic sphere -- are at least partially contradictory, a fact which will impede complete attainment of the country's trade-related goals. For example, the country is embarked on a course of rapid democratization, characterized by an increase in the influence of the Legislative Yuan and the formation of independent opposition parties. This process will strengthen the hand of protectionist elements in Taiwanese society and increasingly hamper the ability of government planners to implement smoothly the liberalization policies which it has embraced as a fundamental economic objective. Similarly, the internationalization of Taiwan's trade regime, and particularly the adoption of GATT MFN principles, will hamper the government's ability to diversify its trade; most importantly, Taiwan will be increasingly unable to discriminate against imports from Japan and in favor of those from the United States, at the very time when it is seeking to increase U.S. imports and contain imports from Japan. Finally, the government places considerable importance on maintaining a higher degree of economic, social, and political stability -- "social harmony" -- than do most western democracies, the financial instability which has followed the loosening of exchange controls and the newfound militancy of the farmers in the face of trade liberalization have alarmed the government; further indicators that the opening of the economy is throwing the country into turmoil may cause the government to moderate or defer its current goals.[77]

TRADE STRATEGIES

Overhaul of the Trade Regime

At the heart of Taiwan's efforts to meet its trade-related objectives in the 1990s is its efforts to liberalize its trade regime by both opening the economy to a larger volume of imports and reducing export subsidies,

---

[76]CEPD, *Perspective of the Taiwan Economy,* Part III.B.2.(a).

[77]Interview with a senior Central Bank of China official.

while shifting the burden of import-relief to GATT-compatible trade remedies. Taiwan plans to "eliminate in principle all prior licensing requirements," with limited exceptions for reasons of "national security, public order, cultural, educational, public health considerations and environmental protection." Under a new system to be established, Taiwan will maintain "negative lists" for three types of products: (a) prohibited products, such as drugs and hazardous chemicals; (b) products subject to import permits, which include agricultural and medicines; and (c) products with no permit requirements, but which must comply with certain stipulated conditions. Products not listed on the negative lists will be freely importable.[78] Imports of some agricultural products, such as rice, are banned altogether, and this is unlikely to change in the coming decade.[79]

Taiwan has had an antidumping and countervailing duty regulation since 1984, and is planning to establish a "trade investigation committee" to administer these regulations.[80] Nevertheless, the government "takes a very cautious attitude" toward the application of these remedies in light of Taiwan's export dependency. Despite periodic outcries from domestic firms over dumping, the government has never imposed antidumping or countervailing duties against any foreign company. That pattern is unlikely to change very much, if at all, in the 1990s.[81]

The government is currently drafting legislation which would provide import relief pursuant to GATT Article XIX (the escape clause). The same legislation provides that BOFT can impose import restrictions or controls on foreign imports when its exports are subject to unfair or illicit foreign trade practices, a remedy comparable to Section 301 of the U.S. Trade Act of 1974.[82] There is no precedent for Taiwan's use of such measures, and it is difficult to predict the extent to which these remedies, once enacted, may be used; however the import relief provision may well be invoked by domestic industries adversely affected by the current liberalization program. The government would probably augment import relief -- implemented in a GATT-compatible manner -- with a variety of financial support measures to facilitate restructuring.

---

[78]*GATT Memorandum*, pp. 119-20.

[79]Interview with a Council of Agriculture deputy director.

[80]CEPD *Highlights of the 1989 Economic Development Plan*, Part III.2.(a).

[81]BOFT, *The Trade Policy of the Republic of China - Taiwan* (mimeo, 1990).

[82]*GATT Memorandum*, p. 21.

Despite Taiwan's current policy of liberalizing trade and investment, the government is unlikely to surrender this ability to act as a gatekeeper to foreign investment. The limitations imposed by space, shortages of labor, and environmental problems will make even a very liberal government very reluctant to allow completely unregulated investment; the government clearly wants foreign investment, but of the right kind. Financial services firms that may pump additional liquidity into the securities markets are not seen as needed; nor are new petrochemical complexes or steel mills. Political factors will preclude opening up investment in agriculture, and national security concerns will prevent the government from allowing foreign investment in sectors with defense implications, such as telecommunications, electrical utilities, railroads, and defense production.

One of Taiwan's most pervasive sources of trade friction has been the misappropriation of foreign intellectual property by Taiwanese enterprises. While this problem will not disappear in the 1990s, it will decline in severity and scope. Many counterfeit operations are moving to Thailand, the PRC, and elsewhere in Asia to escape the strengthening NT$ and increased government enforcement. Anti-counterfeit investigators in Taiwan who cooperate with local authorities in breaking up counterfeiting operations say that "we are gradually putting ourselves out of business." The political climate is also gradually turning against counterfeiting -- consumer groups oppose counterfeiting despite the lower resulting prices because the practice deceives consumers. Numerous trade and industrial associations have taken positions in favor of stronger intellectual property protection. Perhaps most importantly, there is a recognition by Taiwan's economic leaders that it will be difficult for the country to attract the technology it needs to become a high-technology economy if it cannot provide adequate protection for foreign technology.

Taiwan and the GATT

On January 1, 1990, Taiwan formally applied to join the GATT;[83] pursuit of GATT membership is currently Taiwan's number one multilateral priority and is central to Taiwan's overall trade strategy. One local U.S. businessman commented that "they will do almost anything to

---

[83]*GATT Memorandum.*

get into the GATT -- they've put their 'face' on the line for this."[84] In January 1990 the PRC "solemnly requested" the GATT not to accept Taiwan's application.[85]

Taiwan's decision to seek GATT membership represents the culmination of a three-year process of internal deliberation and consensus building within the government, with BOFT the principal advocate of accession. Its principal arguments emphasized the role GATT institutions could play in enhancing and sustaining Taiwan's access to foreign markets. As a GATT non-member, Taiwan does not benefit from GATT-bound tariffs in many countries; this would change with accession -- "98 doors would be opened to us simultaneously."[86] Similarly, Taiwanese exports have frequently been subject to unilateral restrictions; outside of GATT "there is no official channel through which to complain" and GATT is seen as affording some protection against such measures.[87] Finally, the government views the trend toward regional trading blocs, particularly in Europe, as an extremely dangerous development, and the GATT, particularly the most-favored nation provisions of the GATT, are perceived as a partial counter to this trend.[88]

Taiwanese officials place great emphasis on their view that the current GATT application is "legally correct."[89] Taiwan's application for

---

[84]Interview with an official at the U.S. Chamber of Commerce in Taiwan. Currently Taiwan maintains a liaison with the GATT Uruguay Round negotiations by monitoring U.S. negotiations in Geneva and buttonholing them for status reports and comments. This process is "useful," but cumbersome and fundamentally inadequate. Interview with a senior MOFA official.

[85]OECD Working Party Report (1990). GATT delegates from non-aligned countries, speaking anonymously, have expressed surprise at the acrimony with which the PRC has opposed Taiwan's application. Bureau of National Affairs, *International Trade Reporter* (February 28, 1990).

[86]Interview with a MOEA official.

[87]Interview with a MOEA official.

[88]BOFT, "New Forms of Competition and New Protectionism."

[89]The Republic of China was one of the original signatories of the GATT protocol in 1948, but shortly after the fall of the mainland, Chiang Kai-shek's government withdrew from the GATT. Beijing subsequently notified the contracting parties that it, rather than Taipei, was the sole legal representative of China, and that any "return" to the GATT would be by the Beijing government, not the so-called

(continued...)

accession is made pursuant to GATT Article 23 as a "customs territory" rather than as a government purporting to represent all of China. The government points out that regardless of the ongoing dispute with the PRC over which is the legitimate government of China, it has effectively exercised full autonomy in the formulation and implementation of its economic, financial, and trade policies.[90] It distinguishes its current application from its status prior to 1971, when it held GATT "observer" status for the whole of China; now, it simply applies for membership on behalf of "a separate customs territory over which we are currently in control."[91] Taiwan argues that its accession would thus not raise broader issues of sovereignty over China; that its accession would be "in conformity with GATT's idea of pragmatism;"[92] and that it could belong to the GATT without being formally recognized by the GATT contracting parties.[93] Finally, the colonies of Macao and Hong Kong have been admitted as full GATT members despite their prospective reversion to the

[89](...continued)
Republic of China. Taipei received "observer" status in the GATT in 1965, but this was revoked in 1971, in the wake of the U.N.'s recognition of the PRC as the only China. Since then, the PRC's position within the GATT has grown progressively stronger. The PRC belongs to the U.N. Organization for the International Trade Organization, whose sole function is to appoint the GATT Secretariat, and it has exercised a role in selecting the Secretariat. The PRC received permanent observer status in 1984 and can attend GATT Council meetings and those of associated GATT organizations. In 1984, the PRC joined the Multifiber Arrangement, and in 1986, it applied for full GATT membership.

[90]*GATT Memorandum*, p. 1.

[91]BOFT, "The Trade Policy of the Republic of China on Taiwan" (mimeo by 3rd Department (multilateral organizations) staff, 1990).

[92]BOFT cites an EC legal opinion which states that for GATT purposes the question of whether a government has *de facto* autonomy to conduct external commercial relations matters more than whether a government is recognized under international law. BOFT, "Trade Policy of the Republic of China on Taiwan."

[93]BOFT also cites a March 9, 1950 memorandum from the Secretary General of the U.N. to the Security Council stating that the members had made clear by "unbroken practice" that a member could properly vote to accept a representative of a government which it did not recognize, and that such a vote did not imply recognition or a readiness to assume diplomatic relations. BOFT, "Trade Policy of the Republic of China on Taiwan."

PRC; "if Hong Kong and Macao are admitted, why not us?" ask the Taiwanese.[94]

Apart from the political concerns raised by the PRC's opposition, there appear to be few, if any, supportable reasons to deny it membership. Taiwan points out that it is rapidly bringing its tariffs and trade policy regime into alignment with GATT rules and principles. As a major trading power it asks to share the burdens and responsibilities of maintaining an open international trading regime in an era of resurgent protectionism. It points out that it has set up a $1.2 billion development fund with which to assist developing countries. It pledges to participate in all future GATT tariff reductions and non-tariff barrier eliminations, and to implement the results of the Uruguay Round.[95]

Nevertheless, the PRC's vehement opposition to Taiwan's accession remains a major complication. In early 1991 a senior GATT official indicated that Taiwan's application was "very much on the back burner and likely to remain so," privately noting that admission for the Soviet Union and the PRC would be accorded priority.[96] The European Community has raised some legal objections; it is clearly not eager to support the initiative. The U.S. government is "considering" Taiwan's request, which may remain in a state of limbo unless a mutual solution accommodating both Taiwan and the PRC can be worked out. U.S. Trade Representatives Carla Hills commented in March 1991 that Taiwan's application was "well drawn," but that if it were put to a vote within the GATT, it would be rejected even with strong U.S. backing, reflecting "political reactions" generated by the PRC's opposition.[97] Absent U.S. leadership, few if any major trading countries are likely to risk the wrath of the PRC by endorsing Taiwan's accession. On the other hand, smaller countries are less reticent. The Taiwanese government is currently contacting the GATT contracting parties to line up support, and it is finding that its "little friends" are less concerned about pressure from the PRC and more likely to be disposed to supporting Taiwan's application.[98]

---

[94]BNA *International Trade Reporter* (January 30, 1991).

[95]*GATT Memorandum* pp. 1-2; BOFT, "Trade Policy of the Republic of China on Taiwan."

[96]BNA *International Trade Reporter* (January 30, 1991).

[97]BNA *International Trade Reporter* (March 27, 1991).

[98]Interview with a senior MOFA official.

Regardless of whether Taiwan is admitted to the GATT, the mere process of pursuing membership has served to strengthen the GATT system because in so doing, Taiwan is seeking to conform its trade policies and practices to GATT standards, making them more transparent, predictable, and liberal. Advocates of free trade within the Taiwanese government are using and will continue to use Taiwan's GATT application as an effective bureaucratic lever against protectionist elements, enhancing the prospects for liberalization of Taiwan's own trade over the next decade. There is a domestic consensus that GATT membership is in the overall national interest, and that some sacrifices are necessary to conform to the GATT rules; even the Council of Agriculture acknowledges this.[99]

Regional Trade Strategy

Taiwanese private sector investment is currently pouring into Southeast Asia. The Taiwanese government cannot track the investment flows and admits it has no idea exactly how much money is involved, although the amounts are conceded to be large, if not huge. some of this investment involves speculative real estate purchases and the establishment of large plants which would have raised environmental concerns in Taiwan (paper mills, petrochemical complexes), but the bulk of Taiwanese investment in this region is dominated by small and medium enterprises with relatively portable manufacturing and assembling operations -- industries such as toys, sporting goods, Christmas tree lights, consumer electronics products, garments, and footwear that are traditionally associated with Taiwan.

Taiwanese investment in Southeast Asia is attributable for several factors. Most importantly, the region offers in abundance the resources which are becoming scarce in Taiwan -- primarily cheap land and labor; in addition, Southeast Asian governments generally have a lower level of concern over environmental, intellectual property and worker-rights issues -- factors which make possible the continuation of the sort of light manufacturing and assembly operations traditionally associated with Taiwan, but which are becoming more difficult to sustain in Taiwan itself. The strengthening of the NT$ makes resources less expensive in the Southeast Asian countries and enhances their value as export platforms, particularly because they retain the GSP status which Taiwan lost in 1989. Finally, the presence throughout Southeast Asia of a network of overseas Chinese facilitates Taiwanese investment and the establishment of manufacturing and distribution operations.

---

[99]Interview with a Council of Agriculture official, March 1990.

Taiwan's private sector is driving the investment thrust into Southeast Asia, but the government is supporting the effort. It has sought to negotiate investment and tax agreements with Southeast Asian governments and provided direct support for Taiwanese investment in forms such as counselling of prospective investors and the purchase of land in Malaysia for a "Taiwan Electronics Industrial Park," which will provide sites for Taiwanese electronics firms.[100] Government officials, however, express concern over what they see as over-concentration by Taiwanese business on Southeast Asia at a time when it is trying to encourage investment in the EC in anticipation of the Single Market and expansion of exports toward Japan. Taiwan's rival, Korea, it is noted, has been directing its investments toward "getting closer to markets and forestalling protectionism, especially in the European Community," in sharp contrast to Taiwan.[101] The official lament is that Chinese business wants to go "where there are already other Chinese" rather than where the national interest may warrant.[102]

If current Taiwanese investment trends continue, an economic structure is likely to evolve under which Taiwan in effect has transferred the low end of its manufacturing sector to Southeast Asia, retaining mainly the high end (such as electric components, software services, and precision machinery) at home. With Taiwanese investment spurring the region's development, and with Taiwanese businesses integrating the "low" and "high" end of the manufacturing process, Taiwan would rival Japan as an economic power in this region.

Taiwan and the United States

Taiwan has always had an ambiguous relationship with the United States. U.S. military guarantees have prevented the PRC from occupying the island; U.S. aid provided much of the basis for Taiwan's economic expansion in the 1950s and 1960s; and at present U.S. imports of Taiwanese products account for much of its prosperity. On the other hand, Taiwan has been angered by a series of U.S. "betrayals" -- the Cairo Declaration of 1943, which guaranteed that Formosa (then a Japanese colony) would be handed over to China after Japan's defeat; the Nixon-

---

[100]*Central News Agency* (February 15, 1990); CEPD, *Highlights of 1989 Economic Development Plan*, Part III.2(13).

[101]*Far Eastern Economic Review* (March 16, 1989).

[102]Interview with a senior CETRA official.

Kissinger contacts with the PRC in 1971-72, which ignored Taiwan; and most importantly, U.S. recognition of Beijing as "China" in 1979[103]

In the 1980s the political tensions inherent in the U.S. moves to expand relations with Beijing were augmented by a series of acrimonious trade disputes. With the United States no longer confronting the PRC as a potential military adversary, Taiwan's strategic importance has diminished dramatically; at the same time Taiwan has emerged as a major trade rival and a perceived practitioner of "unfair" trade. Taiwan was regularly singled out by U.S. congressmen and trade officials as a practitioner of "adversarial trade," and the U.S. government began pressing Taiwan to modify its policies in a number of specific sectors. The United States withdrew GSP treatment for Taiwan in January 1989.

Because of its extreme dependency on the U.S. relationship, Taiwan has not considered itself in a strong bargaining position, and its principal approach has consisted of concessions. Beginning with the U.S. recognition of the PRC in 1979, government officials began speculating internally that continued over-reliance on the bilateral U.S. tie was dangerous; this concern became more urgent in the late 1980s with U.S. retaliatory actions against Japan, passage of the 1988 trade legislation, and the withdrawal of GSP treatment. In the spring of 1989, Taiwan adopted an official policy of diversifying export trade away from the United States, and announced a sweeping "Action Plan" for improving trade relations with the United States, featuring a sweeping army of concessions. These measures have been unpopular domestically, have fostered intense anti-Americanism, and in some cases, have led to civil disturbances.

Strategies Toward the United States. Many, but not all of Taiwan's initiatives to reduce the surplus with the United States are set forth in the four-year Action Plan generated by CEPD in March 1989. The overall objective of the Plan is to reduce the trade surplus with the United States by 10 percent per year. The government feels that it has been successful in this effort thus far. The main elements being pursued in the plan may be summarized as follows:

- *Procurement.* The government organizes one or two procurement missions to the United States per year; this has resulted in $10

[103]Economist Intelligence Unit (1989) p. 21.

billion in procurements during the past 14 years.[104] Historically public procurements have heavily favored the United States and discriminated against Japan; however, there is a clear sense that the days of this type of practice are numbered.[105] Such discrimination is GATT-inconsistent, and the government is concerned over the domestic political implications of Taiwan's favoritism toward the United States.

- *Import liberalization.* The government has formally committed to review remaining trade restrictions on an annual basis, to simplify import procedures, and to investigate and (where appropriate) remedy alleged unfair trading measures and non-tariff barriers reported by the United States.[106] Because these measures will primarily benefit Japan rather than the United States, liberalization is regarded as a concession to U.S. demands rather than a policy that will actually reduce the bilateral trade surplus.
- *Promotion of U.S. products.* The government of Taiwan is providing a number of services to encourage increased sales of U.S. products in Taiwan. These include free office and exhibition space for American Institute in Taiwan (AIT) in Taipei; free space for U.S. exhibitors in the Taipei World Trade Center; and organization of a U.S. product exhibition twice annually in which the government provides free space and free advertising for U.S. products. These benefits are available to U.S. firms only.[107]
- *Liberalization of the services sector.* The Action Plan calls for the "gradual" opening of the services sector to U.S. companies, including transportation, banking, insurance, and securities. The Plan is vague as to the nature and extent of liberalization of these sectors.
- *Encouragement of domestic demand.* Domestic enterprises, including state-owned companies and farms will be encouraged to intensify

---

[104]Interview with an MOEA official; Action Plan, Part II. Most public procurements are made by a few entities, notably China Petroleum Corp., Taiwan Power Company, and the Director-General of Telecommunications.

[105]Interview with a senior MOEA official.

[106]Action Plan, Part II.

[107]Interview with a senior MOEA official.

their capital investments, a measure which is expected to increase capital equipment imports from the United States.[108]

- *Intellectual property.* The government will take a variety of measures to enhance protection of intellectual property, including amendments to the ROC Copyright Act; establishment of a Department of Copyright responsible for copyright protection; prohibition of the performance of counterfeit movies, videos, and TV and radio programs; and amendments to the ROC Patent Act and Trademark Act, providing, among other things, for confiscation of counterfeit products.[109]
- *U.S. lobbying.* While not explicitly part of the Action Plan, Taiwan's extensive lobbying effort in the United States will continue. Taiwan's lobbying operation in the United States is one of the largest maintained by any foreign country. This effort is directed toward cultivating relationships with senators and congressmen, journalists, small-town mayors and scholars, who are offered junkets to view Taiwan's economic progress first hand. Friendly U.S. localities may find their local economies supported through export orders and deposits of Taiwanese foreign exchange reserves in local banks. Taiwanese companies have channeled large sums into influential Washington think tanks ($3 million for the Heritage Foundation since 1981, $300 to $400 thousand annually to the American Enterprise Institute). These efforts have resulted in the establishment of links (such as trade offices) between Taiwan and 32 U.S. states and 107 cities.[110]

The Exchange Rate Issue. The United States complained during the 1980s that Taiwan's exchange rate was being manipulated by the Central Bank of China to keep the NT$ artificially weak against the dollar; in October 1988, the U.S. Treasury made a formal finding that the government of Taiwan was manipulating the exchange rate to achieve an unfair advantage in international trade. In April 1989, the Central Bank implemented a new system which allows some daily fluctuation in the

---

[108]Action Plan, Part VI.

[109]Action Plan, Part VIII.

[110]*Wall Street Journal* (November 7, 1989).

exchange rate to reflect market forces.[111] The U.S. Treasury Department expressed initial satisfaction with this system but is continuing to monitor the exchange rate; Taiwanese officials cite with satisfaction Treasury's complimentary comments on Taiwan's recent policies.[112]

U.S. pressure on the exchange rate issue, however, and the impact of adjustment have been traumatic for Taiwan's leadership due to wild swings in capital flows which have resulted from concessions to U.S. demands. For many years, during the period of tight exchange controls, Taiwanese businesses pursued various avenues to get their earnings out of the country. Because the NT$ was weak and depreciating, it was in their interest to establish overseas accounts denominated in foreign currency.[113] Over time, this led to the buildup of large overseas foreign currency reserves; the government has only the vaguest idea how much Taiwanese business actually has invested abroad.[114] When the NT$ suddenly appreciated after U.S. pressure on the Central Bank, these overseas accounts began to lose value rapidly, and there was a rush to convert them back into NT$. "All of the overseas money built up during

---

[111]Under the old system, the Central Bank set exchange rates by fixing a daily "mid-rate;" banks trading in NT$ were required to buy and sell NT$ within a 2.25 percent range of the set mid-rate. The Central Bank directed its agent banks, the Bank of Taiwan and the International Commercial Bank of China, to buy or sell a given amount of U.S. dollars at the end of each day; the Central Bank conceded that through these measures it "intervenes somewhat" to protect exporters from a rapid appreciation of the NT$. The new rules eliminate the 2.25 percent range and the mid-rate and permits a group of nine banks to set the rate for the day at a morning meeting, but applicable only to trades under $US30,000. (*GATT Application*, pp. 28-29) For trades over $30,000, banks have hailed these measures as freeing them to set exchange rates, others have termed them mere window-dressing, pointing out that the Central Bank is installing direct telephone lines to all of the trading banks to monitor their exchange transactions -- "like Big Brother, with a big baseball bat." *Far Eastern Economic Review* (April 6, 1989).

[112]Interview with a senior Central Bank of China official.

[113]There were various ways to do this despite exchange controls. For example, under the exchange control regime, exporters were allowed to pay 3 percent commissions to overseas sales agents without securing clearance from the Central Bank of China. Many exporters regularly paid 3 percent "commissions" even though no agents existed to receive them; instead, the money was deposited in foreign banks. Interview with an official at the U.S. Chamber of Commerce in Taiwan.

[114]Interview with a senior MOFA official.

20 years of development came home in three to four months, hitting the market all at once. The stock market went wild; ultimately every cab driver and maid jumped in, wanting to buy stock. The government was totally unprepared."[115]

The government is now placing a strong emphasis on stability. The currency should be held where it is for the time being, until the stock market "acts like a market and not a casino."[116] The Governor of the Central Bank emphasizes the need for "dynamic stability" in the exchange rate. He indicates that the NT$ might fluctuate further against the dollar, but that if this occurs it should reflect economic realities; for example, an adjustment to the level of domestic economic development and foreign trade. Market forces would serve as a "guidepost" for setting the exchange rate.[117] Outside of the Central Bank itself, Taiwan's leaders believe that the NT$ has appreciated "enough" against the dollar. Continuing U.S. pressure on this issue is a source of official and growing popular anger, and may lead to a significant growth in anti-U.S. sentiment.[118] The turmoil which followed the U.S. exchange rate initiative led to comments in the press that the United States was trying to destabilize the currency through a variety of subterfuges which "unnerve the market."[119]

The U.S. and Taiwan Free Trade Area Initiative. In 1988-89, the government of Taiwan mounted an initiative to persuade the U.S.

---

[115]Interview with an official at the U.S. Chamber of Commerce in Taiwan.

[116]Interview with an official at the U.S. Chamber of Commerce in Taiwan.

[117]Interview with a senior Bank of China official. In May, 1990, the NT$ experienced a record one-day fall and established a 14-month low against the U.S. dollar. Taiwan officials warned that the depreciation could increase the trade surplus with the United States. (*Reuter Library Report*, May 16, 1990, Wednesday, BC Cycle). In March the Governor the Central Bank took the unusual step of urging faith in the NT$.

[118]Interview with an American academic.

[119]These include "forecasts" by foreign experts ("unschooled in the Taiwan economy") over how much Taiwan's currency should rise, leaks by U.S. officials to Taiwanese reporters during exchange rate talks, and cultivation of the Taiwanese press by U.S. negotiators to "talk up" the exchange rate. *Tsai Hsun* (December 1, 1988) (JPRS-CAR-89-023); *Ching-Chi Jih Pal* (February 14, 1989) (JPRS-CAR-89-030).

government to enter into a Free Trade Area (FTA) with Taiwan.[120] This proposal was given a substantial airing in Washington but has languished since mid-1989.[121] Taiwanese officials recognize that the FTA initiative has made little progress with the U.S. government, but they remain interested in the proposal -- "we are discouraged, but like a boy courting a girl, we will ask you again and again."[122] Taiwan's principal apparent motive in pressing for an FTA did not emerge in the public discussion of the issue. The government would like to continue treating the United States on a preferential basis with respect to procurement, autos, and other aspects of trade, while containing Japanese penetration of the local market. This is becoming increasingly difficult as Taiwan moves toward an MFN-based trade regime based on GATT principles. To put it baldly, an FTA would permit Taiwan to give benefits exclusively to the United States, but not Japan, and GATT Article 24 would permit this derogation from general MFN principles. Because of U.S. opposition, this initiative is likely to languish indefinitely.

Potential Problems. Taiwan has taken a sweeping series of measures designed to placate the United States and defuse trade tensions; however, several concerns exist. Taiwan's liberalization and internationalization measures, while strongly sought by the U.S. government, will primarily benefit Japanese business, exacerbating Taiwan's other major trade problem, the deficit with Japan. Japanese firms are investing rapidly in Taiwan and are using it as an export platform directed at the United States, particularly for assembly of machinery and other products for which the core components are manufactured in Japan. "Unless we stop Japanese investment here, the bilateral surplus with the United States will worsen."[123] In addition, with the market open to imports of most products, the focus of bilateral trade discussions will increasingly fall on a "hard core" of sectors where liberalization is particularly difficult for

---

[120]BOFT indicates that the FTA was its idea. Interview with a senior BOFT official.

[121]Concerns raised in the United States included the implications for relations with the PRC, outstanding unresolved U.S.-Taiwan bilateral issues, and Taiwan's apparent motive of securing exemption from U.S. trade remedies. See William H. Cooper, Congressional Research Service, *Taiwan-U.S. Free Trade Area: Economic Effects and Related Issues* (February 9, 1989).

[122]Interview with an official at U.S. Chamber of Commerce in Taiwan.

[123]Interview with a senior MOEA official.

political and policy reasons (agriculture, liquor, tobacco, intellectual property, and financial services).

Taiwan and the European Community

Taiwan has not been able to develop trade with the EC commensurate with the Community's size as a potential market and as a potential supplier. No EC country maintains diplomatic relations with Taiwan, and the EC has used Taiwan's lack of GATT standing to restrict its trade fairly harshly. In 1982 the Community sharply curtailed Taiwanese textile exports on a unilateral basis, reflecting the fact that Taiwan is not a party to the Multifiber Arrangement and not subject to its constraints on actions by developed country importers. Taiwanese trade officials complain of preferential treatment for the EC's Mediterranean association partners, high tariffs, and a variety of other restrictions. Nevertheless, Taiwan has expanded its annual exports to the Community to about $8 billion (larger than its exports to Japan) and is developing a major campaign to increase the volume of its EC trade.

There is a consensus within the Taiwan government that the European Community is becoming more protectionist on trade. Government officials are emphatic, if not bitter, as they see the Europeans trying to curtail market access for Asian products. Their criticism of the European Community's current course is more severe than that offered with respect to any other major trading partner. BOFT officials comment that "fortress Europe" is not something that will occur in 1992 -- "it's there already, and has been since 1987." They cite a tightening of the European Community's antidumping regime since 1987 and the unilateral imposition of quotas ("through mere publication of an Official Journal notice"). In addition to these problems, several areas of future concerns were:

- *Harmonization.* The concern is that harmonization of the EC's technical standards and inspection requirements will result in a net increase in technical barriers to trade. Taiwanese industries perceived as particularly vulnerable include motor parts, machinery, and toys.
- *Rules of origin.* The concern is that peripheral countries (EFTA and Eastern Europe) will decrease their sourcing of Taiwan products in order to qualify for preferential treatment in their exports to the Community.

- *Consolidation of national quotas.* The concern is that as national quotas are consolidated at the EC level, the aggregate level of protection will increase.[124]

The situation in the European Community poses a considerable dilemma for Taiwan. On the one hand, Taiwan's trade strategy calls for an expansion of trade with the European Community as it diversifies its trade away from the bilateral relationship with the United States. On the other hand, the European Community appears embarked on a course which will curtail current levels of market access. Taiwanese officials and businessmen feel highly vulnerable in this situation because of their virtually total lack of leverage. They point out that they have no influence in the Community -- Taiwan is not recognized by the European Community, and as a GATT nonmember it is not subject to the GATT's protection. Consequently, the European Community can impose quantitative restraints and other restrictions without any legal constraints.[125]

Trade Strategy. Taiwan's trade strategy toward the European Community has not been as formally structured as its strategy toward the United States, but it is discernible in a recent action plan drawn up by MOEA and through discussions with government officials.[126] It has several main principal elements.

---

[124]National quotas on Taiwan exports include: France (color televisions, footwear); Britain (music centers, color televisions, monochrome TVs, footwear); Italy (footwear). GATT Doc. L/6530 (July 31, 1989).

[125]Taiwan's official contacts with the EC are limited. Once a year the Director General of BOFT meets with the Commission. The consultations are limited in scope; individual problem areas are discussed (such as avoidance of double taxation on shipping). A few sectors, such as textiles, are handled through separate meetings, although they are also discussed in the annual consultations. The Taiwanese view is that such infrequent contacts "are not enough." Interview with a senior MOFA official.

[126]BOFT, MOEA, *Guideline for Strengthening Economic and Trade Ties with Europe.* In contrast to the action plan for improving trade ties with the United States, which was drawn up by CEPD, MOEA has been given responsibility as the supervisory body for the plan and for coordination of all international actions. (Plan, part 3.B.) Virtually all of the actions called for in the plan are trade and investment promotion matters which fall within the jurisdiction of subordinate bodies of MOEA (the Industrial Development and Investment Center and CETRA). (Plan, part 3.B.)

Improve Taiwan's legal position. Taiwan's current trade with the European Community takes place in a virtual legal vacuum. The MOEA action plan seeks to establish a variety of formal commercial legal ties with the EC countries governing various aspects of trade. These include exchanges of air landing rights; conclusion of agreements on maritime and air transportation; signing of a protocol on income tax exemption for shipping enterprises; signing of the ATA Carnet Agreement with EC nations; conclusion of agreements on the reciprocal protection of intellectual property rights; and participation in international organizations to which the European Community and/or the member states are parties, particularly, of course, the GATT.[127] Considerable resources are being devoted to monitoring legal developments within the Community. Specific measures include: (1) monitoring of the development of the EC single market by MOEA overseas offices, collecting relevant laws and regulations for study and consideration of countermeasures; (2) participating in academic projects studying and translating EC laws and regulations; (3) gathering and analysis of countermeasures against EC 1992 being taken by other countries; (4) inviting local and foreign scholars to brief MOEA on EC 1992 at seminars sponsored by the Ministry; (5) sending specialized agriculture, transportation, finance and trade fact-finding missions to Europe. MOEA *Guideline*, Part 4A.

Encourage selected Taiwanese investments. The government will "actively assist" Taiwanese enterprises to invest in the European Community to circumvent anticipated increased import barriers. There is a recognition that such investment must be selective and does not represent an across-the-board solution; for example, "we can't move our footwear or textile industry into the European Community."[128] On the other hand, it may be possible to establish some labor-intensive industries in the ACP countries and Eastern Europe, which enjoy or are likely to enjoy association arrangements with the Community.[129] Government assistance to Taiwanese businesses for investment in the European Community is seen as necessary because if left to themselves, "Chinese businessmen tend to invest in countries where there is already an established Chinese community." This phenomenon would result in the concentration of Taiwanese investment in Southeast Asia at a time when

---

127 MOEA *Guidelines*, Part 4.E.

128 Interview with a senior BOFT official.

129 Interview with a senior BOFT official.

the need exists to establish a presence in the European Community and in the preferential states on the periphery of the Community.[130]

Encourage reciprocal commercial ties. The government will encourage two-way business ties, particularly by seeking to stimulate European investment and technology exchange with Taiwan. European firms will receive financial incentives and "administrative assistance" in order to overcome difficulties they may encounter in setting up business in Taiwan. Taiwan's research institutes and public and private enterprises will be encouraged to support European firms establishing high technology activities in Taiwan. European firms will be encouraged to hold commercial and industrial exhibitions in Taiwan.[131]

Strengthen Taiwan's commercial infrastructure in Europe. The government is placing considerable emphasis on providing infrastructural support for Taiwanese firms in Europe; this reflects the fact that Taiwan's small and medium enterprises (unlike Korea's *chaebol*) require such support, as well as Chinese businessmen's reluctance to make a major commitment to a relatively unfamiliar market lacking an existing network of indigenous ethnic Chinese. The government will encourage Taiwanese firms to set up sales networks in Europe (such as delivery warehouses and product display centers). A "computer industrial park" will be established by BOFT and the RET-SER Engineering Agency in Cork, Ireland for use by Taiwanese computer firms seeking to penetrate the European Community.[132] CETRA will establish a Taiwan Trade Center in Rotterdam, which will provide display facilities, gather market information, concentrate offices, and seek to improve warehouse services for Taiwanese firms. Taiwanese banks will be encouraged to open branch offices in the European Community.[133] The Central Bank of China will deposit a portion of Taiwan's foreign exchange reserves in these overseas branches both to enable them to compete in the EC financial markets and to serve as a source of investment and operating capital for Taiwanese enterprises operating in the EC market.[134] The manpower and financial resources of the ROC's trade offices in Europe will be upgraded. Market

---

[130]Interview with a senior CETRA official.

[131]MOEA *Guideline* Parts 4.B.d. and 4.C.

[132]*China News Agency* (February 15, 1990).

[133]MOEA *Guideline*, Parts 4.B.g. and h.

[134]Interview with a senior official of the Central Bank of China.

research on Europe for the benefit of Taiwanese businesses will be intensified.[135]

Improve ties with EC officials and politicians. The government will attempt to "upgrade" existing official communication channels with the European Community and with member states, and to engage in "regular or irregular" official contacts. EC officials, parliamentarians and "influential civilian groups" will be invited to visit Taiwan. Economic cooperation conferences will be organized on a regular basis with European countries. Communication channels with EFTA will be established. European countries which do not have trade offices in Taipei will be urged to establish them.[136]

Taiwan and Japan

Taiwan was a colony of Japan between 1895 and 1945. Japanese colonial administration was relatively enlightened and engendered little of the antipathy toward Japan that is found elsewhere in East Asia as a result of the Greater East Asia Co-Prosperity Sphere. Nevertheless, Japanese government officials and businessmen still treat Taiwan in a rather patronizing fashion. The government downplays Taiwan because it is not a sovereign state; in contrast to the United States, which has improvised an institutional structure for maintaining relations with Taiwan, Japan not only bans official contacts with the island but strictly enforces that ban. Taiwanese officials are sometimes denied visas to travel to Japan, which in turn only allows low-ranking Japanese officials to travel to Taiwan. The Japanese government allows only one bank, Dai-ichi Kangyo, to offer commercial services in Taiwan. President Lee complained in 1990 that "we have many problems, but no place to solve them. I hope the Japanese government realizes that even without diplomatic relations, there can be contact." A Taiwanese trade association executive commented in 1991 that "Japan is very timid toward Beijing, but very stern towards us."[137] Japanese businessmen tend to disparage Taiwanese competitive capabilities and product quality. One Japanese electronics executive illustrated this attitude with an anecdote at a conference in 1990:

---

[135]MOEA *Guideline*, Part 4.A.e.

[136]MOEA *Guideline*, Part 4.D.

[137]*Far Eastern Economic Review* (February 21, 1991).

> *A [Taiwanese] who had worked for a Japanese company in Taiwan for the past 10 years resigned. When asked what he would be doing after he quit, he said that he wanted to open a snack bar. A Japanese in the same situation, having made enough money and wanting to change jobs, would be moving on within the industry instead. . . . In the case of the Taiwanese, however, he decided to resign suddenly one day in order to open a snack bar or a karaoke bar. His knowledge and skills in electronics, acquired during the 10 years with the company, evaporates into thin air right then and there. How can we transfer technology to a country composed of such people?*[138]

Notwithstanding such attitudes, the bilateral economic relationship has undergone a significant transformation from the colonial era. A generation ago, Taiwan was primarily a plantation economy exporting agricultural products and seafood to Japan, its leading export market. As Taiwan's product mix has shifted toward industrial products, it has been unable to achieve a significant penetration of the Japanese market. Meanwhile, Japan has become the largest single source of Taiwan's imports, and the bilateral deficit with Japan has become progressively larger. Taiwan had a $7 billion deficit with Japan in 1989, and between 1986 and 1989, Taiwan's imports from Japan doubled from $8 to $16 billion.[139] Partially offsetting this imbalance, Taiwan has cut into Japanese export markets in areas such as steel, textiles, and electronics products, and is vying with Japanese businesses for influence in Southeast Asia.

Taiwan's principal failure has been its firms' relative lack of success in penetrating the Japanese market. They encounter "the same problems as U.S. firms" exporting to Japan. There is no problem with respect to sectors where there are no domestic Japanese competitors (eels, flowers, and simple agricultural products); in all other sectors, however, it is "very difficult" to penetrate the Japanese market.[140] Japanese trading

---

[138]Katsutaro Kataoka in *Denshi* (November 1990) (JPRS-JST).

[139]Interview with a senior MOEA official.

[140]Interview with a senior MOEA official. Japanese barriers cited by Taiwanese exporters include "industrial and sanitary standards that are incompatible with international norms, stringent certification procedures that are time-consuming and painstaking for the applicants, import quotas, excessive administrative directions, protective measures for structurally and cyclically declining industries, and the complicated marketing system itself, which rests firmly on Japanese customs and business culture."

companies dominate distribution channels and regulate the quantities of Taiwanese goods sold in the market, preventing Taiwanese firms from acquiring market knowledge or brand recognition with consumers; thus while Taiwan "supplies Japan with most of its golf clubs, electric fans, telephones and wood furniture, most Japanese are unaware that they are made in Taiwan."[141] While most Taiwanese officials are reluctant to criticize Japan or single out specific sectoral concerns, some "ridiculous" restrictions are noted -- highly restrictive standards for imported ski equipment and the requirement that a Taiwanese quarantine official accompany each boatload of bananas exported to Japan.[142] Absent fundamental restricting of the Japanese market itself, the outlook for changes in these patterns is not seen as encouraging.

On the import side, Taiwan maintains a number of discriminatory restrictions against Japan, although these are usually based on formal government measures rather than embedded barriers. Taiwan traditionally prohibited imports of full-sized automobiles, but in the late 1970s it liberalized imports of U.S. and European cars -- it maintained the ban only on imports of cars from Japan (and, more recently, Korea, although it allows some Korean cars in under quota). The Japanese automakers are reportedly circumventing this restriction by exporting cars to Taiwan manufactured by Japanese subsidiaries based in the United States.[143]

Taiwan's trade deficit with Japan is closely linked to its surplus with the United States. A substantial proportion of the Japan deficit and the U.S. surplus consists of intermediate goods imported to Taiwan from Japan and assembled for export to the United States. Curtailing imports from Japan, therefore, is seen as a way to contain the deficit with the United States.

Strategy Toward Japan. In June 1989 Taiwan's Ministry of Economic Affairs engaged a Japanese management consulting company (the Japanese office of McKinsey and Co.) to work with a Ministry task force on Japan

---

[141]Far Eastern Economic Review (February 21, 1991).

[142]Interview with a senior official within the Department of American Affairs, BOFT.

[143]Interview with a senior official within the Department of American Affairs, BOFT.

trade to suggest ways to reduce the trade deficit with Japan.[144] The MOEA action plan which was generated with the consultants emphasizes a series self-help and market-oriented projects rather than government-to-government pressure. These include:

- *Technology induction.* The government (MOEA) is spending about $77 million to purchase advanced Japanese technologies for introduction into Taiwan. Taiwanese firms will be encouraged to extract Japanese technology -- particularly that relating to factory automation and the information industries -- for domestic use.
- *Takeover of a trading company.* Only two of Taiwan's leading 20 trading companies even have offices in Japan.[145] The McKinsey group suggested that one way to crack the Japanese market would be to buy a big Japanese trading company outright, since Japanese wholesalers and retailers are reluctant to buy directly from Taiwan producers. While such a dramatic and unprecedented move seems improbably, given the keiretsu ties of the big trading houses, the idea intrigues government officials and it is not impossible to foresee such an acquisition bid mounted by a Taiwanese consortium, backed by government funds, sometime during the next decade.[146]
- *Key components project.* Currently, Taiwan imports critical components from Japan for a large number of its main industrial products -- items such as facsimile machines, bicycles and motorbikes, and consumer durables and electronics products. Under the plan MOEA will seek to persuade Taiwanese companies which import these products to produce them internally or secure them from a local supplier.
- *Market development project.* Taiwanese businessmen and government officials will visit Japanese factories and urge them to buy Taiwanese products. This initiative will target Japanese firms which buy nothing from Taiwan.
- *European project.* The government will invite European companies to establish factories and assembly sites in Taiwan, using the island as an export platform directed at Japan. The notion underlying this

---

[144]The task force itself consisted of senior industrialists and scholars, and ranking government officials. *Free China Review* (March 1989)

[145]*Far Eastern Economic Review* (February 21, 1991).

[146]Interview with a senior MOEA official.

effort is the fact that Japanese consumers tend to like the status and quality associated with upscale European products.

- *Quality guarantee program.* The government will use standards and inspection to guarantee the quality of Taiwanese industrial products, bearing in mind Japanese consumers' concern with product quality.
- *Training effort.* Typically, a Taiwanese firm opens an office in Japan intending to penetrate the local market, but as difficulties pile up, the firm gives up on selling and begins concentrating on buying, a phenomenon attributed primarily to lack of knowledge as to how the market works, and the shortage of Japanese-speaking personnel.[147] The government will sponsor 2-year Japanese language training programs for 1000 Taiwanese per year; it will also sponsor the dispatch of 60 people per year to Japan to study market conditions.
- *Osaka Trade Center.* The government is establishing a Taiwan trade center in Osaka. This is designed in particular to enable small and medium Taiwanese enterprises to overcome the obstacles to market entry.[148] Taiwan will also host a series of trade shows throughout Japan to highlight Taiwanese products.

Outlook for Relations with Japan. For a small country, the effort being directed by Taiwan to break into the Japanese market for industrial goods is a substantial undertaking. Nevertheless, it is unclear that Taiwan will succeed in reducing, or even containing, its current bilateral deficit with Japan. Even under the most favorable assumptions, export growth to Japan will be slow, and Japan appears poised to substantially expand its sales in Taiwan. Japanese businesses enjoy a natural advantage in Taiwan as a result of geographic proximity. In addition, Taiwan's "business community is heavily infiltrated by Japanese business interests."[149] Japanese trading companies have made impressive efforts to develop local trading networks,[150] and Japanese trading firms' international

---

[147]*Far Eastern Economic Review* (February 21, 1991).

[148]Interview with a senior MOEA official.

[149]Interview with a senior MOEA official.

[150]Typically the big Japanese trading houses employ hundreds of Taiwanese to maintain daily contact with potential importers and end users of Japanese products, (continued...)

distribution networks are so important to local small and medium enterprises that they may be telling Taiwanese firms what to produce for the world market.[151] Finally, Japanese products are perceived as superior in quality to those of other industrialized countries, including the United States. Japan's current exports to Taiwan are constrained by government policy measures rather than embedded structural barriers; as the formal restrictions are lifted -- under U.S. pressure -- Japanese exports to Taiwan are virtually certain to increase substantially. Should this occur, the Taiwanese worry that the island "could remain a second-rate manufacturer and a dumping ground for Japanese goods."[152]

Taiwan and the PRC

Taiwanese businessmen and investors have begun to establish what amounts to an economic sphere of influence in South China. Taiwanese capital, management skills and technology are arguably becoming the dominant economic forces in Guangdung and Fujian Provinces. Taipei adopted a new policy in 1988 to dramatically expand its indirect trade with China, indicating that Taiwanese could freely export their products to the PRC and that Taiwan would liberalize its imports of PRC products (except agriculture and light industry products).[153] The "unofficial" trade with the mainland is now estimated at $4.0 billion, most of which moves through Hong Kong via middlemen; there is also some illicit direct trade carried on through exchanges by boats in the Fujian Straits.[154] Officially, reported Taiwanese investments in the PRC totaled $650 million in 1991, with the true total estimated at about twice that amount.[155] Taiwan permits "indirect" investments by Taiwanese businesses in the PRC in a list of 3,600 product areas, and provides legal advice and tax benefits for firms undertaking them; on the other hand it imposed fines and other

---

[150](...continued)
particularly machinery. Their efforts surpass in scale and quality those of the U.S. and EC business communities. Interview with a CETRA official.

[151]Interview with an American academic familiar with the issue.

[152]*Far Eastern Economic Review* (February 21, 1991).

[153]*Kyodo* (February 13, 1988).

[154]*Far Eastern Economic Review* (June 6, 1991).

[155]*Far Eastern Economic Review* (May 9, 1991).

disincentives on mainland investments which it regards as undesirable.[156] Investments have been particularly heavy in labor-intensive sectors which have been affected by Taiwan's labor shortage; Taiwan's shoe industry, beset by rising labor costs, has largely relocated to the Xiamen area on the mainland, where costs are substantially lower. The PRC has encouraged Taiwanese trade and investment through special incentives, and has set up a department specifically to handle trade with Taiwan in its Ministry of Foreign Economic Relations.[157]

Taiwan-PRC trade relations will expand substantially over the next five years despite unresolved political issues because it is in the interests of both countries that it does so. The expansion of trade and other economic ties with the mainland is seen as inevitable and desirable by most Taiwanese officials.[158] The PRC, they note, has cheap resources -- labor, coal, cotton and other items needed by Taiwanese industry. It is also a market, especially for the light industrial consumer goods that are still the mainstay of Taiwan's manufacturing sector. "So we allow third-country trade. We can't control such trade anyway."[159] For its part, the PRC needs the capital, technology, and management skills that Taiwan can provide. Significantly, the Tiananmen Square episode did not cause Taiwan to depart from its established policy of easing tension with Beijing, which in turn has sought to allay concerns that internal repression will disrupt its growing trade links with Taiwan. PRC officials have pointed out that during the turmoil production proceeded normally at Taiwanese-owned plants in Guangdong and Fujian provinces and that a number of agreements were concluded between Taiwanese and PRC investors with respect to large construction projects after the violence in Beijing.[160]

Taiwan and Korea

Taiwan perceives Korea as a rival, and there is a substantial amount of overt and covert competition between the two countries. They compete directly in some of their most important export lines: textiles, apparel,

---

156 *Far Eastern Economic Review* (May 9, 1991).

157 *Xinhua* (February 1, 1989).

158 Interview with a senior MOEA official.

159 Interview with a senior MOEA official.

160 *Xinhua* (June 29, 1989).

plastics and electronics products. Taiwanese officials take care not to speak ill of Korea, but express concerns such as the notion that if their own population loses the work ethic, Taiwan will be surpassed by the hardworking Koreans.[161] They gauge their country, to a degree, against Korea and frequently ask U.S. trade officials "how are you treating Korea on this?" -- seeking at least equal treatment;[162] they measure their own liberalization program in a similar manner.[163] Taiwan's own trade strategy may be driven, in part, by a desire to counter Korean initiatives; its move into Eastern Europe, for example, is probably partially a response to a similar Korean move.[164] The loosening of restrictions on commercial dealings with the PRC may reflect the fact that Korea is rapidly developing investment and trade ties with the PRC; Korean firms have a cost advantage on the mainland since they do not need to use Hong Kong middlemen as do Taiwanese firms, and the large size of the *chaebol* (in contrast to Taiwan's small- and medium-sized businesses) has given them an advantage in arranging deals with the PRC. Korea has done little to support Taiwan's bid for GATT entry; in fact it has taken the position that Taiwan should join as a developed country.[165]

Sectoral Trade Strategies

Taiwan's industrial development policies have always been explicitly sectoral in character, with the government selecting specific sectors for promotion. This will remain the case in the 1990s, but the government will largely abandon protection as a promotional tool. It will use border measures and investment restrictions to protect only a few sectors (portions of the agricultural sector, financial services, and telecommunication industries); in addition, a few ailing traditional sectors may receive temporary import relief pursuant to GATT escape clause (Article XIX) procedures. The instruments of industrial promotion will be tax incentives, provision of capital (both equity and debt) on favorable

---

[161]Interview with a senior MOEA official.

[162]Interview with a U.S. official familiar with the issues.

[163]In discussing Taiwan's liberalization program, a senior MOEA official pointed out that Taiwan has import controls on 265 items at the 7-digit level, while Korea still controls about 700.

[164]Interview with an American academic familiar with the issue.

[165]Interview with a U.S. official familiar with the issues.

terms, provision of land to key industries, government matching funds for R&D, provision of venture capital to high technology firms, government export promotion services (CETRA), and the deployment of foreign exchange reserves to support strategic Taiwanese investments overseas.[166]

High Technology. The government of Taiwan's decision to promote an array of high technology industries could portend an increase in trade friction with the advanced industrial nations, but several aspects of Taiwan's promotional effort will mitigate this prospect. Most importantly, rather than seeking to build up domestic champions that will eventually seek to "shoot their way" into the international arena, possibly displacing foreign high technology products, the Taiwanese strategy emphasizes an intertwining of foreign and Taiwanese interests. The government has sought to "marry" local and multinational firms through a complex web of capital, technology and personal ties. The country's fledgling semiconductor industry, for example, has been developed with the assistance of U.S. advisers, U.S. technology, and U.S. and European capital; many Taiwanese manufacturing ventures are being established which will provide "foundry" services for U.S. semiconductor design houses. This approach is partially based on international political considerations; to the extent that influential foreign multinationals are drawn into complex commercial and manufacturing relationships based on Taiwan, they are likely to develop an immediate commercial interest in Taiwan's security concerns and be sensitive to Taiwan's position as the two-China issue. The Taiwanese "multinational" approach to high technology industrial promotion is also based on Taiwan's continuing dependency on foreign advanced technology. However, the fact that many Taiwanese high technology firms are partially foreign-capitalized (TSMC), are subsidiaries of U.S.-based firms (Vitelec), are foundries for U.S. design houses, or are U.S.-Taiwan joint ventures (TI-Acer) is likely to reduce the prospect of serious trade friction.

A second factor with militates against trade friction in high technology is the nature of the promotional tools being employed by the Taiwan government. The cruder neomercantilist methods most commonly associated with "industrial targeting" have been largely abandoned in favor of more sophisticated policies. The domestic market is open for most high technology imports and investment. The *Statute for Encouragement of Investment*, which provided tax breaks for designated

---

[166]See generally CEPD, *Perspective of the Taiwan Economy*; CEPD, *Highlights of 1989 Economic Development Plan.*

priority industries, has been replaced by the *Statute for Upgrading Industries*, which does not single out any specific industry for special tax treatment, but will provide tax benefits to all industries for certain generic types of investments, such as R&D, manpower training, and antipollution measures. The new statute is arguably no larger a "targeting" measure at all, since it will make benefits available to all industries. It represents the culmination of a year-long negotiation by the Finance Ministry to persuade the MOEA's Industrial Development Bureau to abandon the industry-specific scheme.

If Taiwan's high technology promotion strategy appears carefully crafted to avoid conflict with the U.S. and other major trading partners, however, its policies in agriculture and financial services are virtually certain to produce additional friction in the 1990s. Underlying Taiwan's reluctance to open its farm and financial markets is the traumatic memory of the loss of the mainland, which is particularly acute among senior officials. The collapse of KMT authority in the late 1940s was preceded by rebellion in the countryside and financial chaos in the cities, particularly runaway inflation. There is a consideration reluctance to risk a repetition of either phenomenon, even in the radically changed world of the 1990s.

Agriculture. Taiwan's farm sector is not competitive by international standards, and portions of this sector remain heavily protected through high tariffs, quotas, and outright import prohibitions (rice, sugar, fresh milk, peanuts, fresh animal offal, small red (adzuki) beans, wheat flour, chicken meat, some cuts of pork and some kinds of fruit). Persistent pressure by the United States has led to a series of piecemeal liberalization measures, and Taiwan is currently a significant market for U.S. grain and sorghum. However, U.S. pressure and Taiwanese concessions have begun to produce a significant political backlash. Taiwan's farmers are resentful of the effects of government policies on their position in the society and have become increasingly well-organized and vocal. In May 1988 Taiwan experienced one of its largest civil disturbances since Chiang Kai-shek left the mainland, a riot which began with farmers' protests over imports of U.S. turkey parts and citrus products (which had been liberalized in 1986-87). In July 1989, inaccurate reports that U.S. agricultural products were contaminated with the carcinogen Alar were given dramatic play in Taiwan's press (although government tests put the rumor to rest.)[167] The U.S., for its part, has been annoyed with Taiwan's barriers to some of its principal potential exports given the overall bilateral trade deficit.

[167]*Far Eastern Economic Review* (August 17, 1989).

Rice is one major area of potential friction. Taiwan, which produces large rice surpluses, bans rice imports and maintains huge stockpiles of surplus rice. An OMA governing rice trade between the U.S. and Taiwan expired in December 1988, causing the U.S. rice producers to warn that Taiwanese dumping of its surpluses could deprive U.S. firms of sales in third markets. The industry has threatened Section 301 action (based on market access as well as third country dumping) and is currently pressing for renegotiation of the OMA. A related potential problem area is wheat. Taiwan imposes a "variable levy" on wheat, which is designed to protect the domestic rice industry by preventing the differential between the price of imported wheat (NT 4,700 in early 1989) from becoming too great with respect to the price for domestic rice (NT 28,000 during the same period). The U.S. government reportedly raised this issue as a possible Super 301 target in early 1989.[168]

Although Taiwan's farmers account for only 10 percent of the population, they have a political strength out of all proportion to their numbers. In part, this reflects the fact that many city dwellers are themselves migrants from rural areas, or retain close ties to relatives who remain on the farm, and many urban dwellers sympathize with farmers' concerns. In addition, the spatial distribution of Taiwan's urban and rural areas tends to intersperse urban zones and farms in a checkered fashion, so that farm concerns are a major issue for Legislative Yuan members in every district of Taiwan except for Taipei itself. The system of representation in the Legislative Yuan, which provides for representation by geographic areas and by occupational groups, gives rural voters a disproportionately large representation.[169] United States demands in some product areas are seen as unreasonable.[170] Finally, the farmers'

---

[168]Taipei *CNA* (15:09 GMT, April 1, 1989) (FBIS-CHI-89-064).

[169]Provinces with under 3,000,000 population are allowed to elect 5 members each, whereas if the population exceeds 3,000,000, only one additional member is allowed per additional 1,000,000. This allocation of seats provides a disproportionate representation for the more sparsely populated rural provinces. Compounding the distortion, the Yuan also provides 89 seats to various designated "occupational groups." Roughly 25 percent of these seats are allocated to farmers, who account for about 10 percent of the population. Additional occupational seats are held by fishermen, who tend to sympathize with farm concerns.

[170]For example, U.S. pressure to open the market for poultry offal (chicken giblets, intestines, and livers) is seen as insulting -- "U.S. chicken traders are trying to sell us what the domestic market discards. . . . [Americans] treat us as inferior people."

(continued...)

willingness to engage in confrontational activity has increased their clout. By all accounts outbursts such as the turkey parts riot have shocked and unsettled government leaders, but instead of provoking a law-and-order backlash, they have induced concessions and a greater degree of official concern for farmers' problems. In May, 1988, for example, a farmers' riot in front of the Legislative Yuan led to a pilot medical insurance program for farmers. Similarly, in 1989, beef farmers unhappy over a proposed liberalization measure staged a protest in front of the Legislative Yuan; farmers also threatened to free hundreds of head of cattle on the Taipei streets. The result was the imposition of an import ban by BOFT. A BOFT plan to liberalize garlic imports was shelved indefinitely following a farmers' protest in front of the Legislative Yuan.[171]

Over the short run, the farmers' political power is likely to increase. The growing influence of the Legislative Yuan, in which the farmers are well represented, works in their favor. In addition, COA is currently seeking to promote the formation of a national farmers' union, an initiative which will almost certainly strengthen its hand bureaucratically. At present there is an informal national farm association, but no formal group; the farmers are represented by a diversity of organizations, including local farmers' associations (which combine economic activities like credit extension and livestock insurance with political activities) agricultural cooperatives (which principally perform marketing functions) and irrigation societies. Politically, the farmers' voice is fragmented; "all kinds of groups are raising all kinds of issues through all kinds of channels -- local, provincial and national."[172] There is no politically powerful association comparable to the Nokyo in Japan or the DBV in Germany; but it is COA's objective to establish a national union so that "the political activities of all the little groups can be channeled into one big organization."[173] Should such an organization be formed, its voice will necessarily carry considerable weight with the government.

Taiwan has indicated that it will adopt a more market-oriented agricultural policy over the long run, including gradual market opening

---

[170](...continued)
Chien-Shien Wang, former Vice Minister of MOEA, in *Wall Street Journal* (March 16, 1987).

[171]Interviews with a Director within the Council of Agriculture; a senior official in the CEPD; and a senior MOEA official.

[172]Interview with a senior Council of Agriculture official.

[173]Interview with a senior Council of Agriculture official.

and a phased reduction in tariffs. It has also indicated that if an agreement in agriculture is reached in the Uruguay Round, it "will endeavor to implement progressively the results taking into account its own situation."[174] To a degree, the impact of liberalization may be softened by subsidies, price supports, and diversification. COA itself is not absolutely rigid on the issue of market protection; its Chairman Yu-hsien Yu, has warned farmers on a weekly television news program not to expect to be protected forever given foreign pressure and the government's strong commitment to trade internationalization and liberalization. However, COA officials indicate that "liberalization of rice is not possible in ten years."[175] While they refused to indicate other sectors which will be similarly protected, they indicated that the criteria was simple -- if a region's economy is organized around a dominant crop or livestock item and no viable economic substitutes are available for displaced farmers, protection will be retained.[176]

In addition, it is likely that protectionism will be manifested in forms other than tariffs and quotas. U.S. Department of Agriculture officials report that intimidation of importers remains a problem.[177] In addition, COA will soon be elevated to Ministerial status. Taiwanese officials (including those at COA) do not believe that this change will have any impact on COA's relative influence within the government. However, under the reorganization the Bureau of Commodity Inspection and Quarantine (BCIQ), a technical agency which is responsible for administering health regulations, will be transferred from the Ministry of

---

[174]*GATT Memorandum*, pp. 26-27.

[175]Interview with a senior Council of Agriculture official. A continued hard line on rice will affect U.S. wheat exports as well as rice.

[176]Interview with a senior Council of Agriculture official. The example given was peanuts, which are heavily concentrated in Yunlin Prefecture, in particular, and Hualien, Changhua and Chiayi provinces as well. If the peanut farmers are forced out of business, they cannot turn to rice production since rice is already in surplus. There is no other readily available commercial opportunity for the peanut farmers; hence, protection is likely to be retained. Rice production is concentrated in the west coastal provinces of Taoyuan, Hsinchu, Miaoli, Taichung, Changhua, Yunlin, Chiayi and Tainan.

[177]COA maintains a list of 124 agricultural items that require prior approval in order to be imported. When importers apply for a license for these products, their name is given to farmers' organizations who harass them and lobby them not to import the product. Interview with U.S. official familiar with the issue.

Finance to the new Ministry of Agriculture. This will put the Ministry in a position to block imports on health and sanitary grounds even if import liberalization has occurred. All Taiwanese officials deny that sanitary/quarantine measures will be used for protectionist purposes,[178] but the transfer of BCIQ to the new Ministry of Agriculture will "put the fox in charge of the henhouse."[179] Significantly, COA officials are currently pushing for a study on coddling moth infestation; Korea has recently used the coddling moth as grounds for insisting that apples imported from the United States be quarantined and fumigated before entry, and the U.S. Department of Agriculture is concerned that COA may be preparing to follow Korea's example.[180] Taiwanese authorities have agreed to open the Turkey market completely by September 1, 1990, but unconfirmed press reports have warned of stricter-than-normal inspection of turkey meat imports.[181]

Nevertheless, U.S. pressure (and, increasingly, pressure from the European Community as well)[182] will continue not only because Taiwan is seen as an excellent export market -- indeed, the number one potential export market for the United States, according to USDA -- but because a substantial indigenous food importing infrastructure will encourage import growth. There are currently hundreds of food importers in Taiwan; hotels and supermarkets buy directly from these importers or wholesalers. Some of the big supermarket chains have begun to import directly themselves, and most Taiwan supermarkets carry an extensive selection of U.S. canned food, wine, fruit, fruit juice, candy and nuts. The proliferation of convenience food outlets like 7-Eleven, Welcome, and AM-PM will serve to draw in U.S. products.

The prospect for the coming decade is one of continued U.S. government pressure for liberalization, which will be met by a protracted rear-guard action led by the Council (soon to be Ministry) of Agriculture, featuring a gradual schedule of concessions in most crop and livestock

---

[178]Taiwanese officials mainly stress that BCIQ is staffed with technicians who don't have positions on trade issues. Interview with a senior CEPD official.

[179]Interview with U.S. official familiar with the issue.

[180]Interview with U.S. official familiar with the issue.

[181]Ken Howland, AIT Taipei, *1989 Agricultural Situation Annual Report.*

[182]The Europeans are utilizing weekly cargo flights from Amsterdam to bring in cut flowers, cheese, and wine from the EC. Hungary has begun to export canned apple juice to Taiwan.

areas. Few if any concessions will be given, however, on certain "core" commodities, particularly rice and grains which compete with rice. Meanwhile, the government's agricultural reform program, the slow erosion of the farmer's political power, and the rising price of land (which will create incentives for farmers to sell land for non-agricultural purposes) will make liberalization measures more politically feasible over the longer term.[183] The Council of Agriculture is drafting a series of support measures to buffer the impact of trade liberalization.[184]

Financial Services. Taiwan's political leadership is under pressure from several sources to liberalize the financial services sector, which traditionally has been highly restricted through limits on new entry, regulatory controls on permitted activities, and government ownership of the dominant financial institutions.

- Taiwan's high savings-to-investment ratio reflects a lack of attractive investment opportunities. The local stock market lists only about 200 companies, and investment in foreign securities is cumbersome. The bond market is underdeveloped and largely limited to government instruments. Bank interest rates have been set lower for large deposits, to discourage accumulation. It is

---

[183]Taiwan's arable land is limited and its farms are extremely small. There are far too many farms to permit substantial increases in productivity; farmers' income is far too low to sustain most families, and currently two-thirds of farm families' income is derived from non-farm income. The farm population is aging as young people move to the cities. These problems have led the Council of Agriculture to map out a long term development plan through the year 2000 whose objective is to reduce the number of farms from 800,000 to 100,000 and increase average farm size from 1-1/2 to 10 hectares. Productivity will be enhanced through infrastructural improvements and upgrading of technology. Still, even if these reforms are achieved, it is unlikely that much of Taiwan's farm sector will be competitive by international standards. The draft development plan also calls for a change in product mix; creation of a national farmers' organization; land use reform; and productivity enhancement. U.S. Department of Agriculture observers regard the plan as extremely optimistic, and believe that there is a good chance that it will not work. Interview with a senior Council of Agriculture official and a U.S. official familiar with the issue.

[184]COA is reportedly considering plans for assistance in production planning, marketing, processing and storage for farmers whose crop sales are adversely affected by imported products. Funding would come from markups by parastatal importers, tariffs, and license fees. Ken Howland, AIT Taipei, *1989 Agricultural Situation Report*.

evident that a partial solution of this problem would be deregulation, new entry and stimulation of competition among financial intermediaries.

- The United States government is pressing Taiwan to allow market entry on a nondiscriminatory basis by U.S. financial institutions.
- Taiwan's leaders have entertained the idea that Taipei may become a "new Hong Kong," or at least share that status with Singapore, if communist rule destroys Hong Kong's viability as a regional financial center after 1997. They realize, however, that this will be impossible without a radical liberalization and restructuring of the country's underdeveloped financial system.

Acceding to these pressures, the government has been pursuing a policy of piecemeal liberalization, emphasizing special concessions to U.S. firms, rather than wholesale liberalization. The slow pace of financial liberalization is attributable to several factors: (a) fear of loss of control of the financial system, which could result in economic chaos; (b) desire to prevent wholesale capital flight into unproductive overseas investments; (c) desire to prevent Taiwan's developing financial services sector from being destroyed by full exposure to foreign competition; (d) lack of pressure by established foreign banks for further liberalization (they have no desire to open themselves to further competition).

Taiwan's securities market remains subject to significant restrictions on foreign firms. Investment in Taiwanese Securities firms is permitted under the Securities and Exchange Law, but not to an extent that permits foreign majority restricted, and there is no effective system for marketing foreign securities in Taiwan.[185] In June 1989, the Securities and Exchange Commission indicated it would grant three foreign brokerage houses licenses to open branch offices in Taipei, although their activities would be limited to selling stocks and bonds listed on the New York, Tokyo and London stock exchanges. Their licenses do not permit them to underwrite local securities issues. The SEC's criteria for these licenses were so strict that only about a dozen firms worldwide were eligible; most of these were Japanese firms which could not secure approval from Japan's Ministry of Finance to acquire the licenses. Eventually two brokerage firms, Merrill

---

[185]Local foreign investment firms have been permitted to promote overseas mutual funds to local investors, but payment for the units has been required to be made outside of Taiwan. *Far Eastern Economic Review* (February 8, 1990).

Lynch and Shearson Lehman Hutton opened branches in Taipei.[186] The purpose of permitting these branch openings was to give Taiwanese investors an opportunity to purchase securities in other markets. Taiwan authorities indicate that three such branches are sufficient; there will be "no more at the moment."[187]

U.S. pressure on Taiwan to liberalize its securities market seeks to enable U.S. citizens to invest in the Taiwan stock market, sell overseas securities to Taiwanese investors, and to permit U.S. firms to participate in the various intermediary services such as brokerage and underwriting. Taiwanese financial officials reportedly oppose U.S. objectives because of a "stuff it in the mattress" mentality; they have been trying to stabilize financial markets by extracting liquidity from the system ("stuffing in the mattress"). The U.S. demands for entry are seen as opening the door for additional large volumes of funds which will be used to "gamble" on the stock market, and further destabilize capital markets. In addition, further liberalization could facilitate the rapid flight of Taiwan's foreign exchange overseas into investments (such as foreign securities) which do little to advance Taiwan's economic development.[188] The wild gyration of the Tokyo stock exchange in March 1990 underscores these concerns. Japan has recently liberalized its financial markets under U.S. pressure.

The banking system, until now dominated by the government, is in a state of upheaval. The government has traditionally limited the number of banks through denial of new licenses; in 1989, Taiwan had 24 major domestic commercial banks, of which the government held a majority share in 13. There were also a number of large, underground institutions whose extent, size and holdings were unknown. This year, pursuant to new legislation, the government will privatize the three largest commercial banks and permit the licensing of new domestic banks; numerous

---

[186]As a general matter foreign securities firms are not particularly interested in the local brokerage business; rather, they are interested in acting as intermediaries for foreign funds flowing into Taiwan and for Taiwanese investment moving abroad. The local brokerage business is seen as tainted with a variety of shady practices, such as illegal underground lending; because foreigners cannot engage in such activities, they are not competitive with local firms. Interview with an official with the U.S. Chamber of Commerce in Taiwan.

[187]Interview with a senior official with the Central Bank of China.

[188]Many Taiwanese officials excoriate the "gambling mentality" of their countrymen, currently reflected in the wild swings in stock prices, which is seen as a fundamental national weakness.

consortia are being formed by industrialists eager to enter the banking business.

The liberalization of domestic banking has been paralleled by a reduction in the restrictions on branches of foreign commercial banks in Taiwan (there are currently 35). The gap between the types of activities in which domestic banks and foreign branches can engage has progressively narrowed.[189] The new banking law permits the foreign branches to set up savings departments, with which they can accept passbook savings deposits and extend long-term loans, and trust departments, which can apply for licenses of securities underwriters, brokers and dealers (although these are likely to be issued sparingly).[190] The current pace of liberalization, coupled with the lack of enthusiasm by established foreign banks for further liberalization that would bring new competition, suggests that the banking sector will not be a source of major trade friction with the United States.

Taiwan limits entry into the insurance market for both domestic and foreign firms by restricting the issuance of licenses. Under U.S. pressure, Taiwan has permitted the issuance of licenses to two U.S. non-life and two U.S. life insurance companies per year.[191] Several Taiwanese officials noted that because the government was not issuing new licenses to domestic firms, this policy actually discriminated in favor of the United States and could cause a political furor if the facts became known -- "we issue you new licenses which are denied even to our own companies, and yet you still ask for more."[192] In fact, U.S. firms cannot engage in some activities that are permitted for local rivals;[193] in addition, some of the conditions for new licenses are considered burdensome.[194] The United

---

189 Interview with an official with the U.S. Chamber of Commerce in Taiwan.

190 Interview with a senior Central Bank of China official.

191 BOFT, *Talking Points on Trade Series.*

192 Interview with a senior MOFA official.

193 U.S. insurance firms cannot establish subsidiaries and joint ventures with non-insurance firms, and cannot establish multiple branch offices in Taiwan. Unlike national firms, foreign firms cannot hold real estate in their portfolios. USTR, *Foreign Trade Barriers* (1990).

194 To receive a license a U.S. firm must be an incorporated, not a mutual insurer and must have been in existence for ten years. Interview with an official at the U.S. Chamber of Commerce in Taiwan.

States' mutual insurance companies are not allowed to open branches in Taiwan. The U.S. government and insurance industry would like to see these restrictions removed and "more licenses issued, faster."[195]

Taiwan's 15-year plan adopted in 1986 calls for the government to "gradually allow foreign insurance companies to establish branches in the ROC to promote the internationalization of the domestic insurance industry.'[196] This approach is likely to continue into the 1990s -- phased issuance of new licenses and a gradual removal of restrictions on existing foreign branches under continued U.S. pressure. The United States' retaliation in insurance might lead to a slight increase in the tempo of liberalization, but is unlikely to produce an "overnight" opening of the market.

---

[195]Interview with an official at the U.S. Chamber of Commerce in Taiwan.

[196]CEPD, *Perspective of the Taiwan Economy,* Part V.C.2.(c)(3).

6

Brazil

Jesse G. Kreier

The inauguration of Brazilian President Fernando Collor in 1990 represented a milestone in the evolution of Brazilian international trade policy. After a decade of economic crisis marked by hyperinflation, budget deficits, massive foreign indebtedness and declining international competitiveness, Collor proposed a fundamental change of course for the Brazilian economy. The new President advocated a less interventionist approach in which market tools would restore the economy to macroeconomic stability and improved competitiveness. In the trade arena, this meant rejection of the doctrine of import substitution in favor of a policy of import liberalization and the integration of Brazil into the world trading system.

The new approach seems to have taken root. While the Collor agenda has experienced a number of setbacks, Brazil appears committed to a course of economic liberalization which can be expected gradually to reshape the manner in which the country interacts with the world economy. However, this process of economic reform does not imply an overnight shift from the strictly-regulated international trading regime of the 1980s to a laissez-faire system. The objective constraints limiting such a dramatic swing are significant -- an enormous foreign debt that must somehow be serviced, at least in part; a legacy of state dominance in many key industries that cannot, regardless of intentions, be eliminated quickly; vulnerable sectors for which the price of full trade liberalization, both politically and economically, would be higher than any government could bear.

Yet the limits on reform go deeper than the economic dilemma which Brazil currently faces. Brazil has a long tradition of state intervention in the economy, and that intervention historically has played a central role in the country's economic development.[1] Although Brazilians generally accept that the present trade regime has failed, many continue to believe that state intervention, including trade controls, can play an important role in advancing national interests. In industrialized nations, this willingness to resort to the use of trade barriers, while not uncommon, is tempered by regard for international norms or, in any event, concern that deviation from those norms could provoke retaliation. Brazilian decision-makers, on the other hand, tend to believe that developing nations such as Brazil should operate under special international trading rules more lenient than those applicable to developed nations. So long as this view persists, Brazil's trade policy is likely to differ significantly from that of the leading industrial nations.

TRADE POLICY BACKGROUND

Pressures for Trade Reform

From 1974 (when the first oil shock rocked the Brazilian economy) until last year, Brazilian trade policy followed the import substitution model.[2] The strategy was to impose barriers to imports so high that any product Brazil was capable of producing, at whatever cost, could not be imported.

---

[1] See, e.g., T.J. Trebat, *Brazil's State-Owned Enterprises: A Case Study of the State as Entrepreneur* (Cambridge University Press, 1983).

[2] See generally, Werner Baer, *The Brazilian Economy* (Praeger, 1989), pp. 197-212. This was not, of course, the first time Brazil had turned to import substitution. Such a policy was followed vigorously and successfully during the 1950s and early 1960s. By the later 1960s, however, much of the benefit to be obtained by replacing imported consumer goods with domestic production had been achieved, and, in the face of deteriorating economic conditions, the military government simultaneously liberalized imports (within limits) and implemented an ambitious export promotion program. It was this policy which Brazil was forced to abandon as a result of the oil shock of 1974. The post-1974 import substitution program, unlike its predecessors, focused on development of the capital goods and basic intermediate industrial sector, metals, fertilizers, petrochemicals, etc. J. Ray Kennedy and Robert Gianetti da Fonseca, "Brazilian Trade Politics and the Uruguay Round," in *Domestic Trade Politics and the Uruguay Round*, ed. Henry N. Nau (Columbia University Press, 1989), pp. 30-34.

There were several reasons for this policy. First, an ideology of autonomy was pervasive. Government officials in general, and military and Foreign Ministry officials, in particular, believed that national sovereignty demanded self-sufficiency. This ideology can be traced from the founding of the Volta Redonda steel mill in the 1940s and the creation of the Petrobrás monopoly in the 1950s, through the formulation of an informatics policy in the 1970s and 1980s.[3] Second, the foreign debt required Brazil to generate a huge trade surplus. To achieve this end, Brazil suppressed imports to as low a level as possible, and provided a wide range of incentives so that Brazilian industry could export, regardless of its international competitiveness.[4]

In the late 1980s, however, the pressures on Brazil to liberalize its economy generally, and its trade regime in particular, intensified. Among the key forces were:

- *Consumer dissatisfaction.* As a result of the import substitution policy, Brazilian consumers found that they were in many cases paying several times world market prices for such essential goods as textiles, as well as for automobiles, consumer electronics, appliances and other luxury items.
- *Macroeconomic instability.* Fueled in part by a restrictive import policy and the high cost of subsidies, Brazil suffered ever higher inflation rates. Brazil's annual inflation rate had reached 4,653 percent by the date of President Collor's inauguration in March, 1990.[5]

---

[3] As one observer noted with respect to informatics, "the issue [enactment of the 1984 informatics law] was presented as a dilemma between national autonomy and self-determination, on the one hand, and control of the country's resources by international companies and their local associates, on the other." Simon Schwartzman, "High Technology Versus Self-Reliance: Brazil Enters the Computer Age," in *Brazil's Economic and Political Future,* ed. Julian M. Chacel, Pamela S. Falk and David V. Fleischer (Westview, 1988), p. 67.

[4] See Benedict J. Clements and J. Scott McClain, "The Political Economy of Export Promotion in Brazil," in *The Political Economy of Brazil,* ed. Lawrence S. Graham and Robert H. Wilson (University of Texas Press, 1990), pp. 69-70. Clements and McClain argue that the only alternative means to cut imports, an economic slowdown, was unacceptable to a military government that had been sharply criticized for failing to improve the living standards of the average Brazilian.

[5] Economic Intelligence Unit, *Brazil Country Profile, 1990-91,* p. 17.

- *Declining competitiveness.* Brazilian industry, unchallenged by foreign competition and deprived of access to new technology, machinery and reasonably priced inputs, suffered from declining international competitiveness. One observer noted in 1989 that, "because of the delicate situation of the balance of payments, even imports of essential equipment, spare parts and raw materials are being rationed. There is an awareness among most businessmen that this situation is untenable in the long run, since equipment would become increasingly outdated and dilapidated."[6]
- *Foreign pressure.* Brazil found itself under increasing international pressure to reform its trade policies. In the United States, the European Community and other developed country markets, Brazilian products were subjected to numerous antidumping and countervailing duty actions. The United States brought section 301 and related investigations demanding market access.[7]
- *Global trends.* A perception developed that Brazil was becoming economically isolated and marginalized. Liberal economic policies were advancing in Eastern Europe and throughout Latin America, and countries such as Spain and Mexico were benefiting from admission to trading systems from which Brazil was excluded.

As an outgrowth of these pressures, some think tanks and government agencies began to advocate a major economic restructuring, which would include a radically new trade policy,[8] and the Sarney Administration in

---

[6] J. Ray Kennedy and Roberto Bianetti da Fonseca, "Brazilian Trade Policy and the Uruguay Round," in *Domestic Trade Politics and the Uruguay Round*, ed. Henry R. Nau (Columbia University Press, 1989), p. 36.

[7] In 1985 the U.S. government took the unusual step of self-initiating a section 301 investigation relating to Brazilian informatics policy. *Daily Report for Executives* (October 10, 1989). A second section 301 case, this time regarding intellectual property protection for pharmaceutical, was initiated at the request of the U.S. Pharmaceutical Manufacturers Association in 1987, resulting in the imposition of retaliatory sanctions against $40 million in Brazilian exports to the United States. *International Trade Reporter* (October 26, 1988). The pressure reached a climax with the identification of Brazil as a "priority country" under the so-called Super 301 provision of the 1988 Trade Act. 54 Fed. Reg. 24438 (June 7, 1989).

[8] For example, Marcio Fortes, President of the National Bank for Economic and Social Development, in 1989 expressed the view that Brazil must follow a policy of "competitive integration" with the developed world, rather than act as a "kamikaze

(continued...)

principle acknowledged the need for change. As a practical matter, however, little real progress was made until the inauguration of President Collor. The Collor Administration has undertaken an economic reform program of dramatic proportions, a key element of which is the liberalization of trade policy. This new policy was first clearly elaborated in an Industrial and Foreign Trade Plan released in June 1990.[9]

Economic Challenges

The future of Brazilian trade reform will depend heavily on three broad economic factors. First, the success of the reform effort is contingent on a satisfactory means of handling Brazil's large foreign debt, which is widely believed to be unsustainable. Second, reform will depend on the ability of Brazil to attract new foreign investment. Third, reform will succeed only if Brazil can reestablish macroeconomic stability. These economic factors are only partially within the control of Brazilian policy makers. Ironically, trade reform may itself be a necessary condition to meeting these economic challenges.

Foreign Debt. Brazil currently has an external debt of $114 billion, some 90 percent of which is owed by the public sector.[10] To meet the service costs on this debt in an environment of limited or no access to international capital markets, Brazil must run an enormous trade surplus. In an effort to meet these obligations, Brazil exported almost twice as much as it imported in 1989.

This situation has tremendous ramifications for Brazilian trade policy. First, the need for a surplus was the primary intellectual justification for the import-restrictive policies of the past two decades. If Brazil's trade balance falls significantly and it is no longer generating a surplus to repay the debt, Brazil may be forced to reimpose some form of import controls.[11] Second, until Brazil reestablishes its credentials as a

---

8 (...continued)
exporter," to overcome its debt crisis and modernize its industry. "BNDES Head Views Privatization Projects," in *Veja* (March 22, 1989) (FBIS-LAT-89-084).

9 Ministry of Economy, Treasury and Planning, *General Directives for Industrial and Foreign Trade Policy* (June 28, 1990) (hereafter, *General Directives*).

10 *Estado de São Paulo* (July 25, 1990) (FBIS-LAT-90-145).

11 Interview with senior trade policy official in the Ministry of Foreign Affairs, July 1990.

borrower, it will lack access to foreign credit. Not only does this situation make it difficult for industry to obtain long-term financing to import the capital equipment and technology needed to modernize and export, but it increasingly precludes access even to short-term export financing needed to sell many products abroad.[12]

There is broad consensus in Brazil that the country's economic reforms will not succeed unless and until Brazil's foreign debt service is cut down to a "sustainable" level through reductions in principal.[13] Brazilians welcomed the Brady Plan because it was the first recognition of this, and judged the reduction of principal on government loans the most significant element of President Bush's Enterprise for the Americas Initiative, announced in June 1990.[14] Brazil is unlikely to resume repayment of its debt in earnest until it achieves an agreement that significantly lightens its debt burden.

Foreign Investment. The government of Brazil is well aware that its economic reforms and, indeed, the very health of its economy depends on attracting foreign investment.[15] Brazil is counting on the new economic and trade policy, which includes a liberalization of investment policy, to achieve this end. The Industrial and Foreign Trade Plan proposed a "new approach" to foreign investment, which will include "the elimination of anachronistic sectorial restrictions and of residual prejudices."[16] The Collor government has taken some steps to implement this policy, such as

---

12 Interview with a senior official of a major Brazilian import-export concern, July 1990.

13 Interviews with senior officials responsible for foreign debt matters in the Foreign Ministry and the Ministry of Economy, Treasury, and Planning. In the latter interview, the official suggested that $7-8 billion per year might be a sustainable rate of repayment.

14 Interview with Foreign Ministry official. For a discussion of the Enterprise for the Americas Initiative, see p. 362.

15 The Industrial and Foreign Trade Plan states that "direct foreign investment will represent an important factor to the Country in restoring the investment rate, in the expansion of international trade and the access to technology." *General Directives*, Section 4.

16 *General Directives*, Section 4.

the repeal of a progressive tax on the remittance abroad of profit earned in Brazil by foreign companies.[17]

This liberalized approach to foreign investment represents a dramatic shift from the attitudes prevailing when the Constitution was drafted in 1988. The tone of the Brazilian Constitution of 1988 is one of economic nationalism. Article 170 identifies "national sovereignty" first on the list of principles for the country's "Economic Order." Consistent with this approach, the Constitution explicitly authorizes the reservation of key sectors to companies of "national capital," (Article 171), provides for the regulation of profit remittances by foreign companies (Article 172), restricts foreign investment in extractive industries (Article 176) and requires the government to grant preferential treatment to companies of national capital in its procurement practices (Article 171).[18]

Although the Brazilian government should be able to minimize the effect of these Constitutional provisions through statutory and/or administrative interpretations, some private observers are skeptical that any major new inflow of capital is likely to result.[19] In addition to Brazil's spotty record as a borrower, the Collor government's actions in sequestering funds and freezing profit remittances, although later renounced, served to further undermine investor confidence. Yet unless Brazil can attract new funds, it will be unable to restore the ability of many lagging industries to compete in world markets.

Macroeconomic Stability. The defeat of inflation is Collor's overriding goal, and even the trade reform itself is intended first and foremost to

---

17 *Estado de São Paulo* (November 2, 1991) (FBIS-LAT-91-214). The 1968 Foreign Investment law was intended to deter "excessive" profit remittances by imposing a progressive tax on remittances. The rate of taxation began at 25 percent for remittances up to 12 percent of a remitting firm's registered capital in Brazil, and rose to 60 percent as remittances increased in proportion to capital. *Brazil Watch* (August 12-23, 1991), pp. 11-12.

18 For a more detailed discussion, see George Charles Fischer and Susan Christina Foster, "Brazilian Companies and Preferential Treatment Under the New Constitution," in *AmCham News Update* (May 1, 1989) (printed by American Chamber of Commerce for Brazil - São Paulo).

19 Interviews with a senior executive of a major import-export concern, and an independent Brazilian economic consultant, July 1990.

help restore price stability through foreign competition.[20] A key component of the stabilization plan is the effort to balance the federal budget, which has important ramifications for sectoral policy generally and for levels of subsidization specifically. Ultimately, the success of the Collor Administration's economic and trade reforms will depend in part on the outcome of the fight against inflation. Should that battle be lost, it is uncertain whether the other components of the program will survive.[21]

TRADE STRATEGY

Brazil's trade strategy for the 1990s is based on a new model for its participation in the world economy. The central reform, from a trade perspective, is an ambitious program to gradually open the country to foreign goods and services. Under this program, import barriers gradually will be lowered and made transparent through tariffication.

This program reflects a widespread belief in Brazil that undiscriminating import substitution is no longer a viable policy for the country. It is generally acknowledged that protectionist trade policies impose high costs on the Brazilian economy. Not only have these policies resulted in higher prices, thereby feeding inflation, but they have, in the eyes of many Brazilians, ultimately undermined the competitiveness of the industries they were intended to promote.[22]

The explanations for this paradox are several. First, trade restrictions insulated Brazilian industry from the pressures of the market place. The new strategy therefore calls for exposing Brazilian industry to competitive forces, both foreign (through trade liberalization) and domestic (through the elimination of cartels and the enactment of new antitrust legislation). Second, trade restrictions have curtailed access to new capital and technology, due to the difficulty of importing new plant and equipment, the reduced need of competitors to provide state-of-the-art products, and impediments to technology transfer. To help Brazilian industry to

---

20 Interview with an official in the Industry and Commerce Department, National Secretariat of Economy, Ministry of Economy, Treasury and Planning, July 1990.

21 Interview with an independent Brazilian consultant, July 1990.

22 Interviews with officials from the Ministry of Foreign Affairs and the Ministry of Economy, Treasury, and Planning, July 1990. Both officials cited recent studies indicating that Brazilian industry is rapidly falling behind that of other developing nations.

respond to the new competitive environment, the Government intends to promote the incorporation of foreign technology, both through technology transfers and foreign direct investment. Government credits will be focused on enhancing the technological capabilities of Brazilian industry. Intellectual property protection will be improved in a bid to encourage increased research and development. State industries will be privatized, in the hope that private enterprise can provide necessary investment funds that the State lacks.

Brazil is seeking gradually to insert itself more fully into the world economy. While some sectors of Brazilian industry may falter, the more competitive sectors of the Brazilian economy are expected to respond to the new climate of openness by upgrading their capabilities and expanding exports. The government hopes to facilitate this trend by securing improved market access abroad through regional trade agreements, enhanced cooperation with the industrialized nations, and more aggressive use of multilateral institutions.

TRADE POLICY ACTORS

The Foreign Ministry is the most important single agency in Brazil's foreign policy decision-making process, and it has sought to maintain this primacy in the field of international economic policy-making as well. The Foreign Ministry's position has not gone unchallenged -- the Ministry of Finance, in particular, has sought to assert a greater role in the process -- but to date the Foreign Ministry has generally come out of such fights the winner.[23] This traditional dominance may be undercut by Collor's administrative reforms, including the formation of several "Super Ministries." However, the professionalism and competence of the Foreign Ministry, combined with the strong presence of Brazilian diplomats on the Presidential staff and throughout the bureaucracy, suggest that it will continue to play a leading role in trade policy matters for years to come.

The Foreign Ministry

Perhaps the best-trained and most competent organization in the Brazilian bureaucracy is the Foreign Ministry, also referred to as Itamaraty. Brazil does not have a separate trade representative, and the

---

23 Michelle O'Neil, "Itamaraty -- Rio Branco, Modernization and diffusion in Brazil's Foreign Policy Decisionmaking Process," *Policymaking in a Newly Industrialized Nation*, eds. Lawrence Graham and Robert Wilson (University of Texas, 1988), p. 20.

Foreign Ministry plays the leading role in trade matters requiring government-to-government contact. The Ministry has chief responsibility for all bilateral and multinational negotiations, except those related to external debt and financing.[24]

In addition to its central role in negotiations, Ministry personnel are on long-term assignment to other agencies throughout the government, where they play a key part in many decisions. This is in part a carry-over from the pre-Collor period, when every agency had a Foreign Ministry representative assigned to it to handle foreign matters. Yet, the Collor government actually has increased the presence of professional diplomats throughout the bureaucracy. At the present time, for example, both the Minister of Economy, Treasury and Planning and the head of that Ministry's Foreign Trade Department are professional diplomats, and President Collor employs nearly thirty diplomats in the Planalto Palace itself, including his chief of staff.[25]

Itamaraty recruits are trained at their own academy, the Rio Branco Institute. As a result, most Foreign Ministry officials share a coherent world view, which tends to be nationalistic, reflecting distrust of the First World, and placing emphasis on national sovereignty.[26] The desire for economic autonomy often leads the Ministry to oppose import and investment liberalization, and to encourage market reserve programs calculated to develop indigenous technologies. Itamaraty has pursued an active Third World policy. Although these attitudes are evolving, they are unlikely to change drastically in the short run, particularly at the second and third echelons of the Ministry.[27]

Nevertheless, the response of the Foreign Ministry to the current reforms has been more positive than might have been expected. Many Foreign Ministry Officials, including some of the nation's leading

---

24 J. Ray Kennedy and Roberto Giannetti da Fonseca, "Brazilian Trade Policy and the Uruguay Round," in *Domestic Trade Policies and the Uruguay Round,* ed. Henry R. Nau (Columbia University Press, 1989), p. 40.

25 *Correio Braziliense* (May 13, 1991) (FBIS-LAT-91-114).

26 Although the current Foreign Minister is not a career Itamaraty diplomat, he has taught law at the Rio Branco Institute for many years and appears to share the traditional Itamaraty world view. See *Estado de São Paulo* (July 29, 1990) (FBIS-LAT-90-168).

27 Interview with an official with the U.S. Chambers of Commerce in Brazil, July 1990 and an American official familiar with the issue.

diplomats, acknowledge that Brazil's trade reform measures are necessary.[28] One official who works closely with Itamaraty on GATT issues asserts, perhaps hyperbolically, that the Foreign Ministry has changed its mind set on trade reform "180 degrees."[29] Thus, while it is likely that the Foreign Ministry will seek to moderate the pace of trade reform, it may not offer the same level of opposition to trade liberalization that it has in the past.

Ministry of Economy, Treasury and Planning

Another key decision-making entity in the trade policy arena in the Collor Administration is the Ministry of Economy, Treasury and Planning. Within this new "Super Ministry," the result of a Collor Administration reorganization joining three independent agencies, are a number of important trade policy decision-making bodies. The reorganization concentrated the trade policy decision-making power of the three agencies in the hands of one Minister, who is undoubtedly among the most influential persons in the government after the President.[30]

The Foreign Trade Department of the Economy Secretariat (Decex) is the lead trade-policy decision-maker in the Ministry. The Department includes the Coordenadoria de Intercambio Comercial (CIC), formerly known as Cacex. CIC, the organization responsible for issuing import licenses, was transferred to the Ministry from the Bank of Brazil.[31] Traditionally very powerful and strongly opposed to liberalization, its separation from the Bank of Brazil is perceived by some as an effort to reduce its independence. CIC has experienced drastic personnel cuts and its influence may be on the wane. Also folded into Decex is the former Council of Foreign Commerce (Concex).

The Department of Industry and Commerce of the Economy Secretariat, while not a trade entity per se, inevitably becomes involved in trade policy as a key element in Brazil's broader industrial policy. The Department was the primary author of the Industrial and Foreign Trade Plan issued in June, 1990.

---

28 Interviews with officials of the Commercial Policy Division of the Ministry of Foreign Affairs, July 1990.

29 Interview with a senior private sector executive, July 1990.

30 *Estado de São Paulo* (March 16, 1990) (FBIS-LAT-90-058).

31 *Brazil Watch* (April 30-May 14, 1990).

The National Bank for Economic and Social Development (BNDES) is a key source of momentum for the import liberalization and privatization programs. The Bank administers much of Brazil's state credit through programs such as Financiamento de Maquinaria e Equipamentos (FINAME). As lender of last resort, BNDES has borne the responsibility for rehabilitating and re-privatizing failing companies. The technocrats of BNDES have long advocated economic reforms, and the June 1990 Industrial and Foreign Trade Plan represents a major victory for them.[32]

The Central Bank is responsible for foreign exchange matters. As such, it wields substantial power over imports, especially as traditional barriers fall away. In addition, it is involved in the administration of export financing programs.[33] It also plays a critical role in the foreign debt negotiations, providing the technical and staff support for the foreign debt negotiator.

Although it is difficult to generalize about a Ministry as diverse as the Ministry of Economy, Treasury and Planning, the Ministry at its highest levels is the key institution in the implementation of the Collor economic reform, including its trade liberalization efforts. Nevertheless, there are undoubtedly many mid-level bureaucrats within the Ministry who will resist all efforts at reform. Further, the long-term influence of this new Ministry can not yet be predicted with certainty.

The Ministry of Infrastructure

Another "Super Ministry" created by the Collor administrative reforms is the Ministry of Infrastructure. This Ministry was formed through the merger of the Ministries of Transportation, Communications, and Mines and Energy. Although the Ministry does not have a direct role in trade policy decision-making, it is responsible for administering most of Brazil's parastatal companies, including the former Siderbrás companies, Eletrobrás, CVRD, Embratel and Portobrás. It has been assigned an important role in the privatization process, and its policies towards the parastatals will affect trade-related domestic subsidies. It can also be expected to have a significant say in trade policies relating to those sectors, such as energy, steel and mining, in which its parastatal companies are dominant.

---

[32] Interviews with officials at the National Bank for Economic and Social Development, July 1990.

[33] "Central Bank Creates Rules to Finance Exports," *Estado de São Paulo* (August 3, 1991) (FBIS-LAT-91-157).

In its upper echelons, the Infrastructure Ministry is a key supporter of Collor's economic reforms and can be expected to play a positive role in the trade liberalization process. On the other hand, many lower-level officials, and especially employees of the state-run companies, will ferociously resist the economic reform effort to protect their jobs. Therefore, the long-term institutional role of the Ministry in trade-related decision-making is difficult to predict.

Private Sector

The direct role of the private sector in trade policy is generally a limited one. For example, only one of the twelve Commissions appointed to develop proposals under the Industrial and Foreign Trade Plan has private sector representatives,[34] although the Executive Groups for Sectoral Policy (GEPS), which, among other things, make recommendations regarding tariffs, are joint public/private bodies.[35] Further, the Collor Administration has been criticized for its lack of openness to input from business people.[36] In the opinion of one U.S. diplomat, the government is moving certain agencies, such as CIC, to Brasília in an effort to insulate them from private sector pressures as much as possible. Collor also has sought to insure government control over joint government-industry bodies, such as the National Council For Informatics and Automation (Conin), apparently in the belief that industry would use its power to block reforms if it could.[37]

---

34 The exception is the Commission studying the Export-Import Bank, for which the government is seeking private participation. Interviews several senior officials and advisors at the National Bank for Economic and Social Development, July 1990.

35 Concern has been expressed that the GEPS could become pressure groups advocating subsidies and tax incentives for their sectors. *Exame* (July 11, 1990) (FBIS-LAT-90-167).

36 According to one observer, Collor treats business people as "bandits" and refuses to see even the CEOs of major corporations. Interview with a private economic consultant in Brazil, July 1990.

37 *Gazeta Mercantil* (October 25, 1991) (FBIS-LAT-91-226) Conin was responsible for overseeing the implementation of many of the market-reserve rules in informatics. A new law will curb that authority as of October 1992. Collor vetoed a provision of that law that would have increased industry representation on Conin. Interview with a private economic consultant in Brazil, July 1990.

In spite of its limited formal role, business can be expected to play an important role in determining the shape and pace of trade reform. As a general rule, its contribution will not be positive. Mainstream industry associations, such as the Industrial Association of São Paulo (FIESP), the Brazilian Association of Basic Industries and the Brazilian Association of Electric and Electronics Associations, generally have benefitted from trade barriers and thus have supported protection in the past.[38] There is broad agreement that industry generally is fearful of liberalization, which forces it to compete and deprives it of guaranteed markets and profits. It is widely believed that the supportive stance of most industry associations can not be taken at face value.[39] In the words of one executive, industry publicly supports reform but is lobbying against it behind the scenes.[40]

At least one observer takes a different view, however. According to economist James Wygand, there are modern, rational managers throughout the economy who support economic reform. While they may not be as visible as the old guard, which prefers an environment of government influence and economic protection, these reformers rapidly are winning the battle for a more open economy.[41] In any event, the government will be able to take advantage of divisions within industry, as some companies that seek access to imported inputs will support liberalization.[42] An early example is textiles, where the opposition of cloth manufacturers to import liberalization has been offset by support from clothing producers.

---

38 J. Ray Kennedy and Roberto Giannetti da Fonseca, "Brazilian Trade Policy and the Uruguay Round," in *Domestic Trade Policy and the Uruguay Round*, Columbia University Press, 1989), p. 41.

39 Interview with a Ministry of Foreign Affairs official, July 1990. An exception is the Instituto de Estudos de Desenvolvimento Industrial (IEDI), a group of businessmen dissatisfied with FIESP that has pushed strongly for trade reform.

40 Interview with a Ministry of Foreign Affairs official, July 1990. The resistance will be directed not at the policy generally, but rather with respect to the specific measures applicable to a given industry. Interviews with a private consultant and an official at the Ministry of Economy, Treasury and Planning, July 1990.

41 *Brazil Watch* (October 21-November 4, 1991), p. 14.

42 This industrialist favors liberalization because he wants to import sheet for his plant. Interview, July 1990.

TRADE REGIME

The Collor Administration has a straightforward plan for Brazil's overall trade regime. To facilitate imports, the widespread non-tariff barriers will be replaced with import tariffs which, in turn, will be gradually reduced. Surges of imports will then be addressed with GATT-sanctioned trade remedies, such as antidumping and countervailing duty investigations (although reversion to foreign-exchange allocation is possible in times of difficulty). Export promotion will be further constrained, with most existing export subsidies phased out and GATT-consistent export assistance programs created to take their place.

Tariffs

The key tool in Brazil's import liberalization effort is the elimination of quantitative restrictions and their replacement with tariffs which are to be gradually reduced over a five-year period. As of 1990, Brazilian tariffs ranged from zero percent to 105 percent, with a trade-weighted average tariff of 35 percent. The Industrial and Foreign Trade Plan provided that the tariff structure at the end of 1994 would be as follows:

- The trade-weighted average tariff would be 20 percent.
- The "normal" tariff rate would be 20 percent.
- A zero tariff would apply to inputs, capital goods and products not made in Brazil.
- A 40 percent tariff could be applied, temporarily and exceptionally, to certain emerging high technology products or to products in need of special protection.[43]

The Collor government moved promptly to implement the tariff reduction program. Under the tariff reduction process, duties on machines, equipment, parts and components, raw materials and intermediate products, not produced in Brazil, fell to zero percent on July 1, 1990. In early February 1991 a Tariff Review Commission, chaired by the Chief of the Foreign Trade Division of the Ministry of Economy, Treasury and Planning, released a five-year tariff reduction schedule based on the criteria set forth in the Plan.[44] Under the schedule, tariffs are set

---

43 *General Directives*, Section 6.3.

44 *Journal of Commerce* (February 4, 1991).

to fall to an average of 14 percent by 1994.[45] The rates will fall most rapidly on capital goods, while tariffs cuts on consumer goods will be phased in more gradually from a higher base. See Table 6.1.

In spite of the significant cuts now contemplated, the impact of the tariff reduction program should not be overstated. Tariffs will generally continue to be high by developed country standards.[46] Many imported products can not compete over a 20 percent duty, much less the 40 percent duty applicable to high technology and other special sectors. Further, the actual rate of protection is much higher than the nominal tariff due to the cumulative imposition of the 18 percent Industrial Products Tax (IPI) and the ICM tax, not to mention freight, insurance and port taxes.[47] In addition, those products most likely to come in at a zero duty rate under the new tariff schedule were likely to enter duty-free previously under one of many incentive programs exempting import duties.

Although the government appears committed to the tariff reduction program at this time, it will not be bound by law or treaty to maintain the rates established by the Commission. In Brazil, legislation only sets out the parameters within which tariff rates must fall, and it is up to the administering agencies to decide actual rates. Further, Brazil is not expected to bind its forthcoming tariff reductions at the GATT. Rather, it has so far offered only to reduce its bound rates modestly from a 1986 base year.[48] Thus, it would be relatively easy for the government to reverse its tariff cuts if it desired to do so. Officials are adamant, however, that the tariff cuts will not be reversed. In fact, it is likely that any renewed protection would come in the form of foreign exchange allocation or other, less transparent measures, rather than through tariff increases.

Non-Tariff Barriers

The current emphasis on tariffs is a new development. In the past, tariffs have been virtually irrelevant to import protection in Brazil due to the comprehensive application of a series of highly effective non-tariff barriers. For example, Brazil imposed a tax on many foreign exchange

---

45 *Gazeta Mercantil* (June 14, 1991).

46 *Brazil Watch* (February 11-25, 1991).

47 Interviews with an official in Brazil's Tariff Policy Commission and an official of the American Chambers of Commerce for Brazil, July 1990.

48 Interview with a Brazilian Foreign Ministry Official, July 1990.

TABLE 6.1 Selected Import Tariff Reductions 1990-1994 (%)

	1990	1991	1992	1993	1994
Capital Goods					
Machinery	40	30	25	20	20
Digital Machinery	65	50	45	35	25
Tractors	45	40	45	30	20
Agricultural Equipment	25	25	25	20	20
Computers	--	65	60	50	40
Consumer Durables					
Cars & Trucks	85	60	50	40	35
VCRs	85	65	50	40	30
Bicycles	85	60	50	35	20
Toys	105	85	65	40	20
Consumer Goods					
Beer	85	55	40	30	20
Whiskey	85	75	65	40	20
Shampoos, Perfumes	85	60	40	30	20

Source: *Brazil Watch* (February 11-25, 1991).

purchases (the "tax on financial operations" or IOF), which ranged as high as 25 percent for some products.[49] It required an import license for virtually all imports, and under the "law of similars" denied licenses for any product that could be made in Brazil.[50] Under company import plans, each company was required to submit for approval an import plan for the following year. The Central Bank would not issue any import licenses outside the context of the plans.[51]

Many of these barriers now have been eliminated by Presidential decree. On March 15, 1990, before the new trade and industrial policy itself was announced, Brazil eliminated the Annex C list of prohibited imports[52] and the company import plans.[53] Subsequently, the "law of similars" was also eliminated (although, as always, the general rules are not applicable in the informatics sector).[54] In response to the elimination of Annex C and related barriers, the U.S. Government terminated its "Super 301" investigation of Brazilian non-tariff barriers to trade.[55]

However, certain barriers remain in effect or could be activated on short notice should they once again be deemed necessary. Import licenses are still required, for example. The present policy is that such licenses are to be issued automatically, within five days, and are required solely for statistical purposes.[56] This policy is currently being observed,[57] but

---

49 United States Trade Representative, *National Trade Estimate Report on Foreign Trade Barriers* (1987), p. 30.

50 United States Trade Representative, *National Trade Estimate Report on Foreign Trade Barriers* (1987), p. 32.

51 United States Trade Representative, *National Trade Estimate Report on Foreign Trade Barriers* (1987), p. 32.

52 Ministerial Resolution 56 (March 15, 1990) in *O Globo* (March 17, 1990) (FBIS-LAT-90-059).

53 *Business Latin America* (May 21, 1991).

54 Maria Christina Carvalho, "Guia para Importer: Liberdade para Pessoas Juridícas e Fisicas," *Gazeta Mercantil* (June 14, 1991), p. 2.

55 55 Fed. Reg. 22876 (June 4, 1990).

56 United States Trade Representative, *National Trade Estimate Report on Foreign Trade Barriers* (1991), p. 20.

there is nothing to prevent the government from reversing itself and delaying the processing of licenses, as it has done in the past. In the opinion of one observer, these regulations are being maintained as a kind of "insurance" against unacceptable import levels.[58]

The elimination of many import barriers has not meant the elimination of all policies favoring domestic production over imports. For example, domestic content tests must be met to obtain government capital goods financing under FINAME, or to sell capital goods to the government. (The domestic content level has gradually been reduced from 85 percent to 60 percent, however.)[59] In addition, although the law of similars has been eliminated for private parties, government entities at all levels are prohibited from importing products where a comparable domestic product exists.[60] With respect to procurement generally, preferential treatment for companies of "national capital" is required by the Constitution.[61]

Foreign Exchange

One likely instrument to be used in case of import surges is foreign exchange and financing controls. As of this writing, Brazil maintains a dual exchange system, with a tourist rate that fluctuates freely and a commercial rate -- the rate at which all import and export transactions must be conducted -- that "floats" in theory but at the moment overvalues the cruzeiro by an estimated 15-50 percent. The government's stated intention is to unify the two rates[62] (which are in fact closer at present than they have been for many years), but some government officials are skeptical that this goal will prove achievable.[63] Meanwhile, the dual

---

57 (...continued)

57 Interviews with two top executives of a Brazilian steel producer, July 1990.

58 Interview with a private Brazilian economic consultant, July 1990.

59 Ministry of Economy, Treasury and Planning, Portaria No. 123 (February 27, 1991) ("Program of Industrial Competitiveness").

60 *Gazeta Mercantil* (June 14, 1991), p. 2.

61 *Constitution of the Federative Republic of Brazil*, Article 171 (1988).

62 Text of letter from Economy, Finance and Planning Minister Zelia Cardoso de Mello and Central Bank President Ibraham Eris to IMF Managing Director Michal Camdessus, item 25, reprinted in *Estado de São Paulo* (September 14, 1990).

63 Interview with a financial policy official in the Foreign Ministry, July 1990.

rates, while permitting the government access to foreign exchange at unrealistically low cost, serve as a disincentive to exports.[64]

The dilemma facing the government is that, while it is dependent on floating exchange rates to generate balanced trade, devaluation would have an inflationary effect that may prove unacceptable. Yet failure to devalue the currency reduces the ability of domestic industry to survive as import barriers are reduced. In the view of some economists, therefore, Brazil's stabilization and trade liberalization programs are incompatible and can not both be carried through.[65] Although this is probably an overstatement of the problem, there is a tension between fighting inflation and permitting devaluation of the cruzeiro, and this tension makes an equalization of the parallel exchange rates difficult.

Brazil may in the future consider it necessary to impose import restrictions on occasion. If so, these restrictions are likely to come in the form of foreign exchange controls. Currently, exporters are still required to convert their export earnings to cruzeiros, leaving the government in control of all foreign exchange. Although most officials deny that the government would resort to foreign exchange controls to restrict imports,[66] there seems to be a widespread perception that foreign exchange allocation can and will be used, where necessary, to restrict imports.[67]

GATT-Sanctioned Trade Remedies

Brazil currently is a signatory of the GATT Dumping, Subsidies and Valuation Codes. Until recently, however, the existence of effective discretionary import restrictions has made the use of GATT-sanctioned trade remedies unnecessary. In fact, Brazil did not even incorporate the Codes into domestic law until 1988. There have been only a handful of

---

64 One producer termed the situation a "negative subsidy" for exports. Interview with a senior executive of a major Brazilian corporation, July 1990.

65 Professors Simão David Silber, Universidade de São Paulo, and Francisco Eduardo Pires de Souza, Universidade Federal de Rio de Janeiro, in *Estado de São Paulo* (July 19, 1990).

66 Interviews with officials from the Commercial Policy Division of the Ministry of Foreign Affairs, July 1990.

67 Interviews with an independent Brazilian consultant, and an official of the Tariff Policy Commission, July 1990.

antidumping/countervailing duty cases since that time. To this day there is no safeguards provision in Brazilian law.

In light of the liberalization process, Brazil clearly intends to make greater use of unfair trade remedies in the future than it has in the past. The 1990 Industrial and Foreign Trade Policy called for "special emphasis" to be given to legislation "protecting national industry from unfair trade practices, such as dumping,"[68] and the Brazilian government in 1990 was preparing to update its system through the issuance of new *portarias*, to set forth a clear set of procedures and timetable for unfair trade cases.[69] Both in the government and the private sector, most believe that the unfair trade laws will assume increasing importance over the next few years.[70] According to one government official, countervailing duty cases against EC agricultural products are already being prepared.[71]

Some observers believe, however, that the Brazilian government lacks the ability or inclination to vigorously implement the unfair trade laws. One businessman who has observed U.S. Commerce Department verifications expressed doubt that Brazilian bureaucrats have the expertise to perform the task, and suggested the government may have to hire international accounting firms.[72] Another observer noted that, in addition to lack of competence, the government in its role as reducer of tariffs has an institutional bias against imposing duties. He indicated that a campaign for a comprehensive trade act is now underway and will likely succeed in a few years after a few firms fail due to import competition.[73]

Export Promotion

Through the 1970s and much of the 1980s, Brazil provided its industries with a wide range of export subsidies. Many of these subsidies

---

68 *General Directives*, Article 6.3.

69 Interview with an official of the Foreign Trade Section of the Ministry of Economy, Treasury, and Planning, July 1990.

70 Interviews with an official at the Foreign Trade Section of the Ministry of Economy, Treasury, and Planning and several private sector executives, July 1990.

71 Interview with an official of the Companhia de Financiamento da Produção, July 1990.

72 Interview with a Brazilian corporate executive.

73 Interview with a private sector official based in Rio de Janeiro, July 1990.

came in the form of fiscal incentives, such as exemptions from taxes on imported inputs used to produce export goods, exemption from the Industrial Products (IPI) and State Sales (ICM) taxes, and an exemption from income taxes for profits earned through exporting. Exporters also benefitted from an export tax credit (the "crédito prêmio") and from a variety of export financing programs.[74] As Table 6.2 indicates, these export incentives amounted to as much as 69 percent of the FOB value of manufactured exports.[75]

Beginning in the late 1970s, however, Brazil came under intense pressure to eliminate its export subsidy programs. Not only did the United States repeatedly impose high countervailing duties on Brazilian exports, but the International Monetary Fund demanded the reduction of export subsidies (along with exchange rate devaluation), as a condition for assistance in servicing Brazil's debt.[76] As a result, Brazil undertook gradually to phase out its export subsidy programs as the decade progressed.

Although Brazil had reduced or eliminated many export subsidy programs by 1990, it had by no means abolished all of them. The Collor Administration, however, was committed to complete the process. In one of its first acts, the government in March 1990 subjected export income to the same income tax rate as income earned from domestic sales.[77] It also ended the practice of granting exemptions from tariffs and Industrial Products taxes to companies which committed under the Befiex program to maintain 3:1 export ratios in exchange for tax exemptions on

---

[74] Benedict J. Clements and J. Scott McClain, "The Political Economy of Export Promotion in Brazil," in *The Political Economy of Brazil*, ed. Lawrence S. Graham and Robert H. Wilson (University of Texas Press, 1990), pp. 66-68.

[75] According to Clements and McClain, however, the high domestic prices resulting from import barriers created an "anti-export" bias that offset export subsidies and encourage producers to sell domestically. See, Benedict J. Clements and J. Scott McClain, "The Political Economy of Export Promotion in Brazil," in *The Political Economy of Brazil*, ed. Lawrence S. Graham and Robert H. Wilson (University of Texas Press, 1990), pp. 70-71.

[76] Benedict J. Clements and J. Scott McClain, "The Political Economy of Export Promotion in Brazil," in *The Political Economy of Brazil*, ed. Lawrence S. Graham and Robert H. Wilson (University of Texas Press, 1990), pp. 74-75.

[77] Provisional Measure No. 161 (March 15, 1990), in *O Globo* (March 17, 1990) (FBIS-LAT-90-058).

TABLE 6.2 Brazilian Export Incentives for Manufactured Products, 1969-1985
(In % of FOB Value of Manufactured Exports)

Year	"Drawback"	"Crédito Premio"	Income Tax Exemption	ICM Exemption[a]	IPI Exemption[b]	Credit Subsidies[c]	Total Incentives
1969	4.00	6.69	--	20.50	7.41	4.07	42.67
1970	4.00	13.50	--	20.50	7.18	7.51	52.69
1971	4.00	13.15	1.30	19.80	7.09	7.80	53.14
1972	4.90	16.26	1.30	19.10	9.04	8.22	58.82
1973	7.20	16.16	1.30	18.30	8.86	6.45	58.27
1974	12.60	11.95	1.80	17.70	4.97	6.14	55.16
1975	8.30	12.06	1.70	17.00	5.43	11.51	56.00
1976	11.80	11.72	1.30	16.30	5.17	15.88	62.17
1977	12.60	12.41	1.50	16.30	5.43	19.63	67.87
1978	9.10	12.79	1.80	16.30	6.13	17.00	63.12
1979	10.50	12.78	2.10	16.30	6.52	13.88	62.08
1980	9.00	0.00	1.90	17.70	6.34	2.04	36.98
1981	9.40	6.51	1.80	18.30	6.83	18.73	61.57
1982	10.30	9.11	1.60	19.10	7.16	21.69	68.96
1983	8.60	7.79	1.60	19.10	7.17	9.31	53.57
1984	9.10	7.84	1.60	20.50	6.99	2.67	48.70
1985	9.10	1.36	1.60	20.50	7.19	3.63	43.38

Source: Renato Bauman and Heloiza C. Moreira, "Os Incentivos Ās Exportações Brasileiras de Produtos Manufaturados -- 1969 a 1985" in *Pesquisa e Planejamento Econômico* (August 1987), reprinted in Benedict J. Clements, *Foreign Trade Strategies, Employment and Income Distribution in Brazil* (New York: Praeger, 1988), pp. 15-17.

[a]Refers to exemption from the state sales tax.

[b]Refers to exemption from the industrial value-added tax.

[c]Includes both preexport and postexport financing subsidies.

imports.[78] Finally, it announced that no new funds would be provided for the Finex subsidized export credit program, so that the volume of Finex lending would gradually decline towards zero.[79]

Brazil initially planned to replace its existing export financing programs with an Export-Import Bank. The Bank was intended to be a private entity, although the government was to make a capital contribution; the government asserted that foreign investors, including Germany's Commerzbank, were interested in participating.[80] However, little progress was made in establishing such a Bank, and Brazilian businessmen began to clamor for some form of financing to aid their export efforts. In response, the government announced in February 1991 that it would seek enactment of a replacement for the now defunct Finex program.[81] This replacement "Proex" program, which was approved by Congress in June 1991, will provide $570 million in subsidized loans in 1991.[82] Because of limited resources, the program reportedly will be available only for a short list of capital goods and services exports.[83]

BRAZIL AND THE GATT

Although Brazil has sought to utilize the GATT to protect market access in developed nations, its posture has generally been defensive.

---

78 Some 542 existing contracts, covering $40 billion in imports and $140 billion in exports, are still being honored. The majority of these contracts are scheduled to expire within two to three years. Some, however, will continue until the year 2000. Interview with an official in the Department of Industry and Commerce, National Secretariat of Economy, Ministry of Economy, Treasury, and Planning, July 1990.

79 Interviews with a Foreign Trade Section official and an official with Fundacão Centro de Estudos do Comercio Exterior, July 1990.

80 Interviews with officials in the National Bank for Economic and Social Development and Fundacão Centro de Estudos do Comercio Exterior, July 1990.

81 Ministry of Economy, Treasury and Planning, Portaria No. 123 (February 27, 1991) ("Program of Industrial Competitiveness").

82 U.S. Department of State Unclassified Cable No. 6628 (June 1991); *Journal of Commerce* (July 22, 1991).

83 *Estado de São Paulo* (August 3, 1991) (FBIS-LAT-91-157).

Because many of its policies were potentially inconsistent with GATT principles, it has sought to maintain special exemptions from GATT disciplines (balance of payment rules, differential treatment). In fact, Brazil has used the balance of payments exception as the primary legal justification for its non-tariff restrictions on imports, an approach which has been sharply criticized by Brazil's trading partners.[84] Brazil also has resisted the tightening of disciplines or the extension of GATT rules into new areas. Brazil and India, for example, headed up the largely unsuccessful efforts by the developing countries to prevent negotiations on services in the Uruguay Round.[85]

For a number of reasons, however, Brazil is likely in the 1990s both to play a more constructive role in the GATT process and to make more aggressive use of the GATT to advance its own interests. First, the trade and economic liberalization should make Brazil less defensive in the GATT arena. For example, the dismantling of many import barriers, elimination of export subsidies, and extension of intellectual property protection should lessen somewhat Brazilian vulnerability to criticism in the GATT and will align it more closely with the interests of the developed world.

Second, events have shown that Brazil needs multilateral rules. For example, Brazil has used the GATT to attack Section 301 actions by the United States, and may be realizing that more such actions are likely if strong multilateral rules are not developed. According to Foreign Ministry officials, Brazil expects to use dispute resolution to challenge the application of antidumping and countervailing duties by the United States, the EC and other nations. Further, a strong GATT is seen as one way to counter the threat presented by regional trading blocs.[86]

Finally, Brazil's commitment to a Third World ideology has weakened. The Collor government prefers to view Brazil as a First World nation,

---

84 In the GATT Committee on Balance of Payments Restrictions, which reviews the use of such measures by GATT signatories, "Doubts were exposed on whether [Brazilian] trade restrictions could make more than a temporary and limited contribution to resolving the country's balance of payments situation. In this regard, the long-standing nature of many of the restrictions was viewed with concern." General Agreement on Tariffs and Trade, *Activities 1987*, p. 89.

85 Ubaldo Cesar Balthazar, "Le Bresil et les Negociations Sur le Commerce de Services dans le Cadre du GATT," *Revue du Marché Comun*, No. 317 (May 1988).

86 Interview with a senior official of the Department of Industry and Commerce, National Secretariat of Economy, Ministry of Economy, Treasury, and Planning, July 1990.

however far behind the other developed nations, than as a Third World leader[87] (although President Collor's speeches and interviews in the summer of 1991 regarding the "Empire of the North" have fueled speculation that he may be undergoing a gradual shift in attitudes.[88]) Even in Itamaraty, the strongest advocate of Brazil's Third-World policy, more pragmatic views regarding cooperation with the developed world are coming to the fore.

The shift of Brazilian policy is reflected to some degree in its stance in the Uruguay Round. Brazil has two key priorities in the Round, discipline over agricultural subsidies and restrictions on the use of national trade laws. With respect to agriculture, Brazil has been severely injured by EC agricultural subsidies and the United States response they have evoked, and this has given Brazil a major reason to participate actively in the Uruguay Round. (President Collor has remarked that a European cow earns a per capita income higher than that of 60 percent of the human race.[89]) As a leader of the Cairns Group of agricultural exporters, Brazil has transcended traditional North-South divisions, finding itself allied with developed nations, including the United States, in advocating the imposition of multilateral disciplines over agricultural subsidies and market access measures.[90] With respect to national trade laws, Brazil is aligned with Asian exporters in seeking changes in the antidumping and countervailing duty laws of the United States and EC.

In order to achieve its goals, Brazil has made compromises on a number of other Uruguay Round issues. For example, it has abandoned its wholesale opposition to the services negotiations, and is now willing to consider a Services Code in exchange for gains on agriculture, market access and textiles, according to one Foreign Ministry official. Similarly, Brazil has reportedly softened its stance in the Trade-Related Intellectual Property (TRIPs) talks, and has agreed to certain U.S. proposals to

---

87 Interview with a foreign business official in Brazil, July 1990.

88 "The End of Bipolarity Created the Great Empire of the North," *Excelsior* (Mexico City) (July 16, 1991) (FBIS-LAT-91-148).

89 "The End of Bipolarity Created the Great Empire of the North," *Excelsior* (Mexico City) (July 16, 1991) (FBIS-LAT-91-148).

90 The Cairns Group, comprised of Argentina, Australia, Brazil, Canada, Chile, Colombia, Hungary, Indonesia, Malaysia, New Zealand, the Philippines, Thailand and Uruguay, has pressed for sweeping liberalization in the agricultural sector. See, "Comprehensive Proposal for the Long-Term Reform of Agricultural Trade," reprinted in *Inside U.S. Trade* (December 1, 1989).

strengthen the dispute resolution process. There are limits to this new flexibility, however. It is not likely to extend to the Trade-Related Investment Measure talks, for example, where Brazil is unwilling to abandon measures it deems essential to the promotion of such sectors as high technology and to regional development. Nor has it changed Brazil's posture on balance of payments measures. While Brazil recently disinvoked its use of balance of payment measures under GATT Article XVIII(B), it continues to believe that developing countries should retain the right to invoke such measures when necessary, and has not renounced possible future use.[91]

More fundamentally, Brazil and the United States will continue to disagree regarding the need for universal rules applicable to all GATT signatories. Brazil's position at the GATT continues to rest on the belief that developing countries are entitled to "differential treatment" under the international trading regime. Even the Cairns Group proposal on agriculture reiterates the need for differential treatment.[92]

This principle of "differential treatment," while recognized in the GATT and in the Punta del Este Declaration,[93] is fundamentally at odds with the United States' view of fairness in the world trading system, and has

---

[91] Statement by Ambassador Rubens Ricupero, Permanent Representative of Brazil, to the Meeting of the Council of Representatives of the GATT (July 11, 1991).

[92] The Proposal states that "[g]overnment measures on assistance, whether direct or indirect, to encourage agricultural and rural development are an integral part of the development programs of developing countries," and that, inter alia, "[t]he timeframe for implementation of the reform commitments for developing countries must be extended, "[t]he depths of cuts in import access barriers will be lower than generally accepted targets, and "[c]ommitments to reduce internal part of the development programs of developing nations will not be required. . . ." "Comprehensive Proposal for the Long-Term Reform of Agricultural Trade," reprinted in *Inside U.S. Trade* (December 1, 1989).

[93] Among other things, the GATT provides that (a) developed nations do not expect reciprocal trade concessions from LDCs in negotiations; (b) LDCs may grant each other preferences and may be given preferences by developed nations without violating the MFN principle; and (c) LDCs may generally subsidize their industries, including export industries. G. Lacharriere, "The Legal Framework for International Trade," in *Trade Policies for a Better Future* (Nijhoff: 1987) pp. 104-108.

been sharply criticized by U.S. trade officials.[94] So long as such divergent perceptions exist, the United States and Brazil are bound to clash in the GATT.[95]

BILATERAL TRADE RELATIONS

Brazil's two most important trading relationships are with the United States, which is likely to improve in the 1990s, and the European Community, which has been historically viewed by Brazilians as an alternative to the U.S. trade connection. Although there are significant economic ties between Brazil and Japan, the development of a strong trading relationship commensurate with Japan's global economic power is restrained by Brazil's foreign debt problem.

Brazil and the United States

Dependence and Diversification. During the 1950s, the United States absorbed 45 percent of all Brazil's exports and provided 34.5 percent of its imports. Although the relative importance of U.S. trade has declined somewhat as the economies of the European Community and Japan prospered, the United States still absorbed 24.4 percent of Brazil's exports and provided 21.4 percent of its imports in 1990. See Figures 6.1 and 6.2. Further, the United States has been more receptive to the import of

---

94 United States Trade Representative Carla Hills, has noted that developing countries say "'Who, Me? I get special treatment. I don't have to abide by these rules, Right?' We think that's wrong." *Daily Report for Executives* (November 24, 1989).

95 One senior government official in the Sarney Administration asked rhetorically whether "Pittsburgh [should] be allowed to defend itself against the inroads of its young Korean and Brazilian competitors with the same weapons that are granted to the nascent minicomputer industries of São Paulo and Manaus to protect themselves against the power of their U.S. and Japanese counterparts?" Sérgio B. Serra, "Brazil's Trade: A View from the South," in *Brazil's Economic and Political Future*, ed. Julian M. Chacel, Pamela S. Falk and David V. Fleischer (Westview, 1988), p. 93. Most Americans assume that Pittsburgh is entitled to equal treatment with São Paulo.

developing country manufactured goods, Brazil's most dynamic export sector, than either the European Community or Japan.[96]

Brazil's access to the U.S. market has been perceived as a mixed blessing by Brazilian policy makers. On the one hand, the U.S. market is important to Brazil and access to it has allowed Brazil to generate substantial export earnings. On the other hand Brazil feels vulnerable to the vagaries of U.S. trade and foreign policy. Brazilian decision makers are well aware that while trade with the United States is vital to their country, Brazilian trade is an extremely small fraction of U.S. foreign commerce. This gross disproportionality makes Brazil the more vulnerable trading partner. Policy makers in Brazil would like to diversify the nation's patterns of trade so as to lessen dependence on the United States, although they realize that no single substitute market is available to them.

Access to the U.S. Market. Like it or not, Brazil remains heavily dependent on the U.S. market. During the 1980's, Brazilian exports to the United States shifted away from raw materials and now consist in large part of manufactured and processed goods. The volume of exports to the United States grew rapidly, assisted by low labor costs, dramatic capacity and productivity gains, an overvalued dollar and some of the most generous export incentive programs in the world. In response, beleaguered U.S. manufacturers sought protection from Brazilian competition, both through unfair trade complaints and through the political process.

Efforts by the Brazilian government to phase out domestic and export subsidies will, in the long term, reduce the country's exposure to U.S. countervailing duties. These results will not be as dramatic or immediate as Brazil might like, however. For one thing, there will likely be exceptions to the subsidy elimination. For example, struggling state-owned companies will probably continue to receive government support.[97] The gradual phase-out of some key export subsidy programs,

---

[96] International Finance Corporation, *Exporting to Industrial Countries* (Discussion Paper No. 8) (1990). The United States imported $122 billion in developing country manufactures in 1988, as compared to $90 billion by the EC and only $40 billion by Japan. On a per capita basis, the United States imported twice as much of these products as the EC and two and a quarter times as much as Japan. pp. 8-9. The United States also has demonstrated a greater propensity to import non-traditional developing country manufactures (i.e., data processing equipment, passenger vehicles) as opposed to textiles, footwear and other traditional products. p. 11.

[97] Interview with an official in the Ministry of Infrastructure, July 1990.

Figure 6.1 1990 Brazilian Exports by Destination*

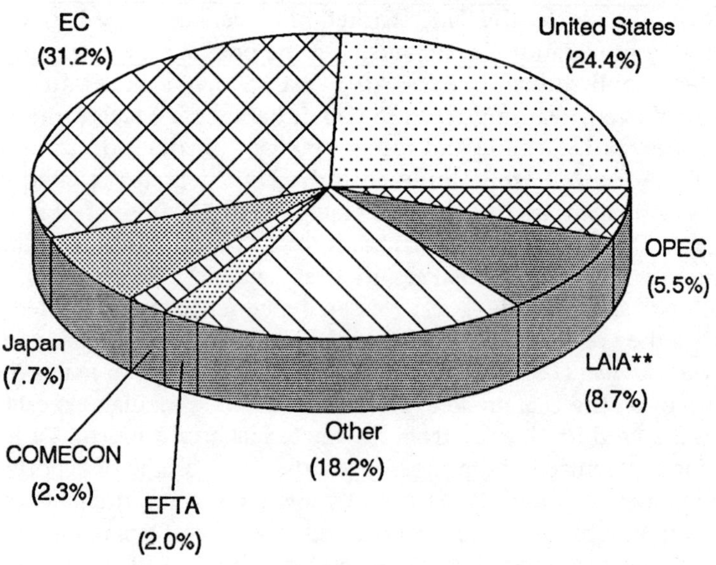

Figure 6.2 1990 Brazilian Imports by Origin*

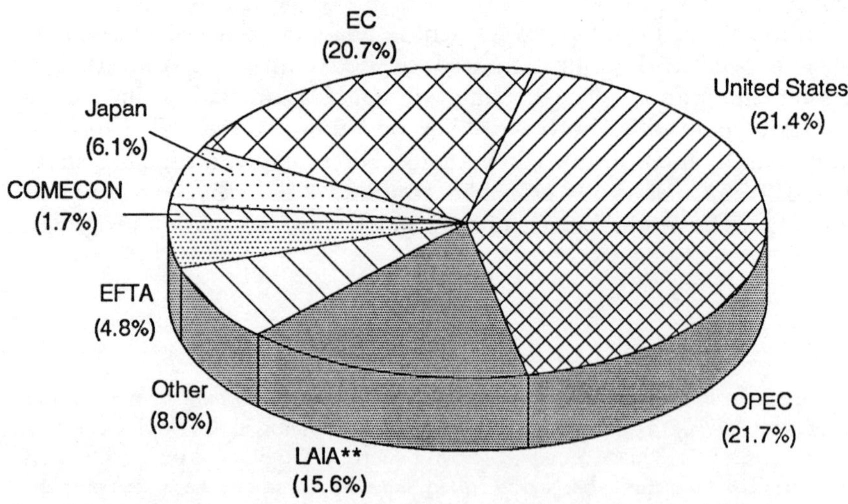

* Source: Federal Republic of Brazil. Preliminary data based on first eleven months of 1990.

**Venezuela, Ecuador included in OPEC, not LAIA figures.

such as Befiex, implies further exposure for beneficiaries for some years to come.[98] Even if all subsidies were eliminated immediately, many past subsidies are of a non-recurring type, which under U.S. law confer countervailable benefits for many years from the date of receipt.[99] As a result, countervailing duty investigations will continue to be brought for years to come.

Access to the Brazilian Market. The United States generally responded favorably to Brazilian trade liberalization efforts. In 1990, the USTR determined that Brazilian efforts to eliminate quantitative restrictions on imports warranted the termination of the Super 301 investigation.[100] As noted above, however, the United States should not anticipate that the Brazilian economy will be opened to imports to the same extent as those of Western nations. The continuing structural need of Brazil to generate a trade surplus to make payments on its foreign debt will result in trade restrictions, which in turn will give rise to Section 301 complaints. U.S. producers of consumer goods will be particularly affected, as these "superfluous" imports are the most likely to be excluded.[101]

Brazilians resent the use by the United States of "unilateral" trade measures such as Section 301. They assert that solutions to trade disputes must be reached through compromise, rather than through confrontation.[102] Nevertheless, some Brazilians suggest privately that the Section 301 actions against Brazil had an impact in bringing the pressures for trade liberalization to a head. As one executive remarked, U.S. pressure helped bring Brazil to the realization that it could not continue on as it had in the past.[103]

---

[98] Interview with an official in the National Secretariat of Economy, July 1990.

[99] U.S. Department of Commerce, Countervailing Duty Regulations (proposed), 54 Fed. Reg. 23373 (May 31, 1989).

[100] 55 Fed. Reg. 22876 (June 4, 1990).

[101] Interview with a Tariff Policy Commission official, July 1990. In the words of one official, "No one has said that Brazil will import like the United Arab Emirates." Interview with a senior official of the Commercial Policy Division of the Ministry of Foreign Affairs, July 1990.

[102] For example, *Folha de São Paulo* (April 30, 1990) (FBIS-LAT-90-084).

[103] Interview with the chief executive officer of a major Brazilian export-import company, July 1990.

Free Trade Agreement Proposals. On June 27, 1990, President Bush announced the first major U.S. economic program for Latin America since the Alliance for Progress in the early 1960s. The Enterprise for the Americas Initiative rests on three "pillars": trade expansion, investment promotion, and debt relief. On the investment front, the Initiative envisions creation of an Enterprise for the Americas Investment Fund to be administered by the Inter-American Development Bank. In the debt area, the Initiative would reduce or eliminate certain government-to-government debt (i.e., Agency for International Development, Food for Peace and Export-Import Bank loans), either through cancellation or debt-for-equity/debt-for-nature swaps. Most importantly from a trade perspective, however, the Initiative calls for the negotiation of framework agreements leading to free trade agreements and ultimately to a hemispheric free trade system.[104]

The reaction in Brazil to the Enterprise for the Americas Initiative was generally positive. President Collor termed it "broad, bold and innovative."[105] Leading dailies, such as O Estado de São Paulo, Jornal do Brasil and O Globo, praised the Initiative.[106] Fundamentally, however, the Brazilians were pleased more because the Initiative seemed to recognize the importance of Latin America than because they expected any tangible results from it in the short term.[107] Almost every person interviewed on the topic pointed out that any Free Trade Agreement with the United States would take many decades to work out.[108]

These attitudes may be shifting somewhat, as Brazil watches Mexico, the United States, and Canada move rapidly to negotiate a North American Free Trade Agreement. On June 18, 1991, Brazil and its partners in the incipient "Southern Cone Common Market," (Mercosur) signed a "framework" Agreement with the United States that could provide a starting point for greater economic cooperation. The Agreement calls for creation of a "Consultative Council of Trade and Investment," with the

---

104 U.S. Department of State press release, *Enterprise for the Americas Initiative* (September 21, 1990).

105 *DYN* (Buenos Aires) (June 28, 1990) (FBIS-LAT-90-126).

106 *Estado de São Paulo* (June 29, 1990); *Jornal do Brasil* (June 29, 1990); *O Globo* (June 29, 1990) (FBIS-LAT-90-127).

107 Interview with a former Brazilian ambassador to the GATT, July 1990.

108 Interviews with an official of the American Chamber of Commerce for Brazil, July 1990.

objective of liberalizing trade and investment among the parties.[109] Its effectiveness will of course depend, in the short-term, on the willingness and ability of all parties to compromise and, in the longer term, on the continued convergence of economic policy among the parties. Economic integration among the five countries cannot move forward unless and until the governments of Mercosur succeed in drastically reducing state intervention in their economies.

Technology Transfer. United States-Brazil relations have been complicated over the past several decades by the United States' attempts to restrict Brazilian access to sensitive technologies, including technologies with military nuclear applications and, more recently, those that can be used in the development of ballistic missiles. These tensions may deepen as the focus of U.S. foreign policy attention swings from the cold war to such issues as nuclear proliferation. The ramifications of Brazil's close relationship with Iraq, and its reported cooperation with Iraq in the development of missile systems and other military technologies, were not lost on the United States during the Persian Gulf war.

Brazil has placed great emphasis on obtaining new technology from the industrial world to modernize its industrial base, and will be sorely disappointed if restrictions are placed on such access.[110] However, some in the Foreign Ministry continue to equate technology transfer generally with access to nuclear and other military technologies, and consider any restrictions on access to be part of a conspiracy by the superpowers to deprive the Third World of important instruments of national policy.[111] Similarly, the Brazilian military has viewed efforts by the United States to inspect or otherwise supervise the use of U.S.-

---

109 *Agreement Among the Governments of the Argentine Republic, the Federative Republic of Brazil, the Republic of Paraguay, the Oriental Republic of Uruguay, and the Government of the United States of America Concerning a Council on Trade and Investment,* Articles, 1, 5 (June 18, 1991).

110 *General Directives.*

111 "The New Foreign Policy, in *Estado de São Paulo* (July 31, August 1, 4, and 5, 1990). The article presents a critical look at the Brazil's foreign policy as reflected in a July address by then Foreign Minister Rezek to the Superior War College. Similarly, at a press conference in March 1990, then Foreign Minister asserted Brazil's right to develop nuclear weapons and condemned efforts to link access to high technology to adherence to the NPT. *Folha de São Paulo* (March 15, 1990).

origin products as "an intolerable affront to national sovereignty".[112] Unless some type of accommodation can be reached, the situation will remain a source of bilateral tensions.

There recently have been signs that such an accommodation may be possible. Over the past several years President Collor has made efforts to narrow the prerogatives of the military, and in particular has curtailed nuclear weapons research. Collor recently has pledged to allow the on-site inspection of nuclear facilities by the International Atomic Energy Agency[113] and, according to one report, may agree to comply with the Missile Technology Control Regime.[114] Most recently, the Collor Administration reportedly is drafting legislation to control the export of strategic technology based on the COCOM model.[115] In the interim, however, industrial nations continue to restrict the flow of products and technology to Brazil.[116]

Intellectual Property Protection. A prime source of U.S.-Brazil trade tension in the 1980s has been Brazil's failure to provide a level of intellectual property protection satisfactory to the United States.[117] Brazilian intellectual property protections generally have been considered to fall far short of those of developed nations. Among the most serious

---

112 *O Globo* (April 14, 1991).

113 Statement by Press Secretary Fitzwater on Argentine and Brazilian Compliance with Nuclear Safeguards and Nonproliferation Regimes (November 29, 1990), in *Weekly Compilation of Presidential Documents,* Vol. 26, No. 48 (December 3, 1990), p. 1939.

114 *Brazil Watch* (July 8-22, 1991). Collor reportedly was motivated in part by the need to attract foreign participation in the ownership and operation of such troubled state-owned arms producers as Engesa, Embraer and Avibrás.

115 *Gazeta Mercantil* (August 2, 1991) (FBIS-LAT-91-167).

116 For example, *Estado de São Paulo* (November 2, 1991) (FBIS-LAT-91-214) (reporting a multilateral "embargo" on sales of sensitive products and technologies for use in the Brazilian "satellite launch vehicle" (VLS project.)

117 The 1990 edition of the USTR's annual publication, *Foreign Trade Barriers,* identified a half-dozen intellectual property issues, including the total absence of protection for chemicals and pharmaceuticals, a compulsory licensing provision, a relatively short period of patent protection, and lax enforcement of copyright laws, that adversely affect U.S. companies. United States Trade Representative, *1990 National Trade Estimate Report on Foreign Trade Barriers,* p. 19.

deficiencies historically have been the exclusion of certain key sectors from coverage,[118] requirements that patent holders "work" their patent or lose it,[119] and penalties for infringement that are both weak and poorly enforced.[120] The U.S. Government's concern on this subject is reflected in its decision to put Brazil on the "priority watch list" under the "special 301" intellectual property provision of the 1988 Trade Act,[121] as well as individual section 301 investigations relating to lack of protection for software and pharmaceuticals.

In the late 1980s, the Sarney Administration made some significant efforts to address U.S. concerns, especially in the software area. In December 1987, Brazil implemented a law extending copyright protection to foreign software and allowing foreign companies to market their software in Brazil under some circumstances.[122] In 1989, Brazil established more transparent rules for importing and selling foreign software,[123] and the country's National Monetary Council agreed to permit repatriation of profits earned from imported software.[124] These

---

118 Traditionally, patent protection has been unavailable for the food, pharmaceutical, chemicals, certain metal alloys and biotechnology products. Timothy J. Richards, "Brazil," in *Intellectual Property Rights: Global Consensus, Global Conflict?*, ed. R. Michael Gadbaw and Timothy J. Richards (Westview, 1988), pp. 168-169.

119 Under Brazilian law, the government can force compulsory licensing if a patent holder fails to "effectively exploit" his patent in Brazil, and importation does not constitute effective exploitation. Even if the patent is being "exploited", compulsory licensing can be ordered if it does not meet the demand of the market. Gadbaw and Richards (1988), pp. 169-170.

120 Gadbaw and Richards (1988), pp. 170-171.

121 The "Special 301" provision requires the Administration to identify those countries whose intellectual property practices caused the most serious injury to U.S. companies, and to enter into negotiations to change these practices under threat of retaliation. Omnibus Trade and Competitiveness Act of 1988, Sections 1988, Sections 1371. Brazil consistently has been identified as "priority watch" country, meaning it meets some but not all the criteria for the initiation of an investigation. *International Trade Reporter* (May 1, 1991).

122 Law No. 7646 (December 22, 1987).

123 *Business Latin America* (October 30, 1989).

124 *International Trade Reporter* (September 27, 1989).

changes caused the U.S. government to drop its section 301 investigation relating to software,[125] but they did not resolve the broader problems surrounding the Brazilian intellectual property regime.

The Collor Administration has introduced in Congress a new intellectual property law which would, among other things, provide protection for pharmaceutical and chemical process patents, extend patent coverage to twenty years, modify the requirement that a patent be "worked" or forfeited, and reduce the power of the National Institute for Industrial Property (INPI) to control the terms of technology transfer arrangements.[126] In the interim, it also has taken steps to facilitate the transfer of technology from abroad by simplifying the procedures for obtaining technology transfer approvals.[127] Collor's reformist approach can be attributed in part to pressure from the United States, but it also reflects the concern of the government both to foster indigenous technological development[128] and to encourage the inflow of new technology from abroad. Resistance in Congress to the proposals has been strong,[129] but it is widely expected that some form of legislation will ultimately be enacted.

Brazil and the European Community

Brazilians view Western Europe as an important alternative to the United States in the trade and investment areas.[130] In the 1960s and early 1970s, Brazil-EC trade boomed, as European countries demanded

---

125 *Daily Report for Executives* (October 10, 1989).

126 "Projeto Facilita Investimento Estrangeiro," in *Estado de São Paulo* (March 30, 1991), p. 1.

127 Ministry of Economics, Treasury and Planning, Portaria No. 123 (February 27, 1991), Art. 3.4.1; Ministry of Justice, National Institute of Industrial Property, Resolution No. 22 (February 27, 1991). An English language translation of Resolution No. 22 was kindly provided by Fischer and Foster Advogados of São Paulo.

128 In a recent survey, more than half of the 1800 Brazilian businessmen asked reported they had suffered from the theft of trade secrets, and 25 percent said they would undertake more R&D if there were better protection. Interview B-23.

129 *Estado de São Paulo* (May 22, 1991) (FBIS-LAT-91-109).

130 Coffey and Corrêa (1988) p. x.

increasing quantities of Brazilian raw materials and supplied the capital equipment needed by the expanding Brazilian industrial economy. Today, the European Community has become Brazil's most important trading partner, supplying 20.7 percent of its imports and absorbing 31.2 percent of its exports. See Figures 6.1 and 6.2. The EC is also Brazil's largest source of foreign investment, supplying 36.2 percent of private investment funds. See Figure 6.3. When the significant participation of EFTA and other European nations in these categories is factored in, the key role of Europe in Brazilian trade and investment becomes clear.

In spite of the importance of Brazilian-European ties, there are problems in the trading relationship. The Community's seeming unwillingness to accept a large volume of Brazilian manufactured goods is a particular concern for Brazil. While manufactured products have comprised a steadily increasing share of total Brazilian exports (See Figure 6.4), only 38 percent of the EC imports of Brazilian goods were manufactured products in 1984.[131] The trends can be explained in part by the prevalence of quantitative restrictions on Brazilian exports, as well as the widespread use of antidumping actions by EC producers. In 1983, 52.2 percent of all Brazilian manufactured exports to the European Community were affected by trade measures in the European Community, versus 37.3 percent in the United States.[132]

The European Community's Common Agricultural Policy (CAP) has presented comparable difficulties for Brazilian agriculturalists. The CAP has made it extremely difficult for Brazil to sell a wide range of agricultural products in the European Community, including such potentially important products as beef and sugar. Brazilians believe that subsidized European agricultural products are displacing Brazilian products in Brazilian and third country markets, and countervailing duty/dumping actions by Brazil can be expected.[133]

---

131 This should be contrasted with Brazilian exports to the United States, 74.6 percent of which were manufactures. In fact, four commodities (coffee, animal feed, iron ore and orange juice) represented 55 percent of Brazil's total exports to the Community. Pochet and Praet, "Trade Relations Between Brazil and the European Community," in Coffey and Corrêa (1988). According to Brazilian government statistics, industrial products accounted for 61.5 percent of Brazil's total exports to all countries in the first eleven months of 1990.

132 Pochet and Praet (1988) p. 125.

133 Interview with an official of the Companhia de Financiamento da Produção, July 1990.

Figure 6.3 Sources of Foreign Investment in Brazil

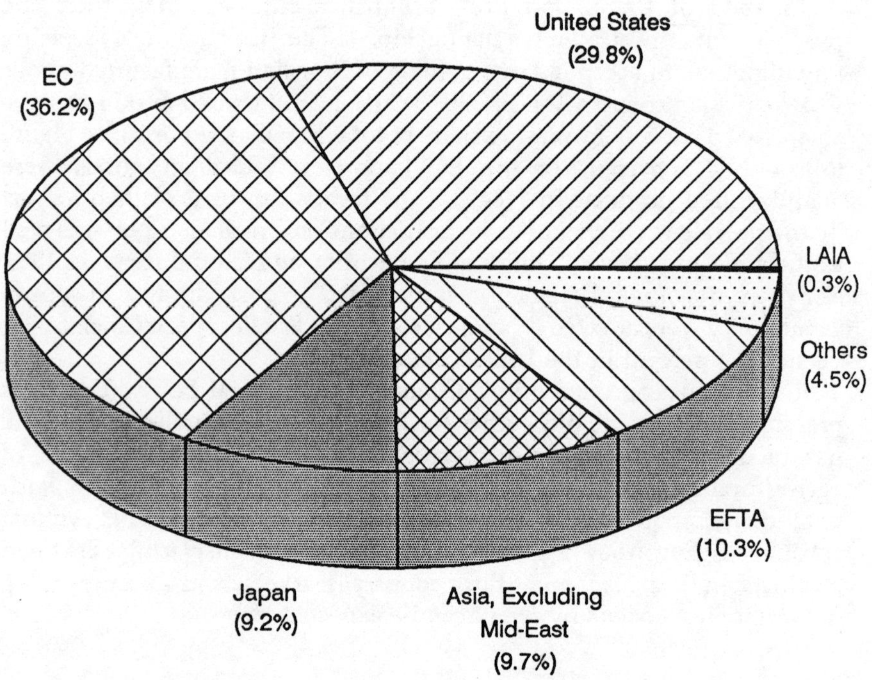

Source: Central Bank of Brazil. Data as of December 31, 1989.

Figure 6.4 1990 Brazilian Exports by Product

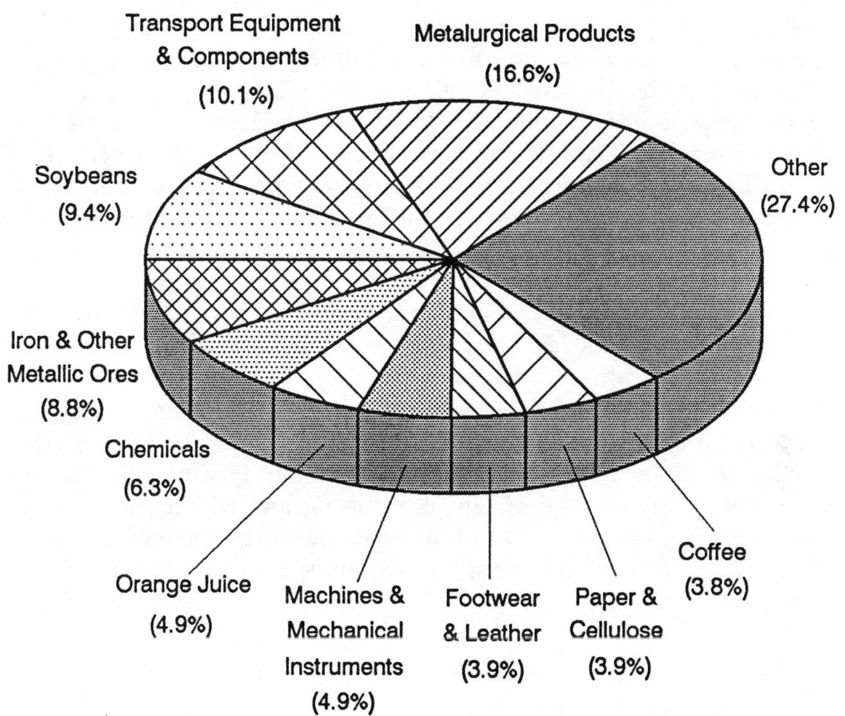

Source: Federal Republic of Brazil. Preliminary data based on first eleven months of 1990.

Special EC preferences for some developing nations tend to disfavor Brazil. The Lomé convention grants certain former colonies of the EC member states (the "African, Caribbean and Pacific Group," or "ACP") special access to EC markets. In essence, access to the EC market is governed by a "pyramid of privileges" under which ACP countries are entitled to preference not only over industrial nations but also over non-ACP LDCs.[134] The EC has steadily diminished the importance of GSP benefits to Brazil through country-specific quotas designed to ensure that no single country derives a disproportionate share of the benefit.

Brazil, as a former Portuguese colony, has sought to take advantage of Portugal's entry into the Community to obtain improved access to the EC market. Some Brazilian companies have invested in Portugal in the hope of using it as beachhead for selling in the EC.[135] However, the likely significance of the "Lusophone" connection should not be overstated. The ties between Brazil and Portugal are much weaker than those between EC countries and their former colonies in the Lomé group. Further, the political strength of Portugal in the European Community will not be significant. Most importantly, Brazil presents a competitive threat to EC industries quite unlike any presented by the ACP countries. In fact, the expansion of the European Community may well have a negative impact on Brazilian exports, as Brazil will be shut out of the Spanish and Portuguese agricultural markets by the CAP.[136]

The EC and some Latin American countries, including Brazil, have recently taken steps to enhance their trading relationship. Manifestations of this trend include the signing in December 1990 of a "cooperation agreement" between the EC and the Rio Group, which entails, among other things, twice-yearly Ministerial meetings between the two groups,[137] and of an inter-institutional agreement between the EC and

---

134 Pochet and Praet (1988) p. 107.

135 Brazil is the fourth largest foreign direct investor in Portugal. Special credit arrangements between the Portuguese and Brazilian Central Banks are intended to encourage this process. *Estado de São Paulo* (July 15, 1990) (FBIS-LAT-90-167).

136 Braga and Santiago, "The Entry of Portugal and Spain into the EEC and Euro-Brazilian Trade," in Coffey and Corrêa (1988).

137 *European Reports*, No. 1640 (December 22, 1990). The members of the Rio Group, in addition to Brazil, are Argentina, Bolivia, Chile, Columbia, Ecuador, Mexico, Paraguay, Peru, Uruguay and Venezuela. *Daily Report for Executives* (December 21, 1990).

LAIA on April 27, 1991.[138] This flurry of new activity between the EC and Latin America reflects new concerns on both sides of the Atlantic. From the European perspective, U.S. efforts to strengthen economic ties with its hemispheric neighbors raise the specter of a relative increase in U.S. influence and ultimately, perhaps, of a regional trading block that disadvantages European trade and investment.[139] From the Latin American perspective, these efforts reflect a desire to attract renewed EC attention in the face of EC 1992 and a perceived European preoccupation with Eastern Europe.[140] European unwillingness to include market access provisions in the accords is an indication of the limits of cooperation, however. In the final analysis, Latin America remains a relatively low-priority item on the European agenda.

Brazil and Japan

Japanese economic relations with Brazil, while significant, have yet to reach a depth commensurate with Japan's steadily advancing role in the world economy. In 1990 Japan absorbed only 7.7 percent of Brazil's exports and provided 6.1 percent of its imports.[141] This is a mere fraction of Brazil's trade with the United States or the European Community. The level of Japanese foreign direct investment in Brazil also is relatively low: Japan accounted for only 9.2 percent of such investments as of 1989, as contrasted to 29.8 percent for the United States and 36.2 percent for the European Community. See Figure 6.3.

Although on first consideration Japan's relatively limited role in the Brazilian economy is surprising, especially in light of the 900,000 persons of Japanese descent that live in Brazil, a number of circumstances combine

---

138 *European Reports,* No. 1672 (April 27, 1991).

139 Italian Foreign minister De Michelis, who announced the Agreement on behalf of the EC, stated that it represented a "European Initiative for the Americas" parallel to the Bush Initiative. *Daily Report for Executives* (December 21, 1990).

140 *European Reports,* No. 1640 (December 22, 1990). The Latin Americans emphasized these themes in the first Ministerial between the two groups, "expressing their concern" about the impact EC 1992 could have on their exports and resuming their request for access to European Investment Bank Funds (now available to Eastern Europe). *Conclusions of the First Institutionalized Ministerial Meeting Between the European Community and the Rio Group,* (April 27, 1991) (EC Press Release 5813/91).

141 See Figures 6.1 and 6.2.

to limit trade. Japan's relatively low propensity to import manufactured goods, which now constitute the greater share of Brazilian exports,[142] has been widely noted. In 1988, Japan imported only $840 million in Brazilian manufactures (the United States imported $6.1 billion, and the EC $3.4 billion, in that year).[143] At the same time, the immense distance between Brazil and Japan discourages the shipment of high-bulk, low-value commodities (although Japan is a significant importer of Brazilian iron ore, soybeans and other commodities). These two circumstances combine to inhibit Brazilian exports to Japan. Meanwhile, the Brazilian market remains relatively closed to the import of consumer items, such as electronics and autos, products in which Japan excels. See Figure 6.5. While both countries gradually may be opening to imports of manufacturers, the process is likely to be a slow one.

With respect to direct foreign investment, other factors are at work. Japanese investors are deterred by the unstable macroeconomic and political environment, overburdened infrastructure, large foreign debt and stagnant market. They were also unsettled by the sequestration of savings implemented at the initiation of the Collor Administration.[144] This low level of investment retards trade in several ways. First, multinational companies (MNCs) producing for the domestic market tend to import capital equipment and inputs from their home country.[145] Second, MNCs often use Brazil as a production base for exports.[146]

---

142 In 1990, approximately 54 percent of Brazilian exports were manufactures, 16 percent were semimanufactures (e.g., steel, aluminum, soybean oil) and only 28 percent were primary products (the balance falls in the "other" category). Calculated from statistics provided by Economic Intelligence Unit, *Brazil Country Report* (1991), No. 1, pp. 26-27.

143 International Finance Corporation, *Exporting to Industrial Countries* (Discussion Paper No. 8) (1990), p. 11.

144 "Factors Inhibiting Japanese Investments Viewed," *Exame* (May 20, 1990) (FBIS-LAT-90-130).

145 The importance of German trade with Brazil, for example, can be explained in part by direct investments by its multinationals. Five companies operating in Brazil (Bayer, BASF, Hoescht, VW and Mercedes-Benz) accounted for 17 percent of all Brazilian imports from Germany in 1984. Pochet and Praet (1988) p. 108.

146 Subsidiaries of U.S. firms accounted for 18 percent of all Brazilian manufactured exports in 1981. Serra (1988) p. 91.

Figure 6.5 1990 Brazilian Imports by Product

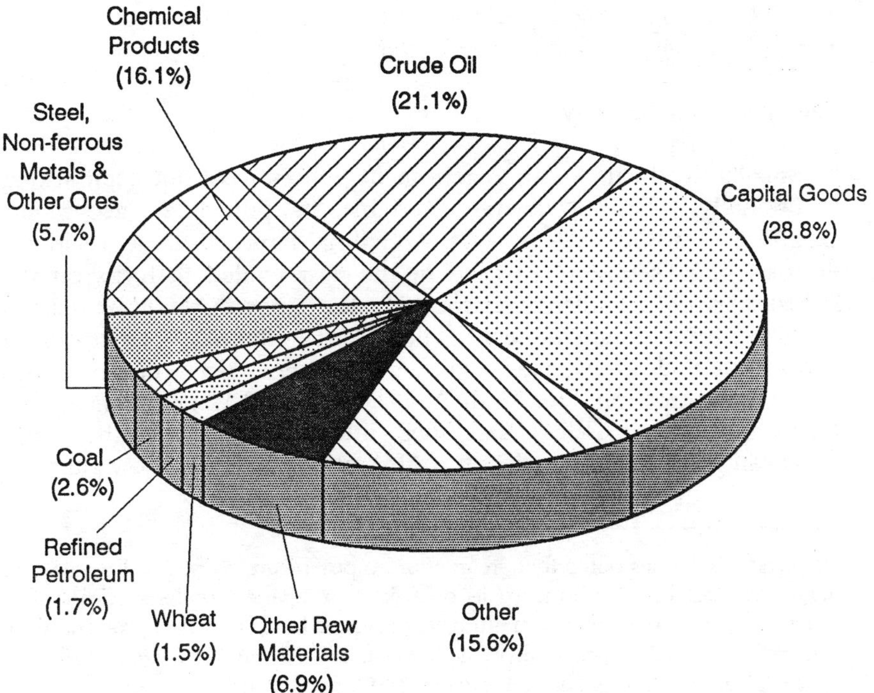

Source: Federal Republic of Brazil. Preliminary data based on first eleven months of 1990.

The Brazilians continue to seek Japanese trade and investment as a means to reduce their economic dependency on the United States.[147] For example, President Collor has actively sought to bring a Japanese automobile manufacturer into the country. There is some hope that the liberalization process will encourage an increase in Japanese participation, although Brazilians recognize that the conditions that inhibit Japanese investment have not changed dramatically. In particular, they know that new Japanese investment must await a resolution of the debt problem, and that this may be a long time in coming.[148]

Regional Trade Strategy

Brazil's ties to its South American neighbors have not been strong traditionally. Brazil's divergent origins, its process of geographic expansion, and its rivalry with Argentina impeded close relations. Further, Brazil's trading patterns in the past tended to focus on the industrial world, a tendency reinforced by the import-substitution policies in place throughout the continent. Past efforts to participate in multilateral trade arrangements with other Latin American countries, such as the Latin American Free Trade Association (LAFTA), proved markedly unsuccessful.[149] A less ambitious integration project, the Latin American Integration Association (LAIA), also got off to a slow start. In

---

[147] One scholar has noted that, in an effort to pursue an "economic diplomacy of diversification," Brazil has muted its objections to Japanese trade policies that, if pursued by the United States, might have provoked loud charges of protectionism, Georges A. Fauriol, "Extrahemispheric Interests and Actions" in *South America into the 1990s*, ed. G. Pope Adams (Westview, 1990), pp. 153-154.

[148] Interviews with a former Brazilian diplomat and an official with the National Bank for Economic and Social Development, July 1990. The President of Brazil's Central Bank, on returning from a July 1991 trip to Tokyo, remarked that new Japanese investments were conditioned on the repayment of overdue debt. *Estado de São Paulo* (July 31, 1991) (FBIS-LAT-91-149).

[149] Brazil was an original signatory to the Montevideo Treaty, which in 1960 established the Latin American Free Trade Association ("LAFTA"). LAFTA was a failure, in good part because its focus on eliminating tariffs would have benefitted primarily the three most developed signatories (Brazil, Argentina and Mexico) at the expense of other members. In 1980, LAFTA was replaced by the Latin American Integration Association, a much less ambitious project aimed at facilitating bilateral tariff reductions between its members. Mario I. Blejer, "Regional Economic Integration in Latin America," in *Economic Development in Latin America and the Debt Problem*, S. Rpt. 100-54 (1987).

the later 1980s, however, trade among LAIA countries began to increase after years of decline.[150] This trend was bolstered by new agreements whereby LAIA member states extended preferential tariff rates to one another.[151]

As part of its trade diversification effort, Brazil recently has placed renewed emphasis on economic integration with other South American nations. Even before the Collor administration assumed power, the Latin American economic integration effort showed some signs of renewed vitality. Collor's predecessor, José Sarney, indicated his belief that "the Brazilian Constitution defines Latin American integration as a national goal."[152]

Unlike the LAFTA and LAIA agreements, however, Brazil's new efforts have focused on bilateral and subregional arrangements. For example, Brazil forged new links with a number of its smaller neighbors. The massive Itaipú hydroelectric project, undertaken jointly with Paraguay, drew Paraguay into Brazil's economic orbit. Bolivia and Brazil entered into an Economic Cooperation and Complementation Act intended to facilitate trade.[153] Brazil has undertaken a series of joint projects in the energy, mining and agriculture fields with Peru.[154] It also has signed

---

150 Brazilian exports to LAIA countries hit nearly $3.7 billion in 1988, after falling to $2.2 billion in 1985. InterAmerican Development Bank, *Economic & Social Progress in Latin America 1989 Report*, pp. 74-75.

151 Under the Program of Recuperation and Expansion of Commerce of the LAIA, the members agreed to intraregional tariffs that are preferential relative to third country tariffs. Under the program, LAIA member states are put into three tiers based on levels of development. The extent of the preference as a proportion of each country's third country tariff will vary depending on the development level both of the importing and exporting nations. For instance, the biggest tariff preference (80%) will be extended by the most developed countries (including Brazil) to the least developed; the smallest preference (40%) by the least developed countries to the most advanced. Instituto para la Integración de América Latina, *El Processo de Integración en America Latina en 1988* (Buenos Aires; 1989), pp. 34-35.

152 *Radio Nacional da Amazonia* (December 1, 1988).

153 *El Mundo* (Santa Cruz, Bolivia), January 5, 1989 (FBIS-LAT-89-030); General Agreement on Tariffs and Trade, *Review of Developments in the Trading System September 1988-February 1989*.

154 *Business Latin America* (November 20, 1989), p. 336. Contacts with Brazil's western and northern neighbors likely will increase as Brazil opens its hinterland to development.

a bilateral agreement with Venezuela to reduce tariffs between the two countries.[155] With respect to these smaller nations, Brazil is to a certain extent replacing other developed countries as an investor, purchaser of raw materials and supplier of manufactured products.

Much more significant is the economic integration taking place between Argentina and Brazil, two relatively advanced nations with manufacturing industries that have long been isolated from one another. While efforts to integrate the two economies preceded the Collor Administration, the process began in earnest as a result of the convergence of the economic policies of Presidents Menem of Argentina and Collor of Brazil.[156] Both Presidents seem to recognize that an integrated market will allow valuable efficiencies of scale, and have therefore undertaken such major ventures as the integration of Brazilian and Argentine auto industries and proposed joint activities in such areas as steel, aircraft and custom capital goods.

These integration efforts culminated in the signing on March 26, 1991 of an agreement for the creation of a Southern Cone Common Market ("Mercosur") by Brazil, Argentina, Paraguay and Uruguay.[157] The Treaty of Assunción sets forth an ambitious agenda for the four signatories. It calls, inter alia, for the elimination of all tariff and non-tariff barriers by December 31, 1994; the erection of a common external tariff; the adoption of a common external commercial policy; and the harmonization of national legislation on a broad range of topics from tax to agricultural policy.[158]

Unlike the United States/Canada Free Trade Agreement, however, the Treaty of Asunción leaves the difficult problems regarding implementation of these goals for later negotiations. In fact, implementation will be difficult to achieve unless and until Brazil and other Mercosur members

---

155 *Estado de São Paulo* (November 19, 1991) (FBIS-LAT-91-225).

156 As one former Brazilian government official noted, integration between countries following import substitution policies is "bull. . . ."

157 I.B. Teixeira, "A Busca de un Grande Mercado," in *Conjuntura Econômica* (April 1991), p. 78. Chile reportedly has expressed interest in joining Mercosur as well. *Radio Nacional da Amazonia* (October 29, 1991) (FBIS-LAT-91-210).

158 *Treaty of Asunción* (March 26, 1991), reprinted in *Conjuntura Econômica* (April 1991), pp. 80-82.

defeat hyperinflation and achieve some degree of macroeconomic stability.[159] It would be unrealistic to expect that Latin American trade will assume a central role for Brazil in the near future. All of Brazil's trading partners in Latin America are heavily in debt and none can afford to run a significant trade deficit with its trading partners. Brazil, on the other hand, must generate a huge trade surplus to service its own debt. Therefore, intraregional trade will operate under severe restraints and in any event cannot satisfy fully the needs of Brazil.[160]

In addition to these economy-wide problems, sectoral issues will plague integration efforts. The Brazilian government has sought to get business actively involved in a process that up till now has been the sphere of diplomats. In spite of the hope that businessmen, particularly in the south of Brazil, will see tangible benefits in specific projects and therefore get involved in the process, business people remain generally cool.[161] Outright resistance can be expected in vulnerable sectors in both countries, such as Brazilian agriculture (where Argentine meat and grains could drastically undersell those of inefficient Brazilian producers),[162] and Argentine manufacturing.[163] A recent survey by Coopers and Lybrand indicated that a majority of private sector companies in all four countries think their country (and presumably their sector) is not yet ready for a fully competitive regional market.

---

159 Argentina, which brought inflation down dramatically in 1991 to low double-digits, reportedly is especially concerned with Brazil's failure to make comparable gains, and Brazil's Foreign Minister has recognized that "[w]e cannot promote Mercosur properly with a high inflation rate." *Brasília Voz do Brasil Network* (October 29, 1991) (FBIS-LAT-91-211); *Gazeta Mercantil* (October 4, 1991) (FBIS-LAT-91-212).

160 The dilemma is demonstrated by tensions between Brazil and Argentina regarding the latter's $US400 million trade deficit with Brazil in 1988. Brazil agreed to reduce tariffs on Argentine products, especially foodstuffs, in an effort to reduce the deficit. *Siderurgia Latinoamericana* (October 1989) p. 25.

161 Interviews with an official of the Secretariat of the Economy and with a private sector executive, July 1990.

162 Interview with an official of the Companhia de Financiamento da Producão, July 1990.

163 Wayne A. Selcher, "Brazil and the Southern Cone Subsystem," in *South America into the 1990s*, ed. G. Pope Adams (Westview, 1990), p. 106.

Confidence was greatest among Brazilian companies and lowest in Uruguay and Paraguay.[164]

In the words of one study, "progress at the speed proposed in the integration agreement between Argentina and Brazil [is] doubtful of attainment despite understandably high expectations . . ."[165] This assessment is true more broadly of Brazil's trading prospects with Latin America. Although there is some gain to be had from Latin American integration, the state of common crisis, indebtedness and relative technological weakness of Latin America means that regional integration will be difficult to implement and in any event is no substitute for close ties with the United States, Europe and Japan.

SECTORAL TRADE POLICIES

The Brazilian government's new economic policy is intended to de-emphasize the country's traditional intervention on behalf of promoted sectors. In the Administration's view, the proper role of government is to promote social goals, such as health and education, and to provide the infrastructure necessary for private enterprise to compete successfully both at home and in world markets. To this end, the government has undertaken to reduce and ultimately eliminate direct state participation in most industrial activities and to phase out domestic subsidies and export incentives. When asked what sectors the government is likely to favor, officials tend to respond that the government is out of the process of sectoral promotion and that any aid provided will be based on the competitiveness of individual projects.[166]

While this must be taken with a grain of salt -- the process of reducing government participation in the economy will be a slow one -- there is no reason to doubt the underlying sincerity of the basic approach. As a practical matter, however, two factors may tend actually to maintain or actually increase the sectoral focus of the Brazilian government. First, the renunciation of import substitution -- under which Brazil attempted to produce everything -- will entail the directing of scarce government resources to those industries most likely to succeed in a competitive

---

164 *Gazeta Mercantil* (October 19-21, 1991) (FBIS-LAT-91-226).

165 InterAmerican Development Bank, *Economic and Social Progress in Latin America: 1989 Report*, p. 80.

166 Interviews with researchers at the National Bank for Economic and Social Development, July 1990.

environment. In short, the government is forced, in industrial policy parlance, to pick winners and losers. Although the volume of assistance may drop, aid is likely to be more focused. Second, the promotion of advanced technology remains a key government goal. As a result, special policies will continue for informatics and other high technologies sectors. Ironically, a restrictive high technology policy could impair efforts to make industry as a whole more technologically capable.

Three sectors have been selected for review in this chapter. The first, informatics, is covered because of its importance for U.S.-Brazil relations, its importance to Brazil, and the exceptional treatment it will receive. The other steel and textiles, have been chosen because they are traditional manufacturing sectors, one state-dominated and the other private, that will be dramatically impacted by economic and trade reform.

Informatics

No sector of the Brazilian economy has received greater attention from its government than informatics. Although the early impulse for an indigenous informatics industry arose out of the military's national security concerns, the policy is now based more broadly on the belief that without an informatics industry Brazil will be trapped in a position of technological dependency. As explained by Foreign Minister Rezek, Brazil must reject an "international division of work in which developing countries. . .specialize in the exportation of traditional manufactured products, while developed countries specialize in advanced technologies."[167] Thus, Brazil has implemented a comprehensive industrial strategy in informatics which differs in degree, if not in kind, from any other sectoral assistance program in the country.

Brazil's traditional informatics policy is based on a system of "market reserve," under which participation in the Brazilian market for a wide range of products, including microcomputers, small computer systems and data communications products, is restricted to Brazilian companies. Foreign firms (firms with 30 percent or more foreign equity, or de facto controlled by foreigners) have been essentially "excluded from production even within Brazil for the range of goods reserved to Brazilian firms."[168] Brazil also has offered subsidies such as fiscal incentives both for investments by informatics companies and for purchasers of

---

167 *Estado de São Paulo* (August 5, 1990) (FBIS-LAT-90-153).

168 William Cline, *Informatics and Development* (Economics International, 1987), p. 34.

indigenous equipment, loans from government credit institutions such as BNDES, research and development grants and equity injections for state-owned companies.[169] The import of informatics equipment required a license and had to be offset by exports. Imports were banned outright to the extent a comparable domestic product was available.[170]

Brazil's traditional informatics policy was fundamentally at odds with the principles underlying the Collor government's economic strategy. That strategy relies on trade liberalization to permit Brazilian industry access to foreign technology required to restore its international competitiveness and increase competition, thereby holding down prices and fostering macroeconomic stability. The restrictive informatics policy effectively prevented Brazilian industry from obtaining advanced and cost-effective foreign technologies needed to compete at home and abroad.[171] As Table 6.3 indicates, it also drives up prices astronomically in an increasingly important sector of the economy. Accordingly, the Collor government made reform of the informatics policy a key priority.[172]

There are strong forces arrayed against informatics reform. As previously noted, the Foreign Ministry at the highest levels is committed to Brazilian autonomy in high technology policy. While Secretary of Science and Technology Goldemberg is pro-reform, much of the informatics bureaucracy remains strongly committed to existing

---

169 For example, *Gazeta Mercantil* (December 21, 1987) (FBIS-ELS-88-005). The article reports new BNDES loans to the electronics industry.

170 Latin American Monitor, Ltd., *Brazil 1989*, p. 103.

171 For example, Brazilian automobiles generally lack fuel injection systems because the technology is unavailable locally and, until recently, could not be imported. *Business Latin America* (August 6, 1990).

172 The President last year told his Cabinet that "[t]he market reserve cannot be a useful tool in the economic policy, especially when it is used with oligopolistic distortions, as was the case with Brazil. If we seek competitiveness and efficiency, we must gradually expose Brazilian production to the international market." *Rede Globo Television* (September 10, 1990). This attitude is shared by many in the Brazilian private sector. Interviews with the chief executive of a major Brazilian corporation, July 1990 ("Some informatics companies will fail as a result of the reforms, but they deserve to."); a former senior Brazilian diplomat, July 1990, ("The policy will change; consumers are amazed at the $200 electronic typewriters available in the U[nited] S[tates]."); and a foreign business consultant in Brazil, July 1990 (There is a "growing unhappiness" with the informatics laws, especially among those who travel abroad.)

TABLE 6.3 Informatics Products: Price Differentials (in Cruzeiros)

Product	Brazil	United States	Difference (times U.S. price)
PC's (keyboard, monitor, 5 1/4" disk drive)			
XT Winchester 20 Mb	265,000	113,000	2.30
286 Winchester 40 Mb	650,000	247,000	2.63
386 Winchester 80 Mb	1,075,000	385,000	2.79
Printers (characters per second [cps])			
180 cps	145,000	43,000	3.30
220 cps	190,000	52,000	3.60
300 cps	250,000	78,000	3.10
Fax machines (personal model)			
Without telephone	190,000	79,000	2.40
With telephone	360,000	122,000	2.90

Note: Product prices in the United States were converted at the commercial dollar rate (175 cruzeiros).

Source: *O Globo* (January 7, 1991) (FBIS-LAT-91-040).

policies.[173] Although the military role in economic policy decision-making has been reduced substantially under Collor, it is still a force to be reckoned with, and one that strongly backs the informatics policy.[174] Finally, there are powerful vested interests in the informatics industry itself -- including both Brazilian and foreign companies -- that oppose any reform.

In the face of this opposition, the Collor government first took steps that did not require legislation. On an institutional level, it attempted to weaken the ability of industry to oppose reform by reformulating the National Council on Informatics and Automatization ("Conin") from a body equally divided between government and industry to an entity with 12 officials and 8 private sector representatives. It also downgraded the Special Informatics Secretariat (SEI), which had been one of the strongest supporters of the market reserve, from an independent entity to a department of the Secretariat of Science and Technology.[175] Substantively, the government proposed, and Conin approved, a measure permitting foreign companies to provide both capital (up to 30 percent) and technology to joint ventures with Brazilian companies, thereby overturning an earlier SEI decision banning technological joint ventures.[176] It also issued a decree permitting the importation of all information products not specifically banned by Conin; however, the

---

173 Interview with a Secretariat of Science and Technology official, July 1990. Officials from the Special Informatics Secretariat declined to be interviewed. It should be noted, however, that months after Collor was inaugurated SEI was still headed by the Kiwal Weber, the same official who held the post in the Sarney government.

174 Brazil's emphasis on informatics had its origin in the navy's need for on-board computers, its aviation industry is closely linked to the requirements of the air force, and a central goal in the development of the nuclear power industry was to develop the technologies necessary for indigenous atomic weapons, nuclear-powered submarines, etc. As the military became involved with these sectors, it developed a vested interest in the preservation of certain enterprises. Army officers established and managed state enterprises, both as tools of nationalist politics and as pension systems for themselves and their subordinates. The military continues to exercise significant power in those sectors it considers essential to national security, i.e., the nuclear energy program, the weapons industry, and the informatics and high-tech industries.

175 "Brazil's Computer Market Verges on Liberalization," in *Business Latin America* (September 17, 1990).

176 *Brazil Watch* (September 24, 1990).

prohibited list includes, inter alia, personal computers, microcomputers, monitors, keyboards, hard drives, floppy drives, printers, fax machines.[177]

While the Collor Administration's rather modest initial steps could be taken without legislation, however, steps to ensure elimination of the market reserve, further liberalization of joint ventures, and reduced discrimination against foreign companies manufacturing in Brazil required the enactment of legislation. In this effort, the Collor government confronted ferocious opposition in Congress. When the Administration introduced informatics legislation in the Chamber of Deputies, opponents of reform substituted a bill that would extend the market reserve until 1994, require foreign informatics companies to invest 8 percent of their profits in Brazilian research and development and to export 50 percent of production, grant special tax incentives to "companies of national capital," and give such companies exclusive access to the Brazilian government procurement market.[178]

The bill ultimately enacted into law represented a middle course between the Administration and the hard-liners (although President Collor was forced to exercise his power to veto certain specific provisions which he deemed unacceptable).[179] In a major achievement for reform, the law provides for the elimination of the market reserve in 1992. Technology joint ventures with up to 49 percent foreign participation will be permitted, and Conin will no longer be tasked with reviewing and approving such ventures. Until October 1992,[180] however, the Secretariat of Science and Technology must approve all plans to manufacture informatics products.[181] The government will continue to give a procurement preference to Brazilian companies first and to local production second, taking into account equivalency of price, quality, etc.,

---

177 *Daily Report for Executives* (October 26, 1991).

178 *Brazil Watch* (June 24-July 8, 1991); *Radio Nacional da Amazonia Network* (May 24, 1991) (FBIS-LAT-91-104); *Estado de São Paulo* (May 18, 1991) (FBIS-LAT-91-103).

179 Bill No. 5804-B.

180 *Gazeta Mercantil* (October 25, 1991) (FBIS-LAT-91-226); *Brazil Watch* (November 4-18, 1991).

181 *Gazeta Mercantil* (October 25, 1991) (FBIS-LAT-91-226); *Brazil Watch* (November 4-18, 1991).

and a range of tax and financial benefits will be restricted to companies of "national capital."[182]

The struggle over informatics policy presents a valuable paradigm for Brazilian trade policy as a whole. As in many other sectors, trade restrictions helped to generate significant development in the informatics sector. However, much of the sector cannot compete internationally, and consumers -- including other producing sectors -- have been harmed by the higher prices and less advanced technology of the protected industry. Realizing the need for change, the Collor Administration has pressed for reform, and has convinced or compelled its opponents to support its program. Yet, as in many sectors, the change will be gradual, and many barriers to full liberalization -- high tariffs, preferential procurement, restrictions on foreign investment and special incentives for local companies -- will remain for the foreseeable future.

Steel

The Brazilian steel industry is deeply troubled. The rapid expansion by the state sector was funded with enormous borrowings. The companies of Siderbrás (the recently eliminated state holding company for the steel sector) are laboring under $17.2 billion in debt, $15 billion of which is to foreign creditors.[183] Exports to the United States and other developed markets, critical to the generation of foreign exchange needed to repay foreign loans, have been limited by quantitative restrictions. Labor strife, quality control problems at some facilities, late deliveries, relatively low productivity, and domestic price controls have had the combined effect of generating enormous losses for the state sector.[184]

---

182 *Gazeta Mercantil* (October 25, 1991) (FBIS-LAT-91-226); *Brazil Watch* (November 4-18, 1991). Fischer and Foster Advogados of São Paulo kindly provided an English translations of informatics legislation, as well as invaluable analysis regarding interpretation of the legislation.

183 Latin American Monitor, Ltd., *Brazil 1989*, p. 107.

184 Industrialists constantly complain about the poor quality and lack of dependability of some of the state producers. One São Paulo-based industrialist we spoke to buys his steel from USIMINAS, in spite of the proximity of CSN, because the quality of CSN steel was unacceptable to the U.S. purchasers of his product. Another industrialist indicated that his company in 1989 put in place a "strategic" plan to purchase imported steel because the state-owned companies could not be counted on to deliver on time and provided low-quality steel.

The steel industry has been a test case for the government's reform programs. Among the first steps in Collor's governmental reorganization was the announced elimination of Siderbrás, and privatization of the steel industry. Two steel companies -- USIMINAS and COSINOR -- were among the first companies to be privatized.[185] The process of privatization has been an extremely difficult one, both politically and commercially. Not only have labor unions and powerful congressional delegations resisted the sales through strikes, court challenges and political maneuvering,[186] but privatization has been hindered by the precarious financial condition of many of the companies, a shortage of capital at home, and limited interest from abroad. Thus, while the first privatizations generated little or no new cash for the government and attracted many other parastatal and few foreign investors, the privatization of USIMINAS, in particular, represents a triumph for the beleaguered privatization program.[187] Whether other, less attractive steel companies can be as effectively privatized will rely, in large part, on the ability of the Collor government to control inflation, reduce government regulation (especially price controls) and restore the domestic economy generally and the steel market in particular to health.

Textiles

The Brazilian textile and clothing industry is one of the nation's oldest manufacturing industries as well as one of its leading employers (430,000 employees in 1988).[188] The industry has been plagued in recent years by dramatic swings in domestic demand and is troubled by antiquated plants and equipment. Laws that prohibit the import of most items where a comparable item is available domestically (the so-called "law of national similars") limited producers' access to state-of-the-art production equipment, and high levels of protection effectively excluded foreign competition from the Brazilian market.[189] As a result, Brazilian clothing costs have been among the highest in the world.

---

185 *Brasília Voz do Brasil Network* (November 14, 1991) (FBIS-LAT-91-221).

186 See "Usiminas Sale Set For October 24," *Metal Bulletin* (October 10, 1991).

187 *Brazil Watch* (November 18-December 2, 1991).

188 Latin American Monitor, Ltd., *Brazil 1989*, pp. 98-99.

189 *Financial Times* (September 15, 1988).

Not surprisingly, the government chose to cut tariffs on cloth immediately (from 65 percent to 40 percent) as one of the first concrete steps under its new industrial and trade policy. Cotia Trading promptly formed an association with the Brazilian Clothing Association, Abravest, to help small and medium clothing manufacturers achieve volume imports of cloth.[190] At the same time, the new industrial policy is supposed to make it possible for cloth manufacturers to modernize and become competitive. Yet the ability of the industry to make the huge investments necessary to become competitive is doubtful. As one observer pointed out, 125,000 of Brazil's 165,000 looms are obsolete and should be replaced. Yet the entire world production of looms is only 100,000 units per year.[191] In a recent survey, 62.3 percent of Brazilian textiles producers indicated that they consider their industry unprepared for competition with foreign imports.[192]

While Brazilian textile producers face the prospect of heightened foreign competition at home, Brazilian export opportunities have been impeded by import quotas in major Western markets. While a new quota agreement with the United States in 1988 allowed Brazilian producers to increase their exports of textiles and apparel substantially,[193] the ability of the Brazilian textile and clothing industries to compete effectively in world markets is by no means clear. Accordingly, while Brazil has made the elimination of the MFA a key goal in the Uruguay Round, the benefits of such an achievement may be elusive. As a practical matter, Brazil's interests may be better served by a system that assures it a share of developed country markets through quotas and does not force it into head-to-head competition with its Far East competitors.

Restricted Investment Sectors

In a number of sectors, foreign investment will continue to be restricted in the 1990s. Leaving aside the special case of informatics, the restrictions will come in one of two forms: restrictions on direct foreign participation in a sector per se, and reservation of a sector to the state. The government is now attempting to eliminate many sectoral restrictions.

---

190 *Journal of Commerce* (July 5, 1990).

191 Interview with a foreign business consultant in Rio de Janeiro, July 1990.

192 Carlos Franco, "Metade das Industrias Cre Que Não Pode Vencer Importados," in *Folha de São Paulo* (May 17, 1991).

193 *Women's Wear Daily* (June 14, 1988).

The combined effect of Constitutional restraints and Congressional opposition will preclude foreign participation in some sectors, however. The Constitution explicitly authorizes the government to concede "protection and special temporary benefits" to sectors considered strategic for the defense or necessary to national development.[194] In addition, it requires the government to limit the exploitation of mineral reserves to Brazilian companies.[195]

The dominance of state-owned companies poses a much broader limit on the role of foreign companies in many sectors. The government has announced a broad privatization program, and has successfully privatized several major companies. However, the hurdles facing the program are great, and its utlimate success remains a question.[196] The State dominates such sectors as energy, telecommunications, steel, and aircraft. A number of these sectors, such as oil, electricity, and telecommunications are reserved to the State by Constitutional mandate and have a "mystique" that precludes their consideration for privatization in the short term.[197] But even those sectors that can be successfully privatized without running afoul of the Constitution will face restraints on foreign participation, since the privatization law, as amended by Congress, prevents more than 40 percent of the voting capital of any privatized company from being sold to non-Brazilians.[198]

---

194 Article 171. It further requires the government to give companies of national capital preference with respect to procurement. This procurement preference, which is manifested in domestic content rules, will not change in the near future. Interview with an official of the Department of Industry and Commerce, National Secretariat of Economy, Ministry of Economy, Treasury, and Planning, July 1990.

195 Article 176.

196 Privatization has been strongly resisted by the companies' management and employees, by the military, by the unions (particularly CUT, which has unions in many parastatals), and by many in Congress. Interviews with a private business consultant in Brazil, an official with National Bank for Economic and Social Development, and a sociologist at Central Unica de Trabalhadores, July 1990. Even Infrastructure Ministry officials actively involved in privatization concede that the schedule of privatization is overly optimistic. Interview with a Ministry of Infrastructure official, July 1990.

197 Interviews with an official at the National Bank for Economic and Social Development and the Ministry of Infrastructure, July 1990.

198 Interview with an official at the National Bank for Economic and Social Development, July 1990.

7

European Community

Thomas R. Howell, Rosemary E. Gwynn,
and R. Michael Gadbaw

With the adoption of the Single European Act in 1987 the European Community sought to reverse a long pattern of stagnation and competitive decline. The consolidation of the economic systems of the current twelve Members, coupled with initiatives designed to integrate, to a greater or lesser degree, those of numerous states on the periphery of the Community, raise the prospect that an economic colossus may be forming which will embrace 600 million or more people and which would dominate the world economy.[1] While it remains to be seen whether the Single Market Initiative will restore Europe to the position of world economic leadership that it enjoyed in the first half of this century, it has already set forces in motion which will fundamentally alter the world trading system in the 1990s and beyond. It has prompted an extraordinary surge of investment in the Community by U.S. and Japanese firms fearful of being excluded from a "fortress Europe," and it has induced the nations of the European Free Trade Association (EFTA) and Eastern Europe to press for closer association with, if not full accession to, the Community.

---

[1]The current Community of twelve members, with 321 million people, already accounts for 38 percent of all merchandise traded internationally (including trade between Member States). Report by the GATT Secretariat in GATT *Trade Policy Review: The European Communities* (Geneva: GATT, 1991), p. 1 (hereafter, "GATT *Trade Policy Review*").

The most dramatic effects of European integration, however, will be felt later in the 1990s and are a source of some apprehension on the part of the EC's trading partners, notwithstanding the reassurances offered by its leadership.[2] For better or worse, economic, monetary and possibly political union will make the Community much more assertive within the international trading system. The Single Market Initiative has been guided thus far by Commissioners with liberal economic vision who are committed to the reduction of external as well as internal trade barriers and to the strengthening of the GATT system, and, as the GATT Secretariat concluded in 1991, "there is little evidence of any recent major intensification of protective measures on the part of the EC."[3] But the Initiative is creating a centralized system of trade and industrial policy tools that can be wielded to achieve liberal or neomercantilist objectives, or even some hybrid mix of the two. The Commission itself, while sometimes viewed as an apolitical body of technocrats pursuing rational policy outcomes, is in fact driven by the "vagaries of power politics between member states and their political leaders; by states jostling for position and comparative advantage; by statesmen having a long term vision of Europe's future; and by those blinded by short-term calculations."[4] At the end of 1991, the economic liberals held the upper hand within the Commission's policy apparatus, but this could change; during past periods of economic dislocation and stagnation, advocates of more interventionist policies have come to the fore within the Commission, and in 1991, with many key European industries falling into disarray, calls for a more protectionist European posture were becoming stronger.[5] One such voice was that of Alain Gomez, the influential Chairman of France's Thomson group, who articulated the case as follows:

> *[I]f you reread economic history you will see that no power has ever been accumulated without protection. There is not one example to the contrary. England? Beginning in 1789, it surrounded itself with massive barriers that allowed it not only to control merchandise imports but also to prohibit*

---

[2]See generally the comments of the Chairman of the GATT Council and the First and Second Discussants in GATT *Trade Policy Review* (1991) Vol. II, p. 121.

[3]GATT *Trade Policy Review* (1991) Vol. II, p. 134.

[4]Juliet Lodge, "EC Policymaking: Institutional Considerations," in J. Lodge (ed.), *The European Community and the Challenge of the Future* (New York: St. Martin's Press, 1989), p. 31.

[5]See *Le Monde* (April 20, 1991); *The Economist* (June 8, 1991).

exports of English machinery -- what today we would call technology. When the English industrial machine became dominant, the barriers were lowered. Germany? Germany was virtually created by the Zollverein of 1834, which was basically a customs union. . .America? America emerged as a power between the War of Secession and 1914, while it was protected by a 50 percent tariff. The most recent example, of course, is Japan.[6]

Because of the Community's sheer economic weight, even slight tilts in a liberal or protectionist direction can have an enormous impact on world trade patterns and on the trading system itself; indeed, by the end of the 1990s, the Community rather than the U.S. or Japan may be the principal actor in the international trading system. But if the Community is to lead the system itself, specific aspects of its trade policy and policymaking process are of serious worry to other trading states whose destinies are linked to that system. The Commission's opaque, "complex and multi-layered process of trade policy formulation and implementation" is a source of concern for all of the Community's trading partners.[7] Its emphasis on preferential regional trading arrangements, and its tendency to give "a less than central role for the [most-favored nation] principle" arguably weakens -- and could possibly destroy -- the GATT system.[8] Finally, the Community, by its own admission, has "no specific trade policy objective. . .in the agriculture sector,"[9] a fact which, given the "appalling"[10] effects EC farm policies have on the trading system and the world economy, raises questions about the depth and strength of the EC's commitment to a liberal, multilateral trading order.[11]

The negative aspects of the Community's trade policies are known; the positives have not yet become fully apparent. The question is whether the entity representing the world's largest market will be able to accept a leadership role in maintaining an open multilateral trading system. The

---

[6]Interview in *Le Monde* (April 20, 1991) (FBIS-WEU-91-095).

[7]Concluding Remarks by Chairman of the GATT Council Lars Anell (April 15-16, 1991) in GATT *Trade Policy Review* (1991) Vol. II, p. 3.

[8]GATT *Trade Policy Review* (1991) Vol. II, p. 5.

[9]"Report by the Commission of the European Community" in GATT *Trade Policy Review* (1991) p. 31.

[10]*Deutsches Allgemeines Sonntagsblatt* (June 21, 1991) (FBIS-WEU-91-147).

[11]Statement by the First Discussant in GATT *Trade Policy Review* (1991).

balance of the current Commission leans in this direction, backed, for the most part, by a dedicated (and overworked) bureaucracy. But the Community is still a confederation in which difficult decisions that impose costs on members for the benefit of nonmembers -- as many trade decisions do -- face at best an uncertain resolution.

TRADE POLICY BACKGROUND

The International Political Context

Since its inception the European Community has been politically overshadowed by the international institutional arrangements established under U.S. leadership to provide security and stability during the Cold War. While NATO was successfully countering increased Soviet pressure in the early 1980s through higher arms spending and the deployment of intermediate range missiles in Western Europe, the Community institutions were generally perceived to be in a state of decay, unable to make progress on the reduction of internal barriers, racked by acrimonious debates over the Common Agricultural Policy, and powerless to arrest what appeared to be the inexorable competitive decline of European industry -- "stuck in its own institutional morass."[12] To the astonishment even of many Europeans, the Single Market Initiative not only restored momentum to the process of European integration, but by the late 1980s had fostered predictions of a comprehensive economic union which would provide a basis for political integration and common European security arrangements, perhaps even supplanting, at some future point, the Atlantic Alliance. Europe's leaders had "talked life back into [the] old idea" of European political union.[13]

Beginning in 1989, however, a number of unanticipated developments threatened to derail the process of European integration. Within a span of less than two years, all of the communist regimes in Eastern Europe collapsed, Germany was reunified, a major war was fought in the Middle East, the Soviet Union began to break up, and Yugoslavia was descending into civil war. Against the background of these events, the disengagement of the Soviets and the Americans from their traditional Cold War posture of confrontation in central Europe raised the prospect

---

[12]Graham Hall, *European Industrial Policy* (New York: St. Martin's Press, 1986), p. 4.

[13]Nicholas Colchester and David Buchan, *Europower* (New York, Economist Books Ltd. 1990) p. 7.

of a political void in the region and corresponding anxiety over what sort of arrangements would be made to fill it. Germany's enhanced size, its longstanding economic and ethnic ties with Eastern Europe, and Bonn's early support for autonomous regimes in its former satellites of Croatia and Slovenia raised fears of an emerging "Teutonic bloc" that would upset the existing equilibrium of the Community. While such concerns were perhaps unfounded, the Community's apparent inability to act decisively in several foreign crises involving its own vital interests -- notably the Gulf War and Yugoslavia -- underscored its abiding lack of influence in international matters outside the economic arena and raised questions about its ability to evolve into a true federal state. Finally, the onset of a recession in 1991, the high cost and irrationality of the Common Agricultural Policy, and the dramatic competitive inroads being made by Japanese transplant operations raised fundamental, potentially divisive questions about the soundness of the Single Market strategy itself.

Despite the internal fault lines and historical anxieties that have been revealed by events since 1989, the fluid political situation created by the end of the Cold War in Europe is likely to culminate in the emergence of common European political and security arrangements which are not dominated by the United States and which eventually extend well into the former Soviet sphere in the East. NATO is already restructuring itself on the basis of a diminished U.S. troop presence, while simultaneously extending its area of "concern" (if not an actual "European Security Shield" as reported by some sources) to embrace Poland, Czechoslovakia and Hungary.[14] France is lobbying for the formation of a large, strategic European force that is capable of operating independently of NATO in areas outside of Europe.

The Internal Political Context

The European Community is a grouping of states which have consented to surrender a portion of their sovereignty in the economic sphere to supranational institutions as a means of enhancing their mutual prosperity. The "deepening" of the Community -- that is, the extent to which further delegations of sovereignty are to be made to the EC

---

[14]Nato Secretary General Woerner expressed this new position as follows: "There are not final security guarantees. . .[But in 1991] we went on step further. We have always said we do not remain indifferent toward the desire for security of these states. Now we have expressly formulated our strategic interest in their security and make it clear that we expect the USSR to respect the desire for security of these states. . . . *Köln Deutschlandfunk Network* (09:00 GMT June 16, 1991) (Foreign Broadcast Information Service).

institutions, and to what end -- has become a matter of controversy because of the momentum toward greater integration that has developed since 1985. Prior to the Single European Act, the actual loss of sovereignty by Member States was quite limited; while they were required to conform their laws to those of the Community, any Member State could wield an absolute veto over any particular piece of Community legislation, and was thus in a position to block adoption of any laws or rules that were fundamentally at odds with national policy. The Single European Act replaced this system with one in which decisions can now be made -- with exceptions in the areas of tax, employment policies, and movement of people -- by a qualified majority, with votes roughly allocated according to a country's population.[15] Recalcitrant Member States can be overridden, and, at least in theory, compelled to accept EC policies which they regard as obnoxious.

The nature of the EC's decisionmaking process -- with votes cast by Member States as entities rather than by representatives directly elected by the European population at large -- minimizes the immediate significance of voter opinion and places a premium on the particular alignments of groups of Member States on a given issue. Perhaps fortunately for European integration, there are no blocs of Member States that vote together across the whole gamut of issues confronting the Community. Through the late 1980s the special relationship between France and Germany was the axis around which the Community's affairs have turned; in addition, the original six Member States shared a certain sense of cohesion and "European" identity that was not present among the "outer" members, based on large Catholic populations and legal systems rooted in the Napoleonic Code.[16] Britain, in particular, bridled at proposals that would curtail her sovereignty and has resisted proposals to "deepen" the Community and extend economic integration to the political sphere; "the 'f' word, federalism, is. . .considered an obscenity in

---

[15]Article 18 of the Single European Act, amending Article 100 of the Treaty of Rome. A qualified majority is 54 votes; at least 23 votes are needed for a blocking minority. Germany, France, Britain and Italy have 10 votes each; Spain, 8; Belgium, Netherlands, Portugal and Greece, 5; Ireland and Denmark 3; and Luxembourg, 2. While an attempt has been made to correlate the numbers of votes with population, some European populations -- notably the Germans -- are underrepresented. The Benelux countries, for example, have 12 votes while the reunified Germany, with three times the population, has 10. *NRC Handelsblad* (June 29, 1991).

[16]Nicholas Colchester and David Buchan, *Europower* (New York: Random House, 1990), p. 181.

Britain."[17] But there are major divisions even among the "original six" core group, and between France and Germany. The Germans have supported Austrian accession to the Community, and, it is feared by the French, may in the future seek to sponsor accession by additional EFTA members and Eastern European countries, all of which would be drawn into a constellation supporting German positions. The French have countered by efforts to defer accession of new members; their proposed alternative is to offer preferential arrangements to such countries stopping short of membership, while Germany itself is more fully integrated and "anchored" in the EC through new political and perhaps security arrangements. Britain has thus far supported Germany's efforts to "widen" the Community simply because to do so makes further "deepening" -- and surrender of sovereignty -- less feasible and therefore less likely. Somewhat surprisingly, as of 1991 there had been no revival of the old Anglo-French "Entente Cordiale" as a counterweight to growing German influence, although this is believed by some EC observers to be a function of particular personalties.[18]

With respect to the trade and industrial policy issues which are the subject of this study, the "original six" core group and the "outer six" are split along a rough north-south axis. The affluent northern states (Germany, Denmark, Netherlands and sometimes Luxembourg) tend to advocate liberal trade policies and limits on government support for industry, whereas the southern Member States (Italy and France) have advocated trade protection and limits on foreign investment, and have used large scale subsidies to promote key industries. Belgium is divided between its Flemish population, whose sympathies lie with the northern group, and the Walloons, who tend to support the southern group. Under Labour Britain generally supported the interventionist group, but has sided strongly with the liberals since the Conservative ascendancy in 1979. The southern group has been greatly strengthened by the accession of Spain, Portugal and Greece, all of whom tend to be protectionist in outlook. The balance is expected to tilt decisively toward the liberal group, however, when the EFTA countries become members.[19]

---

[17]*NRC Handelsblad* (June 29, 1991).

[18]Interview with an EC trade official, March 1990.

[19]The above generalizations about country alignments do not necessarily hold in every case involving trade and industrial policy matters. Britain and Company, for example, see eye to eye on matters of broad economic philosophy but are at loggerheads over farm issues, with Germany strongly supporting the Common (continued...)

The Ideological Context: Liberalism Ascendant

The Community's current liberal posture on trade and industrial policy matters reflects the philosophy of the influential troika of Commissioners Frans Andriessen, Martin Bangemann and Sir Leon Brittan. These three have been able to develop a mandate for a liberal agenda not so much because their views are universally shared but because those who favor a more interventionist approach have been unable to unite around any coherent system of neomercantilism. Many EC policymakers believe that protectionism cannot be successfully implemented at the Member State level if the internal market is open, and that it is irrational to break down internal barriers without a concurrent opening to the world.[20] Although protectionist leanings are common in many Member States, trade protection is generally opposed (outside of agriculture) by the political leadership in West Germany, Great Britain, the Netherlands and Denmark, a grouping which is strong enough to block most major restrictive initiatives.

Notwithstanding the liberal inclination of its leadership, EC officials at the working level frequently take formal and informal measures that are inconsistent with the Commission's own stated policies. This is not a reflection of hypocrisy on the part of the EC leadership or even a deliberate strategy but of the sheer complexity of the Community's bureaucratic machinery, which is characterized by conflict between individuals, between directorates within the Commission, with most key decisions subject to review by the Council, that is, the Member States between Commissioners themselves. At the bureaucratic level, Commission officials are frequently influenced by the industries with which they interact, and may implement specific policies that benefit those industries; as one spokesman for a GATT contracting party commented in 1991, "there seems to be a considerable capacity for catering to special trade interests in different sectors of the member states level and in

[19](...continued)
Agricultural Policy and trade protection in the face of vehement British criticism. Germany is generally critical of industrial subsidies but makes dramatic use of them in areas deemed to be of vital national importance, notably the establishment of a commercial aviation industry.

[20]Interview with a senior trade official with the Organization for Economic Cooperation and Development, November 1989.

respect of individual policy instruments."[21] Even within the top leadership, liberalism is circumscribed by pragmatism. The Commission is striving to pull trade and industrial policy authority away from the Member States and it cannot do so if it appears to be indifferent to European commercial interests. It has already demonstrated a willingness to implement managed trade policies toward Japan and the Korea at the Community level in the 1990s that are similar to those practiced by the Member States in past decades; the most dramatic example being the 1991 negotiation of restrictions on imports of Japanese autos. As one Commission official put it, "We must show the Member States that the EC Commission is made up of tough guys."[22] Even Mr. Bangemann, one of the liberal troika, reportedly told Japanese officials in 1989 that "the four industries of automobiles, steel, shipbuilding and textiles embrace problems that cannot be left to the principle of market competition."[23]

The complex cross-currents formed by contending liberal and mercantilist forces within a multi-tiered decision structure result in an entity that officially embraces GATT principles as well as those of laissez-faire liberalism, but in practice engages in a substantial amount of managed trade, industrial promotion, and outright trade protection. Nevertheless, overall, the trend is clearly toward greater openness, and if trends evident in 1990-91 continue, the Community market will be considerably more open by the end of the current decade. The centralization of trade policy functions at the Community level and the corresponding phaseout of national gray measures will produce a net reduction in the level of protection. In addition, should the Uruguay Round succeed, many of the new GATT rules will constrain the Community's ability to undertake protectionist actions at both the policy and the bureaucratic level.

The Economic Context

European leaders have been engaged in a spirited debate over the European economy and industrial competitiveness since the early 1980s. At that time, European industry had reached a nadir; after years of slipping export performance and declining competitiveness relative to Japan and the U.S., the EC experienced a severe recession which forced

---

[21]Statement by First Discussant in GATT *Trade Policy Review* (1991) Vol. II, p. 132.

[22]Interview with an EC diplomat, March 1990.

[23]*Nihon Keizai Shimbun* (February 8, 1989) p.5.

a painful restructuring on a number of mainstay industries (coal, shipbuilding, steel). A number of the Community's older industrial regions were devastated in the process -- the Ruhr, the Saar, Wales, the Nord, Lorraine, and Belgian Wallonia. Global recovery subsequently helped to pull European industry out of this recession, and the Community economy showed strong growth for the remainder of the decade, with GDP increasing by 3 percent per year, but the debate over what came to be labeled "Eurosclerosis," a uniquely European tangle of competitive ills, continued.[24] European leaders acknowledged that part of the Community's competitive problem was attributable to deeply rooted cultural, attitudinal and quality-of-life factors -- the fondness of European workers for frequent and lengthy vacations, for example, and an embedded resistance to automation, which was seen by many as a threat to job security.[25] However, they diagnosed the principal source of the Community's stagnation as its continuing segmentation into national markets, divided by standards differences, regulatory barriers, and national protectionist measures in key areas like telecommunications and energy. Fragmentation was blamed for European industry's failure to achieve international economies of scale, lagging investment and innovation, and a wide range of other competitive failings. The Single Market Initiative was designed to sweep away Europe's internal barriers and facilitate a boom in investment, and through 1990 the strategy appeared to be working. Agreements were reached which dismantled many of the national regulatory and standards impediments to integration with a speed which surprised many observers,[26] and European companies engaged in a veritable frenzy of transnational acquisitions, mergers and joint ventures in an effort to create "European" and "global" competitive enterprises.[27] Investment in the Community industry,

---

[24]EC Commission, *Industrial Policy in an Open and Competitive Environment*, COM (90) 565 final (November 16, 1990); *Industrie* (June 19, 1985); *Official Journal* No. C. 321 (November 26, 1983).

[25]Essen *Elektro-Anzeiger* (February 1983).

[26]EC Commission, *Fifth Report of the Commission to the Council and the European Parliament Concerning the Implementation of the White Paper on the Completion of the Internal Market*, COM (90) 90 (Final), March 28, 1990.

[27]For example, Siemens of Germany and GEC of the United Kingdom jointly acquired Plessey of Britain; Thomson of France and SGS-ATES of Italy, merged their semiconductor divisions; Carnaud (France) and Metal Box (U.K.) merged to form CMB Packaging.

which had actually declined between 1980 and 1983, grew by 8 percent in 1988 and again in 1989.[28]

However, it remained unclear whether the Single Market Initiative heralded the onset of a European industrial resurgence or merely opened a new chapter in a long chronicle of decline. In 1991, economic growth slowed. Several major European enterprises in key industries -- Groupe Bull, Philips, Olivetti -- were reportedly in serious economic trouble. Planned investments were being postponed or canceled across a range of industries.[29] With key sectors like autos and electronics suffering from overcapacity, questions were raised about the wisdom of the Single Market strategy of attracting Japanese and other foreign transplant facilities to the EC market; these entities not only contributed to the capacity surplus confronting the Community, but appeared better positioned to exploit the Single Market and survive a shakeout than many EC firms. *The Economist* commented (June 8, 1991) that "if Project 1992 overturns barriers according to plan, European businesses are in for a shock."

Current Trade Regime

The Community possesses far and away the most complex and variegated trade regime of any major trading entity.[30] The Treaty of Rome vests jurisdiction in the European Community over many aspects of external trade policy, including tariffs, the conclusion of association and trade agreements with nonmembers, export policy, negotiations with international economic organizations, and antidumping and countervailing duties. Following the formation of the Community, however, Member States were permitted to maintain and renew pre-existing bilateral trade agreements, understandings, and arrangements with nonmembers, subject to periodic Community authorization. These agreements, which eventually numbered in the hundreds, regulated much of the Community's trade, particularly with Asia. Member States have also been permitted to enter into cooperation arrangements with Eastern European

---

[28]EC Commission *Industrial Policy* (1991).

[29]"Industrial Investments: Forced Pause," in *L'Usine Nouvelle* (June 6, 1991).

[30]For a detailed synopsis of the EC trade regime, see "Report by the GATT Secretariat," in GATT *Trade Policy Review* (1990), Vol. I.

countries.[31] The result of this incomplete centralization of authority was a patchwork of trade arrangements concluded at the Community and the national level, and in some cases (e.g., textiles), at both levels, which frequently established different categories of treatment for different classes of countries. Characterizing these arrangements as either protectionist or liberal is difficult as both elements were present; for example, a system of tariff preferences was established with the EFTA countries, a tier of Mediterranean countries, and the so-called ACP (Lomé Convention) countries in Africa, but these preferences were tempered by an array of specific restrictions, usually in the form of quotas, in sensitive areas.[32] The Commission has established comprehensive systems of protection at the European level in textiles and steel, designed to permit imports into the Community in a manner that does not inordinately disrupt the internal market.[33] Tariffs excepted, conditions of relatively free trade have prevailed with respect to highly developed Western market economies such as the United States, Canada, and Australia, but have been subject to de jure and de facto restrictions in some protected sectors and areas (i.e., agriculture, many services sectors, energy and public procurement).

THE TRADE POLICY PROCESS

An old cliche in the Community is that the "Commission proposes and the Council disposes," and in fact, while the Council of Ministers holds the formal authority to make all important policy decisions, in virtually every case the Council only acts on the basis of a Commission proposal. The Commission functions not only as the executive branch of the

---

[31]Many of the gray bilaterals, which involve import quotas on products into the Community, are summarized in annexes to GATT *Review of Developments in the Trading System* (issued biannually).

[32]Examples of the latter include voluntary restraint arrangements in textiles (outside the framework of the MFA) with Turkey, Malta, Tunisia, and Morocco. Notwithstanding free trade agreements with the EFTA countries, bilateral steel agreements commit both parties to observe "normal patterns of trade," a euphemism for traditional market share. This clause is periodically invoked when import volume threatens a change in the status quo. *Metal Bulletin* (February 4, 1988).

[33]See European Commission, *External Commercial Policy in the Steel Sector*, Com (86) 585 final, November 13, 1986, pp. 24-25.

Community but as the "engine of policy," originating, shaping and advocating proposals for new laws, regulations, and policies. The Council represents the status quo, the Commission, a vision of the future.[34]

The Commission presents a peculiar profile to non-EC countries as policy is formulated; input from such sources, if not unwelcome, is not expected or sought, and internal policy debates are carried on largely behind closed doors, with only occasional, imperfect glimpses of the process afforded by leaked documents, comments by those party to the deliberations, and the occasional eruption of a public row. Complexity, ambiguity, and constant compromise are hallmarks of the process. As the Commission observed in 1991,

> *a complex set of checks and balances exist and, in the most usual cases, the result is a network of countervailing forces which can cancel each other out. . . . Some will be in favour of action which is felt to be justified, e.g., by injury to specific interests and which is desirable to achieve a limited objective, while others will consider that this would be contrary to a more global set of Community interests, would risk escalation of the situation thus affecting Community exports, or is not adequately justified. Decisions are therefore very often the result of hard fought internal negotiation and ultimately of compromise.*[35]

The internal struggles that characterize policy formation tend to ensure that the Community rarely adopts extreme policies; on the other hand, the policies which it does adopt, reflecting as they do a difficult process of compromise, are very difficult to change once they are finalized, particularly if the only objections to them are by disgruntled non-EC companies and governments. The Commission's deliberation over proposed trade and trade-related policies thus take on the aspect of a moving train which must be boarded by outsiders before it is too late; at the same time, access to the process is unpredictable and dependent, to a significant degree, on the discretion of the Commission and its staff. The Commission, recognizing this dynamic, has been able to utilize and manipulate its own internal debates as a source of external trade leverage.

---

[34]Interview with a senior DG-I official, April 1990.

[35]EC Commission, "Report by the Commission of the European Communities," in GATT *Trade Policy Review* (1991) Vol. II, p. 35.

The Legal Framework

The European Community derives its trade policy authority from the 1951 Treaty of Paris, which created the European Coal and Steel Community, and the 1957 Treaty of Rome, which established the European Economic Community (EEC) and the European Atomic Energy Community.[36] The EEC Treaty, the most important from a trade policy standpoint, provides for the establishment of a customs union among the Member States with a common external tariff and the progressive elimination of intra-Community barriers to the free movement of goods, services, persons and capital (the four freedoms).[37] The treaty also provides for the adoption of common policies in a number of areas, including agriculture and transport, and for the establishment of a common commercial policy towards third countries,[38] the latter provisions forming the principal source of the Community's jurisdiction

---

[36]In 1967, the institutions of the three Communities were merged to form the basic structure of the European Community as it now exists. The term "European Community" is used in this paper as a collective designation for all three of the Communities.

[37]Although the EEC Treaty envisioned the eventual integration of the member state economies, progress toward that goal stalled following the completion of a customs union. Momentum was regained during the 1980s with the adoption of the 1985 White Paper, which set forth a comprehensive program for completing the internal market by December 1992, and the 1987 *Single European Act* (SEA), which amended the basic treaties in several respects. Most importantly, it allowed accelerated consideration of measures related to the internal market by permitting the Council to adopt most such measures by a qualified majority vote, rather than by unanimous consent. The SEA also reaffirmed the Member States' commitment to completing the internal market and required the Community to adopt measures with the aim of achieving this goal by December 31, 1992. These two documents -- the White Paper and the SEA -- launched the massive undertaking, popularly known as "Europe 1992", that is now the Community's principal preoccupation (and whose completion and refinement will continue to dominate the EC policy agenda throughout the coming decade).

[38]See EEC Treaty, Article 3(a-e). Other important trade-related powers granted by the EEC Treaty include Community control over competition policy (Article 3(f)) and a residual authority that authorizes Community institutions to take action necessary to attain the objectives of the Community even where the Treaty has not provided the necessary specific powers. EEC Treaty, Article 235.

in the field of external trade.[39] Article 113 authorizes Community action "based on uniform principles" in a number of specific areas, including tariffs, antidumping, trade agreements, and trade liberalization. Actions taken under Article 113 to implement the common commercial policy are proposed by the Commission to the Council and must be adopted by the Council by a qualified majority. Where agreements with third countries need to be negotiated, the Commission makes recommendations to the Council, which authorizes the Commission to open the necessary negotiations. The Commission must conduct its negotiations in consultation with a special committee of Member States' representatives appointed by the Council (the Article 113 Committee). Since Article 113 does not limit the type of action that may be taken, the Community may use any form of legislative act authorized under Article 189 -- regulations, directives, or decisions -- to implement policies in this area.[40]

The Players

Decisionmaking in the Community centers on the four governing institutions, the Commission, the Council of Ministers, the European Parliament, and the European Court of Justice (ECJ). In trade, the Commission is far and away the most important; it proposes legislation, oversees its implementation, recommends the negotiation of trade agreements, conducts the negotiations, and represents the Community's

---

[39]The treaty provisions that establish the Community's competence in external trade include Articles 3(b) and 110-116, dealing with the common commercial policy; Articles 9-29, dealing with the common external tariff; Articles 131-136, 228 and 238, which provide for the conclusion of trade and association agreements with non-member countries and organizations; and Article 237 on the accession of new members to the Community. The Preamble to the EEC Treaty indicates that the desire of the founding Member States in establishing a common commercial policy was "to contribute. . .to the progressive abolition of restrictions on international trade." Preamble, par. 6. The breadth of the EC's power to regulate trade and enter into agreements on behalf of the Member States has been further defined in case law and subsequent treaty revisions (e.g., in the Single European Act, which did not, however, specifically address the common commercial policy). See Anna Murphy, *The European Community and the International Trading System,* CEPS Paper no. 48, Centre for European Policy Studies (1990) pp. 40-41; 56-60, and 62-64.

[40]A regulation becomes Community law directly; a decision is binding only on the parties (Member States, companies or individuals) to whom it is addressed; and a directive sets compulsory objectives that Member States must translate into national legislation.

interests in dealings with third countries and international organizations. The Commission also has independent decisionmaking powers in certain areas; for example, it can initiate antidumping and countervailing duty investigations and impose provisional duties without Council approval.[41] The Commission holds authority to enforce the Treaties: it can sue Member States in the European Court for failing to comply with their Treaty obligations, a power that is important in ensuring timely and effective Member State implementation of GATT commitments. The Commission can also formulate recommendations and opinions on both external and internal policy issues; although these have no binding force, they can be influential in shaping Community law and policy. Organizationally, the Commission consists of 17 Commissioners -- political appointees from the Member States -- including one President and six Vice Presidents.[42] France in particular has appointed highly capable officials to Commission posts, and so enjoys a disproportionate influence; other Members often appoint officials to the Commission "to get rid of them," as a form of semi-retirement, or to get their European tickets punched prior to their return to another domestic position.[43] Each Commissioner is assigned responsibility for a portfolio comprising one or more substantive areas and assumes the leadership of one or more of the Commission's major subdivisions, the Directorates General (DGs).[44] Responsibility for external trade policy resides primarily with DG-I

---

[41]These powers may be conferred either by the Treaty or pursuant to a Council delegation of authority. Outside the external trade arena, the Commission's independent decisionmaking powers include implementation of the Common Agricultural Policy and authority over competition policy (including the power to investigate and impose fines for antitrust violations). Audrey Winter et. al., *Europe Without Frontiers: A Lawyer's Guide* (Washington: Bureau of National Affairs, 1989).

[42]The Commissioners are appointed by mutual agreement of the member state governments to serve renewable four-year terms. Germany, France, Italy, Spain, and the United Kingdom each nominate two Commissioners, and each of the remaining Member States nominates one.

[43]Interview with a senior U.S. State Department official responsible for U.S.-EC affairs, March 1990.

[44]The Commissioners' substantive responsibilities may not correspond precisely to those of the Directorates General; thus, there may be several Commissioners overseeing different activities within a single DG. Winter (1989) p. 26 n. 12.

(External Affairs and Trade Negotiations),[45] and to a lesser extent DG-XXI (Customs Union and Indirect Tax), but other DGs often have a significant influence on the content of trade policy, notably, DG-III (Internal Market and Industrial Affairs), DG-VI (Agriculture), DG-IV (Competition) and DG-XIII (Information Technology and Telecommunications).

In drafting proposals the DGs usually consult other institutions and affected interests, but they are not required to do so, nor is the Commission itself legally obligated to consider the views of Parliament or the private sector in formulating and implementing negotiating strategy. Even within the Commission bureaucracy, the massive welter of technical rules and directives being drafted and implemented tends to defy comprehensive oversight; new rules can be made at the working level and become a fait accompli before the political level is even aware of them.[46] The real power brokers are the officials at the director general and director level whose mandate is to reconcile political and technical level considerations. Their relatively small number, insularity, and comparative anonymity contribute to the public perception a mysterious decisionmaking process orchestrated by faceless technocrats. On the other hand, as one EC official observed in 1990, notwithstanding the lack of transparency and perhaps because of it, "it is far easier [than in the United States] to target places to influence the decisionmaking process."[47]

Curiously, the Commission, an intensely political body, is less subject to many of the political pressures that drive decisionmaking in ordinary nation-states, a fact which has fostered stability and continuity in policy formulation in trade and trade-related matters. One British analyst recently castigated the Commission as an "utterly undemocratic body,"[48] and in fact the Commission is largely immune to the pressures of electoral politics; its leadership is never voted out and replaced with new leaders with an entirely different agenda, as occurs in parliamentary democracies. Party politics are largely irrelevant -- apart from broad issues such as enlargement, political union, and agriculture, the political parties at the

---

[45]One of the most important offices in DG-I is one created to manage the "external aspects of the Single Market Initiative," which was created in response to the concerns and potential reaction of third countries to the potentially discriminatory effects of the 1992 initiative.

[46]Interview with a senior DG-I official, April 1990.

[47]Interview with a senior EC diplomat, January 1990.

[48]*NRC Handelsblad* (July 18, 1991).

Member State level seldom take a substantial interest in European issues, particularly in complex and obscure economic concerns, thereby reflecting a general public apathy toward bureaucratic matters handled by the Commission.[49] Lobbying of the Commission by interest groups is uneven by U.S. standards.[50] Although some European industries have developed effective organizations for affecting policy at the Community level (i.e., textiles, agriculture, chemicals),[51] most EC industries are poorly organized at the European level, and historically, have tended to concentrate lobbying efforts on the Member States' governments, utilizing

---

[49]See e.g., Simon Bulmer and William Paterson, *The Federal Republic of Germany and the European Community* (Allen & Unwin: 1987) pp. 123-163.

[50]Murphy notes that "[t]he dialogue between the Commission and industry is unstructured and quite ad hoc. The issue of establishing formal consultation mechanisms. . .has been considered inside the Commission, but officials are generally reluctant to add another layer to the already complex decision-making process. They tend to take the view that it is up to the industry itself to approach it with its views." The absence of formal consultative mechanisms between the Commission and industry on trade issues can lead to "a patchy view of the industrial landscape with regard to certain sectors, which can lead to a false appreciation of the relative strengths and weaknesses of the industry." Anna Murphy (1990) Vol. II p. 128.

[51]The Union of Industrial and Employers Confederation of Europe (UNICE) is well-connected and can be quite influential, but the breadth of its membership and its consensus approach tend to dilute the strength of its positions. John Goodman, "Do All Roads Lead to Brussels? Economic Policymaking in the European Community," American Enterprise Institute, The United States and Europe in the 1990s Conference Paper (March 5-8, 1990) p. 19. See Murphy (1990) p. 127. Other EC-wide interest groups that the Commission consults on a regular basis are ETUC (the European Trade Union Confederation), COPA (Committee of Professional Agricultural Organizations of the European Community), Federation Bancaire (Banking Federation of the European Community), EEB (European Environmental Bureau), BEUC (European Bureau of Consumer Unions) and CEEP (European Centre of Public Enterprises). Winter (1989) p. 54. One of the key groups of businessmen interested in trade policy is the European Business Roundtable. Interview with a senior DG-I official, April 1990. The Roundtable, which includes representatives of major European corporations such as Philips, Volvo, Hoechst and Saint Gobain, tends to maintain a fairly low profile, "eschewing public statements in favour of quiet diplomacy with senior trade officials [in its approach to the Uruguay Round negotiations]." Murphy (1990) p. 127. Influential European-wide business associations in specific sectors include the European Textile Bureau, CEFIC (the Chemicals Industry Federation), and EECA (the European Electronic Component Manufacturers Association).

what limited lobbying resources they possess in Brussels to address integration issues rather than trade-related matters.[52]

The Commission must operate under the political direction of the Council of Ministers. While this can occasionally prove cumbersome in international negotiations; in multilateral trade talks it often finds itself engaged in negotiations on two fronts -- with the Article 113 Committee (representing the Council of Ministers) and with representatives of foreign countries, with the former often proving more complex and exhausting than the latter. More generally, however, the Commission enjoys a relatively wide latitude in trade. Trade policy questions are complex and other institutions tend to defer to the Commission's expertise.[53] Its bureaucracy is characterized by a high degree of professionalism, skill, and independent judgment. While technically required to secure a mandate for negotiations from the Council, the Commission frequently negotiates without one, ostensibly simply conducting "talks" in its area of competence but actually addressing and resolving trade issues. The Council has delegated a number of powers to the Commission in trade, notably in the area of import remedies; while it has sought to retain authority to review Commission actions, that authority is often limited in its effectiveness by the terms under which the delegation is made.[54] For example, the committee procedure applicable to the issuance of special origin rules imposes a fairly high threshold on the Member States to

---

[52]The infrastructure for special interest lobbying the Parliament or the Commission is not well developed. Although Brussels has been home to hundreds of European trade associations, few of these have come to exercise significant influence in the process. In part, this weakness is a function of the unwillingness of national trade associations to give the European-wide organization a sufficient mandate to become effective. The Commission, on the other hand, has the option to bypass the European-level organizations and deal directly with Member State-level groups. See generally Murphy (1990) pp. 126-130.

[53]Interviews with a DG-I official and a senior administration official with the EC Commission, April 1990.

[54]Under the so-called *comitology* process, the Council can qualify a delegation of authority by requiring the Commission to cooperate with a committee of experts representing each of the Member States. Different types of committees may be used, ranging from consultation committees to rule-making committees that can prevent Commission action, thereby forcing the Commission to make a proposal to the Council. In the latter case, the Council can provide for the Commission's decision to take effect if the Council does not act by a qualified majority within a certain period of time, or it can retain the power to prevent (by simply majority) the acting from returning to the Commission. See Winter (1989) pp. 46-49.

override Commission initiatives.[55] A key mechanism for Council oversight of Commission activities is the use of various types of "consultative committees" composed of Member States' representatives; during trade negotiations, for example, the Commission must consult with the Article 113 committee, which is the main contact point between the Commission and the Member States in the Uruguay Round negotiations.[56]

The Community's other institutions, Parliament and the Court of Justice, play a much smaller role in trade. Parliament, the Community's only directly elected body, has a largely advisory role, although its influence over the legislative process with respect to most internal market initiatives was strengthened under new cooperation procedures established by the Single European Act.[57] While it lacks a formal role in most external trade matters, pressure is building to expand its role, and Commission officials note that there is an increasing need to be responsive

---

[55]The committee established under the regulation concerning the common origin of goods must approve a proposed Commission action by a qualified majority vote. If the committee gives no opinion or rejects the Commission's decision, the Commission must refer the proposal to the Council, which can adopt the Commission's proposal by qualified majority. If the Commission does not act within three months, the Commission may implement the decision. This procedure proved to be a decisive factor in the resolution of recent controversies over the Commission's promulgation of product-specific origin rules. In the photocopier case (discussed later in this book), the absence of a blocking vote among the Member States allowed the Commission to implement a controversial origin rule that effectively forced Ricoh to alter its production methods for photocopiers exported from its U.S. manufacturing subsidiary to the EC in order to avoid designation of those products as Japanese-origin (which would have subjected them to antidumping duties).

[56]Other committees may be created in connection with delegations of authority to the Commission. Examples include the committee established to assist the Commission in implementing the regulation concerning the common definition of origin (see below) and an advisory committee on dumping and subsidies.

[57]Under the new procedures, the Council can only reject amendments made by the Commission at Parliament's request by unanimous vote. One interviewee, commenting on the Parliament's growing influence, noted that thirty-eight percent of all Commission single market proposals have been amended by the Parliament. He also opined that (1) foreigners, particularly the Americans, are better at lobbying the Parliament than Europeans, and (2) the fact that the Commission is increasingly overburdened will lead to a greater role for the Parliament. Interview with senior EC diplomat, January 1990.

to it;[58] it has, for example, amended over one third of the Commission's Single Market directives. The Court serves as the final arbiter of the EC treaties, defining the Community's powers and the obligations of the Member States thereunder; while the ECJ has been quite aggressive in its perceived role as the "guarantor of the integration process,"[59] it has been considerably less inclined to meddle in the external trade arena, particularly when dealing with technical issues such as antidumping determinations. Limitations on access to the judicial process make it difficult to bring legal challenges to EC actions in this area.[60]

---

[58]In practice, however, the Commission tries to keep Parliament informed of developments (e.g., the status of Uruguay Round negotiations) and to take account of its interests (to some degree). See Murphy (1990) pp. 125-26. One interviewee indicated that the role of the Parliament is being raised in the civil aviation area where the question of its role in external relations is tied to an interpretation of Treaty Articles 113, 228 and 84. Commission officials, including Commissioner Andriessen and President Delors, recognize the need to address concerns that the Commission is becoming too powerful and lacks accountability to any elected European body, and have therefore come to support those who are calling for a greater parliamentary role in external trade policy. One interviewee noted that currently, the 113 Committee consults with Parliament as a matter of comity, but that Commissioner Andriessen now supports formalizing the role of the Parliament in the process. According to one EC official, it is not clear which direction the EC will take in institutional reform; it could decide to upgrade the Council rather than strengthening the Parliament. (Remarks of Andreas van Agt at Brookings Forum on EC 1992 (June 26, 1990).) Others have opined that there will be a strengthening of the Parliament, at the expense of the Member States. Whether that would have any effect on the EC's trade policy orientation is the real question. While one might expect Parliament to be more protectionist -- as it has been in examining internal directives -- the complexity of the issues involved is likely to make it difficult (as is the case in other countries) for a legislative body to significantly alter the shape of trade policy or wrest its control from the executive. Interview with a DG-I official, November 1989.

[59]See Winter (1989) p. 34.

[60]See generally, Ivo van Bael and Jean-Francois Bellis, *Anti-Dumping and Other Trade Protection Laws of the EEC* (Commerce Clearinghouse: 1990) pp. 8-12, 218-21, 327-28, and 358-59. One commentator has stated that: "The foreign trade law of the European Community is already characterized by the delegation of broad and exclusive discretionary trade-policy powers by the European executive unconstrained by specific guiding standards (cf. Article 113 of the Treaty of Rome) and without effective parliamentary and judicial control of trade restrictions in violation of GATT law." Petersmann, *Economic, Legal and Political Functions of the*

(continued...)

Old and New Policy Tools

In the first decades of its existence, the Commission's implementation of trade policy did not differ dramatically from the prior practices of some of the larger Member States; that is to say, it used the tools of managed trade in a freewheeling manner. It concluded preferential, Community-wide agreements with former European colonies which superseded comparable arrangements between the colonies and the mother countries; it reached discriminatory bilateral arrangements restricting trade with a number of important third countries; and it utilized little-publicized "understandings" to regulate market shares and pricing policies in a number of key sectors. One critic charged in the early 1980s that the Commission's "propensity to work out bilateral and sectoral deals" constituted "a potentially fatal challenge for the present multilateral trading system whose value and benefits are regularly extolled by European authorities."[61] However, in the late 1980s, concurrently with the Single Market Initiative and the ascendancy of economic liberals within the Commission's bureaucracy, the Commission began to modify its mix of policy tools, shifting perceptibly away from a trade diplomacy dominated by back-room deals toward a regime emphasizing legal mechanisms with a greater, although by no means absolute, degree of transparency. An array of new trade and trade-related rules were put in place and existing mechanisms, notably the antidumping law, were utilized more vigorously. These legal tools, coupled with informal "advice" to interested foreign governments and companies, will be the principal instruments with which the Community will conduct its trade policy in the 1990s.

In the strictest sense, if one excludes the ability to conclude trade agreements, the trade policy instruments at the Commission's disposal are actually rather limited, consisting primarily of the ability to utilize rules of origin, the antidumping law, the Common External Tariff, and, with respect to industries in serious difficulty, the ability to adopt safeguards and surveillance measures -- all in all, "the [EC's] arsenal of trade measures

---

[60](...continued)
Principle of Non-Discrimination, 9 World Economy (1986) p. 113, quoted in Van Bael and Bellis (1990) pp. 290 n. 14.

[61]Gardner Paterson, "The European Community as a Threat to the System," in William R. Cline (ed.), *Trade Policy in the 1980s* (Cambridge and London; MIT Press, 1983), pp. 230-31.

. . .is not truly impressive."[62] The Commission has the legal authority to impose countervailing duties on subsidized imports, but rarely does so, probably because of the EC's own vulnerability on this score;[63] likewise, its so-called New Commercial Policy Instrument, patterned on the U.S. Section 301 of the Trade Act of 1974 and aimed at "illicit commercial practices" by third countries, is used very sparingly.[64] But while the Commission's trade tools are few, it also administers domestic policies that can be employed to shape the terms of international competition. As one EC official commented in 1990, "One of your problems [in the United States] is that you don't have an alternative to using trade policy. We have other tools. . . . Innovation policy is important to us and is a preferable means of competition compared with the use of trade policy measures."[65] The Commission has become quite skilled at utilizing internal measures in conjunction with trade policies to achieve trade objectives, and, for that matter, in using trade measures to advance its domestic agenda. Some Commission policies and practices, notably its promulgation of rules completing the internal market, constitute some of its most principal trade policies.

The most important and most strategic trade policy tool at the Community's disposal is the Single Market Initiative itself. The Community has already derived enormous trade leverage from the 1992 process, and will continue to do so as its trading partners and foreign-based suppliers maneuver to ensure that their interests are not prejudiced by European integration. As it eliminates its internal barriers, the Community has called for "reciprocity" and "balance" in the conduct of its external trade,[66] the notion being that third countries will be allowed to participate in the Single Market only to the extent that the EC enjoys

---

[62]Karl M. Meessen, "Europe en Route to 1992; The Completion of the Internal Market and its Impact on the Non-European", in the *International Lawyer* (Summer 1989).

[63]Ivo van Bael and Jean-Francois Bellis, *Antidumping and Other Trade Protection Laws of the EEC* (Commerce Clearinghouse, 1990).

[64]Council Regulation 2641/84, *Official Journal* No. L.252 (September 20, 1984). Between 1984 and 1989 the NCPI was invoked by EC industry only four times, and two of these complaints were rejected.

[65]Interview with a senior DG-I official, March 1990.

[66]See, for example, Commission of the European Communities, *XXIInd General Report on the Activities of the European Communities 1988*, point 831.

reciprocal access to the markets of those countries. In banking, the Commission took the initial position that reciprocity meant mirror-image type treatment, but it adopted a less stringent "national treatment" standard (treatment no less favorable than domestic firms) after strong U.S. protests. Reciprocity provisions have cropped up in Commission directives implementing the Single Market in a number of other areas, including other financial services, public procurement in the excluded sectors (water, telecommunications, energy and transport), competition policy, and testing and certification.[67] In effect, the Commission is using changes in the Community's internal rules to compel non-European countries to open their markets more fully.

Rules of Origin

Any system that is designed to establish gradations of preference among trading partners requires a mechanism for linking products, components and materials which move in commerce to their country of origin; they can then be accorded treatment which is more or less preferential, depending on the Community's relationship with that country. For this reason, rules of origin are emerging as a very significant trade policy instrument whose use is likely to increase over the next decade. One EC official commented that "Rules of origin bear watching. They are cleverly manipulated and can have surprisingly restrictive effect. They are the coming thing. They start out as proposals at the working level, and those at the political level have no idea they are coming up -- and there they are."[68] Origin rules are "the coming thing" because of the key interactive role they play in the implementation of other trade and industrial policy measures. The origin of a product and/or its components must be established, to determine whether a product is subject to restrictions imposed against goods having a certain origin (e.g.,

[67]Observers have speculated that the Community's objective in the area of testing and certification is to use its leverage "to bring about a fundamental change in the private sector-oriented standards system of the United States." United States Government Task Force on the EC Internal Market, EC 1992: *An Assessment of Economic Policy Issues Raised by the European Community's Single Market Program* (May 1990) p. 9.

[68]Interview with a senior EC diplomat, March 1990.

antidumping duties or quotas);[69] to evaluate compliance with local content requirements established for government procurement or provision of state aid; to implement the Community's screwdriver assembly antidumping rules; and to prevent circumvention of preferential programs (e.g., the use of satellite countries as export platforms to avoid EC tariff and other restrictions).[70] In the late 1980s, regulations established special origin rules for a number of electronics products.[71] Their interaction with various preferential and restrictive measures allowed the Community to establish, in effect, a hierarchy of differential treatment for certain classes of imported products, provoking widespread criticism that EC officials were using origin rules to force high-value investment in the Community.[72] U.S. and Japanese criticism of EC

---

[69]For example, the new photocopier origin rule was designed to address concerns that Ricoh was using its U.S. assembly plant to circumvent EC antidumping duties against Japanese photocopiers; and France, in a notorious dispute concerning Nissan Bluebirds assembled in the UK, insisted on subjecting these cars to quotas on Japanese imports unless their EC content was raised significantly.

[70]Maintaining the effectiveness of tariffs can be a factor even outside the context of preferential arrangements. For example, efforts by EC industry to secure a 45 percent value-added test for determining the origin of VCRs reportedly were prompted by concerns that Japanese firms were undermining the protective effect of a 14 percent tariff on finished VCRs by importing the key parts at a lower duty rate (5.8 percent) for "screwdriver" assembly in the Community. Issuance of such a rule would mean that these EC-assembled products would be treated as Japanese (and subjected to the higher duty rate) unless their EC content was increased. (Another option that the EC industry reportedly was considering was to seek to raise the parts tariff.) *European Report* No. 1239 (July 15, 1986).

[71]Integrated circuits, photocopiers and printed circuit boards have all been the subject of special origin regulations or proposed regulations during the past two years, and development of special rules reportedly has been considered for VCRs, motor vehicles and software.

[72]This criticism would appear to be justified, when one considers that (1) all of the new rules were promulgated in connection with antidumping actions; (2) all of them condition EC origin on the performance of certain "core" manufacturing operations in the Community or the attainment of a specified percentage of EC value-added, and (3) all are difficult to reconcile with the test prescribed by the basic EC origin regulation, under which the location in which the "last substantial process" is performed normally confers origin on a product. This inconsistency is, in fact, what necessitates the promulgation of "special" origin regulations that allow the EC to override the basic rule. Use of such product-specific origin rules before

(continued...)

actions, coupled with an adverse GATT panel ruling,[73] appeared as of 1991 to have deferred further EC initiatives on rules of origin until the conclusion of the Uruguay Round. Nevertheless, the Community expands its use of measures that discriminate against, or favor, certain classes of imports, origin rules will play an increasingly important role in ensuring the effectiveness of those measures.

Antidumping Law

Commission officials view the antidumping law as a key policy tool, particularly in sectors where they feel Community industry is most vulnerable to foreign competition; one Community official even called it "the only trade policy instrument available."[74] Despite some procedural improvements during the past decade, the process by which dumping determinations are made remains on the whole a "black box", into which the public has little insight; consequently, EC bureaucrats have a great deal of leeway in making dumping determinations, and little accountability for their actions. Access to judicial review is quite limited, and the European Court of Justice has not, to date, been inclined to second-guess the Commission's judgments.[75] As a result, even antidumping actions which are arguably illegal under Community law, such as the use of antidumping settlements to extract local content commitments from foreign subsidiaries in the EC, have not been challenged in Court.[76] Criticism of the Community's antidumping law -- both internal and external -- has intensified in recent years as the Commission has adopted interpretations of the law which have had an increasingly trade-restrictive effect, fueling the perception that it uses the

---

[72](...continued)
1989, when the rule for integrated circuits was issued, was rare (although one can find precedents in the electronics sector dating back to the early 1970s, when the Commission issued special rules for tape recorders and for radio and television receivers that utilized a 45 percent value-added test for determining origin).

[73]GATT L/6657 of March 22, 1990.

[74]Interview with a DG-XIII official, April 1990.

[75]Van Bael and Bellis (1990) pp. 218-21.

[76]*Official Journal* No. L.291/52 (October 10, 1989).

law as a tool of industrial policy.[77] Perhaps the most controversial actions have involved a screwdriver assembly anti-circumvention provision adopted in 1987; the Commission was accused of using the anti-circumvention rule as a means of forcing high-value investment in the Community by companies seeking to escape antidumping duties.[78] A

[77]The *Financial Times* and a number of European economists are continually at odds with the Commission over its use of this particular measure, and it is very much at the heart of the struggle between liberals and conservatives over what constitutes an appropriate trade and economic policy. Consumers of products subject to antidumping restrictions and certain Member States (Germany, the United Kingdom, and the Netherlands) are becoming increasingly hostile to antidumping actions. Also on the rise are concerns regarding the implications (for example, potential overcapacity) of the surge in foreign investment that has been stimulated by the EC's use of its antidumping law. Some of the Commission's legal interpretations are said to bias the calculation in favor of finding dumping, particularly in cases involving exporters that market their products through related sales subsidiaries in the Community (a class which includes many Japanese and Far Eastern exporters). See Van Bael and Bellis (1990) p. 37; Peter Montagnon, "EC Trade Policy: The Anti-Dumping Test," *Financial Times* (July 2, 1990); Brian Hindley, "The Design of Fortress Europe," *Financial Times* (January 6, 1989); Michael Davenport, "The Charybdis of Anti-Dumping: A New Form of Industrial Policy?", *RIIA Discussion Papers* 22 (Royal Institute of International Affairs, London: 1989) pp. 14-16, 24.

[78]The screwdriver assembly provision provides for the extension of antidumping duties to products assembled in the Community under certain conditions, one of which is that the value of parts and materials originating in the dumping country represent at least 60 percent of the total value of the parts and materials used in the EC assembly operation. In a recent case brought under this provision, the Commission -- in a violation of its own regulations -- required Japanese printer manufacturers to sign undertakings that stipulated that their printers assembled in the Community would contain a specified percentage of parts originating in the Community (i.e., local content). Commission officials later acknowledged that this was an error (while dismissing it as having minor significance). In the meantime, however, several U.S. semiconductor manufacturers had lost important supply contracts with these printer manufacturers. The Commission's stated intentions were irrelevant, in any event, since the design-out was also prompted by several recent Commission rulings on origin. Not only did the U.S. companies' semiconductors not qualify for EC origin under the new integrated circuit (IC) origin regulation, but they were in effect treated as if they had originated in the dumping country (Japan). In essence, the interaction of two different value-based rules (the 60-40 test applied to determine the dumping country content of the printers, and the 45 percent test used to determine the origin of the printed circuit

(continued...)

GATT challenge brought by Japan resulted in a GATT panel finding to the effect that the Community's use of this provision violated its GATT obligations, requiring some modification of the Community's anti-circumvention rule.[79]

Local Content Requirements

Local content requirements and their equivalents have appeared with some frequency in the rules being adopted to implement the Single Market. A proposed directive on government procurement requiring Member States to liberalize procurement in the four so-called excluded sectors -- areas of procurement not covered by the GATT Procurement Code -- would establish preferences for bids containing at least 50 percent EC-origin manufactured products and allow discrimination against bids that do not meet this test. Although negotiations in the Uruguay Round may change this result by extending the preferences to other Code signatories, at least until the end of the Round, the directive will deter suppliers of non-EC products from preparing bids, or encourage them to increase the EC content of their bids, limiting access by many non-EC suppliers to European government contracts. Local content considerations have crept into areas such as antidumping investigations, rules of origin, administration of quotas, provision of state aids, and ad hoc measures (e.g., the television broadcast directive). Regulatory pressure was brought on "screwdriver plants," which were made subject to a rule that made their products subject to antidumping duties unless at least 40 percent of the value of a product assembled at the facility was "non-dumped," e.g., from a country not subject to the order.[80] At least two EC antidumping actions against Japanese firms, involving ball bearings and dot matrix printers, were settled when Japanese companies based in Europe gave an undertaking to increase the percentage of EC content in their products

---

[78](...continued)
boards (PCBs) used in their assembly) allowed the Japanese printer companies to escape antidumping duties on their EC-assembled printers simply by replacing U.S. with EC-origin semiconductors in the PCBs used in their manufacture (without reducing the number of Japanese components therein).

[79]GATT L/6657 of March 22, 1990.

[80]*Official Journal L.* 123 (May 17, 1988); GATT Doc. L/6366 (August 12, 1988) point 164; GATT Doc. L/6205, points 343-45.

assembled in the Community.[81] While the Commission subsequently modified some of these policies under the pressure of public scrutiny (or, in the case of electric typewriters, an adverse GATT panel decision), the message to Japanese companies was clear -- become more European, increase your local content, or risk exclusion from the Single Market.[82]

In addition, EC officials have used jawboning and subtle threats (backed by the documented willingness to adapt existing tools to desired ends, or to create new tools) to induce a massive wave of foreign investment and increased EC sourcing by subsidiaries of foreign firms.[83] In most cases EC officials simply "advised" foreign executives that in light of the uncertainty attendant on the numerous regulatory changes accompanying the Single Market Initiative, they would do well to increase their local content. In 1990 the Director General of DG-I warned Japanese firms investing in the Community that they should "increase their participation in local economies" through such means as "taking an European subcontractors" or risk being viewed as a "Trojan horse sent in to wipe out European industry."[84] U.S. components manufacturers were told by European subsidiaries of non-European firms that "if you don't

---

[81]*Official Journal* L. 291 (October 10, 1989); GATT Doc. L/7530 (July 31, 1989) points 336 and 330.

[82]As of 1991, EC officials took the public position that the undertakings by Japanese subsidiaries to increase their EC content in response to the settlement of an antidumping case were no longer in effect -- the policy had been a mistake and had been changed. Representatives of the affected Japanese firms, however, indicate that whatever the Commission's public statements to the contrary, they are still being held to their original local content commitment.

[83]See, for example, "92 Presses IC Firms," *Electronics News* (November 27, 1989); "U.S. and Japanese Chip Makers Face Pressure to Build in EC," *Financial Times* (January 9, 1989); "EC Announces New Chip Rules to Gain Plants," *Journal of Commerce* (February 7, 1989); "Japan Moves Into Europe," *Financial Times* (February 7, 1989); "Japan Will Transfer Technology to EC in Response to 1992," *Financial Times* (April 8, 1989); "Car Makers Drive Into Europe," *Financial Times* (April 19, 1989); "Europe's Agonizing Over Japan," *New York Times* (April 30, 1989); "Seoul Searching," *Far Eastern Economic Review* (May 18, 1989); "Local Chip Production Key to European Mart," *Japan Economic Journal* (September 30, 1989). Advertising campaigns seek to capitalize on these perceptions: NEC has advertised its DRAMs as "Made in Europe. . .our European facility near Edinburgh will help our customers meet new local content regulations when they buy NEC made-in-Europe DRAMs." *Electronic Buyers' News* (March 5, 1990).

[84]*1992* (October 5, 1990).

manufacture in Europe we will buy from somebody else."[85] NEC, which built a semiconductor plant in Scotland to manufacture dynamic random access memories (DRAMs) ran ads which proclaimed "our European facility near Edinburgh will help our customers meet new local content regulations when they buy NEC made-in-Europe DRAMs."[86] The use of rumors and off-the-record warnings to induce companies to achieve specific local content targets is inconsistent with the spirit, at least, of the GATT, but as one Commission official remarked, "GATT does not have the political clout to prevent Europeans from doing what is necessary to control unruly situations. There will be new gray areas, if necessary outside the system."[87] One Japanese observer remarked in 1990 that:

> *There are no [local content] regulations at all on automobiles. And yet there is this 80 percent thing, walking around as big as life. Unless local procurement is 80 percent or more, it's not an EC automobile. This is not written down anywhere, and yet it is there, alive and well. It is not in any current GATT regulations. . . . How can this unspoken 80 percent rule be in effect? It is in effect because it has become established as a kind of unwritten law.*[88]

Quantitative Restrictions

The Commission is clearly seeking to move away from reliance on one of its principal traditional instruments, quantitative import restrictions based on unilateral quotas or voluntary export restraint by third countries, in favor of more sophisticated, less controversial measures. Nevertheless, quantitative restraints will remain a weapon in the Commission's trade arsenal; it has fought to preserve its freedom of action in this area in the Uruguay Round safeguards negotiations.[89] The new Community-wide restrictions on Japanese auto imports negotiated in 1991 are based on a quantitative formula, and the Commission has adopted a "non-binding"

---

[85]Intel executive in *Electronic News* (August 27, 1990).

[86]*Electronic Buyer's News* (March 5, 1990).

[87]Interview with a senior Belgian diplomat, April 1990.

[88]Takao Negishi in *Denshi* (September 1990) (JPRS-JST-91-031-L).

[89]Interview with a senior DG-I official, March 1990.

quota on non-European television programs.[90] The Commission may, however, make greater use of "surveillance" of imports in lieu of outright quotas -- that is the Commission would signal exporters, by monitoring their products, that more restrictive measures could be forthcoming if they fail to moderate their shipments. Surveillance measures are potentially attractive not only because they are less overtly protectionist, but because the Commission has the authority to initiate surveillance without Council approval.

Tariffs

The importance of tariffs in the EC's trade policy regime has been declining for decades, but tariff protection is regarded as important by several key industries, including electronics, chemicals, pharmaceuticals, and wood and paper products (farm products are a special case, protected by a "variable levy" discussed below). The Commission has shown that it will raise tariffs on sensitive products, GATT bindings notwithstanding, to protect beleaguered product areas, and was under pressure to do so in 1991 by some European electronics firms with respect to computers and semiconductors. However, a more important use of the tariff in the 1990s may be as a mechanism for establishing gradations of privilege with the ring of states on the Community's periphery; the extension to these states of a greater degree of duty-free treatment will partially compensate for refusal to admit them as full members, and will serve to bind them more closely economically to the Community.[91] Origin rules may also be tightened as preferential tariff arrangements are expanded, so that the integrity of the external tariff is maintained.[92] Other tariff tools that could be employed in the future to trade-restrictive ends include tariff classification (as in the case of kraft paper and paperboard, the subject of a longstanding dispute between the Community and the United States), and tariff escalation (i.e., raising the effective tariff rate on a product by

---

[90]*Europe No. 5547* (New Series) (August 2, 1991).

[91]Sensitive sectors -- in particular, agriculture -- will remain largely outside the scope of these preferences for some time to come. While liberalization will occur over time, the EC will carefully control its pace to avoid the disruptions that a massive influx of cheap agricultural imports from Eastern Europe would cause.

[92]The EC already employs special origin rules for goods subject to preferential arrangements, that are more restrictive than the origin rules used for other purposes. Recently, however, the EC has begun to tighten its non-preferential origin rules, as discussed earlier.

lowering the duty on intermediate goods).[93] The Community has shown a propensity to use technical rules to protect certain industries, and there may be a temptation to narrow tariff concessions made in the Uruguay Round through such means, as has occurred in previous Rounds.[94]

Subsidies

Subsidies have long been a mainstay of European industrial policy. The ascendancy of the market liberals within the Commission and the gross distortions which occurred in heavily-subsidized sectors like steel have fostered a rough consensus that certain types of subsidies regarded as harmful should be curbed -- particularly subsidies for operating losses and for ordinary investments.[95] The Community has adopted a formal Code in the steel sector limiting state aids, and has been more aggressive in bringing enforcement actions against subsidies by Member States deemed to be inconsistent with the EEC Treaty. On the other hand, certain types of subsidies are regarded not only as acceptable, but as an essential aspect of the Community's economic policies. Large scale EC and Member State government aid is being poured into research and development in the advanced industrial sectors (aerospace, information technology, factory automation, telecommunications.)[96] The 1990s are

---

[93]The EC maintains a lower duty rate (6 percent) on kraft paper and paperboard containing at least 80 percent softwood content than on imports that do not meet that test (which pay a 9 percent duty). Many U.S. exports do not meet the 80 percent test. The United States has complained that the retention of this discriminatory classification violates an EC commitment made during the Tokyo Round and negates the benefit of a tariff concession made by the EC during that Round. In a more recent example, the European press last year reported that Commission officials were proposing to classify camescopes as videoplayers, a move that would raise the tariff from 4.9 percent to 14 percent. *European Report* No. 1499 (May 27, 1989).

[94]Interview with a trade association official dealing with EC affairs, March 1990.

[95]See Communication of the Commission to the Council and the Parliament, *Industrial Policy to an Open and Competitive Environment*, COM (90) 656 Final (November 16, 1990), p. 8.

[96]One EC official noted that "[w]e will increase the amount of aid to high technology and the amount of regional aid. We will continue to wind down agricultural subsidies. The more we save however in agriculture, the more it will (continued...)

likely to see national and EC-level subsidy programs to facilitate environmentally "clean" technologies on an unprecedented scale, despite a general EC principle that the "polluter pays" such costs. Finally, subsidies will be used to facilitate adjustment by traditional industries affected by trade liberalization, in particular autos and textiles.

Competition Policy

Some observers fear that the wave of restructuring that is now taking place as companies seek to hedge against the risks of a 1992 shakeout by merging and allying with former rivals may actually serve to reduce competition within the Community, and to heighten pressures for transitional measures and other forms of protection against more dynamic outside challengers.[97] The European Community and its Member States' governments thus far have encouraged such consolidation. If they continue to maintain a relaxed antitrust attitude, the result could be a single European market dominated by large, politically powerful companies in highly concentrated markets that are difficult for outsiders to penetrate.[98]

Environmental Policies

The greening of Europe will inevitably heighten pressures to restrict imports of products that do not conform to internal measures to protect the environment or respond to consumer calls for cleaner, safer products. Incidents like the 1988 ban on imports of beef containing hormones are likely to recur, particularly in such areas as agriculture, biotechnology,

---

[96](...continued)
go into other things that Americans won't like, such as subsidies to poorer regions." Interview with a senior EC diplomat, August 1990. Another official noted that "there is a strong tendency toward joint research funded by the EC." Interview with a senior DG-III official, April 1990.

[97]See, e.g., "Europe's Companies After 1992: Don't Collaborate, Compete," *The Economist* (June 9, 1990).

[98]For example, although the evaluation standard in the EC's new merger and acquisition regulation focuses primarily on competitive factors, the Commission can consider "contribution to Community technical and economic progress" in deciding whether to rule against a proposed action. Moreover, the competitive factors could be applied in ways that permit concentration at the national or European level (e.g., considering the relevant market to be global).

chemicals and pharmaceuticals.[99] Heavy industrial goods, particularly those produced by pollution-intensive industries, may also become the subject of pressures for import restrictions to protect EC industries whose competitiveness has declined as a consequence of stricter environmental regulation.

Harmonization of Standards

One of the central elements of the Single Market Initiative is "harmonization" -- the replacement of national standards with uniform European ones. Harmonization affects trade because standards can function as de facto trade barriers, preventing foreign firms from securing approval to sell their products in a given market or, in some cases, requiring them to undertake costly conversion and adaptation measures. At some future point, the Community will establish a uniform set of EC standards and testing and certification procedures. In the interim, the Single Market directives stipulate "essential" requirements needed to protect consumers and the environment with respect to various products; based on the concept of mutual recognition, if a product is certified in one Member State as satisfying such requirements, it can circulate freely in all of the others. The EC's trading partners have not complained about these arrangements, per se, but have expressed concern about their inability to participate in standards-making bodies, refusals to accept foreign test data, excessively costly testing and certification procedures, and unnecessarily specific standards.[100]

---

[99]Some Commission officials and members of Parliament (e.g., the Chairman of the European Parliament's Environment Committee) have called for socioeconomic factors to be added to the existing criteria (safety, efficacy, quality) used to approve new drugs and biotech products. This concept of a "fourth hurdle" that would allow discrimination against imports based on socioeconomic grounds could be expanded into other areas. Recent proposals to ban the use of bovine somatotropin (BST), a growth hormone which increases dairy cattle milk yields, reportedly were prompted in part by concern that small farmers could be put out of business by the consequent decrease in milk prices.

[100]USTR, *Foreign Trade Barriers* (1991) p. 71: GATT *Trade Policy Review* (1991), Vol. I., p. 126.

TRADE STRATEGIES

Although many exceptions to the general pattern can be cited, by the end of the 1980s the emphasis in the Community's approach to trade was undergoing a gradual shift away from a system based heavily on complex, individuated and often clandestine bilateral and sectoral arrangements toward uniform, transparent, cross-sectoral regional arrangements and multilateral rules and codes of general applicability. This is a departure which holds out both promise and risk for the international system. The EC's shift away from bilateralism is likely to be universally viewed as a positive development, but its evolving regional arrangements are a source of widespread apprehension. In 1991, a number of GATT Council members commented with concern on the "complex hierarchy of preferential trade arrangements and trade schemes developed by the EC . . .there ha[s] been an increase in the proportion of the Communities external trade covered by such arrangements. The various preference schemes implied a considerable degree of differentiation in the treatment given to different suppliers."[101]

Historically, in the eyes of its trading partners, "bilateralism" has been the Community's cardinal sin. Notwithstanding its often-reiterated commitment to GATT-based multilateralism, EC negotiators, and in some cases trade officials from the Member States have displayed a "propensity to work out bilateral and sectoral deals [with] willing partners."[102] Typically these arrangements, "lacked transparency and were discriminatory, being usually targeted on the most competitive third-country suppliers. Many [GATT members] regarded this area as a particularly worrying feature of EC trade policies, being at odds with the EC commitment to a free and open international trading system.[103] Bilateralism found favor with the Europeans in substantial part because they enjoyed superior leverage in bilateral discussions with any particular

---

[101]Remarks by Chairman of the GATT Council in GATT *Trade Policy Report* (1991) Vol. II, p.5.

[102]Patterson (1983) p. 231.

[103]Concluding Remarks by Chairman of the GATT Council on GATT *Trade Policy Report* (1991) Vol. II, p. 5.

trading partner.[104] As Hong Kong observers commented after a particularly rough textile negotiation with the EC in 1982, "Hong Kong was 'bullied into the agreement' by the EC,[105] and the Colony's chief negotiator commented:

> *I have no doubt at all that an organization such as the Community builds up a momentum towards a particular objective, regardless of whether it is legal or illegal. It just cannot be stopped, and eventually it will secure the objective by one means or another. That's one of the realities of life, and one that has to be recognized. After all, the [Multifiber Arrangement] is made of paper and the Community is a steamroller. . .we managed to [slow it down] although a few toes got squashed in the process.*[106]

The Community began to shift in the late 1980s toward emphasis on a more uniform system of regional arrangements and the strengthening of the multilateral trading regime, a change which had several bases. The ascendancy of market liberals in the Commission hierarchy brought traditional bilateral gray measures, which were recognized as generally protectionist, into disfavor. The centralization of trade authority in Brussels resulted in replacement of national bilaterals in favor of new arrangements which are more legalistic and which, in effect, placed trade authority in the hands of those who administered the rules in Brussels. In addition, the Single Market Initiative and the growing clamor of peripheral European states for closer affiliation with the EC placed pressure on the Community to deal with them as broad classes receiving a rough uniformity of consideration rather than through particularist and obscure bilateral understandings. Finally, Community leaders have modified their view of the GATT as a potential impediment to their own freedom of action and begun to see it as a potentially important constraint on the actions of its main rivals, the United States and Japan. Accordingly, they have placed greater emphasis on strengthening the

---

[104]"Smaller trading partners were in an unequal position in dealing with demands for restraints from a trading power like the EC." Concluding Remarks by Chairman of GATT Council on GATT Trade Policy Review (1991), Vol. II, p.5.

[105]*South China Morning Post* (December 1, 1982).

[106]*Textile Asia* (January 1983).

GATT system and casting multilateral rules to the Community's advantage.[107]

Regional Trade Strategy

The most important trade policy question confronting the Community in the 1990s is the definition of its relationship with the ring of European and Mediterranean states on its periphery, with which it conducts the greatest portion of its trade. The prospect that the Community will eventually absorb these countries holds out the promise of enormous long run benefits; enlargement will enhance the size of the internal market, the economies of scale which can be achieved by European industry, and the economic and political weight of Europe in the world. More immediately, however, the admission of new members confronts the EC with difficult, if not intractable questions.[108] A number of the peripheral states are economically underdeveloped and in some cases politically unstable, and their admission could not be achieved without fundamentally altering the character of the Community. But even a limited expansion of the Community to include a few of the wealthy democracies, such as Austria and Sweden -- both of which have applied -- raises basic questions about the future direction of the Community. The deeply held commitment to

---

[107]One continuing manifestation of the Community's changing trade priorities is rather mundane -- that is, where it assigns its staff. Notwithstanding the popular view that Brussels is overrun with bureaucrats, the Commission's work force is relatively small -- its Secretariat of 12,000 officials, translators and interpreters (of which the latter group is most numerous) is not as large as the municipal bureaucracy in many European cities. The staff available to work on trade and trade-related matters was already overstretched by the concurrent Single Market Initiative and Uruguay Round negotiations when a series of major new demands arose in 1989-90 -- German reunification, the need to coordinate aid to and negotiate association agreements with Eastern Europe, and a major negotiation with EFTA over the so-called European Economic Area. While the strain on Commission resources could be ended by expanding its staff, the Member States have tended to hold its power in check by refusing to allocate additional resources even as the Community's responsibilities expand. Measured by this crude standard, as of this writing the Commission appeared to be staffing both multilateral and regional negotiations adequately; if anything, bilateral relations were most likely to receive short shrift, at least in the first part of the 1990s. Lodge (1989) p. 34; Interview with a senior DG-I official, April 1990.

[108]Turkey applied for membership in 1987, but was rejected on the grounds that its economy and political system were not suitably mature. Austria applied in 1989, Malta and Cyprus in 1990, and Sweden in 1991.

political neutrality of several of these state countries may constitute an obstacle to the eventual deepening of the Community into a political entity with a security role, and the accession of the prosperous northern countries is likely to tip the balance among the Member States toward the liberal economic policies favored by Germany and the Netherlands. France, Italy, and the Benelux countries favor deepening over broadening -- that is, the further evolution of a federal political structure in the Community and deferral of new members until this is achieved. Conversely, Britain would like to see further broadening of the EC at an early date, precisely because it believes that this would impede further moves toward political unification. Germany favors simultaneous deepening of the EC institutions and admission of new members from EFTA and Eastern Europe, most of which could be expected to align with Germany. Spain, Portugal and Greece are primarily concerned that no broadening of the Community divert development aid from their own to other regions, such as Eastern Europe.[109]

As of 1991 the Commission's official position was congruent with that of France, Italy and Benelux, that is, that its priority should be deepening, not broadening. This still posed the question of how the Community was to respond to the peripheral states seeking to participate in the benefits of the Single Market. The alternative to broadening, articulated by EC President Jacques Delors, would arrange Europe in a series of concentric circles, with the Community at the core, and each outer circle differentiated by trade agreements providing for varying degrees of integration with the EC stopping short of full membership. The first ring would consist of the European Economic Area (EEA) (originally dubbed the "European Economic Space" by Delors) which would embrace the EC and the EFTA countries. Within the EEA, the Community's Four Freedoms would prevail (free movement of goods, persons, services and capital); research, education, environmental and consumer protection policies would be integrated; and some common institutional arrangements would be established that would not, however, subject the EFTA countries to the full *acquis communautaire*, the body of Community law. The next ring would embrace the nations of Eastern Europe, which would be linked to the EC through the association agreements establishing so-called "reciprocal free trade" between these nations and the Community. The third and outer ring would consist of an aggregation of Mediterranean countries with whom a customs union would be established. Such arrangements would, at best, defer rather than forestall additional

---

[109]Interview with a senior Swedish diplomat, November 1989; *Washington Post* (July 28, 1991).

enlargements of the Community, which are virtually inevitable in the 1990s. In 1990, one EC diplomat predicted the following sequence:

> *Austria, followed by Sweden and Switzerland, will attempt, probably successfully, to join the Community within the next three to five years. If these three are in, then they will only be the first. Norway and a number of others will follow -- Cyprus and Malta being not very serious questions. Then, later on will Czechoslovakia and Hungary. Later still, Poland.*[110]

The process of broader European integration, with or without Community enlargement, is fraught with potential for trade conflict. The inescapable corollary to providing sufficiently attractive intermediate alternatives to full Community membership is that for such intermediate status to have any real meaning, all other non-intermediate countries must be accorded treatment that is considerably less favorable, a sort of third class citizenship. Such differentiation of trade privileges would arguably be antithetical to the most-favored national principle which underlies the GATT system, and would further weaken that system, which has already experienced considerable stress as a result of Community policies over the past thirty years.[111] Moreover, in order to protect the Community's competitive position, the extension of varying degrees of preferential status to the peripheral states is likely to be linked to measures that will prevent other countries (mainly Japan, Korea, and the United States) from using them to penetrate the Community in an unacceptable manner (i.e., by establishing screwdriver assembly plants in or transshipping goods through them.) The Community will probably tighten its rules of origin, perhaps requiring a certain level of EC content, and may also insist that the peripheral states adopt protective measures, including, perhaps, part or all of the Common External Tariff directed against third countries, thereby extending the Community's external protective net around these countries.[112] Such measures will certainly provoke a conflict with the United States, which has already lost markets as a result of the successive expansions of the Community.

---

[110]Interview with an EC diplomat, March 1990.

[111]See Paterson, in Cline (1983), pp. 234-37.

[112]*Far Eastern Economic Review* (March 9, 1989).

The First Ring: EFTA and the European Economic Area. The inner ring of Delors' proposed system would consist of the wealthy democracies that comprise the European Free Trade Association. EFTA was established in 1960 by the leading Western European non-EC members as a sort of counterpoise to the Community -- an association of countries with common economic interests, but with no Community-style supranational regulatory institutions.[113] Over time, the EFTA grouping has grown progressively weaker as the Community has grown in size and economic power; Britain, Ireland, Denmark and Portugal ultimately left EFTA and joined the Community. The Single Market Initiative confronted the remaining EFTA countries -- Sweden, Norway, Iceland, Finland, Austria and Switzerland -- with the question of how to avoid loss of markets and other economic dislocation as the nations of the Community proceeded to implement policies which would harmonize standards, achieve economies of scale, and integrate the internal market. As a practical matter it appeared that there were only two real alternatives, full membership or some closer association which, while stopping short of membership, would permit the EFTA countries to achieve a degree of integration with the EC sufficient to prevent dislocation, that is, some variant of the proposed European Economic Area (EEA). EFTA and the EC reached agreement on the EEA in October 1991, with the agreement to go into effect on January 1, 1993.

Many of the stumbling blocks to full accession were revealed in the negotiations over an EEA, which proved more difficult and protracted than anticipated.[114] Because the EFTA institutions are weak, the negotiations were heavily influenced by the positions and concerns of the individual EFTA countries. The issue of political neutrality, already noted, has proven quite emotional in several EFTA countries which have applied for admission or are contemplating doing so. Austria actually conditioned its application for membership on preservation of its neutrality, and a 1991 poll showed that 64 percent of Austrians would oppose full membership if it meant an end to the country's traditional nonalignment.[115] Similar concerns exist in Finland, which worries about being drawn into a future war and about antagonizing the Soviets.[116] An equally difficult issue is the prospective surrender of sovereignty by the EFTA countries which,

[113]Stockholm Convention of January 4, 1960, 370 U.N.T.S. 3.

[114]*Financial Times* (July 31, 1991).

[115]*Die Presse* (May 11-12, 1991).

[116]*Helsingin Sanomat* (May 27, 1991); *Dagens Nyheter* (May 28, 1991).

they fear, would subsume them in a huge political-economic entity in which they would lose their say over their own affairs. In the case of full accession, the smaller EFTA countries worry that they would have no voice in trade matters;[117] the Helsinki *Hufvudstadsbladet* editorialized on March 11, 1991 that

> *Germany and France dominate. If they came to terms with Italy and/or Great Britain, the mice must applaud when the elephants dance. . . . Can our EC friends guarantee that the Germans, French, British and Italians will ever find out about our interests (compared to their own) in negotiations in GATT, or with another third party?*

Even the limited loss of sovereignty entailed by the EEA caused some EFTA countries to balk at further moves toward integration; Community negotiators have sought an EEA institutional structure in which the EC was responsible for decision-making while EFTA was to be content with what is euphemistically called "decision-shaping"[118] -- difficult to distinguish from having no real say in the trade policies which affect their economies. The EFTA countries have asked for a separate and independent EEA court system -- divorced from the EC court system -- which would be the only institution competent to settle disputes relating to EEA legislation. Switzerland is particularly adamant on this point; it "banished foreign judges 700 years ago and [will] not tolerate them now,"[119] -- but from the Community's perspective, the EFTA countries were asking for too many exceptions to the *acquis communautaire.*[120] North-South issues have emerged; Spain, Portugal, Greece and Ireland have demanded that the EFTA countries establish a so-called "cohesion fund" which would be used to finance economic development in their own countries, asking for "at least 1.2 billion ECUs from EFTA in the form of straight grants."[121] The EFTA countries objected to the idea of an "entrance fee" to the EEA and questioned the need for such a fund, given the continued trade protection enjoyed by the poorer Member States, but

---

[117]*Journal de Geneve* (November 26, 1990).

[118]Interview with a senior EC diplomatic official to the United States, August 1990.

[119]*Arbeiderbladet* (April 26, 1991).

[120]*European Report* (July 28, 1990).

[121]*European Report* (June 27, 1991).

eventually agreed to contribute about $1.8 billion in soft loans and $600 million in grants to a special regional development fund.

In addition to such broad political concerns, the EEA negotiations generated a surprising degree of controversy over local issues which had initially seemed relatively unimportant.[122] Iceland and Norway reacted vehemently when EC negotiators insisted on opening these countries' fisheries to trawlers from the EC (mainly Spain) in return for allowing free access for Norwegian and Icelandic processed fish products in the Community.[123] Iceland "only cares about fishing,"[124] which accounts for 75 percent of its economic activity; the EC fishing fleet, with an overcapacity of 40 percent, and with modern technology and rhomboid-mesh nets, could decimate the fisheries off Iceland's coasts.[125] This issue was momentarily finessed in the EEA negotiations when Norway agreed to allow Spanish fishermen a larger quota in Norwegian waters in return for improvements in access to the EC for Norwegian processed fish products. In agriculture, the EFTA countries worried that inclusion in the Common Agricultural Policy would wreck national systems of food production representing a fine-tuned balance between food self-sufficiency, environmental concerns, and the provision of a viable income for farmers; these issues were ultimately broken out of the EEA negotiations for later resolution. The Swiss and Austrians want to continue restricting environmentally-damaging truck movements across the Alps, a position which the EC regards as an unacceptable constraint on the free movement of goods.[126]

In the face of such complications, the principal force driving the EC-EFTA integration process forward is Sweden's apparent determination to join the Community at an early date. Its position is partially attributable to a campaign by Denmark,[127] but Swedish leaders themselves perceive

---

[122] *European Report* (June 27, 1991).

[123] *Aftenposten* (March 5, 1991); *Financial Times* (July 31, 1991).

[124] Interview with U.S. State Department official, March 1990.

[125] *Reykjavik Morgunbladid* (March 19, 1991); *Hufvudstadsbladet* (March 11, 1991).

[126] *Journal de Geneve* (March 30-31, 1991). In the EEA agreement reached in October 1991, Greece received a special quota for truck movements over the Alps; in return the EC agreed to reduce truck emissions in Austria by 60 percent over 12 years and to make greater use of rail transport in Switzerland.

[127] *Svenska Dagbladet* (May 7, 1991).

a strong rationale for joining; they reason that by virtue of its geographic position, Sweden will be dependent upon the politics and economics of the Community, and "only membership will make it possible to balance that dependency with contributory influence. The sooner Sweden joins the better, because Community policies are being formulated now to which Sweden will have to adjust without having participated in them."[128] Sweden's drive to join the EC, itself an effort to jump on the moving train of EC integration, has created a moving train of its own within EFTA. Other EFTA Members are concerned that if Sweden joins the EC first, they will either be left out in the cold or "stuck" with carbon copies of the accession agreement hammered out between the Swedes and the Community, without having participated in its negotiation.[129] Sweden's enthusiasm for EC membership has thus prompted a good deal of criticism and hand-wringing in the northern countries, but apart from vague proposals for creation of a Nordic bloc, no one has been able to advance a clear alternative.[130] Significantly, the Swedes have rationalized the potential implications of accession for their country's neutrality by observing that their country's traditional nonparticipation in military alliances is only an instrument of security policy, not an end in itself; therefore, in light of the end of the Cold War, Sweden could conceivably take part in an "all European security system."[131] Sweden's flexibility on this point may point the way to an accommodation between the other EFTA neutrals and the EC on security policy.

Despite the numerous problems of integration that became apparent in the EEA negotiations, it is highly likely that the 1990s will see full accession by all of the EFTA states will occur by the end of the decade. The EEA negotiations have cleared away many of the obstacles that would confront attempts at full membership; indeed, the EEA, once established, may prove such a tenuous concept -- "the doormat of the EC" -- that accession will follow relatively quickly. A number of EC officials believe that because the EFTA countries tend to "travel en masse," the Community will expand from twelve to eighteen very quickly; Austria is expected to join in 1993 or 1994, and Sweden, Norway and Switzerland will follow

---

[128]*Dagens Nyheter* (February 22, June 15, 1991).

[129]*Arbeiderbladet* (June 22, 1991); *Svenska Dagbladet* (May 7, 1991); *Aftenposten* (March 20, 1991).

[130]See *Huvfudstudsbladet* (February 22, 1991); *Helsingin Sanomat* (March 14, 1991).

[131]Foreign Minister Sten Andersson in *Wochenpresse* (June 6, 1991).

shortly thereafter.[132] While issues such as fishing and agriculture have complicated the negotiations, similarly difficult problems characterized the negotiations on Spanish and Portuguese accession, and were overcome. One EC official commented in 1990 that "the new countries are irresistible. They are permitted in by the Treaty of Rome; therefore the Community has no real choice in the matter."[133]

The Second Ring: Eastern Europe. Until the 1980s the development of trade relations between the Community and Eastern Europe was impeded by the Cold War and Soviet emphasis on maintaining "bloc-to-bloc" relations between the EC and its own economic bloc, the Council for Mutual Economic Assistance (CMEA or COMECON). Although the Soviets generally opposed bilateral agreements between individual CMEA members and the Community, over time a number of such bilaterals were worked out on a sectoral basis when CMEA exports caused disruption in sensitive EC areas such as steel, agriculture, and textiles. In the 1980s, with Gorbachev's "new thinking", CMEA relaxed its constraints on individual bilateral arrangements, and in 1988 Hungary signed a broad agreement covering trade and economic relations with the EC.[134] The abrupt disintegration of communism in 1989, culminating in the dissolution of the CMEA itself in 1991, confronted the Community with a ring of states pressing for closer economic relations with whom an incomplete set of institutional arrangements existed. Community negotiators moved with a surprising degree of speed to grant trade concessions and sign trade and economic cooperation agreements, and many EC barriers to Eastern European products vanished virtually overnight -- a transition which required considerable pressure by the Commission on some Member States to moderate or eliminate old national quantitative restraints.[135] Accords were signed with Poland in 1989 and Bulgaria and Czechoslovakia in 1990, and since the original agreements were reached, they were repeatedly modified and expanded as the pace of political and economic reform in the former CMEA countries accelerated. By 1991 the Community was concentrating on the establish-

---

[132]Interviews with two senior EC diplomats to the United States, January and May 1990, and an interview with a senior DG-I official, May 1990.

[133]Interview with a senior EC diplomat, August 1990.

[134]See Susan Senior Nello, "Some Recent Developments in EC-East European Economic Relations," in 24 *Journal of World Trade Law* 5 (1990).

[135]Interview with a U.S. State Department official, March 1990.

ment of comprehensive association agreements with each Eastern European country which would provide for "reciprocal" free trade with the EC.[136]

The Commission favors association agreements with the former communist states for several reasons. The Community, and particularly the Commission, has a jurisdictional interest in negotiating such agreements, which provide for the elimination of numerous residual Member-State restrictions, clearing away these vestiges of national trade policymaking and strengthening the Commission's own role.[137] The prospect of association is expected to provide an incentive to the Eastern European nations to implement political and economic reforms, since democratic structures and a market economy are prerequisites to such agreements. Finally, as tariff and non-tariff barriers between the Community and Eastern Europe fall, the volume of trade will increase; the Community would realize the economic benefits of trade creation, although not without some costs and dislocation associated with greater economic integration.

The Eastern European countries view the association agreements as stepping stones to EC membership,[138] a perspective that is not unanimously welcomed or shared in the EC itself.[139] The French take the position that these countries cannot be admitted at an early date due to their "worrying state of decay," although another motive appears to be to prevent accession of what they fear would become a bloc of German satellites. There is a more general concern that early accession of these states would disrupt the process of "deepening" European integration and would make it more difficult to assimilate the new members already waiting in the wings, such as Austria and Sweden. "It is not like a line waiting outside a store in which the 10th person is very hungry so you allow the first nine in very quickly. The community must first define how it sees itself after the realization of the 1992 objective."[140] In the initial

---

[136]"There will be a new generation of association agreements." Interview with a DG-I official, May 1990. The previous generation of association agreements was signed in the 1960s and early 1970s with Greece, Turkey, Malta, and Cyprus.

[137]Interview with a senior DG-I official, March 1990.

[138]See interview with Polish negotiator Jaroslaw Mulewicz in *Polityka* (January 26, 1991) (FBIS-EEU-91-027).

[139]*European Report* (March 24, 1990).

[140]President Delors in *Liberation* (September 6, 1991) (JPRS-WEU-91-175).

negotiations on the association agreements, the EC took the position that the new agreements, unlike those signed with the Mediterranean countries in the 1960s, would not contain any mention or promise of membership.[141] In 1991, however, the Council of Ministers agreed to a compromise which provided that the agreements with Czechoslovakia, Hungary and Poland would specify full EC membership as a "final objective," but that membership would not be "automatic" at the end of a 10-year "transition period" to phase in the free movement of merchandise.[142] Yet, as with EFTA, key EC policymakers believe that East European membership in the Community is just a matter of time.[143] In 1991 the Poles, Czechs and Hungarians envisioned a period of 8-10 years as associate members, at the end of which they would be admitted to the Community.[144]

Leaving aside the broader political issues raised by the potential accession of the Eastern European states -- deepening versus broadening, the fear of a dominant Germany and the like -- the negotiations have highlighted some prosaic trade-related obstacles to further integration. The Community's sensitive steel and textile industries have traditionally been protected from imports of these products Eastern Europe by quantitative restrictions. Under the accords being negotiated with Poland in mid-1991 -- likely to serve as a model for other agreements -- these sectors would be liberalized in phases, years for steel, 10 for textiles, rather than immediately.[145] The Eastern countries possess substantial production potential in these industries and a demonstrated propensity to use it; it is unclear whether even a 5-10 year phase-in of free trade can be achieved, particularly if market conditions are stagnant. Agricultural products present a thornier problem; the Eastern European countries, which possess enormous tracts of arable land, are already competitive in some product areas, and will inevitably become more so, with the potential to cause enormous disruption of the finely-tuned production and price support arrangements that constitute the foundation of the

---

[141]Commission of the European Communities, *EC-Eastern Europe Relations,* ICC Background Brief (May 29, 1990).

[142]AFP (23:08 GMT, April 15, 1991) (FBIS).

[143]Interviews with a senior EC diplomat, August 1990, and a senior DG-III official, April 1990.

[144]*Polityka* (January 26, 1991) (FBIS-WEU-91-027).

[145]*Europe* No. 5477 (New Series) (April, 22/23, 1991).

Common Agricultural Policy.[146] Poland indicated in mid-1991 that it would agree to a phased liberalization of agriculture trade to the EC market, with some products liberalized immediately, some within five years (including cereals, flour, beef, butter, pork, lamb and eggs), and the remaining products within ten years.[147] Perhaps significantly, however, French farmers have already reacted vehemently against the prospect of increased farm imports from the east.

The Third Ring: The Mediterranean. Since the inception of the Community, the states bordering on the Mediterranean have confronted it with a mosaic of particular concerns. When the EC was formed, Algeria was still legally a part of metropolitan France, and Tunisia and Morocco, formerly French colonies, were members of the old franc zone. Many of the nations on the southern and eastern rim of the Mediterranean were former colonies or current dependencies of Member States. Greece and Turkey were politically shaky but vital members of NATO's southern flank. The Community was interested in maintaining political stability around the entire Mediterranean littoral and also wished to maintain and if possible expand at least some aspects of the preferential economic arrangements that had been inherited from the colonial era. As a result, it developed a patchwork of "complex and differential" ties with the Mediterranean countries, consisting of association agreements, cooperation agreements, and "preferential" and "non-preferential" trade agreements.[148] These arrangements tended to provide some preferential access to the EC market for these countries while maintaining a degree of

---

146Interview with a DG-VI official, April 1990.

147*European Report* (June 27, 1991).

148See generally Kevin Featherstone, "The Mediterranean Challenge; Cohesion and External Preferences," in Lodge (1989) p. 187. The EC has concluded association agreements with Turkey (1963), Malta (1970) and Cyprus (1972) which provide for an eventual customs union for industrial products according to a time table. Significant restrictions remain in agriculture and textiles. An additional protocol was signed with Turkey in 1970 providing for a specific phase-in of a customs union to be achieved by 1995. An agreement with Israel (1975) provides for abolition of most tariffs on industrial products. Cooperation agreements were reached in 1975 and 1976 with Egypt, Jordan, Syria, Morocco, Tunisia and Lebanon providing for unrestricted access to the EC market for all raw materials and industrial products, as well as for financial and technical cooperation. Notwithstanding these arrangements, the EC has maintained some restrictions on textile imports. GATT Secretariat "Report by the GATT Secretariat," in GATT *Trade Policy Review* (1991) Vol. I, p. 27.

protection for sensitive EC sectors like agriculture and textiles. Three "Mediterranean preferentials", Spain, Portugal and Greece, ultimately become full members of the Community and three others, Turkey, Malta and Cyprus, have applied for membership. Many of the remaining preferentials are economic satellites of the Community, serving as convenient platforms for labor-intensive offshore manufacturing and assembly operations for EC-based firms.

The significance of the Mediterranean preferentials to the EC has been eclipsed, for the moment, by the EFTA negotiations and events in Eastern Europe. The Community is likely to retain existing arrangements with most of the preferential states, and any new initiative will serve primarily as a foil for attempts at accession. Now that Greece, Portugal and Spain have joined the EC, there is very little support within the Community for further southward expansion over the near term (although Malta and Cyprus are so inconsequential that they could be absorbed without major effort). The latter three have all been net recipients under the Community's budget, and any new members from the Mediterranean region would increase the drain on the EC's resources even further. The demands of integrating the former East Germany, Austria, possibly other EFTA states and ultimately some Eastern European country's will absorb the Community's attention and resources. In addition, the prospect of increased immigration from these countries to the "rich" northern states is a strong deterrent in Member States where immigration and ethnic minorities are becoming a major social and political issue. Accordingly, the Community's strategy toward the more persistent Mediterranean states will remain one of deferring their requests indefinitely, attempting to placate them with additional preferences which stop well short of full member status.

Turkey, in particular, which has pressed hardest to join the EC and whose first membership application was rejected on the basis of its inadequate level of development, is extremely unlikely to be offered Community membership in the next decade. Greece vehemently opposes Turkish membership and Greek representatives in the EC institutions are attempting to block Community aid to Turkey in order to secure a resolution of Greek concerns over the Turkish occupation of northeastern Cyprus.[149] As an alternative to membership, the Commission has proposed formation of a customs union under which trade barriers between the two countries would be eliminated, and Turkey would adopt the Community's conditions for a common trade policy (i.e., common

[149]See interview with Greek EC Commissioner Vaso Papandreou in *Elevtherotipia* (March 11, 1991).

external tariff, antidumping regulations, etc.); on the other hand, the Commission would not permit the customs union to apply to agricultural products covered by the Common Agricultural Policy, and it might also exclude textiles, one of Turkey's most competitive export products.[150] Turkish leaders periodically denounce the Community for its "negative attitude," citing a variety of grievances ranging from inadequate aid, failure to expand commercial ties, textile quotas, and failure to implement the existing association agreement in an adequate manner.[151] However, the Community has decided that such political costs are preferable to any of the alternatives, and Turkey does not appear to entertain much expectation of change over the near term; a 1991 survey of 32 Turkish leaders and intellectuals published by the journal Cumhuriyet revealed that less than one third expected that Turkey will have become a member of the EC by the year 2020.[152]

Multilateral Trade Strategy

The EC and the GATT: An Ambivalent Legacy. Although the Community has always been strongly supportive of the GATT system as a matter of general principle, tensions between the GATT and the EC are as old as the Community itself. The Treaty of Rome, providing for establishment of a common market among the signatories, arguably conflicts with the basic

---

[150]Turkish textile imports have been a chronic problem for the Community. Given the enormity of Turkey's production potential, EC policymakers fear that unchecked Turkish shipments could decisively affect the position of the EC industry. Turkish exports to the Community have grown rapidly, but the Turkish government has consistently refused to negotiate quantitative limits with the Commission, arguing that under the terms of their preferential agreement, all Turkish industrial products are free to enter the Community unrestricted. The Commission has periodically imposed unilateral restrictions on textile imports from Turkey, prompting Turkish retaliation. Frustrated by the Turkish position, the Commission has taken the extraordinary step of bypassing the government altogether and negotiating a series of quantitative restraint arrangements directly with Turkish textile industrialists. *Community-Turkey Relations*, Memo 73/89 (December 18, 1989).

[151]Letter from President Turgut Ozal to EC Foreign Ministers summarized on *Bayrak Radio* (20:30 GMT, March 4, 1991).

[152]The survey appeared in *Cumhuriyet* on March 2-5, 26-30 and April 9-13, 1991.

principle of nondiscrimination upon which the GATT system rests.[153] This conflict was played down, for political reasons, when the EC was formed, but the "pragmatic" approach taken by the contracting parties to the EC was a "turning point" in the evolution of the GATT system, "acting as an incentive for a number of further 'pragmatic departures' from the GATT rules after 1958."[154] The contracting parties never legally resolved the issue of the Community's compatibility with the GATT regime, and the issue has arisen in other guises as the Community has enlarged and built its "complex hierarchy of preferential arrangements," reaching preferential tariff arrangements with a constellation of Mediterranean countries and former colonies in Africa. The Community has enjoyed sufficient strength within the GATT to block decisions finding these discriminatory arrangements inconsistent with GATT rules, and has not hesitated to do so when those rules appeared to conflict with the Community's regional arrangements.[155] The Commission has also participated in the administration and expansion of a web of discriminatory, restrictive bilateral agreements with the nations of Eastern Europe and East Asia; the Commission's preference for such arrangements, rather

---

[153]See generally John Jackson, *World Trade and the Law of GATT* (Charlottesville: Michie Publishers, 1969) pp. 607-618.

[154]Ernst-Ulrich Petersmann, "The EC as a GATT Member -- Legal Conflicts Between GATT Law and European Community Law," in N. Hilf, F. G. Jaróles and E. V. Petersmann, *The European Community and the GATT* (Deventer: Kluwer, 1986) p. 40; see also John Jackson (1969), p. 759.

[155]In 1982 the United States formally challenged the legality of the EC's preferential arrangements with Mediterranean countries as they affected citrus fruits. The GATT panel did not rule on the question of whether the EC's preferential arrangements were inconsistent with GATT Article XXIV, but concluded that the EC's tariff, preferences had been granted without a free trade or customs union having been established with the beneficiaries, and that the U.S. right to find the most-favored nation treatment was being impaired. However, the Community blocked adoption of the panel report. In 1986, the U.S. brought a complaint against the EC arising out of the accession of Spain and Portugal, which, the U.S. alleged, resulted in a net increase in Spanish and Portuguese tariffs after accession. The working party's report noted that many of its members believed that the evidence pointed to higher duties being applied after accession, as well as more restrictive quantitative restraints. The EC, however, strongly rejected these conclusions, and "because of the divergent views expressed," the working party could not reach a decision. See USITC, *Effects of Greater Economic Integration within the European Community on the United States* (USITC Pub. No. 2204, July 1989) p. 14-8; GATT Doc. L/6405 (October 5, 1988).

than GATT-sanctioned dispute-resolution, has been "construed as reflecting a preference of the EC for handling its disputes through 'power-oriented' bilateral negotiations, rather than 'rule-oriented' impartial third-party determinations based on GATT rules.[156] A member of the GATT Secretariat observed in 1985 that

> *In the whole process [the perceived decline of GATT discipline] the Community, with her special proclivity for discriminatory arrangements, played the main role. With active support from Europe, the United States would have remained a safe bulwark of non-discrimination in international trade -- for the single reason that it does not have an alternative political tradition. For the last two decades, American administrators were torn between awareness of the practical value to them. . .of the most-favored nation principle and the need to keep together NATO, at the European end of which discrimination became the acme of statesmanship.*[157]

The Community's traditional posture began to change in the late 1980s. The EC, while placing priority on internal integration, nevertheless made a substantial commitment to strengthening the GATT system in the Uruguay Round negotiations. It began to utilize GATT dispute resolution procedures more actively. The new Community attitude reflected a widespread -- although not universal -- view within the Commission that the GATT regime can be utilized effectively not only to improve market opportunities abound for European firms, but to advance the process of European integration.[158]

The Internal Debate. EC policymakers agree that the Community's role in the international system will change in the 1990s, but they differ as to the nature of this change, with each of the two key directorates seeking to nudge the Community in the direction over which it has greatest

---

[156]Petersmann (1986) p 45.

[157]Jan Tumlir, "GATT Rules and Community Law -- A Comparison of Economic and Legal Functions," in Hilf, et. al. (1986), p. 15.

[158]For example, the adoption of GATT disciplines on restrictive national procurement policies and certain types of state aid measures regarded by the Commission as pernicious will strengthen the Community's own rules in these areas. Similarly, the anticipated phaseout of the Multifiber Arrangement is regarded by the Commission liberals as sound economic policy since the European textile industry is arguably healthy and capable of competing in a more open trading environment. Interview with a DG-I official, April 1990.

competence. In general, officials in the Internal Market Directorate (DG-III) believed that the Community, preoccupied with European integration, would play a relatively passive role, while officials in the External Affairs Directorate (DG-I) expected that the Community would exert a greater degree of leadership.[159] Officials in DG-III, the chief architects of the Single Market effort, anticipate that the Community will not have the time or the energy to devote more than cursory attention to the multilateral system given the demands of European integration, which includes not only the Single Market Initiative but German reunification, the European Economic Area, the negotiation of association agreements with Eastern Europe, and the membership applications by Sweden, Austria, and possibly others.[160] DG-I policymakers, who have already largely succeeded in winning from the Member States the right to speak on behalf of Europe in the trade arena, now expect the Community to provide the impetus for multilateral trade initiatives. These officials point with some pride to the Commission's participation, albeit as an observer, in the annual G-7 Summits,[161] and believe that as the world becomes increasingly multipolar, their own stature as leaders of the world's largest trading bloc will increase.[162] They see the Community taking a greater leadership role in future GATT negotiations in order to secure improvements in the GATT system, citing the Community's actions on intellectual property rights during the Uruguay Round as an example; in that case the Community initially adopted a very passive role, but beginning in 1990, it became actively engaged in creating an Intellectual Property Rights Code.[163] DG-I policymakers are already looking ahead to another round of multilateral trade talks, which would include issues such as competition policy and a broadening of disciplines in services and trade-related investment measures.[164]

The differences in perspective of the two directorates should not be construed as a fundamental disagreements. The issue is in significant part

---

[159]Interviews with two DG-I officials, November 1989 and April 1990, and two DG-III officials, April 1990.

[160]Interviews with two DG-I officials, April 1990.

[161]*European Report* (July 15, 1989).

[162]Interviews with two DG-I officials, November 1989 and April 1990.

[163]Interview with a senior DG-I official, November 1989.

[164]Interview April 1990.

one of administrative resources, which were spread very thin as the 1990s began. Each directorate is aware that its own position is strengthened by the achievements of the other; DG-III's progress in advancing the Single Market has given DG-I substantial additional negotiating leverage in the trade area, and DG-I's actions in multilateral trade negotiations are a useful foil for critics who charge that the Community in its preoccupation with internal integration, neglecting the international system. As a result, EC policymakers believe that while the Community's priority in the 1990s will be European integration, it will reserve enough administrative resources to remain a leading player in the international system.

Negotiating Objectives and Strategy. When asked individually, most of the Commission's leaders and trade officials believe that the Community should make substantial concessions in agriculture in order to ensure a successful outcome in the Uruguay Round; however, these views, even if widely held, will not necessarily produce such an outcome. The internal political opposition to the proposed reductions in farm subsidies and levels of trade protection has been intense. Officially, the Community simply has not stated trade objectives in agriculture and rejects any attempt to link the Uruguay Round negotiations with its own internal deliberations on farm policy reform.[165] Accordingly, the Commission has sought, to the extent possible, to de-emphasize the importance of farm issues to the Round as a whole and to seek to advance other objectives. In particular, the Community has pressed hard for new GATT codes governing trade-related intellectual property rights (TRIPs) and in services.[166] In addition, the Community would like to establish multilateral dispute resolution procedures that constrain the ability of individual contracting parties (mainly the United States) from acting unilaterally using domestic trade remedies -- "Section 301 must be changed . . .the U.S. must not have the unilateral ability to go ahead and act against us."[167] A principal aspect of the Community's negotiating strategy has been to insist on the principal of "overall reciprocity" -- that

---

[165]"There is no specific trade policy objective in a formal sense, in the agricultural sector." Report by the Commission of the European Communities, GATT *Trade Policy Review* (1991) Vol. II, p. 31.

[166]*European Report* No. 1693 (July 13, 1991) and No. 1684 (June 12, 1981).

[167]On this point, French leaders reportedly favor U.S. actions against Japan under Section 301 while the Germans and most of the rest of the Community oppose use of Section 301 as a general proposition. Interview with an EC diplomat, January 1990.

is, that it should not extend the benefits of liberalization of its internal market to third countries without concessions from those countries which establish a "mutually advantageous balance of benefits for all parties." Unilateral liberalization will not be undertaken in areas not yet covered by GATT rules, such as services.[168] The Commission had indicated that it regards it "as foolish to extend unilaterally to third countries from whom it would be reasonable to expect comparable liberalization measures, the benefit of its own liberalization process."[169]

The European Community and the United States

At the beginning of the 1990s many observers predicted that relations between the United States and the Community were headed for trouble. Long-festering differences in agriculture were being augmented by other actual and potential points of major conflict over subsidies for high technology industries, the future of the GATT, and over the prospective enlargement of the Community. Moreover, not only was a resurgent Community becoming more self-confident and assertive, but the old security concerns that had offset trade differences in the past appeared to be fading away.

Arguably it is the United States, not any other nation or group of nations, or even the GATT itself, which has served as the principal constraint on the Community's freedom of action in the international trade arena. Because of its sheer size and economic power, the EC has been able to compel most other trading partners, including Japan, to accept the bilateral and regional arrangements which it has devised. The EC has -- depending on one's perspective -- ignored, or taken a narrow approach to interpretation of its GATT obligations when those obligations have appeared to conflict with its key objectives, and, where necessary, has used its political muscle to block adoption of adverse GATT panel decisions.[170] The Americans, however, have challenged the Community's actions in many areas on the trade equivalent of moral grounds, castigating the EC for protectionism, discrimination, bilateralism, and other sins. Even worse, from the Community's perspective, has been

---

[168]GATT Secretariat, "Report by the GATT Secretariat", in GATT *Trade Policy Review* (1991) Vol. I, p. 37.

[169]EC Commission, Europe -- World Partner, Questions and Answers (October 19, 1988), cited in GATT *Trade Policy Review* (1991) Vol. I, p. 37.

[170]In general, see Gardner Patterson, "The European Community as a Threat to the System," in Cline (1983), and Petersmann (1986).

the American propensity to take unilateral retaliatory action when the U.S. has failed to obtain satisfaction through negotiations or the international dispute settlement process. In the 1990s, as the Community's self confidence has grown, Europeans have signaled that they will no longer readily accept what they regard as American meddling in their affairs. A Bundesbank official, bridling at U.S. pressure on interest rates in 1991, commented that "we'll cut our rates when we want to;" French Prime Minister Edith Cresson, defiant of U.S. criticism of European subsidies to Airbus, stated that "united with a faultless solidarity, we Europeans will not let our civilian aviation industry be dismantled."[171]

There have always been, to be sure, significant limits on the United States' ability to cajole, persuade or coerce the Community into a particular course of action. In contrast to Japan, where U.S. pressure virtually always becomes a key element in that government's decisionmaking process, Community institutions generally do not take U.S. concerns into account in the first instance and are capable of shrugging them off even when the U.S. raises serious objections. The EC is not particularly vulnerable to trade retaliation by the U.S. and has repeatedly shown that it will counter-retaliate if the U.S. decides to use the big stick. Nowhere have the limits of U.S. influence been more evident than in agriculture. The original formation of the Common Market and the subsequent implementation of the Common Agricultural Policy (CAP) not only caused a massive loss of U.S. farm export markets in Europe, but fostered huge European surpluses which were dumped onto international markets through the use of export subsidies. Yet despite nearly thirty years of U.S. threats, pleas, and occasional use of sanctions, it has arguably had a marginal impact on any aspect of the CAP.[172] In the early 1990s, despite the fact that the U.S. had staked its

---

[171]*Wall Street Journal* (July 15, 1991).

[172]In the so-called "Chicken War" of 1963-64, the U.S., in retaliation for new CAP restrictions on poultry imports imposed stiff retaliatory duties on EC products (brandy, "automobile trucks", potato starch, dextrine), but this did not prevent the subsequent extension of CAP import restrictions to many other agricultural commodities. In the 1985 "Citrus War" the Reagan Administration retaliated against EC pasta imports in response to the Community's establishment of tariff preferences for Mediterranean fruit, but the EC counter-retaliated against U.S. exports of walnuts and lemons. In the same year, the U.S. retaliated against EC pasta exports to the U.S. to protest EC export subsidies of the durum wheat component in pasta, but in response the EC actually increased the disputed subsidies. In a more general response to EC farm export subsidies, the U.S. began

(continued...)

prospects for a successful Uruguay Round on achieving reform of EC farm policies, internal Community discussions of the CAP scarcely took note of U.S. concerns -- as always, these frequently-heated debates primarily turned around internal budget issues and farmers' demands for adequate incomes.[173]

While the Europeans are frequently annoyed by the American propensity for unilateral measures taken to compel a desired European response, from a U.S. perspective there is often no clear alternative. No overarching set of formal or informal institutional arrangements exists regulating U.S.-EC trade other than the GATT itself, whose limitations have repeatedly been demonstrated, and bilateral agreements covering a few product sectors. Historically, there has been little comprehensive bilateral collaboration on trade between the United States and the European Community; as one observer recently noted, the U.S. does not have a coherent EC policy and the Community lacks a coherent U.S. policy, although each has well-formed policies toward other world states and regions.[174] The United States has no formal mechanism for participating in the Single Market Initiative,[175] and the Community is usually not consulted when the United States formulates trade policy which may affect EC interests; the U.S. notion that it might participate in the formulation of EC Directives is regarded by the Europeans as an affront and the notion that the Europeans might play a role in shaping

---

[172](...continued)
in 1985 to give exporters free surplus farm products held by the Department of Agriculture for sale in competition with EC products in third country export markets; the accession of Spain and Portugal led to a protracted, bitter wrangle over loss of U.S. markets for corn and sorghum, characterized by brinkmanship on both sides in the form of threatened retaliation and counter-retaliation. See Roy Ginsberg, "U.S.-EC Relations," in J. Lodge (1989), pp. 266-77.

[173]When Commissioner McSharry advanced a CAP reform proposal in 1991 which met with some U.S. approval, that fact appeared to be serendipitous rather than a response to external pressure -- U.S. Trade Representative Carla Hills observed that the McSharry proposal was a "result of EEC budgetary problems rather than. . .a conscious effort to help GATT talks." See *European Report* No. 1693 (July 13, 1991); No. 1694 (July 17, 1991).

[174]Ginsberg (1989).

[175]In February 1989, Secretary of Commerce Robert Mosbacher demanded a seat at the EC negotiating table; his request was rejected, although joint consultations were later held to discuss mutual arrangements on standards and certification procedures. Murphy (1990) Vol. II, p. 22.

U.S. trade legislation would be dismissed by most Americans as unacceptable. Bilateral joint ministerial cabinet meetings are concerned with how the United States and the Community will coordinate in external matters of the broadest sort, such as the Uruguay Round, followed by a laundry list of sectoral irritants. Status summaries of the bilateral trade relationship at any given point in time consist largely of compilations of unresolved complaints and ad hoc arrangements (such as VRAs in steel) that were implemented to resolve specific disputes.

At the same time, U.S. ties with the Community are arguably stronger and more diverse than with any other trading partner except Canada; these ties are not so much institutional as commercial, attitudinal, and cultural.[176] One of the most significant ties is the enormous two-way trade and investment flow, which is now characterized by increasing interpenetration of the two economies by U.S. and European multinationals. Although there are many problem areas in the bilateral economic relationship, on a net basis, neither party has reason to feel strongly disadvantaged or exploited by the other. In contrast to the U.S.-Japan trade balance, the U.S.-EC balance has proven responsive to macroeconomic policies such as shifts in the exchange rate, indicating a relatively low prevalence of structural impediments -- indeed, the EC market has been an important factor offsetting the growth of the U.S trade deficit. Underlying the trading relationship is a rough consensus on many of the broad principles which should govern it, so that while U.S. and European business and political leaders may not always agree on trade matters, they at least talk the same language. In the area of trade and economic policy, the views of the Bush Administration and of the Commission's leadership have been more often than not congruent. The Commission, like the U.S. Administration, is dominated by economic liberals committed to free trade and open markets. The Commission and the U.S. government are strongly supportive of the GATT system and the extension of GATT disciplines to areas like services, intellectual property and investment, and the U.S. and the EC share a particular interest in

---

[176]George Kennan, one of the principal architects of postwar U.S. foreign policy, described the Western Europeans in words that many Europeans would no doubt echo: "For all [their] edginess and for all their criticism of us, these people are, for the most part, our best friends -- not in the sense that they like us, individually or collectively, but in the sense that they know us well, after so many mutual involvements; that they are aware, as are few others in the world, of their stake in the existence and the prospering. . .of our society; they are conscious, in other words, of the community of fate that binds us all together. . . ." George Kennan, *The Cloud of Danger: Current Realities of American Foreign Policy* (Little Brown, 1977), pp. 126-27.

sustaining a strong international antidumping regime. Given these numerous areas of common interest and shared attitudes, it is possible to regard the periodic bilateral disputes that erupt in trade as mere manifestations of integration as two complex, interrelated economic systems come into closer contact with each other.

But this view is too sanguine. Trends under way at the beginning of the 1990s have the potential for producing conflict that is more serious and less manageable than any of the disputes of the 1970s and 1980s. The development with perhaps the most significant potential for trouble -- which has, as yet, been overshadowed by issues arising out of the Single Market Initiative -- is the imminent enlargement of the Community. At some point in the 1990s the Community will expand to include some or all of the current EFTA countries, and may also absorb several Eastern European nations, which will adopt the Common External Tariff with respect to third countries. If the history of past enlargements is any guide -- and there is no reason to believe otherwise -- this looming, greatest-of-all enlargements may entail a huge net loss of export markets to the United States, a prospect which the U.S. is unlikely to accept passively. The bilateral row which erupted over the accession of Spain and Portugal is a harbinger of the sort of serious conflict which could occur if the accession of EFTA and other states in the 1990s is not managed skillfully. That earlier enlargement triggered one of the nastiest rounds of U.S.-EC disputes. One observer commented that

> *While settled in early 1987, the tenor of future bilateral relations is bound to suffer because the two came to the brink of a full-scale trade war. Threats of punitive action, counter threats, actual punitive action and more retaliation are bound to unleash the kinds of centrifugal forces that could throw the relationship off balance, perhaps to the point of no return.*[177]

A second source of serious conflict arises out of the Community's large scale support to several strategic industries, notably commercial aviation, space, and the information technologies. Such assistance is already having a major adverse effect on at least one key U.S. industry, commercial aircraft manufacturing, where European government subsidies have enabled the Airbus consortium to cut into the market position of U.S. manufacturers. But this is probably only the beginning. In the 1990s, U.S. firms will experience further erosion of their position in commercial aircraft, but may also begin to lose markets to subsidized European

---

[177]Roy H. Ginsberg in Lodge, (1989) pp. 271-72.

competitors in strategic product areas like advanced consumer electronics, new materials, factory automation systems, software, commercial satellite launch services, and biotechnology. The fact that the U.S. government itself provides some support to these industries, mainly in the area of defense-related R&D, will in no way mitigate the intensity of U.S. outrage at the EC's particular brand of industrial policy, which is considerably more heavily weighted toward support for explicit commercial objectives. U.S.-EC disputes over industrial subsidies underscore the fact that while there is much commonality in U.S. and European thinking on economic matters, there is an important divergence over the proper role of the government in the economy. That fact was at the root of the major sectoral disputes of the 1980s (agriculture, steel, shipbuilding, Airbus) and will drive the sectoral disputes of the 1990s as well. For their part, the Europeans have shown no sign of backing off on this issue; as one EC diplomat remarked in 1990,

> *The Americans want us to abolish EC subsidies. The European Community cannot. We have poor people and poor regions. We can move to common ground on JESSI and SEMATECH, but Airbus will still have to be partially financed. We will have to retain our subsidies. . . . We will increase the amount of aid to high technology and the amount of regional aid. We will continue to wind down agricultural subsidies. The more we save, however, in agriculture, the more it will go into other things that the Americans won't like, such as subsidies to poorer regions.*[178]

The U.S. and the Community are each becoming more exasperated with the other's particular brand of unilateralism. The Community, preoccupied with the completion of the internal market, has repeatedly shown what the U.S. regards as insensitivity to its concerns; as one EC policymaker commented in 1990, "in the coming years we will not be thinking of the external aspects of the [internal] policies we adopt. We will be concentrating on how to get measures passed. The burden will lie on our partners to get external considerations considered early in the decision-making process."[179] The Community's distraction with its own internal processes places a continuing burden on the U.S. government and U.S. companies to monitor a policy formation process in Brussels which can by turns be opaque, baffling, and discriminatory, and which may

---

[178]Interview with an EC trade official, January 1990.

[179]Interview with a senior EC diplomat, January 1990.

result in the introduction of policies which, by the time they are unveiled, cannot be modified, especially in response to complaints of outsiders. But the Community has similar criticisms of the United States. It has repeatedly expressed its concern for what is perceived to be a freewheeling and occasionally belligerent unilateralism on the part of the United States. Europeans like to point out that the Community is a "school in sharing sovereignty;" the United States, in their view, tends to throw its weight around against trade practices it regards as "unfair" relatively unmoored by any sense of deference to multilateral rules or discipline. A 1990 EC report on trade barriers and unfair trade practices by the U.S. complained of "the often arbitrary and unilateral nature of much of U.S. trade legislation," with Section 301 of the Trade Act of 1975 singled out for particularly severe treatment:

> *Unilateral action under Section 301 on the basis of unilateral determination without authorization from the GATT contracting parties is illegal under GATT. Such unilateral action runs counter to basis GATT principles and is in clear violation of specific provisions of the General Agreement.*[180]

U.S.-E.C. philosophical differences are exacerbated in virtually every dispute by the manner in which the issue is cast, usually by the United States. The U.S. government rejects industrial policy and the panoply of measures associated with it (subsidies, cartels, government-driven rationalization) as "unfair," and uses its trade policy measures to deliver what the Europeans perceive as moral judgments on their own policies. European irritation is increased by the perception that U.S. negotiators define success in negotiations in terms of their ability to score debating points and to cast their opposite numbers in a bad light vis-a-vis international rules rather than in terms of reaching agreements on what they regard as fundamental U.S. interests. Such differences in American and European perspectives and style have complicated transatlantic relations since the days of Wilson and Clemenceau; however, in the 1990s the Commission will be far more assertive in challenging the United States on the high moral ground that it has long regarded as its own. In response to the U.S. Trade Representative's annual catalog of unfair foreign trade practices (in which the Community is prominently featured), the EC has begun publishing its own large annual compendium of "unfair" trade practices by the United States, which is laced with harsh

---

[180]EC Commission, *Report on the United States Trade Barriers and Unfair Trade Practices* (1990).

criticism of U.S. "unilateralism," "protectionism," an alleged lack of commitment to the GATT system.[181] In the late 1980s, uncharacteristically, the Community successfully brought GATT challenges against U.S. policies which it regarded as objectionable, the 1986 U.S.-Japan Semiconductor Arrangement and the U.S. use of Section 337 against infringements of intellectual property rights.

The Uruguay Round negotiations themselves have underscored certain important differences in the vision of the U.S. and the EC with respect to the future of the GATT system. The U.S. has sought to strengthen the GATT Subsidies Code, in substantial part, to compel the Community to curtail the subsidies which have formed an integral part of its industrial policy. Similarly, it wants a GATT agreement on agriculture that would make it impossible for the EC to continue subsidizing and protecting its farm sector. The Community, with significant backing from some other GATT contracting parties, has sought not only to legitimize some categories of subsidies under GATT rules -- particularly research, environmental and regional subsidies, which will be particularly important to the Europeans in the 1990s -- but to establish GATT mechanisms which would restrict and in some cases eliminate U.S. ability to offset injurious subsidies through the use of countervailing duties, Section 301 of the Trade Act of 1974 and other "unilateral" measures. The fact that the two largest participants in the GATT system were deadlocked over these basic questions was responsible for the deadlock in several key areas of the Uruguay Round negotiations that became evident in late 1990 (subsidies, dispute settlement). Even if the Round is ultimately brought to a close, it is unclear that the U.S. and the EC will be capable of collaborating on further strengthening of the GATT system.

The European Community and Japan

Concern about Japan has been and remains an important element in European policymaking. The single greatest external motive for the Single Market Initiative may very well have been the Community's perceived need to respond to Japan's growing economic and technological power. Most of the more controversial measures being implemented by the Community in connection with EC 1992 relate directly or indirectly to the challenge from East Asia -- quantitative restrictions being developed at the Community level, restrictions on internal sales by Japanese auto "transplant" facilities, reciprocity requirements, rules of origin, local content requirements imposed on EC subsidiaries of foreign firms, and a

[181] EC Commission (1990).

wide range of subsidized high-tech research and development projects. The Japanese have responded to what they perceive as protectionist, occasionally strong-arm tactics by the European Community with massive direct investment, joint ventures, and a divide-and-conquer approach to Member States and regions. Japanese investment in the Community virtually exploded in the late 1980s, from $6.6 billion in the 1987 to $42 billion at the end of March 1990.[182] By 1991, Japanese "transplant" operations had become extremely prominent in the Community and, under the pressure of recession, many of Europe's largest indigenous firms were experiencing severe competitive difficulties, with a few apparently on the verge of collapse. Concern about Japan appeared to be on the rise not only in France and Italy but even in Germany,[183] where a number of observers questioned whether Germany could prevail against Japanese competition over the long run.[184] As Japanese inroads in the EC market became more pronounced, the perception of a growing economic and competitive crisis led a number of business and government leaders began to question not only the soundness of the Community's policies toward Japan, but the premises underlying the entire Single Market Initiative; "A backlash against 1992 is growing. . .from the very people who were supposed to be the Single Market's firmest friends -- captains of European industry."[185]

Historically, Japan has been viewed by the Europeans with "suspicion and hostility" arising out of the memory of pre-war trade wars, bitter recollection of Japanese actions in Southeast Asia during World War II, and, according to some observers, a goodly amount of racial prejudice.[186] Japan has certainly received hard treatment at the hands of the Europeans, who initially obstructed its accession to and full participation in the GATT, and, in the so-called "Doko shock" of 1976, subjected a visiting delegation of Japanese leaders to a barrage of virulent

---

[182]*The Economist* (June 8, 1991).

[183]*Le Monde* (April 20, 1991); *Wirtschaftswoche* (April 5, 1991); *The Economist* (June 8, 1991); *Business Week* (June 3, 1991).

[184]See interview with Konrad Seitz, Planning Staff Chief of the Foreign Ministry, in *Wirtschaftswoche* (April 5, 1991).

[185]*The Economist* (June 8, 1991).

[186]"There is a racial overtone, a bias, to the EC's attitude toward Japan. This comes from the French." Interview with EC diplomats (1990); see also Gordon Daniels, "EC-Japan: Past, Present and Future," in J. Lodge. pp. 279-80.

criticism and threats.[187] Individual Member States restricted imports of Japanese products through a web of quantitative restraints based on "gray" bilateral agreements, with the most significant restrictions occurring in the areas of greatest Japanese strength -- autos, steel, consumer electronics products, machine tools.[188] The Commission also imposed quantitative limits on imports of some Japanese products such as VCRs, motorcycles, televisions, forklift trucks, machine tools and quartz watches,[189] and vigorously applied antidumping measures against imported Japanese products.[190]

The defects inherent in the Community's trade policy toward Japan -- essentially a mishmash of ad hoc border measures imposed in response to specific sectoral threats -- was evident by the mid-1980s. While trade restrictions were numerous, they did not constitute elements of a broader strategy; one EC diplomat observed that "there is no policy toward Japan . . .the actions, taken one at a time, are defensive."[191] Merely excluding, or trying to exclude, certain Japanese products from the European market had done little to prevent the erosion of the European competitive position. Accordingly, concurrently with the formation of the Single Market, the Commission began a more comprehensive and sophisticated policy toward Japan. Although not explicitly spelled out officially the main elements of this strategy appear to be as follows:

- Traditional "gray" quantitative import restrictions were retained to protect a few sensitive sectors (autos, televisions), but border measures were deemphasized in favor of the use of legal tools and informal pressure to channel Japanese inward investment in a manner regarded as advantageous (e.g., featuring local R&D and design, local engineering, local manufacturing, local sourcing). Manifestations of what was regarded as Japanese economic aggression -- notably dumping and screwdriver plants -- were attacked through vigorous regulatory actions.

187Daniels (1989) p. 279.

188GATT Doc. L/6530, July 31, 1989, Point 259; *Nihon Keizai Shimbun* (February 8, 1989).

189GATT Doc. L/6530, July 31, 1989, Point 73.

190*European Report* No. 1500 (May 31, 1989); No. 1511 (July 8, 1989); No. 1519 (September 2, 1989); No. 1479 (March 11, 1989).

191Interview with a U.S. official, March 1990.

- EC negotiators sought to utilize the leverage arising out of the Single Market Initiative to secure improved market access for EC products in Japan.
- The Commission sponsored a panoply of R&D projects designed to enhance the competitiveness of EC industries relative to Japan. Institutions such as the European Investment Bank, which had traditionally channeled its resources to regional development, began making subsidized loans to facilitate the establishment of "spearhead" technologies such as communications satellites, personal computers, and semiconductor manufacturing facilities.[192]

The Commission's policy of encouraging channeled Japanese investment in the Community has proven controversial, with the Member States divided over the desirability of such investment and the degree to which it should be regulated. Member States like Britain, Ireland and Belgium have actively sought to attract Japanese manufacturing and distribution activity through tax incentives, negotiated land and financial packages, and a variety of other enticements. These actions have angered the French and Italians; while not in favor of total exclusion of Japanese investment, leaders in these countries would limit it to sectors where there is no significant European competition, or restrict Japanese investment to a small equity position in existing European firms (such as France's Bull) so that continuing European control can be ensured. The Commission has straddled the gap between these two camps. On the one hand, it has consistently supported the basic freedom of Japanese firms to invest in the EC provided that Japanese firms assume a sufficiently "European" aspect. On the other hand, it has sought to curb the use of subsidy incentives to attract transplants,[193] and has clearly let the Japanese know that "screwdriver plants" -- local facilities that merely assemble components made in Japan -- are not welcome in the Community. A Japanese analyst commented in 1990 that

> *[W]e now find capital moving into foreign countries, where we build factories. So far so good. Until we start getting complaints about how we're running those factories. We already see this happening with the screwdriver operation problem. Japanese factories on European soil are not doing enough local procuring. And we are using Europeans as coolies, subjecting them to hard physical labor, while the head, the top, is back in*

---

[192]European Investment Bank *Annual Reports* (1987, 1988, 1989).

[193]*European Report* No. 1475 (February 25, 1989).

Japan. . . . To put it bluntly, Japan is treating Europe like an undeveloped region. So "transfer your R&D operations to Europe." We are already hearing such complaints, and such demands.[194]

The Commission's effort to encourage Japanese investment and "localization" of production and procurement appears to have succeeded brilliantly; indeed, if anything, it underestimated Japanese industrial groups' ability and willingness to comply with the various local content, R&D and manufacturing requirements. However, the question increasingly being posed by the Europeans was whether the basic strategy of encouraging inward Japanese investment was a sound one to begin with. By 1991 Japanese auto and electronics firms not only were establishing complete manufacturing facilities in the Community, but transplanting entire supplier systems and distribution organizations, and beginning production operations in related "upstream" process industries like chemicals and steel;[195] the transplants not only typically utilized a high percentage of EC content but boasted that they were "more European than the European" firms, utilizing a higher percentage of EC components and materials than indigenous enterprises. The Single Market Initiative, by reducing internal barriers, appears to have greatly facilitated Japanese market penetration. *Business Week* observed on June 3, 1991,

From metal fasteners to memory chips, the Japanese are suddenly everywhere. Europe's fearsome fortress is beginning to look like Swiss cheese. Japanese investors are pouring in their dollars and yen, totaling $54 billion as of April, leaping over Europe's hurdles and establishing manufacturing footholds from Manchester to Milan.

By 1991 a reassessment of the EC strategy toward foreign investment generally, but Japanese investment in particular, was under way. "In every government and every country, and in the EC Commission, there are people now who are very prejudiced against Japanese production oriented investment."[196] In an historic agreement in 1991, the Commission concluded a bilateral arrangement with Japan which will restrict the automobile sales of Japanese transplants in the Community through 1999 -- a clear derogation from the principal of national treatment

---

[194]Takao Negishi in *Denshi* (September 30, 1990) (JPRS-JST-91-031-L).

[195]*Handelsblatt* (March 14, 1991).

[196]Takao Negishi in *Denshi* (September 1990) (JPRS-JST-91-031-L).

for local subsidiaries of foreign firms. The Japanese government vigorously denied that it had agreed to limit its transplant sales, but this was probably attributable to its concern that if its concession were to be acknowledged, the same principal could be applied by the Europeans and other trading partners to Japanese transplant operations all over the world; as the Europeans described the arrangements, Japan agreed to freeze its direct exports of autos to the EC between 1992 and 1989 at 1.23 million units, and to limit its transplant output under a gradually-increasing ceiling that would hit 1.2 million units by 1999. If transplant output exceeds the indicative ceiling, the Europeans indicate that they can reduce Japan's direct export quotas by a corresponding amount. In addition to departing from the principal of national treatment, the EC-Japan auto arrangements are not fully consistent with the notion of a single market, since they also establish informal quotas for individual Member States.[197]

Growing European resistance to Japanese investment has been manifested in other key sectors. In electronics, Britain's leading computer firm, ICL, was expelled from JESSI and several industry groups after its acquisition by Fujitsu, and some EC electronics officials were calling for restrictions on Japanese electronics firms in Europe.[198] As the rationale for this strategy was articulated by Alain Gomez, President of Thomson, in 1991:

> *Without radical change, Japanese pressure will prove fatal in the fields of computers, televisions and semiconductors, well before the end of the decade. The only good solution is to turn Europe into a protected area. Once external protection is established, total deregulation of the internal market -- the biggest in the world -- would guarantee optimum efficiency.*[199]

SECTORAL TRADE STRATEGIES

The Commission has no Treaty mandate to conduct sector-specific industrial policies, but it possesses enough discrete powers in areas like spending, trade, and competition policy that it is capable of implementing

---

[197] *Europe No.* 5547 (New Series) (August 2, 1991); *New York Times* (August 12, 1991).

[198] *The Economist* (June 8, 1991).

[199] *Le Monde* (April 20, 1991).

such policies if the inclination and political support for them exists. Historically the Member States preferred to pursue their own promotional policies in what were perceived as growth sectors (aerospace, computers, telecommunications, and, until 1974, steel) while turning to the Commission when international conditions rendered such national policies ineffectual. Thus, in the 1970s and 1980s the Commission administered comprehensive regimes in crisis sectors such as textiles, steel, and shipbuilding, and, in the 1990s, as the inadequacy of national measures in the information sector has become evident, is now implementing a "European" strategy in this industry. However, the division among the Member States over approach -- Colbertism versus a more liberal mix of policies featuring research and training -- has limited and will continue to limit the depth of the Commission's intervention in any particular sector.[200] From the perspective of he world trading system of the 1990s, by far the most important sector-specific policy measures are likely to be manifested in agriculture and the electronic information technologies.

Agriculture

The Common Agricultural Policy (CAP) is arguably the single greatest trade distorting measure implemented by any Western state since the end of World War II. As the *Deutsches Allgemeines Sonntagsblatt* observed on June 21, 1991, the CAP

> *stores the surplus [farm] products, and dumps them at given periods onto the world market at giveaway prices. The consequences are appalling. On the one hand, agriculture in the countries of the Third World cannot stand up for itself in its own markets when confronted with these dumping practices on the part of the Europeans, and on the other hand, all the rules and agreements of free trade are undercut. . .thirdly and finally, in this way surplus production is spurred on again.*[201]

The CAP exists because the Community's farms are capable of producing far more food than its consumers can absorb. If market forces were allowed free play, surplus production and imports would drive EC prices down to levels that would render many farms, particularly smaller ones, unviable, and would produce a wholesale restructuring of the farm sector. Such an outcome has been regarded as politically unacceptable in most

---

[200]Graham Hall, *European Industrial Policy* (New York: St. Martin's Press, 1968).

[201]FBIS-WEU-91-147.

Member States (See the discussion of the politics of agriculture in Chapter 3.) Thus, while the CAP has produced distortions in internal and external agricultural markets, fostered deep divisions among Member States, and entailed major foreign policy costs for the EC, the Community has not been able to abandon it. Its strategy has been, and is likely to remain, an effort to delay foreign pressure for change while attempting to encourage a phased rationalization of the farm sector.

The CAP is a system of price supports, trade protection and subsidies designed to ensure Europe's food security and to maintain the standard of living of the Community's farmers.[202] The CAP essentially creates a high-priced European island in a world market characterized by lower prices for agricultural products. As of mid-1991, the price of butter in the community was 2600 ECU per ton versus a world price of 900 ECU; the disparity for beef was 2600 ECU per ton in the EC versus a world price of 600 ECU; for cereals EC prices of 155 ECU per ton compared with world prices of 55 to 65 ECU.[203] The so-called "intervention price" is a minimum floor price guaranteed to EC producers; the "target" price is the upper end of the range within which prices can fluctuate, and the "threshold price" is a floor price for imported agricultural products. Variable import levies are imposed on imports to raise them to the threshold price,[204] and variable subsidies (known as "restitution payments") are used to make EC products competitive with world prices -- that is, they are export subsidies. Because the world price of farm commodities is often only a fraction of the CAP price, the export subsidy paid to EC producers often exceeds the sale price of the commodity several times over, so that the net effect is the dumping of large volumes of EC farm products in markets outside the Community to the substantial detriment of all other major agricultural exporting nations.[205] Subsidized EC farm exports "exert downward pressure on world agricultural prices and reduce the rate of return for all agricultural

---

[202]Other stated objectives are to enhance agricultural productivity and ensure adequate supplies to consumers at reasonable prices, although considerable tension exists between the latter two objectives and the first.

[203]Commission official cited in *BNA International Trade Reporter* (July 17, 1991).

[204]Variable levies apply to grains, sugar, dairy products, eggs, poultry, beef, pork, and processed products made from these items.

[205]Restitutions are paid for exports of wheat, wheat flour, beef, dairy products, poultry, some fruits, and some processed products such as pasta.

producers,"[206] and U.S. producers have lost substantial markets in third countries as the EC share of world agricultural markets increased.[207] With respect to the tariffs on the several products which the Community is committed to hold at GATT-bound levels, EC processors of such products receive a subsidy if they use EC-grown products "to ensure that Community growers can still sell their produce despite competition from cheap imports."[208] The EC has also implemented restrictions on the imports of meat on health grounds.[209]

The CAP has always been the principal source of trade friction between the EC and the United States and has fostered major disputes with other EC trading partners, primarily the so-called Cairns Group of agricultural exporting countries.[210] When the Common Market was initially formed, and the system of variable import levies put in place, the U.S. lost significant markets in Europe; it has lost additional export markets with each expansion of the Community. It has invoked GATT dispute-resolution procedures, with little effect. Of the 21 GATT actions initiated by the U.S. against the EC between 1960 and 1985, 17 involved agricultural or fisheries products.[211] In a number of cases, the

---

[206]USTR, *Foreign Trade Barriers* (1991) p. 73.

[207]Between 1970 and 1985, the EC-10's share of OECD agricultural exports grew from 45.2 percent to 55.9 percent while the U.S. share fell from 25.0 to 20.1 percent during the same period. IMF, *The Common Agricultural Policy of the European Community* (November 1988), p. 31.

[208]These products include rapeseed, cottonseed, sunflower seed and protein plants such as peas and field beans. European Communities, *A Common Agricultural Policy for the 1990s* (Luxembourg: European Communities, 1989).

[209]Pursuant to the Third Country Meat Directive (TCMD) EC veterinarians must individually inspect and certify individual foreign meat plants from which exports are made to the EC. With respect to the U.S., the Community has applied strict standards and in some cases, de-listed U.S. plants for noncompliance with the TCMD. In the late 1980s the EC imposed a ban on imports of meat treated with hormones. GATT Doc. L/6366, Point 53; USTR *Foreign Trade Barriers* (1991) p. 74-76.

[210]The Cairns Group includes Australia, Argentina, Chile, Colombia, Hungary, Indonesia, Canada, New Zealand, Brazil, Uruguay, Malaysia, Thailand, and the Philippines.

[211]Gary Hufbauer, *Europe 1992: An American Perspective* (Washington, D.C: Brookings, 1990), p. 29.

Community has blocked GATT adoption of adverse panel decisions, leading to retaliatory action by the U.S. against EC products.[212]

The Internal Political Impasse. Very few EC trade officials have anything good to say about the CAP, which is the subject of intense criticism in virtually every Member State. The issue is not so much the CAP's distortion of world trade as its cost to the taxpayer -- the annual cost of farm subsidies in the EC is estimated at a staggering $49 billion annually.[213] In 1991 the Community reportedly had surplus stocks of 20 million tons of grain, 750,000 tons of beef, and 450,000 tons each of butter and powdered skim milk.[214] Because of price supports set to satisfy the political needs of the high cost producer countries as well as improvements in agricultural productivity, domestic agricultural production has continued to increase despite falling world prices. As a result, expenditures by the European Agricultural Guidance and Guarantee Fund (EAGGF) have skyrocketed, leading non-farm dependent constituencies to question whether these huge sums of public money might not be put to better use. Britain, a net contributor to the EC budget which abandoned the notion of agricultural self-sufficiency with the repeal of the Corn Laws 150 years ago, has been particularly harsh in its criticism of the CAP, which is seen as a massive, irrational transfer of wealth from Britain to farmers on the continent. Nevertheless, most of the major continental Member States have politically well-entrenched farm lobbies that make it difficult, if not impossible, for national governments to show much flexibility on the issue (one such national lobby is described in Chapter 3.) Cognizant of the farmers' clout, whatever their private thoughts on the subject of the CAP may be, the Prime Minister of France and the German Chancellor frequently telephone the President of the EC to complain about the plight of their farmers and to lobby for support measures.

---

[212]For example, the U.S. brought a complaint before the GATT Standards Code Committee in 1987 over the EC's ban on imports of hormone treated meat. The EC blocked action by the Committee on the U.S. complaint, so the U.S. imposed 100 percent tariffs on imports of EC agricultural products. An "interim" U.S.-EC agreement allows U.S. producers to ship meat not treated with hormones to the EC, and exempts pet food from the hormone ban. USTR, *Foreign Trade Barriers* (1991), pp. 74-75.

[213]*The Economist* (March 23, 1991).

[214]*NRC Handelsblad* (July 23, 1991) (FBIS-WEU-91-15a).

Agriculture interests are represented in Brussels not only by key Member State governments but by very effective direct lobbying groups, the Committee of Agriculture Organizations (COPA), an umbrella group to which over 30 national farm organizations belong, and COGECA, representing the EC's agricultural cooperatives. COPA is one of the oldest Brussels lobbying groups and has a reputation for securing most of its objectives from the Commission.[215] By the late 1980s COPA's effectiveness was being somewhat diminished by internal divisions and its own decisionmaking procedures, which often compelled it either to adopt watered-down positions to maintain consensus or to permit delegation reserves in which individual members oppose the COPA position. The internal divisions were particularly acute over fundamental issues like trade policy, with the members roughly split between "realists," (Dutch, British, Irish) who urge compromises to retain COPA's credibility and hard liners (Italy, France) who supported a more rigid defense of virtually every aspect of the CAP system.[216] Notwithstanding these problems, however, COPA remains a powerful force for protection.

The Community institutions have proven too cumbersome to effectuate meaningful reform of the farm sector. Most key Council decisions involving the CAP, such as approving a Commission proposal, require a qualified majority vote, or 54 out of a total of 76 votes. A blocking minority is thus 23 votes, and can be mustered whenever any two of the big four Member States can secure the support of 1-2 smaller states. Ultimately, the "package deals" that emerge from this process are so politically delicate that the EC trade negotiators sent to Geneva do not have the authority to agree to any significant changes in the CAP.

The biases and interests of the Council of Agricultural Ministers also help sustain the status quo. Although policy proposals originate with the Commission,[217] they are approved, amended or rejected by this Council, which consists of the Ministers of Agriculture of each Member State. The Agriculture Council meets more often than virtually all other EC Councils, and its decisions have generally not been constrained by those of other councils with partially overlapping jurisdictional concerns (Budget, General Affairs). The Agriculture Council has been characterized as a "club" whose members are committed to the CAP, even when their own

---

[215]It has a large staff and meets regularly with the Commission both formally and informally. COPA has a staff of 44. Its "Presidium" meets twice annually with the Commission and its staff maintains numerous informal contacts.

[216]*Financial Times* (March 2, 1989).

[217]Primarily the Special Committee on Agriculture.

national positions may diverge, although this has been hotly denied by Agriculture Ministers who insist that they do not take positions in the Council not fully consistent with the negotiating mandate from their own governments. Nevertheless, the impression is periodically given, with good reason, that individual Agriculture Ministers are pursuing a policy course which diverges from that of their home governments.[218] Their ability to act as an autonomous force is enhanced by the fact that the agricultural bureaucracies of the Member States are very much understaffed, particularly in southern Europe.[219]

The most significant force for change of the CAP is simply the irrational financial and commercial results which it produces; the CAP's opponents in the Community sometimes express the hope that its costs will rise dramatically, imposing such a crushing burden that reform will follow. The Agriculture Ministers have grappled with the need for reform for a number of years. In February 1988 they agreed to expand the use of "stabilizers," or ceilings on spending per product, and to begin disposing of some of the Community's grotesque pile of surplus stocks -- the "butter mountains" and "milk lakes." In 1990, they agreed in principle on a 30 percent reduction in farm subsidies for a ten-year period running from 1988 to 1998. In July 1991 the Agriculture Minsters, recognizing that if current trends continued they would find themselves "in a intolerable situation regarding surplus production and budgetary spending,"[220] agreed on a proposal for reform drafted by Commissioner MacSharry, featuring a reduction in intervention prices and a sliding scale of compensation payments to farmers to set aside usable land. This proposal, which was cautiously praised by the United States, drew virtually universal criticism from the Ministers.[221] The basic controversy -- wholly unresolved as of this writing -- was between Member States who saw the CAP as a mechanism for enhancing farm efficiency, which would suggest a progressive equalization of EC and world prices, and those that saw the CAP's purpose as one of guaranteeing minimum income levels for

---

[218]See, for example, Chapter 3 (Germany).

[219]Interview with a U.S. Department of Agriculture official, March 1990.

[220]*BNA International Trade Reporter* (July 17, 1991).

[221]*Journal of Commerce* (July 15, 1991); *Europe* No. 5535 (new series) (July 15/16, 1991). The MacSharry Plan would cut cereal intervention prices by 35 percent and those for beef, butter, poultry and pork by 15 percent.

farmers.[222] COPA and COGECA backed the latter position and vowed to press their views in opposition to the McSharry Plan with national governments, the European Parliament, and the Council of Ministers.

The External Impasse. The collapse of the Uruguay Round negotiations in December 1990 was largely a consequence of the inability of the U.S. and the EC to reach any common ground on issues relating to reform of the CAP. The centerpiece of United States' original position, formulated under President Reagan, was a proposal that GATT rules be adopted mandating a complete elimination of all trade-distorting policies in agriculture by the year 2000. The Bush Administration tabled proposals to phase out all export subsidies over a five year period, to convert all trade barriers to tariffs and reduce those tariffs over ten years, and to ban or bring under GATT disciplines domestic support measures. The EC offered a commitment to reduce subsidies by 30 percent by 1998 but rejected the basic U.S. demand, calling instead for "gradualism" in the phaseout of farm support policies.[223] If only because of the internal political imperatives, the Community is unlikely to capitulate to U.S. trade demands in agriculture. Instead, it is likely to seek to establish broad "green light" and "amber light" categories of support measures for farmers -- that is, measures which are permissible or conditionally permissible under international rules -- and seek an arrangement pursuant to which it can its "red" (prohibited) measures into "green" or "amber" measures, and secure GATT sanction for a long, gradual phaseout of "red" measures.[224] Such a program would be designed to dovetail with the Community's fiscal objective of reducing the net cost of the CAP. Thus, the Community is likely to try to reorient the CAP away from production and price supports through set-aside schemes, the replacement of price supports with direct income supports, rural development projects, and increased emphasis on environmental and public health concerns.[225] The Parliament would like to impose production controls, and may succeed in

---

[222]Dutch Minister cited in *BNA International Trade Reporter* (July 17, 1991).

[223]GATT Doc. L/6530, Point 15; *Financial Times* (April 11, 1989).

[224]This scheme is based on the notion that farm support measures are divisible into those which distort trade, those which do not, and those which may or may not have distorting effects depending on circumstances (the amber category).

[225]Interviews with DG-VI and Committee of Agricultural Organizations (COPA) officials, April 1990. See also Murphy (1990).

this endeavor -- farmer resistance notwithstanding -- once its influence on the EC policy-making process is enhanced.[226]

Information Technology

The electronic information technologies are the Achilles heel of the Community's aspirations to overtake Japan and the U.S. in the international competitive arena. Europeans recognize that the cluster of industrial sectors which electronically manipulate, store and transmit data are strategic, in the sense that "the basic freedoms -- political, industrial, economic, social and cultural -- depend on their survival."[227] The Commission, governments of the Member States, and Europe's leading electronics firms have poured resources into efforts to enhance the technological level and manufacturing competitiveness of the information sector, but the results to date have been worse than disappointing. While EC-based electronics firms achieved a slight increase in their world market share in 1990, this followed two decades of steady decline, with the result that in 1991 European firms held only 10 percent of the world's semiconductor market, 20 percent of the consumer electronics markets (mostly in the older product areas) and 15 percent of the market for computer peripherals. European computer production covered only about two thirds of EC demand, and of this 60 percent was accounted for by EC subsidiaries of U.S. firms.[228] Some of the largest EC electronics firms were in trouble; Philips, for example, lost $2.5 billion in 1990 and announced plans to lay off 40,000 workers. The Commission itself was sharply critical of the EC information industry, stating that "the industrial strategy of Community firms has failed to take sufficient account of the Community's dimension and long term prospects. . .[They] fail to bring enough innovative products onto the market quickly enough."[229] A Japanese electronics industry spokesman was even more blunt;

---

[226]Interview with a Committee of Agricultural Organizations (COPA) official, April 1990.

[227]Jean Caillot, Chairman of French Electronics Industry Association, "Europe 1992: How Will Europe's Electronics Industry Change?" See also interview with Konrad Seitz in *Wirtschaftswoche* (April 5, 1991) (JPRS-EST-91-014).

[228]EC Commission, *The European Electronics and Information Technology; Industry: State of Play, Issues at Stake, and Proposals for Action* (March 26, 1991) (hereafter, EC Commission, *European Information Technology*).

[229]EC Commission, *European Information Technology.*

> *[I]t is hardly an exaggeration to say that Europe has no information industry, and that means no computer industry. . . . The computer industry is almost a total disaster [and] the semiconductor industry is also a total disaster. . . . Why is [a leading EC firm] losing money on its components? The reason, quite simply, is that its semiconductors are no good.*[230]

The European information industry is dominated by several large European-capitalized firms, notably Siemens, Philips, Thomson, Bull and SGS-ATES, and by European subsidiaries of foreign firms, primarily American, but now increasingly Japanese. The old line European firms have been the beneficiaries of "national champion" promotional efforts, preferential telecommunications procurement practices, and a variety of protective measures, particularly in consumer electronics. At the Community level, the Commission has sponsored a wide range of expensive joint research and development efforts -- notably ESPRIT, JESSI, RACE -- which seek to stimulate transnational R&D efforts. It has also maintained a controversial inverted tariff structure, with duties of 14 percent on semiconductors and 4.9 percent on computers; the regressive effect of this input tariff on the EC computer industry has, however, been partially offset by widespread use of duty suspensions.[231] The Commission has negotiated quantitative restraints with Japan with respect to televisions and VCRs, and has negotiated "floor price" arrangement with Japan in two critical semiconductor products areas, DRAMs and EPROMs.

With the notable exception of agriculture, no industrial policy issue has engendered more controversy within the Community than what should be done about the EC's trailing position in the information technologies.[232] A laissez-faire school, whose proponents are strongest in the U.K. and in Germany's Ministry of Economics, argue that it does not matter if Japan and perhaps the U.S. dominate the European information field as long as their products remain widely available in Europe at competitive prices; Britain has given its blessing to the

---

[230]Takao Negishi, "From Speech Made to Import-Export Committee," in *Denshi* (September 16, 1990) pp. 16-28 (JPRS-JST-91-031-L).

[231]The tariff structure does not reflect a rational policy decision, but an historical accident; it continues to exist because the Community has not yet devised a way to rationalize the structure in light of the internal and external complexities involved.

[232]*Der Spiegel* (April 24, 1989).

acquisition of its leading computer producer, ICL, by Fujitsu, and has encouraged the establishment of U.S. and Japanese production facilities on its soil.[233] A second school, with its strength concentrated in the governments of France, Italy, Germany's Ministry of Research, and the large European electronics firms themselves, favors major intervention measures to maintain European competitiveness in the information sector. Thomson, Philips, SGS and Siemens -- each headed by ebullient, articulate CEOs -- have been outspoken and effective in urging a comprehensive European response to the challenge from East Asia. The Commission itself is divided between these two schools: DG XIII (Information Technology and Telecommunications) favors an activist policy and has implemented high-visibility R&D projects like ESPRIT and RACE; DG I (External Relations) has tended to support this position with trade policies that protect elements of the electronics sector; while DG III (Internal Market) and DG IV (Competition Policy) support a more laissez-faire approach. Arguably one reason that the Community has allocated such large resources to basic R&D efforts like ESPRIT is that such support measures are less controversial than intervention measures which are closer to the market, such as trade protection and direct subsidization of operations and investment.[234]

---

[233]See *Le Monde* (March 26, 1991); *Enterprises et Telecommunications* (April-May, 1991) (JPRS-EST-91-014).

[234]These opposing perspectives were reflected, if not reconciled, in a major paper by the Commission on the information technologies released on March 26, 1991. EC Commission, *European Information Technology.* The paper, which was considerably more liberal in tone than any prior Commission document on the subject, was the product of considerable tussling by the interventionist and laissez-faire camps within the Commission bureaucracy. In November 1990 the Council of Ministers approved a new Community approach to industrial policy which was characterized as "minimalist" and "a victory of the Community's free marketeers." DG XIII subsequently produced a draft paper on information technology policy, however, which called for "special help" for the computer and electronics sector because of their "strategic important." Leaks of the working drafts of this document from DG XIII "aroused the ire of Brussels free-marketeers, who object[ed] to the protectionist, interventionist tone of the policy paper." Commissioners Bangemann (DG III) and Brittan (DG IV) criticized the paper's interventionist recommendations and "thinly veiled Japanophobia." The paper ultimately was revised to add more of a laissez-faire flavor, while not wholly dispensing with prescriptions for government policy measures. EC Commission, Communication from the Commission to the Council and to the European Parliament, *Industrial Policy in an Open and Competitive Environment*, Com (90) 556 final (November 16, 1990); *The Economist* (February 16, 1991); *Financial Times* (March 11, 1991).

Even the European political and business leaders who advocate an interventionist approach to competition in the information field disagree on the nature of the measures which should be taken. The Commission bureaucracy, not surprisingly, believes that a European information industry strategy should be devised and implemented primarily under the rubric of the Community institutions.[235] The largest EC Member States and electronics firms, however, have bridled at what is viewed as the Commission's excessive bureaucracy, insistence that small businesses and poorer Member States participate in joint R&D projects, and its antipathy to R&D efforts that are directed at the market rather than basic research themes.[236] As a result, in the mid-1980s, some of the large Member States and national governments initiated a range of joint projects completely outside the EC joint R&D framework, an effort that was ultimately organized under the acronym EUREKA.[237] The EC programs like ESPRIT and EUREKA programs like JESSI have co-existed somewhat uneasily; the division of effort is alternatively criticized as "duplicative" and a dispersal of effort and praised as an enlightened division between basic and commercial themes. Experience has shown that the EUREKA projects, while favored over the EC efforts by Europe's most competitive firms, have experienced chronic difficulty in extracting funding from the Member State governments, whereas the EC projects, which can be funded directly by the Commission from the proceeds of the Community value-added tax, do not encounter similar difficulties.[238] However, more fundamentally, it remains unclear whether any of these programs, inside or outside of the Commission's ambit, and regardless of funding levels, can reverse Europe's long competitive slide; critics charge that while the Community has spent $6.2 billion on high-technology R&D since 1987, "the money padded payrolls but did little to boost Europe's competitive status."[239] A Japanese observer commented in this regard that "Europeans love to make programs. They also love to advertise their

---

[235]NRC *Handelsblad* (July 15, 1985).

[236]NRC *Handelsblad* (December 6, 1986).

[237]Government of France, *La Renaissance Technologie de l'Europe* (June, 1985).

[238]*Polytechnisch Weekblad* (November 15, 1990); *Zero Un Informatique* (May 9, 1988); *Wirtschaftswache* (September 14, 1990).

[239]*Business Week* (March 25, 1991).

programs. Except in rare cases, however, their deeds do not match their words."[240]

From the perspective of non-Europeans, the internal debate over research policy -- ESPRIT, EUREKA and so on -- is perhaps of less interest than European divisions over trade and foreign investment policy, which will ultimately determine the degree of foreign access to the EC market. Several firms, most notably Siemens, have determined to implement a "global" competitive strategy based on strategic alliances with first-rank U.S. and Japanese firms (IBM, Mitsubishi); for a firm pursuing such a strategy, overt government protectionist measures tend to be an embarrassment and an encumbrance. The leading Franco-Italian firms, by contrast, have openly advocated a virtual sealing off of the European information market, creating "a protected European space" to permit European firms to achieve the necessary economies of scale.[241] Philips of the Netherlands has not been as open a proponent of such measures but has maneuvered behind the scenes to secure a degree of protection.[242] A less-than-clear attitude exists toward the best approach to foreign investment in the EC; initially, a number of those in the protectionist camp favored measures to compel Japanese and U.S. firms establishing facilities in the EC to adopt a high level of EC content.[243] However, the ease with which Japanese firms satisfied this de facto requirement and established manufacturing facilities in the Community,[244] coupled with their outright acquisition of ICL, fostered a growing unease over foreign investment in this strategic sector.

However, notwithstanding a growing sentiment within the Community to establish a "protected European space" in the information sector, a new trade regime based on increased levels of protection at the border, perhaps coupled with restrictions on foreign subsidiaries operating in Europe, is unlikely to come into being. Not only are the liberal forces within the Commission and among the Member States strong enough to block such an outcome, but the neomercantilist camp is probably too

---

[240]Takao Negishi in *Denshi* (September 1990) (JPRS-JST-91-031-L).

[241]Thomson President Alain Gomez in *Washington Post* (April 21, 1991).

[242]"from voluntary restraint agreement on exports to Europe, tariff hikes and now antidumping measures, you can see the hand of Philips." Alan Lawson, University of Sussex, in *New York Times* (June 4, 1989).

[243]*Business Week* (February 9, 1987).

[244]*Nikkan Kogyo* (January 16, 1991) (JPRS-JST-91-033-L).

divided over the nature of the protective measures required to unite around any coherent program. The 1990s are likely to see a continuation of the trends of the 1980s, that is, an increase in the volume of subsidies for R&D -- a relatively uncontroversial measures -- and the continued use of subtle procedures and rules to protect key product sectors from the full brunt of Japanese competitive pressure. The latter will consist of measures such as the manipulation of tariffs (through unbindings and suspensions); rules of origin; and antidumping actions to restrict imports directly or to compel "voluntary" restraints; preferential procurement; the redirection of competition policy either as an offensive treatment against foreign anticompetitive practices or as a defensive tool to permit certain collusive practices by EC firms; and formal and informal local content requirements. As a French government official put it in 1990, "We have ways to take care of the Japanese that are quite effective. You [the U.S.] have your tools that are quite public. But our ways are more effective. We would not allow them to do here what you allow them to do in the United States."[245]

CONCLUSION

Throughout the postwar era, the world trading system has been led by the United States. In the 1990s and beyond, the United States will no longer be able to drive the system on its own, but will be required to co-manage it, primarily with another large democratic federation, the Community. To date, on the U.S. side, there has been a chronic failure of pragmatism, a propensity to make moral judgements, and a failure to understand the art of diplomacy, which requires seeing the other side's point of view as a means of moving them toward one's own. On the EC side, the overwhelming preoccupation with internal processes and the frequent appearance of indifference to the concerns of outsiders invites the "unilateralism" that Europeans regard as the most offensive aspect of U.S. behavior. Even leaving aside specific sectoral irritants like agriculture, the poor communication which has characterized this relationship to date is potentially highly problematic. The developments of the past several years within the Community are encouraging -- a clear move toward liberalism, openness, and more active support for the GATT system. Should these trends continue, and should the U.S. government find ways to engage the Community at a practical level to help manage the world trading system, then the fears raised about a "fortress Europe"

[245]Interview with a French official, February 1990.

and the breakup of the system into regional blocs will prove to have been misplaced. Given the history of the relationship, however, and the complexity of the internal policy process on both sides of the Atlantic, it is premature to view such an outcome as inevitable or even probable.

8

The Failure of American Trade Policy

Alan Wm. Wolff

I think you can only analyze fairly and honestly what you have been a part of. Otherwise you are an outsider, and while your analysis might be intellectually acute, it is not formed by experience. Only once you've been there can you say what it was like and how it could be better. I make my living in this culture and I am one of its chief critics. Those of us in government should be the chief critics of government. And those of us who are patriots should be the chief critics of our country. Patriotism to me is critical analysis applied in love to that which nurtures you. I have always been an in-house critic. I know my mother's faults better than anyone else since my father died. And I tell her all the time how she can improve herself, but it is done through love.[1]

-- Bill Moyers

---

[1]"Moyers on Washington," *Washington Post*, Sunday, September 1, 1991. There is some truth in what Bill Moyers has said. And yet if one accepted the proposition he advances as conferring an exclusive right on insiders (and one-time insiders) to offer criticism, the world would be impoverished by being deprived of the analysis of those whose careers are spent in reviewing the efforts of others. The principle enunciated would, for example, invalidate some of the analysis contained in this book. I have included this quotation not because it is wholly correct, but as an apologia for being at once part of the process in varying roles and at the same time a demanding critic of U.S. trade policy and the process by which it is made.

DIFFERING PERSPECTIVES IN AN INTERDEPENDENT WORLD

In June 1991, Margaret Thatcher, former Prime Minister of Great Britain, stood before the New York Economic Club, answering questions about trade policy. For example: what was her reaction to recent statements of the new French Prime Minister, Edith Cresson, about competition from Japan? Predictably, she condemned the statements as further evidence of French protectionism. She told the audience about French efforts to limit exports from Britain of Nissan Bluebird autos from a Nissan plant in Britain, the French having insisted that very high European content requirements be met before they would allow these autos entry into France. Speaking with passion, Mrs. Thatcher deplored this approach, recalling the fact that she had herself cut the ribbon that opened that British Nissan plant.

When asked about the utility of economic sanctions against South Africa, she condemned these measures in unequivocal terms, saying that the United States had been mistaken in thinking that the measures had a positive effect. She cited the case of a plant owned by a friend of hers which had been forced to close, leaving 1700 workers unemployed and 17,000 dependents destitute. She spoke with knowledge and precision. She could have been asked, and answered equally well, questions about sales of British telecommunications equipment in Korea, or British business interests in Hong Kong.

Her American audience took little notice of the depth of her knowledge of, and intense interest in, matters distinctly commercial, but none of them would have thought to have asked an American President similar questions. The kind of knowledge Mrs. Thatcher has was very different than that which any American head of state would have had or could have displayed. Commercial matters, as a general proposition, fall outside of the frame of reference of America's leaders.

Dominant political and military status has not always meant according commercial interests a very low order of priority. Imperial Britain in its time, was also a superpower. It used its political and military muscle very often for commercial ends. The original motive for British imperial expansion was commerce, whether in India or in Hudson's Bay. These roots of British policy are still evident today. Its leaders still address with great feeling Britain's foreign trade interests. This has not been the case for America's leaders. American presidents see their role in international relations as primarily (if not solely) dealing with political issues, nearly precluding them from becoming involved in questions of commerce.[2] Yet Great Britain achieved its status as a world power for the purpose of, as well as by, minding its commercial interests.

This chapter describes America's frame of reference for approaching trade policy, how it came into being, and the implications for international trading relations of the way in which the American government conducts itself with respect to trade policy.

THE DETERMINANTS OF U.S. TRADE POLICY

Form of Government

> *The powers delegated by the proposed constitution to the federal government are few and defined. Those which are to remain in the State governments are numerous and indefinite.*
>
> *It will not be denied that power is of an encroaching nature and that it ought to be effectually restrained from passing the limits assigned to it.*
>
> *. . .the defect must be supplied, by so contriving the interior structure of the government as that its several constituent parts may, by their mutual relations, be the means of keeping each other in their proper places.*
>
> Madison, *Federalist Nos. 45, 48, and 51.*

The United States was founded with a federal government designed to be limited in its powers. In this respect, it differs from the more traditional forms of government of the other countries with which it principally trades, with the exception, perhaps, of the federal democracies of Canada and Germany. Those powers not expressly granted to the Federal government are generally reserved to the several states. A system of checks and balances has been constructed that divides the executive, legislative and judicial branches, and often sets them against each other. The Reagan Administration's theme of avoiding government involvement in most issues has been one of the central themes of American political life since the founding of the Republic. As Barber Conable, the respected

---

[2]To his credit, President Bush placed a priority on commercial matters in his visit to Japan in January 1992. This could be dismissed as reflecting the pressures of an upcoming election year. However, his actions were widely criticized in the U.S. as novel and inappropriate; the President should not, it was argued, be a "car salesman."

former ranking minority member of the House Committee on Ways and Means said on his retirement, in defense of the conservative view that he had taken from Congress of the role of that body: "Remember, if we could have done more *for* you (businesses seeking Congressional action), we could have done more *to* you."

Throughout our history, the intrusion by government in commercial matters has been controversial whenever it has been proactive. It has been welcomed only as a mechanism for protecting the public against the excesses of private behavior. The greater part of Franklin Roosevelt's experiment in industrial policy did not survive challenges by the courts, despite the desperate need to combat the disastrous economic conditions of the Great Depression.[3] His regulatory agencies remain with us today. The wartime systems of price controls, administered production and rationing implemented during the First and Second World Wars were enthusiastically scrapped when these national emergencies ended. Even loan guarantees to important firms such as Lockheed and Chrysler stand out in modern American economic history primarily because they are exceptions to America's rule of segregating the industrial or commercial from America's national policies.

There is, to be sure, an American tradition of government support for certain forms of economic activity, but only so long as they involve pursuit of objectives that are one step removed from backing particular commercial interests. In the nineteenth century the federal and state governments underwrote the construction of canals, roads and railroads, and in the twentieth century government has provided similar support for infrastructural activities such as highway and airport construction, and generation and transmission of electrical and nuclear power; but these activities have been directed at enhancing the general welfare rather than the promotion of any individual competitors or groups of competitors. Government intervention in the farm sector -- where, curiously, free trade ideology is strongest -- has been more pervasive than in any other sector where goods are traded, but here the government's objective has been not so much the promotion of commercial objectives as the preservation of the way of life of the small farmer.[4] U.S. government preparations for

---

[3]See generally Ellis W. Hawley, *The New Deal and the Problem of Monopoly* (Princeton: Princeton University Press, 1966).

[4]Throughout most of U.S. history, farmers -- the heirs to the Jeffersonian tradition -- regarded themselves as virtually indistinguishable from "the people." William Jennings Bryan and other agrarian populist spokesmen extolled the notion that the independent farmer was the nation's real businessman, an exemplar of the truest (continued...)

national defense have spawned entire new industries, -- the dyestuffs industry, an offshoot of U.S. mobilization for World War I, the titanium industry for the Korean War, and the semiconductor industry, which benefitted from the U.S. Minuteman missile and Apollo programs of the 1960s. But these spinoffs have remained unacknowledged children to policymakers rather than recognized as conscious products of national policy. With these exceptions, the role of the Federal government in the economic arena has been primarily to regulate, not to promote, U.S. commerce.

In this century the federal government's public policy emphasis has been on the promotion of "competition" as an end in itself rather than the promotion of individual competitors. This philosophy can be traced back to the 1880s and 1890s, when public alarm over industrial concentration and the abuse of private power fostered an antitrust movement which culminated in the enactment of federal antitrust legislation and the creation of the Federal Trade Commission.[5] Since the days of Theodore

---

4(...continued)
commercial virtues. It is not without irony, therefore, that U.S. farmers organized this country's first and arguably most successful foray into industrial policy, securing their own cabinet post in 1889 and lobbying successfully for federal legislation establishing grass-roots R&D facilities (the Federal experimental stations), subsidies for education in agronomy, and land-grant colleges; by the 1920s, farmers had won general acceptance of the notion that agriculture was "a special national interest requiring a special public policy." Under the New Deal, the federal government began administering a system of price supports making the government a partner in a comprehensive system of production regulation. At present, various U.S. farm sectors benefit from export subsidies, preferential loans from the Commodity Credit Corporation, import protection (sugar, dairy products, livestock) research and development assistance, and price supports (grains, dairy products). All of these activities have coexisted with an enthusiastic embrace of free trade, laissez-faire principles by many spokesmen for the farm sector. See generally Saloutes and Hicks, *Agricultural Discontent in the Midwest, 1900-1939* (Madison, 1951), cited in Hofstadter (1955), pp. 122-29; Robert H. Wiebe, *The Search for Order, 1877-1920* (New York; Hill and Wang, 1967) pp. 126-27.

5In the years after the Civil War, the United States experienced a virtual explosion of entrepreneurial activity, much of it driven by individuals and small businesses. Concurrently, enormous concentrations of economic power occurred as railroads acquired a quasi-monopoly grip on many agrarian regions in the West and the Midwest, holding companies facilitated the consolidation of manufacturing sectors into "trusts" (cartels), and large financial empires were built. The onset of a succession of depressions (in 1883-85 and the depression which followed the Panic

(continued...)

Roosevelt and William Howard Taft, U.S. presidents have jousted with "big business," breaking up "trusts" and concentrations of industrial power in the name of the public interest.[6] This anti-big business tradition remained alive and well in the America of the 1970s and 1980s, although the long-ago world in which such attitudes had germinated and taken root -- in which the United States was isolated from other economies, to a considerable degree, by two oceans and a high tariff wall -- had ceased to exist. This heritage explains the longstanding federal policy of confrontation with America's foremost companies and industries -- Franklin Roosevelt's battles with the "Money Power" of Wall Street; General Motors' circumspect behavior in the 1960s when it felt that it could not increase market share without provoking an antitrust challenge; the Justice Department's efforts to curb IBM in the 1970s, the break-up by the courts of AT&T; and the dismemberment of America's largest international airline under the "open skies" policies of the 1970s.

During the same era that antitrust principles were becoming embedded in the American political, commercial and legal landscape, systems of industrial organization which were quite different were evolving in Europe and East Asia, without provoking the sort of popular reaction that

---

[5](...continued)
of 1893) saw the failure of many small businesses and short line railroads, and in many cases their absorption by big business. These developments produced a backlash against big business which not only drove the politics of that era but became firmly and perhaps permanently embedded in the American political tradition. A curious duality of attitude toward economic endeavor evolved, which continued to extol unbridled entrepreneuralism and economic growth but condemned its natural consequence, "bigness." An Illinois Central Railroad official observed ruefully at the end of the last century that "The people are in favor of building a new road and do what they can to promote it [but] after it is built and fixed, then the policy of the people is usually in opposition." The Sherman Antitrust Act, "seeming to appear from nowhere. . .outlawed monopoly in stern, sweeping, imprecise language" reflecting a consensus which had formed during the preceding decade. The Sherman Act became law in 1890, and was buttressed by enactment of the Clayton Act and the Federal Trade Commission Act in 1914. Wiebe, *Search for Order* (1967) p. 46.

[6]In 1911, a watershed year in the development of American industrial organization, enforcement of the Sherman Act broke up three major industrial groups -- American *keiretsu*, as it were -- Standard Oil of New Jersey, the American Tobacco Company, and Du Pont Nemours. In the election of 1912, the demand for federal regulation of business was the single most important issue in the campaign.. Alfred D. Chandler, *Scale and Scope: The Dynamics of Industrial Capitalism*(Cambridge and London: Harvard University Press, 1990) p. 78.

occurred in this country.[7] In Germany, particularly after World War I, so-called I.G.s (cartels) and *Konzerne* were consolidating the most important manufacturing sectors (steel, chemicals, shipping, shipbuilding, machinery, nonferrous metals) into enormous, diversified, vertically and horizontally integrated conglomerates which were able to dominate regional markets and raise massive pools of capital.[8] Similarly, in Japan, at virtually the same moment that the Sherman Act became law in the U.S., the Meiji government was providing extensive commercial benefits to large merchant houses which helped them to evolve into sprawling industrial groups, the so-called *zaibatsu*, that dominated Japan's strategic industries through the end of World War II.[9] To be sure, there was a parallel contemporaneous movement in the United States to promote comparable concentrations of economic power, but it foundered during the New Deal, largely as a result of the divisions within American society and of the separation of powers within the U.S. government.[10] The

---

[7]The most marked similar reaction abroad has been the student demonstrations against the power of the *chaebols* in Korea in recent years.

[8]The *Konzerne* were combinations of entities bound together through cross-shareholdings of stock; the *Interessengemeinschaften* (I.G.s) or "communities of interest" were cartels affiliated through agreements. Both types of entities cooperated in marketing, research, and materials acquisition. The I.G.s also pooled profits. Chandler, *Scale and Scope*, p. 506-07.

[9]The government provided these entities (Mitsui, Mitsubishi, Sumitomo, Furukawa and others) with monopoly licenses and other commercial privileges, capital, and occasionally with pilot plants to facilitate entry into new industries. Johnson, *MITI and the Japanese Miracle*, p. 85.

[10]The experience of government planning and management of the economy by the War Industries Board during World War I fostered a group of advocates for systematic, rational organization and planning of the economy and the creation of large entities capable of maximizing scale economies. This movement was split, however -- hopelessly as it turned out -- between left-leaning individuals who saw the direction of such activity as the proper role of the government, and industrialists and businessmen who believed that such results should be achieved not by the State but by "associations" of businessmen who could reduce "cutthroat" competition and make rational planning decisions. Oscillating between these two camps, and cognizant of an intense public antipathy to organized business interests blamed for the Depression, the Roosevelt administration was never able to develop an "intellectually coherent and logically consistent set of business policies." Most of its excursions into industrial policy were struck down by a hostile Supreme Court. Hawley (1966) pp. 13-14.

enactment of the Glass-Steagall Act in 1934, which barred commercial banks from investment banking, made it more difficult for U.S. banks to speculate with "other Peoples' money," but it also ensured that no U.S. counterpart of the bank-led Japanese and German industrial groups could evolve. By the mid-1940s, proponents of antitrust had prevailed over industrial concentration not only in the U.S., but momentarily, at least, in Japan and Germany as well, where the U.S. occupation authorities dismembered the *zaibatsu* and *Konzerne* and established antitrust regimes patterned on the U.S. mode. Both countries -- Japan in particular -- experienced something of a counter-reformation thereafter, but in the immediate postwar decades of American hegemony it was politic to pay at least public obeisance to U.S. antitrust doctrine, while industrial groups analogous to the *zaibatsu, Konzerne,* and I.G.s were quietly and gradually reconstituted.[11] During the same period a move toward industrial concentration was evident throughout most of the advanced and developing world, as governments sought to promote large entities -- national champions -- to compete in the international arena. By the 1990s, the American policy and business communities were beginning to awaken to the existence of a series of interconnected problems that had been fermenting for a long time -- the challenge of the *keiretsu*, the gobbling up of small U.S. firms by European and Japanese industrial groups, and the lack of agreed international rules governing competition policy. Our less than coherent response to these challenges, to date, is as reflective of

[11]MITI Vice Minister Naohiro Amaya's famous comment in 1980 that the Antimonopoly Law was an alien protein injected into the body of Japan -- producing an allergic reaction -- is shared by many Japanese businessmen. (*Bungei Shungei*, December 1980). The prewar *zaibatsu* were partially reconstituted (as strengthened *keiretsu*) with government encouragement as a response to the liberalization of foreign investment after 1967. The German federal government has enforced a strict antitrust policy since the early postwar era, but its business community never fully accepted what one German executive characterized as a process of "fragmentation and unravelling" of the industrial structure as a result of such policies. With the coming of the Single Market, the German Cartel Office has lost much of its authority, and huge German industrial groups have engaged in an intense period of consolidation and expansion. See "Die Absatzpolitik der Deutschen Stahlindustrie" in *Continentaler Stahlmarkt* (June 1976); *Die Zeit* (November 11, 1988) (JPRS-EST-89-018); *Hamburger Abendblatt* (September 9, 1989); *Kölner Stadt-Anzeiger* (November 15, 1988); "Cartel Germany: Competition in our Own Ranks is Being Curbed", in *Der Spiegel* (August 26, 1991) (FBIS-WEU-91-192).

longstanding, unresolved contradictions in American attitudes toward industrial organization as it is of "unfair" foreign actions.[12]

The United States does not lack government entities or public officials cognizant of these issues, or of the need to develop a response to international competitive pressures. They are most commonly found at the state level, or in the Congress representing constituent interests.[13] To a degree, the divisions between the States and the Federal government, between the Congress and the Executive, and between the government and the business community -- which differentiates the U.S. government from those of most other major trading countries with respect to the institutional foundations of its policies -- are impediments to developing a rational approach. But one must not judge our institutions or traditions too harshly[14]; our historical experience would not, by itself, necessarily have produced a government which is generally oblivious, and sometimes hostile, to its own international commercial interests; the United States, is somewhat similar in its structure to the Federal Republic of Germany, yet it differs in this regard from the Federal Republic. Other factors are obviously also at work.

---

[12]The problem, in a nutshell, is how to "reconcile the practical necessity with the individualistic ideal, some arrangement that would preserve the industrial order, necessarily based on a high degree of collective organization, and yet would preserve America's democratic heritage at the same time." Hawley (1966) p. 473.

[13]At the local level, employment matters -- not only the numbers employed, but the kind of employment. State universities, publicly funded research centers, and cooperation with private companies are all the subject of intensive state programs. At the federal level, however, while Congressional initiatives exist to set up commercially relevant technology programs with federal funding, most of the research actually being funded at the federal level must, as a matter of policy, have no direct commercial applicability. See generally U.S. Office of Technology Assessment, *Technology, Innovation and Regional Economic Development* (Washington, D.C.: U.S. Government Printing Office, 1984).

[14]Indeed, the inefficient, disorganized seeming chaos which is our form of government is also a guarantor of our pluralistic (some would say atomistic) way of life. Churchill called democracy the worst form of government but for all the others. Nevertheless, in terms of the impact on competitiveness, our form of democracy, with its marked dislike of collective action, is a distinct disadvantage, in competition with the other democracies.

Philosophical Precepts

The Doctrine of Laissez-Faire. The manner in which democracy is manifested in the United States, with a limited central government circumscribed by checks and balances, has over time become merged in our national consciousness with our guiding laissez-faire economic philosophy.[15] Michael Novak has written of the close interrelationship of the free operation of the marketplace and the rise of democracy.[16] The events in Eastern Europe in the last few years appear to validate this view, and to us it is altogether natural that a democratic system and a laissez-faire ideology should emerge simultaneously in countries like Poland and Hungary. But democracy and laissez-faire are separable concepts. The nations whose trade policies are the subject of this study are all democracies, yet all differ substantially from the United States in their view of the proper role of the government in the commercial arena. Indeed, for a country known for its pragmatism, the United States is remarkably doctrinaire when it comes to its trade policy and to policies affecting industry, and has become more so during the past several decades. This philosophy not only guides actions but colors its view of how others conduct their policies.[17] In contrast to the 1920s and 1930s,

---

[15]One recent observer points out that since World War II an "extremely potent alliance" of Cold Warriors, businessmen and traditionalist economists has combined to produce a rigid adherence to laissez-faire principles in successive U.S. administrations: "The Cold Warriors like American markets to be as open as possible because this is part of the glue of alliance, in which the low politics of trade takes second place to the high politics of national security. . . . The private capitalists like global laissez-faire for the obvious reason: they wish to escape the discipline of national regulation. Orthodox economists complete the triad by preaching that the least regulated market is the most efficient one, and they certify the scientific soundness of laissez-faire. Neoclassical economists, industrialists and investment bankers flow in and out of government jobs, where they share the premises of the Cold Warriors about America's hegemonic responsibilities. American industry, in turn, supports researchers known for respectable, internationalist thinking, which is to say laissez-faire. All these links create a club of like-minded people that marginalizes or excludes heretics." Robert Kuttner, *The End of Laissez-Faire* (New York: Albert Knopf, 1991), p. 20.

[16]Michael Novak, *The Spirit of Democratic Capitalism* (Lanham, Md.: Madison Books, 1991.

[17] The elevation of laissez-faire ideology over empirical observation produces a peculiar analytic tautology -- that is, that because laissez-faire competition

(continued...)

when a freewheeling debate over industrial policy and economic organization was waged by some of the best American minds of that era, the debate in our own time has been stuck fast in the hardened concrete of laissez-faire doctrine. Many issues simply cannot be discussed without provoking an outcry; the utterance of the words "industrial policy," for example, usually provokes a chorus of criticism that this is an inappropriate term to use in a discussion of U.S. public policies. The impact of this doctrinaire rigidity can be seen in America's handling of trade issue after trade issue. The United States automobile industry has faced competitive difficulties since the end of the 1970's, but, for ideological reasons, there could be no real inquiry by the government into the various causes of this problem -- this was regarded as an inappropriate subject for the government to discuss. The government would not permit itself to consider whether environmental or safety regulation, antitrust policy or even lapses in management judgment, had an impact on the international competitive position of the industry; instead, it merely analyzed whether imports were causing injury; if so, the sole remedy was import restrictions. Even this narrow analysis divided different kinds of trade-related injury -- injury from imports that are unfairly traded, injury from imports whether or not unfairly traded, and injury from the closure of foreign markets preventing exports from the United States.

The central irony of this restrictive analytical framework is that it causes this free-trading country to rely solely on trade policy instruments in seeking remedies for industry. As a result, the system tends to be "protectionist" in its purest form, undiluted by the admixture of other policy tools. This is true even though the protection is ineffective. But because the problems which exist in fact as well as in political reality must

---

[17](...continued)
supposedly produces optimal results, if an industry or even a country enjoys economic success, it can only be because that country or industry is a good exemplar of the laissez-faire model. Factual observations and evidence which may contradict this view are dismissed as "anecdotes." The results, from an intellectual perspective, have been bizarre; for example, orthodox economists, viewing the rapid growth of neomercantilist states in East Asia -- which have been characterized by extensive government intervention and high levels of trade protection -- have concluded, often with little first-based knowledge of these countries' policies, that success must be attributable to open markets and government noninvolvement in the economy, because only through the rigid and uncompromising application of laissez-faire doctrine could such spectacular results have been achieved. For a critique of such thinking, see Robert Wade, *Governing the Market: Economic Theory and the Role of Government in East Asian Industrialization* (Princeton: Princeton University Press, 1990).

be dealt with by some action, and trade restrictions often are the only policy tool available. Thus, a free trade intent yields all too often a protectionist result, in the purest sense of that term, with protection forming not an element in a conscious industrial policy, but simply a substitute for such a policy. In the case of automobiles, the inability of successive administrations to admit publicly that there was an industrial problem as well as a trade problem -- or even that a trade remedy had been put into place at the request of the United States -- has resulted in the anomaly that the government of the exporting country, Japan, periodically makes the determination as to how much of what kind of exports are politically tolerable in the United States at a given time. American automobile manufacturers are deprived of any certainty as to the duration or the efficacy of even this remedy, making planning of investments difficult, if not impossible, to the extent that public policy determines the investment environment.

The Provision of Equity. The American embrace of laissez-faire is powerfully reinforced by another embedded view, that of the proper role of government as an impartial arbiter of "fairness" between competing individuals, groups and enterprises, rather than as a promoter of any particular interest or cause. An integral part of the American democratic system is that rights and obligations are the product of adjustments between competing interests, often achieved through litigation, rather than through government regulation (as in Europe) or administrative guidance (Japan). Americans resist the ordering of their lives by government fiat, and they also harbor a very strong belief in the provision of equality of opportunity -- that there should be no government-enforced hierarchy of preferences or privilege, whether among classes of individuals (other than to remedy past inequities) or among industrial sectors. The notion of the government as an impartial referee has roots in the American past which are centuries old, but it became firmly enshrined in American economic thinking during the presidency of Theodore Roosevelt, where it has remained ever since, with homage being duly paid by successive Republican and Democratic administrations down to our own time.[18] The idea of the neutrality of the state has become

---

[18]Although Roosevelt was the first major U.S. leader to articulate the concept of the "neutrality of the powerful state," the ideal of free competition, without state backing of any particular group, was already widely accepted in American life. The concept is based on the competitive model of classic economics, a system advocated by Adam Smith, John Stuart Mill, Alfred Marshall, John Bates Clark and others; it was "reinforced by the frontier process and eventually became embedded

(continued...)

merged with economic laissez-faire concepts to produce an appealing, but not necessarily accurate conclusion -- that if competition among enterprises is "free" *and* is waged according to rules that are "fair" (enforced by an impartial state), the result will not only be equitable, but an optimal economic outcome. As Herbert Hoover articulated this notion in the election campaign of 1928:

> *It is as if we set a race. We through free and universal education provide the training for the runners; we give to them an equal start; we provide in the government the umpire of the fairness of the race. The winner is he who shows the most conscientious training, the greatest ability, and the greatest character.*[19]

The political ideology of government neutrality, merged with hands-off economic ideology, has fostered a policy climate which yields statements imputed to Administration sources such as "it doesn't matter whether this country produces computer chips or potato chips." While individual policymakers deny articulating or endorsing this particular sentiment, the record of recent U.S. government action (and inaction) suggests that our trade policy could be accurately represented by the statue of Justice, blind to all who come before her, save only for the unwelcome (to policy makers) intrusion of political reality (of which more is said below).

Distrust of Government. Distrust of government, or in this case, more accurately, the distrust of the legislative and executive branches, each for the other, has led to the evolution of a rigid and legalistic framework for considering which trade actions should be taken. Congress, which is generally regarded as an institution incapable of taking individual decisions without excessive influence being brought to bear on behalf of constituents, or of exercising any policy leadership at all, is considered by itself as well as by the Executive Branch as a reckless and unstoppable juggernaut in the field of trade. It is believed that the political dynamic of Congress' representation of constituencies leads to protectionist horsetrading of votes in favor of restrictions, and that the ghost of the

---

[18](...continued)
in American folklore. Economists taught it to their students; politicians paid homage to it; businessmen gave it lip service when they engaged in oratory for public consumption. . . ." Ellis W. Hawley, *The New Deal and the Problem of Monopoly* (Princeton, 1966) p. 47; Richard Hofstadter, *The Age of Reform* (Vantage, 1955) pp. 234-51.

[19]Cited in R. Hofstadter, *The American Political Tradition* (1947) p. 38.

Smoot-Hawley tariff is ever ready to rise from the grave into which it was consigned four years after its enactment (in the creation of the Reciprocal Trade Agreements Program in 1934).

It is far from clear that this picture of the Congress is accurate. There has been no serious move to impose across-the-board trade restrictions since the Mills Bill in 1970.[20] Even the trade-restrictive legislation which has passed both houses in recent decades has arguably been designed to enhance the Executive's negotiating leverage rather than to actually result in a legislated comprehensive program of protection (although such initiatives have been served as rallying points for groups seeking more general protection.)[21] Even at the height of concern over the United States trade imbalance in the 1980s, the chief Congressional vehicle for bringing about import restrictions (the Gephardt amendment) never received Congressional approval. In fact, it could be argued that the effect of the amendment was positive, as it served to force the Executive and America's trading partners to reach an agreement for a realignment of exchange rates, widely considered by the economics profession and the business community as a very favorable development.[22]

Nevertheless, the fear of a Congress run amok, and more practically the wish of the elected representatives themselves to divert pressures from

---

[20]The Mills Bill, which would have placed direct restrictions on textiles and footwear imports, and contained a mathematical trigger to impose quotas on other imported goods, was actually a gambit by Ways and Means Committee Chairman Mills -- generally a free trade advocate -- to generate pressure on Japan to negotiate a VRA in textiles that would obviate the need for protectionist legislation. The Mills Bill was ultimately killed by the Congress itself through the addition of sweeping social security and welfare titles that made it too massive to survive the legislative conference process. For an account of the Mills Bill see I.M. Destler, H. Fukui and H. Sato, *The Textile Wrangle; Conflict in Japanese-American Relations*, 1969-71 (Ithaca: Cornell University Press 1979), Chapter 11.

[21]In 1986, a textile industry bill that would reduce existing quota levels passed the House and Senate, but this bill was originally designed to stiffen the Administration's position in upcoming negotiations over the Multifiber Arrangement. Protectionist provisions were later added for copper and footwear; the legislation, as was anticipated by one and by all, was ultimately vetoed by the President.

[22]Secretary of the Treasury Jim Baker was able to negotiate the Plaza Accord among key Western powers both because the specter of "Congressional protectionism" freed his hand within a highly ideological Administration and because the other trading nations required continued unimpeded access to the U.S. market. See note 24.

protection away from the hallways outside their offices, has resulted in the delegation of authority to the Executive Branch to put trade restrictions in place. However, the Executive Branch is known to worry primarily about broad concerns and not to dwell too much on the health of any given industry. This issue it considers outside of its terms of reference. Other concerns, such as consumer impact, inflation, and the conduct foreign relations occupy it. Thus, Congress and the Executive can rely on any given Administration not to grant excessive protection (at least not knowingly). The common wisdom is that the Administration will be more resistant to taking protectionist (or even aggressive) trade actions than would the Congress.

However, this tendency toward inaction on the part of the Executive leads to a buildup of political pressures on the Congress for action. Congress in turn responds by granting the Executive Branch authority (which it does not seek or perhaps even need) to deal with trade problems. It inserts into these trade laws time limits and requirements for action (always with an escape) which tries to make the Administration more aggressive. As in the creation of a court system, the Congress has attempted to deal with the pressures that it feels from constituents by creating rights of action -- procedures for relief -- with access criteria under which relief is more or less mandatory. It is the result of these pressures for action that the rest of the world views as the United States penchant for "unilateral" action.

At this point it is worth a word or two about America's legalistic approach to problem solving. It is often said that America has too many lawyers. This is true primarily because America's people do not wish to be regulated by government fiat, whether by Executive decree or by legislation. It was the intent of the framers of the Constitution that most rights and obligations should be left to be determined by litigation as a final resort.[23] This leaves much more scope for individualism, although

---

[23]Article III of the Constitution, which established a separate judiciary branch of government, was part of an effort to secure the support of "men of property" for the Constitution. These gentlemen wanted to ensure that their property rights would be protected by an independent judiciary which would ensure the sanctity of contracts and to settle private disputes impartially, based on mutually agreed principles and procedures, whose decisions would be accepted by all parties. Similarly, the establishment of diversity jurisdiction in the federal courts (which enabled out-of-state litigants to remove cases from state courts to a federal court for a presumably more neutral adjudication) has been viewed as an attempt to open the way for commercial expansion beyond the Appalachians by providing a safeguard for outside commercial interests against local and class biases. Frank, (continued...)

there may be frustration over the degree of litigiousness of the society and over the inability of its leaders (even its judicial leaders) to make choices, to draw lines, to distinguish between those kinds of conduct that will be permissible, those which will be encouraged, and those which will be proscribed. This aspect of the American experience is an important one; one of the secrets of the healthy functioning of our society, not unlike the way group loyalty explains the effective functioning of Japanese society. However, this does not mean that this legalistic approach is appropriate in all circumstances; when it is applied excessively in the area of the conduct of trade policy, it can result, quite simply, in the virtual abdication of governmental function. The granting of equity becomes a substitute for decision-making. It excuses intervention by the government notwithstanding laissez-faire philosophy; however, given the context and nature of such interventions -- essentially adjudicative, and remedial -- such actions have haphazard results when viewed from the perspective of the nation's commercial interests.

The Role of Politics

At one time this section would have occupied a much larger portion of this text, dealing extensively with trade policy for benzenoid chemicals, scotch whiskey bottled in the United States, dairy products, footwear, steel, textiles and apparel, peanuts, and other products having strong domestic constituencies reflected in powerful lobbies in the Congress. But over time, and with the effects of adjustment within the United States as the world economy has become increasingly integrated, the special programs for individual industries with special cases to argue has diminished. This has also evolved because over the course of the last 61 years the Congress has become increasingly disengaged from directly legislating the level of trade barriers. In the place of legislated protection, the Congress has increasingly enacted special, but usually generic (that is, not product-sector specific) provisions to prod the Executive into being more aggressive in implementing the nation's trade laws. This process was fueled in the mid-1980s by the very large over-valuation of the dollar and the consequent enormity of the nation's trade deficit. Business leaders who approached the Administration complaining about an exchange rate which gave their competitors a 30-40 percent cost edge generally were brushed off, "told, in essence, that they were cry-babies

---

[23](...continued)
"Historical Bases of the Federal Judicial System" in 13 *Law and Contemporary Problems* (1948).

and should stop asking for government help against the workings of the marketplace."[24] Not surprisingly, not finding a hearing at the White House, many of those executives turned to the Congress. The Congressional reaction was to offer the Gephardt amendment, which would have imposed across-the-board restrictions on several trade surplus nations to force down the bilateral imbalances. The Administration's reaction was to avoid losing control over setting the direction of trade policy by taking dramatic action to rectify the exchange rate misalignment and by self-initiating several "Section 301" cases in September, 1985, directed against market barriers in several foreign countries.[25]

The initial movement toward easing of the trade imbalance was not followed by a lessening of Congressional concern over obtaining further market access abroad, however. Rather, interest has intensified. The 1984 Trade Act had put into place a requirement for reporting on foreign barriers in the form a report from the Executive to the Congress called the National Trade Estimates.[26] In the 1988 Trade and Competitiveness Act, Congress put this document to practical use. It was to form the basis for the Administration to consider which barriers or other trade distortions would be ripe for 301 cases.[27] This process, which mandated the initiation of 301 cases was known as "Super-301", and for one year the Administration followed its prescription. As a result of Congress' decisions in the 1980s, Special-301 provisions were put into place in order to protect intellectual property and access to foreign telecommunications markets. It was the Congress' intent that these provisions be utilized.

If the Executive could not find its way clear to use the tools Congress had provided to it, an additional source of Congressional pressure was

---

[24] I.M. Destler, *American Trade Politics: System Under Stress* (Washington and New York; Institute for International Economics, 1986) p. 105.

[25] Secretary of the Treasury Baker secured a commitment from the Finance Minister of Japan, Germany, France and the U.K. to work for a weaker dollar, and to intervene jointly in foreign exchange market to make this happen. Announcement of the *Ministers of Finance and Central Bank Governors of France, Germany, Japan, the United Kingdom and the United States* (September 22, 1985).

[26] Section 303, Trade and Tariff Act of 1984. USTR compiles the National Trade Estimates based on information gathered from other government agencies, U.S. embassies abroad, and the private sector. An idea of Senator Lloyd Bentsen, this initiative was based on the national intelligence estimates used for purposes of formulating foreign and defense policies.

[27] Section 1304, Omnibus Trade and Competitiveness Act of 1988.

found, grounded in the fact that all significant trade agreements (that is, those which require implementation) must be approved either in advance by the Congress or approved in implementing legislation. This requirement stems from the Constitutionally mandated division of powers among the different branches of the Federal Government. Only the President can negotiate international agreements for the United States. But it is the Congress which has been given the Commerce Power. Thus, to a large degree, only Congress can implement what the President commits to in negotiations with other countries. Since most aspects of trade policy are influenced to some degree by international agreement which must be implemented through legislation, the Congress is given an additional means of shaping American trade policy. But experience with this procedure has indicated that, under the system of checks and balances, the Congress can only influence, not fully control, the direction of policy.

Thus, even with the lesser role of Congress in the trade field generally deriving from the diminution of the level of tariffs -- once a significant source of legislative power -- and despite a committee system grown increasingly unwieldy, there is still the potential for Congress influencing U.S. trade policy to a greater extent than it does now. There is no immediate sign that it is about to organize itself to do so, however.[28] But the Executive must be ever conscious that if it strays too far from the politically acceptable path, there may be a price to pay with the Congress in terms of failure to get its agreements passed[29] or that it might attract further Congressionally-mandated constraints in future legislation.

---

[28]There is no Congressional Trade Office similar to the Congressional Budget Office which gives Congress the full ability to deal with details of the Federal Budget. It must rely on a highly talented, but very small, group of professional trade staff. But even more important than lack of staff is Congressional self-restraint, which is considerable. Congressmen and Senators generally wish to influence the direction of Executive Branch leadership. They do not wish to supplant it.

[29]It should be remembered that for a long period in the history of the President's trade agreements program, most agreements that were not approved by the Congress in advance failed to be accepted at all, and remained a dead letter or were neutered. This was true of the International Trade Organization (ITO) in the 1940s, the World Trade Organization (WTO) in the 1950s, the two nontariff trade agreements entered into by the United States in the Kennedy Round of Trade Negotiations in the 1970s (relating to the American Selling Price system of customs valuation and the Antidumping Code), and the U.S.-USSR trade agreement also in the 1970s.

One should not over-emphasize points of difference among the countries studied in this book, nor the differences between those countries and the United States. All countries' governments, for example, feel political pressures and must react to them to some degree. All of the countries which are the subject of this study suffer from some twinges of laissez-faire idealism, some much more so than others, and feel a need to justify or hide what they do that departs too far from the precepts shared by most mainstream academic economists. But no country has a mix of forces at work quite like that characteristic of the United States. Few are divided against themselves by internal organization to the extent that we are. Nowhere else is there the same devotion to legalistic mechanisms for making policy choices, which most others would consider an abdication of governmental responsibility. None believe more fully in the sanctity of allowing market forces to work, while aggressively intervening to prevent interruption or distortion of those forces by private combinations. Few have resisted domestic political pressures more successfully. When examining the policies of others, it is necessary to remember that however correct we view our own policies, that these are, when compared with those of others, arrived at in a most unique manner and are therefore, as could be expected, highly idiosyncratic as viewed by others. The prism through which we view their decisions introduces some distortions of its own. These differences give rise on many occasions to substantial conflicts. Thus, it is not only what we do and what they do that brings about confrontations, but how we go about the conduct of policy, and how we and others view each other's actions.

AN ASSESSMENT OF HOW WELL THE U.S. SYSTEM OF TRADE LAWS HAS WORKED

The GATT system, which is a reflection of U.S. domestic trade laws, is designed to provide a balance. The system is designed to foster trade liberalization, but if there are rapid, injurious changes in trade flows, and adjustments are required by industries, temporary protection can be granted.[30] Moreover, if there are instances of injurious subsidization or dumping, self-help measures in the form of additional or offsetting duties may be imposed on imports.[31] With few other exceptions, including national security and protection of intellectual property, barriers at the

---

[30]GATT Article XIX, the "Escape Clause".

[31]GATT Article VI, Antidumping and Countervailing Duties.

border to trade in goods are to be eliminated. Quotas are banned.[32] Tariffs are reduced through negotiations and contractually bound at what are -- after decades of negotiations -- very low levels (averaging about 3% in the major industrialized countries). The GATT framework is permissive, in that it *allows* restrictions to be placed on imports in the exceptional circumstances outlined above, it does not *require* its contracting parties to do so when the conditions are met. Notionally, there is not a lot involved in the formulation of trade policy under either the GATT or the U.S. system. The reigning ideology provides that it is imperative to maintain open borders, particularly one's own, but provides little, if any, additional direction.

This has led inadvertently, in effect, to the privatization of trade policy formulation in the United States. Although the statutes provide that the Secretary of Commerce must initiate an investigation whenever he or she has reason to believe that there is injury being caused by foreign subsidies or by dumping[33], it is extremely rare that this is done other than on the basis of a complaint by a domestic industry. Laissez-faire philosophy does not provide guidance as to what should be done so much as guidance as to what should not be done. A series of administrations have been passive, awaiting events. Trade policy could be said to be based on whatever comes into the Executive Branch's in-basket. Like the court system after which it is modeled, in fact (although this is not required by law) there must be a case or controversy before the Executive will act. This passivity is supported by an implicit political rationale as well. It is much harder for a bureaucrat or a political appointee to get into trouble for inaction or omission than it is for acting. What may be seen as gratuitous interference by a public official in economic matters carries high risks; if there is not a successful competitive outcome, the government must then accept some of the responsibility. This it is reluctant to do.

The United States lost its color television industry in the 1960s and 1970s due to a series of factors, including unfair trade acts such as dumping and anticompetitive practices, but there was never a court of inquiry to determine what failures in public policy might have contributed to the demise of this U.S. industry, nor will there be. It is not considered the business of government to mind the country's industrial base (unless there is a strikingly clear connection to immediate national security needs). Private parties choose when to approach the government

---

[32]GATT Article XI.

[33]19 U.S.C. § 1671; 19 U.S.C. § 1673.

on an issue concerning harm due to foreign competition and they choose the method of redress which they wish to seek. The highly legalistic trade policy system provides several individual windows at which a complaint may be filed.

Some companies, for their own reasons, decide not to utilize the system of trade remedies at all, reaching their own accommodations with the realities of foreign competition. An individual firm can prosper by exiting an industry, by joint venturing, by selling out to a foreign firm, or licensing its technology. Such decisions may be colored because the firm in question views it as inappropriate to work with the government on trade issues, reflecting the general feeling of antagonism between industry and government. This is a natural condition, perhaps, between those regulated for domestic policy purposes and the regulators. However, it has also been fueled by a canard spread by several American presidents that government is certainly a part of the problem but does not have much to offer in the way of being part of the solution. Thus, where no petition to the government is presented, whatever issues might arise, it is generally considered that these must be matters in which there is no public interest involved. Without a petition, all that is involved is private transaction.[34] Thus, in trade matters, the firms in an industry (and sometimes the unions representing workers in the industry) are left the threshold determination of whether the public interest is involved in a particular area of loss to foreign competition. Unfortunately, the past several decades have given us many cases which underscore the inadequacies inherent in this mode of dealing with competitive problems.

The Loss of the Indigenous Color Television Industry

In the case of color televisions, the U.S. industry faced what proved to be a lethal threat -- a group of Japanese producers who worked at times in concert, and arguably in violation of both Japanese and U.S. law, to penetrate the U.S. market through a variety of anticompetitive acts, including price fixing in the Japanese and U.S. markets, market allocation,

---

[34]There has been some shifts in recent years. With the enactment of the Omnibus Trade and Competitiveness Act of 1988, the President may prohibit foreign acquisitions of U.S. companies which might adversely affect national security. (Section 5021 of the Act, amending the Defense Production Act of 1950, 50 U.S.C. App. 2158 et.seq.).

dumping, and circumvention of U.S. customs rules.[35] Confronting this challenge, not only did some key private American players absent themselves from the fray, but those that did invoke trade remedies did so on a piecemeal and not always well-conceived basis rather than as part of an industry-wide action plan. By one count, a total of fifty-seven separate administrative proceedings were conducted between 1962 and 1981 arising out of the U.S.-Japan conflict in color televisions; at one point, in 1976, U.S. imports of televisions were being investigated under five different U.S. remedial statutes.[36]

The quantity of litigation, by itself, proved to have no significant bearing on events, reflecting industry fragmentation, bureaucratic inertia and lack of knowledge, and the inadequacy of the remedies themselves. Three U.S. television companies attacked Japan's rebate of indirect taxes on exports (the so-called commodities tax) as a countervailable subsidy.[37] Most persons knowledgeable with the GATT and U.S. trade law felt that this was a case which should never have been filed because of the futility of doing so; the GATT permitted the application of countervailing duties to the rebate of direct taxes (taxes on income and property) but not necessarily of indirect taxes (e.g., state and local sales taxes, value added taxes). The countervailing duty action was not only doomed but divisive;[38] the Japanese rebate of the commodity tax was uncomfortably similar to tax benefits enjoyed by some U.S. television producers with respect to their offshore operations in Mexico and Taiwan, and the petition was the overture for a bitter internecine fight over the tax treatment of offshore assembly operations which pitted American

---

[35]These activities were exhaustively detailed in documents seized from the companies by the Japan Fair Trade Commission and in JFTC analyses. For a synopsis, see Kozo Yamamura and Jay Vandenburg, "Japan's Rapid Growth Policy on Trial: The Television Case," in K. Yamamura, ed. *Policy and Law Issues of the Japanese Economy* (Seattle: University of Washington, 1987).

[36]Yamamura and Vandenberg (1986), p. 263.

[37]The petition was filed by Zenith, Magnavox and Sylvania. "Indirect" taxes are taxes on goods as distinguished from taxes on people which, under the accepted taxonomy, are considered direct taxes.

[38]See generally John Jackson, *World Trade and the Law of GATT* (Charlottesville: Michie, 1969) pp. 384-85.

management and unions against each other.[39] The Treasury Department rejected the countervailing duty petition in 1976. The fact the petitioners may have had a valid argument that the U.S. law and the GATT were not based on sound economic analysis was largely irrelevant in the forum chosen, in this case the Treasury Department; the Administration was not about to try through this case to overturn the GATT system, and would have had no hope of re-negotiating the world's trading rules over the short term. The issue raised by the petition was not a new one. The only solution practical as a matter of living with the existing system of international trading rules was for the United States to switch over to its own indirect tax system and adopt its own system of rebates at the border. This it was not prepared to do.

Another group of domestic television companies brought an antidumping case. This should have met with success, but because the Treasury Department had an inadequate commitment to the administration of this law, and therefore devoted little in the way of resources to it, there never was an adequate response. The case was filed in 1968; in 1971 the Tariff Commission made an affirmative finding of dumping and transmitted the case to the Treasury Department for calculation of the duties to be assessed; "amidst confusion and legal maneuvering, the Department grappled for seven years with the question of how much to assess."[40] In 1978, Treasury decided on the duties to be paid for the years 1972-73, but the decision was protested and the duties were not collected. In 1980, jurisdiction over the case and the administration of the statute were transferred to the Commerce Department, and under a negotiated settlement agreement, Japanese firms were directed to pay $66 million ($440 million was actually owed), but collection was delayed by further litigation. "In sum, the Japanese were found guilty of dumping under the [antidumping law] but the actual collection of duties had not, eleven years later, been made."[41]

---

[39]See James E. Millstein, "Decline in an Expanding Industry: Japanese Competition in Color Television" in J. Zysman and C. Tyson, eds. *American Industry in International Competition* (Ithaca and London: Cornell University Press, 1983), pp. 125-26.

[40]Yamamura and Vandenburg (1986) pp. 263-64.

[41]Yamamura and Vandenburg (1986) p. 264. Even then, dumping duties would not have made the industry whole. The duties are paid to the government. Price margins are ultimately limited. But market share, if not the entire market itself, has been ceded.

In 1970, still another group of petitioners brought an antitrust action against Japanese television producers in federal district court under an obscure statute enacted during World War I to provide a private right of action against predatory dumping.[42] In 1982, twelve years after the inception of the action, the federal district court dismissed the action on the grounds that the evidence presented by the petitioners was inadmissible under federal rules of evidence.[43] In 1983 this ruling was reversed by the U.S. Court of Appeals for the Third Circuit. The Japanese defendants sought review by the Supreme Court and in 1986, the Court reversed the Court of Appeals decision, effectively ending the case. By this time, sixteen years after the case had been initiated, the litigation had outlived much of the U.S. industry it had been intended to defend. Despite the existence of substantial evidence pointing to a concerted effort on the part of Japanese television producers to increase their share of the U.S. market through a pattern of anticompetitive conduct, the U.S. court system never gave the case a hearing on the merits.

In still another legal arena, three major television industry labor unions filed for import relief in 1971 pursuant to the Trade Expansion Act of 1962, but their petition -- while receiving a sympathetic hearing from the Tariff Commission -- was rejected on the grounds that it failed to meet narrowly-drafted, difficult-to-satisfy statutory standard.[44] Several years

---

[42]National Union Electric filed an action under the Antidumping Act of 1916 in Federal District Court in New Jersey. The Act provides for the recovery of damages by firms injured by dumping undertaken with predatory intent. Zenith subsequently brought an action under the same statute in Federal District Court in Pennsylvania. The cases were consolidated in 1975. Yamamura and Vandenburg (1986) p. 264.

[43]The petitioners' case had been based in substantial part on documents seized by the Japan Fair Trade Commission from Japanese television manufacturers, on legal documents prepared by the JFTC describing a pattern of anticompetitive conduct by the defendant firms, and on official proceedings of the U.S. International Trade Commission. The court found that all of this evidence was untrustworthy and prejudicial, and therefore inadmissible. This evidence, however, which consisted of findings by U.S. and Japanese government agencies and evidence gathered by them, clearly demonstrated a pattern of anticompetitive behavior as the part of the Japanese electronics industry. The court's ruling effectively eliminated a substantial part of the evidence supporting the plaintiffs' case and consigned it to failure. See Yamamura (1986) p. 264.

[44]Although import volume had increased from virtually nothing in 1961 to over 4.5 million units in 1970, the statute required that petitioners show that this

(continued...)

later, in the Trade Reform Act of 1974, a broader statutory provision was enacted giving import-injured industries a right to seek import relief, and in 1976 a coalition of U.S. television producers and unions successfully petitioned for relief under this statute. An orderly marketing agreement was negotiated, and quantitative limits on shipments to the United States were thus imposed. But this was very late in the competitive struggle of this industry, and the U.S. television industry as it had existed in the mid 1960s had largely disappeared; most U.S. firms had been forced to liquidate, been acquired by foreign firms, or had moved all manufacturing activities offshore. Today the U.S. has only one indigenous, U.S.-owned television manufacturer, Zenith,[45] and an estimated 60-70,000 skilled jobs have disappeared from the U.S. economy. Foreign observers watched the passivity of U.S. institutions with a mixture of fascination and incredulity as the television industry disintegrated under concerted foreign assault; one European executive joked in 1986 that "there is no engineer left in America that knows how to make a shortwave radio"; that the Americans had "given away their marketing position in their home market for a mess of pottage."[46]

No post-mortem was conducted by the Administration as to what had caused the demise of this part of the U.S. economy. In addition to the failings of government (which were many, if poorly understood), there were undoubtedly also questions to be put about failures on the part of the private sector actors, about the skills of the U.S. industry in the areas of design capability and manufacturing technology. But whatever the answers to those questions, there is probably not a more sorry chapter in the history of U.S. trade policy than the color television episode. The result was the creation of a hole in the fabric of the U.S. economy which weakened the entire electronics sector, the largest industrial employer in the United States, the consequences of which are even now not yet completely known -- although the absence of American ability to produce

---

[44](...continued)
increase was a result of "concessions granted under trade agreements." Since the tariff on television, receivers had only been ratedly reduced during the period under review to 6 percent ad valorem (from 10 percent) the Commission ruled that it could not make the requisite finding. Tariff Commission Pub. No. 436, p. 4, cited in Millstein (1983), p. 123.

[45]Zenith, together with Thomson (GE/RCA) and Philips (Magnavox) constitute the current domestic American color television industry.

[46]*NRC Handelsblad* (April 23, 1986); *De Standaard* (April 22, 1986) (JPRS-EST-86-015).

state-of-the-art flat panel displays which is a current topic of concern is undoubtedly linked to the trade policy failures of the prior decades.[47]

Since the television debacle, the Treasury has been relieved of its trade remedy responsibilities. The Congress shifted these functions to the Commerce Department in the 1979 Trade Act, as a reaction in large part to Treasury's ineptitude and lack of interest in the administration of these laws. But the defects in the U.S. trade policy process illustrated by the handling of the color television problem have not by any means been eliminated.

Automobiles

Automobiles are a large part of the industrial base of any modern industrialized nation. It is amongst the largest consumers of steel, fabrics, plastics, glass, rubber, chemicals, paints and electronics. In any input-output analysis of an economy, the automotive industry would form the nexus of many of strands of productive capability, and an analysis of this sector is essential to understanding the basic trends affecting the manufacturing economy.

At present the U.S. companies hold a declining share of their own market and of the world market. The U.S. government trade policy response has been awkward even in its best moments, and overall must be considered to be a massive failure. In the late 1970s, American car manufacturers realized that they were not cost-competitive with their Japanese competitors; they came to the U.S. government with this information, but had no particular requests to make, nor did they invoke any particular statutory relief provisions. The U.S. officials, told some of the facts, but provided with no basis on which to act, nor with any request for action, did nothing.[48] Finally, in 1980, Ford and the UAW

---

[47]A final depressing footnote on the failure of U.S. policy relates to the workers whose jobs were lost when the U.S. television industry was destroyed in the 1960s and 1970s. Under U.S. law American workers displaced by import competition were eligible for Trade Adjustment Assistance (TAA) and between 1970 and 1973 workers in the television and associated component industries filed eleven petitions for TAA, more than in any industrial sector. Every one of these petitions was denied on the grounds that the statutory criteria for relief, which were too restrictive, could not be met. Tariff Commission Pub. No. 502, cited in Millstein (1983) p. 125n.

[48]A few years earlier, there had been a dumping complaint brought by a Congressman and the United Autoworkers, but at the time, the Treasury

(continued...)

brought an import relief case, charging that imports (primarily from Japan) were increasing in such quantities as to be an important cause of serious injury, but by a 3-2 vote, the International Trade Commission found that recession rather than imports was a greater cause of injury, and on this technicality, the trade law mechanism jammed. Politics then took over as the guiding force behind U.S. trade policy; a normally free-trade Senator introduced a quota bill, and under this pressure the Japanese voluntarily agreed that the number of autos from Japan should not exceed 1.68 million units per year.[49] The VRA (voluntary restraint agreement) assured that the Japanese could continue to ship cars into the United States at a profit, could shift the value of the cars to the upper ranges, and could substitute investment in the United States for direct exports.

However, eleven years later, Detroit is still in difficulty, the Japanese car makers now have substantial manufacturing facilities in the United States, and the voluntary limits on direct exports are still in effect. In this case, from the beginning the United States government prepared no particularly useful analysis, and dealt with the issue as if it were first just a legal problem, then as if it were just a political problem, and finally as if it were solely the government of Japan's problem. If any government has had a coherent policy role in this affair, it was the Government of Japan; it wished to continue to increase its producers' share of the U.S. market without provoking a backlash, and to upgrade its product mix and profitability. It is most likely that Japan simply backed into a policy of accommodation. In any event, the result served Japan's commercial interests; at the end of 11 years of trade restrictions, its firms are stronger, and America's firms are weaker.

---

[48](...continued)
Department found that rather than selling at less than fair value in the United States, the Japanese producers were overstating their costs and thus depriving the United States Treasury of revenue. Since antidumping was administered by the same Department that was responsible for the collection of income taxes, the information was turned over to the IRS for action. If the Treasury had difficulty handling the administration of the dumping law, it understood fully how to extract tax revenues and began the lengthy process of doing so.

[49]The 1.68 million figure was set for the first year of the program. In the second year, the figure was to be 1.68 million units plus 16.5 percent of any increase in the U.S. market for autos. After that, Japan was to monitor export volume to the U.S. to avoid surges. Japan has annually announced the volume it will ship in the coming year. U.S.I.T.C. *Operation of the Trade Agreements Program*, 34th Report, USITC Pub. No. 1414 (1983), p.182.

Whether a different set of U.S. policies would have succeeded is open to question; what is certain is that it would have been difficult to do a worse job of policymaking. Through the establishment of a de facto quota under the VRA, America's consumers have been taxed an unbelievably large amount of money -- a one time a premium of about $3000 per car (when average wholesale car prices were $10,000), most of which has gone to Japan. There was no serious attempt by the industry and government to work together, and no dialogue to try to ascertain how the competitiveness of the U.S. industry could have been enhanced -- this would have been, in the eyes of the Administration, an unwarranted intrusion into the affairs of the private sector. Instead, a policy of implicitly pure protectionism -- that is, trade restrictions as the exclusive policy instrument -- was employed, although not acknowledged. This was a bastard trade policy that benefitted foreign producers, did not leave the U.S. industry better off, cost the American consumer billions of dollars, and resulted in the importation into the United States of the anticompetitive Japanese auto parts supply structure. Were it not for cases such as color televisions steel, commercial airlines and telecommunications vying for the honor, the automobile case would arguably represent the most dramatic sectoral indictment of U.S. trade policy management.

It has been said facetiously of U.S. trade negotiations that they go through five stages: (1) careful analysis and planning; (2) consultation with those affected; (3) intensive negotiations; (4) evaluation; and (5) the search for those responsible. But none of these stages occurred in the case of autos. This was the largest industry in the United States, with by far the most important production in terms of dollar amount of sales and importance as regards its place within the industrial economy; next to housing and tax payments, the car industry generated the largest flow of individual consumer dollars to a single purpose -- and, without a word of reproach, the U.S. government stood by while another hole was torn in the fabric of the American economy. The political appointees and the civil servants did not consider it their responsibility to try to affect this result, nor did industry inform the government the calamity which was befalling it. Industry executives certainly knew what was happening; perhaps they felt that Washington would not understand or had nothing useful to offer.[50] John Dunne wrote about the individual that "No man is an island, entire of itself; everyman is a piece of the continent. No man stands alone. Each man is part of me. If a clod is washed away, it diminishes us all. Do not send for whom the bell tolls, it tolls for thee."

---

[50]There were some very belated visits to the government in 1991. But these came very late in this story.

In the case of autos, mainstream American economists, the U.S. government, and the media did not consider that the erosion of a major part of the American manufacturing economy touched them directly. The consumer, perhaps wistfully, bought what he or she felt was the better, less expensive car. While the whole country was thereby hurt, American trade policy remained oblivious to the loss.

Steel

A dramatic aspect of the history of the post-World War II period has been the re-industrialization of Europe and Japan and the industrialization of much of the developing world. An essential element of this process was the construction of integrated steel mills, which were widely seen as prerequisites to a modern manufacturing economy. Outside the U.S., the postwar growth in steelmaking capacity was driven, to an extraordinary degree, by the decisions of government planners often pursuing objectives only tangentially related to market conditions -- promotion of what was traditionally regarded as a "strategic" industry linked to national security, national and regional development, job creation, bureaucratic empire-building and sheer national aggrandizement.[51] Whatever the rationales, the result of many simultaneous decisions by governments to promote the steel industry was a dramatic expansion in capacity which, as world demand leveled off in the stagnant economic environment of the mid-1970s, created conditions of "structural" recession in this industry -- that is, massive overcapacity and the enormous operating deficits associated with low utilization rates in a capital-intensive industry.[52] Government intervention, which had helped to precipitate the crisis, increased dramatically after the onset of

[51]U.S. Department of Commerce, "Foreign Import Restraints and Unfair Practices in Steel" (Washington, D.C.: U.S. Department of Commerce, September 18, 1981). This study showed that if one excluded Japan and the U.S., 75 percent of the world's raw steel production capacity was state owned.

[52]Western world raw steel production increased phenomenally, from 153.0 million metric tons in 1950 to 494.9 million tons in 1974. After 1974, western world consumption stagnated, and in 1986 was actually 7 percent below 1974 levels. Capacity kept on expanding, however, and by 1986 was 72 million metric tons greater than in 1974. Reflecting a gross imbalance between steelmaking capacity and demand, world steelmaking capacity utilization was below 75 percent for virtually the entire period 1975-87. American Iron and Steel Institute, *Annual Statistical Reports* (various issues); Peter F. Marcus and Karlis M. Kirsis, *World Steel Dynamics, Core Report BB* (PaineWebber, Inc., January 1988), Exhibit BB-1-5.

the structural recession. After 1975 a truly staggering volume of government subsidies was poured into steel enterprises to prevent their collapse; cartels were formed or reinforced to stabilize markets; and virtually all major steel producing nation established trade restrictions at the border.[53] Producers suffering from excess capacity desperately sought to export their surpluses to maintain operating rates, with the result that the more open markets -- the U.S. and initially, the EC -- experienced surges of low-priced imported steel.[54]

The U.S. steel industry, which in the mid-1970s possessed facilities which were older and less advantageously sited than many of the new foreign mills, were simultaneously confronted with the need to restructure and a massive influx of imported steel, much of its sold below the cost of production or at subsidized prices. The industry experienced a severe - contraction; over 25 steel firms filed for bankruptcy, the industry lost $12 billion between 1982 and 1986, and capacity utilization rates reached their lowest level since the Great Depression. The work force shrank from 500 thousand in 1974 to 163 thousand in 1987.

The U.S. government had no industrial policy in steel and, for that matter, no trade policy other than to react to successive crises as they developed. In the decade following the onset of the structural recession in 1975, a recognizable policy cycle was played out: first, import levels would rise, prompting the filing of antidumping and countervailing duty actions by the U.S. industry;[55] second, as the cases proceeded, it would become apparent that relief, if granted, would entail prohibitive

---

[53]Between 1980 and 1985, according to the EC Commission, Community steelmakers received $37.4 billion in subsidies from governments of the Member States. *Report from the Commission to the Council on Application of the Rules on Aids to the Steel Industry,* Com (86) 235 final, August 6, 1986. See generally T.R. Howell, W.A. Noellert, J.G. Kreier and A. Wm. Wolff, *Steel and the State: Government Intervention and Steel's Structural Crisis* (Boulder and London : Westview, 1988).

[54]The European Community market was seriously disrupted by imports in 1975-77, with the result that a comprehensive system of bilateral restraint arrangements were established in 1978. The U.S. market experienced major import surges between 1976 and 1988. EC Commission, Summary of *Arrangements for Iron and Steel Products* (Brussels, April 5, 1983).

[55]Between the beginning of the structural crisis in 1974 and the phasing in of the Reagan VRAs in 1984-86, roughly 250 antidumping and countervailing duty cases were filed in the steel sector. Major rounds of litigation took place in 1977, 1980, 1981-82, and 1984-85. For a listing of steel cases since 1981 (which omits, however, many cases involving the EC) see U.S. Department of Commerce, *Summary of Steel Cases Since 1981.* (June 15, 1988).

international political costs;[56] third, the U.S. administration would negotiate a political settlement with the main steel exporting nations, most commonly in the form of voluntary restraint arrangements, as an alternative to cases;[57] fourth, after a period of time, these arrangements would expire, come unraveled, or be scrapped, resulting in another import influx -- and the cycle would begin again with another round of antidumping and countervailing duty cases.[58] With each cycle the U.S. industry contracted and U.S. self-sufficiency in this basic industry was further eroded.[59] Thus while the U.S. steel sector was characterized by extensive government attention and intervention for much of the decade between 1975 and 1985, the measures taken were improvised, tentative, ad hoc actions designed to respond to immediate problems; at no time until President Reagan established a steel program based on voluntary restraint arrangements in 1985-86 did the industry receive anything approximating effective comprehensive relief from dumped and subsidized steel. At that point, the erosion of the U.S. industry was halted, with import penetration declining from an all time six-month high of 26.2 percent in the first half

---

[56]To cite an example, major cases filed by the U.S. industry in March 1980 against the EC coincided roughly with the Iran hostage crisis and the Soviet invasion of Afghanistan. From a political perspective, the cases against the steel industries of the leading U.S. European allies were an embarrassment for the Carter Administration, which was seeking to strengthen the solidarity of the Western alliance. See H. Patrick and H. Sato, "The Political Economy of U.S.- Japan Trade in Steel," in K. Yamamura, ed. *Policy and Trade Issues of the Japanese Economy* (Seattle: University of Washington Press, 1982).

[57]Japanese steelmakers began unilaterally restraining exports to the U.S. in 1978 although this action was not based on a formal commitment. In 1978-80, the U.S. experimented unsuccessfully with the so-called Trigger Price Mechanism, designed to provide an early warning of dumping, as an alternative to relief under the trade laws. In 1982, the U.S. government negotiated VRAs with the EC, and after 1984, VRAs were concluded with the majority of U.S. trading partners.

[58]See Howell, et al.; (1988) pp. 517-34.

[59]For example, in the 1981 import surge, a massive influx of low-priced foreign steel, mainly from the EC, was accompanied by the closure of 23 steel plants in the U.S. and the elimination of approximately 50,000 jobs -- a result characterized by one U.S. analyst as "an economic tragedy of epic proportions." *Metal Bulletin* (October 9, 1981); *American Metal Market* (September 16, October 12, 1981); *Wall Street Journal* (October 19, 1981).

of 1985 to 21.3 percent in 1987 and 16.2 percent in the first half of 1990.[60] The industry got a breathing space in which it modernized, by 1987 becoming one of the world's most efficient steel producers measured in terms of man-hours per ton produced.[61] However, the world steel trade problem was not solved; surplus capacity remained in the world's main steel producing regions, much of it built or sustained with subsidies.[62] Large scale subsidization of steel production continued in Italy, Indonesia, Brazil, Mexico, and other countries, although a number of nations were moving to privatize state steel producers and to renounce subsidization.

The Bush Administration decided in 1989 that the twenty year history of VRAs was interventionist and protectionist, and that the cycle of negotiated restraints had to end; it therefore announced that the VRA regime would expire in 1992 and that thereafter the U.S. would no longer utilize VRAs in this sector. Further, as part of a "President's Steel Program", the United States announced that it would seek a negotiated "Multilateral Steel Agreement" (MSA) which would bind signatory countries to prevent them from concluding VRAs in the future.[63] Thus the traditional tool by which the world and successive Administrations had managed their steel trade problems would be foresworn; in its place would be steel trade litigation (according to the Administration) and an agreement under which steel producing countries would, more or less,

---

[60]American Iron and Steel Institute.

[61]Peter F. Marcus and Karlis M. Kirsis, World Steel Dynamics: *Steel Strategist 14* (December 10, 1987), Exhibit D. It should be noted, however, that exchange rate fluctuations make it virtually impossible for any steel producer to maintain either the lowest or the highest cost position over a period of time. The Japanese steel industry, for example, by every measure a very efficient industry, has among the highest costs in the world, reflecting the strong yen. Marcus and Kirsis (1987), Exhibit D.

[62]See generally EC Commission *Communication from the Commission to the Council Amending Com (87) 388 final*/2 of September 17, 1987, Com (87) 640 final, November 26, 1987.

[63]A multilateral agreement precluding VRAs is more likely to limit U.S. actions in this regard than those of other countries. The U.S. has historically concluded most of its VRAs in an open manner, and any action of this kind would be immediately challenged under the MSA. Governments and producers in Japan, the European countries and other major steel trading states often make clandestine arrangements or reach unwritten agreements and understandings that would not be difficult to subject to comparable international scrutiny. See Howell, et. al. (1988) pp. 52; 211-14; 244-46; 416.

end subsidization. In the event, renouncing subsidies was easier said than done; as the negotiations proceeded, it became evident other subsidies (for research, environmental compliance and worker adjustment) would be given a "green light," that is, treated as permissible. Moreover, while it was fine in principle to state that there would be no further subsidization, there was a demand that yesteryear's and yesterday's subsidies be free of discipline. Thus a plant built with state funds which began production one day before the Agreement was signed, or under a program existing at the time the Agreement was entered into would be "grandfathered", that is, permitted as an exception for pre-existing practices. At the time of this writing the negotiations are stalled, the VRAs are scheduled to expire in March, 1992, and the cycle of intermittent protection, broken from time to time by periods of litigation accompanied by further industry erosion, is set to repeat itself.

Could U.S. trade policy have done a better job with respect to steel? Yes. This is a proposition to which all would agree, whether those who feel that too much protection was granted or those who feel that there was too little. There was never a comprehensive, long term program for dealing with steel trade issues. The industry never could rely on a given set of policies being in effect for more than a few years at a time. It did not know what to expect of government, nor what government expected of it (with the exception of a re-investment requirement in the implementing legislation of the next to the last series of VRAs). It will be argued that this was a lesson in the evils of U.S. government intervention in trade. It could as readily, and more compellingly, be argued, however, that the result was an inconsistent series of half-measures,[64] crafted with little understanding of the industry's needs or problems. This phenomenon is still with us; the evident failure of the MSA talks has not led to a re-examination of the decision to terminate the restraints once and for all, nor has there been an inquiry into what distortions remain, or the extent to which an extension of restrictions might be justified.

Automobiles, steel and consumer electronics form a very large portion of America's productive capability. It would in many ways suffice to stop here and let conclusions be drawn as to the efficacy of American trade policy. But a few words on other sectors is appropriate. There is an old joke about the surgeon who states that an operation was a great success but unfortunately the patient died. There is much about U.S. trade policy that falls into this unfortunate category; each attempt made to solve a

---

[64]It is worth stressing, especially when the language used in this chapter is so critical, that many of the individuals in government are striving earnestly to do the best that they can within the policy framework in which they must operate. The results are nevertheless, ultimately disappointing.

trade policy problem is self-contained, most often as part of a trade case under a given trade remedy statute. The object in each instance is to administer a statute -- that is, to counter a subsidy in one instance or to counter dumping in another, but not to mix the two together. It is certainly not to leave an industry necessarily better off for the experience. This is a consideration which plays virtually no formal part in evaluating whether or not the exercise has been of value. The chronicle of U.S. policy management of major trade problems over the past several decades illustrates the limits inherent in such a narrow approach.

Machine Tools

This industry petitioned for relief from import pressure under a variety of U.S. statutes. It was a highly fragmented industry unable to compete effectively with the onslaught of foreign competition. One machine tool producer, Houdaille Industries took one of the first runs at getting relief, filing a case in 1982 under section 103 of the Revenue Act of 1971, an obscure and never-utilized remedy, which would have resulted in the denial of the investment tax credit to American investors utilizing imported machinery. Houdaille charged that the Japanese government had promoted the expansion of its machine tool industry with subsidies, loans and other financial incentives, home market protection and an administered cartel, all of which had adversely affected Houdaille and other U.S. machine tool firms. The Houdaille case was extremely well documented. But like Zenith in the color television case, involving the rebate of the Japanese commodities tax, Houdaille did not recognize that no American administration would take the action requested -- in this case to deny the investment tax credit to foreign machinery, an act which would have violated America's national treatment obligations. The United States has several dead letter statutes, and it was Houdaille's ill-luck to fail to appreciate that section 103 was one of these. There never was a possibility of relief being granted in the case that was brought. Following an extraordinarily protracted, enfeebling internal debate within the Administration, relief was denied, and Houdaille exited the machine tool industry in 1984.[65] That ended the matter, as far as the Administration was concerned. Under the U.S. system, the petitioner is merely a litigant who must live or die by the choices it makes; Houdaille chose improperly and was consigned to commercial extinction. The fact that machine tools

---

[65]For an insiders' account of the paralysis which characterized the Reagan Administration's deliberating over the Houdaille case, see Clyde Prestowitz, *Trading Places: How We Allowed Japan to Take the Lead* (New York; Basic Books; 1988) pp. 213-29.

are absolutely vital to a modern national economy was simply not regarded as relevant to any aspect of the exercise. The statue of American trade policy, were there one, would wear a blindfold. Not only does it grant equity occasionally without regard to the importance of the question or industry before it, but most often it does not deign to even re-direct a petitioner to some other course of action if the one embarked upon turns out to be a (dead-end even if the Executive knows this from the outset). Instead, it went through the panoply of a full hearing before determining that -- of course -- no relief could be provided under the statute.

After the Houdaille debacle, the U.S. machine tool industry was still in desperate straits. Ultimately, it fell back on one of America's statutes of last resort, bringing a case under section 232 of the Trade Expansion Act of 1962, which permits the imposition of import restrictions to protect industries deemed essential to the nation's security.[66] National security having been found threatened, voluntary restraint agreements were negotiated with Japan and Taiwan.[67] But this was a policy adopted very late in the day insofar as being of assistance to the machine tool industry was concerned -- something of a half policy, decided on very late, and very uncertain of producing an adequate result.

Commercial Airline Service

In the immediate post-World War II period, America had the only international passenger airline capability of any significance. Pan Am and TWA served over a hundred foreign points and operated the most efficient and modern aircraft fleets. Pan Am was in fact so highly competitive that it was barred by U.S. regulators from building up a domestic route network in the continental U.S., the notion being that its modern aircraft and international routes would give it such a competitive edge that it would stifle the growth of domestic competitors. But in the decades after the war, foreign flag carriers began expanding their own systems, and the number of such carriers grew because of the many new

---

[66]19 U.S.C. § 1862. Section 232 has been used very sparingly by the President, generally in connection with imposition of quotas, fees, or sanctions on imported petroleum products. U.S. International Trade Commission, *Operation of the Trade Agreements Program* (42d Report, 1990), p. 172.

[67]Japan and Taiwan agreed in 1986 to five years of export restraint to the U.S. machine tool market. Germany and Switzerland refused to enter into comparable arrangements. U.S.I.T.C. *Trade Agreements Programs*, p. 172; Presidential Notice dated December 16, 1986 on Machine Tool Revitalization Program.

nations coming into existence. It was assumed that every country worthy of the name had to have its own flag airline. These carriers not only enjoyed their own domestic feeder systems (there being less concern with fostering domestic competition and more with required service and international competitiveness) but were usually state-owned and subsidized. Given the generally lax foreign antitrust standards, the foreign flag lines could enter into revenue-pooling arrangements with each other that enabled them to lock out U.S. carriers from access to much of the passenger traffic moving in international commerce.[68] But most significantly, while foreign governments generally prioritized negotiation of "hard" rights for their carriers -- that is route rights to foreign gateway cities -- the U.S. government, particularly in the Carter Administration, emphasized the fostering of "competition" itself, seeking to multiply the number of carriers serving various markets and to increase fare discount competition in order to maximize consumer welfare. While foreign countries were arranging monopoly rights, cash infusions and other competitive benefits for their flag carriers, America gave its carriers increased competition, eventually fragmenting the U.S. international network. Thus, with a blind eye to what made foreign carriers strong, American policy -- what might be described as an unconscious trade policy -- produced international carriers which were fit only for Chapter 11. Pan Am went into liquidation in 1991. While domestic carriers like United, American, Delta and Northwest have successfully extended their operations overseas, the U.S. international airline system is now primarily an out-and-back system serving major foreign hubs and a few beyond points from major U.S. cities. The globe-girdling system built by Pan Am is gone -- its Round-the-World service was ended in the 1980s -- replaced by comparable systems operated by European and Asian carriers, whose governments have adhered to different priorities. While U.S. government policy is not the only factor underlying this change, it has been a primary contributing factor.

Construction Engineering

Another service industry in which America has had a world leadership role, construction engineering, has faced a largely closed market in Japan.

---

[68]Under pooling arrangements, two or more foreign carriers serving a route would agree to do so jointly, meshing their schedules to provide the optimum pattern of service (rather than competing with each other by scheduling head-to-head flights), selling seats on each others' flights (but not on U.S. flag flights) pooling revenues received from ticket sales, and dividing the revenues according to an agreed formula.

A system of bid-rigging called *dango* bars access to virtually the entire Japanese market for foreign construction firms, conferring a large protected home base on America's Japanese competitors.[69] The potential market foreclosed is huge -- $350 billion annually, or about 15 percent of Japan's GNP. Moreover, the loss of contracts involves more than just foregoing income from a particular transaction; it means that the purchase of machinery and supplies, and the technology used, most often Japanese as well, sets a pattern for future procurements once the original construction contract is concluded. Large Japanese construction firms, protected at home, are now making significant inroads in the U.S. construction market and the U.S. share of foreign markets.

Here again, U.S. trade policy has failed to resolve the basic problem, an imbalance in the relative openness of the U.S. and Japanese markets which is now working to the competitive disadvantage of U.S. firms. Japan's Kansai International Airport project has been the principal focus of U.S. negotiating efforts to open the Japanese construction market. These negotiations underscore the limitations inherent in U.S. policy to date. Construction of the airport is being managed by the Kansai International Airport Corp. (KIAC), which invited a consortium of Japanese construction firms to participate in the planning of the airport. U.S. firms were excluded, giving the Japanese firms the inside track on subsequent bidding on construction projects.[70] After some prodding by the U.S. government, KIAC allowed U.S. firms to register for competitive bids on all four phases of the project, but in 1986, shortly after this apparent concession, KIAC announced that "phase one" of the project would be contracted entirely to Japanese firms.[71] In 1987, three U.S. firms were awarded contracts to supply services to the Kansai project, but

---

[69]See Chapter 2.

[70]A principal U.S. concern was the Japanese practice of "designated bidding," under which KIAC gave selected suppliers access to design specifications to enable them to submit their bids. Japanese firms "privy to these specifications could line up subcontractors and equipment suppliers in order to present more responsive bids." USITC, *Operation of the Trade Agreements Program, 39th Report* (July 1988), p. 4-27.

[71]Phase one included construction of an offshore island, a sea wall, and a bridge connecting the island to the mainland. KIAC contended that to permit U.S. firms to bid on this phase of the project would "delay construction." As KIAC was rebuffing U.S. attempts to take part on the project, Prime Minister Nakasone "continued to assure U.S. officials that American firms would be provided timely information on procurement plans, bid procedures and award criteria." USITC, *Operation of the Trade Agreements Program, 39th Report* (July 1988), p. 4-27.

these amounted to less than one percent of the project's value, and further bilateral negotiations on bidding procedures remained deadlocked. The Congress, meanwhile, was becoming increasingly frustrated with the lack of progress on the Kansai issue. In 1987 it took the symbolic step of barring Japan from participating in federally-funded construction projects having a value of over $500,000 during FY 1988.[72] In February 1988 the Trade Policy Review Group (TPRG), a subcabinet-level interagency group advising the President, recommended self-initiation of a Section 301 action against Japan in the construction sector. A confrontation was averted, however, through an agreement pursuant to which Japan agreed to move to transparent procurement procedures for 17 public works projects, including Kansai Airport.[73]

The Omnibus Trade and Competitiveness Act of 1988 contained a provision which required USTR to initiate a Section 301 investigation of Japanese market barriers in the construction sector, and an investigation began on November 1988 -- fizzling a year later when USTR concluded that while "unreasonable"[74] practices worked to exclude U.S. construction firms, no action would be taken because "promises made by the government of Japan to address these and other U.S. concerns were sufficient to defer the decision on whether to take retaliatory action until May 1990, when the bilateral agreement was to be reviewed."[75]This deadline passed, however, with no U.S. retaliatory action, and in July 1990 a new dispute erupted when KIAC awarded a contract for a people-mover transit system to two Japanese firms who had bid $22 million more than

---

[72]Senator Murkowski of Alaska attached amendments to six authorization bills prohibiting foreign firms from participating in federally-funded public works projects if their governments did not grant reciprocal access to U.S. firms. The final measure adopted was added to the continuing resolution at the end of 1987. USITC, *39th Report*, p. 4-28.

[73]Exchange of Letters between Commerce Secretary Verity and Japanese Ambassador Matsunaga, May 25, 1988.

[74]The "unreasonable" practices cited included inadequate government action to prevent bid rigging, requiring that foreign firms have experience in Japan before being eligible to participate in public projects, and discriminatory access to project information. USITC, *Operation of the Trade Agreements Program,* 41st Report, USITC Pub. No. 2317 (September 1990), p. 110.

[75]USITC, *Operation of the Trade Agreements Program,* 41st Report, USITC Pub. No. 2317 (September 1990), p. 110.

the foreign competitor, AEG-Westinghouse Transportation Systems Inc.[76] The Commerce Department notified Japan's Ministry of Foreign Affairs of its belief that "irregularities" had characterized the award of the project, and gave Japan a deadline of January 15, 1991 to resolve these "procedural problems."[77] At the end of 1990, the U.S. government requested that Japan broaden the scope of the 1988 agreement on bidding procedures to cover all public works projects and to cover projects with a design aspect, a proposal that was rejected by the Japanese government.[78] Finally, in mid-1991, with Japan confronting the prospect of legislated retaliation under Omnibus Trade Act provisions sponsored by Senator Murkowski, a new agreement was reached which brought 17 more projects under the bidding procedures established in the 1988 agreement,but which fell short of the U.S. objective of bringing all public procurement projects under these procedures.[79] Senator Murkowski indicated he was not "personally satisfied" that the matter was resolved, and Commerce Secretary Mossbacher indicated that while the shortfall from original U.S. objectives was a "step in the right direction," it was "somewhat disappointing."[80]

In this as in other instances, the U.S. government has proven unable to pursue an effective remedial course in a prompt fashion. Part of the problem, to be sure, has been a lack of consensus on the part of the U.S. industry as to which course is appropriate; moreover, it must be acknowledged that the current, highly motivated negotiating team at the Commerce Department, working with Congressional supporters such as Senator Murkowski, has succeeded against the odds in opening 34 major projects to foreign bids. But this result has been achieved many years after the problem was identified, may not lead to significantly increased

---

[76]AEG-Westinghouse was an experienced supplier which had an 80-percent share of the world market for people-mover systems, whereas the winning Japanese firms had never built a people-mover system and did not meet the technical specifications for the project. BNA International Trade Reporter, (November 28, 1990); USITC, *Operation of the Trade Agreements Program, 42nd Report*, USITC Pub. No. 2403 (July 1991), p. 122.

[77]USITC Pub. No. 2403 (July 1991), p. 122.

[78]*BNA International Trade Reporter* (January 9, 1991).

[79]U.S.-Japan Major Projects Arrangements (July 31, 1991).

[80]*NNA International Trade Reporter* (August 7, 1991).

U.S. participation, and affects only a tiny fraction of the total Japanese market, which for the most part remains closed to U.S. firms.

Commercial Aircraft

The U.S. has led the world in the manufacture of commercial aircraft throughout the postwar era. This industry remains one of the mainstays of our economy. But it has suffered a sharp and continuing loss of market share during the past decade. This is another industrial sector in which warning signs were received early, but in which the response has been wholly ineffectual. The potential for trouble first surfaced in the 1970s, when the governments of France and the U.K. decided to subsidize the development of a supersonic civilian passenger jet; the derisive initial U.S. reaction to the Concorde is now a thing of the past.[81] It was said, defensively, by Europeans at the time, that what was important was not so much the commercial success of such ventures, but the very fact of the creation of a pan-European modern industrial effort at the cutting edge of technology. This philosophy continued to drive European efforts in this field, and with the advent of Airbus Industrie, the Europeans have begun to make serious inroads into the U.S. market position. The sales generated by Airbus for the European economy are huge, as, for that matter, are the subsidies which have enabled Airbus to arrive at its current position challenging the U.S. industry.[82] The erosion of the U.S. competitive position in the international market has been dramatic. U.S. trade policymakers have faced a series of impasses. They have lodged protests against European subsidies to Airbus in various bilateral fora

---

[81]The Concorde program ultimately led to the delivery of less than two dozen aircraft. The Concorde's fuel inefficiency and noise have precluded the aircraft's widespread use. and in financial terms, the program was a fiasco. Technically, however, it was arguably a success, and it laid the psychological and technological groundwork for the Airbus initiative.

[82]In 1990, the Commerce Department released a study which concluded that U.S. market share for orders of large commercial aircraft decreased from 87 percent in 1980 to 64 percent in 1989, while Airbus' share grew from about 7 percent in 1980 to 27 percent in 1989. In 1990, the Office of the U.S. Trade Representative estimated European subsidies to Airbus to be at least $12 billion between 1970 and 1990; the Commerce Department puts the figure at $13.5 billion. *The Economist* (February 16, 1991); USTR, *1990 National Trade Estimate Report on Foreign Trade Barriers*; Gellman Research Associates, Inc., for the U.S. Department of commerce, *An Economic and Financial Review of Airbus* (September 4, 1990).

since 1984 with virtually no effect to date on European actions.[83] The European position is that Europe will have a large commercial aircraft industry, even if this means massive subsidies; the United States government, understanding of European aspirations, not clear of how far to press its own commercial interests, and with its own industry unsure as to how to proceed, has found no answers.

Heavy Electrical Generating Equipment

This sector, in contrast to others cited in this study, has not been the subject of much public controversy -- but it also illustrates the shortcomings of U.S. trade policy. Heavy electrical equipment is a product area in which U.S. firms are highly competitive, yet they have achieved virtually no sales at all in the European Community since 1960, and have been marginalized in most world export markets. The public utilities and other procurement authorities in the EC prefer to purchase from indigenous EC producers or firms based in Switzerland and Sweden, nations which are closely linked to the EC through financial ties. The procurement bidding process in the EC is closed to outside suppliers. U.S.

---

[83]The U.S. filed a complaint against European government subsidies to Airbus in the GATT Committee on Trade in Civil Aircraft in March 1987. This action and subsequent U.S. protests had no perceptible effect on the commitment of large additional subsidies to Airbus by European governments, including a highly controversial guarantee by the German government designed to protect the consortium against exchange rate fluctuations. In 1988, the U.S. International Trade Commission summarized the past years' negotiations with the EC: "Continuous delays and lack of progress at meetings frustrated U.S. negotiators." The U.S. began proceedings against the German exchange rate guarantee pursuant to the GATT Subsidies Code in 1991. Airbus' director reportedly "shrugged off" this most recent U.S. action, stating that "there will be no major concessions." The Community also indicated that it might seek parallel arbitration pursuant to the GATT Code on Trade in Civil Aircraft, which it viewed as a more favorable forum for its position. In the fall of 1991,the U.S. was reportedly preparing to seek "conciliation" before the GATT Subsidies Committee, but community officials indicated they would block this initiative unless the U.S. showed that it was prepared to make "major concessions." One EC official commented that "we just don't see the point of going to the Subsidies Committee once again with the same old arguments." At this writing, the EC and U.S. were reportedly exploring settlement options which would involve a "cap" on EC subsidies to Airbus, but not their abolition. *The Economist* (February 16, 1991); BNA *International Trade Reporter* (September 18, 1991); USITC, *Operations of the Trade Agreements Program, 40th Report* (July, 1989) U.S.I.T.C. Pub. No. 2208; *Inside U.S. Trade* (September 27, October 4, 1991).

firms like GE and Westinghouse have received inadequate notice of procurements, have been asked by procuring authorities not to bid on contracts, and have seen their bids rejected without any reason given.[84] The U.S. International Trade Commission observed in 1983 that a "high degree of nationalistic procurement is a leading characteristic of the oligopolistic [EC] power plant markets."[85] The EC Commission was even more blunt; in 1988 it commented that the national "markets are essentially closed to suppliers or contractors from other Member States, however competitive they may be. Indeed, the result in some cases appears to be a firmly closed, vicious circle in which outside firms do not even try, since to do so would be a waste of resources and impossible for a responsible manager to justify."[86] In contrast to the EC market, the U.S. market for heavy electrical equipment is relatively open, and by the mid-1980s, imports accounted for about 20 percent of domestic consumption.[87] Approximately one half of this total was accounted for by European producers, having been able to obtain high prices in their noncompetitive domestic markets, price very aggressively in export markets.[88] By 1985,

---

[84]USITC, *The Effects of Greater Economic Integration Within the European Community on the United States*, USITC Pub No. 220Y (July, 1989) pp. 4-32, 4-33.

[85]USITC, Foreign Industrial Targeting (European Community and Member States), (1984) p. 134. The USITC noted that the French government reportedly assisted its industry through R&D subsidies of up to 50 percent of project costs and through investment subsidies. USITC (1984), p. 134.

[86]EC Commission, *Proposal for a Council Directive on the Procurement Procedures of Entities Providing Water, Energy and Transport Services* (October 11, 1988).

[87]The Buy America Act has benefitted U.S. producers of heavy electrical equipment, "but only with respect to business solicited by federally operated power authorities," where U.S. firms get a 6 percent preference on bids against foreign firms. (USITC *European Targeting*, pp. 209). Most of the U.S. market for heavy electrical equipment consists of private and non-federal public utilities.

[88]In 1972, the U.S. government imposed antidumping duties on large power transformers from France, Italy, Switzerland, Japan, and Britain. Suspension agreements were later negotiated with Britain and Switzerland. The antidumping duties remained in effect against the other countries and periodic administrative reviews of this order revealed continued dumping at extraordinary margins (70 percent from France, 92 percent from Italy). Treasury Decision No. 72-162, 37 F.R. 11772 (1972). European governments have also utilized export credits to stimulate sales of their national producers. Office of U.S. Trade Representative, *Export Financing for the Heavy Electric Power Generating Equipment* (October 1984).

European firms held 45 percent of world export markets in large power transformers, and U.S. firms only 3 percent.[89]

The problems confronting this industry have been known to U.S. policymakers for a long time, but have never been pressed with much vigor. During the Tokyo Round negotiations in the 1970s, the U.S. government tried unsuccessfully to secure coverage of the foreign entities which procure heavy electrical equipment in the new GATT Procurement Code. In the legislation implementing the Tokyo Round agreements, Congress directed the President to study the adverse effects of closed procurement of these products on U.S. firms, and to recommend a course of action.[90] In 1981, USTR issued a report suggesting three measures for rectifying the lack of reciprocity in this sector, and warned sternly that if foreign countries did not agree to bring their heavy electrical equipment procurement authorities under the GATT Code by January 1, 1985, USTR would "recommend appropriate actions to Congress to achieve reciprocity."[91] This admonition apparently failed to produce the desired effect on the Europeans. Renegotiation of the Procurement Code began in 1984, and in March 1985 -- after the January 1, 1985 deadline had come and gone with no U.S. action -- USTR acknowledged that "if the renegotiations do not produce satisfactory results, we will have to reconsider our options."[92] The "first phase" of the Procurement Code renegotiations ended at the end of 1986, with no expansion of code coverage to procurement of heavy electrical equipment purchases. Three years later, a U.S. industry group asked USTR to designate the EC's procurement practices in heavy electrical equipment as a U.S. trade liberalization priority under the new "Super 301" provisions of the Omnibus Trade and Competitiveness Act of 1988. USTR declined to do so.[93] The issue was eventually folded into the Uruguay Round

---

[89]U.S. Department of Commerce, *A Competitive Assessment of the U.S. Transformer Industry* (February 1986) pp. 6, 22, 24.

[90]Section 302(e) and (d), Trade Agreements of 1979.

[91]USTR, *Report to the Congress Pursuant to Section* 304(d)(1) of the Trade Agreements Act of 1979 *(November 17, 1981).*

[92]USTR, *Report to the Congress Pursuant to Section 304(d)(1) of the Trade Agreement Act of 1979* (March 29, 1985).

[93]Petition of the National Electrical Manufacturers Association (March 23, 1989).

negotiations and, as of mid-1991, no resolution was in sight.[94] As a U.S. industry paper commented in 1988, over a decade of "consultations and negotiations have yielded no tangible result for this industry."[95] While negotiations have failed to produce any real progress, the U.S. industry, with substantial investments in Europe, presumably has found it impolitic to invoke U.S. unilateral trade remedies against the Community. U.S. policymakers, awaiting the filing of a case to become activated, have remained paralyzed. The result is a shrinking U.S. world market position in this industry.

Semiconductors

The American semiconductor industry began to be seriously concerned in an organized way with Japanese competition in 1977; the reason that the date can be identified with some precision is because the industry created a separate trade association in that year due in large part to these concerns.[96] The Japanese had created an industrial policy initiative in the early 1970s that ranks with government-industry efforts in Korea and Japan in shipbuilding and steel. MITI, which had already gained a reputation for what it had accomplished with respect to heavy industry, turned its attention to microelectronics-based technologies, working closely with industry to craft a program to make Japan a leader in information technologies.[97] One of the main themes of these efforts was

---

[94]In 1988, the U.S. began "fact-finding" consultations with the EC with respect to procurement procedures affecting heavy electrical equipment. The EC has indicated the Single Market Initiative will result in the adoption of Community-wide procurement rules which will make the process more transparent but which will not necessarily result in increased U.S. sales. Moreover, in order to qualify for nondiscriminatory treatment, a supplier must be able to demonstrate 50 percent EC content. The U.S. government is currently seeking to bring GATT "excluded sectors" (including many areas of public procurement) within the scope of the GATT Procurement Code.

[95]Petition of the National Electrical Manufacturers Association (March 23, 1989).

[96]The Semiconductor Industry Association (SIA) was established in 1977 as a stand-alone trade association, effectively replacing the electronic components division of the Electronic Industries Association.

[97]The principal promotional measures were set forth in a series of special laws which authorized MITI to undertake industry rationalization and the extension of financial assistance. In 1957, the Diet enacted the *Law Concerning Special Measures*

(continued...)

to create a computer industry. Before this could get fully off the ground, IBM launched a new generation of computers (the 360 series) and MITI and its major electronics firms had to go back to the drawing boards. The result was a plan developed to bring about entry and then dominance in the production of semiconductors -- the small computer chips called integrated circuits, in which thousands of microscopic circuits enabled the computer to gain greater and greater capabilities in less and less space. The Japanese chose dynamic random access memories (DRAMs) as one of the main points of entry.[98]

The U.S. industry came to Washington in the late 1970s to attempt to determine what could be done to counter what it called Japanese "industrial targeting." This was a term used in testimony by L.J. Sevin, the Chief Executive Officer of Mostek Corporation, one of the first producers of DRAMs. He testified before the Joint Economic Committee in October, 1979, and succeeded only in mystifying his listeners; no one in the Washington trade policy establishment understood what industrial targeting was. The business of Washington was not, by and large, the promotion of American commerce, nor its defense, save in very narrow circumstances. The plight of these California entrepreneurs was therefore little comprehended.

The American industry's first instinct was to build some mechanism which would preserve it against the extensive dumping which it was expected -- correctly -- would have to follow the vast capacity expansion in which Japan was engaged. Industry leaders such as Bob Galvin of Motorola and L.J. Sevin saw the build-up with government organization and assistance, and expected a *tsunami*-like wave of products to follow. They were not mistaken. Within a few years, Mostek went into bankruptcy and Motorola and five other American producers exited the DRAM market by the end of 1985.[99] The Japanese cornered the

---

[97](...continued)
for the Promotion of Specific Electronic Industries. This was replaced by Law No. 17 of 1971, the *Extraordinary Measures Law for the Promotion of Specific Electronic and Machinery Industries (Kidenho),* which was in turn replaced by Law No. 84, the *Law for Provisional Measures for the Promotion of Specific Machinery and Information Industries (Kijoho).* These laws provided the basis for MITI's promotional aid to the semiconductor and computer industries.

[98]*Japan Economic Journal* (May 30, 1978); *Nihon Keizai Shimbun* (February 16, 1980); *Nikkei Sangyo Shimbun* (December 16-17, 1981).

[99]USITC, *Dynamic Random Access Memory Comments from Japan,* USITC Publ. No. 1862, final (June 1986); *Electronics News* (October 14, 1985).

merchant market for DRAMs, losing some $4 billion dollars over two years to achieve this position. The American producers, having very different industrial organizations, could not withstand losses -- which they sustained -- of roughly half this magnitude. By 1986, Japan controlled 90% of the world market for the current generation 256K DRAM.

The U.S. government tried to be responsive within its own very pronounced limits. The Administration in 1979 accepted some language which the industry wished to place in the legislative history of the Antidumping Act amendments, recognizing that threat of injury could occur rapidly in short product life cycle products. This was not terribly useful as the sole response to the kind of competitive threat which Japan posed. It was followed by the establishment of a consultative mechanism called the High Tech Work Group in 1983 through which the U.S. government sought to understand better what the Japanese industrial and trade practices were and what effects they had. This resulted in a High Tech Work Group accord between the two governments on semiconductors.[100] This effort was hortatory. It was hoped that the Japanese government would open its market further, and that its companies would refrain from dumping. These hopes proved to be vain however, and a formal five year Semiconductor Agreement was finally negotiated in September 1986.[101]

This formal accord was possible only after there had been extensive erosion of the U.S. industry, whose world market share had been reduced from nearly 60 percent to under 45 percent by the government-supported competition from Japan. It was also only possible after a formal section 301 complaint had been filed against Japan's closure of its market and after EPROM (another computer memory chip) and DRAM antidumping cases had been filed, all in 1985. Once the problem had been understood, once weaker measures (the failed High Tech Work Group agreement on semiconductors) had been shown to be wholly ineffective, once cases were filed, once the Congress had become adamant that something be done by executive, only then could the United States formulate a response -- and this response really only became truly effective not when the Agreement was signed, but when the President of the United States imposed sanctions in the spring of 1987, for Japan's failure to accord market access

---

[100] *Recommendations of the U.S.-Japan Work Group on High Technology Industries* (November 2, 1983).

[101] *Arrangement Between the Government of Japan and the Government of the United States of America Concerning Trade in Semiconductor Products* (September 2, 1986).

to foreign semiconductors and for its failure to prevent continued dumping in third country markets (that is outside the United States).[102]

It can be said that the semiconductor story is a major "success" in U.S. trade policy, but this is not saying as much as one might hope. Relief was not delivered until a full ten years after the industry had first identified the nature of the problem, and in this case, to a large degree, relief delayed was tantamount to relief denied; the microelectronics leadership of the United States had been severely damaged, and remains precarious even at this writing. There were other elements of response through this period. One of the most notable was the creation of a Semiconductor Manufacturing Technology Initiative (SEMATECH), to provide a Defense Department co-funded cooperative research facility in which industry could improve its manufacturing techniques and attempt to save its manufacturing equipment infrastructure. But the semiconductor equipment and materials industries had by the mid-1980s become very seriously undermined by foreign competition; it too lost market share very sharply.[103] By the beginning of the 1990s, American industry had become increasingly dependent on companies affiliated with its foreign competitors for the tools with which to make semiconductors as well as the semiconductors themselves.[104] The long-run national implications of dependency on foreign sources for such critical products should be obvious; in 1991 the General Accounting Office released a report which indicated that nearly half of 52 U.S. firms surveyed had encountered "difficulty getting advanced equipment and parts from Japanese suppliers," and that seven of these firms "had experienced pressure from Japanese suppliers to take certain actions in order to obtain products."[105]

The final verdict is not in on America's policy responses to foreign competition in the microelectronics sector. The grade that would have to be given at this stage might most charitably be an "incomplete." The

---

[102]Proclamation by the President, *Increase in the Rates of Duty for Certain Articles from Japan* (April 17, 1987).

[103]In 1979 all of the world's top five semiconductor equipment firms were American. In 1989 four of the five top firms were Japanese, including the top two, Nikon and Tokyo Electron. General Accounting Office, *Sematech's Efforts to Strengthen the U.S. Semiconductor Industry* (September 1990).

[104]See generally National Advisory Commission on Semiconductors, *Preserving the Vital Base: America's Semiconductor Equipment and Materials Industry* (1990).

[105]General Accounting Office, *U.S. Business Access to Certain Foreign State-of-the-Art Technology* (September 1991).

failure is not as certain as in automobiles, steel or in color televisions. Some innovative policies were followed. But they were instituted so late, and are sufficiently inadequate to the task at hand, that it must be conclude that they at best stabilized a situation of rapid decline. Further measures are needed.

Softwood Lumber

Canada lies on the border of the United States, seen by Canadians and Americans alike as a vast storehouse of basic natural resources and, therefore, natural resource-based industries. For years, a large portion of the trade between the two countries has been, as one might expect, in forest products. By the mid-1980s, Canadian mills accounted for one-third of the softwood lumber consumed in the United States. But the simple existence of a resource base does not by itself determine the share of a market which any given supplier will have. This will depend upon a number of factors. One is distance; lumber is a product which has a low value to weight ratio. Thus, transportation to distant markets with competitive indigenous lumber mills would tend to be limited, absent special factors. Yet Canadian lumber from British Columbia not only found its way into the United States in large quantities, but by 1985 accounted for half of the lumber sold in two Southeastern lumber producing states! This extraordinary fact was not due to Canadian wage rates -- so often a determining factor in international trade. In fact, Canadian wages in the forests and in the lumber mills were slightly higher than in the industry of their neighbor to the south.[106] It was not due to superior efficiency -- an International Trade Commission study found that U.S. and Canadian mills cutting comparable products had comparable efficiency.[107]

The key factor that increased Canadian share of the U.S. lumber market from the low 20 % range to 33% was the cost to the mills of the trees that they cut. Most of the timber lands in Canada are in the hands of the provinces. The price paid for the right to cut timber on these lands is called a "stumpage fee". Canadian stumpage fees were (and are), on the

---

[106]In 1984 the average hourly wages for production workers in the Canadian softwood lumber industry was $10.24; for comparable U.S. workers the figure was $9.26. USITC, *Softwood Lumber Investigation* (1985) p. 84.

[107]Refined U.S. and Canadian Softwood Lumber Employment Data, USITC (January 1986).

whole, allocated administratively rather than being competitively bid.[108] The price disparity on the two sides of the border was enormous; Canadian mills paid prices averaging $10 to $12 per 1000 board feet in 1984, compared to an average of $100 per board feet paid by U.S. mills.[109] Canadian timber prices were a small fraction of the competitive value of timber in Canada. The Canadian administered timber pricing system was specifically intended to foster jobs that would not have otherwise existed. Unfortunately, those jobs came at the expense of otherwise competitive U.S. firms. The result was the domination of much of the U.S. market by Canadian subsidized lumber, cut uneconomically from the lands of Canada's provinces, and shipped thousands of miles south. The net effect -- due more to the presence of subsidized Canadian lumber than to any other single factor -- was the closure of approximately 600 U.S. mills between 1974 and 1984, and the elimination of one in every four American jobs in this industry during the same period.[110]

American trade policy was again ignorant of the problem as it developed. It awaited the bringing of a case and once a case was filed, legal cant prevailed over both common sense and national commercial interest. A countervailing duty action was filed with the Department of Commerce which decided in 1983 that there was no countervailable subsidy. Its reasoning was that the subsidy was "generally available" -- as the road system or education or police protection is generally available to the populace at large.[111] The rule barring the granting of relief when a subsidy is generally available might make some logical sense in the abstract. But the fact that there is an injury test which must be met before a subsidy may be offset by countervailing subsidies really excludes the possibility that a very general subsidy would be met with a countervailing duty in any event. However, when a foreign industry is only one of several which benefits from a less than market priced resource -- such as natural gas or oil, or in this case, timber, it is not clear why a

---

[108]Standing timber on public land in the U.S. is usually sold at auction to the highest bidder at a price which is usually higher than the appraised price. In Canada, timber had offered under license to private firms who pay an appraised price set by the Provinces. USITC *Softwood Lumber Investigations* (1985) pp. x-xi. Today, while the Canadian pricing system has changed, it is still based upon a low, administered price.

[109]USITC *Trade Agreements Program, 38th Report*, p. 4-18.

[110]USITC *Trade Agreements Program, 38th Report*, p. 4-18.

[111]*Certain Softwood Products from Canada*, 48 F.R. 24, 159 (1983).

U.S. industry should suffer injury due to this state-granted competitive advantage just because a few other foreign-industries may be advantaged at the same time. In the case of lumber, the timber resource was supplied to make pulp (but the trees were different, and generally unsuitable for making lumber), and was also used for other comparatively insignificant, industries (fence posts, turpentine, and charcoal were examples given). It was the fact that those other, comparatively minor, alternative uses for trees exist, which resulted in hundreds of U.S. mills being closed and thousands of jobs lost.

The economic pain being too much to accept, the industry still wandered the corridors of the government looking for relief. In 1985, a Senator from a forest product state asked the International Trade Commission to examine the competitiveness of the Canadian and U.S. industries. The Commission found that the U.S. industry was certainly as competitive as the Canadian.[112] Why then was it losing so much share to its northern neighbor? The answer had to be subsidy, and the industry decided to file another countervailing duty case. Moreover, in the interim, the U.S. carbon black industry had been forced to seek relief from subsidized Mexican imports and, after an initial negative finding, the Commerce Department recognized in that case that natural resource subsidies, while nominally generally available, could be subsidizing a specific industry.[113]

In the second lumber case, faced with obvious facts, with serious injury, with new legal precedent, high-level Canadian officials' admissions that their timber was undervalued, and with an irate Congress, the Department of Commerce found as a preliminary matter that there was a subsidy averaging 15% on Canadian lumber entering the United States (the amount would in reality vary by province, as some subsidized sales of stumpage more than others). Canada, while maintaining that its Provinces could choose to sell stumpage at whatever prices they wished as a matter of sovereign choice, bowed to the fact that the United States would now impose additional import duties on Canadian lumber.

Canada determined that it would rather apply an export tax than suffer additional import duties.[114] This way the provinces could replace the Federal export tax with increased stumpage fees and Canada could keep

---

[112]U.S.I.T.C., *Conditions Relating to the Importation of Softwood Lumber in the United States, (hereafter Softwood Lumber Investigation*, USITC Pub. No. 1765 (October 1985).

[113]Carbon Black from Mexico, 51 Red. Reg. 13269 (Department of Commerce 1986).

[114]The tax became effective in January 1987. USITC *Operation of the Trade Agreements Program, 38th Report*, USITC Pub. No. 1995 (July 1987) p. 5-10.

the revenues at home. In many respects this was a good settlement of the issue. The Canadian provinces got to increase their revenues. With more appropriate stumpage fees, the market mechanism caused Provincial forest management practices to become more responsible, pleasing both Canadian environmentalists and those who feared that the Provinces and their forest products companies were sacrificing too much of the future for the present. It also gave the American mills a chance to compete on fairer terms.[115]

This did not mean that the settlement had not been highly political. The Department of Commerce and the Canadian government accepted a 15% adjustment that changed Canada's resource price. But competitively-bid timber in British Columbia and in the United States still outsold British Columbia Provincial stumpage so that B.C. lumber had as much as a 12% to 35% advantage *after* the 15% adjustment was made; the U.S. government had presumably made a judgment that it would cut another policy baby in half, giving the Canadians the right to subsidize after the 15% correction. But this was not just a decision about policy. It was a decision about where mills and jobs would be located. And while Canada smarted under the agreement which it felt had been exacted under duress (not only with the threat of an import duty but with the possible loss of the U.S.-Canada Free Trade Agreement), it was the American economy which made the sacrifice for additional Canadian profits and employment, above and beyond what the operation of the market would have provided.[116]

There is much to be learned from the softwood lumber case about how the U.S. trade policy process does and does not work. The U.S. trade policy mechanism had been paralyzed for years, during which the U.S. economy suffered much in the way of dislocations, until the domestic industry was able to muster both the legal arguments and the political support to permit those arguments to be accepted. It also had to overcome the reluctance of its government to get involved and to use trade measures -- strong aversions that pervade American trade policy.

---

[115]52 F.R. 229, January 2, 1987.

[116]Five years later, Canada, running into electoral problems in British Columbia, denounced the Agreement, noting that its stumpage fees covered silviculture costs. Of course, this had never been the issue. If it costs a government only $1/ounce to mine gold, this is not its value to those industries which use gold. If a government mine were to sell gold to Canadian eyeglass frame manufacturers for the cost of production of the raw material, that industry would expand its world market share very rapidly, at the expense of other countries' industries, however competitive they might have been prior to the subsidy being granted.

The measures imposed, once decided, were nevertheless still seen by some as being "protectionist" since there would be some limited additional taxes or duties placed on trade.[117] This knee-jerk reaction occurred regardless of the character of the foreign act which gives rise to the U.S. response; Canadian protectionism in the form of subsidization (and the resulting loss of thousands of otherwise competitive U.S. jobs) was simply not as compelling a subject for censure by free-trade critics of America's trade policies as was America's response.

CONCLUSIONS TO BE DRAWN FROM THIS EXPERIENCE

The foregoing recitation of sectoral case studies is not just a regrettable record, it is a tragedy in terms of the costs to the U.S. economy and the unnecessary personal hardships inflicted on hundreds of thousands of workers and their families and communities.[118] It deserves scathing condemnation. More importantly, however, certain features of the system need to be well understood with a view toward reforming it.

Congress and the Trade Remedies

The fact that U.S. trade policy is driven, to a significant degree, by a haphazard welter of trade litigation, reflects, to a significant degree, the frustration of a Congress which is aware of a fundamental problem but which lacks the executive authority to deal with it and -- always cognizant of the Smoot-Hawley disaster -- is reluctant to legislate solutions that usurp what is now perceived to be the President's prerogative of implementing trade policy. For several decades the Executive's reactive posture has been too passive for the Congress, which hears daily from constituents who face problems of denial of market access abroad or trade-related injury at home. Thus, the Congress continually prods the Executive -- largely through successive changes in the trade laws, to become more proactive, a reiterative process that has been underway since the enactment of the Trade Expansion Act of 1962 and the Trade Act of 1974. In these statutes, Congress has provided the private sector with the means to trigger investigations that promise relief

---

[117]The Canadian government characterized the settlement as a "calculated protectionist action." USITC *Trade Agreements Program, 38th Report,* p. 4-17.

[118]In the early 1970s, a young law clerk, new to the Office of the Special Trade Representative, wrote, somewhat unwittingly, "When the Government makes trade policy, it is the public that suffers." This is all too true.

from foreign unfair trade practices. Every four or five years, the Congress has looked at its handiwork and made adjustments to seek to make the trade remedy machinery more effective and resulting relief more certain.[119] In this regard, however, it has had only very limited success. To some degree equity has been provided. In those areas of the law where there is to be little or no discretion exercised, such as in recent years the provision of relief from dumping (through the provision of antidumping duties) and the countering of foreign subsidization which causes injury (through the application of countervailing duties), all those sophisticated enough to seek relief under these statutory remedies may (at least in theory) in like degree find it, regardless of the size of the industry or its importance to the American economy.

Unfortunately, most problems in international competition are more complex than is suggested by the statutory framework, or than can be addressed through the application of penalties following an adjudicative procedure. Dumping or subsidization may be present in any given trade problem, but they are usually just one symptom of a larger failure to deal with complex issues of industrial policy and international competition.[120] Since the problem is broader and deeper than can be addressed within the scope of the trade remedies, the provision of antidumping or countervailing duty relief may at best deliver only a palliative, or temporary relief. And, sadly, relying solely on trade measures alone to deal with problems of international competition more often than not results in a purely protectionist outcome -- trade restrictions and even slower adjustment by the affected U.S. industries.

---

[119]Adjustments were made to the U.S. trade remedies in the Trade Agreements Act of 1979, the Trade and Tariff Act of 1984, and the Omnibus Trade and Competitiveness Act of 1988.

[120]Dumping for example, is more often a symptom of competitive problems than the root cause. Typically, dumping may occur when foreign producers enjoy market power in their own market -- that is, they are protected by import barriers from external competition, and are able to restrict internal competition through inter firm arrangements or even formal legal cartels. They can then maintain high domestic prices and export surpluses at or just above the variable cost of production, so that export prices are much lower than domestic prices (e.g., dumping). The root problem, however, is not dumping, but the existence of a protected market and anticompetitive arrangements within that market.

U.S. Trade Policy and Relations with Others

Ironically, the quest for fairness and equity has not yielded smoother trade relations with America's trading partners -- quite the contrary. Viewing it from the outside, foreigners find the American system very hard either to predict or to understand. Since the government largely awaits a complaint to be filed by the private sector before it becomes engaged in an issue, U.S. government action often comes very late from a petitioning industry's perspective, so that for the foreign exporters and their government, trade measures are imposed abruptly, without much forewarning, after months or years of inaction. The United States appears to move very quickly from taking formal notice of a problem to threatening retaliation or imposition of other trade measures, despite the fact that trade problems, like glaciers, do not tend to just show up unexpectedly in one's backyard on a given morning, as House Ways and Means Trade Subcommittee Chairman Sam Gibbons is fond of saying. Most trade disputes are predictable, were the government of a mind to gaze toward the future.

Ironically, despite all the public attention given to the imposition of U.S. trade remedies, the agonizing that goes into the decision to impose them, and the adverse reaction from abroad when they are announced, the restrictions put into place are almost always less onerous than the prosaic trade restrictions of other trading nations. For example in steel or automobiles, the United States allows much higher levels of import penetration than would be tolerated or even considered in other markets. At least one reason for the adverse reaction abroad to America's trade actions is that the United States almost always acts overtly, after an opportunity for public comment and after public notice has been given. This very transparency tends to give rise to more of an international outcry over American trade policy than over the policies of other countries. Inter-industry arrangements and informal quotas are ignored by the international trading system because they are deniable. What does not occur officially does not exist officially, and need not be complained of, especially as the informal barriers are products of negotiation. The United States almost always acts officially and overtly, and is thus often considered a menace to the trade interests of others. It is accused of engaging in unfettered unilateralism. But generally, its sins are noisy but small.

In addition, this country's legalistic approach, in contrast to the pragmatism with which most other countries have approached trade policy problems, gives rise to irritation wholly apart from the substance of the trade action contemplated. The U.S. government has built a system which puts on trial -- in a quasi-judicial sense -- the activities of foreign countries. Because the Congress cannot get the Executive to act simply when it feels that the latter should understand that the country's commercial interests warrant action, it has larded the statute books with legal requirements for hearings, public findings, timetables for decision, reports to the Congress and the like. Much of this process involves labeling foreign behavior, both private and official, as "unfair." Not surprisingly, this does not sit well with those so labeled. Oddly enough, they state a preference to deal with the pragmatists in other countries who give less access to their markets, who can strike deals but who do not render moral judgments. This is certainly the case with Japan, which has stormy relations with the United States and more tranquil relations with Europe, despite the far more protectionist and discriminatory approach which has been taken toward Japan by the Europeans.[121]

The U.S. system also causes abrasions abroad because the United States is the world's largest single market (and will be so well past 1992). More than any other country (although the European Community is a not too distant second) America has a tendency to affect a large number of interests abroad in each action it takes, if not always in terms of current trade interests, then by way of adverse precedent for future occasions. Thus, foreigners need be concerned even when the specific case may not involve them directly -- this time. There is also more of an outcry over American trade actions because the United States system of trade policy formation tends to take greater cognizance of foreign criticism than do the trade policymaking apparatuses of other countries. Thus, just as some in the Middle East seem to think that it makes more sense to take U.S. rather than Soviet hostages, because a greater impression is made, there is more reason to complain long, hard and loudly about U.S. trade actions than Japanese or European actions. Complaints are more likely to effect a change in policy here than abroad.

Success Without Satisfaction

If foreigners are displeased with American trade policies, and they are, American industry and their representatives in Congress feel aggrieved as well. This feeling of dissatisfaction at home is somewhat ironic in light of the fact that American policy has been largely successful at what it has sought to achieve. Since 1934, the United States government has sought through international negotiation to remove all tariffs and official quantitative restrictions on trade. In this respect, there can hardly have been a greater success. Tariffs in developed countries are on average

---

[121]See Chapter 2.

nominal (although there are important product-specific exceptions to this generalization) and official quantitative restrictions are largely nonexistent. Even among the many of the key developing countries, liberalization is taking hold -- in Mexico, Brazil, Taiwan and (fitfully) in Korea.

But what American industry wants and what its government has achieved are now two separate things, although this was not the case originally. The U.S. government is still primarily trying to create a system of international rules which builds on its domestic experience with the rule of law. Its policymakers overlook the fact that countries with differing economic systems and differing goals may not coexist easily with one set of rules without an unacceptably high level of sacrifice of the perceived and real interests of some of the participants. American firms seek in their government an ally in defending their -- and they suppose, their nation's -- commercial interests. The two may or may not be divergent in fact. However, U.S. government policymakers often act in a manner suggesting that they are oblivious to either set of interests.

It is an immutable rule governing human affairs that individuals, groups and -- it must necessarily follow -- governments, are more likely to succeed at what they are attempting to accomplish than at tasks they have not consciously set for themselves. At the grander level of geopolitical strategy, what the United States wished to achieve was to prevent a recurrence of the Great Depression, to halt the spread of communism abroad (or less consciously, the resurgence of the breeding grounds of the most virulent forms of fascism), and to foster world prosperity by creating a liberal international trading system, one without barriers at any national border. Its strategic foreign policy goals were seen to be served by this trade policy. Its senior Cabinet officials -- the Secretaries of State and Treasury -- were actively involved in the fostering of this policy. There are certainly vestiges of this policy theme to be found today, even if the strength of belief is not as strong today.

This fostering of a multilateral trading system was a central tenet of post-war American Administrations through the mid-1970s. Then, as the U.S. trade surplus ebbed and its international accounts position turned to deficit, and as the tide of world communism reached its high water mark and the specter of the Depression faded, America's concerns began to shift. This has been a slow process. The principal focus of activity under the trade laws has begun to be the opening foreign markets rather than protecting the home market against unfairly traded or otherwise injurious imports. Section 301, long an insignificant provision of the U.S. trade laws (it was first enacted in 1962 as section 252 of the Trade Expansion Act of that year), moved to center stage, displacing the escape clause or import relief provisions as the focal point of U.S. trade policy deliberations.

As the U.S. trade surplus disappeared, other concerns arose. It should not have to be stated, but policy makers seems to forget, that trade balances are made up of specific goods and services. While economists were looking at the overall balances, and at equations that dictate a trade deficit if there is a shortfall in domestic savings, others -- primarily in the private sector (who had to live with the consequences of trade for their enterprises) -- were looking for more sophisticated answers. U.S. industries which had not known competition for decades (either because of high tariffs before the Second World War or because other countries had largely lost their productive capacity during the War) found themselves embattled and, in all too many instances, losing. The emerging issue became the international competitiveness of America's industries. In the 1980s, Commissions and Councils were formed to examine the reasons for America's declining performance in internationally-traded goods. Many diagnoses were advanced. Lists of prescriptions were drawn up. But these were, by and large, ignored by the policy-making process.

The U.S. Executive Branch was not very receptive to these inquiries and policy recommendations. It had its eye fixed upon perfecting the multilateral trading system by extending the coverage of the rules to new areas -- trade in services, the protection of intellectual property, and trade-related investment restrictions, and by bringing agriculture within the disciplines of the GATT. It was also concerned with the removal of barriers to trade within the North American region, through the negotiation of two free trade areas with the nations on its northern and southern borders, in preparation for hemispheric free trade.

As noted at the beginning of this chapter, the approach of American officials to trade questions has differed markedly from that of corresponding officials in other governments. In addition to the Constitutional reasons for these differences is the fact that other governments had as a central purpose promotion of industry -- in Europe and in Japan the focus was on reconstruction, while in Korea, Taiwan and Brazil, the central tenet has been economic development. Not since the century of Alexander Hamilton have American policymakers thought in these terms. They might create an industry by publishing a Federal Register notice asking for bids for its development at the expense of the Federal treasury,[122] but this extreme aberration in their conduct would

---

[122]Creation of the titanium industry during the Korean war, pursuant to the Defense Production Act.

only occur for reasons of national security in time of war.[123] Otherwise, they were indifferent to the composition of the American economy and certainly not interested in the commercial success of any given industry -- by and large, America's commerce was not their business.

If United States' trade policy is judged on the basis of how well American industry is doing in international competition, the policy must be held to have been a failure over the last few decades. But this judgment would bring the immediate rejoinder that this is not what American policy has been designed to achieve. Both are accurate statements. The commercial success of its industry has not been of interest to America's government. The success of its agriculture, its space program, and its military, has been. Therefore, while only the United States would be capable of launching and prosecuting successfully and Operation Desert Storm, putting Americans on the moon, or, perhaps, causing a green revolution, America's industries have not achieved the capability to produce the computer notebook on which the manuscript for this chapter has been prepared.

All policies at the national level of any country are designed in the first instance to maintain a nation's security and economic welfare. This was seen, as has been noted previously, by the architects of the post World War II international economic system as constructing a multilateral trade and payments system that would provide the necessary basis for reconstruction of countries whose economies had been destroyed in the war and to permit the development of those countries (largely former colonies) which had not yet industrialized. In this regard, America's policies succeeded. These policies ceased to serve America as well in the 1970s and 1980s. They will not serve America as well in the 1990s. Their failings will lead not only to a further disappointments in results for American industry but increasing friction between America and its trading partners.

The following chapters examine what is wrong with American trade policy and what might be done to correct these defects, as well as whether support of the GATT and of multilateralism have outlived their usefulness as the central tenets of American policy, as some believe, and finally, outlines the challenges to be faced in the remaining years of this decade.

---

[123]The United States found itself uncomfortably dependent on foreign, not necessarily friendly, sources of supply of titanium at the outset of the Korean War.

9

Improving United States Trade Policy

Alan Wm. Wolff

If we could first know where we are, and whither we are tending, we could better judge what to do, and how to do it.

-- Abraham Lincoln[1]

THE IMPORTANCE OF THE SUBJECT AT HAND

A formative experience of the current generation has been the triumph of the concepts of individual freedom and the market economy over those of communism and command economies. The success of this Western form of social and economic organization is not solely a victory of a set of ideas; it has occurred because democracy and capitalism were seen to produce better results, a fact which was evident to almost everyone -- including all those in Eastern Europe whose reason was left even partially unclouded by communist ideology. Absent a military conflict in which communism had the edge, it can now be said with perfect hindsight that it had to lose in the long run. The final results on the Nixon-Khrushchev kitchen debate are now in; the result was Darwinian, the fittest survived.

---

[1]Acceptance speech, June 1857 Illinois Republican State Convention, quoted in Shelby Foote, *The Civil War*, Vol 1, at p 30, Vintage Books, 1986.

This was a contest in which the winning side was led by the United States. In mid-century, it was this country's form of government and market organization that replaced the fascist regimes of Europe and brought sweeping changes to Japan and to its former colonies, Korea and Taiwan. It was the United States, with help principally from Great Britain, which, in the postwar era, shaped the international economic institutions governing trade, reconstruction and development aid, and payments. These efforts have now been crowned with success.

But this was not the "end of history." The contest is not over, nor will it ever be. Future generations of Americans will, of course, applaud the result of the long struggle of the last seventy-five years against the threat of communism, but they will judge this generation of Americans primarily by another test. Knowing how America fared in the competition that began in the late 1960s -- the commercial competition among the Western allies -- they will examine the 1990s as the turning point, and will examine the record of this decade for clues to the successes or failures which lie ahead for America in the 21st century.

This newer competition is not military, nor is it life threatening, as far as we can judge. The issue should not be framed, as the American public has done in recent public opinion polls, as a matter of Japan replacing the Soviet Union as the number one security threat to the United States. This is a peaceful competition among those who are fated by their natures to be economic rivals. It is a result of that internal drive which caused Europe to decide to become an exporter of steel and large commercial aircraft, and Japan of steel, televisions, automobiles, semiconductors and computers. More is at stake in this competition than employment; were that the sole issue, macroeconomic means might well accomplish the desired results. The large industrial efforts of the other major trading nations are not evenly spread among the various product sectors for purposes of job creation. They are targeted at certain sectors viewed as strategic. Governments believe that the futures of their countries depend on the composition of their economies, and for the most part they see their success as nations as defined by their relative success in these specific efforts.[2]

The rationale for these national endeavors is usually unspoken, although it is odd that something this important is generally left unarticulated. In part, this reticence may be due to the lip service paid by

---

[2]See generally EC Commission, Directorate-General, Internal Market and Industrial Affairs, *Industrial Consequences of Targeting Strategies, With Particular Reference to the Electronics Industry* (Working Paper, January 1990); see also U.S. International Trade Commission, *Foreign Industrial Targeting and Its Effects on U.S. Industries* (Three volumes).

each of the foreign governments studied in this book to leaving commercial outcomes to the market, even when in reality the market is being influenced greatly by conscious government and government-industry programs. The reason governments seek to influence commercial outcomes through sectoral intervention is their natural concern for national security and their peoples' standard of living. The United States is not immune from this set of interests, however oblivious it may be to the fact that other nations pursue very different courses in trying to serve them.

With the demise of the Soviet Union as a superpower it will be argued by some that national security is no longer a pressing U.S. concern. But this requires one to put aside the current military capabilities of the former Soviet Republics, and to forget Tiananmen Square -- which should serve as a reminder that a large part of humanity is still in the grip of an ideology that preaches the destruction of our way of life. It would also require us to forget the recent Gulf War -- which dramatically demonstrated how regional conflicts can erupt unexpectedly, threatening our security. Moreover, history teaches us that nations which are longstanding friends can become bitter enemies within a relatively short time. While this is not a credible concern to today's citizen, it should be -- Americans have several times in this century felt the same complacence about the implausibility of threats that were to prove only too real a short time later.[3] Thus, while the United States should seek a decline in the level of global armaments, it must retain strong defensive capabilities.

In this time of harmony between what was the Eastern bloc and the West, a more satisfying reason for keeping a dominant, or, as it is evolving, a first-among-equals position in the world, is to maintain our ability to do good as we are given the vision to do good. If we are to continue to play a major role in the work of feeding the world's hungry, fighting the world's diseases, improving the economic lot of others, or protecting the global environment, we must maintain our economic strength. This is not due solely, nor even mainly, to altruism; it is required in order to serve the United States' broader economic and security interests. Our own prosperity depends in part on the extent to

---

[3]This is not meant to suggest unfaithfulness on the part of our current friends. But the world is an unpredictable and sometimes dangerous place. In the last century, reflecting political changes in other countries, we have abruptly found ourselves in a position of armed confrontation, and in some cases outright warfare, with countries with which we had enjoyed cordial relations only a short time before -- Italy, France (under the Vichy regime), China, Cuba, Iran, Nicaragua, Panama, Iraq. From tomorrow forward, we do not know the tests to which any generation may be put.

which the international environment is one in which economic growth continues. In order for the United States to retain the capability to influence this environment, U.S. industries must remain internationally competitive. Whatever the objectives -- altruistic or self-serving, military or pacific -- the ability of the United States economy to excel at making advanced technology goods and providing complex services is vitally important.

The Gulf War should be particularly instructive of our national security needs. Watching the arcade game-like flight of guided missiles and tallying the miraculously small loss of American lives in that conflict, the importance of advanced technologies was not lost on the military, and should not be lost on the rest of us. Remarkably, and to some degree it must be noted with some distress, the microelectronics technologies that brought a quick and relatively bloodless victory for the allies were ten to fifteen years old. This was due to a variety of factors that would be relevant in a broader discussion of U.S. competitiveness, such as the government's inability to be a first class customer. While the United States still possesses the competitive position in microelectronics to make the leading edge chips necessary for future weaponry, its leadership position has been eroded, in part because U.S. computer chipmakers lost downstream markets twenty years ago, particularly in consumer electronics. In effect, this country's capabilities in future armed conflicts has been diminished, to some degree, by the failures of U.S. trade policy -- in this case, the loss of the color television battle, with a resultant loss of capabilities in microelectronics. The consequences of acts and omissions in the field of trade are more far-reaching than past and present policymakers have readily understood.

If writing in anticipation of future wars seems negative and mean-spirited, and if our capacity to assist other countries in their development seems too lofty and remote an objective to guide day-to-day policies, there is still another set of reasons why we should be concerned with the composition of the nation's economy. These strike much closer to home -- they concern our standard of living. Here we can be less Darwinian; it is not necessary to triumph over others, but to be, on average, at least their equals, ahead in some things, close in others. If we fail at this, the way we live will suffer. The grand American experiment in democracy is inextricably interwoven with economic success; communism would have been far more robust, even if still oppressive, had it delivered material prosperity.

To be successful, any system must, at the most basic level, provide "freedom from want."[4] But this is not enough for advanced modern nations. We are fortunate that with the exception of those whom our societies have failed, the primary concern of the governments of the industrialized nations of the world goes beyond the issue of providing the bare necessities. At the next level, it is the number of jobs, and ultimately, the kind of jobs that is the focus of policy. In the most basic terms, at issue is the nature of the problems which future generations will be given to solve in their work. A new school of economic thought has grown up in recent years which points out that dynamic rather than static comparative advantage governs national economic success. Bruce Scott, of the Harvard Business School, argues that David Riccardo's model was somewhat flawed.[5] Riccardo pointed out the benefits to Great Britain and to Portugal of trading cloth for port. He did not point out that the benefits to Great Britain of producing cloth, in terms of the knowledge gained (or externalities), far outweighed any benefits that Portugal could extract from the production of wine; indeed the punch cards of the Jacquard loom are the intellectual predecessor of the software of today's computers. In the industrial revolution, England gave its workers intellectual challenges unrivaled in all the world. The result, ultimately, was a continuation of power and prosperity that was great in both absolute and comparative terms.

We are currently concerned over whether Americans in this generation will be better off materially than their parents were, and the answer to this question is uncomfortably far from clear. To avoid stagnation, we need to increase productivity, which does not mean simply producing things more efficiently; it means producing them differently, more cleverly. The Europeans and the Japanese seem to have grasped intuitively the fact that it is vital to current employment and the future well-being of their peoples that their scientists, engineers, administrators and other workers be challenged by the greatest intellectual tests possible to devise. Thus the Europeans have decided that they must excel not only in chemicals and mechanical devices but in large commercial aircraft, information technologies, new materials, and biotechnology. In both Japan and Europe, policymakers and politicians are seeking to improve the

---

[4]One of the four freedoms cited by Franklin Delano Roosevelt.

[5]Bruce R. Scott and George C. Lodge (eds.), *U.S. Competitiveness in the World Economy* (Boston: Harvard Business School Press, 1985).

material well-being of their peoples and economic strength of their nations.[6]

This book addresses only a subset of the problems which require resolution if the United States is to maintain its competitive edge. It is designed solely to give a brief overview of the prospective trade policies (or, as relevant, trade and industrial policies) of seven of the most important contestants -- the European Community, Japan, Germany, Brazil, Korea, Taiwan, and the United States -- and draw some of the inferences available.[7] Trade policy is just a subset of the many policy

---

[6]See generally the French government's blueprint for what later became the Eureka initiative, *La Renaissance Technologique de L'Europe* (1985); Japan's Ministry of International Trade and Industry, *Trends and Future Tasks in Industrial Technology (a.k.a. White Paper on Industrial Technology)* (September 1988); West German Ministry of Research, *Informationstechnik* (1984).

[7]To conduct any analysis, it is necessary to define one's terms. The threshold question is what is "trade policy". Breaking this phrase down, "trade" is simply the flow of goods and services across national borders. Explicit "trade policy" is any decision of government that intends to influence these flows of goods and services, whether in direction, amount, or composition. Acts of government which inadvertently affect trade have an implicit trade policy component. It may be a semantic nuance but "policy," which one might think inherently cannot be unconscious, nevertheless often is. Thus, for example, a decision to protect the spotted owl may sharply reduce timber availability, and therefore curtail the possibility for exporting wood products. That policy is seen as being solely environmental or ecological, and not a trade policy decision, but to some extent, it is. At the other extreme, a much clearer case is a decision to subsidize airframes, engines, or aeronautical instruments for Airbus. These measures are not called "trade policies" but are by design not primarily for the creation of a product for home consumption, and therefore must be viewed as major trade policy decisions, of which the trade effect was an intended result. The purpose was and is to conquer world markets. It would be a wholly artificial distinction to limit an inquiry into trade policies to those government decisions which are labeled as such. In today's world, which has been scrubbed of most border measures -- tariffs and quotas -- at least in developed countries, few important trade policy decisions actually involve border controls on trade. Taking this analysis one step further, a decision which reserves a market for the producers of one's own country -- such as through a decision not to enforce rules regarding competition -- can also be the making of trade policy. Primary examples often occur in the case of Japan, which often regulates its trade with little or no overt government intervention. At a microeconomic level (which nevertheless has macroeconomic effects), examples would include the failure to allow competition to develop in the form of chains of large retail stores, slowing greatly the import penetration of consumer goods

(continued...)

questions facing government. Those engaged in making the many policy decisions required daily in government -- for example procurement of goods for the Defense Department or deciding whether or not to investigate a transaction for antitrust concerns -- are very often also making trade policy decisions, although in this country they are usually unaware of it. Similarly, those making trade policy decisions perforce are acting within the context of factors which are not solely related to questions of regulating imports or exports. It is the thesis of this chapter that there are a whole range of policy decisions made by the U.S. government that must begin to take into account their impact on the competitiveness of American industries, including services and agriculture.

Those who make trade policy must begin to be recognize that the seemingly remote objectives of serving national security and enhancement of this nation's standard of living will be affected by the many, often mundane, decisions which they make. This does not mean that every trade issue is freighted with these broader considerations. But it is imperative to recognize them when they do occur.

EIGHT CHALLENGES

Recognizing That There Is a Problem

"My name is Ozymandias, King of Kings,
Look on my Works, ye Mighty, and despair!
Nothing beside remains. Round the decay
Of that colossal Wreck, boundless and bare
The lone and level sands stretch far away."

"Ozymandias," by
Percy Bysshe Shelley, 1817

---

[7](...continued)
generally both by dampening effective demand because unavailability of goods raises prices and by the fact that the complex distribution system is tied in many cases to domestic producers (The Large Retail Store Law), and the nonenforcement of antitrust laws with respect to distribution. These examples have become, in effect, central elements of Japanese trade policy. Indeed, the protective effects, if originally unintended, are now relied upon: Japan need not impose direct import restrictions on apparel, for example, because those Japanese interests which control trade and the distribution of goods do not wish them to enter into Japanese commerce. Trade has been curtailed by either government action or conscious inaction. But there are no border measures.

Shelley was writing about the great statue of the pharaoh that we know as Ramses. He was telling us that no civilization, no nation, retains its vitality forever -- all pass. Thus passed Sumer, Akkad, Egypt of the Pharaohs, Athens, Rome, the dynasties of China, the Japan of Shoguns, and the empires of the Mayas and Incas, Spain, Portugal, Imperial Britain, and countless others. America's Founding Fathers realized that they had in this country a delicate experiment with a precarious future.[8] They proceeded with infinite care to build institutions, and exercised policy options with great regard for their effects. Arguably we lost that sense of the importance of our actions, and the perils of inaction, when the country began to expand across a boundless Western frontier. A feeling of invulnerability was reinforced by our victories in two World Wars, and now by the collapse of the USSR and its empire. And yet there is a gnawing suspicion that not all is well. Thus, perhaps, this is not so irrelevant a time and place -- in a book on trade policy in the 1990s -- to be quoting Shelley. There is now a problem facing the United States whose proportions are worthy of the sweeping comparisons of the preceding sentences. The central problem of our time, however, is that we need to feel the challenge before we can properly look after our interests, and we do not feel it.

The United States has periodically shown that it can be roused to action given the right circumstances. The challenge of Nazi Germany was not initially perceived by the majority of Americans as a threat that required action, but the need to respond to the bombing of Pearl Harbor was undeniable, and we did so with a stupendous national effort. Likewise, the need to respond to the launch of the first Soviet space satellite sounded a tocsin throughout the United States; the resources of the scientific community were mobilized, and the educational system was reformed. Four years after Sputnik, President Kennedy was to declare that America would put astronauts on the moon, and in 1969, we did.

The central problem today is not that the resources are not present to respond to the competitive challenge which exists, but that the challenge itself is not perceived. It is as if instead of the Capitoline geese giving the warning that called forth Rome's defenders, one goose called at a time and was ignored. One such call is the periodic announcement of math test scores in which United States high school children do not place within the ranking of the first dozen countries; another occurs as the market shares of key industries decline vis-a-vis their foreign competitors. It was well enough to accept the fact that the United States would lose share naturally as other countries went through reconstruction or development

---

[8]See Jay, *Federalist* Nos. 3-5; Hamilton, *Federalist* Nos. 6-8.

after the Second World War, but what is being witnessed now is not merely a statistical phenomenon; the United States' leading position in industry after industry is disappearing or on its way disappearing. Gordon Moore and Andrew Grove, the Chairman and President of Intel Corporation, have illustrated this trend graphically in a series of "x-curves," showing for industry after industry the declining slope of the U.S. market share in an industry plotted against the rising curve of market share of the competing Japanese industry.[9] None of these events is Sputnik-like. There is no dramatic announcement for the televised evening news, merely an accretion of lost contracts, lost jobs, closed plants, and lost opportunities. These are not events that touch our collective consciousness, but they are nevertheless very real, and their impact will be felt far into the future. The philosophers of the Middle Ages kept a human skull on their desks to remind themselves of their mortality. America's official policy makers might do well to keep on their desks a set of the Grove/Moore x-curves of the decline of key American industries. It may be that like Ozymandias, one must despair of our system of government and society lasting through the millennia, but that is no excuse to allow America to decline during our own period of stewardship, particularly when remedies are at hand that would alter the near and mid-term results. We do not require a cry of despair, but a call for action. More likely than not, we must await a President who will provide the necessary leadership to enable us to overcome our complacency.

Correcting the Internal Compass

At the beginning of this chapter, Abraham Lincoln is quoted as stating "If we could first know where we are, and whither we are tending, we could better judge what to do, and how to do it." Knowing where we are and whither we are tending is in large part a function of self-knowledge as well as of knowledge of one's surroundings. Horace Greeley was not in doubt about the country's direction of growth and opportunity when he told a generation "Go West, young man." This was the period of "manifest destiny." It cannot be held that national direction was clearer

[9]A.S. Grove, *Silicon Valley; The Next Techno-Colony?* (Mimeo, September 26, 1990). These curves show, for example, the U.S. machine tool industry declining from a world market share of around 18 percent in 1975 to around 6 percent by 1988, while Japan's went from 29 percent to the vicinity of 50 percent during the same period; and a decline of U.S. share of the world semiconductor equipment market from over 80 percent in 1979 to around 30 percent in 1988, while Japan went about from 10 percent to over 40 percent during the same period.

Policy Failures Underlying America's Competitiveness Plight

- ***Failure to recognize the challenge and the absence of political will.*** *None of the problems faced are insoluble. Few of them are recognized for what they are by more than a small minority of observers. The challenges not being apparent, the will to deal with them is absent. The consequences for America's security and standard of living are grievous.*

- ***Failure of the conceptual framework.*** *U.S. Government policy makers lack a relevant internal compass. Being devoted to free trade and subscribing to a laissez-faire ideology do not provide a guidance mechanism sufficient to the policy decisions currently required to meet international competition. As a group, U.S. officials charged with conducting economic policies have not recognized that the United States has national commercial interests.*

- ***Failure to have an adequate analytical capability.*** *Beyond the philosophical predisposition to ignore the policy questions raised by failures to meet international competition, there is a deficit in the skills and experience in government needed to understand problems and craft responses. There is also is a lack of continuity of policy-level officials, resulting in a lack of institutional memory. These deficiencies are in direct contrast to the situation of foreign governments.*

- ***Failure to organize a collective response.*** *The relationship between industry and government is adversarial, as are relationships within the business community. The foreign competition is often better organized and this can confer a major advantage. The fact that the operations of foreign enterprises may not be profitable over extended periods of time, and therefore are not by our measures considered successful, does not mean that they cannot do great damage to American industry.*

- ***Failure of trade policy.*** *American trade policy compartmentalizes the analysis of competitive problems. It asks whether there is dumping or subsidization or violation of intellectual property rights, or just massive injury -- each in the alternative. It provides partial remedies after great delay. It is not integrated with any other of the nation's policies (in industry as opposed to agriculture). It is preoccupied with process rather than results. It has no response to private restraints on trade or to foreign industrial targeting. We have not recognized that nations generally succeed at the objectives they set, and that these may be at odds with America's commercial interests.*

- ***Failure to invest for the future.*** *No solutions have been implemented with respect to the shortfall in American savings and investment. According to OECD statistics, as of 1988 Japan was investing at twice the rate of the United States in plant and equipment. That this will make a telling difference in future results of international competition cannot be doubted, but we are blind to it. U.S. tax policy is set as a matter of adjusting equities among domestic interests without considering international competitive effects.*

- ***Failure to exploit America's strengths in technology.*** *U.S. educational, government and private R & D capabilities, taken together, outmatch that of any competitor. Disorganization and lack of focus severely dilute what should be an unbeatable advantage.*

- ***Failure of America's educational system.*** *We are lagging behind our major foreign competitors in investment in human capital. This is one of the most serious problems we face. The solution lies in a greater degree of public commitment to seeing that the problem is remedied. It is a question of recognizing the challenge and generating the political will to provide a response.*

- ***Failure of manufacturing quality and process.*** *American firms lag behind the leading edge of foreign manufacturing capability. Public policy can highlight the problems and catalyze and clear the way for more effective responses.*

(These are issues beyond the scope of this work, but of equal importance.)

then because life was far simpler; in fact it was much more encumbered with risks to health, safety and to livelihood. But the American people did seem to know what they were about.

There was a general sense of loss of purpose in the 1950s. President Eisenhower even went so far as to appoint a Presidential Commission on the subject; it issued a report entitled "Goals for Americans." However, this national aimlessness was not true of trade policy.[10]

Opening Markets. There was a certainty of purpose in U.S. trade policy that began in 1934 and continued well into the recent past with the launching of the Uruguay Round of Multilateral Trade Negotiations.[11] From the outset of Franklin Roosevelt's and Cordell Hull's Trade Agreements Program, this nation was dedicated to tearing away, on a reciprocal basis, the barriers that, while not causing, had deepened and prolonged the Great Depression. National policy starting in 1934 was pragmatism clothed in idealism; the Administration was clear in its judgment that it was in the national interest that world trade grow to prior levels. This was the earliest and most successful plank of an internationalist economic program that turned its back on American isolationism.

To this general goal of improving the economic condition of the world through increased trade, President Kennedy, in the Trade Expansion Act of 1962, added two further purposes. First, trade was to be used as a weapon in the effort to halt the spread of communism. Poverty in third world countries provided a breeding ground for unrest on which communism fed; trade, it was felt, could help remedy that poverty. It was also President Kennedy's intent that the newly formed European Economic Community not be allowed to become a European fortress against American goods. Global tariff negotiations were to dilute the discrimination inherent in the Common Market. The Kennedy Round of GATT negotiations brought tariffs down further and sought the reduction of nontariff barriers. Regrettably this latter, nontariff effort met with little success at the time, as it was rejected by the Congress. This task was left for the Tokyo Round, concluded in 1979, which adopted codes of conduct governing subsidies, customs valuation, product standards, government

---

[10]With the collapse of the Soviet Union, the 1990s will bring refocussing of public attention on national purpose. However, with high national debt and related economic problems, there is a risk that economic isolationism might blunt the adoption of more worthy objectives.

[11]GATT, *Ministerial Declaration on the Uruguay Round* (Min. Dec., September 26, 1986) ("Punta del Este Declaration").

procurement, and a variety of other areas of governmental protection largely unrelated to tariffs.[12] In the Uruguay Round, the United States sought the extension of the GATT to entirely new areas -- to trade in services, trade-related investment, and intellectual property protection, as well as for the first time to give meaningful application of the international trading rules to agriculture.

There was great continuity to this stream of trade negotiating efforts. The central theme was the broadening and deepening of the international rules in a way that brought about increase in trade. Priorities had to be set, and they were; in international negotiations, one cannot get everything one would like, and one cannot give up that which is too dear in political and/or economic terms. In its preparations for the Tokyo Round, the Administration worked hand-in-glove with the private sector to define American interests. This was not, at the first, done wholly willingly. An elaborate private sector advisory process was created by the Congress that encompassed business, agriculture, and labor leaders as well as technical experts, about one thousand in all. These advisors were closely consulted, as opposed to the generally light duty to which the roster of 300 or so advisors in the Kennedy Round had been put.[13] The Congressional pressure to work with the private sector was reinforced by the memory that the two nontariff barrier agreements entered into by the Kennedy Administration did not receive Congressional approval.[14] This time, the Administration knew, the entire results of the Round would require approval by the Congress. And at that stage, the Congress would turn to the private sector advisors and ask for their opinions on the merits of the deals struck.[15] Moreover, as negotiations became increasingly technical (it was one thing to cut tariffs by 33%, it was another to create

[12]President of the United States, *Agreements Reached in the Tokyo Round of Multilateral Trade Negotiations*, 96th Cong., 1st Sess., House Doc. No. 96-153.

[13]I.M.Destler, *American Trade Politics; System Under Stress* (Washington and New York; Institute for International Economics, 1986), pp. 94-96.

[14]One was never ratified, regarding the American selling price (ASP) of customs valuation, and the other was seemingly gutted (the Antidumping Code). Renegotiation Amendments Act of 1968, Pub.L.No. 90-634; S.Rep. 1385, 90th Cong., 2d Sess., pt. 2 (1968).

[15]The investment in time spent with advisors paid dividends -- the package of trade agreements passed the Congress by overwhelming majorities, 90 to 4 in the Senate, 395 to 7 in the House.

rules governing product standards), the U.S. negotiators of necessity became more dependent on private sector expertise.

Thus, within the context of seeking open markets generally, the dynamics of broad, multilateral trade negotiations had several favorable effects in the policy-making process: It forced the setting of priorities. This required close working relations with the private sector, and analysis of where the greatest gains could be made. Analysis and advice were also sought from the International Trade Commission and from the line departments. Politics had something of a role to play, too, but did not overwhelm the general thrust of what was being sought to be achieved. The system worked. This process of setting priorities -- making choices -- in broad trade negotiations is now well understood and causes little or no philosophical objection. But outside of broad negotiations, the government is ill-equipped to come to any trade decisions. Being in favor of openness gives no direction as to where to start, or how to accomplish anything once an objective is identified.

Granting equity. Overlaid on this general feeling that the world would be a better place if markets were open -- allowing the market to allocate tasks in accordance with the dictates of efficiency -- is the desire to grant equity under the trade laws. By and large, the U.S. government does not pick its targets, so much as it is thrust against them by private litigants. This may result in efforts directed at the right priorities from the viewpoint of the national interest, or, alternatively, in a certain amount of tilting at windmills, accomplishing little or achieving objectives not worthy of the effort expended.[16] This part of U.S. trade policy has been privatized. The central irony is that the private sector, which was deputized to choose the targets of trade policy actions, has become so dissatisfied. Trade policymakers found that while they antagonized foreigners, they did not satisfy domestic interests very much either. But if upholding laissez-faire ideals and providing equity does not provide sufficient guidance for concerted action toward worthwhile objectives, there should be a more sensible approach.

---

[16]In 1990, the U.S. government conducted countervailing duty investigations, with respect to sodium sulfur compounds from Turkey, leather from Argentina, limousines and pork from Canada, butt-weld pipe fittings from Thailand, silicon metal from Brazil, salmon from Norway, steel wire rope from Israel and India and a number of other products. (U.S. Department of Commerce, International Trade Administration). The affirmative findings reached in a number of these cases make it clear that the petitioners had legitimate concerns with foreign subsidies. Arguably, however, the sum of these cases does not constitute a coherent national policy on the issue of foreign subsidies.

More fundamental objectives. First, there should be recognition that trade policy should seek to foster the nation's security and its people's standard of living.[17] This is not a call for protectionism or neo-mercantilism, nor does it mean an abandonment of the search for the holy grail of free markets as the best organizing principle. It does mean that trade policy efforts must, at a minimum, concentrate consciously on curbing distortions which injure the industrial base.[18] Second, it must be acknowledged that the composition of our own economy matters -- it can never be a sufficient goal of policy simply to maintain employment, or GNP growth alone. What the nation produces, and the degree of skill required to produce it, are important as well. Third, it follows from a recognition that trade issues matter to the nation's safety and well-being (both in macroeconomic and compositional terms) that there are national commercial interests. The success of American manufacturers in world markets must be a matter for more than passing commendation by the Secretary of Commerce. The Secretaries of State and Treasury, as well as the President, must be concerned with how the country fares in trade. They need not applaud every transaction, but they must support them in the aggregate, and individually where there is a specific national purpose served. The removal of barriers and unfair advantages granted to foreign competitors by governments abroad should become national priorities.

For the United States, as with other governments, it must be recognized that the national interest is not divorced from the success or failure of the nation's businesses. It seems too simple a concept, but there would be a vast change in trade policy were there recognition of this fact. This does not mean that national interest is served by too large a role for government. Nor does it mean that caring about trade must mean cosseting industry with protection. But it does indicate a need for identifying the nation's commercial interests as policies are made. This recognition does not have to be at the expense of foreign countries' interests, because this competition can be a mutually beneficial one -- all can gain from it. Nor is a return to xenophobia, isolationism, or protectionism called for. Foreign investment which is positive should still be entirely welcome, for example, but the purchase of U.S. companies simply to strip them and remove technology should not.

A President who cares about what is being made in the United States -- about not only how many people are employed, but how they are

---

[17]This may seen painfully obvious. But current U.S. policies have only a remote and tenuous connection to these basic premises.

[18]In this context, "industry" must be defined broadly to include traded services and agribusiness.

employed -- will be practicing the new and improved trade policy that is needed for meeting the challenges of the 21st century. It will be his or her responsibility, along with that of those who shape opinion elsewhere in government, in business, labor, academia and the media, to readjust the national internal compass by which trade policy will be set. U.S. trade policy will more often than not result in failure until this shift in thinking takes place. This change requires no adjustment in U.S. law or in international rules. It simply means changing our national attitude, a difficult but not impossible task -- a challenge for those who would lead the country in the coming years.

One cannot help but feel somewhat defensive in advocating a position that must be taken by most mainstream, one-world, internationalist, rules-oriented (or foreign) observers as one of excessive American chauvinism. There is, in fact, another model which could serve for organizing international affairs. In an ideal world, why should national borders matter at all? Companies would operate without real citizenship, doing what they could for shareholder returns, and placing their operations wherever economic efficiency dictated. All countries would simply be good, selfless hosts. They would be wholly neutral toward investment, provide a rich medium (an educated work force, modern infrastructure, and the like) to investors. Alas, although many have argued that we are on the threshold of such a world, the world not only does not now work this way but possibly never will. Competition and pursuit of advantage appears to be the organizing principle of nature. This we may regard philosophically as being good, but it does not work out in the way that Adam Smith envisaged it:

> *Every man, as long as he does not violate the laws of justice, is left perfectly free to pursue his own interest his own way, and to bring both his industry and capital into competition with those of any other man or order of men. The sovereign is completely discharged from a duty, in the attempt to perform which he must always be exposed to innumerable delusions, and for the proper performance of which no human wisdom or knowledge could ever be sufficient: the duty of superintending the industry of private people.*[19]

In fact, firms compete for resources, as do educational institutions and governments. Firms locating in a given nation will tend to reach out to and ally themselves with universities and government agencies, to strengthen their ability to compete. The foreign government may refrain

---

[19]Adam Smith, *The Wealth of Nations*, 1776, bk IV, ch. 9.

from trying to superintend the private industry, but usually it will not be deaf to a call for assistance, and in some cases it will initiate the intervention. Such government actions may benefit an industry or firm or may prove costly and unwise, but in either case, competing firms in other countries may be harmed. In these cases, the U.S. government must understand what is taking place and seek to counter the effects of the intervention. It is unlikely to be wholly successful, because every foreign government may decide that it needs a steel industry, an airline industry, or an information industry, regardless of how the U.S. government feels about it. Consequently, while U.S. policymakers may try to move the world toward the Adam Smith model which they admire, they must watch for the harm that others may do, and to nurture, where necessary, the growth of industries that serve the national interests set forth above.

Improving the Government's Analytical Capability

If you are an official at the U.S. Department of Agriculture, you are concerned about the loss of a sale of American wheat in the North Africa market. You will be alert to the fact that the loss has occurred in the first place. You can call down into the Department's professional staff, and ask what the Argentines are selling their wheat for that day, or what the French are selling their flour for. You can find out within the Department what the terms of sale are for competitive American products (if wheat, it was probably financed by your program). If there are foreign subsidies, you will know how much they are, and how they are given. You will be able to plan an American response without a legal complaint. You are motivated, you are knowledgeable, and you have the policy tools, relatively speaking, to deal with the foreign competition.

Not all aspects of agricultural trade are worth emulating, but the fact that the U.S. government's trade officials have a body of factual data about foreign markets and trade at least allows policy to be made on an informed basis. The senior officials at the Commerce Department are less well-equipped -- but there is no expectation that they be otherwise. Many of their analysts are assigned to cover a broad swath of industrial product sectors with which the government generally has little contact. The State Department, Foreign Commercial Service, the National Technical Information Service, the International Trade Commission, the International Trade Administration, the Office of the U.S. Trade Representative and the Central Intelligence Agency all gather massive quantities of data on foreign trade and industrial policies, but this information is imperfectly disseminated, analyzed and understood within the government and is often unavailable or not readily available to the private potential litigants that have been invested by our system with the role of initiators of trade policy actions. As a result, there are large gaps in the government's knowledge of where the United States is competitive, and what makes it more or less so, and what the market conditions abroad are like for the product.[20]

Key U.S. trade decisions are made, or often are simply not made at all, on the basis of very limited information. To some extent, this suits the government's temperament. Because it views itself in trade policy most often as a judge and not a party, if it bases its judgments largely on the facts supplied by the contestants in a proceeding -- the foreign government and foreign companies on the one hand and the U.S. industry on the other -- there is little feeling that much is missing. If the terms of the inquiry are sufficiently narrow, and the response similarly limited, the absence of the facts necessary to determine national interest in any broader sense does not generate any particular sense of loss.

There is also sometimes a perverse influence at work: to seek to know more about a trade problem is to imply that something can or should be done about it. There is thus no substantial effort within the U.S. government, or within the GATT or the OECD, to study the effects of industrial targeting programs on trade and investment decisions generally. There has never been an in-depth study by the Commerce Department of the competitive effect of various subsidies, perhaps because this could trigger the statutory responsibility of the Secretary to initiate countervailing duty cases.[21] To be sure, if a Secretary engaged in gratuitous intervention, the results could be chaotic and politically costly. On the other hand, a large burden is placed on the domestic industry to gather basic information for the government before any decision can be taken.

The lack of a sufficient information base in the government is partly attributable to the lack of the institutional memory of the U.S. government and, ultimately, on the manner in which it is staffed. When American and Japanese negotiating teams sit down across the table from each other, it often becomes apparent that the kinds of people involved differ in a number of significant respects. The typical Japanese negotiator has already spent about 20 years in the Ministry of International Trade and

---

[20]This problem has been improved through the creation of the Foreign Commercial Service, and the International Trade Administration. But the officers in these agencies and the trade policy officials serving outside the United States (at the U.S. Mission to the European Communities in Brussels and in the GATT Mission in Geneva) are too few given the size of the task.

[21]He is to do so when he has reason to believe that the statutory evidentiary standard has been reached. 19 U.S.C. § 1671(a).

Industry. He (almost never she) will have been a top graduate of the University of Tokyo, who has served in a wide variety of assignments in different bureaus and divisions -- General Trade Policy, Basic Industries, Science and Technology, Energy, Machinery and Information Industries, and the like. He will have moved up in the ranks, having worked around the clock and often six days a week with various segments of MITI, other Japanese ministries, and very extensively with the larger Japanese industrial companies. He may have served in a key position in a MITI office abroad, may have been an aide to the MITI minister and worked closely with the Diet (legislature), or may have served as the MITI aide in the Prime Minister's office. Because of MITI's important role in key sectors of Japanese manufacturing, he will be intimately familiar with the inner-politics of the industry as well as its prospects. He will have participated in or be very familiar with industrial policy councils, and therefore knowledgeable about where the industry is headed. He will have participated in writing the annual MITI "visions" from one perspective or another, and will understand where national priorities lie. Lastly, he will know that in the future, he may become the dominant official in the agency, the Administrative Vice Minister, and retire in a "descent from heaven" (*amakudari*), to be employed in a very comfortable way in a MITI-regulated industry, after a two-year cooling off period.

His American counterpart, if he or she is an Undersecretary level official, will likely as not have had no prior experience in the trade field, may or may not have had other government service, and will have a length of service life-expectancy of about two years in his or her current position. He/she will often have taken a cut in pay to come into the job or will be sacrificing better opportunities in the private sector. He or she may or may not trust the civil servants who surround him or her. The latter are underpaid and feel under-appreciated, which they in fact are.[22] The lack of comparability of compensation with the private sector means that an increasing number of civil servants cannot contemplate a lifetime career in the Federal service. If these factors were not enough, these individuals know that public service has become highly politicized, and that advancement is increasingly very difficult because even middle level jobs in some departments have become the preserve of political appointments. Economic pressures and frustrations over the possibilities of advancement make a lifetime career in government rare -- although there are some dedicated individuals who make this sacrifice. The

---

[22]Indeed, there have been several recent Democratic and Republican Presidents who have "run against Washington"; they have succeeded in denigrating the government -- branding it part of the problem rather than part of the solution. They have thereby made public service less attractive as well.

number of "revolving door" appearances of impropriety grow, bringing further discredit on public service, although the standard of integrity in government service generally remains very high. With a high degree of turnover, policy becomes disjointed. What is learned by one crop of Presidential appointees may be lost with their departure, as in the MOSS talks (market-oriented-sector selective = MOSS). Naive approaches appear sensible; that which has gone before is completely forgotten.[23]

Creating a Career Trade Service. A career trade service is needed, featuring systematic training of highly talented individuals with a full exposure to foreign and domestic economic issues. This ought to begin with an intensive, university-level series of foundation courses, which would give members of this group the grounding which they need to perform their functions. Training and service ought to be combined in the form of service on detail in a variety of capacities in the other agencies of government, such as the Commerce Department (International Trade Administration), the Office of the United States Trade Representative (USTR), the State Department (primarily the Economic and Business Affairs Bureau), the Treasury (Office of the Assistant Secretary for International Affairs), the Labor Department (International Labor Affairs), the Environmental Protection Agency, the Central Intelligence agency, as well as in several state development agencies. Congressional internship experience would also be beneficial, and a systematic program should be arranged. There should be continuing education available at an advanced level at institutions such as the National War College; this should include case method teaching of what was done correctly, and less than optimally, with respect to major trade issues in the past. (Those who litigate before the government might impart some useful lessons as well). Travel and experience in intensive briefing sessions with the European Community or MITI for the Japanese Ministry of Foreign Affairs ought to be appropriately funded out of U.S. appropriations rather than -- as at present -- sponsored by foreign governments.

A professional trade service could be confined to the middle to senior ranks of government, or begin at an entry level. The emphasis should be on creating a prestige service where integrity and professionalism is stressed and valued. Tours of duty could be committed in return for a higher level of compensation and/or benefits. Other career systems should be examined, such as the France's elite *inspecteur des finances* to identify the elements that work best. Very senior jobs in government

---

[23]On this point, see generally Senate Finance Committee, Trade Agreements Act of 1979, 96th Cong. 1st Sess., July 17, 1979, S. Rept. 96-249, pp. 268-69.

which are now political appointments should be open to this trained corps of men and women. Additional career posts should be available abroad. Continuity and expertise can be assured with the right incentives. The nation would benefit, rather than having to depend entirely on the continued self-sacrifice of those praiseworthy individuals who are willing to put up with today's conditions of service.

Congressional oversight of the trade program can be enhanced through personnel interchange. There is highly competent staffing of the oversight committees already; these individuals could benefit by the opportunity to serve on occasion in senior jobs in the Executive Branch. Care should be taken to organize Executive Branch and Congressional inspection of plants abroad and at home, together with briefings, so that Congress not only conducts oversight of government functions but relates this oversight to the interaction of government and private sector activity. This would contribute to a decision-making process that would be better informed about the practical results of policy decisions.

A major benefit of the introduction of a rigorous program of improving the knowledge of the U.S. government on trade and competitiveness issues would be that economic and political systems that differ from America's will become more understandable, and continuity of policy can be achieved with respect to them. In the case of Japan, for example, there is much that each successive wave of U.S. negotiators has learned and then has taken with them when they left government service, leaving the government none the wiser. We can ill afford to continue the amateurish approach that U.S.-Japan negotiations have too often taken in the past. "Japan 101" should be taught at Fletcher, the Kennedy School, Berkeley or the National War College -- not at the negotiating table. A side benefit of this use of the nation's educational facilities is that the schools, being market driven, will perforce improve their ability to teach about the subjects which the government officials need to learn. What has been the history of U.S. trade policy? What has been the history of U.S. efforts to open the Japanese market? What are the sources of aggregate trade flows? What are the trade interests of each of the major trading countries? More knowledge and analytical skill is needed by trade policy officials than the international economics learned in the half year devoted to trade and monetary policy in many graduate programs. If there were a continuing stream of government students who wished this specialized training, these courses would also begin to be utilized by those seeking MBAs and other advanced degrees, creating more understanding of basic trade policy issues in the business, labor and academic communities at large, as well as in the media.

Organizing a Collective Response

Living with Diversity. Pluralism is at one and the same time our national strength and weakness. We put a premium in our national folklore on the contribution of the individual; history is not seen as being about classes of people, but about particular personalities -- George Washington, James Madison, Thomas Jefferson, Thomas Edison, Alexander Graham Bell, Andrew Carnegie, and John D. Rockefeller. In more recent times, we are fascinated by the story of Edwin Land of Polaroid, Bill Hewlett and George Packard, and Bob Noyce of Intel and Silicon Valley, or of Steve Jobs formerly of Apple. Presidential elections are far less elections of party slates than they are of particular candidates. In this the U.S. differs from most other nations. But in large, complex technical endeavors, it is not the individual that stands out or determines success, but the quality of the organization. The Space Shuttle program is an example; we can identify the astronauts who fly the shuttle, but we all realize that it is a group effort that gets them into space. Organization makes the larger projects of mankind successful -- the building of pyramids or bringing to commercial reality a complicated new computer.

Common efforts require not only an agreed common objective, but an organization worthy of the name, and in these respects the American political system, absent very special circumstances, all too often breaks down -- designed as it is more to prevent the abuse of power than to enable it to be wielded effectively. If one were going to decide to build pyramids or space stations, creating effective checks and balances to restrain those engaged in the effort would not be first on anyone's list of requirements. While the preservation of liberty is worth the costs associated with the division of power within our system, it is necessary to develop a consensus among the various components of our system in order to attain specific goals. This is never easy; a national ethic that maximizes individualism over group accomplishment reinforces the tendency toward fragmentation.

To counter the centrifugal tendencies inherent in our system, we require national leadership, which must come in the first instance from the President. However, a President (or Presidential candidate) cannot lead successfully until a consensus for movement in that direction begins to form.[24] Fortunately, that is exactly what is occurring now in the United States. There is increasing concern over an erosion of American

---

[24]As the Congress became less and less able to accomplish its legislative functions, the complaint went up about a lack of leadership, to which the members of the leadership on both sides of the political aisle decried the lack of "followership."

competitiveness, about the losses that are being sustained in trade. There is no agreement as to the solutions to be tried, but a majority would concur that there is a problem. That is a beginning.

Organizing the Federal Government to Solve the Problems Identified. There is nothing quite as likely to provoke ennui among trade buffs or government watchers than to call for a reorganization of government functions.[25] There is never a right time to do it -- either the tasks at hand will not allow a pause to tie one's laces, or there are individuals already ensconced in the relevant Cabinet positions and their feelings would be hurt by loss of their current employment, or the Congress is seen to have a vested interest in the status quo. Moreover, there are many in the private sector who like things the way they are. It is said that a combination of functions will either be clearly protectionist, or dominated by multinational firms and thus be doctrinairely free trade -- and such statements are typically made about the same reorganization proposal. However, the current organization of U.S. trade functions does not make a great deal of sense. Is there any way to organize the functions more effectively?

A Department of Technology, Trade and Industry (DTTI) should be created. The trade functions of government are now divided amongst a variety of agencies, of which the principal ones are the Office of the United States Trade Representative (USTR) and the Department of Commerce. Within Commerce, a sizable establishment has grown up in the International Trade Administration (ITA), which is concerned with industrial analysis, export promotion, trade negotiation, and the administration of import remedies for subsidies and dumping. A separate bureau administers the export control functions. At USTR, a principal function is chairing interagency negotiating teams at trade talks, although some bilateral issues may be chaired by other agencies. USTR also administers section 301 (foreign unfair trade practice remedies), and related statutes -- the so-called special and super-301 provisions, all of which are largely aimed at opening foreign markets. Since the trade laws and trade negotiations are split between two agencies -- Commerce and USTR -- if both agency heads are assertive, there will almost unavoidably be conflicts and dissention.[26]

---

[25]See generally I.M. Destler, *America Trade Politics* (1986) pp. 98-106.

[26]It will be objected that the trade negotiating function will infect quasi-judicial trade law administration. Regrettably, this has already occurred. Fragmentation of functions cannot overcome the deficiency of purpose which afflicts U.S. trade (continued...)

USTR is also charged with trade policy coordination, although this is more easily said than done. The statutory Trade Policy Committee created in the 1974 Trade Act no longer meets. While the law calls for this Cabinet level committee to set the government's direction in trade policy, it is not the will of more powerful agencies, such as Treasury and State, that this organization function at all at a Cabinet level. The failure of this Committee even to be able to meet underscores the fact that trade policy is subordinated to other policies, e.g., foreign policy, or domestic or international financial policy. Trade policy coordination is managed at the Under Secretary and Assistant Secretary levels under the leadership of a Deputy U.S. Trade Representative,[27] and at the Office Director and Deputy Assistant Secretary level by an interagency committee chaired by an Assistant U.S. Trade Representative.[28] Interagency recommendations reach the President through a Cabinet-level Economic Policy Council, chaired by the Secretary of the Treasury and staffed in the White House. The USTR and Secretary of Commerce are not the senior or most influential Cabinet officers serving on this Committee.

Whether form is following substance or helping to shape it, the current organization of functions is just another indication that trade policy is something of a stepchild in the overall policy process. Central policies of the government are to maintain amicable relations with other nations and to limit U.S. government involvement in trade issues. Thus, the form suits the policy. Trade issues (other than the fate of Uruguay Round multilateral negotiations) have been considered less as serious problems affecting the national economic interest than as inconvenient economic and/or political predicaments that require some sort of fix so that policymakers can get back to more important matters. The current organization is neither efficient nor conducive to making good policy. It is for the President to recognize this and, if he or she cares about how American industry fares, to organize the institutional instruments of policy to deliver the results sought. A useful initial step would be to recognize why the current organization of functions does not work.

First, there is a failure to address trade and competitiveness issues together, comprehensively. Various extremities of the Federal bureaucracy may be seized with aspects of a problem, but it is very difficult to craft a

---

[26](...continued)
policy. A unification of functions makes sense, but only in a reformed policy context.

[27]The Trade Policy Review Group (TPRG).

[28]The Trade Policy Staff Committee (TPSC).

coherent approach. Today's problems tend to be complex. If elements of the problem are subsidization and closed markets abroad, and inadequately coordinated regulatory and technology policies at home, it is highly unlikely that the U.S. government can find more than the odd disparate element of a solution. Having a single department for technology, trade and industry is not a guarantee of successful coordination, nor are turf wars unknown within departments, but there is greater likelihood of a productive intramural solution than an intermural one. Secondly, currently there is a division between the analysts and those charged with setting policy. This leads to differing priorities, or even an absence of priorities, in the analytical portions of government. Third, a policy based on fragmentary measures may be more easily rendered ineffective. If one unfair trade practice is halted but another persists, or if a domestic policy component of a solution is missing, a partial solution may well turn out to be more costly and worse policy than if no assistance had been rendered.[29] Fourth, foreign competitors are able to profit by the irresolution inherent in so disorganized a process, when, for example, a policy response is required at home but none is forthcoming, or when squabbling U.S. agencies can be played off against each other.

It would not be a bad test of U.S. government organization to apply to the Government the same tests as businesses must meet that is, bottom line results: Are the results which should be sought actually achieved? Are the means devised well-suited to the challenges at hand? And in the case of a nation, are the objectives sought consonant with assuring the continued security and prosperity of the community?

The same arguments that favor consolidation of the technology, trade and industry functions in a single department also suggest the need for a return to the statutory framework of a trade agency led interagency policy coordination process. At a minimum, there should not be a duplication of agency roles. If the trade policy committee is to coordinate trade policy, there should be no need for National Security Council (NSC) participation, for example. Presumably, State and Defense can represent NSC views in an interagency discussion. Similarly, if the Office of Management and Budget (OMB), the Council of Economic Advisors (CEA), the Justice Department, and Treasury all seek to look out for the consumer's interests, are they all necessary participants in the policy discussion, or is just one enough? One could even ask the heretical question, if international economic policy (e.g. exchange rate policy) can be set by the Treasury acting alone, and if foreign policy can often be set

---

[29]A probable example is the flat panel display antidumping case. See pp. 563-64.

by the Department of State acting only with the guidance of the President, need trade and competitiveness policies be subjected to a broad interagency committee, often dominated by agencies having constituent interests distant from or not in sympathy with trade policy needs? It is not surprising that policy tends to be senile. If the policymaking mechanism cannot be trimmed to a single department acting under presidential guidance, there is something to be said for reducing participation to those agencies with an immediate and essential interest, adding such agencies as the Department of Agriculture, the Environmental Protection Agency, or the Justice Department, when a product, industry, or other policy interest within its purview is directly at issue.

One thing is certain: there has been an increase in interagency deliberation over the years and a decrease in output from the process. The private sector has learned that an excessive bureaucracy is reducing the capability of the organization to function effectively.[30] The government's trade policy formulation process is in need of thorough review and reform. The organization which was suitable for what seemed simpler times, in the 1960s and 1970s, when tariffs and discrete nontariff barriers were seen as the main distortions of international trade, is not equal to today's tasks. Fragmentation and dispersal of responsibilities have undermined the vitality of the process. It must have its sense of purpose restored. It must set priorities against known objectives, and not primarily serve as an aloof judge of seemingly private altercations. It must have a better capacity to formulate and implement policy.

Government vs. Industry. Mr. Lincoln noted that "A house divided against itself cannot stand." This truth, which was self-evident in 1860, has become obscured in the last decade of U.S. politics. The same self-fulfilling campaign slogans denigrating the Federal government, which have made government a less attractive career option for the best and brightest, have also increased the gulf between the government and the private sector which it exists to serve. Industries seeking public policies supportive of their future growth are too often met with something between suspicion and apathy, and generally, a complete lack of understanding. It is as if the government does not comprehend that the fate of the country and its industries is intertwined. As a result, most chances for marshalling existing resources needed to advance the competitiveness of industry have been lost. The national laboratories, for example, pursue their objectives independently from those of industry,

---

[30]One might learn from the reorganization of the Union Pacific since 1987.

although the two have much that they could usefully do together.[31] Again, the result is that trade policy consists solely of the granting of import restrictions, a form of ineffective protectionism. What is needed is a change of attitude to the point where government and industry work towards common goals, together.[32]

Industries Divided. In a society and a private sector which so prizes individual initiative, diversity, and competition, there are still times when a collective effort is needed. At these times, government can and should act as a catalyst. This does not call for coercion, but leadership, and occasionally contribution. The television disaster, in which various segments of the U.S. industry were fighting each other, and the government was standing by as Japanese firms mounted a concerted drive against the U.S. market position, has been described in the preceding chapter. This would have been a time for joint action, or at least consideration of it, had either industry or government had the wit to envision it. More recently, the near-total loss of the U.S. DRAM (dynamic random access memory) industry offers a comparable example of internal division. The government was willing to take several measures to help the industry when it was clear that it faced a massive onslaught of foreign dumped chips, but the primary measure taken, a self-initiated antidumping action, was too little and too late -- the first relief measures did not become available until most of the U.S. industry, after experiencing horrific losses, had ceased to exist. Thereafter, government officials periodically wished that the U.S. firms which had witnessed and in some cases experienced this debacle would enter or reenter the DRAM

---

[31]A panel headed by David Packard of Hewlett-Packard reviewed the work of the federal research laboratories in 1983 and concluded that "they perceived industry as an awkward partner with a different value system. . . . . The current federal procurement system discourages agencies and [government] laboratories from contracting with universities and industry." *Report of the White House Science Counsel Federal Laboratory Review Panel* (Washington, D.C.: Office of Science and Technology Policy, May 20, 1983).

[32]The creation of the Malcolm Baldrige Award for manufacturing excellence is a good example of how government can work creatively to foster international competitiveness. It is a program uniformly and widely applauded by the private sector. It advances the national interest as well. Oddly enough, it is solely a process of picking or at least identifying winners (and, by negative implication, losers, too.) There must be other creative ideas for cooperation between government and industry which merit adoption, and these could be found if the prevailing attitude, shaped by the President, were that government and industry have more in the way of common interests than issues which divide the two.

market, but there were few takers. After several years of DRAM shortages and high prices reflecting the manipulation of DRAM supplies by the dominant Japanese suppliers, several U.S. chip producers and consumers did attempt to band together to form a U.S. company to produce DRAMs (a venture to be called "U.S. Memories"), but this effort failed. The government was emphatic that it wished the venture well but wanted no direct involvement. The short term economic interests of the participants did not warrant the investments on the scale necessary for success.[33]

How does one create a public good, in the interest of all in the long term? This has been the role of government since the times in pre-history when organization was needed to build canals to irrigate agricultural lands. The government can invest public funds, or in some cases, as in this example, it might have been enough simply to contribute leadership -- a Secretary of Technology, Trade and Industry could have called together the chief executive officers of the leading companies involved, users and producers alike, and helped them see jointly a vision of their common interest.[34] In DRAMs, the government -- to the extent it understood the problem -- did not perceive this to be its role. It had created a price-monitoring system intended to prevent future dumping,[35] in itself important, but not nearly enough to revive an industry mortally wounded by past dumping. More was needed; nothing more was forthcoming.

---

[33]The verdict rendered by one U.S. industry publication on the demise of U.S. Memories was as follows: "The people of the United States have never mastered the ability to work together in a consortium except in times of dire national risks. In the brief period of [U.S. Memories'] existence, North American companies' worldwide semiconductor market share declined from 37 percent to 35 percent. How much worse do matters have to get before the leaders of the U.S. government and industry realize that a national crisis is at hand?" *DQ Monday* (January 15, 1990).

[34]In the Sematech initiative, which stands in contrast to the failure of U.S. Memories, the government contributed capital to an industry-driven R&D consortium designed to improve U.S. semiconductor manufacturing technology and to strengthen the U.S. semiconductor materials and equipment industries. By most accounts the private sector would not have united alone, without a government investment; it was not so much the money that mattered as the government's vote of confidence in the collective effort.

[35]Subsequently replaced by a Japanese company data collection system.

The Failure of Trade Policy: Import Restrictions

One of the greatest defects in the trade policy responses provided by the U.S. government to date has been the over-specialization of remedies. As pointed out in many of the cases cited in the previous chapter, an industry which knows that it is having difficulties with foreign competition is usually aware that the source of the trouble is usually not a single factor, such as a foreign tax or a subsidy program. Industrial targeting features a combination of policy tools to achieve its trade objectives. But the current state of U.S. trade law is not much different than that of English law in prior centuries, which had various writs (requests for remedy) for very specific purposes. If one cited the wrong writ, that is, pleaded incorrectly, the case was thrown out. This form of archaic jurisprudence has become a thing of the past in the U.S. court system, but its spirit lives on in the administration of the U.S. trade laws. These remedies do not comprise a coherent system but an accretion of separate measures built up over the last century to deal with a variety of supposedly unrelated problems, based on differing theories as to why import relief should be granted. Countervailing duties originated in 1892 as a response to subsidies which sought to subvert the U.S. tariff structure (the problem at the time was sugar rebates paid by the governments of Austria-Hungary, the German Empire, Czarist Russia and several other European powers). The Antidumping Act of 1916 was designed to protect U.S. industries from a "destructive flood" of European products when, it was feared, the end of World War I would free up European productive capacity for trade.[36] The Antidumping Act of 1921 was enacted to prevent private price discrimination from continuing to cause material injury.[37] The "escape clause" (import relief) was designed to permit general trade liberalization, by providing a temporary pause that was industry-specific when rapid increases in imports caused serious injury. Section 301 was a battering ram designed to open foreign markets, but it generally has no international analog available as a matter of right, and is therefore difficult to use within the international trading rules.[38]

Apart from the immediate rationale for the various remedies, there is a more general reason why these formal remedial arrangements have come

---

[36]53 Cong. Rec. App. 1938, 1911, 13061 (1916).

[37]H.R. Rep. No. 1, 67th Cong. 1st Sess. (1921); S. Rep. No. 16, 67th Cong. 1st Sess. (1921)

[38]Article XXIII of the GATT requires permission of the GATT Contracting Parties before it may be used as authority for retaliation.

into being and been periodically refined. Each time the Congress has been has been asked to make a grant of its Commerce Clause powers to the Executive to allow the latter to negotiate further reciprocal reductions in trade barriers, it has in effect been told by the Executive, "If your constituents get into trouble from what we are doing, there are excellent remedies which will be readily available". Thus was a political bargain struck -- but the remedies did not in fact prove to be readily available. Any number of cases demonstrated that the system was not predictable (or, all too predictable -- no timely relief was forthcoming). A succession of Democratic and Republican Administrations considered having been insufficiently vigorous in administering the trade laws, Congress has tightened and made them increasingly mandatory in a succession of legislative enactments over the last twenty years. The growing rigidity in the laws, and the narrowing of discretion allowed to the administrators, is due to a fundamental sense of distrust. For example, if one were to ask the lumber state Senators and Congressmen if they would allow greater discretion to the Executive Branch in the matter of countering Canadian timber subsidies, the answer would be clear: absolutely not. The same replies would be given by automobile or steel state Congressmen. While, theoretically, discretion might allow the President greater leeway in fashioning an effective, comprehensive response, in practice, it is feared, greater discretion simply increases the likelihood that no significant action of any kind will be taken. The U.S. Executive Branch historically has often shown greater concern for the domestic politics of its major trading partners than over U.S. economic interests -- in the case of lumber, Canada, in which the unfettered right to give large subsidies is very important.

Is there a way through the impasse arising out of Congressional distrust and an arthritic set of trade remedies? There has been some thought given from time to time to a one-stop shopping approach to trade remedies, particularly in connection with industries made up of small businesses, which may lack the resources to pick their way through the complexities of the various requirements of the trade statutes. However, it is really generally the larger industries that require comprehensive analysis and creative, multifaceted solutions. Given the history of inter-branch and private sector distrust of the Executive Branch, if a central filing point were constructed, at this stage, it would probably have to be an alternative track to relief rather than a replacement for the existing remedies. If the Executive Branch proved that it had an interest in being more effectively reactive, or even occasionally proactive, it might over time find that the new system could be an avenue to obtaining discretion in the use of the existing remedies.[39]

The most creative response would be to analyze trade problems in the first instance without reference to the stock of traditional remedies available. One might find a foreign market closed due to anticompetitive practices, giving rise to price discrimination, as well as some degree of subsidization, a cost of capital differential, a different financial structure (patient capital), and some lesser factors. This is in fact what faced the U.S. semiconductor industry in the 1980s. As a response, it sought improvement of the dumping injury test, elimination of tariffs here and in Canada and Japan (a cost saving action), an R&D tax credit (cost saving and focussing resources where needed), a new statutory form of intellectual property protection, an amendment to the antitrust laws providing for joint R & D consortia; a government industry joint manufacturing research project (SEMATECH), a pooling of funds for university research (the Semiconductor Research Corporation), and a trade agreement to provide access to the Japanese market and a deterrent to a resumption of dumping (under the U.S.-Japan Semiconductor Arrangements of 1986 and 1991). Taken all together, this is an implicit, somewhat coherent (if still inadequate) U.S. semiconductor policy. However, it did not arise as a coherent package of government policy decisions arrived at as a consequence of informed debate. It was the product of a series of individual decisions, spread over nearly a decade, linked to some degree by a common perception shared by both industry and government of the competitive problem. What was and is needed is a comprehensive approach, based on ongoing analysis and evaluation of policies that would assist in meeting the competitive challenges faced, at least to the extent of remedying the unfair trade practices encountered.

To move away from what academic economists consider protectionism, part of any solution must involve domestic measures such as, to take one example, more relevant work being done in government laboratories through a re-ordering of government research and development priorities. If the future is to be bright, both in terms of how U.S. industries fare in international competition, as well as in reducing conflicts among nations

---

[39]It would also be complicated to substitute the new unified remedy provision completely for the old, given the fact that the international trading rules which permit use of trade measures are crafted to fit the formal remedy tracks that currently exist. Thus, even if the Congress decided to confer more discretion on the Executive, most of the other nations of the world would not wish to see a U.S. Executive Branch given freedom to confer import remedies with full discretion. America's trading partners generally want greater formal curbs placed on American trade remedies, not fewer.

over commercial matters, there will have to be more resort to domestic measures and greater efforts at preventing injury before it occurs -- such as through opening foreign markets and eliminating foreign anticompetitive practices. But this greater degree of harmony among trading nations will not occur unless part of this policy deliberation includes an inward look at the defects within this country's borders for which we must hold ourselves accountable.

The Failure of the Trade Policy: Export Controls

The collapse of communism in the Soviet Union and Eastern Europe revealed societies and economies which were woefully deficient in modern technology, reflecting, to a substantial degree, a longstanding Western effort led by the United States to restrict the flow of sensitive technologies to the Soviet Bloc.[40] However, recognizing the contribution of export controls to national security does not mean that these policies have performed well, or even adequately, for the nation. The United States has maintained far more stringent controls on its own firms' technology exports than have its leading allies. U.S. technology exports are governed by a rigid and highly complex system of laws and regulations; the government enjoys (and historically has exercised) broad discretion to restrict exports, with no meaningful avenue of appeal for affected private parties.[41] National security concerns have been given priority and the commercial interests of U.S. firms have been treated as a matter of secondary importance. The controls maintained by U.S. allies

---

[40]Although Soviet technological shortcomings were far less pronounced in the military sector than elsewhere, by the 1980s the Warsaw Pact forces clearly faced a broad technological disadvantage of strategic proportions relative to NATO. The Gulf War, in which a modern Allied force easily defeated a numerically superior Soviet-armed and equipped Iraq, demonstrated the significance and character of this technology gap. Controls on the export of advanced technologies played a material role in sustaining the strategy of containment that eventually won the Cold War.

[41]In the United States, administration and enforcement of export controls engages the attention of a much larger government bureaucracy with less input from and consultation with the private sector. The United States has developed technical expertise within the government and relied on extensive participation from the Defense Department; the various government departments have their own private sector advisers, but they are kept at arms length and consulted only on technical matters, not policy.

are far more sensitive to commercial concerns, more flexible, and, as events have repeatedly demonstrated, more porous.[42]

U.S. government restrictions on exports are a relatively recent phenomenon in our national life. Although there is no right to export, Americans have historically enjoyed great freedom to do so.[43] No regime of permanent broad-based export regulation existed until World War II.[44] After the fall of France in 1940 the President was empowered broadly to curtail exports from the United States of all commodities and

---

[42]The allies enforce only those controls upon which there is multilateral agreement and there is no attempt to control an item once it has crossed the national border. They generally maintain a very small administrative capability with, until recently, no involvement with the military. Private industry advisers play a central role in formulating the rules and collaborate in detail with their governments about matters under negotiation with COCOM. In Germany, which has been embroiled in a series of scandals involving sales of nuclear, chemical weapons, and missile technology to various unfriendly countries, the agency charged with monitoring exports of sensitive technologies (BAW) has been so ineffective that one German politician declared in 1989 that "we simply have an open door." Hermann Bachmaier, SPD, Chairman of the Nuclear Research Committee in Bonn, in *Der Spiegel* (June 12, 1989) (FBIS-WEU-89-130). *Der Spiegel* reported that "customs investigators, state attorneys and intelligence officers have the same complaint -- that the [BAW] is purely an institute for promoting exports and frequently hinders investigations of companies." The President of the BAW reportedly "drummed into" his employees the notion that any legal restrictions on exports were to be applied in practice so "that freedom of economic activity is to be interfered with as little as possible." *Der Spiegel* (June 12, 1989). See also *Der Spiegel* (June 19, 1989) (FBIS-WEU-89-134); January 23, 1989) (FBIS-WEU-89-014). For comparisons of U.S. export controls policies with those of U.S. allies, see President's council on Competitiveness, *Global Competition: The New Reality* (Washington, D.C.: U.S. Government Printing Office, 1985), Exhibits 11 and 12; National Academy of Sciences, Balancing the National Interest (Washington, DC: National Academy Press, 1987).

[43]The Constitution grants the Congress the power to regulate commerce with foreign nations. U.S. Constitution, Art. I, § 8, cl.3. This power is qualified by a prohibition against the imposition of a tax or duty on exports from any state. U.S. Constitution, Art. I, § 9

[44]Export restrictions or embargoes have been extraordinary measures related to armed conflicts or the export of munitions. The trade embargo imposed against England and France before the War of 1812 and the prohibition against the export of coal and other war materials enacted just prior to the Spanish-American War are examples of the exceptional nature of U.S. export controls. Even in World War I, trade restrictions were authorized only against designated enemies.

later, of technical data.[45] This authority and the licensing system that accompanied it have been more or less renewed or extended to the present day.[46] During the Cold War U.S. export controls were integrated into a system of multilateral controls on exports to the Soviet bloc conducted through an organization consisting of 15 Western allies, the Coordinating Committee on Multilateral Export Controls (COCOM). Under this system, export authorization is required for virtually all exports; where a general license or standing authority is not available, exporters must file an application and obtain an individual license. For large volume exporters in the high technology sector, so-called bulk licenses have been introduced to approve multiple transactions on an on-going basis. Use of such licenses, however, generally requires maintenance of an internal control system that can be quite costly to an exporter.[47]

---

[45]This broad control system is distinct from regulations aimed at a particular category of exports such as munitions or nuclear items. It is the predecessor of the Export Administration Regulations administered by the Commerce Department. The original wartime purpose of national security was expanded to include foreign policy due to the diplomatic considerations surrounding the start of the Cold War and domestic shortages due to the economic disruptions continuing after the World War II. With a few notable exceptions such as restrictions on domestic oil following the Arab Oil Boycott of 1973, domestic supply concerns have not had much effect on the export control regime.

[46]The Cold War provided a strong consensus for continued regulation of exports. In one of the periodic reauthorization of this authority, the House Committee on Banking and Currency emphasized that "the act gives the President the widest possible discretion to limit, restrict or prohibit entirely exports to any person or to any nation of any or all commodities or articles, whether or not, and to whatever extent they are of military, industrial, or economic significance, if limitation, restriction, or prohibition is found to be in the interest of our national security or our foreign policy or necessary because of domestic shortages." Extension of Export Control Act of 1949, House Committee on Banking and Currency, H.Rep. 1836, 87th Cong., 2d Sess., 1962, p.4.

[47]The U.S. regulations are applied by the United States on an extraterritorial basis -- any amount of U.S. origin in the form of components or technology can subject a reexport in a foreign country to U.S. control, a policy which has made U.S. controls applicable to the activities of foreign companies outside the United States. It has resulted in bitter political disputes with U.S. allies, especially when, as in the Soviet oil pipeline case, the United States imposed controls for foreign policy rather than national security purposes. It also created a strong incentive for foreign manufacturers to "design out" U.S. components, such as semiconductors, so as to

(continued...)

During the height of the Cold War in the 1950s and early 1960s, U.S. national security export controls not only had little competitive impact (because of U.S. economic and technological preeminence), but were arguably essential to the containment strategy that was being implemented (and which ultimately prevailed) against the Soviet Bloc. But those circumstances have now changed beyond recognition. The Soviet threat has receded substantially; at the same time, U.S. technological preeminence has eroded and, in areas such as advanced ceramics and optical components, disappeared altogether. Under these changed circumstances, the perpetuation of export controls that are not observed by U.S. allies (and competitors) undermines U.S. competitiveness and, ironically, our national security.

In light of the momentous changes in the Soviet Union and Eastern Europe, U.S. export controls should be more discriminating in the future.[48] They should be tailored to address more limited but still compelling issues affecting national security and foreign policy, such as

---

[47](...continued)
avoid U.S. controls on their own end-products. U.S. regulations also imposed controls on a variety of items that were not controlled by COCOM countries or others. These unilateral controls were often devised when the U.S. product was unique, but as the technology spread internationally, other nations seldom imposed comparable controls.

[48]Statutory changes attempting to reorient U.S. export controls have been enacted by the Congress since the late 1960s. As a general proposition, the Congressional initiatives have attempted to respond to the realities of the marketplace and the inherent limitations of any multilateral system of export controls. Beginning with the renewal of the Export Administration Act in 1969, political pressures from the Congress began to alter the system. The Congress declared for the first time that unwarranted restrictions of exports could be harmful and controls should be applied to the maximum extent in cooperation with other nations. From this modest beginning, Congress has proceeded to realign the statutory basis for export controls with each renewal of the Export Administration Act. By 1990, the law placed a "high priority on exports." Exports to COCOM nations would no longer require an individual license. Unilateral national security controls were outlawed. Unconstrained foreign availability of a particular item should eventually result in elimination of controls. A *de minimis* threshold was placed on the extraterritorial application of controls on parts and components used in foreign-end products. Even foreign policy controls are to be weighed against the effect on the economic performance of the United States.

proliferation of nuclear, chemical and biological weapons, and terrorism. In reformulating existing regulations, U.S. officials should be leery of using as a point of departure the comprehensive system of controls born in the 1940s. Instead the cost to U.S. industry of export controls should be explicitly calculated and carefully weighed. Unilateral controls should be shunned and extraterritorial reach should be achieved through multilateral agreement. U.S. industry should be provided a full opportunity to consult with government officials in connection with international negotiations and the formulation of export control policy. To the extent the U.S. government takes account of the trade and economic impact of U.S. export controls, U.S. interests will benefit and the controls themselves will likely be more effective in achieving their purpose.

Investing for the Future

In reviewing the tangle of competitive problems confronting U.S. industries which have suffered competitive reversals in the international arena, one theme that runs with regularity throughout the case studies is capital -- its comparatively high cost, its limited availability at key junctures, and perhaps most importantly, its tendency to migrate elsewhere at the worst possible moment, that is, when competitive challenges are encountered by U.S. firms. As individual U.S. industrial sectors have come under foreign competitive pressure, they have often found themselves unable to keep pace within their competitors' level of capital spending. In some market segments, U.S. companies have fought for market share by maintaining high levels of investment in the face of major losses, but this has more often been the exception than the rule -- the U.S. economic system does not encourage or support such a response.[49] More commonly, encountering mounting difficulty in raising debt and equity investment capital for product areas where returns are chronically low or negative, U.S. firms tend to shift their investments to other product lines and other industries in order to obtain more

[49]Examples include the decision by Zenith to contest the television receiver business with Asian firms and the stand taken by U.S. producers of EPROMs in 1985, when they matched Japanese dumping with their own price reductions. Such actions frequently entail -- as in the case of EPROMs -- "significant financial losses." *Erasable Programmable Read Only Memories from Japan* (U.S.I.T.C. Pub. No. 1927, final, December 1986).

acceptable rates of return.[50] This phenomenon is usually portrayed as a failure of U.S. management and its obsession with short-run, bottom-line results, but it is actually a reflection of differences in national systems of capital allocation.

In 1990 a Wall Street analyst commented to a group of U.S. semiconductor executives that "the goal of people investing in stocks is to make money. . . . That's what capitalism is all about. It's not a charity. . . . I can't tell [my brokers] 'Gee, I'm sorry about your client, but investing in the semiconductor [industry] is good for the country.'"[51] While this individual was stating a truth so obvious that it verges on the banal, he was touching on a fundamental dilemma confronting U.S. industry today -- in light of the investor sentiment expressed above, how is a company to maintain the level of investment needed to remain competitive over the long term, particularly if there is no prospect of a short run payoff or if foreign competition has destroyed the prospect of earning a return on that investment? A few U.S. firms -- family owned and managed companies like Motorola and Corning, and some very large firms like IBM and GE -- have on occasion proven capable of undertaking long range strategic investments on a regular basis, and, in some cases, of meeting foreign below-cost price offensives head on for a sustained period. More often, however, a company's "internal" investors -- the executives who allocate capital -- have no choice but to invest in areas that are likely to produce a high return on investment over the short run. They know they are accountable to lenders and shareholders who can simply redirect their investments elsewhere if the firm persists in committing to areas where returns are low or negative, or are perceived to be forthcoming only in the distant future.

U.S. economic doctrine holds that this country's market-driven method of capital allocation is more nearly perfect than any alternative mechanism which could be devised. However, beginning in the 1960s and occurring with increasing frequency in the 1970s, 1980s and 1990, U.S. industries have come into collision with foreign industries whose capital has been allocated, in whole or in part, by governments, and by financial and industrial leaders on the basis of government directives or

---

[50]The *New York Times* noted on February 6, 1987 that U.S. venture capital investment, which had been an important source of capital for U.S. high technology industries, was shifting away from high tech to areas where greater returns were anticipated, such as leveraged buyouts of existing companies, pizza shops, and athletic apparel concerns.

[51]Speech by Steven J. Bulog, Shearson Lehman Hutton, "Wall Street's View of the Semiconductor Equipment Industry." (January 2, 1990).

industry-government understandings that capital should flow to sectors and products regarded as strategic, regardless of the prospect for short or medium run returns. In many cases, the result has been dominance of those sectors by foreign firms. In Japan, Korea and Taiwan, an array of fiscal and tax policies have encouraged savings, limited the ability of those savings to more offshore, and have served to channel those savings toward investment in designated industries.[52] Government resources (usually modest) are amplified by parapublic and private financial institutions and industrial organizations (the *keiretsu* and the *chaebol*) which are structured to channel capital into the areas deemed important from a national perspective. Capital for these sectors is not only abundant but cheap, often extraordinarily so.[53] One result of this system of capital allocation is a high level of investment in technologies and products that are unlikely to reach commercial fruition for 10 years or more; another is bursts of investment in product sectors deemed strategic, regardless of short term market conditions, a phenomenon which has produced the massive overcapacity and dumping which have characterized many electronics products sectors since the 1970s.

The periodic competitive "bloodbaths" that have occurred in strategic sectors since entry by East Asian firms look very different from a U.S. and from an East Asian perspective. To a Japanese or Korean producer, staggering losses on a strategic product are regrettable, to be sure, but can

---

[52]For analyses of East Asian systems of capital allocation see Wade, *Governing the Market* (1990); Alice Amsden, *Asia's Next Giant; South Korea and Late Industrialization* (Oxford and New York: Oxford University Press, 1989); Okimoto, *Between MITI and the Market* (1989).

[53]Numerous analyses by macroeconomic economists have argued that, net of inflation and corporate tax rates, the cost of capital in the U.S. and Japan are comparable. Other analysis dispute this and argue that Japanese firms enjoy a significantly lower cost of capital. Macroeconomic analyses, however, miss the point -- regardless of the average cost of capital for all firms in the economy, East Asian firms in *priority* sectors enjoy artificially low, e.g., subsidized rates of capital, as well as greater availability of capital. Korean firms in priority sectors, for example, have been able to borrow at negative real interest rates for sustained periods despite poor returns and high average interest rates for the Korean economy. (See World Book, Korea: *Managing the Industrial Transition* (1987).) On the macroeconomic cost of capital debate, see Iwao Nakatuni, The Economic Role of Financial Corporate Grouping," in Masuhiko Aoki (ed.) *The Economic Analysis of the Japanese Firm* (Amsterdam: North Holland, 1984); Albert Ando and Alan Auerback, "The Corporate Cost of Capital in Japan and the United States: A Comparison," in John Shoven, ed., *Government Policy Toward Industry in the United States and Japan* (Cambridge, 1988).

be viewed simply as the price to be paid to enter and remain a player in that sector;[54] the losses will usually have little effect on the producers' ability to raise capital or on the cost of that capital, since in many cases they are not accountable, in the Western sense, to their investors.[55] In Korea, the steel industry in the 1970s and 1980s had nearly the lowest rate of return on investment of any industrial sector, but in an economy where government policies limited capital availability, it received a disproportionate share of capital and at rates which were the lowest of those paid by any major Korean sector.[56] To a U.S. producer, massive losses in an industry -- strategic or no -- is likely to trigger an investor exodus and, quite likely, an upheaval in company management. Thus,

---

[54]In the 1984-85 "semiconductor winter," U.S., Japanese and Korean firms suffered multibillion dollar losses on DRAM sales. Most U.S. DRAM firms exited the market, but no Japanese or Korean producer did so. As the government announced new plans to aid the national semiconductor industry, a Korean government official shrugged that "there's no point in making a big deal out of the recent situation. The risk of chipmaking and the immediate loss were well conceived from the beginning." *Business Korea,* August 1985). A Mitsubishi executive commented in 1986 that: "You can imagine the big loss [we had] in semiconductor operations. . . . We use DRAMs as the technology driver for developing new generation integrated circuits. All six major Japanese semiconductor companies are pushing hard to come out with 1-megabit and 4-megabit DRAMs, which will take a major advance in technology to sub-micron line geometries on devices. None of them will drop DRAMs, no matter how unprofitable they may be, because we need that base to develop 1M-bit and 4M-bit DRAMs." *Electronics News* (April 29, 1986).

[55]Japanese *keiretsu* and Korean *chaebol* are characterized by extensive cross-ownership of shares among the members; this gives them considerable discretion in making investments, notwithstanding the concerns of erstwhile "owners" or "stockholders" who have "become invisible to the point that the concept of ownership is no longer means much of anything." Chalmers Johnson, "Trade Revisionism, and the Future of Japanese-American Relations," in K. Yamamura (ed.), *Japan's Economic Structure* 1990), p. 119 (forthcoming, U. of Washington). Creditors are generally large banks and insurance companies who may be members of the same industrial group and who are generally responsible to signalling from the government as to where their lending priorities should lie. In Korea, many banks -- formerly government-owned -- have been privatized, but continue to operate as arms of Korea's industrial policies. *Far Eastern Economic Review* (February 11, 1988).

[56]World Bank, Korea: *Managing the Industrial Transition* (1987); Brent Bartlett, *Preferential Allocation of Credit to the Korean Steel Industry by the Government of Korea* (1989).

instead of upping the ante with further large investments in areas coming under competitive pressure, U.S. managers face strong incentives to redeploy their capital away from areas entered by foreign rivals who enjoy access to abundant capital on preferential terms. That is exactly what has been happening in electronics for over twenty years, as U.S. firms and investors have abandoned an enormous sweep of product sectors entered by East Asian firms:

> *U.S. risks were higher and profits were lower in these contested areas, and the marginal returns on investment were greater elsewhere. . . These retreats by U.S. firms were facilitated by the freedom and fluidity of the U.S. economy, and by talented managers, who have learned to exploit this flexibility in pursuit of [return on investment].*[57]

Capital investment is a function of more than institutional structures. Investment decisions are driven by the sum total of factors that determine a company's short, medium, and long term prospects. In Far Eastern economies, the knowledge that a company in a strategic sector will in many cases enjoy home market protection, de facto antitrust immunity, government financial support, and possibly a government bailout if serious difficulties are encountered, not only serves to reassure investors, but frequently triggers a veritable investment stampede into a designated industry. Conversely, in the U.S., the knowledge that the government takes little interest in commercial outcomes and has, at best, an indifferent, unpredictable record of responding to concerted foreign assaults on key sectors sends its own set of signals to investors. Under such circumstances, it should not be particularly surprising that the mere rumor that Japanese firms are entering a particular product area may suffice to drive U.S. investors out of the field.

The recurrent phenomenon of disinvestment by U.S. firms in the face of large-scale foreign investments is a symptom of the larger failure of U.S.-based market doctrine. During the past decade U.S. companies have been out-invested in key industries like semiconductors, advanced consumer electronics, semiconductor equipment and materials, and advanced displays, while at the same time U.S. investors have spent hundreds of billions of dollars on the construction of new office buildings and condominium complexes, many of which now stand vacant, and on leveraged buyouts of firms that are now in receivership. This outcome

---

[57]MIT Commission on Industrial Productivity, *The Decline of U.S. Consumer Electronics Manufacturing* (Working Paper 1989), p. 11.

was in a sense market-driven, but it was arguably neither "efficient" in any meaningful sense nor in our national interest.

The U.S. government's generic analysis of the effect of the relative cost and availability of capital or commercial outcomes is still badly lagging behind the need for evaluation and response. There is currently an ongoing Commerce-Treasury study of capital as a factor in competitive success. Policy responses have been few, however. Proposed initiatives to help U.S. industries address the capital shortage have been rejected on ideological grounds without any real consideration -- the HDTV project proposal of the American Electronics Association (AEA) and the Consumer Electronics Capital Corporation (CECC) proposal of the National Advisory Committee on Semiconductors. What is distressing is not so much that these ideas met with criticism, some of it deserved, -- this was to be expected -- but that while the proposals addressed real problems, the public and internal government debate as to how better to address those problems never took place.

Today's failure to invest in key technologies is tomorrow's foreign source dependency in critical technology products. Simply exhorting "the market" to invest in technologies deemed important is completely ineffective. Traditional trade policy is not sufficient, and sometimes arguably inappropriate, as the means of trying to address these failures in investment. The flat panel display antidumping case is a good case in point. Despite general recognition of their strategic importance to computers and other industries, the U.S. has seen relatively little investment in advanced flat panel displays,[58] in contrast to Japan, where the government orchestrated a large-scale national developmental effort.[59] As a result, computer makers in this country have become completely dependent for their laptop computer displays on Japanese suppliers. Such indigenous U.S. capability as exists does not produce the right technology nor does it have the necessary capacity to do so in the foreseeable future. Nevertheless, antidumping duties have been imposed on imports of some types of Japanese flat panel displays. The issue cannot be resolved through the imposition of antidumping duties, however, since such action will simply force the entire laptop computer

---

[58]"[A] U.S. flat-panel industry never existed. The U.S. industry largely moved out of solid state displays when they were still relatively simple. The Japanese firms took over this market by making simple consumer displays. These firms have since been largely responsible for the slow and difficult progress that has been made." Congressional Budget Office, *Using R&D Consortia for Commercial Innovation: SEMATECH, X-Ray Lithography and High Resolution Systems* (July 1990), pp. 49-50.

[59]MITI, *Dawn of the Age of Giant Electronics* (September 1988).

to be assembled offshore. Allowing this issue to be litigated as the sole means of establishing national policy on this subject is simply trade and industrial policy by default. While there may be philosophical objections from many academic economists to any change, the current approach is more likely than not to produce the worst possible result -- protection and another devastating industrial failure. If inadequate U.S. investment in key technologies is the malady, it cannot be remedied simply by treating one of the symptoms -- by providing protection.

There is, to be sure, a role for updated traditional trade policy tools; there has to be an awareness of targeting, and the use of measures -- Section 301 and international codes of conduct -- to curb the elements of targeting (such as closed markets and anticompetitive practices) that ultimately contribute to disparities in investment between U.S. and foreign industries. But hand-in-hand with these tools, there has to be the means found to assure that the investment is taking place that industry will require to assure its and the nation's future.

Utilizing America's Technological Strengths

We get all the Nobel prizes, but Japan gets all the profits.

-- Senator Ernest "Fritz" Hollings

In many instances, the United States has not translated its strength in basic research into success in the commercialization of new products and processes. There are many products, such as the VCR and the flat panel displays, which were invented in the United States but are now manufactured overseas. To some extent, this problem could be addressed by refocusing the current federal R&D investment. In 1992, the federal government will spend over $75 billion in R&D, but very little of that expenditure will have any significant industrial application. According to the OECD, only 0.2 percent of the U.S. federal R&D budget is dedicated to industrial development; the comparable figure is 4.8 percent for Japan and 14.5 percent for Germany.

There are some signs that the United States is endeavoring to improve the return on investment of its R&D expenditures. In September 1990, the Bush Administration issued a statement on "U.S. Technology Policy", which recognized a role for government in the funding of "pre-competitive, generic, enabling technologies." In 1991, the Administration unveiled a $638 million High Performance Computer and Communications Initiative. Members of Congress have introduced a number of legislative proposals, such as the National Critical Technologies Act of 1991. This initiative sets specific goals, such as the development of a computer capable of one trillion computations per second, and the deployment of a high-speed data network linking universities and research institutes.

Organizations such as the Council on Competitiveness, the Center for Strategic and International Studies, the Carnegie Commission on Science, Technology and Government, the Computer Systems Policy Project, the Aerospace Industry Association, and the National Advisory Committee on Semiconductors are all working to define the outlines of a more sensible technology policy. Several common themes have emerged:

- At a broad level, there is a consensus as to which technologies are most important to America's economic well-being and national security. The same core group of technologies (electronics and information technology, biotechnology, materials, manufacturing process technology) are recognized as critical by experts in Washington, Brussels and Tokyo.
- For that reason, the percentage of the federal B&D budget devoted to these technologies should be increased. This does not require the government to pick "winners and losers." First, these technologies are important for virtually all industries. Second, the government would sponsor "precompetitive" R&D, as opposed to extending production subsidies to individual firms or industries. Finally, the government could require firms or consortia to "match" the federal investment, which would impose much of the discipline of the market-place on these programs.
- The United States would be stronger, both economically and militarily, if it adopted a "dual-use" strategy for technology development. Now that civilian technologies often surpass defense technologies, integration of the civilian and defense technology base is particularly important.
- With the end of the Cold War, America's national laboratories, particularly the DOE labs such as Sandia, Oak Ridge and Argonne, need to be given a mandate to work with industry. The national labs spend more than $20 billion, with a minimal level of technology transfer to industry.

It is important to put the role of technology policy in perspective. As John Armstrong, IBM's vice president for science and technology has noted, "The problem is in all the steps between research and the customer -- rapid response to the marketplace, continuous improvement in quality of manufacturing, short cycle times in product development. That's where the primary focus of attention should be." As part of a broader strategy, a shift of America's federal R&D priorities could boost U.S. productivity and international competitiveness.

America's vast resources in technology, in company, university and government laboratories, can be used together more often on selected projects. Companies can cooperate to eliminate duplicative research to a greater extent without lessening the amount of competition in the market place. In some instances, joint production will be an attractive option. In both cases, cooperation will make good sense in research, experimentation and production consortia where the risks for any one firm of commercializing a technology do not justify an individual firm's investment, or where, perhaps, foreign firms have an overwhelming lead in an area. Cooperation in selected areas will not change the general pattern of economic activity. Firms will still be vigorous competitors. Sometimes, however, they can only do so if some cooperative activities occurs.

Improving Education and Training

> *When Apple went to Singapore, we weren't looking for cheap labor. We went because, on average, labor there is more trainable and of higher quality.*
>
> -- John Sculley, Chairman, Apple Computer

Beginning with *A Nation At Risk*, which warned of a "rising tide of mediocrity," a flood of studies has documented the shortcomings of America's educational system. The magnitude of the problem is well-known. One million young people drop out of high school every year, with rates approaching 50 percent in inner cities. Roughly 25 percent of those who do graduate cannot read or write at the eighth-grade, or "functionally literate" level. In a recent study of 13-year-olds in the U.S., Korea, Spain, Ireland, the United Kingdom, and Canada, U.S. students were last in average mathematics proficiency, nearly last in science proficiency, and first only in the percent of those watching five or more hours of television each day. The U.S. has no comprehensive system for training skilled workers and craftsmen; there are few significant government training programs, and high labor mobility has made individual employers reluctant to invest in long term training. As a result, the "quality of the U.S. labor force -- and particularly that with only a high school degree or less -- has probably declined relative to that overseas, and notably relative to Japan." The U.S. work force has become sharply segmented into a pool of highly-skilled white-collar workers and a much larger pool of lower-skilled or unskilled workers.[60]

All of this has clear implications for America's ability to compete in global markets. As The Commission on the Skills of the American Workforce recently put it, America faces a choice between "high skills or low wages." Unless the United States wants to compete directly with Third World nations, it will have to create "high performance work organizations." In such organizations, front-line workers are empowered to make rather than follow decisions, workers are given responsibility for tasks such as quality control and production scheduling formerly reserved for middle management, and tasks are performed by a few highly skilled workers as opposed to many unskilled workers.[61]

America's chief economic competitors all "maintain coherent, highly systematic structures to stimulate both the supply of and the demand for highly skilled workforce."[62] These include high academic expectations for all young people, school-to-work transition programs, a commitment to lifelong learning, and labor market agencies with training, information and placement services. In Germany, for example, students begin learning about occupations from local employers in the seventh grade, and at age 15 or 16, about 60 percent of young people enter an apprenticeship program which typically lasts three years, and which combines on-the-job training and classroom instruction.[63] The government works with trade associations and unions to develop standardized curricula, regulations and examinations for apprentices in more than 400 occupations. Large companies maintain training centers, sometimes funded and licensed by the Länder governments, to supplement the vocational school curricula. Apprentices at smaller companies spend time at area training centers

---

[60]Henry Ergas, "Does Technology Policy Matter?" in Bruce R. Gaile and Harvey Brooks (eds.), *Technology and Global Industry* (National Academy Press, 1987), pp. 204-05.

[61]*America's Choice: High Skills or Low Wages!*, National Center on Education and the Economy, June 1990.

[62]*America's Choice: High Skills or Low Wages!*, National Center on Education and the Economy, June 1990, p. 58.

[63]Public vocational schools teach for 1-2 days/week some theoretical aspects of occupational training, as well as some general school coursework. The rest of the week is spent learning practical skills at the workplace. Peter J. Katzenstein's *Industry and Politics in West Germany* (Ithaca and London; Cornell University Press, 1989), pp. 12-13.

supported by local chambers of commerce and the Federal Ministry of Education and Science. This comprehensive apprenticeship program has had a significant impact on the productivity of German workers and firms.[64] Indeed, German industry is characterized by a degree of "overskilling", a surplus of trained human capital which has resulted -- in autos, for example -- in temporary assignments of highly trained individuals to line production jobs.[65] In effect Germany fosters "a very high level of intermediate skills in the working population."[66] It should not be particularly surprising that craftsmanship, design and product quality are the hallmarks of German industry.

There are numerous proposals and initiatives which are designed to strengthen America's education and training system. At a 1990 education summit, President Bush and the nation's governors established six goals for the year 2000. If these goals are realized, all children will enter school ready to learn, the high school graduation rate will increase to 90 percent, U.S. students will demonstrate competency in challenging subjects, U.S. students will be first in the world in math and science, every adult will be literate and possess the skills needed to compete in the global economy, and every school will be drug-free. Elements of the President's strategy for achieving these goals include establishing a system of voluntary national examinations, promoting school choice, sponsoring the design of "New American Schools", and encouraging adult literacy and life-long learning. However, according to the National Education Goals Panel, the United States is very far from reaching these targets and it is increasingly clear, that unless the United States makes a concerted effort to improve its education and training system, declining competitiveness and declining real wages are the likely result.

MANAGING THE WORLD TRADING SYSTEM

National, Bilateral, and Multilateral Approaches

For the first three-quarters of the nation's history, trade policy was dominated by an interest in the impact that trade measures had on the domestic economy. Protection was a tool of industrial and agricultural

---

[64]See *Worker Training: Competing in the New International Economy*, Office of Technology Assessment, September 1990.

[65]Katzenstein (1989) p. 130.

[66]Ergas (1987) pp. 207-08.

policy, as well as a necessary instrument to raise revenue. Alexander Hamilton, as Secretary of the Treasury, did everything in his power to support the manufacturing and commerce of the country. While Jefferson was originally hostile to this view when serving as President, he began to see the practical necessity of accommodating trade policy to the needs of the countries new industries. These policies were considered sound to most of America's outstanding leaders of this formative period. In 1843, Abraham Lincoln defended a Whig resolution which declared "a tariff of duties upon foreign importations, producing sufficient revenue for the support of the General Government, and so adjusted as to protect American industry, to be indispensably necessary to the prosperity of the American people. . .".[67] He quoted with approval a letter of Thomas Jefferson which stated

> *To be independent for the comforts of life, we must fabricate them ourselves. We must now place the manufacturer by the side of the agriculturalist. The grand inquiry now is, shall we make our own comforts, or go without them at the will of a foreign nation?. . . . [E]xperience has taught me that manufactures are now as necessary to our independence as to our comfort.*[68]

He also cited the view of General Andrew Jackson, "It is time we should become a little more Americanized, and instead of feeding the paupers and laborers of England, feed our own;. . . [69] Lincoln writing to the people of Illinois, stated that ". . . th[e] country is extensive enough, its products abundant and varied enough, to answer all the real wants of its people."[70] These were popular sentiments. Political forces as well as national policy played a central role in determining trade policy.

The Twentieth Century witnessed a continuation of a high tariff policy, culminating in the Smoot Hawley Tariff Act of 1930. At a time of economic distress, unrivaled by any the country had previously witnessed, the United States, matching the actions of the nations of Europe, built

---

[67]*Northwestern Gazette and Galena Advertiser*, March 17, 1843, as quoted in The Collected Works of Abraham Lincoln, Rutgers, Brunswick, N.J. 1953, Vol I at p. 309.

[68]The Collected Works of Abraham Lincoln, Rutgers, Brunswick, N.J. 1953, Vol I at p. 311.

[69]The Collected Works of Abraham Lincoln, Rutgers, Brunswick, N.J. 1953, Vol I at p. 310.

[70]The Collected Works of Abraham Lincoln, Rutgers, Brunswick, N.J. 1953, Vol I at p. 310.

even higher tariff walls. Although there is little historical evidence that the Smoot-Hawley tariff either significantly restricted trade or prompted much of a foreign response, its psychological and political importance was profound -- it entered American economic thinking as the primary example of how restrictive trade policies can curtail world trade.[71] The 1930 Tariff Act, together with the Roosevelt Administration's reaction to it contained in the Reciprocal Trade Agreements Act of 1934, provide the watershed of current trade policy: the 1930 Act because it was taken to demonstrate the catastrophic error of protectionism in the modern world, and the 1934 Trade Agreements Program, because it appeared to be a rational way out. The long shadow of the policy of protectionism and the light of reciprocal trade liberalization shade and illuminate every trade major action which every subsequent Administration has taken.

From the 1930s forward, the organizing principle of United States trade policy was not commercial self-interest or the nation's revenue, but the liberalization of international trade for its general benefits for the economy and, after the Second World War, its contribution to America's foreign policy objectives. The framework was the Trade Agreements Program, wholly bilateral through World War II, and almost exclusively multilateral thereafter -- until just these last few years. The trade

---

[71]The percentage increase in the ratio of duties calculated to dutiable imports under Smoot-Hawley (32 percent) was only half that which had been put into effect by the Fordney-McCumber Tariff Act of 1922 (over 60 percent). Even after enactment of Smoot-Hawley, two-thirds of all U.S. imports (in value) entered the U.S. duty free. The economic literature of the Depression gives little importance to the economic effects of Smoot-Hawley on the severity of the Depression. The analysts who have been most critical of the effects of Smoot-Hawley, Kindleberger and Saint-Etienne, cite not so much its economic effects as its role as a catalyst in triggering reciprocal tariff increases by other countries. But Smoot-Hawley was more of a culmination of a world trend toward higher tariffs than an instigating factor. Britain instituted increased tariffs in 1915 (McKenna Act) and again in 1921 (Safeguarding of Industries Act) which placed 33⅓ percent ad valorem duties on all products alleged to be vital to national defense. France, Italy, India and Australia all increased tariffs significantly before Smoot-Hawley was enacted. Concededly, Smoot-Hawley did prompt some retaliatory action (Switzerland increased duties on watches) but it does not deserve the watershed status it has acquired in American economic mythology. See William A. Noellert, *The Smoot-Hawley Act and the Great Depression* (mimeo, May 31, 1985) Joseph M. Jones, *Tariff Retaliation* (Philadelphia: University of Pennsylvania Press, 1934); Joseph Schumpeter, *Business Cycles* (New York: McGraw-Hill, 1939); Ingvar Svennilson, *Growth and Stagnation in the European Economy* (Geneva U.N. Economic Commission for Europe 1954); Herman Van der Wee (ed.) *The Great Depression Revisited* (The Hague; Martinus Nijhoft, 1972).

decisions within this framework were primarily minor adjustments -- where to go a bit further or hold back somewhat in international tariff negotiations, where to pull back for a time (in escape clause cases), and where to offset a specific unfair trade practice (antidumping and countervailing duties).

Domestic political forces played a role, but these diminished over time as the tariff and other forms of protection were reduced. In their place came a belief in the rule of law. As the tariff became a less important (if not, on average, insignificant) form of trade measure, a rules-based international trading system became the objective of U.S. policy. There was no way to eliminate all measures which had trade distorting effects, but these could be hemmed in with international regulations. And as rules were promulgated, it seemed entirely possible to move from a GATT-centered system of mediation to one of adjudication. The notion of world federalism, which in recent years has seemed entirely bankrupt for political purposes, was increasingly seen by the United States as a reasonable method of governing world trade. The trade negotiations would create international trade laws, and a quasi-judicial dispute settlement mechanism would administer them. The third branch of international trade governance, the executive, was left largely unformed, as the cession of sovereignty as overtly as would occur with the creation of a supra-national executive was beyond the politically acceptable or even imaginable. However, a less noticeable cession of sovereignty under the rule of law to international panels of judges was irresistible.

One essential factor in creating a supra-national forum for reaching adjudicated results is simply not being very concerned about outcomes. If the international legal mechanisms limit the use of trade measures against foreign subsidies, for example, there is a sense of frustration but not profound loss, given the fact that the U.S. government does not identify closely with its commercial interests. The difference between the pursuit of political and security interests (as traditionally defined) and the pursuit of commercial interests, could not be more astoundingly different. The invasion of Grenada or Panama, whether in retrospect important or not, would never be put to international adjudication. Yet it is proposed to place all commercial (trade) questions under binding international dispute resolution.

While successive Administrations have put increasing emphasis on organizing world trade through multilateral rules under the regime of the GATT, there have been some counter-tendencies. These have taken the form primarily of an interest in regional bilateral agreements. There has also been some debate about the utility or harmfulness of unilateral action, and the use of bilateral issue-specific or product-specific trade agreements to settle particular disputes. There has been something of a public debate, or at least serious questions raised, about the utility of the United States pursuing policies built largely upon the multilateral foundation of the GATT, especially given the distressing failure of the Uruguay Round to deliver the results anticipated of it within the time frame which had been set aside for its completion.[72]

Are There Alternatives to Multilateralism?

In the late 1970s, a group a Japanese Diet members visited the Office of the U.S. Special Trade Representative. They had come to complain about America's pressing Japan to accept American citrus products more freely. Their case was straightforward. They said that Japan was self-sufficient in citrus, in the form of the mikan (mandarin) orange. These legislators said that Japan did not "need" America's oranges or grapefruit. The Deputy Trade Representative replied, with some irritation, that most of world trade did not take place on the basis of need but on the basis of preference. If Japan did not need American oranges, the United States, applying the same logic, did not need Japanese automobiles, stereos, cameras, or tape recorders. But, the U.S. official concluded, this was not a way to conduct a nation's trade policy.

So when the question is posed, a question often suggested when the GATT round of negotiations was stalled, "Are there alternatives to multilateralism", the answer is clearly, "of course, there are". For most of the history of economic relations among nations, multilateralism did not even exist. For those visiting members of the Japanese Diet in the late 1970s, who represented agricultural interests, their answer was a preference for isolationism, to have no trade at all.[73] This sounds farfetched, but for some elements in the European Green (environmental) parties today as well, it is still preferred policy. Thus, while this is an extreme position, it holds some attraction for identifiable groups. Fortunately, it is a position taken by almost no group in power, or this planet's inhabitants would be a good deal poorer.

The more serious schools of trade policy can be delineated in a few broad categories. First, there are the pure multilateralists. They believe that the GATT is all that is necessary in a world of trading nations assumed somewhat uncritically to be each adhering to and acting on laissez-faire principles. At the opposite philosophical pole, a school which

---

[72]It was to have been concluded at Brussels on December 7, 1990.

[73]They failed to mention that Japan even had a trade surplus in oranges with the United States, an ironic note, even if not of great economic significance to the two countries.

has recently collapsed believed in (or could not find practical alternatives to) the barter arrangements of the Communist countries.

Within the United States, Japan and Europe, there are a number who believe in managed trade. This is not a school represented in any country's official rhetoric. It finds its roots less in any philosophical articulation (except outside of official circles, by someone like Alain Gomez, the chief executive officer of the French firm Thomson). It exists as a matter of pragmatism rather than trade theory. Western Europe's policies toward Japan and Eastern Europe in the 1960s, '70s and most of the '80s fall into this category. The same pragmatism tinged with mercantilism defines much of Japanese trade policy.

The Western Europeans have never embraced any school of trade policy with sufficient definitiveness to fall into a distinct category. Their officials would certainly subscribe officially to multilateralism and, currently, a laissez-faire ideology. But elements of pragmatism, and distinct variations in approach can certainly be found depending on which EC Member State's policies one is reviewing. The constellation of Community politics and interests will produce differing results on individual issues. A determining factor in the past has been the economic state of the Community -- that is, whether there is a prevailing mood of Euro-pessimism or the more recent period of economic growth and consolidation of the single market, characterized by feelings sometimes approaching Euro-euphoria. It is not yet clear what the shape of future EC policies will be, but clearly, economic liberalization is the dominant force currently. However, the triumphalism of the late 1980's has begun to wear off as the EC members encounter economic difficulties and the Community and its prospective members begin pulling themselves together into broader pan-European arrangements.

Free Trade Areas and Customs Unions. The most enduring major deviation from the post World War II multilateral framework has been the Customs Union and Free Trade Area exception to the GATT.[74] There have been other examples of serious discrimination -- "negative," in the case of Europe's treatment of Japan and Eastern Europe, and "positive," in the form of various trade preference schemes for developing countries. But the former has largely been phased out, and the latter have been greatly diluted by the general reduction of tariffs. Thus the most notable example of an organizing principle for international trade that is not multilateral is the European Common Market and its associated free trade areas, until now the chief among these being the European Free Trade

---

[74]GATT Article XXIV.

Agreement (EFTA). While there are theoretical underpinnings to the idea of a customs union and a free trade area,[75] the principal motivation for the acceptance of this discriminatory derogation from GATT principles by the United States was the political benefit attributable to a Europe united in economic interest and therefore less likely to find itself in yet another fratricidal conflict into which the U.S. would again be drawn; a Europe that would be sufficiently economically sound to resist falling into the Communist camp.

With this impressive political and economic example of success before American policy-makers, and with frustration building with the lack of progress in multilateral negotiations, in the 1980s the United States for the first time in the modern era moved away from the multilateral and back to the bilateral approach, entering into its own preferential regional arrangement with Canada. Canada was of course a special case, being America's largest trading partner. Geography dictated the absence of trade barriers between the two countries; more trade moved north-south than east-west (within Canada). Tariff schedules and other regulations were illogical barriers to normal economic flows of goods and services. While this bilateral move could be used by U.S. negotiators to show the rest of the world that the United States had some alternatives if multilateral trade talks bogged down, the principle motivation for the U.S.-Canada Free Trade Area was pragmatism and straight-forward economics, rather than foreign policy. The opposite can be said of the U.S.-Israel Free Trade Agreement. Here politics, both foreign and domestic, dominated. The significance of this arrangement for U.S. trade policy was and is somewhere between slim and none.

The North American Free Trade Agreement (NAFTA) is another matter. The important element for the U.S. is opening up the border to Mexico, not the creation of a North American free trade area (Canada has been included because it wished to be). The principal U.S. motivation was political. The complementarity of the Canadian and U.S. economies was not replicated in the proposed southern tier accord. The essence of the agreement was that a more prosperous and politically stable country on the southern border of the United States was in the nation's foreign policy interests. The fact that there are also arguably significant economic benefits to both countries was almost beside the point. The case for regional economic integration could, of course, be made, and was. This was not necessarily a departure by the United States from the basic multilateral organizing principles of its foreign trade policy. But one cannot redirect major energies (moving much of the attention for a

---

[75] J.Viner, *The Customs Union Issue* (1950).

significant period from a multilateral round of negotiations to bilateral talks) without having an effect on policy. The devotion of the United States to a multilateral world trading framework was beginning to be called into question. In part, this was by design, to show other countries that a stalemate in the GATT talks could have undesirable consequences for them. But the policy was only partially due to the impasse with the Community over agriculture in the GATT talks. The key change in circumstances was the advent of a Mexican President who was an economic liberal and who did not come to power as a sworn enemy of the United States. Stability through investment and growth could be brought to Mexico, and these in turn could be accelerated by the NAFTA.

In the midst of this re-focussing of official attention on the bilateral and regional, the United States reinforced the impression abroad that its interest in the GATT had waned. It did this by the President's announcement, without much internal deliberation within the Administration of a proposed "Enterprise for the Americas", a free trade agreement for the entire Western Hemisphere. This was a political declaration, whether or not intended, that the nations of this hemisphere had a special interest in trading with each other that was not shared between the United States, and, for example, the ASEAN nations (Singapore, Malaysia, Indonesia, the Philippines, and Thailand). In a world in which modern transportation has reduced distances, and the revolution in data processing and communications has allowed American case law digests to be prepared in Korea, one may wonder whether the United States' future economic relations were more importantly centered on Central and South America, than with the rapidly growing economies of East Asia.[76] It is clear that this question did not receive much in the way of analysis. Likewise, the notion that hemispheric economic integration made more sense than a greater degree of integration with Europe was clearly not examined.

Whatever could be considered the motivations of the Administration, it has not been its intent to create a trading bloc to the exclusion of the expansion of other economic contacts. Each of these less-than-multilateral approaches to trade had a variety of reasons why it was considered necessary and appropriate. Each was designed as an exceptional case and not as a new paradigm. But a free trade area has its limits as an appropriate policy mechanism. The idea was put forward a few years ago by the United States Ambassador to Japan, Mike Mansfield, that a U.S.-

---

[76]Brazil is a separate case, for which closer association might well make some sense.

Japan free trade area be negotiated. This did not make any sense, other perhaps than as a political gesture of friendship.[77]

The idea has also been floated from time to time of a "GATT Plus" or an association for trading purposes of the like-minded, an idea which surfaced when the developing countries functioned in international conferences more as a bloc, and a militant one at that. But trade liberalization and decision-making organized on a North versus South basis would have only further polarized the world economically and politically.

Trading blocs are not what the United States should be seeking. Geography and economics argue for a U.S.-Canada Free Trade Agreement, and there are political arguments to be made as well for a U.S.-Mexico FTA. Moreover, regional integration need not imply an exclusionary trading policy. But here, at the boundaries of North America, is where this trend should stop. There is little justification for taking it further.

Bilateral Solutions to Specific Trade Problems. On a less broad scale, there have been other departures from a multilateral approach. Since 1935, whenever a specific trade problem required foreign export restraint, a bilateral agreement, formal or informal, has been utilized. Thus, for example, formal agreements (called orderly marketing agreements or OMAs) have been negotiated to deal with injurious imports of specialty steels, color televisions, and machine tools. Informal understandings (voluntary export restraints, or VERs) have been utilized with respect to automobiles, and many years ago, ceramic tile from Japan. These latter agreements had no statutory basis or acknowledged parentage. Occasionally, U.S. and foreign officials disavowed their very existence.

---

[77]There are a variety of reasons why a free trade area with Japan is an inherently unsound concept. A free trade agreement (FTA) is designed primarily to remove tariffs. Most tariffs between the United States and Japan were already very low. But most importantly, an FTA would not have addressed the underlying sources of conflict in U.S.- Japanese economic relations. Not tariffs and quotas but investment and production incentives, different competition rules, anticompetitive practices, restrictive distribution systems, and the like, that is, largely internal barriers, block access to the Japanese market. A free trade area with Japan would have built up the level of frustration (had the Congress countenanced its negotiation and approved it) as no problems were dealt with successfully once the FTA was concluded. Moreover, a bilateral approach of this magnitude could not help but do great damage to the multilateral trading system. The same could be said of a U.S.-European FTA, which would make greater economic sense. The multilateral trading system could not withstand as great a derogation as either of these inter-regional free trade agreements would create.

Less than fully multilateral approaches have been used in and since the Tokyo Round GATT negotiations, for example, where it proved impractical to include all countries which were parties to the GATT due to their lack of interest or unwillingness to participate in a given agreement. This conditional MFN approach was not so much a derogation from the multilateral trading system as the creation of subcommittees with those of like mind or those with common interests. Thus, all of the GATT codes -- e.g. aircraft, dairy, and government procurement -- have memberships which fall short of the full list of Contracting Parties, but are open to all to sign if they are willing to undertake the requisite obligations. Current attempts are being made to negotiate other codes that would have less than universal membership -- e.g. steel and shipbuilding. This is also not considered to be a serious departure from multilateralism, as a code can in theory and in practice cover all Contracting Parties which have an interest in joining.

There have also been problems that are best negotiated bilaterally even if the benefits are available multilaterally. This has been true of many of the agreements reached after the United States has prosecuted a section 301 case. It is mainly pragmatism that drives the United States to a bilateral solution. The U.S.- Japan Semiconductor Agreement is one such example. The problem was manifested by Japan's market closure and consequent dumping. U.S. trade interests were affected far more directly than those of any other country. It was thus the United States that worked out a solution directly with Japan. Upon review of this Agreement in the GATT, the essential elements were left unmodified. The result was multilateral in effect -- that is, the Agreement is nondiscriminatory.[78]

Issues Which are Inherently Multilateral. The multilateral approach to trade negotiations was designed in the first instance in part to answer practical problems of the negotiation process. One country's tariffs affect more than one exporting/supplying nation. To try to reduce a tariff for only one supplier would run afoul of the most-favored-nation clause. To give benefits to all without their reciprocal participation leads to the problem of rewarding free riders. A major incentive for trade liberalization would be removed if benefits were extended without reciprocal concessions being required.

---

[78]Although the GATT case on the semiconductor trade agreement was technically brought against Japan, it was also a direct challenge to the ability of the United States to work out a trade dispute bilaterally, when the effects of the agreement were seen to extend to other members of the trading system.

The complexity of dealing bilaterally only increases where nontariff barriers are involved. There is the practical problem of two countries drafting rules having potentially broader application and not having taken into account the interests of others. After having concluded a bilateral set of rules, attempting to get others to join may not be possible because renegotiation would constantly be required to obtain further signatories.[79] There is also the "three cornered deal" aspect of trade negotiations. It is often not possible to wrap up an agreement in one area without including other areas because a mutual balance of interests cannot be achieved. For example, suppose that Britain and the United States want to open the world's markets to the sale of insurance, but the two of them alone cannot create a sufficient negotiation. India might wish to sell iron manhole covers or rubies or vacuum bottles or textiles, or inexpensive computers, for which it might agree to accept sales of foreign insurance in its market. India might be pleased with this deal only if it had both Europe and the United States as markets for its products.

There is also the problem of obtaining critical mass. In trade negotiations, it is often impossible to remove a single barrier but quite possible to remove many. The reason is that the overall game becomes sufficiently important for a nation, so that while it cannot overcome its reluctance to make the small deal, if enough has been put on the table it may find that it cannot afford to turn its back on the large deal. Cutting one tariff may be impossible, but cutting many tariffs develops political and economic imperatives of its own. The only alternative to developing critical mass outside of multilateral trade negotiations is broad, across-the-board liberalization contained in a free trade agreement, and, as noted, this latter alternative has nearly run its logical course for the United States (although this has not yet occurred in Europe).

Outside of free trade area negotiations, the sad fact is that leverage in the bilateral context is more often threat than prospective gain. Bilateral negotiations in recent history are most often driven by what the United states might do to another country rather than what the two might gain mutually from a liberalizing exchange of trade concessions. But there are distinct limits to what can be obtained by threats. The improvements in market access are more likely to be narrow, rather than broad changes in barriers or in behavior.

---

[79]However, rules agreed to in a bilateral agreement may have a useful precedental value when a new area of rule-making is covered for the first time.

Unilateralism. As noted, many of the subjects of bilateral agreements are actually compromises reached following the issuance of unilateral threats. Section 301, and "Super 301" have had their uses -- wood products, insurance, super computers, amorphous metals, and semi-conductors, are examples of negotiations which resulted in settlements, motivated by the threat of unilateral measures. But countries cannot go around issuing threats incessantly; in fact, some issues become more intractable if threats are used. For example, it is unlikely that the EC's Common Agricultural Policy would be altered more quickly under a threat of massive retaliation from the United States; at least, no one has been willing to test the proposition that it would.

At the same time, beyond providing an impetus to the solution of individual problems,[80] unilateralism has some broader uses. In a world where the United States market is more open than many others, the possibility that the United States might act unilaterally -- that is, without the benefit of international agreement or the use of internationally agreed procedures -- does motivate other countries to come to the bargaining table to try to establish agreed rules and procedures. The Uruguay Round is in part the product of other countries' concerns, including many developing countries, that the world would be a better place with more rules curbing United States' actions, as opposed to a world in which there were fewer rules and more freedom of action for all. The United States is still a very large actor, and while its leverage has some bounds, it can do a lot of damage to the trade interests of others if it behaves (in their view) somewhat irrationally, that is, outside of international norms.

There is one other aspect of unilateral action worth mentioning. This is that a government, in the final analysis, has a responsibility to its people to protect national interests. In this regard, whether the interest is commercial, environmental, or of a foreign policy nature, it is an attribute of sovereignty that it may well believe that it must act regardless of international approval. True, it may have to pay a price for what others would see as rogue behavior, although the GATT, like the Pope, has no army. Thus weighing the costs and benefits, any country, including the United States should not consider surrendering the option of acting unilaterally. Agreeing to submit to international rules must have some limits.

In this regard, it should be noted that sometimes a fervent belief in multilateralism obscures some of the defects of the international system.

---

[80]The fact is that the U.S.-Japan Semiconductor Trade Agreement was not being implemented materially until President Reagan actually did impose retaliatory tariffs.

This is particularly true with respect to international dispute settlement. Disputes can only be settled in accordance with agreed substantive rules. As opposed to a national court system, the GATT panel structure and the GATT Council are not empowered to extend the applicability of the GATT rules beyond what was explicitly agreed. The GATT is a contract, not a constitutional government. It is not the place of the GATT Secretariat to choose, for example, to advise panels to construe countervailing duty or antidumping actions as narrow exceptions to the GATT. It is not the place of GATT panels to substitute their judgment for those of national decision-making bodies unless an international rule is clearly infringed. Deference must be paid to national decision-making bodies. The creation of mandatory jurisdiction vested in GATT panels is a major error in any area in which there is no real consensus as to the substantive rules which are to be applied. This amounts to a haphazard cession of sovereignty. There are limits to the GATT, and however disagreeable unilateralism may be to other trading nations, the GATT will lose respect and credibility if it seeks to legislate, rather than simply to apply, existing rules within the limits of that which has been negotiated.

Some Conclusions to Be Drawn. In implementing its trade policy, the United States should continue to utilize a combination of approaches. The right to act unilaterally -- America's principal and ultimate leverage -- must not be yielded in Uruguay Round or in any other negotiation. Where this right is curtailed in any way, this must be done with the greatest of caution, and certainly not in the absence of achieving clearly superior alternatives. While free trade areas should be pursued in Europe and North America, the limitations of regional trade liberalization should be recognized. These free trade areas are not an adequate substitute for multilateral approaches. Bilateral negotiations will remain an indispensable method for resolving specific issues that are truly not of general international concern, but they are supplements to the multilateral scheme of global management, not a substitute for it. There is also a place for plurilateral efforts, that is agreements among groups of countries that are not all-inclusive. The OECD (Organization for Economic Cooperation and Development) and the GATT codes, like the attempted Multilateral Steel Agreement, provide examples of tackling concerns which are widespread but not universal.

But the central thrust of American policy must of necessity still be multilateral. To those who are ready to condemn the GATT as being ineffective, the retort must be made that the GATT serves a useful purpose for the United States. It is a good management tool for many of the kinds of distortions which afflict international trade, particularly the traditional ones. While it is true that it is not all that it could be, reports of the

GATT's demise are greatly exaggerated. As a general proposition, the GATT does serve America's and others' interests.[81] It has moral force and occasionally can be used as a more direct lever for the opening of markets. It should be extended to new areas of coverage -- such as services, trade-related investment distortions and the protection of intellectual property rights -- as the current U.S. Administration is now attempting to do.

But if the GATT is to serve as a tool for the management of international trade, it too requires some management. In this regard it suffers from a number of defects. It has a secretariat that should be more activist with respect to ferreting out what is actually happening in world trade -- that is, to understand why trade flows in the paths that it currently takes, and why it does not flow in some areas at all. It was suggested once to the Director General of the GATT that the GATT Secretariat be given a subscription to the *London Financial Times* so that it would know what was going on in the world. His reply was that the GATT had the funds to subscribe to this newspaper but that the Contracting Parties would not let the Secretariat read it. It is in the interests of the United States that the GATT know more about the realities of trade and spread this knowledge. The Secretariat's analytical capabilities should be enhanced. The links between the International Monetary Fund, the World Bank, and the GATT should be strengthened, with the GATT being given the lead role on trade policy questions.

But the chief defects in the GATT are not to be found in the institution itself, or in its organization or funding. The GATT can do no more than a consensus of key countries will allow it to do. It is not supra-national, it is multinational. The U.S. and the EC must come to an accord on most fundamental issues if the GATT, or the Uruguay Round and subsequent rounds of negotiations are to be successful. It would be a very fine thing if Japan would, through sufficient liberalization of its own economy to international trade, join this informal management group. Regrettably, however, this is unlikely to occur in the near future. It is impossible for Japan to lead from its current position, being a country substantially deficient in its sharing of the burdens of world trade.[82]

---

[81]On the other hand, it should not become all that some would have it be -- that is, a final decision-making body with respect to the regulation of all nations' foreign trade.

[82]Japan will be more involved in multilateral organizations in the 1990s than at any time before, but in the GATT it is likely that this involvement will be directed primarily at defending Japan's economic interests, not at improving the trading system.

Thus, it is very important that the European Community and the United States compose their major differences -- over, for example, agriculture and industrial subsidies. This should not prove impossible for people of good will on both sides of the Atlantic. The EC and the United States actually have strong common interests, but these have been obscured by high-profile disputes. The two will have to act in a spirit of compromise if the GATT is to fulfill its true potential and if multilateral negotiating rounds are to be brought to successful conclusion. It is time that the United States and Europe forged the necessary partnership. It would be a great error for either to be so preoccupied with regional integration or internal development that the opportunity for cooperation between the two largest trading entities in the world was foregone.[83] The rate of future progress of the international trading system depends on the forging of this transatlantic partnership.

As for the Uruguay Round -- incomplete as of this writing -- it is clearly worth pursuing to a conclusion which has strong and positive results. There is much to be gained, such as the negotiation of an international regime of intellectual property rights protection, that will not be available as a practical matter within bilateral negotiating frameworks. The negotiation has been long and difficult. While it is entirely possible to settle for too little, and there will be a temptation to do so, and this must be resisted. The effort to attain more is worthwhile. A solid foundation must be put down from which further progress is all but inevitable.

TRADE RELATIONS WITH JAPAN

> *. . . he would take a hard line on trade issues toward Japan; "whose adversarial policies undermine much more than the economic prosperity of Americans. Restrictive, purely nationalistic trade policies by developed nations will make life more miserable for the growing number of people on this planet who are unable to support themselves."*[84]

---

[83]An increasing, but still small, number of Japanese are arguing for Japan to adopt a more global outlook. See the discussion of the concept of the new "globalism" by Shinji Fukukawa, former Vice Minister of International Trade at MITI, in "The Role of the Japanese Economy in a Changing Western World," *European Affairs* (Winter 1988) pp. 143-150.

[84]*Washington Post*, September, 1991, story on Senator Bob Kerrey announcing that he will seek the Democratic Presidential nomination.

The Problem

There is no more troubling or politicized subject in U.S. trade policy than "the Japan Problem."[85] No other trade issue has been proven so persistent, so intractable, and so damaging to the U.S. economy. Public commentators hold widely divergent views on the subject, but businessmen have been troubled for years, and therefore their elected representatives in Congress and the trade agencies in the Executive Branch have been grappling with this question since the early 1960s, when the largest issue was textile imports. As the focus of trade disputes moved from textiles and low-priced consumer electronics goods to steel, automobiles, and televisions, increasing attention came to be focused not only on product-specific issues, but on U.S.-Japan trading relations in general. There were bitter recriminations against Japan, largely on the floor of the Senate and the House, but some also in the press.[86] These were often emotional outcries, and many observers said that the case against Japan, such as it was, was not well documented.[87] In the 1990s, public opinion polls for the first time reported that Japan might be the main enemy of America rather than the Soviet Union -- a startling turn of sentiment given Japan's eschewing of any military role in world affairs.

The growing U.S. exasperation with Japan did not in fact reflect memories of Pearl Harbor or spring from racism -- explanations which struck a curious note in American ears but which were common in the Japanese press. As with many other aspects of the U.S. trade policy, the politics of the U.S.-Japan estrangement have been driven by the American sense of fair play. Constituents told their representatives in Congress about the problems they faced in seeking entry into the Japanese market;

---

[85]This is a term coined by Karel Von Wolferen in an article of that title in *Foreign Affairs* (January 1987). There is a separate, but related challenge stemming from the coming Japanese domination of the economies of Southeast Asia which is not yet recognized.

[86]On March 28, 1985, for example, the Senate voted 92-0 to endorse a resolution calling for major sanctions against Japan if it did not take steps to reduce its trade surplus with the U.S. A similar resolution passed the House 394-19. S. Con. Res. 15, 99th Cong., 1st Sess., 131 Cong. Rec. S3573 (daily ed. March 28, 1985); H.R. Con. Res. 107, 99th Cong. 1st Sess. 131 Cong. Rec. H1815-16 (daily ed. April 2, 1985).

[87]Theodore H. White, wrote one such article in the Sunday *New York Times* in the mid-1980s. The article, on an unaccustomed topic for White, trade policy--was broadly considered as intemperate and stemming substantially from White's having been a reporter in Nanking a generation earlier.

the major decades-long accretion of these "horror stories" of those who had tried to sell in Japan but had failed in the attempt generated heated Congressional debates on trade policy.[88] While its own market appeared to be largely impervious to imports, Japanese producers were extraordinarily aggressive. Tidal waves of exports -- *tsunami* -- swept their foreign competitors from product area after area.[89] The enormous bilateral trade deficit, cresting at $57 billion in 1987, created severe pressures for remedial U.S. legislation. The combination of a Japanese home market seen as being largely closed, and very aggressive export sales brought Congress to consider measures such as the Gephardt bill, legislation which would have placed a cap on the bilateral trade deficit with Japan. Instead, the "Super 301" provision was enacted, which required a rifle-shot approach against the worst "unfair trade practices" which the Executive Branch could find from any country. Super 301 was clearly not a cure for the Japan problem -- it was not even aimed explicitly at Japan -- but Japanese trade practices were the chief subject of the Congressional concern that fostered the legislation.

Anyone reviewing this period of U.S.-Japan relations confronts several questions. Why had the decades of Congressional anger and the frustrations of the U.S. business community not resulted in some more direct response to Japanese trade policies earlier? Why, when the response came, was it so seemingly unequal to the nature of the problem?

---

[88]Examples of these stories are legion. A small sampling would include: The President of Champion Spark Plugs who offered free products to Japanese automakers if they would only just try his company's superior products. . . . The Texas cattlemen who when they sought to fill a small quota for imports of high quality beef for hotel use in Japan were given orders for "inside skirts", a cut of meat unlikely to build a market for them in Japan. . . . The inventors of a new, much more efficient electric generator core who could not find any doors open to them despite the lack of competitive alternatives in Japan. . . . The soda ash manufacturers of Wyoming who found their access limited by a producer's cartel, despite superior, less-expensive, more environmentally sound (in the manufacturing process) product. . . . The fireproof wood panel producers whose products failed Japanese tests (withstanding flames for a specified period) because the tumescent coating extinguished the flames before the test period expired. . . . The producers of cherries in the Pacific Northwest whose products were subjected to warm temperature fumigation, depriving the products of salability. . . . The semiconductor producers whose products were promised market entry through formal trade concessions and then had this access taken back through informal, but government-initiated "liberalization countermeasures."

[89]Primary examples were textiles, followed by consumer electronics, steel (in an earlier period) and bearings.

One reason is that critics of Japan were always met by others who pointed to other plausible reasons for unfortunate sectoral outcomes -- e.g., exchange rates, relative rates of savings affecting relative costs of capital, or relative natural resource endowments. Scholarly analysis, both of Japan experts and of academic economists, served as a counter-balance to the politicians and trade policy makers. Most standard economic works had been macroeconomic, theoretical justifications which explained that the Japanese market was not really closed, despite the experience of businessmen.[90] Americans, always ready to engage in introspection, wondered if perhaps they themselves were not the larger part of the competitive problem. Consumers, after all, were voting with their wallets, not only for remarkably inexpensively priced Japanese goods but also for high-priced brand-name goods such as Sony equipment, the Lexus and the Infiniti. There was an outpouring of books on things that the Japanese were doing right.[91] Those who felt that they had grievances against Japan's trade policies were generally regarded by the center of U.S. public opinion in the 1970's and early 1980s as a form of businessman-underachiever; those who took up their cause automatically became "Japan-bashers."

However, the weight of American opinion began to change in the mid-1980s, coinciding with the period of overvaluation of the dollar and its aftermath. With the massive shift in the U.S. trade balance to deficit, a large part of which was accounted for by Japan, books and papers began to appear which were generally critical of Japanese policies; these met a more receptive American public. Those in business who had succeeded in all other markets in the world, but not in Japan, began to have greater credibility. Their reports, which the economics profession in general had regarded as merely "anecdotal" -- facts unsupported by economic theory -- were given greater credence. Journalists were among the first to pull together the individual problems and discern a pattern of Japanese

---

[90]For examples of representative uncritical papers on Japan's trade policies, see the works of Gary Saxonhouse in general; C. Fred Bergsten's and William Kline's *The United States Japan Economic Problem*, (Washington: Institute for Economic Relations, 1985), the annual reports on U.S. Japan Relations of the School of Advanced International Studies, Johns Hopkins; or the columns of Hobart Rowan in the *Washington Post*.

[91]One of the more insightful works was Eza Vogel's *Japan as Number One: Lessons for America* (Cambridge: Harvard University Press, 1989), published in the period of adulatory books about what Japan was doing right. See also William G. Ouchi, *Theory Z: How American Business Can Meet the Japanese Challenge* (Avon, 1982); and James Abegglen, *Kaisha; The Japanese Corporation* (New York, Basic Books, 1985).

behavior.[92] This was followed by articles by other observers whose credentials were such that they could not be dismissed as insufficiently trained observers. Perhaps a turning point in the public debate was Peter Drucker's article, "Adversarial Trade" in the *Wall Street Journal* in 1986. (This article made an even more significant impression in Japan, as it came from a man widely respected if not revered in Japan for his expertise in management.) Until this point, few scholars had explained in depth what Japan was doing or how.[93] Initially these new opinions were not widely read by the public, and tended to be obscured by the weight of opinion on the other side, particularly of the academic economists. However, eventually mainstream economists began to be less oblivious to the Japanese phenomenon. Robert Lawrence wrote a widely-read Brookings paper on the anticompetitive effects of *keiretsu*, and Ed Lincoln published *Japan's Unequal Trade.* By 1988, the center of academic opinion had begun to shift,[94] somewhat late for many U.S. industries, but not too late to produce a more credible response. This coincided with some advance in the learning processes of the U.S. government.

The incoming Bush Administration, compelled to act almost immediately under the mandatory requirements of the 1988 Omnibus Trade and Competitiveness Act, brought three Super 301 cases (supercomputers, wood products, and satellites) against Japan in the first months of 1989. However, in the following year, it announced that it could not find further issues that were worthy of Super 301 treatment that were not already subject to ongoing negotiation, and this legislation became a dead letter. To those in Congress who had hoped to see an organized response to the central issues of U.S. trade relations with Japan, the "Super 301" attempt may have seemed to misfire. But in dealing with the first round of "Super 301" investigations in 1989, U.S. Trade

---

[92]Two of the most notable were James Fallows writing in the *Atlantic* and *The New York Review of Books*, and Karel Van Wolferen, a Dutch journalist, condensing twenty-five years of experience in a single volume, *The Enigma of Japanese Power.* These authors discerned patterns of behavior from the countless stories of failures of outsiders to deal with the Japanese system.

[93]Exceptions included Chalmers Johnson, John Zysman, and Michael Borrus at the University of California at Berkeley, Kent Calder at Princeton, Daniel Okimoto at Stanford; and Kozo Yamamura at the University of Washington in Seattle.

[94]See also Bela Bellassa and Marcus Noland, *Japan and the World Economy* (Washington, D.C.: Institute for International Economics, 1988); Stephen D. Cohen, *Cowboys and Samurais: Why the U.S. is Losing the Battling with the Japanese, and Why it Matters* (Harper, 1991).

Representative Carla Hills took a step which was politically very astute. The Super 301 cases -- in effect self-initiated section 301 cases -- were aimed at a variety of narrow targets around the world, each chosen to be illustrative of the kinds of trade barriers American companies faced abroad. However, it was clear that three sectoral cases filed against Japan would not assuage Congressional ire at what was seen as a much broader pattern of unacceptable Japanese trade behavior. The Administration thus initiated a wide ranging quasi-negotiation aimed at reviewing the attributes of the Japanese economy which were seen to underlie the bulk of the trade complaints. This effort was dubbed the Structural Impediments Initiative (SII).[95] SII was to focus on such problems as the trade-restrictive effects derived from the structure of the Japanese distribution system, interfirm relationships (*keiretsu*) and the inadequate enforcement of Japan's antitrust laws. This approach was an outgrowth of the Reagan Administration's MOSS (market-oriented sector selective) negotiations. Neither MOSS nor SII produced much in terms of immediate results. However, if they did not solve many problems, these kind of talks informed both sides in detail of what some of the underlying problems were.

Despite a certain lack of seriousness on the U.S. side about the review of structural problems in the U.S. economy, the approach taken in the SII talks was a departure from prior efforts, including the MOSS talks. The searching look at the competitive problems foreign firms faced in Japan was to be structured from two points of view--the barriers faced in Japan and the deficiencies within the U.S. economy that undercut American companies' competitiveness. The latter included America's high cost of capital, its low savings rate, and problems caused by the U.S. tax and capital structures, such as the short time horizons of American managers. The two governments had, perhaps somewhat unwittingly, emulated bilaterally in the trade area the function the International Monetary Fund performs in the international monetary field -- they held up a mirror to each country's policies. This provided an opportunity to scrutinize the factors that gave rise to the inability of each to live comfortably in a trading relationship with the other; each could see also itself as the source of many of its trade problems with most of the countries with which it traded.

Regrettably, the SII process cannot be judged a success. Absent strenuous remedial measures, the identification of problems, while a

---

[95]To ease the confrontational nature of the exercise, the Administration paid lip-service to the proposition that the U.S. economy's blemishes would similarly be placed under scrutiny.

potentially useful step, causes the process to degenerate into little more than a graduate seminar in comparative economic and commercial structures. However, the Japanese side can afford to be as critical as the Americans of this outcome, because of the two sides, arguably it was the Americans who took the process less seriously -- disdaining Japanese advice offered regarding defects in how the United States is organized. The exercise of accepting criticism in return for offering it was perhaps considered an empty diplomatic formula by the U.S. negotiators. If that is the case, the Americans ended up learning less than they should have from the exercise. The graduate seminar analogy unfortunately is valid for another reason as well: many of the officials involved, particularly on the U.S. side, simply moved on to new, unrelated, assignments, or left government altogether not that long after the beginning of the process, with most of the problems still left intact.

One of the troubling aspects of the SII experience has been that much of what the U.S. government was learning, and more, had been known to U.S. businessmen for a long time. Zenith was complaining about Japan's restrictive distribution system in the 1960s. Montgomery Ward knew about the effects of the Large Retail Store Law as much as two decades ago. Bob Galvin of Motorola had a very good understanding of Japanese industrial targeting and the impact of *keiretsu* and other interfirm relationships by the early 1970s. Houdaille's experience in the machine tool case, T. Boone Picken's experience in attempting to participate in the board of a Japanese auto parts manufacturer, George Hatsopolis' study on relative cost of capital, the American soda ash industry's experience with Japanese anticompetitive activities -- all these and countless others' experiences had documented in great detail various aspects of the problems of competing with Japan years earlier.[96]

Were this not dismaying enough, to it must be added the most recent discovery of American observers, that Japanese companies are in the aggregate out-investing U.S. companies -- $660 billion compared with $510 billion -- in 1990. This is hardly what anyone would characterize as an

[96]Virtually all of the structural problems in Japan addressed in SII were documented at considerable length by the U.S. General Accounting Office over a decade ago in a comprehensive survey of problem sectors including machine tools, forest products, computers, televisions, farm products and telecommunications equipment. This report, based on extensive field surveys and interviews with U.S. businessmen was reviewed by the State Department, the Office of the U.S. Trade Representative, and other agencies, whereupon it faded into virtually complete oblivion. Report by the Comptroller General of the U.S., *U.S.-Japan Trade: Issues and Problems* (ID-79-53, September 21, 1979).

unfair trade practice. But, as U.S. Ambassador to Japan Michael Armacost has noted, it is a cause for serious concern.

Knowing what we now know, what is to be done?

Analysis

After all these years of dealing with various aspects of the trade problems with Japan, to recommend that there be further analysis will seem to be a somewhat anemic step. However, there is a need to utilize the various sources of intelligence available. For this to occur, there must be a major organizational effort within the U.S. government, leaning heavily on private sector experience and academic study. A first step would be simply to ask a group of clear-eyed government-industry-academic Japan experts to give their recommendation to the Executive Branch and Congress as to how to gather and assess intelligence on trade problems with Japan.[97] This need not be cause for a significant delay in effecting cures. Much of what needs to be known is readily at hand.[98]

Setting Priorities

There being an inherent limitation to government energy and resources, U.S. negotiators must establish clear priorities, after consultation with the Congress.[99] No effort will be successful unless the President and his Cabinet places a higher emphasis on the nation's commercial interests. Once this is done, the effort should be supported by all agencies striving for success of a comprehensive program with clear objectives. This has occurred perhaps once in the last fifteen years, with a cooperative, collegial interagency approach having been taken in the early years of the Carter Administration. It led to an agreement with Japan on macroeconomic Japanese growth targets as well as specific trade concessions.[100] The collaborative effort quickly collapsed, however, and the pressure for further progress abated as a Presidential trip to Japan was

---

[97]The National Association of Manufacturers recommended such an approach in a letter to President Bush on March 13, 1991.

[98]This system could be extended to a broader geographic area at a later date.

[99]A serious effort might well avert mandatory Japan-oriented legislation, which is the predictable consequence of unproductive negotiations.

[100]The Strauss-Ushiba Agreement, January 13, 1978.

scheduled and short-term amity became the immediate goal of U.S. policymakers. Were a set of a long-term policy objectives established, and if the political will existed to achieve them, it just might be possible to sustain a line of policy over a significant period of time and deliver concrete results.

Objectives of Policy

There is no substitute for results. Every business is judged by the bottom line. The trade agreements program, therefore, similarly, ought not to be judged by the number of agreements concluded without much regard to the actual effect on commerce. This has some of the artificiality of the Vietnam War's body count and number of hamlets pacified as measures of progress in winning the war. Success in trade negotiations must be defined as more open markets resulting in more trade -- that is, there must be more sales of U.S. and other countries' products in the foreign market in question.[101] In this light, trade negotiations with Japan have largely been a failure. Imports of manufactured goods are still a very low percentage of Japanese GNP compared to that in all other developed nations. Too often, the United States has sought and concluded process-oriented agreements with Japan -- e.g., requiring open, transparent bidding procedures, public notice, and a right to comment. These are fine as means to an end, but must not be confused with the objective stated above, namely results. U.S. trade policy, particularly with respect to Japan, must be results-oriented if it is to have any chance of being successful.

Putting aside for the moment the structural problems and policy failures at home that condemn some U.S. industries to competitive failures, and concentrating solely on the Japanese side of the equation, what should be required of Japan?

Burden sharing. Japan must bear a proportionate share of the burden of world trade. This means accepting its share, related to its wealth, of the manufactured goods produced by other countries.[102] The United

---

[101]Foreign goods, rather than U.S. goods alone, is the correct measure because trade negotiations' benefits are granted on a non-discriminatory basis.

[102]There is a difficult trap to be avoided here. A significant portion of world trade is intra-company in nature. In the case of Japan, there has been a sharp increase in offshore assembly in Southeast Asia in the last few years. This shift in the placement of Japanese plants gives a distorted picture, indicating that Japan is (continued...)

States will benefit directly, and indirectly through an increase in the capacity of others (such as the ASEAN nations and Korea) themselves to import more. In a new, results-oriented policy, this is a primary measure of success.

Anticompetitive activities. Trade protection in Japan has become largely privatized. There are very few official trade restrictions in the form of border measures. Anticompetitive practices, having an adverse affect on world trade to the extent that they are not suppressed by the Japan Fair Trade Commission, should be dealt with by U.S. (and the EC) directly, through bilateral negotiation, or through multilateral responses (such as a new GATT code or an Article XXIII case under the GATT Articles of Agreement).

Structural reforms. These must continue to be sought. The SII exercise has identified several areas requiring attention. The distribution system and corporate inter-relationships are two that deserve priority. In addition, it is imperative that Japanese businessmen behave to a greater degree in accordance with the dictates of the marketplace. If group loyalty cannot be overcome by market forces, market solutions will not be appropriate to resolve the "Japan problem" over the longer term.

Priority trade interests. The three foregoing objectives are not to be adopted to the exclusion of the pursuit of specific American trade interests. There will always be products for which access must be specifically sought. Where strategic American interests are involved, U.S. negotiators should not accept "no" for an answer. Results are what count.

Policy Alternatives

It has been argued by some that the United States should not seek to reform Japan. If Japan wishes to retain large nonmarket elements within its economy, it is said, that is its business. This would be entirely true were it not for international trade. Our interests in Japan are not what they were in China in the era of gunboat diplomacy; we do not seek an open Japanese market solely as an outlet for our goods, but so that we can

---

[102](...continued)
liberalizing to a greater extent than it is. This is more a form of colonialism than it is trade liberalization. Foreign capital affiliated companies must have an opportunity to sell their competitive goods both to Japanese businesses in Japan and Japanese subsidiaries (dubbed "transplants") overseas. Openness must be measured in sales to Japanese companies by unrelated, non-Japanese companies.

live in harmony with Japan in an open international trading system. If Japan wishes to practice adversarial trade -- refusing to import what it exports -- open trade with Japan will prove unacceptable to other trading nations. We have economic interests that will not allow our continuing to sustain damage to the U.S. economy through current Japanese trading practices. The broad U.S. policy options, therefore, put starkly, are: (1) containment, (2) conversion, or (3) convergence.

Containment. Isolation of Japan -- must be considered a highly undesirable, destructive path, leading to a poorer world, and ultimately a clash of national wills that may extend beyond solely economic conflict. In a sense, this policy has been followed ineffectively and with less than wholly desirable results in export restraint agreement after restraint agreement. However, if either of the following two options does not prove to be feasible, this is the path which is likely to be taken by default.

Conversion. This is the finest of all the options, and the least practical. Japan is unlikely ever to adopt fully our own set of commercial values or attitudes toward government and the economy -- particularly since Japan's system seems to be demonstrating to the Japanese its superiority over ours.

Convergence. This is the hardest of the three choices, and the only acceptable option. It means that both Japan, on the one hand, and the United States and Europe, on the other, must change somewhat in the direction of the other. It means that Japan must become a better consumer of the rest of the world's goods. It means that the United States and Europe must become world-class producers of more classes of goods. What each side must do need not be set forth again here. There are enough compendia now of the steps each must take. (For a start, Americans can look to the reports of the private sector's Council on Competitiveness.) This is not only a path to peaceful coexistence. It is a path to maximizing economic welfare globally. Regrettably, neither side is currently demonstrating the will to make much of a beginning at doing what clearly must be done.

The Necessity for Finding a Solution

There is no guarantee of the nation's economic prosperity or of its remaining powerful if it settles for being second best. Craig Fields, Chief Executive Officer of the Microelectronics and Computer Corporation (MCC), described this phenomenon (in discussing competition among firms) as nonlinearity. "There is only a fraction of a second that separates a racehorse from being a horse destined for the glue factory."[103] The United States and Europe for their own good, need to be broadly competitive with Japan. There are no acceptable alternatives. No trade policy solution will be effective absent U.S. industrial competitiveness. If the U.S. responds solely with trade measures, its attempts to meet Japanese competition will never amount to more than inadequate holding actions. The best that can be said of current policy is that it may be better than doing nothing.

It is not an acceptable policy option to continue to tolerate the status quo in U.S.-Japan trading relations. The test of whether Japan's conduct in international trade is acceptable is merely to ask whether the international economic system would work if all countries followed Japan's policies. For example, not every country can have 9:1 export-import ratio in electronics. This is the adversarial trade of which Peter Drucker has complained. One of the first trade priorities of an incoming Administration must be to find and implement effective responses to the problem of U.S.-Japan relations.

While there are aspects of international competition in other regions that display similarities to the problems experienced in competition with Japan (e.g., Airbus or heavy electrical generating equipment procurement in Europe), there is nowhere else the concentration of market access problems, anticompetitive private combinations, targeting and export drives that characterize competition from Japan. There is little coherent analysis within the government of the challenges posed, and the responses provided are largely ineffectual in any meaningful time frame. Paradoxically, the fact that the current list of bilateral trade issues with Japan is very short indicates not that problems are really solved, but that there has been a failure to come to grips with many of the problems which exist. It is essential that the United States evolve policies which enable industries to remain competitive with Japan, as well as with other major trading countries, in key product sectors.

---

[103]Speech to the Semiconductor Industry Association, October 2, 1991, Santa Clara, California.

10

Conclusion: The Changing Trade Policy Environment and the United States

Alan Wm. Wolff

The United States will be confronted in the 1990s with a paradox: its success in assisting in the establishment of resurgent Japanese and European economies, in the context of a liberal international trading system, has resulted in a challenge to its own role and influence in the world economy. These other two major economic forces have primary objectives which differ from those of the United States. Japan is interested in continuing its industrial development, while the European Community is intent on building a united Europe. The United States is primarily interested in perfecting the multilateral trading system, which it has invested with disproportionately curative powers for the problems that it sees in the world trading environment. In some ways, Japan and the United States are similar, in that they are carried forward by the momentum of policies of an earlier era, without stopping long to re-examine and re-confirm their suitability in the current environment.

In a world in which the United States has a less dominant role than the one to which it is accustomed, and after a series of negotiations in which it has already made many of the concessions that provide access to its markets, it increasingly must rely for leverage on its willingness to act unilaterally, sometimes contrary to international rules. It can no longer exercise influence solely by moral suasion based on unrivalled economic strength or on the promise of granting, or the threat of withholding, future trade concessions. The other major countries of the world economy, together increasingly with the developing countries, are determined to curb what they see as U.S. "unilateralism" in its trade policy and to challenge aggressively U.S. trade actions. At the same time, foreign national strategies to excel in advanced technology products increasingly pose a direct challenge to the dominance of many U.S. industries, increasing pressure on the U.S. government for a trade policy response.

The new trading environment of the 1990s presents the United States with opportunities to both pursue its own particular economic self-interest as well as to advance its longstanding goal of greater openness in the world economy. The corollary of the relative loss of position of the United States in the world trading system is that the United States will become far less tolerant of other countries being "free-riders". Thus while there will be greater demands placed upon the United States to hedge American flexibility to respond to foreign practices by increasing the presence of international dispute settlement procedures, the United States will increasingly argue for greater openness on the part of other countries because of their increased competitive capabilities. The United States bore a disproportionate burden of the liberalization of trade in the last several decades. It will now seek greater burden sharing by others.

Despite the relative decline in the economic position of the United States in the world economy and its relative loss of influence in the GATT, paradoxically, there should be little change in the U.S. leadership role in directing the world trading system in the 1990s. Japan has not shown itself ready to take up its share of the mantle of leadership, which would require a much greater degree of liberalization at home. The Community, for its part, is preoccupied with the process of converting economic confederation into political federation and economic union, as well as drawing the surrounding nations of the European Free Trade Area and of Eastern Europe into a new Community framework. From the viewpoint of the world trading system, whatever the benefits flowing from a more vibrant Europe, the attention of an already overworked bureaucracy in Brussels will be largely absorbed by regional concerns. There will likely be a less unified position among the LDCs as countries such as South Korea, Taiwan and Brazil see themselves more as having distinct interests of their own than as developing nations as such and demand a greater say in the functioning of the trading system. The United States will still have to lead, if only by default. It will be difficult to share fully these responsibilities with others.

Another fact which the United States must confront in the coming years is the limited efficacy of trade policy and border measures, absent other policy measures, in the new environment of the 1990s. The U.S. Government will be forced to reassess its repugnance for the various domestic policy measures that are used by its trading partners as a means of addressing economic problems no longer susceptible to trade policy action.[1] In the near term, there will be no international consensus with respect to the appropriate use of these measures. The U.S. Government will also be likely to be forced to consider measures which are not traditional trade actions to address foreign practices beyond the reach of GATT-sanctioned trade remedies. For example, foreign industrial practices -- such as bid-rigging, price-fixing and organized boycotts -- which are private restrictions on trade, are likely to be addressed by legal proceedings under U.S. laws governing anticompetitive practices.[2] This will eventually bring about a more generally perceived need for a code of conduct with respect to competition policy.

MULTILATERALISM AND THE SHARING OF SOVEREIGNTY

The United States will find it increasingly frustrating to watch the elaboration of international rules curb its ability to respond to foreign industrial, services and agricultural practices which adversely affect American commercial interests. This will be the case because there will be an appearance that the international disciplines are more effective in preventing a U.S. response to foreign unfair trading practices than in preventing the practices themselves. This loss of the ability to respond will coincide with a greater awareness of the need to respond through trade measures, heightened by America's lack of alternative measures more acceptable to others and more likely to obtain better results -- namely domestic policies more supportive of U.S. preeminence in high technology and other industrial activities. Seen from abroad, the United States will present an image of a country wholly unprepared to share sovereignty. The implicit message read by others will be that the United States supports international institutions such as the GATT when they are an instrument of U.S. policy, but that it is less enthusiastic about subordinating its own actions to international authority. This trap will be one of America's own making. It is currently engaged in building a web

---

[1]As one EC official put it, a problem for the United States is that it doesn't have an alternative to using trade policy. The European Community, on the other hand, has other tools it can use to address trade related problems. DG-III and DG-XIII are active in this regard. Innovation policy is seen as a preferable means of competition compared with the use of trade measures. Interview with senior DG-I official.

[2]The initiative for such actions could come from the FTC, the antitrust division of the Justice Department, or from private legal actions.

of supra-national juridical procedures when there is no common understanding of how economies ought to be run or consensus as to which activities designed to promote industrial development are legitimate. This is a recipe for heightened conflicts among the major trading nations.[3]

In the past, many countries were reluctant to challenge the United States over a trade dispute in the GATT, preferring to settle the dispute bilaterally. This is very likely to change in the 1990s. A greater proportion of bilateral trade disputes are likely to be addressed in the GATT and a greater number of U.S. trade actions are likely to be successfully challenged in the GATT. For example, the recent GATT cases brought by the European Community against the United States on Section 337, and concerning the U.S.-Japan Semiconductor Agreement[4] are a harbinger of the future EC approach to the United States. The way in which these cases, and the Swedish steel case (on review of an administrative antidumping finding) were adjudicated underlines the fact that the U.S. government has championed prematurely a system which it is unprepared to utilize effectively. It is a great irony that the most litigious of all nations will be entangled in international legal proceedings for its responses to trade distorting actions, and unable to reach these same practices using the same procedures.

It will be extremely difficult for the United States to prevail on an issue in a multilateral forum without first having formed a key participant consensus on the issue. Thus the United States will need to continue to pursue new initiatives and the expansion of rules governing government actions that affect trade through groups smaller than the GATT, in preparation for broader GATT acceptance. Some quiet, small group such as that which has directed international monetary affairs will need to be created. This is most likely to be a U.S.-EC grouping, with Japan brought along, followed by the involvement of a few other countries as the consensus is broadened. Regional economic integration will be a continuing strong force which will have to be overcome for there to be a

---

[3]One consequence of the relative decline in U.S. ability to manage the trading system and work its will on other countries is that the quality and experience of the people doing trade policy will become much more important. The United States will have to prevail in the 1990s more on the merits of its case and how it is argued than on its dominance over the system.

[4]Although the GATT case on the semiconductor trade agreement was technically brought against Japan, it was also a direct challenge to the ability of the United States to work out a trade dispute bilaterally, when the effects of the agreement were seen to extend to other members of the trading system.

continuation of progress on the multilateral front. Preliminary bilateral or regional agreements may also be reached on sectoral issues such as financial services or R&D subsidies, especially to the extent that progress in the GATT remains blocked.

There will be continued attempts by the United States to drive other countries into new areas of multilateral agreement through exercise of unilateral action in selected instances. This is likely to be less a conscious American plan than a response to Congressional demands for removal of what will be defined in legislation as foreign unfair trade practices. However, such efforts will meet increasing resistance by those countries which view their own actions as legitimate domestic policy. When intransigence abroad is met by the threat or imposition of Congressionally-mandated trade measures, U.S. actions will increasingly be challenged in the GATT, or the subject of OECD review. The United States will thus be placed on the defensive in part because it will seek to utilize an excessively legalistic approach with respect to other countries' policies -- because it has so few alternative policy tools of its own, and because it believes too much in the homogeneity of economic views of the major trading countries.

This is not to say that the U.S. approach cannot produce some positive results. The United States has used the "super 301" process to follow such a strategy with respect to intellectual property protection and telecommunications trade. If used judiciously, this type of strategy can produce some gains. Other countries would like to use multilateral rules to take this tactic out of the U.S. playbook. However the factors outlined above are unlikely to provide the United States with other options for influencing others to pursue new agreements with respect to removing distortions to international trade.

THE CHALLENGE IN HIGH TECHNOLOGY

High technology will be a critical area of trade policy conflicts in the 1990s. While this fact has implications for all countries, it is especially significant for the United States. Most of the efforts of other countries in the high technology area are directed at catching up to or surpassing U.S. capabilities in the high technology area. Thus many of the trade disputes in the 1990s concerning high technology products and industries will involve the United States.

Most of the important disputes will continue to be between the United States and Japan, because Japan is the source of the sharpest competition in these products. It is difficult to envision the United States and Japan avoiding serious trade friction in computers and, a few years later, in aerospace. The concerted efforts of Japan in industrial promotion in these two sectors build on what was done for semiconductors the 1970s. Japan will pursue its industrial policy goals in these two sectors and hope to manage the conflict with the United States when a U.S. response can no longer be put off. In the meantime, the key Japanese aim will be industrial promotion and development.

The United States has not found a method to deal with Japanese competition in high technology. It does not match Japan in industrial policy measures, and has no intent of doing so; nor does it shape and organize even those competitive factors which even it considers acceptable to mount an effective response. As in other sectors, this puts pressure on trade policy to remedy problems that go beyond trade. The relief is symptomatic when granted and rarely very effective. The U.S. is left with slogans and ineffective procedural fixes that bear too little fruit. High technology issues are just a subset of the Japan problem, however, for which the United States has no considered answer or effective response.

Europe will be the second largest source of substantial problems if the United States and Europe cannot find a way to cooperate more closely. Here again, a division over ideological approach blocks progress. There should be much to be gained out of transatlantic cooperation. There are areas of complementarily of skills and resources. Private sector initiatives may lead the way. In contrast to the case of Japan, U.S. companies have been able to invest more freely in Europe, and Europeans have invested heavily in the United States as well. Technology joint ventures may occur with greater mutual confidence than with Japanese companies, because of closer similarities in business practices.

Conflicts with Brazil are still likely despite the path of liberalization being followed by the present Brazilian government. Brazil will proceed very cautiously with liberalization in informatics. Since this area is of great importance to the United States as an area for which market access is desired, this is likely to lead to continued friction. The trade policy dilemma for the United States will be to encourage Brazil to maintain its current plans for rapid trade liberalization while not letting the inevitable disputes in high technology lead to counter-productive trade conflicts and retaliatory measures.

Trade friction with South Korea is likely in several high technology sectors: semiconductors, telecommunications and certain types of advanced capital equipment. The possibility for trade friction in semiconductors may be mitigated to the extent that South Korean firms (primarily Samsung) seek to avoid repeating the Japanese experience of the period from 1985 to the present.

Taiwan is following similar industrial policy objectives to South Korea in several high technology sectors, but it is seeking to engage U.S.

partners in the process. At the same time, Japanese firms are investing heavily in Taiwan to use it as an export platform for component assembly to export finished high technology products such as computers to end-markets such as the United States. If the Taiwanese have their way, the threat of Japanese dominance will be offset by a web of Taiwan-U.S. technological alliances and joint ventures; it remains to be seen, however, how far U.S. industry is prepared to go in this direction.

The United States is likely to try to resolve high technology trade disputes through bilateral or plurilateral agreements aimed at limiting state aids. One such example is the attempt to procure an arrangement concerning the type and level of subsidies that can be given to Airbus that the United States is currently trying to conclude with the European Community. Whether or not this approach solves the current problem with the EC, it is likely to be of limited utility in the future, because the problems go beyond direct subsidization, and any agreement to be successfully concluded must be seen to serve the self-interest of all of the parties. Self-interest, the motivation for others entering into an agreement, can take the form of avoidance of retaliation -- as noted, an increasingly difficult source of leverage to bring to bear; a mutual interest in limiting budgetary exposure (which is partially dependent on whether those granting aids believe that they already have achieved or cannot possibly achieve their objectives); or some mutual gain from cooperation. This last tack is a very difficult one for the United States to take, given its ideological framework. Where leverage does exist, some agreements may well be comprehensive at least insofar as trade measures are concerned. One model would be the 1986 and the 1991 U.S.-Japan Semiconductor Trade Agreements. The principle idea of these Agreements was to remedy dumping and market access in the same agreement as a means of affecting foreign industrial policy through curbing its adverse external effects. At the time of the signing of the first agreement, then U.S. Trade Representative Clayton Yeutter had seen this approach as historic, and a pattern for other agreements. It sought substantive results, as opposed to just changes in process. In the event, this has not been a path chosen by subsequent U.S. negotiators.

The fundamental problem for the United States with respect to trade conflicts in high technology is that most disputes will involve government actions and policies that are not clearly proscribed by international rules. Further, the United States will have few allies in the international community who will support U.S. efforts to exert greater international discipline over the many domestic policy measures that governments use to promote high technology industries.

In some ways U.S. trade policy toward high technology in the 1990s may be a replay of the more aggressive trade policy actions taken in the

1980s, but success may be more limited. In the 1980s, in large part to appease Congressional desires to address the huge imbalance in U.S. trade, the administration pursued a policy of aggressively using section 301 to force other countries to open markets or to take other trade-related actions that would benefit U.S. interests. This approach was later codified in the Omnibus Trade and Competitiveness Act of 1988 with the introduction of concepts such as industrial targeting as actionable practices under section 301 and the addition of the "Super 301" provisions. This more aggressive trade policy did produce positive gains in terms of opening markets and was responsible for helping to get issues like intellectual property protection on the multilateral agenda in the GATT Uruguay Round. But these trade policy actions also produced a negative reaction by America's trading partners. The result is that the United States, assuming that the trade balance doesn't substantially worsen (which would stimulate it to greater aggressiveness) will probably not have the same degree of success if it attempts to pursue a similar policy with respect to high technology trade in the 1990s. Other trading partners will feel more assertive in resisting United States' pressure and challenging it in the GATT where the subject of dispute is not clearly proscribed by the GATT rules.

If this trade policy option is of reduced effectiveness for the United States, alternative courses of action will have to be explored. There are three possible options. The first is to do nothing; this option means that all alternative policy actions were considered and rejected as either being too costly or not in the U.S. interest. A second option is to consider taking domestic policy actions similar to the ones that are the subject of dispute, at least until international consensus is reached over agreed rules covering such measures. The United States has taken this approach in the past with respect to the issue of officially subsidized export credits. Except for the issue of mixed credits, the U.S. strategy of matching other countries' subsidized export credits did produce an agreement in the OECD to tie government export credits to market interest rates. It will be argued that a drawback of this approach is that it could entail significant government expenditures. A third option would be to seek bilateral agreements on cooperation in high technology that might mitigate the trade dispute, and provide some means for cooperation in the product sector. Much of the cause for trade disputes in high technology industries is that a country is giving its national firms a competitive advantage vis-á-vis other national firms by providing some form of assistance not available to firms in other countries. In some instances it may be possible to allow firms from other countries access to programs or assistance provided by host governments. One example of an area where cooperation is possible has been in semiconductor production equipment R&D. Discussions have been held between officials from JESSI (EC) and SEMATECH (U.S.), two R&D consortia devoted to semiconductor manufacturing technology, about mutual cooperation. This approach would only work, however, between two economies which are relatively open.

FACTORS SHAPING U.S. TRADE POLICY

As described earlier, the United States can be expected to maintain its leadership position in the international trading system, in part due to default by others, especially with respect to setting the international agenda for rule-making and supporting continued liberalization of the system. This will require the support of a reinvigorated alliance of domestic forces. The post-war coalition which supported trade liberalization as a bulwark against world communism and an engine of growth through exports has lost the degree of interest it once had in this program. Now, specific rather than general results are required. Fewer corporations back trade talks simply because they believe in the bicycle theory of trade relationships (if one does not keep pedaling -- that is, liberalizing -- calamity follows). They also wish to see results which affect their bottom line -- the protection of intellectual property, the opening of specific markets or the reduction of identified tariffs. It will be increasingly difficult for the United States government to build a consensus behind a common idea of what is in the national interest and consequent trade policy actions unless there is a more direct relationship of these policies to clear economic benefits for the United States. The great exception to this is the North American Free Trade Area, in which the idea, (especially a few years ago for free trade with Canada) was a sufficient cause for the FTA without the need for specific bottom-line justifications. The value of any GATT code in the future is likely to be very much judged on its merits -- what concrete benefits will it contribute, rather than the satisfaction taken of placing a new area nominally within the GATT system.

While the relative position of the United States in the international trading system has been diminished, the United States still retains significant leverage to achieve its policy objectives:

- The United States still has the largest, most open market for goods in the world. While its GATT obligations place limits on how this leverage can be exercised, the United States will have to hold out the issue of access to the U.S. market where significant U.S. interests are at stake.

- The GATT system which the United States has long nurtured, despite its well known weaknesses, will remain the most important instrument for U.S. trade policy. The United States will likely use this GATT leverage to further push countries such as South Korea and Brazil toward trade liberalization and full accession to the obligations of the GATT over time and to press the European Community to keep formation of the single market consistent with the GATT.
- The United States will still be able to rely on groups of countries in the international trading system to support its initiatives in a number of important areas. A clear trade policy objective expressed by officials in South Korea, Taiwan and Brazil was to obtain market access abroad beyond that achieved from the United States. Historically, these countries became dependent on the U.S. market because of barriers to export in other markets. The United States should therefore find itself with natural allies as it seeks to obtain greater burden sharing from Japan and the enlarged European Community.

A premium will increasingly be placed on obtaining the support of at least one other major country or entity for U.S. initiatives. The need to line up allies on any trade policy initiative will likely lead to a more careful assessment of the costs and benefits of individual trade policy initiatives. A prime candidate for reevaluation is likely to be the degree of U.S. policy emphasis with respect to trade in agriculture. There are a number of reasons to expect a reassessment of U.S. trade policy objectives in agriculture:

- Too few countries support America's ambitious objectives for agricultural trade. Five of the six foreign countries studied in this report -- Japan, the European Community, Germany, Taiwan and South Korea -- all face very significant domestic economic and political opposition to any substantial and rapid change in agricultural policies, without counting the United States. Brazil is the only one of the six that is supportive of U.S. goals, because it feels it loses export sales to both the United States and the European Community due to agricultural export subsidies.
- The difficulties and fallout of aggressively challenging other countries to radically change their agricultural policies has arguably had costs for the United States both inside and outside of the agricultural area. The United States expended a large amount of scarce political capital in obtaining what up to now is very marginal

progress in agricultural trade negotiations. The effort has entailed opportunity costs by restricting efforts in other areas.

- A negotiating approach must be formulated in which other countries can identify their self-interest.[5]

The reassessment of U.S. trade policy will have to extend not only to objectives but also to the tools used to achieve those objectives. In the past, private petitioners in the United States have been forced to place too much emphasis on the use of antidumping and countervailing duty laws to address the trade effects of other countries' domestic and industrial policies. The increased resistance of other countries to U.S. application of these laws, and their increased willingness to challenge U.S. administrative decisions in the GATT, will compel a search for alternative policy means to address these trade problems.

Another complicating factor facing U.S. trade policy-makers in the 1990s concerns the increasing difficulty of identifying the "U.S. interest" with respect to any trade policy action. There have always been some U.S. businesses, usually importers, who have a common interest with

---

[5]The United States will not be the only country having difficult defining its national interest. As companies respond to the increasing demands placed upon them to meet national objectives and as the integration of global markets proceed, it will be increasingly difficult for countries to define what the domestic interest is, at least in traditional terms. At the simplest level, what happens when a national champion is suddenly a foreign company as recently occurred when Fujitsu purchased Britain's ICL. Does it matter? There is a sense that it does but this is likely to be a hotly contested issue. The European Community has probably gone the farthest in addressing this issue because there is clearly a well-defined perception by foreign firms operating in the Community that certain things must be done to Europeanize themselves. Companies like IBM and Ford that have moved the farthest along the spectrum are considered virtually European but only because they have achieved European content in their products generally greater than have their homegrown counterparts, their management is European (hence their decision-making is presumed to be) and their R&D is centered in Europe. Even so these companies remind people constantly just how European they are. Japan adds the overlay of the keiretsu on top of all the formerly mentioned factors. To be truly Japanese, a foreign firm would have to become part of a keiretsu family structure and no foreign firm has successfully penetrated that structure, although many of them clearly have strategies aimed at earning them the right some day to be part of the system. Taiwan has taken a different approach; it vigorously encourages inward foreign investment in many key industries, such as the information technologies, but regulates or prohibits investment in sectors where it might produce results viewed as inconsistent with the national interest (such as heavily polluting industries).

foreign producers in a trade dispute. However with the development of worldwide sourcing, especially in the high technology area, many U.S. producers have become increasingly dependent on foreign suppliers for components. For example U.S. computer manufacturers have made common cause with Japanese producers of flat panel displays in the recent antidumping case. On the other hand U.S. firms may be suppliers to foreign producers engaged in trade disputes with the United States. Part of the difficulty the United States has had in the discussions with the European Community over subsidies to Airbus is that major components of Airbus planes are manufactured by U.S. firms, including jet engines by GE and Pratt & Whitney. How is the U.S. government to assess the interests of Boeing and McDonnell Douglas properly compared to the interests of GE and Pratt & Whitney?

Other governments are well aware of the diversity of U.S. interests in any trade dispute and are becoming increasingly sophisticated in using the domestic U.S. interests when they coincide with the foreign country's interests. In a number of the countries studied, an explicit goal was to increase trade lobbying in Washington to influence U.S. policy. A key aspect of this will be to seek ways to tap into the common ground that the foreign firms have with U.S. domestic firms.

To some extent, the effect of the globalization of production is that it will no longer be as easy to identify a clear policy direction for the United States in trade policy because of the polarization which is likely to occur over any potential action. One effect of this trend is to reinforce the likelihood that the United States will be forced to seek to address trade problems in the 1990s through means other than measures taken at the border. Another feature of the landscape may be a revival of nationalistic feeling as the U.S. industries appear to be losing across the board in high technology. Such an outcome could galvanize public support behind a very clear effort to support U.S. industries.

OPPORTUNITIES FOR PROGRESS

The 1990s open a new chapter in trade diplomacy, with major U.S. efforts needed in key capitals abroad to solicit support for U.S. initiatives. The relative growth in importance of Brussels, Tokyo, Berlin, and, to a lesser extent, Brasilia, Seoul, and Taipei, will require major consensus-building efforts to achieve America's broader objectives.

The following opportunities and challenges present themselves for the United States in the coming years:

Obtain Greater Burden Sharing

The major trading countries, the first of which requiring attention being Japan, must participate more equally in the responsibilities of the world trading system. The continuing enlargement of the European Community and the perfection of its internal market must not be at the expense of others. A major challenge for the EC will be the absorption of the products of Eastern Europe. The more advanced developing countries must continue to liberalize their economies, internally in terms of organization and externally, to the goods and services of others.

Integration of Japan into the World Economy

The promise of the Maekawa Report must be realized. There is no more ready source of trade conflict than from this island nation. The problem is its insularity, not in a geographic sense but in terms of its business culture. Either it will become more "westernized" in this respect, and at a far more rapid pace, or there will be continuing conflicts, which may well become increasingly confrontational. Part of the problem stems from the inadequacy of United States policy toward Japan. There is no coherent strategy or consistent approach, and the poverty of the results are the consequence.

Reaching for Pragmatism in Trade Policy

Every policy deserves to be judged solely by the results which it achieves. The results of American trade policy are far from adequate. There are markets that have been closed for years in key areas, with no effective attempts to open them. We have settled too often for process, where market forces were not operating. Procedural agreements in such circumstances are largely exercises in self-delusion. Recently seeking results has been tarred with the accusation that it constitutes "managed trade". America's growth was due in substantial part to its pragmatism. We have to return to basics.

Forming a Partnership with Europe

The United States is not going to be able to manage the international trading system alone, nor will it be able to do so in a large group. The GATT was always an organization in which political rhetoric could largely be put aside and practical people could do practical deals. This trading system worked primarily on the basis of understandings between Europe and the United States -- this was the secret of the conclusion of agreements in the Tokyo Round. The absence of a common view between these two largest players caused the stalling of the Uruguay Round. Thus it is not just global trade policy which requires management, but the bilateral relationship, and more thought needs to be given to strengthening it. If we do not do so, the Europeans will certainly become preoccupied with their internal integration, and our relations with Europe and our ability to influence for the good the world economy will suffer.

Integration of U.S. Policy

Trade policy conducted in isolation from domestic policies is likely to be excessively protectionist. This is a lesson to be drawn from the last twenty years of trade policy decisions. Too much of a burden has been placed on trade measures to achieve adjustment to competition in the world market. This is not to say that the protection has been effective. Trade protection is a weak instrument of policy when used alone, and it need not have been used at all in many cases had a broader menu of options been provided, including opening foreign markets at a stage when this could have been a positive contribution, and providing an domestic environment in which domestic industry, services, agriculture and technology can thrive.

Cooperation on High Technology

It may prove possible to redirect the competition in high technology, at least in terms of basic R&D, into more cooperative areas. One possibility is for Japan and Japanese firms to provide more support for basic science in their own country and for applied R&D programs in the United States and Europe. There will be other major opportunities to exploit complementary strengths between industries, for example, in Europe and the United States, to foster the evolution of stronger competitors and therefore greater competition in the world markets.

The Extension of the GATT to New Areas

The Administration is on the right track in seeking to cover services, intellectual property protection, and trade-related investment measures in the GATT. These areas require liberalization as part of the process of promoting growth in international commerce. However, there are equally important additional subjects that the current GATT negotiations are not addressing. These are anticompetitive activities and industrial targeting. As governments have increasingly subjected themselves to disciplines over the formal trade barriers which they may impose, protection appears to have become increasingly privatized. Non-enforcement of a reasonable competition policy is often as distortive of trade as traditional trade barriers have been. Targeting, the creation of artificial competitive advantage through state and group action is probably not going to be easily susceptible to a code of conduct. It would probably best be handled by creating an internationally recognized right of response on the part of governments whose economies suffer injury from these practices.

Agriculture

This area has been too long neglected by the international trading system, and must be brought within its disciplines. The question is how, and how quickly. The frontal assault on the Common Agricultural Policy has not worked; in any event, the United States could not have lived, as a political matter, with its own proposals. There has to be a gradual phase-in of market forces. In hindsight had the Europeans and the group of agricultural exporters agreed to what then would have seemed an inconceivably long period of adjustment by farmers when the conversations on this subject first began in the 1950s and 1960s, world trade farm would by now already be substantially free of major distortions. This may be an area where patience and process are necessary to obtain the desired results. A first step would be to begin close coordination of agricultural policies, including support levels. This coordination was called by Finn Gundelach and the other negotiators in the Tokyo Round a "cathedral in which persons from all denominations would be welcome." It is time to begin creating the necessary structure.

Transparency in Trade Policy

There exists the opportunity to combine the movement toward greater liberalization in the trading system with more transparency in the trade policy decision-making processes abroad. The public spotlight on these currently restrictive practices can sometimes build public pressures for change in the countries imposing trade measures. The United States has been trying this approach with respect to Japanese anticompetitive practices, the Large Retail Store Law, and specific agricultural quotas, with at best mixed results. It is worth putting the spotlight domestically on the internationally indefensible. It is the beginning of a process of working to inform public opinion in favor of change to a less restrictive regime. At the same time, there is growing interest in many countries by their legislative bodies to take on a more active role in the trade policy process.[6] In most of the countries studied in this book, democratization has reinforced protectionist tendencies, but there is no inherent reason why this should be the case, particularly in countries like Japan whose market barriers have effectively reduced the quality of life of axioms. The United States needs to seek to influence the public debate on trade policy in other countries much as other countries now do in the United States.

Technical Assistance

Countries that heretofore have not used GATT procedures to regulate trade and trade disputes (Brazil, Mexico, South Korea, Taiwan), are now attempting to establish institutional procedures to apply GATT rules regarding such practices as dumping and subsidization. The United States should encourage these efforts by seeking the expansion of GATT resources in order to provide technical assistance to countries with respect to implementing GATT-consistent procedures. It may be argued that this will just encourage the replacement of indiscriminate across-the-board protection with selective procedural protection. This risk is well worth accepting, however; it is part of the process of liberalization. There was always a quid pro quo for liberalization -- if there was injury due to a rapid surge of imports, or injury due to unfair imports, appropriate offsetting measures could be taken. The United States cannot expect to preserve its own trade remedy laws within the GATT framework and not expect those beginning to be more fully integrated into the GATT system to exercise similar rights.

Expansion of GATT Membership

United States support for letting Taiwan, the USSR, the PRC, and countries of Eastern Europe who are not yet members, into the GATT would help sustain the movement toward liberalization in the world trading system. In particular, Taiwan's move to liberalize its economy and implement a GATT-based trade regime warrants a positive response.

---

[6]We do not anticipate that the progress legislative bodies will make in asserting a more active role in trade policy will be very rapid or proceed very far in the 1990s. Progress will be slow because of the complexity of the issues involved and the lack of competent staff. While in theory the greater involvement of the legislature could make trade policy more parochial in some countries, we do not anticipate much influence in this respect in the 1990s.

Integration of the World Bank, the International Monetary Fund, and the GATT

Many trade problems are a result of policies driven by debt or by external imbalances. Trade cannot be used successfully to support the international financial system without provoking an unacceptable level of trade friction. Changes in the international financial system must be geared to supporting an expansion of world trade.

LOOKING FORWARD

Trade policy in the 1990's will play an important role in the preparation of the United States for the challenges of the 21st century. The shape of the U.S. economy and of the external environment will be determined in part by the trade policy decisions taken, and those avoided, in Washington and in other capitals during these next nine years. If the U.S. approach remains ad hoc to each individual trade problem as it arises, and if there is not a more coherent view taken of this nation's commercial interests, then not only will the 1990s be a decade of continuing conflicts, but very likely a precursor of a century of disappointments.

Broader recognition has to be given to the reality that there is an intimate link of the nation's security interests to the health of its industrial base. This is by no means limited to the current production of weapons systems. It extends to the need to have the technologies as well as the manufacturing capability to build weapons. Napoleon said that politicians concern themselves with military strategy and tactics, but generals concern themselves with logistics. But it is not enough to be able to equip our military forces as needed. As important is a strong vibrant American economy, in which advanced manufacturing, related services and agriculture are fully internationally competitive, to provide the foundations of security.

It is imperative for the nation's security that the United States shape the world in which it lives. Wars which either involve or simply affect this country can sometimes be avoided with the application of influence at an early stage. The capacity to affect the international political environment will be directly dependent on the nation's economic strength. This will in turn depend on the assuring ourselves of the competitiveness of American industry. This imperative is undeniable. We wish that we could do more to assist the nations of Eastern Europe. In the 1960s and 1970s, this country spent over $160 billion fighting a war in Vietnam which we did not finance by taxes. We followed that by a decade of fiscal profligacy in the 1980s. We have weakened ourselves, not only through the Vietnam War and the Federal budget deficit, but also in part through the inadequacies of the nation's trade policies. The result is that we must now struggle to provide a few hundred million dollars to the cause of nurturing democracy among countries that were our former adversaries. We are about to be tested but our options have been narrowed. If we cannot be of sufficient assistance to the Soviet Union and Eastern Europe, what could we offer to a more democratic regime, were one to come to power, in China? Nor is foreign policy the sole external purpose for maintaining our economic strength. There is still a huge amount of good that can be done for the health of the peoples of Africa and Asia, through food and medicines, and promotion of economic development. There is an enormous environmental challenge, whether in cleaning up our immediate physical environment, or in assisting others to avoid environmentally unsound practices, such as in the Amazon rain forests. Our well-being is dependent on our ability to affect events in the world around us. This ability to influence the international political and physical environment is dependent on our economic strength, and this is far less in relative terms than it was in earlier years.

To some degree, we have squandered our inheritance. We had, and still have many of the technologies that will improve the lives of humankind. We are not doing as well as we should in commercializing them. Those in government, and those training for government service, like the British elite in the early decades of this century, seem to have forgotten the source of our strength and of our current world role, both founded on an industrial base second to none. Trade policies are a significant part of finding our way again. For the sake of future generations, it is essential that we do better.

Index